Oxford mathematics for the Caribbean 4

New Edition

Examination Level

V Bentt
S Bynoe
N Goldberg
MP Singh
ME Wardle
CJ Weeks

Edited and revised by N Goldberg

Oxford University Press

Oxford University Press, Walton Press, Oxford OX2 6DP

Oxford   New York   Toronto
Delhi   Bombay   Calcutta   Madras   Karachi
Petaling Jaya   Singapore   Hong Kong   Tokyo
Nairobi   Dar es Salaam   Cape Town
Melbourne   Auckland

and associated companies in
Berlin   Ibadan

Oxford is a trade mark of Oxford University Press
ISBN 0 19 914277 7

First published 1981 and 1982
New edition 1989
Reprinted with corrections 1991

Cartoons by Peter Bailey

Printed and bound in Great Britain by
Butler & Tanner Ltd, Frome and London

To the teacher

This new edition of Oxford Mathematics for the Caribbean has been prepared to cater for the needs of the increasing number of students entered for the Caribbean Examinations Council (CXC) examinations.

The First three books provide a self-contained course suitable for a wide range of Junior Secondary and Secondary schools. At the same time they provide a firm foundation for further examination work. The work in the last two years leading to the CXC examinations is covered in the fourth book which completes both the CXC Basic Proficiency and CXC General Proficiency syllabuses.

In this edition, the text has been enlivened with cartoons and simplified to make it easier for the student to use for self-study. More worked examples, more practice at all levels, and more detailed summaries have been provided.
Understanding of basic principles is stressed throughout the course and practical work is used to reinforce these principles. It is important that such practical work is attempted by students as an integral part of the learning process: children learn by doing!

Research has shown that many traditional topics are introduced too quickly into the secondary mathematics curriculum. The inability of many CXC candidates to perform even simple computations is just one indication of this. This new edition attempts to overcome this problem by teaching a number of topics, formerly covered just in Book 1, over a three year period. Better student comprehension should be the result of this innovative approach.

Text questions have been carefully graded: they should be attempted in the order given and at the student's own pace, leaving the teacher free to cope with individual problems. The calculator is introduced early: make use of it if at all possible because it allows the student to concentrate on the ideas rather than the arithmetic.

This Examination Level book covers the requirements of the Basic CXC syllabus in Part 1 and of the General CXC syllabus in Parts 2 and 3. Practice examination papers are included after Part 1 and after Part 3. The optional topics required by higher level students are fully covered in Part 3. Numerical answers to all questions and three-figure tables are provided at the end of the book.

The editor is most grateful to the many schools and individuals throughout the Caribbean who have provided valuable comments on the first edition of this course. He hopes that justice has been done to these comments and that the varied and lively approach will enable more students to enjoy mathematics and become more successful at it.

Nicholas Goldberg
Dominica, May 1989

Contents

Part I Basic syllabus

1 Sets 1
1.1 Revision 2
1.2 More about union and intersection 6
1.3 Problems using two sets 10
1.4 Number of subsets 12

2 Mapping and functions
2.1 Mapping diagrams 14
2.2 Function notation 16
2.3 Relations, equations and graphs 19
2.4 Converting measurements 23

3 Graphs 1
3.1 Revision 25
3.2 Linear relations 28
3.3 Solving simultaneous equations graphically 30
3.4 Gradients 32

4 Computation and number
4.1 Calculating with fractions – revision 35
4.2 Calculating with decimals – revision 36
4.3 Fractions and decimals 37
4.4 Significant figures 38
4.5 Indices 40
4.6 Standard form 42
4.7 Error in measurements 43
4.8 Calculations and degrees of accuracy 45
4.9 Number bases 46

5 Measurement
5.1 Area – revision 49
5.2 Circles 51
5.3 Arcs and sectors 52
5.4 Triangles and quadrilaterals 53
5.5 Solids – surface area 55
5.6 Volume 56
5.7 Measurement and scales 59

6 Geometry
6.1 Constructions 62

6.2 Bisecting 64
6.3 Constructing angles 66
6.4 Ratios and similar triangles 67
6.5 Congruency 69
6.6 Angles in circles 72
6.7 Quadrilaterals 75
6.8 Plans and elevations 76

7 Consumer arithmetic
7.1 Money management 82
7.2 Profit and loss 86
7.3 Interest and investment 88
7.4 Hire purchase and mortgages 90
7.5 Rates and taxes 92

8 Statistics 1
8.1 Bar and pie charts – revision 97
8.2 Histograms 99
8.3 Medians and quartiles 102
8.4 Cumulative frequency 103
8.5 Using cumulative frequency graphs 105

9 Probability 1
9.1 The idea of probability 110
9.2 Experimental probability 111
9.3 Theoretical probability 113
9.4 Using your knowledge 114

10 Algebra 1
10.1 Revision 117
10.2 Binary operations 121
10.3 Linear equations 122
10.4 Linear inequalities 124
10.5 Simultaneous equations 127
10.6 Word problems 129

11 Graphs 2
11.1 Quadratic graphs 133
11.2 Solving quadratic equations graphically 134
11.3 Non-linear relations 136
11.4 Variation 137
11.5 Variation and graphs 139

12 Transformations 1

12.1 Translations	144
12.2 Rotations	145
12.3 Reflections	147
12.4 Enlargements	149

13 Trigonometry 1

13.1 Sine and cosine	153
13.2 Tangent	154
13.3 Bearings	157
13.4 Pythagoras' Theorem	158
13.5 Angles in solids	159

Practice Papers for Basic CXC Examination

Paper A	162
Paper B	164
Papers 1 to 6	168

Part 2 General syllabus (compulsory)

1 Sets 2

1.1 More about sets	176
1.2 Problems using three sets	178
1.3 Sets and logic	181

2 Relations and functions 1

2.1 Facts about functions	185
2.2 Some special functions	187
2.3 The inverse of a function	189
2.4 The composition of functions	191
2.5 Composition and inverses	194

3 Graphs 3

3.1 Revision	199
3.2 Graphs of functions	201
3.3 Graphs of inequalities	202
3.4 Finding roots using graphs	205

4 Gradients

4.1 Gradients of straight lines	209
4.2 Equations of straight lines	212
4.3 Gradients of curves	213
4.4 Rates of change	215

5 Transformations 2

5.1 Revision	218
5.2 Glide reflections	221
5.3 Shears and stretches	223
5.4 Combining transformations	226

6 Trigonometry 2

6.1 Graphs of trigonometric functions	228
6.2 Using tables and calculators	233
6.3 The sine and cosine rules	234
6.4 Radians	239
6.5 Sectors and segments	241

7 Algebra 2

7.1 Revision	244
7.2 Fractional indices	246
7.3 Changing the subject of a formula	247
7.4 The product of two brackets	250
7.5 Completing the square	252
7.6 The difference of two squares	254
7.7 Factorising quadratic expressions	255
7.8 Solving quadratic equations	257
7.9 Word problems	261
7.10 Simultaneous equations	263

8 Statistics 2

8.1 Revision	265
8.2 The mean	267
8.3 Grouped frequencies	269
8.4 Standard deviation	270
8.5 Using standard deviation	271
8.6 Extending your knowledge	276

9 Probability 2

9.1 Revision	278
9.2 Probability of compound events	280
9.3 Using tree diagrams	283
9.4 Mutually exclusive events	285
9.5 Independent and dependent events	287

10 Vectors and matrices 1

10.1 Vectors	291
10.2 Using vectors in geometry	295

10.3 Matrices 299
10.4 Multiplying matrices 301

Part 3 General syllabus (optional)

1 Relations and functions 2
1.1 Lines and regions 306
1.2 Linear programming 308
1.3 Areas under graphs 312
1.4 Using tangents and areas 315

2 Graphs 4
2.1 More about graphs 319
2.2 Quadratic inequalities 323

3 Trigonometry 3
3.1 Lengths and angles in 3-D shapes 328

3.2 Vectors and the real world 331
3.3 Earth distances 333
3.4 Sines, cosines and tangents in surd form 337

4 Vectors and matrices 2
4.1 The inverse of a matrix 340
4.2 Simultaneous equations 343
4.3 Transformation matrices 346
4.4 Combining transformations 351

Practice Papers for General CXC examination
Paper A 356
Paper B 359
Papers 1 to 6 363

Answers 372
Three-figure tables 436

PART I
Basic CXC syllabus

1 Sets 1

1.1 Revision

A set is a collection of distinguishable elements.
A set can be defined by:
   (a) listing the elements
      e.g. {2,4,6,8,10}
   (b) describing the elements precisely
      e.g. {the first five even numbers}

1. Describe the elements of the set:
   (a) {1,3,5,7,9}   (b) {1,4,9,16,25}
   (c) {a,b,c,d,e}   (d) {a,e,i,o,u}

2. List the elements of the set:
   (a) {the first four multiples of 7}
   (b) {the factors of 12}
   (c) {the names of the suits in a pack of cards}
   (d) {the months which have 31 days}

{. . .} is read as *the set of* . . .
ϵ means *belongs to,* or *is an element of*
$\notin$ means *does not belong to,* or *is not an element of*

3. Use ϵ or $\notin$ to complete the statement:
   (a) 6 ____ {2,4,6,8,10}
   (b) 4 ____ {2,3,5,7,11}
   (c) 6 ____ {the factors of 12}
   (d) 4 ____ {the multiples of 3}

4. Say whether the statement is true or not.
   (a) Clive Lloyd ϵ {West Indian Cricketers}
   (b) Mexico $\notin$ {European countries}

We can use a letter to describe a set
e.g. F = {the factors of 12}
     M = {the first four multiples of 3}

5. (a) List the elements of F and M above.
   (b) How many elements are there in F?

In Question 5, the *number* of elements in M is 4.
We can write this as $n(M) = 4$
Using the same notation $n(F) = 6$

6. A = {a,b,c,d}, D = {days of the week}
   Write down:
   (a) $n(A) =$ (b) $n(D) =$

7. Write down:
   (a) $n\{1,3,5,7,9,11\} =$
   (b) $n\{\text{factors of 8}\} =$
   (c) $n\{\text{months of the year}\} =$
   (d) $n\{\text{multiples of 3, less than 20}\} =$

8. How many months have 32 days?

{months with 32 days} has no members.
It is an example of an *empty* set. We use the symbol ϕ
or { } to stand for an empty set. $n(\phi) = 0$

9. Say whether the set is empty or not
   (a) { prime numbers between 24 and 28}
   (b) {multiples of 12, less than 10}

Some elements in {2, 4,6,8,10} are multiples of 4.
We say that 4 and 8 form a *subset*.
i.e. {4,8} is a subset of {2,4,6,8,10}
or {4,8} $\subset$ {2,4,6,8,10}

3 and 6 are not both in {2,4,6,8,10}
so {3,6,} is not a subset of {2,4,6,8,10}
or {3,6,} $\not\subset$ {2,4,6,8,10}

10. Use $\subset$ or $\not\subset$ to complete the statement.
    (a) {2,4,8} ____ {2,4,6,8,10}
    (b) {5,10} ____ {2,4,6,8,10}

11. Say whether the statement is true or not.
    (a) {36,64} $\subset$ {square numbers}
    (b) {5,10} $\not\subset$ {factors of 15}
    (c) {2,3,5} $\subset$ {prime numbers less than 20}
    (d) {prime numbers} $\not\subset$ {odd numbers}

12. U = {1,2,3,4,5,6,7,8,9,10}
Write down these subsets of U:
(a) M = {multiples of 3}
(b) F = {factors of 10}
(c) L = {numbers less than 5}
(d) P = {prime numbers}
(e) S = {square numbers}
(f) T = {the whole numbers from 1 to 10}

13. Using the subsets in question 12, write down:
(a) n(M)   (b) n(F)   (c) n(L)
(d) n(P)   (e) n(S)   (f) n(T)

Venn diagrams

We can show subsets of a set using a Venn diagram.

Whole numbers from 1 to 10

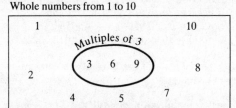

It is important to label each loop.

14. (a) Describe the subset shown below.

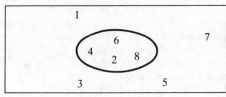

(b) Copy the Venn diagram above and label each loop.

15. Draw a Venn diagram to show the set and the subset.
(a) N = {1,2,3,4,5,6,7,8,9}
   E = {even numbers in set N}
(b) L = {a,b,c,d,e,f,g,h,i,j}
   V = {vowels in set L}

16. Using the sets in Question 15, write down:
(a) n(N)   (b) n(E)
(c) n(L)   (d) n(V)

17. Two subsets are shown in the Venn diagram below.

Whole numbers from 1 to 10

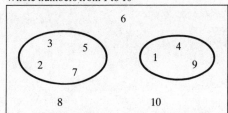

(a) Describe each subset shown above
(b) Copy the Venn diagram and label each loop

The two subsets in Question 17 have no elements in common.
They are called *disjoint* subsets
{1,3,5} and {1,4,9} each contain the element 1.
They are not disjoint subsets.

18. Say whether the two subsets are disjoint or not.
(a) {2,4,6,8}, {1,3,5,7}
(b) {1,2,5,10}, {1,3,5,7}
(c) {days of week beginning with T},
   {days of week beginning with S}
(d) {days of week beginning with S},
   {days of week with 6 letters in name}

19. T is {whole numbers from 1 to 20}
(a) List the elements of the subsets of T:
   (i) F = {multiples of four}
   (ii) N = {numbers which are not multiples
      of 4}
(b) Write down:
   (i) n(T)   (ii) n(F)   (iii) n(N)
(c) Are the subsets F and N disjoint or not?
(d) Draw a Venn diagram to show T, F and N.

20. Say whether n(E) is finite or infinite.
(a) E = {even numbers less than 99}
(b) E = {even numbers between 100 and 200}
(c) E = {even numbers greater than 100}

Complements

A set of quadrilaterals (U)

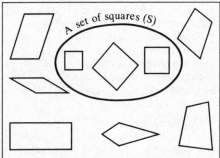

The diagram above shows a set of quadrilaterals and a subset of squares. The shapes outside the loop are the quadrilaterals which are *not* squares.

In this example the *Universal Set* is the set of quadrilaterals.
The quadrilaterals which are not squares form the *complement* of the subset of squares.

The complement of S is denoted by S'.

21. (a) Look at the Venn diagram below and describe:
     (i) the Universal Set
     (ii) the subset V
     (iii) the letters in the shaded region

Universal Set (U)

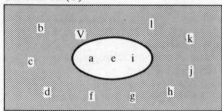

    (b) Do you agree that the letters in the shaded region form the complement of V?

22. (a) Look at the Venn diagram below and describe:
     (i) the Universal Set
     (ii) the subset P
     (iii) the numbers in the shaded region.

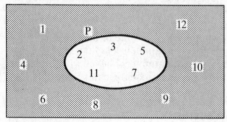

    (b) Do you agree that $P' = \{1,4,6,8,9,10,12\}$?

In Question 22, U = {whole numbers from 1 to 12}
P = {prime numbers less than 12}
P' = {non prime numbers from 1 to 12}

P' is the complement of P, and also
P is the complement of P'.
Together P and P' form the Universal Set (U).

23. Draw a Venn diagram and find T' if:
  (a) $U = \{1,2,3,4,5,6,7,8,9,10\}$, $T = \{3,6,9\}$
  (b) $U = \{a,b,e,y,c,x,o,w,u\}$, $T = \{a,e,o,u\}$
  (c) $U = \{g,h,i,j,k,l,m\}$, $T = \{h,k\}$
  (d) $U = \{2,4,6,8,10,12,14\}$, $T = \{2,14\}$
  (e) $U = \{$days of week$\}$,
      $T = \{$Tuesday, Thursday$\}$

24. If U = {students in form 4} and
B = {boys in form 4}, describe B'.

25. If U = {Bob, Ruth, Ronald, Sally, Marvin},
and G = {girls}, find G'.

26. If $U = \{1,2,3,4,5,6,7,8,9,10\}$ and $E = \{2,4,6,8,10\}$
  (a) list the elements of E'.
  (b) describe the elements of E'.

27. Say whether the statement is true or false, for the subset E in Question 26.
  (a) $6 \in E$ (b) $7 \in E'$ (c) $9 \notin E$
  (d) $9 \in E'$ (e) $2 \notin E'$ (f) $5 \notin E'$

28. (a) Use the subset V in Question 21, and write down:
     (i) $n(U)$ (ii) $n(V)$ (iii) $n(V')$
   (b) What can you say about $n(V) + n(V')$?

29. (a) If U = {whole numbers from 1 to 10} and
     T = {multiples of 3 less than 10} write down:
     (i) $n(U)$ (ii) $n(T)$ (iii) $n(T')$
   (b) Do you agree that $n(T) + n(T') = n(U)$?

30. (a) If $n(U) = 10$ and $n(T) = 7$, find $n(T')$.
  (b) If $n(U) = 20$ and $n(A) = 12$, find $n(A')$.
  (c) If $n(B) = 6$ and $n(B') = 4$, find $n(U)$.
  (d) If $n(U) = 10$ and $n(C') = 9$, find $n(C)$.

31. If $n(U) = 10$ and $n(T) = 10$ what can you say about T'?

32. Show that in Question 25, $n(G') = n(U) - n(G)$.

Intersection

The *intersection* of two sets consists of those elements which are common to *both* the two sets.

The intersection of {1,4,9,16} and {1,3,5,7,9} is {1,9}
The symbol for intersection is $\cap$ so
$\{1,4,9,16\} \cap \{1,3,5,7,9\} = \{1,9\}$

33. (a) Which elements are common to:
     (i) {1,2,3,4,5}; {2,4,6,8,10}
     (ii) {a,b,c,d,e}; {a,e,i,o,u}
     (iii) {days of week with 6 letters}; {days of week beginning with S}?
   (b) What is the intersection of:
     (i) {1,3,5,7,9}; {3,6,9,12}
     (ii) {k,l,m,n,p}; {a,l,p,w}
     (iii) {factors of 12}; {factors of 8}?

34. Copy and complete:
  (a) $\{1,2,3,4,5\} \cap \{1,3,5,7,9\} =$
  (b) $\{a,c,e,g,i\} \cap \{a,e,i,o,u\} =$
  (c) {factors of 12} $\cap$ {multiples of 3} $=$

The diagram below shows the intersection of two subsets.

Whole numbers from 1 to 20

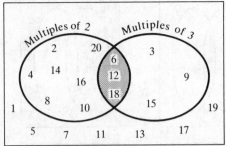

{6,12,18} are the common multiples of 2 and 3
{multiples of 2} ∩ {multiples of 3} = {6,12,18}

35. In the diagram above describe the subset:
(a) {2,4,8,10,14,16,20}
(b) {3,9,15}
(c) {1,5,7,11,13,17,19}

36. (a) Use a Venn diagram like the one above to
show the sets:
U = {whole numbers from 1 to 20}
F = {multiples of 5}
T = {multiples of 2}
(b) Describe the subset in each part of the
diagram.

Union

The *union* of two sets consists of all the elements which
are in *either* set.

The union of {1,4,9,16} and {1,3,5,7,9} is
{1,3,4,5,7,9,16}
The symbol for union is ∪ so
{1,4,9,16} ∪ {1,3,5,7,9} = {1,3,4,5,7,9,16}

37. (a) Write down a list of all the elements which are
in either set.
(i) {1,2,3,4,5}; {2,4,6,8,10}
(ii) {a,b,c,d,e}; {a,e,i,o,u}
(iii) {days of the week with 6 letters}; {days of
the week beginning with S}
(b) What is the union of:
(i) {2,4,6,8,10}; {1,4,9,16}
(ii) {p,q,r,s,t}; {p,r,t,v,x}
(iii) {factors of 6}; {factors of 8}?

38. Copy and complete:
(a) {3,6,9,12,15} ∪ {1,3,5,7,9} =
(b) {a,c,e,g,i} ∪ {a,e,i,o,u} =
(c) {factors of 12} ∪ {factors of 15} =

The diagram below shows the union of two subsets.

Whole numbers from 1 to 20

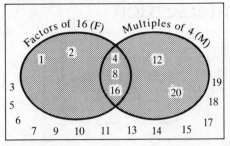

F ∪ M = {1,2,4,8,12,16,20}

39. (a) Use a Venn diagram like the one above to
show the sets:
U = {whole numbers from 1 to 20}
F = {factors of 20}
M = {multiples of 5}
(b) Now write down F ∪ M.

40. Using the diagram above do you agree that:
(a) F′ =
{3,5,6,7,9,10,11,12,13,14,15,17,18,19,20}
(b) M′ = {1,2,3,5,6,7,9,10,11,13,14,15,17,18,19}
(c) $n(F \cap M) = 3$ (d) $n(F \cup M) = 7$
(e) (F ∪ M)′ =
{3,5,6,7,9,10,11,13,14,15,17,18,19}?

1.2 More about union and intersection

Example

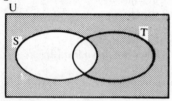

On the Venn diagram above shade the region which represents

$$S' \cap T$$

First shade S'

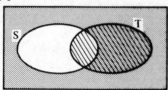

Then shade T

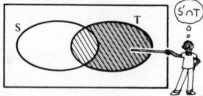

The region which is common to both S' and T i.e. the region that is shaded twice is $S' \cap T$

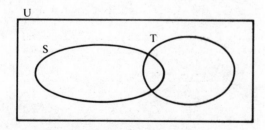

▨ is $S' \cap T$

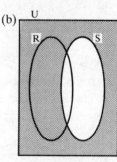

1. On separate copies of the Venn diagram above, use shading to represent the region:
(a) $S \cap T$ (b) $S \cup T$
(c) S *but not* T   (d) T *but not* S
(e) T' (f) $S \cap T'$

2. Use letters and symbols to describe the shaded region below.

(a)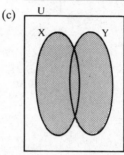

(b)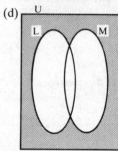

(c) (d)

3. You should have found that the shaded region in Question 2(d) is the complement of the union of L and M. Using symbols, it is written as $(L \cup M)'$. Make two more copies of the diagram and show by shading:
(a) $L \cap M'$ (b) $(L \cap M)'$
Can you see why the brackets are important in part (b)?
The use of brackets in Question 3(b) is important. The brackets tell you to find the intersection of the two sets first and then to find the complement.

4. If U = {1,2,3,4,5,6,7,8,9,10},
     S = {1,4,9} and
     T = {1,3,6,10}, find:
(a) S' (b) T' (c) $S' \cap T'$
(d) $S \cap T$ (e) $S \cup T$ (f) $(S \cup T)'$

5. In Question 4 did you find that $S' \cap T' = (S \cup T)'$?

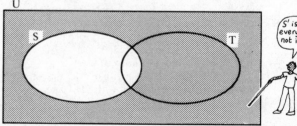

6. Do you agree that the shaded region on the Venn diagram is S'?
(a) Copy the diagram and use a different sort of shading to show T'.
(b) Copy the diagram again, without any shading. On your copy shade only the region $S' \cap T'$.
(c) Do you agree that $S' \cap T' = (S \cup T)'$?

7. If U = { 1,2,3,4,5,6,7,8,9,10},
    E = {2,4,6,8,10}, and
    F = {5, 10}, find:
(a) E′   (b) F′   (c) E′ ∪ F′
(d) E′ ∪ F   (e) E ∩ F   (f) (E ∩ F)′

8. Did you find in Question 7 that E′ ∪ F′ = (E ∩ F)′?

9. Draw a Venn diagram like the others opposite, showing sets E and F. First shade the region E′, then shade F′.
Clearly mark the region E′ ∪ F′. Do you agree that this part of the diagram can also be described as (E ∩ F)′?

(E ∩ F)′ is everything that's not in E ∩ F

We can also represent three subsets on the same Venn diagram as is shown below.

Members of youth club (U)

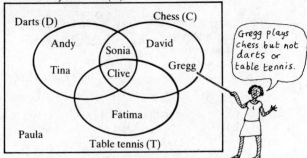

Gregg plays chess but not darts or table tennis.

10. Look at the Venn diagram above. Which members of the youth club play:
(a) Darts, chess and table tennis
(b) Darts and chess but not table tennis
(c) Chess
(d) Darts only
(e) Darts and table tennis but not chess
(f) None of these three activities?

11. Using the Venn diagram above write down.
(a) D ∩ C ∩ T
(b) D ∪ C ∪ T
(c) D ∩ C
(d) C ∩ T
(e) (D ∪ C ∪ T)′

12. (a) Copy and complete the Venn diagram started below by putting in the missing numbers.

Whole numbers from 1 to 20 (U)

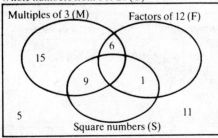

(b) Use your completed diagram to write down:
   (i) M ∩ F ∩ S
   (ii) M ∪ F ∪ S
   (iii) M ∩ F
   (iv) S ∩ F
   (v) (M ∪ F ∪ S)′
(c) Describe the numbers which lie outside the three loops.

13. (a) Draw a three loop Venn diagram to show the following sets.
    U = {whole numbers from 1 to 20}
    M = {multiples of 4}
    S = {square numbers}
    F = {factors of 16}
(b) Use your Venn diagram to write down:
   (i) M ∩ S ∩ F
   (ii) M ∪ S ∪ F
   (iii) (M ∪ S ∪ F)′
   (iv) (M ∩ S ∩ F)′
(c) Describe in words each of the four subsets in (b).

14. (a) If U = {capital letters of the alphabet} list the elements of:
   (i) H = {letters with a horizontal line of symmetry}
   (ii) V = {letters with a vertical line of symmetry}
   (iii) R = {letters which have rotational symmetry}
(b) Use your information from (a) to copy and complete the Venn diagram started below.

Capital letters in the alphabet (U)

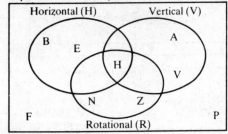

15. (a) Look at your completed diagram in Question 14 and write down:
(i) $H \cap V \cap R$ (ii) $H \cup V \cup R$
(b) Describe in words each of the three empty sets.

16. Use a three loop Venn diagram to show the following sets.
U = {whole numbers from 1 to 50}
T = {multiples of 3}
F = {multiples of 4}
V = {multiples of 5}

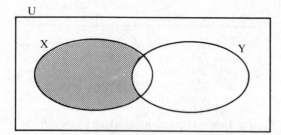

The shaded region in the diagram above can be described as X *but not* Y or $X \cap Y'$.
In the same way we can describe regions on diagrams with three sets.

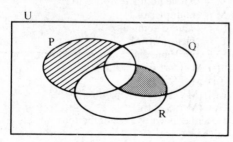

The region shaded ▨ is
$(Q \cap R)$ *but not* P or $(Q \cap R) \cap P'$.

The region shaded ▨ is
P *but not* Q or R or $P \cap (Q \cup R)'$.

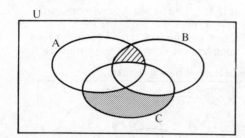

17. (a) Use letters to describe the region:
(i) shaded ▨   (ii) shaded ▨
(b) Make a copy of the diagram, without any shading. Now shade the regions described by:
(i) $(A \cup B)$ *but not* C   (ii) $(B \cup C) \cap A'$

18. Copy and complete the Venn diagram below.

Whole numbers from 2 to 60

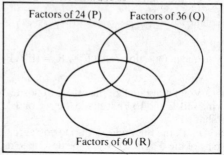

Write down the elements of:
(a) P   (b) Q   (c) R
(d) $P \cap Q$ (e) $P \cup Q$ (f) $(P \cap Q)'$
(g) $(P \cup Q)'$ (h) R' (i) $P \cap R'$
(j) $P \cap Q \cap R'$ (k) $P \cap R \cap Q$
(l) $(P \cup Q)' \cap R$ (m) $(P \cap R)' \cap Q$

19. Find each set listed below on your completed diagram for Question 18. Describe the set using letters and symbols.
(a) {2, 3, 4, 6, 12},   (b) {9, 18, 36}
(c) {8, 24}   (d) {5, 10, 15, 20, 30, 60}

20. Use your completed diagram in Question 18 to say whether the statement is true.
(a) $6 \in (P \cap Q) \cap R$
(b) $9 \in (P \cup R)'$
(c) $8 \in (Q \cap R)' \cap P$
(d) $12 \in (P \cup Q)$ *but not* R
(e) $4 \notin (Q \cup R) \cap P'$
(f) {8, 10, 12} is a subset of $(P \cap R)'$
(g) {7, 11, 18} $\subset \{P \cup R\}'$
(h) $(P \cap Q) \cap R'$ is a null set

21. Describe the shaded part of the diagram below:
(a) in your own words
(b) using symbols and letters

Students in Form Four

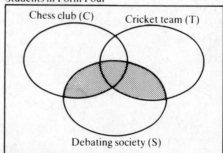

22. For the Venn diagram below, write down the number of elements in:
(a) S   (b) F   (c) S ∩ F
(d) S ∪ F   (e) S *but not* F
(f) F *but not* S   (g) *neither* S *nor* F

Whole numbers from 1 to 16

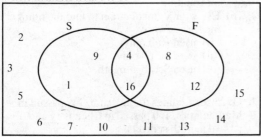

Write phrases to describe sets S and F.

23. Using the information in Question 22, copy and complete:
(a) $n(S) =$ (b) $n(F) =$
(c) $n(S \cap F) =$ (d) $n(S \cup F) =$
(e) $n(S$ *but not* $F) =$ (f) $n(F$ *but not* $S) =$
(g) $n(neither$ S nor F$) =$

24. If U = {whole numbers from 1 to 20},
   T = {multiples of 3},
   S = {square numbers}, find:
(a) $n(T)$ (b) $n(S)$ (c) $n(T \cap S)$
(d) $n(T \cup S)$ (e) $n(T$ *but not* S$)$
(f) $n(S$ *but not* T$)$ (g) $n(U)$
(h) $n(T')$ (i) $n(S')$
(j) $n(T \cap S')$ (k) $n(T \cup S')$

So far when using Venn diagrams we have shown the actual elements of the subsets.
However we can also use a Venn diagram to show the number of elements in each region.

25. $n(A) = 20$, $n(B) = 12$ and $n(A \cap B) = 5$.
   Show this information on a Venn diagram, and use your diagram to find:
(a) $n(A$ *but not* B$)$
(b) $n(B$ *but not* A$)$
(c) $n(A \cup B)$

The diagram below shows the information for Question 25.

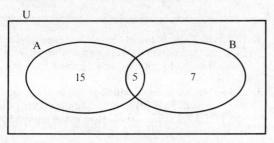

The number written in each region represents the number of elements belonging to that region.
For example:
There are 15 elements in A *but not* B.
There are 5 elements in A ∩ B.

To find the number of elements in A, just add the numbers in these two regions together.
So $n(A) = 15 + 5 = 20$.

26. For the diagram below, write down:

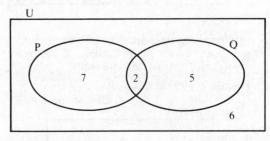

(a) $n(P \cap Q)$ (b) $n(P$ *but not* Q$)$
(c) $n(Q$ *but not* P$)$ (d) $n(neither$ P nor Q$)$
(e) $n(P)$ (f) $n(Q)$
(g) $n(P \cup Q)$ (h) $n(U)$
(i) $n(P')$ (j) $n(Q')$

27. Each dot below represents an element.

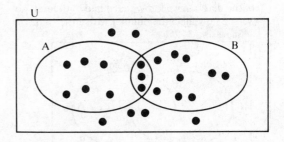

(a) Write down:
   (i) $n(A)$ (ii) $n(B)$ (iii) $n(A \cup B)$
   (iv) $n(A \cap B)$
(b) Do you agree that:
   $n(A \cup B) = n(A) + n(B) - n(A \cap B)$?

1.3 Problems using two sets

Venn diagrams can be used to solve problems and provide extra information.

Example 1

In a factory making shoes, out of 100 tested, 12 were found to have faulty stitching, 15 had faulty gluing and of these 4 had both faults.

Find the number of shoes with:
(i) no faults   (ii) just one fault.

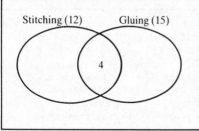

In the diagram we know that 4 had both faults so we can now fill in the number with either fault.

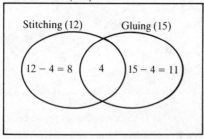

From this we can see that 23 (8 + 4 + 11) had at least one fault so 77 (100 − 23) had no faults.

---

1. In testing 100 bolts produced by a machine, it was found that:
   15 had cracks
   12 were below standard length and
   7 had both faults.
   (a) Draw a Venn diagram to show this information
   (b) Use your Venn diagram to find the number of bolts with:
      (i) cracks only
      (ii) incorrect length
      (iii) no faults
      (iv) just one fault
      (v) at least one fault.

2. In a survey 1000 people were asked which of two detergents Rub and Scrub were used.
   500 used Rub
   100 used both Rub and Scrub
   250 used neither
   (a) Draw a Venn diagram to show this information.
   (b) Use your Venn diagram to find the number in the survey who:
      (i) used Rub only
      (ii) used Scrub only
      (iii) used Scrub altogether.

3. Of 250 candidates for an exam, 149 passed in Mathematics, 160 passed in Chemistry and 87 passed in both subjects.
   (a) Draw a Venn diagram to show this information.
   (b) Use your Venn diagram to find the number of candidates who:
      (i) passed in Mathematics only
      (ii) passed in Chemistry only
      (iii) passed in neither subject
      (iv) passed in only one subject.

Example 2

In a class of 22 students, 18 study Mathematics and 12 study Spanish. How many study both?

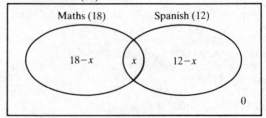

Using x to stand for the number who study both subjects we can find the number who study only one subject as shown above.
From this we can form an equation:
$(18 − x) + x + (12 − x) = 22$ so $x = 8$
The number who study both subjects is 8.

---

4. Of 25 students, 20 are in the football team and 15 are in the cricket team. How many are in both teams if three do not play either game?

5. 100 people were asked which of two programmes they enjoyed. 50 enjoyed one, 72 enjoyed the other and 17 did not enjoy either. How many enjoyed both?

Example 3

In a group of 25 cricket fans, 16 had seen the West Indies play England, 8 had seen them play Australia and 4 had seen neither. How many of the group had seen the West Indies only play Australia?

First, show the information on a Venn diagram.

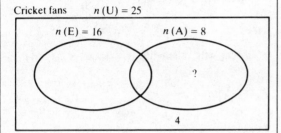

Cricket fans　　　$n(U) = 25$

$n(E) = 16$　　　　　$n(A) = 8$

?

4

Next, let the unknown quantity be x. Then you can describe each region in terms of x.

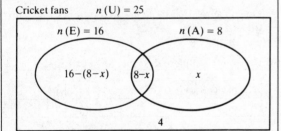

Cricket fans　　　$n(U) = 25$

$n(E) = 16$　　　　　$n(A) = 8$

$16-(8-x)$　$8-x$　　　x

4

The number in the universal set is 25.
The numbers in each of the four regions must therefore add up to 25.
So we can write the equation:
$16-(8-x) + (8-x) + x + 4 = 25$
so $20 + x = 25$
　　　$x = 5$
5 fans saw the West Indies only play Australia.

6. Use the method above to find the number of fans who saw the West Indies only play England. Did you get the answer 13?

7. In a group of 36 cricket fans, 25 had seen Trinidad play India, 17 had seen Trinidad play Pakistan, and 2 had seen neither. How many fans had seen Trinidad play both teams?

8. In a group of 21 students, 17 liked Maths, 13 liked English while 3 did not like either.
　(a) How many students liked both subjects?
　(b) How many students liked English *but not* Maths?

9. Of 40 children in a stamp club, 27 collected American stamps, 31 collected African stamps and 6 collected only West Indian stamps.
　(a) Find how many collected both American and African stamps.
　(b) How many children collected American stamps *but not* African stamps?

10. $n(A) = 17$, $n(B) = 11$ and $n(A \cup B) = 23$.
　Find $n(A \cap B)$.

11. $n(P) = 16$, $n(Q) = 29$ and $n(P \cup Q) = 40$.
　Find $n(P \cap Q)$.

12. Of 30 students in a class, 18 cycle to school and 15 wear glasses.
　(a) What is the least number who might cycle to school *and* wear glasses?
　(b) What is the greatest number who might cycle to school *and* wear glasses?
　(c) What is the greatest number who might *neither* cycle to school *nor* wear glasses?
　(d) What single extra piece of information would you need, to find the number of each type of student?

1.4 Number of subsets

Joyce   Taraben   Joe

1. The picture above shows a set of three children. Write down the names of the children in each of the following subsets:
   (a) {children carrying a bag}
   (b) {children whose name begins with J}
   (c) {girls}
   (d) {children carrying a tennis racket}
   (e) {boys}
   (f) {girls not carrying tennis rackets}
   (g) {children whose names begin with T}
   (h) {boys not carrying a tennis racket}

2. Do you agree that your answer for Question 1 (a) is *the universal set*, and for 1 (h) is *the empty set*?
   What can you say about the number of elements in subsets (b), (c) and (d)?
   What can you say about the number of elements in subsets (e), (f) and (g)?

3. Can you find any subsets of {Joe, Joyce, Taraben} other than those you found in Question 1?
   How many different subsets have you found altogether? (Remember the order of the elements in a subset does not matter.)

You should have been able to find eight different subsets in Question 1.
Remember that the universal set and the empty (null) set are both counted as subsets of the universal set.

4. Write down the eight possible subsets of:
   (a) {p, q, r}   (b) {1, 2, 3}

5. How many different subsets can you make from the set:
   (a) {p, q}?   (b) {1, 2}?

6. Do you agree that the only subsets you can make from {p} are {p} and { }?

7. A list of subsets that can be made from the set {p, q, r, s} has been started below. Copy the list, filling in the missing subsets.
   Subsets with 4 elements   {p, q, r, s}
   Subsets with 3 elements   {p, q, r}
                                    {p, q, s}
                                    . . . .
                                    . . . .
   Subsets with 2 elements   {p, q}
                                    {p, r}
                                    . . . . .
                                    . . . . .
                                    . . . . .
   Subsets with 1 element   {p}
                                    . . .
                                    . . .
                                    . . .
   Subsets with no elements   { }

8. Write down all possible subsets for the set {1, 2, 3, 4}.

9. Do you agree that there are 16 different subsets for the set:
   (a) {p, q, r, s}?   (b) {1, 2, 3, 4}?

10. Copy and complete the table for sets.

No. of elements	1	2	3	4	5	6
No. of subsets	2		8			

Can you find a pattern here?

11. In Question 10 you should have found that *a set of n elements has 2^n possible subsets*.
    Find the number of subsets of a set with:
    (a) 3 elements   (b) 5 elements   (c) 8 elements

12. The subsets of {1, a} are {1, a}, {1}, {a} and { }.
    The subsets of {1, b} are {1, b}, {1}, {b} and { }.
    (a) If A = {subsets of {1, a}} and
        B = {subsets of {1, b}} find A ∩ B and A ∪ B.
    (b) Copy and complete the Venn diagram.

Subsets of {1, a, b}

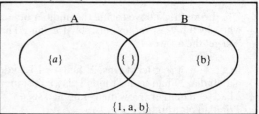

13. (a) Using your results for Question 12 find:
    (i) $n(A)$ (ii) $n(B)$ (iii) $n(A \cap B)$
(b) Show that:
$$n(A \cup B) = n(A) + n(B) - n(A \cap B)$$

14. If P = {subsets of {1, 2, p}} and
Q = {subsets of {1, 2, q}},
list the elements of:
(a) P and find $n(P)$
(b) Q and find $n(Q)$
(c) P $\cap$ Q and find $n(P \cap Q)$
(d) P $\cup$ Q and find $n(P \cup Q)$
Use your results to show that
$$n(P \cup Q) = n(P) + n(Q) - n(P \cap Q)$$

15. Copy and complete the tables, and comment on any patterns you can find.

(a)

$\cap$	{ }	{a}	{b}	{a, b}
{ }				
{a}				
{b}				
{a, b}				

(b)

$\cup$	{ }	{a}	{b}	{a, b}
{ }				
{a}				
{b}				
{a, b}				

Summary

By the end of this chapter, there are things you should know about.

1.1 Revision (pages 2–5)

Defining a set or subset by (i) listing (ii) describing the elements.
The notation { }, ϵ, $\notin$
The number of elements in a set $n(A)$
The empty (or null) set { } or ϕ
The universal set U
The complement of a set A′
The intersection of two sets A $\cap$ B
The union of two sets A $\cup$ B

1.2 More about union and intersection
(pages 6–9)

Showing the union and intersection of subsets by shading parts of a Venn diagram.
Identifying members in the union or intersection of subsets from a Venn diagram.
Showing the number of elements in each subset on a Venn diagram.

1.3 Problems using two sets (pages 10 and 11)

How to work out problems using two loop Venn diagrams.

1.4 Number of subsets (pages 12 and 13)

How to find the number of subsets of a given set.
Remember that two of the subsets of a given set are:
   the set itself
   the empty (or null) set
A set of n elements has 2^n possible subsets.

2 Mapping and functions

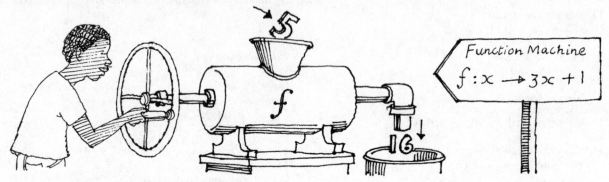

2.1 Mapping diagrams

The relation between two sets of numbers can be shown on a mapping diagram.

Example 1

What is the relation between the two sets below?

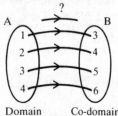

The relation is: *is two less than*.

In the example the first set A is called the domain and the set B the co-domain.
The rule can also be written as a number machine

$$\text{Input} \quad \rightarrow \quad \boxed{+2} \quad \rightarrow \quad \text{Output}$$
$$x \qquad\qquad\qquad\qquad\qquad y$$

or more simply as

$$x \rightarrow x + 2$$

Example 2

Draw a mapping diagram for the map $x \rightarrow 2x$ with domain $\{0, 1, 2, 3\}$

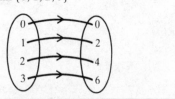

1. Draw mapping diagrams for the maps defined as follows:

Map	Domain
(a) $x \rightarrow x + 1$	$\{0, 1, 2, 3\}$
(b) $x \rightarrow x - 2$	$\{0, 1, 2, 3\}$
(c) $x \rightarrow 6 - x$	$\{0, 1, 2, 3, 4\}$
(d) $x \rightarrow 2x + 1$	$\{0, 1, 2, 3, 4\}$
(e) $x \rightarrow 3x - 2$	$\{^-1, 0, 1, 2\}$
(f) $x \rightarrow x^2$	$\{^-2, ^-1, 0, 1, 2\}$
(g) $x \rightarrow x^2 + 1$	$\{^-2, ^-1, 0, 1, 2\}$
(h) $x \rightarrow \frac{1}{2}x - 4$	$\{^-2, 0, 2, 4\}$
(i) $x \rightarrow 2x^2$	$\{^-3, ^-1, 0, ^-1, 3\}$
(j) $x \rightarrow (2x)^2$	$\{^-3, ^-1, 0, 1, 3\}$

2. Copy and complete the arrow graph. Write down the set of ordered pairs for the relation.

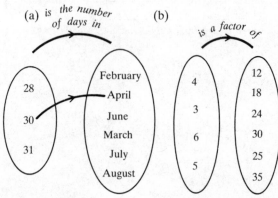

3. Copy and complete the arrow graphs below

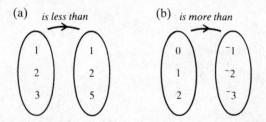

Types of mapping diagram

There are four types of *mapping diagram*.

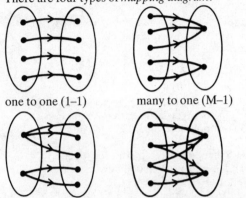

one to one (1–1)   many to one (M–1)

one to many (1–M)   many to many (M–M)

4. Draw a mapping diagram for the two sets using the arrow as defined:
   (a) $\{1, 4, 9, 16, 25\}$, $\{^-3, ^-2, 1, 2, 3, 4, 5\}$
       $: \rightarrow$ *is the square of*
   (b) $\{8, 10, 12, 16, 18\}$, $\{2, 3, 4, 5, 6\}$
       $: \rightarrow$ *is a multiple of*
   (c) $\{1, 2, 3, 4\}$, $\{10, 100, 1000, 10000\}$
       $: \rightarrow$ *is the log of*
   (d) $\{Ahmed, June, Jason, Jill, Andrew\}$,
       $\{A, B, J\}$
       $: \rightarrow$ *has as its first letter*
   In each case say whether the mapping diagram is (1–1), (M–1), (1–M), or (M–M), and write down the corresponding set of ordered pairs.

5. Look at your mapping diagrams for Questions 1, 2 and 3. Write down the type of mapping in each case.

6. What type of mapping is shown in the diagrams below?

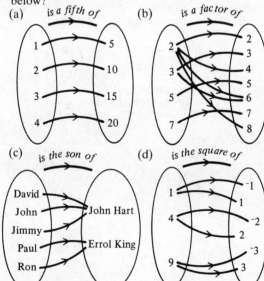

   (a) *is a fifth of*   (b) *is a factor of*

   (c) *is the son of*   (d) *is the square of*

Functions

In Questions 6 (a) and 6 (c) each member of the domain has just one arrow going to the co-domain. Mappings like these which are either *one-one* or *many-one* are called functions.
A function is a many-one or a one-one mapping. Each member of the domain maps to just one member of the co-domain.

Example 3

Which of the arrow diagrams describe functions?

(a)   (b)

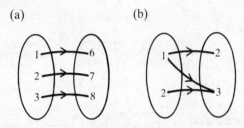

Diagram (b) is not a function because

$$1 \rightarrow 2$$
$$and\ 1 \rightarrow 3$$

In other words, there is no single image point for one member of the domain.

---

7. Complete the open sentences below. Say whether you can find more than one member to make the statement true.
   (a) 16 *is a half of* . . . .
   (b) 16 *is the square of* . . . . .
   (c) 16 *is a factor of* . . . . .
   (d) 16 *is three more than* . . . . .
   (e) 16 *is less than* . . . . .

8. Did you find that Questions 7(a) and 7(d) each had only one possible answer? Did you find that the others had more than one possible answer?

9. Using $\{4, 9, 16, 25\}$ as the domain, draw a mapping for each relationship in Question 6.

10. (a) Do you agree that the mappings for Questions 7(a) and 7(d) are functions?
    (b) Explain why the other three mappings are *not* functions.

11. Look at the number machine below. If there is only one possible output for each input, the machine produces a function.

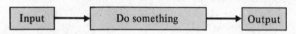

Which of these number machines produce a function?

(a)

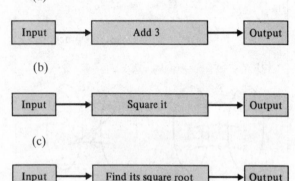

(b)

(c)

12. (a) Copy and complete each mapping below.

(i) + 4   (ii)   × 3

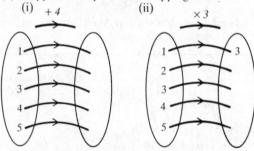

(b) Do you agree that each member of the domain is mapped to just one member of the co-domain?
Do you agree that each represents a function?

13. If x is a member of the domain of each function above, write down the corresponding member of the image set.

14. Using the rule $x \rightarrow x + 5$, draw an arrow graph to show the function, if the domain is:
(a) $\{1, 2, 3, 4, 5\}$ (b) $\{6, 9, 11, 13, 20\}$

15. Draw a mapping to show the function $x \rightarrow x - 2$ for the domain $\{10, 20, 30, 40, 50\}$

16. Draw a mapping to show the function $x \rightarrow 2x$ for the domain $\{1, 2, 3, 4, 5\}$

2.2 Function notation

The relation $x \rightarrow x + 4$ is a function. To save writing we can use a symbol to describe it.
We can write

$$f : x \rightarrow x + 4$$

This is read as:
"f is a function such that x maps to $x + 4$".
The function f is a type of operation. In this case the operation is simply *add four*.

1. Draw a mapping diagram for each function f, g, h, j, k and l over the given domains if:
(a) $f : x \rightarrow x + 1$ where $x \in \{1, 2, 3, 4\}$
(b) $g : x \rightarrow 4x$ where $x \in \{1, 3, 5, 7\}$
(c) $h : x \rightarrow 3x - 1$ where $x \in \{1, 2, 3, 4\}$
(d) $j : x \rightarrow x^2$ where $x \in \{2, 4, 6, 8\}$
(e) $k : x \rightarrow x^2 + 2$ where $x \in \{1, 2, 3, 4\}$
(f) $l : x \rightarrow 2(x + 1)$ where $x \in \{1, 3, 6, 9\}$

2. Functions f and g are represented below.
(i)   (ii)

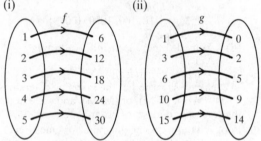

(a) Describe each function in the shorthand way.
(b) For each, write down the image of 3.

3. Make up a function of your own. Describe it in shorthand, then draw a mapping for it.

4. The function f is defined by $f : x \rightarrow 3x + 2$ where $x \in \{1, 2, 3, 4\}$
(a) What number in the image set does 2 map to?
(b) What is the image of 4?
(c) What number in the domain maps to 5?
(d) What number has 11 as its image?

5. (a) Look at the graph below. Write down the set of ordered pairs that describes the points.
(b) List the members of
   (i) the domain   (ii) the image set
(c) Do you agree that this graph represents a function? What is the rule?
(d) Describe the function in a short way.

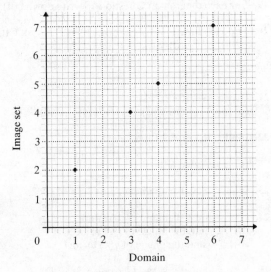

Domain

6. Look again at the graph in Question 5
(a) What number in the image set does 3 map to?
(b) What is the image of 6?
(c) What number in the domain maps to 2?
(d) What number has 5 as its image?

More shorthand

In Question 4 you found that the image of 4 when using $x \to 3x + 2$ was 14. We can write this as:

$$f(4) = 14$$

This is read as:
the image of 4 when using f is 14.

The function f operates on 4 by multiplying it by 3 and adding 2.
In the same way
$f(1) = 3 \times 1 + 2 = 5$ $f(2) = 3 \times 2 + 2 = 8$
$f(3) = 3 \times 3 + 2 = 11$ $f(x) = 3x + 2$

7. For each function, write down $f(1)$ and $f(^-1)$
(a) $f : x \to x + 1$ (b) $f : x \to x^2$
(c) $f : x \to 1 - x$ (d) $f : x \to x^2 - 1$
(e) $f : x \to x^2 + 5x + 6$

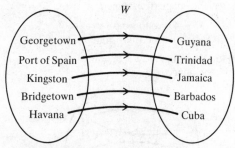

8. Look at the mapping diagram above.
(a) Is it a function? Why?
(b) What is the rule of the function?
(c) Which city is the capital of Trinidad?
(d) What is the image of Kingston?
(e) Which country is Havana the capital of?
(f) Which city has Guyana as its image?
(g) Do you agree that W (Kingston) = Jamaica?
(h) Write down:
   (i) W (Port of Spain)   (ii) W (Bridgetown)

Example

If $g : x \to 5x + 6$, for what value of x is $g(x) = 41$?
$$g(x) = 41$$
$$\Rightarrow\quad 5x + 6 = 41$$
$$\Rightarrow\quad 5x = 35$$
$$\Rightarrow\quad x = 7$$

---

9. The function f is defined by:
$f : x \to x^2 + 3$ where $x \in \{1, 2, 3, 4\}$.
Do you agree that $f(4) = 19$? Write down:
(a) $f(1)$ (b) $f(2)$ (c) $f(3)$
For what value of x is $f(x) = 7$?

10. The function g is defined by $g : x \to 3(x + 2)$ where $x \in \{1, 3, 5, 7\}$
Do you agree that $g(1) = 9$? Write down:
(a) $g(3)$ (b) $g(5)$ (c) $g(7)$
For what value of x is $g(x) = 21$?

11. M is the function in which
month $\to$ the number of days in month.
Write down:
(a) M (January)   (b) M (November)
For what month is M (month) = 28?

12. A function f is described using the information $f(x) = 5x + 1$.
(a) Is this a complete description of the function? Why?
(b) Do you agree that $f(10) = 51$? Write down:
   (i) $f(2)$ (ii) $f(5)$ (iii) $f(100)$
   (iv) $f(\frac{1}{2})$ (v) $f(a)$ (vi) $f(k + 1)$
(c) For what value of x is $f(x) = 41$?

Summary of function notation

f is the name, or label, of a function.

$f(x)$ is the image of x, using f.

$f : x \to x^2 - 4$ is read as
'f is a function such that x maps onto $x^2 - 4$'.

In the diagram below $f(x) = x^2 - 4$.
$f(3)$, the image of 3, is 5.

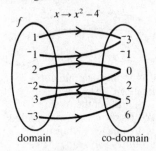

domain   co-domain

13. Using the diagram above, write down:
(a) the image of 2   (b) the image of $^-1$
(c) $f(1)$ (d) $f(^-2)$ (e) $f(^-3)$

14. For each function write down (a) $f(2)$;   (b) $f(7)$;
(c) $f(0)$;   (d) $f(^-3)$:
  (i) $f(x) = 7x - 4$ (ii) $f(x) = 4x + 19$
  (iii) $f(x) = 1 - 5x$ (iv) $f(x) = 4 - 3x$

15. For each function write down (a) $g(1)$;   (b) $g(2)$;
(c) $g(4)$;   (d) $g(\frac{1}{2})$:
  (i) $g(x) = x^2 + 5$ (ii) $g(x) = x^2 - x$
  (iii) $g(x) = 1 - x^3$ (iv) $g(x) = x + 1/x$

16. Copy and complete each diagram using the given
rule and the left-hand set as the domain:

(a) $f(x) = x + 5$ (b) $f(x) = 9x - 4$

2   4   14
3   7   2   33
5   8   9   77
7   10   13   113
           12   117

(c) $f(x) = 6 - 5x$

4   26
$^-2$ 16
2          $^-4$
$^-4$ $^-14$

17. For each diagram in Question 16 write down $f(2)$

18. Draw an arrow graph for the given rule and
domain:
(a) $g(x) = 7x + 11$, $\{0, 1, 4, 9\}$
(b) $g(x) = 1 - 6x$, $\{1, 2, 3, 4, 5\}$
(c) $g(x) = \frac{1}{4}x - 5$, $\{4, 8, 12, 16\}$
(d) $g(x) = x^2 + x$, $\{1, 2, 3, 4, 5\}$

19. For each diagram in Question 18 write down $g(4)$.

20. For each function write down: (a) $f(2)$;   (b) $f(10)$;
(c) $f(-3)$;   (d) $f(0)$:
  (i) $f : x \to 12x + 5$ (ii) $f : x \to 12 - 5x$
  (iii) $f : x \to x^2 - x$

21. If $k : x \to 1/x - 3$, find:
(a) $k(1)$ (b) $k(2)$ (c) $k(\frac{1}{2})$ (d) $k(\frac{1}{3})$

22. Find x, if $f(x) = 20$ and:
(a) $f : x \to 4x$ (b) $f : x \to x + 7$
(c) $f : x \to 3x + 2$

23. Find x, if $g(x) = 15$ and $g : x \to 2(x - 1) + 3$.

24. If $f : x \to x + 3$ and $g : x \to 5x$ find:
(a) $f(2)$ and the image of $f(2)$ using g
(b) $g(4)$ and the image of $g(4)$ using f.

25. Find x, if $h(x) = 40$ and $h : x \to 3(2x + 1) - 5$.

26. If $h : x \to 2x + 3$ and $k : x \to 4x - 1$, find:
(a) $h(7)$ and the image of $h(7)$ using k
(b) $k(11)$ and the image of $k(11)$ using h

2.3 Relations, equations and graphs

You will need . . .
You will need twenty matchsticks, some centimetre squared paper and a pair of scissors.

1. Arrange your matchsticks as in the diagram on the left below.

Second side

A rectangle

First side

Complete the rectangle as shown in the second diagram, using all twenty matchsticks.

We could record the information in the diagrams using the ordered pair (6, 4).
The 6 stands for the number of matches in the first side, the 4 stands for the number of matches in the second side.

2. Use your matchsticks to make a rectangle described by the ordered pair (3, 7).

3. Make as many other rectangles as you can, using all twenty matchsticks. Record each rectangle using an ordered pair like the one above.
Remember, the *First side* is always the one along the bottom.
So (4, 6) represents a different rectangle from (6, 4).

4. What can you say about the two numbers in each ordered pair in Question 3? Can you find a relationship between them?

5. Do your ordered pairs in Question 3 belong to the truth set for $\square \times \triangle = 20$ or for $\square + \triangle = 10$?

6. Do your ordered pairs in Question 3 represent a relation? If so, write down the domain and image set.

You should have found nine different rectangles, described by the nine ordered pairs:
(1, 9), (2, 8), (3, 7), (4, 6), (5, 5), (6, 4), (7, 3), (8, 2), (9, 1)

In each ordered pair, the sum of the two numbers is 10.
Using $\square$ and $\triangle$ for the two numbers, we can write:
$\square + \triangle = 10$.

$\square + \triangle = 10$ is a way of describing the relation, as long as you state the numbers that can be used in the $\square$.

7. The ordered pairs for a relation can be represented as $(\square, \triangle)$.
If you can use any of the numbers $\{1, 2, 3, 4, 5\}$ in the $\square$, write down the ordered pairs for the relation described by:
(a) $\square + \triangle = 8$ (b) $\square + \triangle = 5$ (c) $\square \times \triangle = 60$

8. The domain of each relation in Question 7 is the set of numbers which can be put in the $\square$.
The image set is the corresponding set of numbers used in the $\triangle$.
For each relation in Question 7, state the image set.

9. The ordered pairs in a relation can be represented as points on a graph like the one below, which shows $\square + \triangle = 10$.

Show the three relations in Question 7 in the same way. Use the same axes for all three, but different coloured pencils.

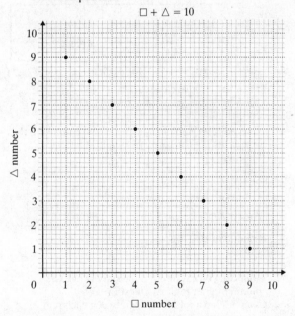

$\square + \triangle = 10$

10. Take some centimetre squared paper and carefully cut out 36 centimetre squares.
Arrange your 36 squares to form a rectangle as shown below.

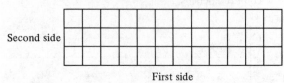

Second side

First side

(a) What is the area of each square?
(b) What is the area of the rectangle?

11. Now make as many rectangles as you can, using the 36 squares. Record each rectangle in a table like this one.

Length of first side (cm)	12			
Length of second side (cm)	3			
Area of rectangle (cm²)	36			

Remember that the *first side* is the one along the bottom.

12. What can you say about the numbers in each column of your table in Question 11?
Can you find a relationship between each pair of lengths, and the area?

13. Write the lengths for each rectangle in Question 8 as an ordered pair. Do the ordered pairs belong to the truth set for $\square + \triangle = 36$ or for $\square \times \triangle = 36$?

14. Do your ordered pairs in Question 13 represent a relation? If so, write down the domain and the image set.

15. Copy and complete the graph below to show the pairs which represent the relation $\square \times \triangle = 36$ in Question 13.

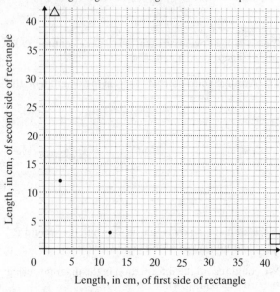

Edge lengths of rectangle made with 36 squares

16. What is the difference in shape between the graphs for Questions 9 and 15?

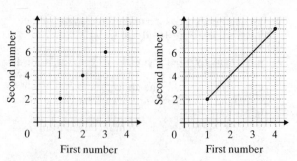

17. Look at the two graphs above.
Each represents a relation.
(a) Write down three ordered pairs for the first and three different ordered pairs for the second.
(b) For each, say what relationship is used.

18. (a) See if you can form a line by drawing lots of points very close together.
(b) Do you agree that a line is made up of an infinite number of points?
(c) Look again at the two graphs in Question 17. The first shows only four ordered pairs. Do you agree that the second shows an infinite number of ordered pairs?

19. (a) For each graph in Question 17 write down:
    (i) the domain of the relation
    (ii) the image set of the relation
  (b) Do you agree that the two relations in Question 17 use the same relationship but have different domains?

20. Draw a graph like those in Question 17 to show the relation defined by the given domain and relationship:
  (a) $\{1, 2, 3, 4\}$: *is a quarter of*
  (b) $\{1, 2, 3, 4\}$: *is two less than*
  (c) $\{any$ number between 1 and 4$\}$: *is a quarter of*
  (d) $\{any$ number between 1 and 4$\}$: *is two less than*

21. Show as a graph the relation whose domain is $\{1, 2, 3, 4, 5\}$ and whose ordered pairs belong to the truth set for:
  (a) $\square + \triangle = 6$ (b) $\square \times \triangle = 120$

22. In Question 21, what difference would it make to your graphs if the domain included *any* number between 1 and 5?

23. You can win a prize on the machine shown above if you score *15*.
To play, you put some money in, and press the handle down. The discs spin round. When they stop spinning, you add the numbers nearest the arrows. In how many ways can you make a score of 15?

24. (a) Write your results for Question 23 as a set of ordered pairs, (F, S). F represents the number on the first disc, and S represents the number on the second disc.
  (b) Write a statement which shows the connection between F and S.

25. The set of ordered pairs in Question 24 defines a relation. Write down:
  (a) the domain   (b) the image set.

26. For the machine in Question 23, write down the ordered pairs which belong to the truth set for:
  (a) $F + S = 12$
  (b) $F + S = 17$
  (c) $F \times S = 24$

27. For each of the relations defined in Question 26 write down:
  (i) the domain   (ii) the image set

28. Show each of your relations in Question 26 as points on a graph. Remember, there should be one point for each member of the domain.

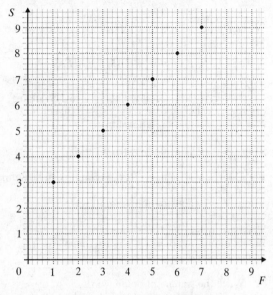

29. (a) Look at the set of points on the graph above. Copy the table below, and complete it for each point on the graph.

F	1	2	3	4	5	6	7
S							

  (b) Write a statement which shows the connection between F and S.

30. (a) Copy the table below and complete it by writing in the S values, if $S = F - 3$.

F	4	5	6	7	8	9
S						

  (b) Draw a graph like the one above to show these ordered pairs.

31. For the relations in Questions 29 and 30 write down: (a) the domain   (b) the image set

Some shorthand for a relation

In Question 24 on page 21, the ordered pairs are obtained by letting F and S take whole number values from 1 to 9, and by using the statement

$$F + S = 15$$

We can write this in a much shorter way using symbols, as shown below.

$$\{(F, S) \quad : \quad F + S = 15, \quad F, S \in N\}$$

a typical   such   statement   F and S belong
ordered   that   of   to set N
pair   relationship

where N = {whole numbers from 1 to 9}.

For Question 29 on page 21, the relation can be defined as $\{(F, S) : S = F + 2, \ F \in V\}$
where V = {whole numbers from 1 to 7}

This is read as:
the set of ordered pairs (F, S) such that $S = F + 2$, where F belongs to set V.

32. Write the statement out in words.
    (a) $\{(F, S) : F + S = 12, \ F, S \in N\}$
    (b) $\{(F, S) : S = F + 2, \ F \in V\}$
    (c) $\{(F, S) : S = 2F, \ F \in V\}$
    (d) $\{(F, S) : S = 2F - 1, \ F, S \in N\}$
    (e) $\{(F, S) : S = 2F - 3, \ F \in N\}$
    (f) $\{(F, S) : S = 0.5F + 1, \ F \in N\}$

33. Write down the ordered pairs for each relation in Question 32, if:
N = {whole numbers from 1 to 9}, and
V = {whole numbers from 1 to 7}

34. Write the statement out in words.
    (a) $\{(x, y) : x + y = 7, \ x \in W\}$
    (b) $\{(x, y) : y = 3x, \ x \in U\}$
    (c) $\{(x, y) : y = x - 1, \ x \in T\}$

35. If T = {whole numbers from 1 to 10}
      U = {0, 1, 2, 3, 4}
      W = {whole numbers from 1 to 6}
list the ordered pairs for each relation in Question 34.

36. x stands for the first number in the ordered pair.
y stands for the second number in the ordered pair.
Write an x, y statement to show the connection between the two numbers in each ordered pair.
    (a) {(0, 0), (1, 1), (2, 4), (3, 9), (4, 16)}
    (b) {(0, 1), (1, 2), (2, 5), (3, 10), (4, 17)}
    (c) {(0, 5), (1, 4), (2, 3), (3, 2), (4, 1)}
    (d) {(0, 0), (1, 4), (2, 8), (3, 12), (4, 16)}

37. Copy and complete for each relation defined in Question 36.
$\{(x, y) : \ldots \ldots \ldots \ldots, \ x \in U\}$
where U = { $\ldots \ldots \ldots \ldots$ }

38. (a) Write down the set of ordered pairs shown by the points on the graph below.
    (b) Show the connection between the two numbers in each ordered pair as an x, y statement.

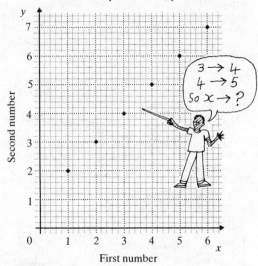

39. For Question 38, list the members of:
    (a) the domain   (b) the image set.

40. Define the relation in Question 38 by completing
$\{(x, y) : y = \ldots \ldots \ldots, \ x \in P\}$
where P = { $\ldots \ldots \ldots \ldots$ }

41. (a) Make up a relation of your own, and define it as in Question 40.
    (b) Write down the ordered pairs for your relation.
    (c) Draw a graph showing the relation.

2.4 Converting measurements

Converting units

1. Draw accurately lines 2″, 4″, 6″ and 8″ long.
   Measure these lines (accurately) in centimetres.
   Use your measurements to complete the mapping:
   2″ → 5.1 cm
   4″ →
   6″ →
   8″ →

2. (a) Does the diagram in Question 1 represent a function? Explain your answer.
   (b) Describe the function, using the shorthand shown on page 22.

3. Show the information in Question 1 as a graph on squared paper.
   (a) Is it correct to join the points? Why?
   (b) What is the domain of the function?
   (c) What is the image set?

4. If the name of the conversion function in Question 1 is V, write down:
   (a) V(2)   (b) V(6)   (c) V(8)
   Use your graph to help you to find:
   (d) V(1)   (e) V(3)   (f) V(7)

5. Use your graph in Question 3 to find the value of x for which V(x) is:
   (a) 4 cm   (b) 7 cm   (c) 12 cm   (d) 17 cm

6. Show the information in Question 5 as a graph for converting centimetres to inches.

7. If the name of the conversion function in Question 5 is W, write down:
   (a) W(4)   (b) W(12)   (c) W(17)
   Use your graph to help you to find:
   (d) W(9)   (e) W(14)   (f) W(22)

8. Check the accuracy of your graph by comparing your answers for questions 1 and 7.

So many dollars to get so few dollars!

FOREIGN EXCHANGE

Converting currencies

9. What is (a) sterling?   (b) the exchange rate for a currency?

10. Some exchange rates for sterling are shown. Below them is a machine for converting $Bd to £ sterling.

Today's rate for sterling
Bd $1 = £0.21
E.C. $1 = £0.16
G $1 = £0.16
J $1 = £0.23
T.T. $1 = £0.17
U.S. $1 = £0.42

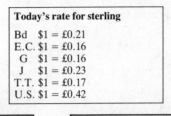

Input in $Bd → Multiply by 0.21 → Output in £

   (a) Check that the machine correctly converts $Bd to £ sterling. Does it produce a function? Explain.
   (b) Write down ordered pairs (input, output) if the domain is {$10, $20, $30, $40, $50}
   (c) Show your results in (b) as points on a graph.
   (d) Would it be correct to join the points with a straight line? Why?
   (e) If the function above is called B, use your graph to find:
       (i) B ($15)   (ii) B ($25)   (iii) B ($42)
   (f) How many Bd$ would you get for:
       (i) £5?   (ii) £2.50?   (iii) £8.75?

11. Draw a function machine for converting:
   (a) E.C. $ to £   (b) T.T. $ to £

12. If the input is {$10, $20, $30, $40, $50}, write a function for each machine in Question 11.

13. (a) Draw a function machine for converting:
       (i) J $ to £   (ii) U.S. $ to £
   (b) Draw a reverse machine, that will convert:
       (i) £ to J $ (ii) £ to U.S. $

14. Use your machines in Question 13 (b) to help you complete, to two decimal places:
   (a) £1 = J $ □   (b) £1 = U.S. $□
   (c) J $1 = U.S. $□

15. (a) Using your results in Question 14, write a function for converting J $ into U.S. $. The domain is {$10, $20, $30, $40, $50}
   (b) Write down the ordered pairs that describe the function.
   (c) Draw a graph showing the function.
   (d) If the function is J, find
       (i) J ($15)   (ii) J ($38)   (iii) J ($47)

Summary

By the end of this chapter, these are the things you should know about.

2.1 Mapping diagrams (pages 14–16)

How to draw an arrow diagram for a mapping over a given domain.

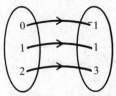

Domain   Co-domain
$$x \to 2x - 1$$

Mappings can be described as **one to one, many-to-one, one-to-many** or **many-to-many.**
A **function** is a one-to-one or many-to-one mapping:

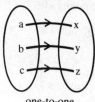   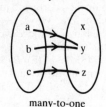

one-to-one   many-to-one
   map   map

2.2 Function notation (pages 16–18)

A function can be described in shorthand.
For example:
$f : x \to x + 5$ where $x \in \{1, 2, 3, 4, 5\}$
This is read as:
f is a function such that x maps to $x + 5$, where x
belongs to the set of whole numbers from 1 to 5. Using
the function f above we can write:
$f(1) = 6, f(2) = 7, f(3) = 8$ and so on.

2.3 Relations and graphs (pages 19–22)

A relation can be shown as:
 (i) one set and arrows showing the relationship between its members.
 (ii) two sets and arrows showing the relationship between their members.
(iii) a set of ordered pairs.
(iv) a set of points on a graph.
 (v) the domain and the relationship – you can then find the image set
(vi) a statement showing the connection between the two numbers in the ordered pair, and the values that the numbers may take.
      For example, $F + S = 15$
      where $F, S \in \{$whole numbers from 1 to 15$\}$

A relation can be written in shorthand. For example:
$\{(F, S) : F + S = 15, \ F, S \in N\}$
where $N = \{$whole numbers from 1 to 9$\}$
This is read as:
the ordered pair (F, S) such that $F + S = 15$,
and both F and S belong to N, the set of whole numbers from 1 to 9.

2.4 Converting measurements (page 23)

How to write a conversion function for converting one set of units to another, or one currency to another.

3 Graphs I

3.I Revision

Reading graphs

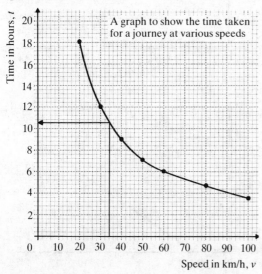

Example 1

The graph shows the time taken to travel 360 km at various speeds. How long is the journey if the speed is 34 km/h?

From the graph, it is seen that the time taken is about 10.5 hours.

1. The graph shows the temperature of a room between 6 a.m. and 6 p.m.

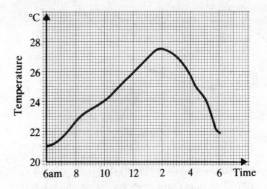

(a) When was the temperature 21°C?
(b) What was the highest temperature?
(c) At what time was the temperature greatest?
(d) At what time was the temperature 25°C?

2. The graph shows the time it takes to roast different masses of chicken.

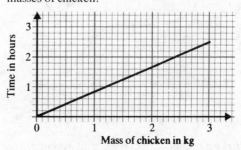

(a) How long does it take to roast 2 kg of chicken?
(b) How much chicken can be roasted in 2 hours?
(c) Estimate the time it would take to roast 4 kg of chicken.

3. The graph shows the distance a man is from his
   home at different times.

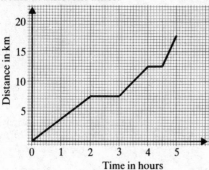

   (a) How far from his home is he after 1 hour?
   (b) What is he doing during the second hour?
   (c) How long does it take him to travel 15 km?
   (d) When is he moving the fastest?

4. The graph shows the number of thousands of
   bacteria present in a dish at different times.

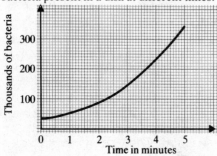

   (a) How many bacteria are in the dish initially?
   (b) How many bacteria are in the dish after
       3 minutes?
   (c) When are there 200 000 bacteria present?
   (d) How many new bacteria are produced during
       the fourth minute?

5. The graph shows the cooling curve of a liquid.

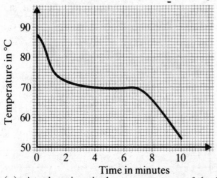

   (a) At what time is the temperature of the liquid
       75°C?
   (b) What is the temperature after 9 minutes?
   (c) When is the temperature drop most rapid?
   (d) Why do you think the temperature may be the
       same between the fourth and sixth minute?
       Ask your science teacher.

Plotting graphs

Example 2

The length in centimetres of a spring which has
different masses placed on it is given in the table.

L (cm)	3.5	5.9	7.4	8.6	13.1
M (kg)	0.4	1.2	1.7	2.1	3.6

Plot a graph of this relation.
First look at the range of values of L and M.
That is
  L varies from about 0 to 14 and
  M varies from about 0 to 4.
Then choose a suitable scale for each axis which
uses these values.
Make sure the scales are linear.
On the horizontal L-axis, a scale of 1 cm is used
to represent 2 cm. On the vertical M-axis, a scale
of 1 cm is used to represent 1 kg.

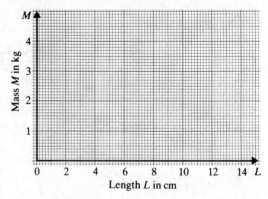

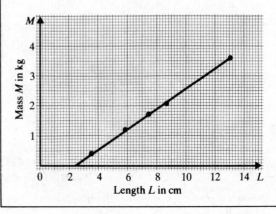

6. The relationship between the potential difference
V across a resistor and the current I passing
through it is shown on the graph.

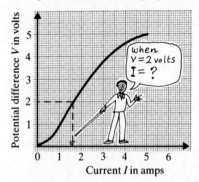

(a) What is the current when $V = 2$ volts?
(b) What is the potential difference when the
current is 3.5 amps?
(c) How much does the potential difference
increase as the current is increased from 2 to
3 amps?

7. A stone travels the following distances when
dropped down a mountain.

time (s)	1	2	3	4	5	6	7	8
distance (m)	0.4	7.2	20.4	40	66	98.4	137.2	182.4

(a) Using a scale of 1 cm to represent 1 s on the
horizontal axis and 1 cm to represent 20 m on
the vertical axis, plot the graph.
(b) Use your graph to find the time the stone takes
to travel 100 m.

8. The cost of spraying bananas per hectare is given in
the table below.

number of hectares	1	2	3	4	5	6	7	8
cost in dollars	22.50	40	57.50	75	92.50	110	127.50	145

(a) Plot the graph using a scale of 1 cm to represent
1 hectare on the horizontal axis and a scale of
1 cm to represent $20 on the vertical axis.
(b) How much will it cost to spray $5\frac{1}{2}$ hectares?
(c) How many hectares of bananas can be sprayed
for $50?

9. The height of a plant at different days after planting
is given in the table below.

days after planting	5	9	17	22	28	36
height (cm)	1.2	2.16	4.08	5.28	6.72	8.64

(a) Plot the graph, using a scale of 1 cm to
represent 5 days on the horizontal axis and 1 cm
to represent 1 cm on the vertical axis.
(b) What was the height of the plant after 15 days?
(c) Estimate how long after planting will the plant
be 10 cm tall?

10. The volumes of different masses of a certain liquid
are shown in the table.

mass (g)	30.6	53.7	85	113	146.7	189
volume (cm³)	35.8	62.8	99.4	132.2	171.6	221.1

(a) Plot the graph, using a scale of 1 cm to
represent 20 g on the horizontal axis and 1 cm
to represent 20 cm³ on the vertical axis.
(b) What is the mass of 100 cm³ of the liquid?
(c) What is the mass of 1 cm³ of the liquid (its
density)?

11. The volume of a certain mass of gas at different
pressures is given in the table below.

volume of gas (cm³)	21	20.6	20.1	19.7	19.2	18.9	18.6
pressure of gas (cm of mercury)	71	72.3	74	75.6	77.3	78.9	80

(a) Plot the graph, using a scale of 2 cm to
represent 1 cm³ on the horizontal axis and 1 cm
to represent 1 cm of mercury on the vertical
axis. (Do not try and put the origin $(0, 0)$ on
your graph!)
(b) What is the volume of gas at atmospheric
pressure (76 cm of mercury)?
(c) Estimate the pressure required to reduce the
volume to 18 cm³.

12. The sine of an angle is given by the table.

angle $x°$	0	10	20	30	40	50	60	70	80	90
sin $x°$	0	0.17	0.34	0.5	0.64	0.77	0.87	0.94	0.98	1.00

(a) Plot the graph of sin x, using a scale of 1 cm to
represent 10° on the horizontal axis and 1 cm to
represent 0.1 on the vertical axis.
(b) Use your trigonometric tables to draw graphs
of cos x and tan x for $0° \leqslant x \leqslant 90°$.

3.2 Linear relations

Linear graphs

A set of points which can be joined by a straight line is called a linear graph.

1. Plot these sets of points
   (a) $(^-2, 1), (^-1, 1), (0, 1), (1, 1), (2, 1)$
   (b) $(1, 4), (2, 5), (3, 6), (4, 7), (5, 8)$
   (c) $(^-1, 11), (0, 10), (1, 9), (2, 8), (3, 7)$
   (d) $(^-2, ^-1), (0, 3), (2, 7), (4, 11), (6, 15)$
   (e) $(^-2, 4), (^-1, 1), (0, 0), (1, 1), (2, 4)$

   Which set represents a linear relation?

Example 3

Find the relationship between the points $(0, 2)$, $(1, 5), (2, 8), (3, 11)$

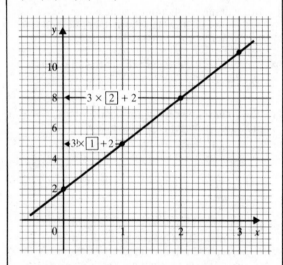

The coordinates are shown on the graph. They lie on a straight line so it is a linear relation.
Each y-coordinate is found by multiplying each x-coordinate by 3 and adding 2.
That is $y = 3x + 2$

---

2. Find the relationships between these sets of points.
   (a) $(0, 0), (1, 2), (2, 4), (3, 6)$
   (b) $(0, 1), (1, 2), (2, 3), (3, 4)$
   (c) $(0, ^-1), (1, 0), (2, 1), (3, 2)$
   (d) $(0, 2), (1, 4), (2, 6), (3, 8)$
   (e) $(0, ^-3), (1, ^-1), (2, 1), (3, 3)$
   (f) $(0, 3), (1, 3), (2, 3), (3, 3)$

Example 4

Plot the graph of the relation $y = 2x - 1$ for $x = ^-2$ to $x = 4$
First complete the table of values for each value of x

x	$^-2$	$^-1$	0	1	2	3	4
$2x$	$^-4$	$^-2$	0	2	4	6	8
$^-1$	$^-1$	$^-1$	$^-1$	$^-1$	$^-1$	$^-1$	$^-1$
y	$^-5$	$^-3$	$^-1$	1	3	5	7

The points which satisfy the relation $y = 2x - 1$ are $(^-2, ^-5), (^-1, ^-3), (0, ^-1), (1, 1), (2, 3), (3, 5), (4, 7)$.
The graph is:

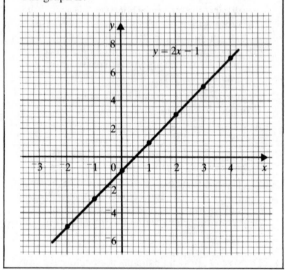

3. Copy and complete the table for $y = 3x + 2$.

   Draw the graph of $y = 3x + 2$ using a scale of 1 cm to represent 1 unit on the x-axis and 1 cm to represent 2 units on the y-axis.

x	$^-2$	$^-1$	0	1	2	3	4
$3x$	$^-6$		0			9	
$+2$	$^+2$		$^+2$		$^+2$		
y	$^-4$						14

4. For each of the following, draw up tables of values for $x = ^-2$ to $x = 4$
   (a) $y = 2x$ (b) $y = x + 4$
   (c) $y = 2x + 4$ (d) $y = 3x - 4$

5. Using a scale of 1 cm to represent 1 unit on the x-axis and 1 cm to represent 2 units on the y-axis, plot the graphs of the relations in Question 4.

6. Using suitable scales, plot the graphs of the following relations for $x = {}^-3$ to $x = 3$.
   (a) $y = 5x - 9$ (b) $y = \frac{1}{2}x + 2$
   (c) $y = 6 - x$ (d) $y = 12 - 2x$

7. (a) Show that the relation $x + y = 8$ can be rewritten as $y = 8 - x$.
   (b) Hence plot the graph of $x + y = 8$ for $x = 0$ to $x = 8$.

8. (a) Show that the relation $x + 2y = 8$ can be rewritten as $y = 4 - \frac{1}{2}x$
   (b) Copy and complete the table for this relation.

x	$^-2$	$^-1$	0	1	2	3	4
	4	4	4				
$-\frac{1}{2}x$	1			$-\frac{1}{2}$			$^-2$
y	5	$4\frac{1}{2}$		3			

   (c) Hence, using a suitable scale, plot the graph of $x + 2y = 8$

9. Using the method of Question 8, plot the graphs of
   (a) $x + 2y = 6$ (b) $2x + y = 10$
   (c) $x - 3y = 9$ (d) $4x + 3y = 12$
   for $x = {}^-2$ to $x = 4$.

10. (a) A gallon of petrol costs $6.50. Copy and complete the table for gas costs.

number of gallons (g)	0	1	2	3	4	5	6
Cost (c) $	0	6.50	13.00				

   (b) Using a suitable scale, plot this graph.
   (c) From your graph find:
      (i) the price of $4\frac{1}{2}$ gallons of petrol
      (ii) how much petrol can be bought for $20.
   (d) Write down the equation of the graph in terms of g and c.

Linear laws

On a certain island, the monthly charge for a telephone is $5, plus 12 cents per unit of telephone time used. The graph below shows the cost of using 0, 100, 200, 300, 400 and 500 units.

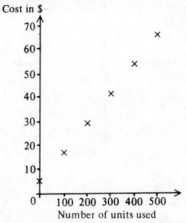

A graph such as this where the points lie on a straight line represents a *linear relation*.

11. Represent the information as a graph and hence find whether the graph represents a linear relation or not.

(a)
Number of litres	Cost of gas in cents
1	22
2	44
3	66
4	88
5	110
6	132

(b)
Number of miles	Cost of hiring taxi in cents
0	50
1	62
2	74
3	86
4	98
5	110
6	122

(c)
Length of side of square in cm	Area of square in cm^2
1.2	1.44
1.7	2.89
2.1	4.41
2.5	6.25
3.0	9.00
3.6	12.96

(d)
Time for journey in hours	Distance travelled in km
1	32
2	64
3	100
4	128
5	160
6	200
7	224

12. In those parts of Question 11 where the graph represents a linear relation, write down the (x, y) equation which describes the information.

13. The information given represents a linear relation. Show this on a graph and hence complete the table.

(a)

Time for journey in hours	Distance travelled in km
1	83
2	166
3	
4	332
5	
6	498
7	

(b)

Number of hectares	Cost of spraying in $
0	5
1	22.50
2	
3	57.50
4	
5	
6	110
7	

(c)

Time taken in hours	Distance from home in km
0	
1	172
2	
3	116
4	
5	60
6	32
7	

14. For each part of Question 13, write down the (x, y) equation which describes the information.

15. A gas station sells gas at a rate of 22 cents per litre. There is a reduction of 2 c per litre if you buy a multiple of 5 litres. Show on a graph: (a) the cost of buying 5, 10, 15, 20, 25, 30, 35 and 40 litres; (b) the cost of buying 6, 12, 18, 24, 30, 36 and 42 litres. Which of these represents a linear relation?

3.3 Solving simultaneous equations graphically

The point $(1, 2)$ lies on the line $y = 2x$.
It also lies on the line $x + y = 3$.
So the values $x = 1, y = 2$ satisfy both the equations $y = 2x$ and $x + y = 3$ at the same time.
Equations like these which have a common solution are called *simultaneous* equations.
The pair of simultaneous equations
$$y = 2x \text{ and } x + y = 3$$
have $x = 1$ and $y = 2$ as their common solution.

Example

Plot the graphs of
$$x + y = 6$$
$$x - y = 2$$
Hence find the solution to this pair of equations.

The table of values for $x = 0$ to $x = 6$ are

$$x + y = 6$$

x	0	1	2	3	4	5	6
y	6	5	4	3	2	1	0

and

$$x - y = 2$$

x	0	1	2	3	4	5	6
y	$^-2$	$^-1$	0	1	2	3	4

Plotting both relations on the same graph gives:

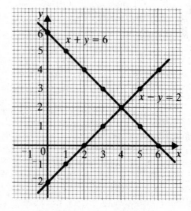

Line Ⓐ gives the solutions to $x + y = 6$ and
Line Ⓑ gives the solutions to $x - y = 2$.
So the points that lie on both lines are solutions to both equations.
Here there is only one point, $(4, 2)$ on both lines.
So the solution to both equations is $x = 4, y = 2$.

1. Plot the graphs of
   $y = 2x - 1$
   $y = x + 1$
   Hence find the solution to this pair of equations.

2. Draw graphs for each pair of equations, and find
   the solution.
   (a) $y = x + 4$
        $y = 6 - x$
   (b) $y = 3 - x$
        $y = 3 - 3x$
   (c) $y = 2x$
        $y = x + 1$
   (d) $y = 2x + 1$
        $y = x - 5$
   (e) $y = 2x$
        $y = x + 2$
   (f) $y = x + 3$
        $y = 2x + 1$

3. Draw each pair of lines on the same graph. Find the
   point of intersection. Show this point satisfies both
   equations.
   (a) $y = 2x$
        $y = 8 - x$
   (b) $y = 2x - 4$
        $y = x + 1$
   (c) $y = 3x - 2$
        $y = x + 4$
   (d) $y = 4x - 3$
        $y = 2x + 2$

4. Draw each pair of lines on the same graph. Find the
   point of intersection. Show this point satisfies both
   equations.
   (a) $y = 5x - 7$
        $y = 5 - x$
   (b) $y = 2x + 3$
        $y = 13 - 3x$
   (c) $y = 5x - 4$
        $y = 3x - 1$
   (d) $y = 7 - x$
        $y = 12 - 3x$

5. Plot the graphs of
   $y = 3x - 1$
   $y = 3x + 2$
   Why is there no solution to this pair of equations?

6. Write down the (x, y) equation which describes
   each set of ordered pairs. Check that the common
   ordered pair satisfies both equations.
   (a) $\{(0, 0), (1, 2), (2, 4), (3, 6), (4, 8), (5, 10)\}$,
        $\{(0, 6), (1, 5), (2, 4), (3, 3), (4, 2), (5, 1),$
        $(6, 0)\}$
   (b) $\{(0, 3), (1, 5), (2, 7), (3, 9), (4, 11), (5, 13)\}$,
        $\{(0, ^-2), (1, 1), (2, 4), (3, 7), (4, 10), (5, 13)\}$

7. Show each set of ordered pairs on the same graph.
   Find the point of intersection of the two lines.
   Write down the (x, y) equation for each line. Show
   that the common point satisfies both equations.
   (a) $\{(1, 6), (2, 5), (3, 4), (4, 3), (5, 2), (6, 1)\}$,
        $\{(1, 4), (2, 7), (3, 10), (4, 13), (5, 16), (6, 19)\}$
   (b) $\{(0, 1), (1, 3), (2, 5), (3, 7), (4, 9), (5, 11)\}$,
        $\{(0, ^-4), (1, 0), (2, 4), (3, 8), (4, 12), (5, 16)\}$

8. Find the point of intersection of the two lines:
   (a) $y = 3x + 1$
        $y = 2x - 3$
   (b) $y = x + 1$
        $y = 2 - x$
   (c) $y = \frac{1}{2}x + \frac{1}{2}$
        $y = 4 - 3x$
   (d) $y = 2x + 1$
        $y = 6 - 2x$

9. The diagram shows the graphs of $y = x - 1$ and
   $y = 10 - 3x$.

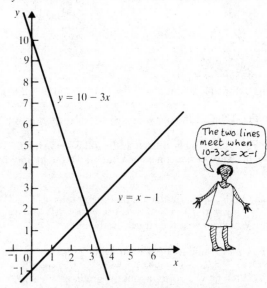

(a) Which of the following is the correct value of x
   where the lines intersect?
   $2\frac{1}{2}, 2\frac{3}{4}, 1\frac{7}{10}, 3\frac{1}{4}, 2\frac{1}{3}$
(b) Find the corresponding value of y.

10. Use the diagram in Question 9 to solve the
    simultaneous equations:
    (a) $y = x - 1$
         $x = 0$
    (b) $y = x - 1$
         $y = 0$
    (c) $y = 10 - 3x$
         $x = 0$
    (d) $y = 10 - 3x$
         $y = 0$

11. Draw graphs for each pair of equations and find
    their solution.
    (a) $2x + y = 9$
         $3x + 2y = 14$
    (b) $x + 3y = 7$
         $3x - 2y = ^-1$

3.4 Gradients

Fig. 1 Small gradient   Fig. 2 Large gradient

In Fig. 1 the incline shown is easy to walk up. It is not very steep.
In Fig. 2 climbing is difficult as the hill is very steep.
We measure the steepness of a hill, or a straight line, by its gradient.

1. On the same set of axes, plot the graphs of:
   (a) $y = x$ (b) $y = 2x$ (c) $y = 3x$ (d) $y = 4x$
   Which line has the largest gradient?

2. On the same set of axes, draw the graphs of:
   (a) $y = 2x - 1$ (b) $y = 2x$ (c) $y = 2x + 1$
   What do you notice about the gradient of each?

We define the steepness of a line, or its gradient, as follows:

$$\text{gradient} = \frac{\text{vertical rise}}{\text{horizontal shift}}$$

Example 1

Find the gradient of the line $y = 2x + 1$.

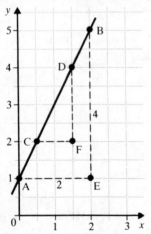

Choose two points A (0, 1) and B (2, 5) on the line.

$$\text{gradient} = \frac{\text{Vertical rise}}{\text{Horizontal shift}} = \frac{\text{BE}}{\text{AE}}$$

$$= \frac{5 - 1}{2 - 0} = \frac{4}{2} = 2$$

Note: In the example it does not matter which two points are chosen on the line.
If we choose, instead, the points C(0.5, 2) and D(1.5,4) the right-angled triangle is CDF, and

$$\text{gradient} = \frac{\text{DF}}{\text{CF}} = \frac{4-2}{1.5-0.5} = \frac{2}{1} = 2$$

3. (a) Find the gradients of the line graphs in Question 1.
   (b) Copy and complete the table

Equation of line	Gradient
$y = x$	
$y = 2x$	
$y = 3x$	
$y = 4x$	

   (c) What do you notice?

4. Find the gradients of the line graphs in Question 2.

5. (a) Plot the points A (1, 2) and B (5, 6) on a suitable pair of axes.
   (b) Join the points with a straight line.
   (c) Find the gradient of this line AB.

In Question 5, the gradient of AB can be found more simply by noting that

$$\text{gradient} = \frac{\text{Vertical rise}}{\text{Horizontal shift}}$$

$$= \frac{\text{increase in value of } y}{\text{corresponding increase in value of } x}$$

$$= \frac{6-2}{5-1} = \frac{4}{4} = 1$$

Example 2

Find the gradient of the line joining (1, 4) to (3, ⁻2).

$$\text{Gradient} = \frac{\text{increase in value of } y}{\text{corresponding increase in value of } x}$$

$$= \frac{^-2 - 4}{3 - 1} = \frac{^-6}{2} = ^-3$$

The negative gradient indicates a downward slope.

---

6. Find the gradients of the lines joining these pairs of points.
   (a) (4, 2) and (8, 10)   (b) (3, 1) and (4, 3)
   (c) (⁻3, ⁻2) and (4, 5)   (d) (4, 2) and (1, ⁻3)
   (e) (⁻2, 3) and (3, 3)   (f) (4, 7) and (4, 3)

7. The Downtown Youth Club found that its committee meetings took longer if more members were present. This table shows how long some meetings took:

Number present (x)	5	10	15	20
Time taken in minutes (y)	25	40	55	70

(a) Draw a graph of the time taken against the number present. Does the graph show a linear relation?
(b) Where does the graph cut the y-axis?
(c) Find the gradient of the graph
(d) What information does the gradient give us?

8. In an experiment, a spring is stretched by hanging weights on its end. Here are the results:

x : Weights (kg)	5	10	20	25
y : Length of spring (cm)	22	24	28	30

(a) Draw a graph of the results of the experiment.
(b) What is the unstretched length of the spring? How can you tell?
(c) Find the gradient of the graph.
(d) By how much is the spring extended for each addition of 1 kg?

Using gradients to find linear laws

The graph below shows a set of measurements collected during an experiment. If a line can be drawn through, or close to all the points it can be used to find the *Linear Law* which the data may satisfy, by reading off the gradient and the intercept on the y-axis.

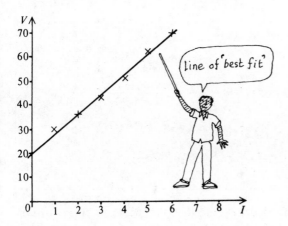

Note: When drawing the line it is usually best to make sure that the same number of points lie on each side of the line: the line of 'best fit'.

9. The data in the graph above approximately satisfies the relation $V = E + IR$. Use the values of the gradient and intercept on the y-axis to find E and R.

10. Show the information given below on a graph. Draw a line to show how the information approximates to a linear law. Use this line to state the likely law connecting s and t.

(a)

t	s
1.2	16.4
2.5	34.1
2.9	39.5
3.4	46.4

(b)

t	s
1.8	6.2
2.3	8.1
3.1	10.8
3.8	13.4
4.7	16.5

11. The values of C and n are connected by the linear relation $C = I + Pn$. The data on the right was collected in an experiment.
Show the information on a graph and hence find the most likely values for I and P.

n	C
2.4	22.6
3.4	27.9
4.3	32.7
5.7	40.1
7.4	49.0
9.5	60.1
11.9	72.7
15.0	89.0

12. Find, by drawing a graph, which of the values given on the right seems to indicate that an error was made when collecting data satisfying the linear law $E = 0.51\,W + 3$.

W	E
12	9.2
15	10.6
19	11.1
23	14.7
28	17.3
31	18.8
36	21.4

Use your graph to find a more likely value for the wrong value of E.

13. Find, by drawing a graph, which two of the values given on the right seem to indicate that an error was made when collecting the data.

W	E
0.2	8.8
0.5	7.7
0.9	6.4
1.1	6.0
1.6	3.9
1.9	2.8
2.4	1.1
2.7	0.6

Assuming the data fits the linear law $E = aW + b$, find from your graph the most likely values of a and b and hence find a better value for the two inaccurate results.

Summary

By the end of this chapter, you should know about
these things.

3.1 Revision (pages 25–27)

How to read and obtain information from a variety of
line graphs.
How to plot graphs from a table of information.
How to choose an appropriate scale to use for your
graph.

3.2 Linear relations (pages 28–30)

That when a set of points can be joined by a straight
line they belong to a linear relation.
Determining whether a set of points represents a linear
relation.
Finding simple relationships when given sets of points.
Completing tables of values and drawing graphs for
$y = 3x + 2$ etc.
Representing information as a graph and finding
whether it is a linear law or not.

3.3 Solving simultaneous equations graphically
(pages 30–31)

The idea that the solution to a pair of equations can be
found by drawing their graphs and finding the point of
intersection.
The idea of finding the common ordered pair which
satisfies both equations.
Solving a pair of simultaneous equations by drawing
their graphs.

3.4 Gradients (pages 32–33)

The idea of the gradient as a measure of the steepness
of a line.
Finding gradients as

$$\frac{\text{vertical rise}}{\text{horizontal shift}}$$

Finding a gradient using the co-ordinates of points.

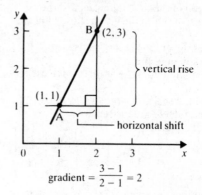

$$\text{gradient} = \frac{3 - 1}{2 - 1} = 2$$

The idea of a negative gradient for a line sloping
backwards i.e.
Using gradients to find information from graphs.

4 Computation and number

4.1 Calculating with fractions – revision

Addition:

$$\frac{2}{3} + \frac{1}{2} = \frac{4}{6} + \frac{3}{6} = \frac{7}{6} = 1\frac{1}{6}$$

Subtraction:

$$\frac{2}{3} - \frac{1}{2} = \frac{4}{6} - \frac{3}{6} = \frac{1}{6}$$

Multiplication:

$$\frac{2}{3} \times \frac{1}{2} = \frac{\cancel{2}^{1}}{3} \times \frac{1}{\cancel{2}_{1}} = \frac{1 \times 1}{3 \times 1} = \frac{1}{3}$$

Division:

$$\frac{2}{3} \div \frac{1}{2} = \frac{2}{3} \times \frac{2}{1} = \frac{2 \times 2}{3 \times 1} = \frac{4}{3} = 1\frac{1}{3}$$

1. Calculate and simplify your answer.
(a) $\frac{3}{8} + \frac{5}{8}$ (b) $\frac{3}{8} + \frac{1}{2}$
(c) $\frac{1}{4} + \frac{2}{3}$ (d) $\frac{1}{5} + \frac{2}{3}$
(e) $\frac{9}{10} - \frac{1}{2}$ (f) $\frac{7}{8} - \frac{1}{4}$
(g) $\frac{7}{8} - \frac{1}{3}$ (h) $\frac{2}{3} - \frac{1}{9}$

2. Calculate and simplify your answer.
(a) $1\frac{1}{4} + 2\frac{1}{5}$ (b) $3\frac{1}{2} + \frac{7}{8}$
(c) $3\frac{1}{2} + 2\frac{2}{3}$ (d) $10\frac{1}{2} + 11\frac{5}{8}$
(e) $2\frac{3}{4} - 2\frac{1}{4}$ (f) $2\frac{3}{4} - 1\frac{1}{8}$
(g) $2\frac{1}{8} - 1\frac{3}{4}$ (h) $2\frac{1}{5} - 1\frac{3}{4}$

3. Multiply and simplify your answer.
(a) $\frac{2}{3} \times \frac{1}{3}$ (b) $\frac{2}{3} \times \frac{1}{2}$ (c) $\frac{3}{4} \times \frac{2}{3}$
(d) $1\frac{1}{2} \times \frac{2}{3}$ (e) $2\frac{1}{2} \times \frac{4}{5}$ (f) $\frac{3}{4} \times 2$

4. Divide and simplify your answer.
(a) $\frac{1}{3} \div \frac{1}{2}$ (b) $\frac{3}{4} \div \frac{2}{3}$ (c) $\frac{1}{5} \div \frac{1}{10}$
(d) $\frac{3}{4} \div 2$ (e) $1\frac{1}{2} \div 3$ (f) $\frac{1}{9} \div \frac{1}{3}$

5. Work out:
(a) $(1\frac{1}{2})^2$ (b) $2\frac{1}{4} \times 1\frac{1}{2} \times \frac{1}{3}$
(c) $6 \times (1\frac{2}{3} + 1\frac{1}{2})$ (d) $(2\frac{5}{6} + 3\frac{1}{4}) \div 4$
(e) $3\frac{3}{4} - 1\frac{7}{8} + \frac{1}{2}$ (f) $\frac{5}{8} - \frac{7}{9} + \frac{1}{3}$

6. Calculate:
(a) $2\frac{7}{10} \div 1\frac{7}{15}$ (b) $\frac{3}{8}$ of $1\frac{1}{2}$
(c) $3\frac{1}{8} \times \frac{4}{5} \div 1\frac{1}{2}$ (d) $2\frac{2}{3} \div 2\frac{2}{5} \times 1\frac{1}{2}$
(e) $\dfrac{3\frac{1}{2}}{1\frac{1}{2} + 2\frac{1}{4}}$ (f) $\dfrac{2\frac{1}{2} \times \frac{7}{8}}{6 - \frac{3}{4}}$
(g) $\dfrac{3\frac{7}{8} - 1\frac{5}{6}}{2\frac{3}{4} - 1\frac{2}{3}}$ (h) $\dfrac{6\frac{7}{9} - 4\frac{8}{9}}{3\frac{1}{2} + 1\frac{3}{5}}$

7. (a) How many lengths of $1\frac{1}{2}$ m may be cut from a length of 18 m?
(b) How many lengths of $1\frac{1}{2}$ m may be cut from a length of 20 m? Is there any left over?

8. (a) How many quarters in 16?
(b) How many thirds in 3?
(c) What is a tenth of ten?
(d) What is three-tenths of three?

9. (a) Find a tenth of three-quarters of $800.
(b) Find three-quarters of a tenth of $800.

4.2 Calculating with decimals – revision

Fractions like ½ or ⅔ are called **common** or **vulgar**. This just means that they are ordinary fractions.

Fractions with a denominator of 10 or 100 or 1000 or any power of 10 are called **decimal fractions** or, simply, **decimals**.

$\frac{3}{10}$ is a decimal fraction.

Decimal fractions can be written in a different way like this:

$$\frac{3}{10} = 0.3 \qquad \frac{3}{100} = 0.03$$

$$\frac{43}{100} = 0.43 \qquad \frac{143}{100} = 1.43$$

Adding and subtracting decimals

It is important to keep the decimal points in a line.

```
   13.26          13.26
    1.59        −  6.59
 +  4.23          ─────
 ───────           6.67
   19.08
```

1. Find:
   (a) 1.7 + 2.1   (b) 2.9 + 3.3
   (c) 2.8 − 1.6   (d) 7.5 − 4.5
   (e) 17.5 + 27.6   (f) 28.3 − 14.7

2. Find:
   (a) 2.36 + 3.23   (b) 5.97 + 1.03
   (c) 8.53 + 7.68   (d) 9.75 − 4.63
   (e) 2.66 − 1.04   (f) 100 − 67.7

3. Find:
   (a) 2.1 + 0.21 + 3.07
   (b) 6.13 + 7.5 + 0.68
   (c) 7.04 + 8.13 − 4.69
   (d) 0.612 + 0.735 + 0.416
   (e) 17.064 − 8.192
   (f) 0.007 + 0.011 + 0.123

Multiplying decimals

Example 1

6.1̲2 × 3.4̲

612 × 34 = 20 808
So the result is 20.8̲0̲8̲

The number of places following the decimal point is 3 because the sum of the number of places in the numbers being multiplied is 3.

It is also useful to check.

$6 \times 3 = 18$.

So an answer of about 20 is the right size.

4. Calculate:
   (a) 0.3 × 7   (b) 1.2 × 4   (c) 6.3 × 8
   (d) 0.21 × 3   (e) 2.76 × 8   (f) 17.26 × 9
   (g) 1.26 × 10   (h) 1.9 × 100   (i) 2.3 × 50

5. Calculate:
   (a) 0.3 × 0.4   (b) 0.6 × 1.2   (c) 3.1 × 0.1
   (d) 1.21 × 3.1   (e) 6.5 × 2.65   (f) 4.2 × 3.2
   (g) 8.04 × 0.04   (h) 7.3 × 0.06   (i) 3.62 × 1.07

Dividing decimals

You first need to make the number you divide by into a whole number.

Example 2

$$\frac{6.88}{1.6} = \frac{68.8}{16} \quad \text{multiply 'top' and 'bottom' by 10}$$

$$= \frac{34.4}{8} \quad \text{cancelling}$$

$$= 4.3$$

6. Find:
   (a) 0.8 ÷ 4   (b) 1.6 ÷ 2   (c) 2.8 ÷ 7
   (d) 0.64 ÷ 4   (e) 0.08 ÷ 4   (f) 2.184 ÷ 7

7. Find:
   (a) 7 ÷ 0.1   (b) 8 ÷ 0.01   (c) 23 ÷ 0.001
   (d) 8 ÷ 0.2   (e) 6 ÷ 0.03   (f) 24 ÷ 0.04

8. Find:
   (a) 0.4 ÷ 0.1   (b) 6.4 ÷ 0.8   (c) 8.4 ÷ 0.7
   (d) 0.4 ÷ 0.01   (e) 5.6 ÷ 0.07   (f) 8.1 ÷ 0.03

9. Find:
   (a) 14.4 ÷ 3.6   (b) 24.3 ÷ 2.7   (c) 0.72 ÷ 1.8
   (d) 0.76 ÷ 0.5   (e) 0.4 ÷ 0.5   (f) 1.3 ÷ 0.04

10. (a) How many lengths of 0.2 m can be cut from 1.2 m?
   (b) How many injections of antibiotic of 0.010 ℓ are contained in a 0.1 ℓ bottle?
   (c) How many feeds of 0.125 kg of the milk powder are contained in a 50 kg sack?

4.3 Fractions and decimals

To convert a number written as a vulgar fraction to a decimal, you do a division.

Example 1

Change $\frac{3}{8}$ to a decimal

$$\begin{array}{r} 0.375 \\ 8\overline{)3.000} \end{array}$$

So, $\frac{3}{8} = 0.375$

---

1. Change to a decimal.
   (a) $\frac{1}{4}$ (b) $\frac{5}{8}$ (c) $\frac{3}{4}$ (d) $\frac{2}{5}$

2. Change to a decimal.
   (a) $\frac{3}{40}$ (b) $\frac{4}{25}$ (c) $\frac{6}{50}$ (d) $\frac{3}{16}$

To convert a number written as a decimal to a vulgar fraction, you need to cancel.

Example 2

Change 0.85 to a vulgar fraction

$0.85 = \frac{85}{100} = \frac{17}{20}$

---

3. Change to a vulgar fraction and simplify:
   (a) 0.35   (b) 0.8   (c) 0.95   (d) 0.24

4. Change to a vulgar fraction and simplify.
   (a) 0.625   (b) 0.075   (c) 0.184   (d) 0.008

5. Find $\frac{1}{8}$ as a decimal.
Use your answer to write down the decimal equivalent of
   (a) $\frac{2}{8}$ (b) $\frac{3}{8}$ (c) $\frac{4}{8}$ (d) $\frac{5}{8}$ (e) $\frac{6}{8}$ (f) $\frac{7}{8}$

6. Find $\frac{1}{16}$ as a decimal.
Use your answer to find the decimal equivalent of
   (a) $\frac{5}{16}$ (b) $\frac{9}{16}$ (c) $\frac{7}{16}$ (d) $\frac{11}{16}$ (e) $\frac{15}{16}$

7. Complete this sequence by dividing by 2 each time:
$\frac{1}{2} = 0.50000$
$\frac{1}{4} = 0.25000$
$\frac{1}{8} = 0.12500$
$\ldots$

and continue to $\frac{1}{32}$
Use your answer to find the decimal form of
   (a) $\frac{3}{32}$ (b) $\frac{31}{32}$ (c) $\frac{3}{64}$ (d) $\frac{3}{128}$

Recurring decimals

Sometimes changing a fraction to a decimal produces a sequence that does not stop. The most simple is

$\frac{1}{3} = 0.3333\ldots$

and this decimal never ends.
It is called a **recurring** decimal.
We usually write $0.\dot{3}$
Sometimes the repetition is two or more figures.
A calculator will give you.

$\frac{1}{37} = 0.027027027\ldots$

We write this as $0.\dot{0}2\dot{7}$

8. Work out the decimal form of these fractions and stop after five decimal places:
   (a) $\frac{2}{3}$ (b) $\frac{1}{6}$ (c) $\frac{5}{6}$ (d) $\frac{4}{9}$ (e) $\frac{1}{12}$

9. Find the decimal form of $\frac{1}{11}$.
Use your answer to write as a vulgar fraction:
   (a) 0.181818...   (b) 0.272727...
   (c) 0.818181...   (d) 0.909090...

10. The decimal 0.3 is not quite equal to $\frac{1}{3}$ as this number line diagram shows.

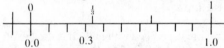

Draw a diagram to show that 0.33 is close to but not exactly $\frac{1}{3}$.

11. Use a calculator or long multiplication to find:
   (a) 1.7^2 and 1.8^2
   (b) 1.73^2 and 1.74^2
   (c) 1.732^2 and 1.733^2
Write down an approximation for $\sqrt{3}$ to four significant figures.

How close can you get?

A number like $\sqrt{3}$ can be written as a decimal as accurately as you wish by repeating the process in Question 11. But the decimal does not end and it is not recurring.
All vulgar fractions, like $\frac{1}{4}$ or $\frac{1}{3}$, and their decimal forms, 0.25 and $0.\dot{3}$ are called **rational** numbers.
Numbers like $\sqrt{3}$ are called **irrational** numbers.

Fraction and decimal problems

12. A piece of ribbon is 50 cm long. How many $10\frac{1}{2}$ cm lengths of ribbon can be cut from it? How much ribbon is left over?

13. I walk $\frac{2}{3}$ km to school then $2\frac{1}{2}$ km to the store and $1\frac{1}{4}$ km back home. How far do I walk altogether?

14. A book weighs 0.42 kg. What is the weight of each page if there are 160 pages and the cover weighs 260 g?

15. A large thermos flask holds sufficient coffee to exactly fill 2 large cups of capacity 0.24 litres and 4 smaller ones of capacity 0.13 litres. What is the capacity of the flask?

16. A crate of 24 soft drinks weighs 17.8 kg. If the empty crate weighs 3.5 kg what is the mass of each full bottle?

17. A matchbox contains 50 matches, each of mass $\frac{2}{10}$ g. What is the mass of the full box if the empty box weighs 6.3 g?

18. On each bounce a ball rises to $\frac{2}{3}$ of its previous height. To what height will it rise after the fourth bounce, if dropped from a height of 81 cm?

19. Liver is sold for $7.16 a kilogram. What is the cost of 0.24 kg of liver?

20. A bottle of juice holds $2\frac{1}{4}$ litres. How many glasses of juice can be poured from the bottle if each glass holds $\frac{3}{8}$ litre?

21. A half litre jug is filled with milk. It is used to fill two cups, one holding $\frac{1}{8}$ litre the other $\frac{2}{7}$ litre. How much milk remains in the jug?

22. A piece of wire is 70 cm long. How much wire is left if 17 lengths of 28 mm are removed? What fraction of the wire is removed?

23. Given $x = 0.2727\ldots$, find
  (a) $100x$
  (b) $99x\ (= 100x - x)$
  (c) the value of x as a fraction.

24. Repeat the method of Question 23 to find these recurring decimals as fractions
  (a) $0.3434\ldots$ (b) $0.8686\ldots$
  (c) $0.3333\ldots$ (d) $0.1111\ldots$

25. Can you think of a method to write these recurring decimals as fractions? Write them as fractions.
  (a) $0.4\dot{1}\dot{4}$ (b) $0.2\dot{1}\dot{7}$

26. Three sons were to inherit their father's camels after his death. The will declared they were to receive $\frac{1}{2}$, $\frac{1}{3}$ and $\frac{1}{6}$ respectively. Unfortunately, there were 25 camels to share and they could not come to an agreement. A wise mullah offered to solve their quarrel. He removed one camel and invited them to divide up the rest. And it worked! He kept the extra camel as payment. How many did each son receive?

4.4 Significant figures

Revision: rounding off numbers

[1] It is not always necessary to give an exact number. For example, in an essay for school, you would not be expected to give the *exact* number of people at a big carnival, or of people living in the city.
Instead you could give an approximate number, rounded off to the nearest thousand or ten thousand.
[2] **Rounding off** a whole number means writing it correct to the nearest ten, hundred, thousand etc. For example 124 is nearer to 120 than to 130.
124 is 120, correct to the nearest ten.

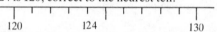

        120   124   130

[3] Here is how to round off a whole number, without drawing a number line:

1. Look at the number, and find the place you want to round it off to – *tens, hundreds* etc.
2. Now look at the digit to the right of this place.
3. If this digit is 0, 1, 2, 3 or 4 the number must be rounded down. If it is 5, 6, 7, 8 or 9 the number must be rounded *up*.

Example 1

(a) Write 372 and 125 correct to the nearest ten.

  The *tens* place is underlined, below.

  $3\,7\,②$ $\xrightarrow{\text{round down}}$ 370 to the nearest ten.

  $1\,2\,⑤$ $\xrightarrow{\text{round up}}$ 130 to the nearest ten.

(b) Write 1378 and 26 425 correct to the nearest hundred.
  The *hundreds* place is underlined, below.

  $1\,3\,⑦\,8$ $\xrightarrow{\text{round up}}$ 1400

  $2\,6\,4\,②\,5$ $\xrightarrow{\text{round down}}$ 26 400

1. Write correct to the nearest ten.
   (a) 56   (b) 45   (c) 71
   (d) 68   (e) 65   (f) 144
   (g) 292   (h) 1411   (i) 1045
   (j) 2542   (k) 13 785   (l) 14 299

2. Write correct to the nearest hundred.
   (a) 173   (b) 809   (c) 1486
   (d) 2545   (e) 4555   (f) 4499
   (g) 11 659   (h) 12 111   (i) 13 011
   (j) 20 068   (k) 130 506   (l) 220 087

3. Look at the newspaper headings opposite. Which
numbers have been reported exactly? Which have
been rounded off? Give reasons for your answers.

Example 2

(a) Write 5.64 and 3.1824 correct to one d.p.

The first decimal place is underlined, below.

5.6④ $\xrightarrow{\text{round down}}$ 5.6 correct to one d.p.

3.1⑧14 $\xrightarrow{\text{round up}}$ 3.2 correct to one d.p.

(b) Write 2.144 and 3.255 correct to two d.p.

The second decimal place is underlined,
below.

2.14④ $\xrightarrow{\text{round down}}$ 2.14 correct to two d.p.

3.25⑤6 $\xrightarrow{\text{round up}}$ 3.26 correct to two d.p.

---

4. Write correct to one d.p.
   (a) 1.31   (b) 1.35   (c) 1.42
   (d) 3.71   (e) 5.461   (f) 2.202
   (g) 12.394   (h) 13.011   (i) 0.057

5. Write correct to two d.p.
   (a) 1.443   (b) 2.504   (c) 10.4001
   (d) 0.3031   (e) 10.089   (f) 0.008
   (g) 0.1084   (h) 13.327   (i) 15.401

Significant figures

When describing large crowds etc., newspapers tend to
round off numbers so that they contain only one or two
other numerals, before the zeros. They give the
numbers to one or two **significant figures**.

Example 3

Written to one significant figure:

20 871 becomes 20 000
 4175 becomes 4000
18 381 becomes 20 000
0.0165 becomes 0.02

Example 4

Written to two significant figures:
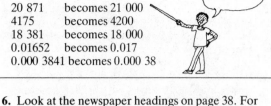

20 871   becomes 21 000
4175   becomes 4200
18 381   becomes 18 000
0.01652   becomes 0.017
0.000 3841 becomes 0.000 38

---

6. Look at the newspaper headings on page 38. For
each number, say how many significant figures have
been used.

7. Write correct to one significant figure:
   (a) 850   (b) 9317   (c) 41 290
   (d) 43 651   (e) 0.763   (f) 0.072
   (g) 0.0065   (h) 8.93   (i) 0.000 398

8. Write correct to two significant figures:
   (a) 537 000   (b) 41 562   (c) 0.037 06
   (d) 0.000 215   (e) 11.931   (f) 1.076
   (g) 0.004 76   (h) 1432   (i) 0.3061

9. Here are some numbers written to three significant
figures. Some of them are wrong. Pick out the
wrong ones and write them down correctly.
   (a) 539 010 $\longrightarrow$ 539 000
   (b) 0.005 706 $\longrightarrow$ 0.005 70
   (c) 0.050 621 $\longrightarrow$ 0.0506
   (d) 508 716 $\longrightarrow$ 508 700
   (e) 15 480 000 $\longrightarrow$ 15 500 000
   (f) 0.010 06 $\longrightarrow$ 0.0100

10. Write correct to three significant figures:
   (a) 18.403   (b) 157 683   (c) 10 467
   (d) 0.030 084   (e) 15.092   (f) 113.387
   (g) 21 547   (h) 13.406   (i) 21.004

11. Imagine your job is to make up headlines for a
newspaper. For each fact below, decide whether
you would write an *approximate* number or the
exact number in your headline. If *approximate*,
write down the number you would use instead.
   (a) West Indies v England: 280 for 6 (94 overs)
   (b) 15 307 people attended political rally
   (c) 2 897 401 left homeless after nuclear attack
   (d) 14 maths students receive prizes
   (e) New world record: mile in 3.172 minutes!
   (f) Banks lost $631 743 through fraud last month
   (g) Distance from earth to moon measured by
        amazing new method: 384 432 km
   (h) Will a black person be president in 1993?

4.5 Indices

1. $3 = 3^1, 3 \times 3 = 3^2, 3 \times 3 \times 3 = 3^3$
In the same way, write using an index:
  (a) 5   (b) 7   (c) 9   (d) 10
  (e) $3 \times 3 \times 3 \times 3$ (f) $7 \times 7 \times 7$
  (g) $5 \times 5 \times 5 \times 5 \times 5$ (h) $p \times p \times p \times p$
  (i) $q \times q \times q$ (j) $y \times y \times y \times y \times y$

2. Write out in its long form:
  (a) 3^5 (b) 7^4 (c) 6^3 (d) 9^2
  (e) p^5 (f) q^4 (g) r^3 (h) y^2

3. Copy and complete:
  (a) $3^4 = 3 \times 3 \times \ldots \ldots = 81$
  (b) $5^4 = 5 \times 5 \times \ldots \ldots = \square$
  (c) $2^7 = 2 \times 2 \times \ldots \ldots = \square$
  (d) $25 = 5^\square = 5 \times \ldots \ldots$
  (e) $49 = 7^\square = 7 \times \ldots \ldots$
  (f) $8 = 2^\square = 2 \times \ldots \ldots$
  (g) $81 = 3^\square = 3 \times \ldots \ldots$
  (h) $10\,000 = 10 \times 10 \times \ldots \ldots = 10^\square$
  (i) $1\,000\,000 = 10 \times 10 \times \ldots \ldots = 10^\square$

4. Copy and complete:
  (a) $5 = 5^\square$ (b) $9 = 9^\square$
  (c) $125 = 5^\square$ (d) $64 = \square^2$
  (e) $27 = 3^\square$ (f) $32 = \square^5$
  (g) $256 = 4^\square$ (h) $1331 = \square^3$

Multiplication and indices

5. Copy and complete:
  (a) $3^2 \times 3^4 = 3 \times 3 \times \ldots \ldots = 3^\square$
  (b) $2^3 \times 2^5 = 2 \times 2 \times \ldots \ldots = 2^\square$
  (c) $7^5 \times 7 = 7 \times 7 \times \ldots \ldots = 7^\square$
  (d) $5^6 \times 5^4 = 5 \times 5 \times \ldots \ldots = 5^\square$

6. Look carefully at your answers to Question 5. Is there a quick way to find the answers? Use your quick way to simplify:
  (a) $2^3 \times 2^4$ (b) $3^5 \times 3^2$ (c) $4^6 \times 4$
  (d) $5^7 \times 5^3$ (e) $6^5 \times 6$ (f) $7^{10} \times 7^5$

In the expression 4^7, 7 is called the **index** or **exponent** and 4 is called the **base**.

From Question 5 you should have found:
When two numbers have the same base you can multiply them by adding their indices. Using symbols:
$a^m \times a^n = a^{m+n}$

Example 1
  (a) $2^3 \times 2^4 = 2^{3+4} = 2^7$
  (b) $2^2 \times 2^5 \times 2^7 = 2^{2+5+7} = 2^{14}$
  (c) $2p \times p^4 = 2p^5$
  (d) $3x \times 4x^2 = 12x^3$

---

7. Simplify:
  (a) $6^2 \times 6^3 \times 6^5$ (b) $7 \times 7^{10} \times 7^{12}$
  (c) $3^2 \times 3^{10} \times 3^5$ (d) $10 \times 10 \times 10^3$

8. Do you agree that $p^3 \times p^2 = p^5$?
In the same way, simplify:
  (a) $a^2 \times a^3$ (b) $q^5 \times q^3$
  (c) $r^4 \times r^6$ (d) $s^{10} \times s^5$
  (e) $p \times p^2 \times p^5$ (f) $j^3 \times j^7 \times j^9$
  (g) $a^m \times a^n$ (h) $p^a \times p^b$
  (i) $m^a \times m^b \times m^c$ (j) $x^a \times x^m \times x^c$

9. Simplify these, if possible, leaving the answer in index form. If not possible, explain why.
  (a) $2^6 \times 2^7$ (b) $2^3 \times 3^2$
  (c) $3^2 \times 4^2 \times 5^2$ (d) $a^2 \times a^3$
  (e) $a^2 \times b^3$ (f) $p^2 \times p^3 \times q^2$
  (g) $2p^2 \times p^3$ (h) $p^2 \times 2p^4 \times q \times q^2$

Division and indices

10. Copy and complete:
  (a) $\dfrac{3^4}{3^2} = \dfrac{3 \times 3 \times \ldots \ldots}{3 \times \ldots \ldots} = 3^\square$

  (b) $\dfrac{5^7}{5^3} = \dfrac{5 \times 5 \times \ldots \ldots}{5 \times \ldots \ldots} = 5^\square$

  (c) $\dfrac{7^{10}}{7^4} = \dfrac{7 \times 7 \times \ldots \ldots}{7 \times \ldots \ldots} = 7^\square$

11. Can you see a quick way of finding the answers, in Question 10? Use this quick method to simplify:
  (a) $\dfrac{2^6}{2^3}$ (b) $\dfrac{3^7}{3^4}$ (c) $\dfrac{4^8}{4^3}$

  (d) $\dfrac{7^{10}}{7^5}$ (e) $\dfrac{9^7}{9}$ (f) $\dfrac{5^{12}}{5^8}$

12. Copy and complete:
  (a) $\dfrac{p^5}{p^2} = \dfrac{p \times \ldots \ldots}{p \times \ldots \ldots} = p^\square$

  (b) $\dfrac{q^8}{q^3} = \dfrac{q \times \ldots \ldots}{q \times \ldots \ldots} = q^\square$

  (c) $\dfrac{r^{21}}{r^7} = \dfrac{r \times \ldots \ldots}{r \times \ldots \ldots} = r^\square$

Does your quick way work here too?

In Questions 10–12 you should have found:
When two numbers have the same base, you can divide them by subtracting their indices. Using symbols:
$a^m \div a^n = a^{m-n}$

Example 2

(a) $5^7 \div 5^3 = 5^{(7-3)} = 5^4$
(b) $a^{12} \div a^{10} = a^{(12-10)} = a^2$
(c) $p^m \div p^n = p^{(m-n)}$

---

13. Simplify, leaving your answer in index form.
  (a) $6^3 \div 6^2$ (b) $5^7 \div 5^4$ (c) $12^6 \div 12^3$
  (d) $7^5 \div 7$ (e) $20^9 \div 20^4$ (f) $q^2 \div q$
  (g) $b^6 \div b^5$ (h) $p^7 \div (p^3 \div p)$ (i) $y^4 \div y^m$

The meaning of a^0 and a^{-1}

14. (a) Do you agree that $4^2 \div 4^2 = 16 \div 16 = 1$?
  (b) Complete: $4^3 \div 4^3 = 4^{3-3} = 4^{\square} = \square$

15. Copy and complete:
  (a) $2^3 \div 2^3 = 2^{\square} = 1$ (b) $3^5 \div 3^5 = 3^{\square} = \square$
  (c) $7^2 \div 7^2 = 7^{\square} = \square$ (d) $9^{10} \div 9^{10} = 9^{\square} = \square$

16. Do you agree that $a^0 = 1$, where a is any number greater than zero?

17. Write down the value of:
  (a) 5^0 (b) 7^0 (c) p^0 (d) m^0

18. Copy and complete:
  (a) $4^5 \div 4^6 = \dfrac{4 \times \ldots\ldots}{4 \times \ldots\ldots} = \dfrac{1}{\square}$

  (b) $4^5 \div 4^6 = 4^{(\ )} = 4^{-1}$ (c) $\dfrac{1}{\square} = 4^{-1}$

19. Copy and complete:
  (a) $5^6 \div 5^7 = \dfrac{5 \times \ldots\ldots}{5 \times \ldots\ldots} = \dfrac{1}{\square}$

  (b) $5^6 \div 5^7 = 5^{(\ )} = 5^{\square}$ (c) $\frac{1}{5} = 5^{\square}$

20. Write as a fraction:
  (a) 7^{-1} (b) 3^{-1} (c) 4^{-1} (d) 8^{-1}

21. Write in index form:
  (a) $\frac{1}{6}$ (b) $\frac{1}{2}$ (c) $\frac{1}{20}$ (d) $\frac{1}{100}$

22. Find: (a) $5^6 \div 5^8$ (b) $p^4 \div p^7$
  What do you think 5^{-2} and p^{-3} mean?

23. By considering $4^7 \div 4^9$, show that $4^{-2} = \dfrac{1}{4^2}$.

24. By considering $p^5 \div p^8$, show that $p^{-3} = \dfrac{1}{p^3}$.

---

25. By considering $a^0 \div a^n$, show that $a^{-n} = \dfrac{1}{a^n}$

26. Simplify and write as a fraction in its lowest form:
  (a) 3×3^{-1} (b) 4×4^{-2}
  (c) 12×2^{-3} (d) $\frac{1}{4} \times 4^2$
  (e) 16×2^{-4} (f) 9×3^{-3}
  (g) $4^{-2} \times 12$ (h) $3^{-2} \times 4^{-1}$
  (i) $(\frac{2}{3})^{-2}$ (j) $6^3 \times 3^{-3}$

27. Simplify:
  (a) $3a(a^{-1} - a)$ (b) $a^2(a - a^{-1})$

  (c) $a^2(a^{-2} - a^2)$ (d) $a^3\left(\dfrac{1}{a^{-2}} + a\right)$

  (e) $\dfrac{a}{3}(3^2 - 3^{-1})$ (f) $4a^{-2}\left(a^2 + \dfrac{a}{4}\right)$

Summary: the laws of indices

[1] $a^m \times a^n = a^{m+n}$ [2] $a^m \div a^n = a^{m-n}$
[3] $a^0 = 1$ [4] $\dfrac{1}{a^n} = a^{-n}$

a, m and n represent any numbers.

28. Look carefully at the first three below. Then copy and complete the list.

$0.1 \quad = \dfrac{1}{10} = 10^{-1}$

$0.01 \quad = \dfrac{1}{100} = 10^{-2}$

Such a small number!

$0.001 \quad = \dfrac{1}{1000} = \square$
$0.0001 = \square = \square$
$0.00001 = \square = \square$

29. Express the fraction using an index.

  (a) $\dfrac{1}{1000}$ (b) $\dfrac{1}{10\,000}$ (c) $\dfrac{1}{1\,000\,000}$

  (d) $\dfrac{1}{10\,000\,000}$ (e) $\dfrac{10}{10\,000}$ (f) $\dfrac{100}{100\,000}$

30. In Question 28, what connection is there between the number of places after the decimal point, and the size of the index?

31. 10^{-4} is 0.0001
  10^{-5} is 0.00001
  In the same way, write in full form:
  (a) 10^{-2} (b) 10^{-6} (c) 10^{-7} (d) 10^{-8}
  (e) 10^{-4} (f) 10^{-10} (g) 10^{-11} (h) 10^{-12}

4.6 Standard form

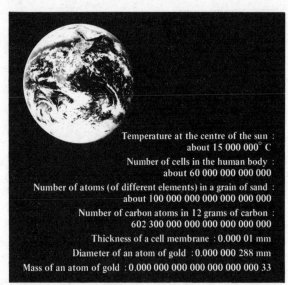

Temperature at the centre of the sun :
about 15 000 000° C

Number of cells in the human body :
about 60 000 000 000 000

Number of atoms (of different elements) in a grain of sand :
about 100 000 000 000 000 000 000

Number of carbon atoms in 12 grams of carbon :
602 300 000 000 000 000 000 000

Thickness of a cell membrane : 0.000 01 mm

Diameter of an atom of gold : 0.000 000 288 mm

Mass of an atom of gold : 0.000 000 000 000 000 000 000 33

Look at the numbers above.
Are they easy to remember? Why?
Are they easy to copy without mistakes?

Scientists often use numbers like those above, in their work.
The numbers are difficult, because they are either very large or very small.
To make them easier to use, they are often written in **standard form**.
In standard form, the number is written as:
(**number between 1 and 10**) × (**ten to a power**)

Example 1

Written in standard form:

(a) $6000 = 6 \times 1000 = \mathbf{6 \times 10^3}$
(b) $8\,000\,000 = 8 \times 1\,000\,000 = \mathbf{8 \times 10^6}$

---

1. Write in standard form:
  (a) 4000   (b) 20 000   (c) 70 000 000
  (d) 300 000   (e) 9000   (f) 10 000
  (g) 80 000   (h) 100 000   (i) 1 000 000

2. Write the number in full.
  (a) 3×10^7 (b) 4×10^6 (c) 7×10^9
  (d) 5×10^4 (e) 3×10^9 (f) 6×10^6

Example 2

(a) $6340 = 6.34 \times 1000 = \mathbf{6.34 \times 10^3}$
(b) $57\,100 = \mathbf{5.71 \times 10^4}$
(c) $6\,820\,000 = \mathbf{6.82 \times 10^6}$

Example 3

$53\,410. = \mathbf{5.341 \times 10^4}$

The index is 4.
Can you see the connection between the size of the index, and the new position of the decimal point?

$4\,780\,000. = \mathbf{4.78 \times 10^6}$

Example 4

(a) $0.53 = \mathbf{5.3 \times 10^{-1}}$
(b) $0.0211 = \mathbf{2.11 \times 10^{-2}}$
(c) $0.004\,168 = \mathbf{4.168 \times 10^{-3}}$

Example 5

$0.003\,4 = \mathbf{3.4 \times 10^{-3}}$

The index is −3.
Can you see the connection between this number, and the movement of the decimal point?

$0.000\,082\,1 = \mathbf{8.21 \times 10^{-5}}$

---

3. Write in standard form:
  (a) 401   (b) 2170   (c) 3401
  (d) 9082   (e) 11 200   (f) 25 000
  (g) 6741   (h) 58 200   (i) 34 761

4. Write in standard form:
  (a) 3270   (b) 4300
  (c) 104 000   (d) 357 000
  (e) 831 400   (f) 1 740 000
  (g) 2 801 000   (h) 13 500 000

5. Write the number in full.
  (a) 1.5×10^3 (b) 6.32×10^2
  (c) 1.628×10^4 (d) 3.94×10^6
  (e) 5.41×10^{10} (f) 9.999×10^{12}

Example 6

(a) $0.4 \;= 4 \times 0.1 \;= \mathbf{4 \times 10^{-1}}$
(b) $0.07 = 7 \times 0.01 = \mathbf{7 \times 10^{-2}}$
(c) $0.009 = 9 \times 0.001 = \mathbf{9 = 10^{-3}}$

---

6. Write in standard form:
  (a) 0.5   (b) 0.8   (c) 0.04
  (d) 0.07   (e) 0.006   (f) 0.003
  (g) 0.001   (h) 0.0005   (i) 0.009

7. Write the number in full.
(a) 7×10^{-1} (b) 3×10^{-2} (c) 4×10^{-3}
(d) 9×10^{-4} (e) 6×10^{-5} (f) 5×10^{-6}

8. Write in standard form:
(a) 0.16 (b) 0.37 (c) 0.022
(d) 0.094 (e) 0.087 (f) 0.0064
(g) 0.0096 (h) 0.0037 (i) 0.000 91

9. Write in standard form:
(a) 0.0032 (b) 0.009 46
(c) 0.000 874 (d) 0.000 003 77
(e) 0.000 000 999 (f) 0.000 000 000 621
(g) 0.000 000 8046 (h) 0.000 000 000 0009

10. Write the number in full.
(a) 3.6×10^{-2} (b) 7.409×10^{-3}
(c) 6.11×10^{-4} (d) 1.999×10^{-2}
(e) 2.6741×10^{-3} (f) 5.47×10^{-6}
(g) 1.677×10^{-8} (h) 3.084×10^{-10}

11. Express all the numbers at the top left of the opposite page in standard form.

12. Pick out the largest number from each group.
(a) 9872, 10^4, 9.423×10^3
(b) 10^7, 371 000, 6.87×10^8
(c) 4 169 000, 5.54×10^9, 10^{10}
(d) 10^{-6}, 0.000 0007, 3.2×10^{-7}

13. Pick out the smallest number from each group.
(a) 0.004, 10^{-3}, 1.2×10^{-2}
(b) 10^{-5}, 0.004 006, 1.009×10^{-6}
(c) 0.000 0001, 6.3×10^{-8}, 10^{-7}
(d) 6.431×10^5, 590 000, 10^6

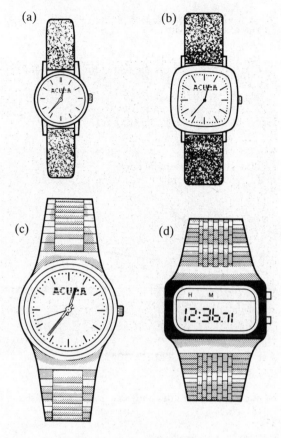

(a) (b)

(c) (d)

4.7 Error in measurements

Accuracy and instruments

1. Each of the four watches above is keeping good time. Write down the time shown on each.

2. (a) With which of the watches can you measure time most accurately?
(b) Do you agree that the accuracy of a time measurement depends on the watch you measure with?

3. Which watch above would be accurate enough for:
(a) measuring the fastest time for the 100 m final on School Sports Day
(b) telling when maths class is nearly over
(c) measuring the time a swimmer takes to swim a length of a pool
(d) measuring how long your friend takes to run two miles
(e) measuring how long you can hold your breath?
Give reasons for your answers.

4. Which of these would you *not* measure with a ruler? Explain why.
   (a) the thickness of a hair
   (b) the length of this book
   (c) the distance from the school to the main Post Office
   (d) the width of your desk
   (e) the length of your foot
   (f) the thickness of a spring bar for a watch

5. Use a ruler to measure each line below. Write down the measurement correct to:
   (a) the nearest cm   (b) the nearest mm

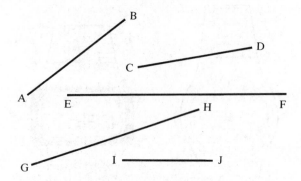

6. Were any of the lines above an *exact* number of:
   (a) cm?   (b) mm?

Error in measuring

In measuring, the word **error** has a special meaning. The error in a measurement is the difference between the result you record and the correct one.

This line is 3.7 cm long. ───────────
Its length is 4 cm, to the nearest cm.
When you read its length to the nearest cm, the error is 0.3 cm or 3 mm. $(4 - 3.7 = 0.3)$

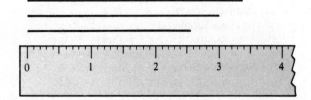

7. Part of the centimetre ruler is shown magnified above. Each small division represents 1 mm.
   (a) Look at the three lines above. Do they all look the same length?
   (b) How long is each line, to the nearest cm?
   (c) Were you answers for part (b) all the same? Do you think your measurements include an error?

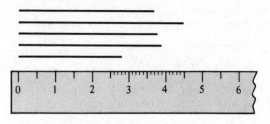

8. Using the ruler drawn above, write down the length of each line correct to:
   (a) the nearest cm   (b) the nearest mm

9. For each line in Question 8, write down the error (in mm) when the answer is given to the nearest cm.

The greatest possible error

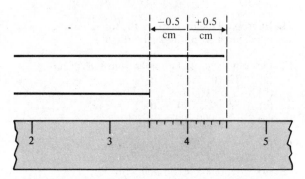

10. Both lines above measure 4 cm to the nearest cm. If a line measures 4 cm to the nearest cm, do you agree that:
   (a) it could be as short as 3.5 cm?
   (b) it could be up to 4.5 cm long?
   (c) the greatest possible errors in giving its length to the nearest cm are $+0.5$ cm and -0.5 cm?

When a line is measured to the nearest cm, the greatest possible errors are $+0.5$ cm and -0.5 cm. This is shortened to ± 0.5 cm.

± 0.5 cm is read as *plus or minus nought point five centimetres*.
In the same way, when a line is measured to the nearest mm, the greatest possible error is ± 0.5 mm.

11. If you are rounding off to the nearest centimetre, how long is the shortest line that could be recorded as:
   (a) 5 cm?   (b) 7 cm?   (c) 12 cm?
   What is the error each time?

12. If you are measuring to one d.p., how long is the shortest line that could be recorded as:
   (a) 5.6 cm?   (b) 4.1 km?   (c) 1.0 m?

13. If you are measuring to two significant figures, what is the shortest measurements that can be recorded as:
(a) 32 min?   (b) 120 miles?
(c) 0.25 s?   (d) 1.3 cm?

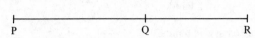

P   Q   R

14. Measure PQ, QR and PR above:
(a) to the nearest mm   (b) to the nearest cm

15. Look at the drawing for Question 14. Do you agree that PQ + QR = PR?
(a) Check the equation using your results for Question 14 (a). Is it correct?
(b) Now check using your results for 14 (b). What do you notice? Explain.

16. In the Olympic Games, the following times were recorded in a heat for the 4 × 100 m relay:
Trinidad   39.13 s
U.S.A.   39.13 s
W. Germany 39.26 s
Trinidad won the heat.
(a) How could the same time be recorded for both Trinidad and U.S.A., even though Trinidad won?
(b) To what accuracy is each time given?
(c) What is the *fastest* time that Trinidad could have run in, to clock up 39.13 s?
(d) What is the *slowest* time the U.S.A. could have run in, to clock up 39.13 s?

4.8 Calculations and degrees of accuracy

1. Which number is the 'odd man out'? Why?
(a) 4.1   (b) 5.7   (c) 6.3   (d) 8.54   (e) 9.1

2. Six students measured each other's heights. They recorded these results:
153 cm   141 cm   149 cm
150.2 cm   159 cm   145.5 cm
Which two measurements would you rewrite? Why?

3. Tani ran 100 m in the following times:
48.3 s, 52.14 s, 50.32 s, 49.8 s, 50.6 s.
(a) Two of the times were measured to a greater **degree of accuracy** than the rest. Which ones were these?
(b) To compare them, should all the times be given to the same degree of accuracy? Why?
(c) Write a new list of Tani's times, each to 1 d.p.
(d) Calculate Tani's average time, from your list in (c). How many significant figures will you give in the answer? Why?

4. Can you see anything wrong with these calculations of measurements? If *yes*, rewrite them correctly.

(a)   3.12 s
      −0.34 s
      ─────
       2.78 s

(b)   5.4 cm
      −1.19 cm
      ─────
       4.21 cm

(c)   11.46 cm
       17.3 cm
       18.2 cm
      ─────────
    3)46.96 cm
    Av. = 15.65 cm

(d)   2.0 kg
        1.7 kg
        2.4 kg
      ────────
     3)6.1
    Av. = 2.0 kg

What does Av. mean in (c) and (d)?

5. The lengths of three metal rods are recorded as 9.3 cm, 10.4 cm and 11.1 cm, to one d.p.
(a) Write down the greatest and least possible values for the length of each rod, to 2 d.p.
(b) Write down the greatest and least possible values for the total length of the three rods.

6. (a) The length of a chain is recorded as 95 cm, to the nearest cm. Write down the greatest and least possible values for the length of chain, to 1 d.p.
(b) A piece 38 cm long is cut from the chain. Write down the greatest and least possible values for the length of the remainder.

7. A sketch of the classroom floor is shown below.

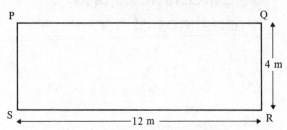

(a) Write down the largest and smallest measurements that can be recorded as 12 m.
(b) Write down the largest and smallest measurements that can be recorded as 4 m.
(c) Draw two more sketches, showing the largest and smallest rectangles that could be recorded as 12 m × 4 m.

8. (a) Find the areas of each of the three rectangles in Question 7.
(b) What is the largest error that could have been made, in calculating the area of the classroom floor?

9. The sides of a sheet of paper measure 3.2 cm and 5.6 cm.
(a) Find the area of the piece of paper.
(b) Find its largest possible area.
(c) Find its smallest possible area.
(d) What is the largest error that could have been made in writing its area as 17.92 cm?

10. For the paper in Question 9:
(a) to what accuracy was each side measured?
(b) do you think it reasonable to give the area to 2 d.p.? Give reason for your answer.

11. The edge-length of a wooden cube is recorded as 4 cm, correct to the nearest cm.
(a) What is the greatest and least possible length, for each edge?
(b) Calculate the volume of the cube, assuming each edge is:
   (i) the greatest possible length
   (ii) the least possible length
(c) If each edge is supposed to be 4.0 cm, what is the greatest possible difference between the supposed volume and the actual volume?

4.9 Number bases

Quintus, like us, uses his fingers to count. He has five fingers on each hand.

He also has five hands.
So 5 fingers = 1 hand
   5 hands = 1 person

When adding, he will set out his work like this.

```
  P H F
  1 3 4
+ 1 2 3
-------
  3 1 2
```

And his number system continues in base five.
Five people are called a gang and five gangs make up a colony.

1. Carry out these additions in base five.

(a)	23 +12	(b)	14 +23	(c)	31 +12
(d)	32 +14	(e)	101 + 14	(f)	312 +144

2. Carry out these subtractions in base five.

(a)	23 −12	(b)	21 − 3	(c)	22 −13
(d)	100 − 11	(e)	241 −113	(f)	201 −112

3. Using Quintus's base five system, find
(a) 10 − 2 (one hand – two fingers)
(b) 100 − 2 (one person – two fingers)
(c) 44 + 1
   (four hands and four fingers + one finger)
(d) 20 + 30 (two hands + three hands)
(e) 1000 − 100 (one gang – one person)

Multiplication tables are different from ours, but there are fewer to learn.
$2 \times 1 = 2$ $2 \times 2 = 4$ $2 \times 3 = 11$ $2 \times 4 = 13$

4. Write out the 3× and 4× tables.
Long multiplication is done in the same way that we do ours.

Example 1	*Example 2*
2 3 × 2 ───── 10_11	2 3 × 1 4 ───── 23 0 $20_2 2$ ───── 43 2

5. Work out these
(a) 13×2 (b) 23×3
(c) 24×21 (d) 211×13
(e) 121×121 (f) 31×14

6. Write down the values, in base five, of
(a) 0^2 (b) 1^2 (c) 2^2 (d) 3^2 (e) 4^2
Is it possible to have a square number in base five ending with a 2 or a 3?

7. A game Quintus likes to play.
See Example 3. Then try some yourself.
Are there any exceptions?

Example 3

Take any two-digit number
with different digits 32
                             -23
                             $\overline{04}$

Reverse the digits and 40
subtract the smaller from -04
the larger   Repeat $\overline{31}$

Whatever number he starts 31
with, he always ends up -13
with 13.   Repeat $\overline{13}$

---

8. Is there a similar result for three-digit numbers? If so, what number do you always finish up with?

Changing base

Quintus works in base five. We work in base ten, sometimes called denary.
Changing from base five to base ten is easy. Just remember the column headings.

Example 4

$$423_{five}$$
$$= 4 \times 25 + 2 \times 5 + 3 \times 1$$
$$= 111$$

---

9. Change these base five numbers to denary.
(a) 14   (b) 32   (c) 103   (d) 121
(e) 304   (f) 230   (g) 1200   (h) 1234

10. In base four, the counting system is based on 4 :
$4^2 = 16$, $4^3 = 64, \dots$
Change these base four numbers to denary.
(a) 13   (b) 22   (c) 103   (d) 221

11. Change these base three numbers to denary.
(a) 11   (b) 21   (c) 101   (d) 212

Changing denary numbers to base five is not quite so easy. You need to find the number of fives, twenty-fives, etc in the number.

Example 5

$$87 = 75 + 10 + 2$$
$$= 3 \times 5^2 + 2 \times 5 + 2 \times 1 = 322_{five}$$

It is not always easy to see the number of twenty-fives in a number. Here is another way of setting out the work. You first keep dividing by five and record the remainders.

$$5 \underline{|87}$$
$$5 \underline{|17} \text{ r } 2$$
$$3 \text{ r } 2$$

Answer 322_{five}

12. Change these denary numbers to base five.
(a) 21   (b) 26   (c) 37   (d) 61
(e) 70   (f) 121   (g) 130   (h) 140
(i) 250   (j) 370   (k) 624   (l) 625

13. Change these denary numbers to base four.
(a) 9   (b) 14   (c) 16   (d) 24
(e) 61   (f) 83   (g) 255   (h) 256

Numbers in base two are called **binary**. These are important in preparing machine code for computers and circuits for calculators. Calculations in binary arithmetic are simpler because you only use two symbols, 0 and 1. But they can be more difficult because there are so many digits in a number.

Example 6

     1011   1011
$+$ 101 $-$ 101
  10000   110

Example 7

$2\underline{|20}$
$2\underline{|10}$ r. 0 $20 = 1010_{two}$
$2\underline{| \ 5}$ r. 1
$2\underline{| \ 2}$ r. 0
    1

---

14. Add:
(a) $11 + 10$ (b) $101 + 11$ (c) $1011 + 1011$

15. Subtract:
(a) $101 - 10$ (b) $1101 - 110$ (c) $1100 - 1$

16. Change these binary numbers to denary.
(a) 111   (b) 10101   (c) 10001   (d) 11111

17. Change these denary numbers to binary.
(a) 4   (b) 16   (c) 23   (d) 32   (e) 60
(f) 63   (g) 127   (h) 128   (i) 500   (j) 1024

18. What is the largest denary number that can be handled by an 8-bit computer chip, that is, one that can use a binary number with eight digits?

Summary

By the end of this chapter, these are the things you should know about.

4.1 Calculating with fractions (page 35)

Revision of addition, subtraction, multiplication and division.

4.2 Calculating with decimals (page 36)

Revision of addition, subtraction, multiplication and division.

4.3 Fractions and decimals (pages 37–38)

Converting vulgar fractions to decimals and decimals to vulgar fractions.
Recurring decimals like $0.3333\ldots$
Another name for numbers which can be written as fractions is **rational**.

4.4 Significant figures (pages 38–39)

How to write a number to a given number of **significant figures**.
53 610 is 50 000 to 1 s.f.
         54 000 to 2 s.f.
0.004 79 is 0.005 to 1 s.f.
           0.0048 to 2 s.f.

4.5 Indices (pages 40–41)

$a^m \times a^n = a^{m+n}$
$a^m \div a^n = a^{m-n}$
The meaning of $a^0 = 1$
The meaning of $a^{-n} = \dfrac{1}{a^n}$

4.6 Standard form (pages 42–43)

How to write any number in standard form.
A number is written in **standard form as**
(number between 1 and 10) × (ten to a power)
$632 = 6.32 \times 10^2$
$0.00\,745 = 7.45 \div 1000$
$= 7.45 \div 10^3$
$= 7.45 \times 10^{-3}$

4.7 Error in measurements (pages 43–45)

The accuracy of a measurement depends on the instrument you measure with.
For example a very accurate watch will measure time to a tenth of a second.
The error in a measurement is the difference between the result you record and the correct one.
If you measure to the nearest cm, the possible error is $\pm\,0.5$ cm.
A book is 17 cm long to the nearest cm.
Its greatest possible length is 17.5 cm.
Its least possible length is 16.5 cm.
Suppose your watch has divisions to show minutes.
Then the possible error in measuring time to the nearest minute will be $\pm\,0.5$ min.
Suppose your watch shows seconds. Measuring to the nearest second, the possible error will be $\pm\,0.5$ s.
Suppose your watch shows tenths of seconds. Measuring to the nearest tenth of a second, the possible error will be $\pm\,0.05$ s.
So there is always a possible error. But the more accurate your watch, the smaller the error will be.

4.8 Calculations and degrees of accuracy (pages 45–46)

Every measurement has a possible error. When you do calculations involving errors, the result also has a possible error.

4.9 Number bases (pages 46–47)

How to add, subtract and multiply in a different base.
How to change a number from one base to base 10.
$134_{\text{five}} = 1 \times 5^2 + 3 \times 5^1 + 4 \times 5^0$
$= 25 + 15 + 4$
$= 44$
How to change a base 10 number to a different base.

$5\,\underline{|44}$
$5\,\underline{|8}\ \ \text{r. } 4$
$5\,\underline{|1}\ \ \text{r. } 3 \qquad 44 = 134_{\text{five}}$
$\ \ \ \ \underline{0}\ \ \text{r. } 1$

5 Measurement

5.1 Area – revision

The area of a shape can be found by counting or estimating the number of unit squares that can cover it.

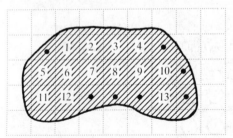

The area of the shape above is about 20 small squares. Only squares at least half a square in size have been counted. Why is this a good method of estimating the area?

1. Estimate the area of the shaded shapes below.

(a)

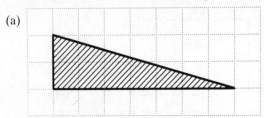

(b)

(c)

(d)

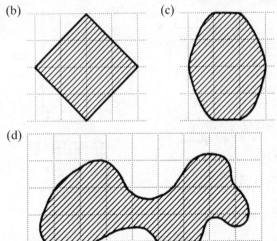

The square centimetre (cm²) is often used as the standard unit to measure area.

2. Draw a shape with area exactly:
   (a) 2cm^2 (b) 5cm^2 (c) $4\frac{1}{2} \text{cm}^2$

3. (a) Count squares to find the exact area of the
rectangles below.

(i)

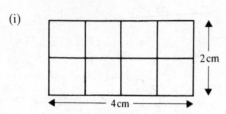

(ii)

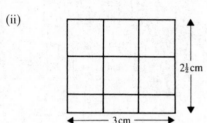

(b) Use your answers to (i) and (ii) to write down
the relationship between the area of the
rectangle to its length and width.

4. Calculate the area of the rectangles below.

(a)

(b)

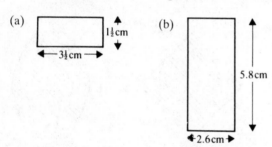

Area is measured in square units

$1\,cm = 10\,mm$

So an area of $1\,cm^2$
is the same as $100\,mm^2$

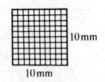

Also $1\,m = 100\,cm$

So an area of $1\,m^2$ is the same as $10\,000\,cm^2$

5. Which of these is correct?
   (a) $1\,m = 10^2\,cm$ (b) $1\,m^2 = 10^4\,cm^2$
   (c) $1\,m = 10^3\,mm$ (d) $1\,m^2 = 10^3\,mm^2$
   (e) $1\,m^2 = 10^6\,mm^2$ (f) $1\,m^2 = 10^9\,mm^2$

6. (a) What is the area of the square above in cm^2?
   (b) What is the area of each small square in
      (i) cm^2?   (ii) mm^2?

7. (a) Find the area of a rectangle 6 cm long and 4 cm
      wide.
   (b) What is its area in mm^2?
   (c) What is its area in m^2?

8. Calculate the area of the shapes below.

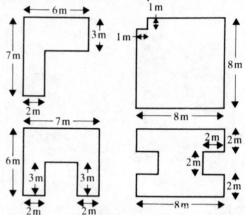

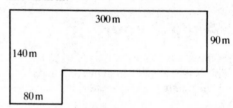

9. In land measure, 1 hectare $= 10^4\,m^2$.
   You know that $1\,km = 10^3\,m$.
   Find the number of hectares in $1\,km^2$.

10. A piece of land shaped like an L has the dimensions
   shown in m.

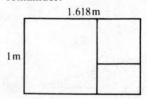

Find the area giving your answer in hectares.

11. Honey bees build their cells as hexagons.

A count of cells shows that there are approximately
420 cells in an area of $100\,cm^2$ of honeycomb.
What is the area of one cell in mm^2?

12. A rectangle measures $1\,m \times 1.618\,m$. A square is
   cut off one end and then a square is cut off the
   remainder.

Find, in cm^2, the area of the remaining rectangle.

5.2 Circles

The names **semi-circle, radius, diameter** and **circumference** are used with circles.

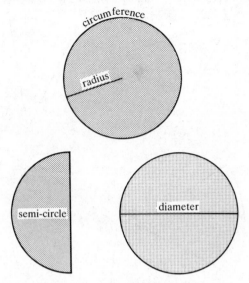

The circumference of a circle is about 3 times its diameter.
We write $C = \pi d$ or $C = 2\pi r$

The Greek letter π (pi) is a number which can be calculated very accurately.
Use $\pi = 3.14$ unless you are told otherwise.

The area of a circle of radius r is given by the formula
$A = \pi r^2$

1. Find the circumference of a circle of radius:
   (a) 2 cm   (b) 5 cm   (c) 10 cm

2. Find the area of each circle in Question **1**.

3. Use $\pi = 3\frac{1}{7}$ to find the area of a semi-circle of radius:
   (a) 7 cm   (b) 56 mm   (c) 35 mm

4. Use $\pi = 3.142$ to find the circumference of a circle of diameter:
   (a) 4 cm   (b) 10 cm   (c) 0.1 m

5. A semi-circle is made from a circle with radius 4 cm. Find:
   (a) its perimeter   (b) its area

6. Find the shaded area.

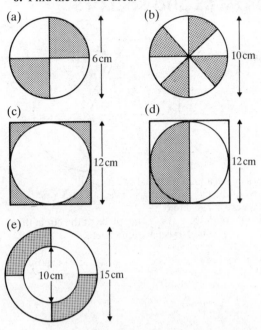

(a)   6 cm
(b)   10 cm
(c)   12 cm
(d)   12 cm
(e)   10 cm   15 cm

7. A swimming pool is made in the shape of a semi-circle. The length of the straight side is 10 m. Find the total length of the perimeter.

8. A large melon is a sphere of radius 14 cm.
   (a) What is the length of the largest circle of wire through which the sphere can just pass?

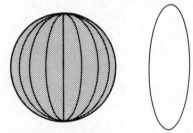

   (b) How much longer must the wire be if there is to be a gap of 1 cm between the melon and the wire?

9. The earth is approximately a sphere of radius 6000 km.
   (a) If it were possible to stretch a length of wire around the equator, what length of wire would be used?
   (b) How much extra wire would need to be added if the wire hoop were to be everywhere 1 m above the equator?

5.3 Arcs and sectors

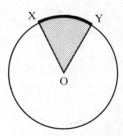 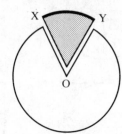

In the diagram above, OX and OY are radii.
The part of the circumference between X and Y is
called an **arc** of the circle.
If you cut along OX and OY, the piece of the circle that
you remove is called a **sector** of the circle.

1. A quarter of a circle is cut out of a circle of radius
   10 cm.

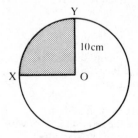

   (a) Find the length of the arc XY.
   (b) Find the area of the circle.
   (c) Find the area of the sector OXY.

Example 1

OAB is a sector of a circle of radius 8 cm.
What is its area?

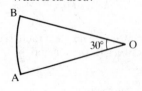

Area of sector
is $\frac{1}{6}\pi \times 8^2$

Sector $OAB = \dfrac{30}{360} = \dfrac{1}{6}$

so sector is $\dfrac{1}{6}$ of complete circle.

Area of complete circle $= \pi r^2$
$\qquad\qquad\qquad\qquad = \pi \times 8^2 \text{ cm}^2$
so area of sector OAB $= \dfrac{1}{6} \times \pi \times 8^2 \text{ cm}^2$
$\qquad\qquad\qquad\qquad = 33.5 \text{ cm}^2$

---

2. A circular cake is of radius 12 cm. It is to be cut into
   eight equal sectors.
   (a) What is the angle at the centre of each sector?
   (b) What is the area of each sector?

3. For each of these, find what fraction it is of a circle.

(a) 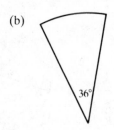   (b)

(c)   (d)

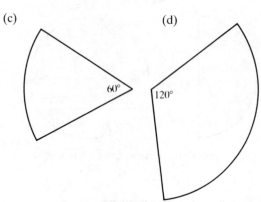

4. What is the circumference of a circle of radius
   2 cm?
   For each sector in Question 3, find the arc length if
   the radius in 2 cm.

5. Calculate the area of each sector in Question 3 if
   the radius is 2 cm.

6. The angle between the sighting of two stars is 2°.
   It is known that they are both approximately
   9×10^{13} km from Earth.
   Obtain an approximation for the distance between
   the stars.

5.4 Triangles and quadrilaterals

Area of a **triangle**
$A = \frac{1}{2}bh$

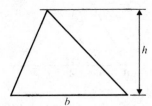

Area of a **parallelogram**
$A = bh$

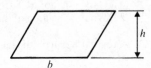

Area of a **trapezium**
$A = \frac{1}{2}(a + b)h$

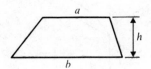

1. Find the area of these triangles.

(a)

(b)

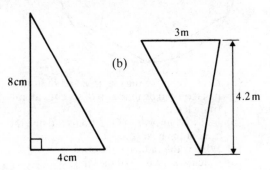

(c)

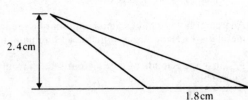

(d)

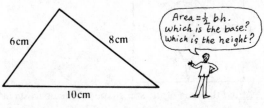

Area = $\frac{1}{2}$ bh.
which is the base?
which is the height?

2. Here are the coordinates of the vertices of a triangle. Draw the triangle on graph paper and find its area.
   (a) $(1, 1), (1, 5), (6, 1)$
   (b) $(0, 0), (0, 7), (3, 2)$
   (c) $(3, 4), (7, 4), (5, 6)$
   (d) $(^-1, 0), (1, 0), (^-4, 3)$

3. Find the area of each of these shapes drawn on a square grid.

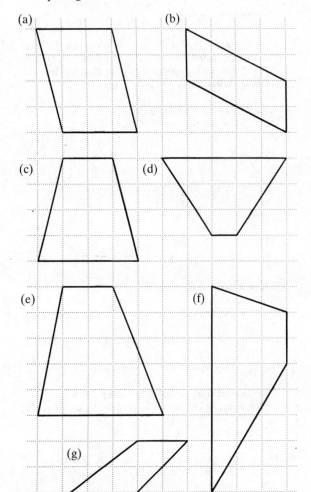

4. Find the area of the quadrilateral with vertices given by the coordinates.
   (a) $(1, 1), (1, 6), (6, 4), (6, 9)$
   (b) $(6, 4), (6, 9), (8, 9), (8, 0)$
   (c) $(2, 10), (4, 10), (6, 4), (0, 4)$
   (d) $(1, 1), (6, 4), (8, 4), (6, 1)$
   (e) $(1, 1), (1, 2), (3, 6), (3, 9)$

5. A quadrilateral ABCD has right angles at A and C.

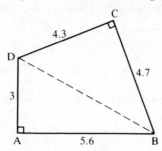

The measurements of the sides to the nearest
0.1 cm are given in the diagram. Find the area of
ABCD by calculating the area of each triangle
ABD and BCD.

6. A quadrilateral ABCD has a right angle at A and
BD̂C is also a right angle.

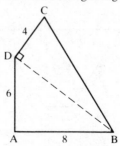

The sides AB, AD, and DC are 8 cm, 6 cm, and
4 cm respectively.
(a) Use Pythagoras' Theorem to find the length
BD.
(b) Find the area of the two triangles ABD and
BCD.
(c) What is the area of the quadrilateral ABCD?

7. Draw a sketch of a quadrilateral ABCD with
AB = 8 cm, BC = 8 cm, CD = 5 cm, DA = 10.1 cm,
and AB̂C = CD̂A = 90°.
Find the area of ABCD.

8. Draw a sketch of a quadrilateral ABCD with
AB = 12 cm, BC = 5 cm, CD = 4 cm and
AB̂C = AĈD = 90°.
(a) Use Pythagoras' Theorem to find the length
AC.
(b) Find the area of the quadrilateral ABCD.

9. In the kite ABCD, the diagonals AC and BD are
perpendicular and cross at the mid-point of BD.
The lengths of the diagonals are AC = 12 cm,
BD = 10 cm.
Find the area of ABCD.

10. The diagonals of a quadrilateral are perpendicular
and of length 8 cm and 5 cm respectively.
Find the area of the quadrilateral.

11. ABC is an equilateral triangle of side 2 cm.

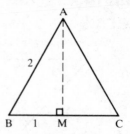

M is the mid-point of BC.
(a) Use Pythagoras' Theorem to find AM.
(b) What is the area of the triangle ABC?

12. A regular hexagon of side 2 cm is inscribed in a
circle.

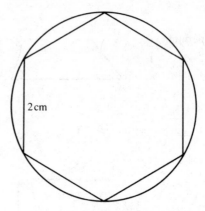

(a) Draw a copy of the diagram and show that the
hexagon can be made up of six equilateral
triangles.
(b) Use your answer to Question 11 to find the
area of the hexagon.
(c) What is the radius of the circle?
(d) Calculate the area of the circle.
(e) How much greater is the area of the circle than
the area of the hexagon?

13. A circular hole of radius 5 cm is cut out of a square
metal plate of side 12 cm. Find the area remaining.

14. A star shape is made by cutting four sectors from a
square plate of side 14 cm.

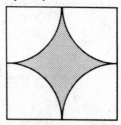

Find the area of the star shape, to the nearest cm².

5.5 Solids – surface area

You have already met solids such as **cuboids, prisms, cylinders** and **spheres**. The area of the total surface of a solid is called its **surface area.**

1. A cube has an edge length of 1 cm.
   (a) What is its surface area?
   (b) A larger cube is built up from eight of these cubes to make a cube of edge length 2 cm.

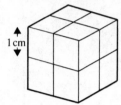

1 cm

What is the surface area of this larger cube?

2. Find the total surface area of cubes of edge length 3 cm and 6 cm.
   What happens to the surface area if the edge length of a cube is doubled?

3. Find the total surface area of a cuboid with dimensions.
   (a) 1 cm × 2 cm × 3 cm
   (b) 3 m × 2.5 m × 10 m
   (c) 20 mm × 35 mm × 40 mm

4. A prism of length 10 cm has a right-angled triangle end-face with edges 3 cm, 4 cm and 5 cm

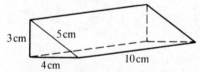

3 cm   5 cm

4 cm   10 cm

   (a) How many faces has the prism?
   (b) Find the total surface area.

5. A triangular prism has a right-angled triangle end-face of edge length 5 cm, 12 cm and 13 cm. The length of the prism is 20 cm.
   (a) Draw a sketch of the prism
   (b) Find its total surface area.

6. A piece of paper 10 cm wide is rolled up to make a cylinder.

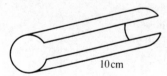

10 cm

The diameter of the circular ends is 7 cm.
(a) What is the circumference of the cylinder?
(b) Find the surface area of the paper.

In Question 6 you used the idea that the curved surface of a cylinder can be formed from a rectangle.

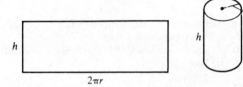

h

$2\pi r$

h   r

If the radius of the cylinder is r and its height is h, then the rectangle measures $2\pi r \times h$. This leads to the formula
Curved surface area = $2\pi rh$
The ends of a cylinder are circles. If these are included, we get
Total surface area   = $2\pi rh + 2\pi r^2$

Example 1

A cylinder has radius 4 cm and height 7 cm.

Curved surface area = $2 \times 3.14 \times 4 \times 7$
                    = 176 cm^2

Total surface area   = $176 + 2 \times 3.14 \times 4 \times 4$
                    = 276 cm^2

---

7. Find the curved surface area of a cylinder with:
   (a) $r = 3$ cm, $h = 10$ cm   (b) $r = 6$ mm, $h = 12$ mm
   (c) $r = 5$ cm, $h = 200$ cm (d) $r = 0.15$ m, $h = 1$ m

8. Find the total surface area of each cylinder in Question 7.

9. A cylinder has both height and diameter equal to 7 cm. Calculate:
   (a) the curved surface area
   (b) the total surface area.

10. A metal cylinder has radius 2 cm and height 3 cm. A second cylinder has radius 4 cm and height 6 cm.
    (a) Find the total surface area of both cylinders.
    (b) How much greater is the surface area of the second cylinder?

The surface area of a **sphere** is given by the formula
$S = 4\pi r^2$
Half a sphere is called a **hemisphere**.

r

Example 2

The diameter of a tennis ball is 7 cm.

The radius $r = \frac{7}{2} = 3.5$ cm
$S = 4\pi r^2 = 4 \times 3.14 \times 3.5^2$
            = 154 cm^2 Its surface area is 154 cm^2.

11. Find the surface area of a sphere with:
    (a) $r = 7$ cm   (b) $r = 2$ cm
    (c) $r = 10$ cm   (d) $r = 5$ mm

12. The radius of the Earth is approximately 6300 km.
    (a) Find its total surface area.
    (b) 71% of the surface of the Earth is water. Find
        the land surface area.

13. Find the surface area of the Moon whose diameter
    is approximately 3500 km.

The curved surface area of a **cone** is given by the
formula

$S = \pi rl$

where r is the radius of the base and l is the slant height.

14. Calculate the curved surface area S of a cone with:
    (a) $r = 1$ cm, $l = 2$ cm   (b) $r = 2$ cm, $l = 4$ cm
    (c) $r = 5$ cm, $l = 7$ cm   (d) $r = 0.5$ m, $l = 3$ m

15. A cone for ice cream is made with a slant height
    15 cm and top diameter 4 cm.
    (a) What is the radius r?
    (b) What is the surface area?

16. A solid cone has a base radius 5 cm and slant height
    12 cm.
    (a) What is the area of the base?
    (b) What is the curved surface area?
    (c) Find the total surface area.

For a solid cone, the total surface area must include the
area of the circular base.
If base radius $= r$ and slant height $= l$, Curved Surface
Area, $C = \pi rl$
Total Surface Area, $S = \pi rl + \pi r^2$

17. Factorise $\pi rl + \pi r^2$.
    Use your answer to find the total surface area of a
    cone of base radius 3 cm and slant height 4 cm.

18. A child's toy is made from a hemisphere of radius
    12 cm surmounted by a cone. The slant height of
    the cone is also 12 cm. Calculate the total surface
    area of the toy.

5.6 Volumes

All the solids like cubes, cuboids, prisms and cylinders
have parallel sides and constant cross sections.
The volume in each case is:
V = area of end face × length

Cube
Area of end face $= a^2$
Volume $= a^2 \times a = a^3$

Cuboid
Area of end face $= ab$
Volume $= ab \times c = abc$

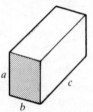

Triangular prism
Area of end face $= A$
Volume $= A \times h = Ah$

Cylinder
Area of end face $= \pi r^2$
Volume $= \pi r^2 \times h = \pi r^2 h$

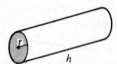

1. A metal cube of edge length 6 cm is melted down
   and recast to form a cuboid whose end is a
   rectangle 4 cm × 3 cm. How long is the cuboid?

2. A tape cassette measures 11 cm × 7 cm × 1.7 cm.
   (a) Draw a sketch to show how a box could be
       made to hold twenty cassettes in two rows of
       ten.
   (b) What are the dimensions and volume of the
       box?

3. Find the volume of the
   L-shaped solid whose
   dimensions are given in
   cm.

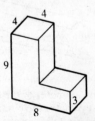

4. The end face of a prism of length 10cm is a right-angled triangle with sides 3cm, 4cm and 5cm.
   (a) Draw a sketch of the prism.
   (b) Find the volume of the prism.

5. The diagram shows a wedge.

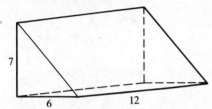

The lengths of the edges are shown in cm. Calculate the volume.

6. Find the volume of the cylinder with:
   (a) $r = 1$cm, $h = 2$cm   (b) $r = 7$cm, $h = 10$cm
   (c) $r = 5$mm, $h = 12$cm   (d) $r = 0.15$m, $h = 1$m

7. A coin has diameter 2cm and thickness 2mm.
   (a) Write down the radius and height of the cylinder using cm.
   (b) What volume of metal is needed to produce 100 coins?

The volume of a **sphere** is given by the formula
$V = \frac{4}{3}\pi r^3$

Example 3

The diameter of a tennis ball is 7cm.

The radius is $r = \frac{7}{2} = 3.5$cm
$V = \frac{4}{3}\pi r^3 = \frac{4}{3} \times 3.14 \times 3.5^3$
$\quad = 180$cm^3 Its volume is 180cm^3.

---

8. Find the volume of a sphere with:
   (a) $r = 1$cm   (b) $r = 3$mm   (c) $r = 0.8$m

9. What is the volume of metal required to make 1000 ball bearings of diameter 2mm?

10. A grapefruit has a diameter of 14cm.
   (a) What is its volume?
   (b) One third of the grapefruit is juice. How much juice can be got from 14 such grapefruit? (Take $\pi = \frac{22}{7}$)

11. (a) What is the volume of a cylinder with base radius 7cm and height 12cm?
   (b) 500cm^3 of water are poured into the cylinder. What is the volume remaining?
   (c) How many metal spheres of radius 7mm can be put into the cylinder before the water overflows? (Take $\pi = \frac{22}{7}$)

12. A plastic water carrier is in the shape of a sphere. The diameter of the carrier is 40cm.
   (a) What is the volume of the carrier?
   (b) How many litres of water does it hold? (1 litre $= 1000$cm^3)
   (c) How many carriers are needed to fill a cylindrical tank with base radius 1m and height 2m?

13. A swimming pool has a cross section made up of a rectangle with two semi-circular ends. The dimensions are shown in the figure below.

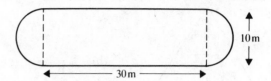

   (a) The depth of the pool is 2m. What is its volume?
   (b) How many litres of water are needed to fill it?

Volumes of cones and pyramids

  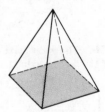

A pyramid with a circle as base – this is called a **cone**.   A pyramid with a triangle as base – this is a **tetrahedron**.   A pyramid with a square as base.

A **pyramid** is a shape whose sides slope upwards from the base to a vertex.

The volume of any pyramid can be written as:
$V = \frac{1}{3} \times$ height $\times$ base area

Example 4

Find the volume of a cone with base radius 8cm and height 10cm.

Base area $= \pi r^2 = 3.14 \times 8^2 = 201$cm^2
Volume of cone $= \frac{1}{3} \times 10$cm $\times 201$cm^2
               $= 670$cm^3

---

14. Find the volume of a cone
with the dimensions
shown on the right.

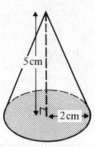

15. Find the volume of a pyramid with the dimensions
shown below.

(a)

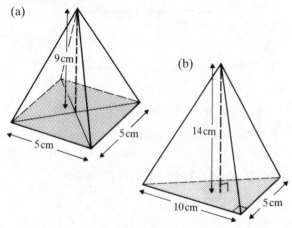

(b)

16. The great pyramid of Cheops in Egypt is 146 m
high, and has a base area of 52 500 m². Calculate its
volume.

Example 5

Look at the cone on the
right. If you know the
values of *l* and *r* you can
calculate *h*, using
Pythagoras' theorem.

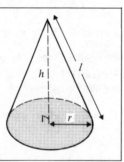

$l^2 = r^2 + h^2$
$h^2 = l^2 - r^2$
$h = \sqrt{(l^2 - r^2)}$

17. A cone has a slant edge of 6 cm and a radius of
3.6 cm. Find:
   (a) the height   (b) the volume

18. The volume of a cone is 12π cm³.
   (a) If its height is 9 cm, find the radius of its circular
       base.
   (b) Find also the length of the slant edge.

19. The pyramid has a square
base. Each slant edge is
the same length. N is the
mid-point of the base.
Find the height of the
pyramid by these steps:

   (i) find AC using Pythagoras's theorem;
   (ii) find AN;
   (iii) find VN, which is one side of triangle VAN.

20. Using your answer from Question 19, calculate the
volume of the pyramid.

21. Find the volume of a pyramid similar to that in
Question 19, but with each edge 10 cm.

22. (a) Find the volume of a pyramid of height 12 cm,
        with a regular hexagon of edge 4 cm as its base.
   (b) Find also the length of the slant edge.

23. Find the volume of the shape with measurements
shown.

(a)

(b)

(c)

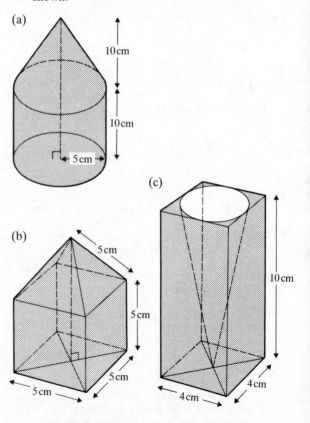

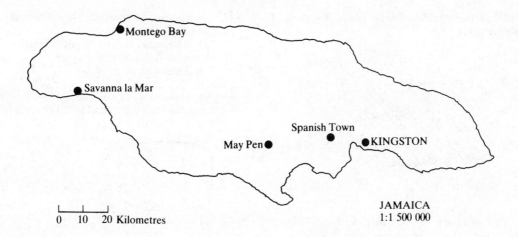

0 10 20 Kilometres

JAMAICA
1:1 500 000

5.7 Measurement and scales

Maps are always drawn to a **scale**. The scale of the sketch map of Jamaica shown above is 1 : 1 500 000. This is the ratio of a length on the map to the actual distance.
If you measure the distance on the map between May Pen and Spanish Town it is 1.8 cm.
Actual distance = 1.8 cm × 1 500 000
= 2 700 000 cm
= 27 000 m
= 27 km
Of course this is the distance 'as the crow flies'. The road distance may well be longer.

1. The distance on the map between Kingston and Spanish Town is 1 cm. What is this distance in km?

2. Use a ruler to measure in cm, the distance from Kingston to:
   (a) Montego Bay   (b) May Pen.
   What are these actual distances in km?

3. Use the sketch map to find, to the nearest km, the greatest length of the island.

4. The distance from Kingston to Savanna la Mar is approximately 125 km. What is this distance on a map with a scale of 1 : 1 500 000?
   Check your answer by measuring.

5. A more detailed map has a scale of 1 : 50 000. Find the actual distance between two places if the distance on the map is:
   (a) 1 cm   (b) 5 cm   (c) $\frac{1}{2}$ cm
   Find the map distance if the actual distance is:
   (d) 5 km   (e) 10 km   (f) 1 km

6. On a map the scale is written 5 cm : 1 km.
   (a) What is the distance, in metres, represented by 1 cm on the map?
   (b) What is the distance, in cm, represented by 1 cm on the map?
   (c) Express the scale as a ratio 1 : n

7. On a road map the scale is sometimes shown as 1 : 100 000 or 1 cm : 1 km.
   Match these scales:

1 : 50 000	1 cm : 1 km
1 : 100 000	2 cm : 25 km
1 : 1 250 000	10 cm : 1 km
1 : 10 000	1 cm : 4 km
1 : 4 000 000	2 cm : 1 km
1 : 400 000	1 cm : 40 km

8. What distance does 1 cm represent on a scale:
   (a) 1 : 50 000   (b) 1 : 200 000   (c) 1 : 5 000
   (d) 1 : 1 250 000   (e) 1 : 5 000 000?

9. The scale on a road map is 1 : 25 000.
   (a) What is the distance, in metres, represented by 3 cm?
   (b) What is the area of a field represented on the map by a rectangle 3 cm long and 4 cm wide?
   (c) What is the area of the field in hectares?
        (10 000 m^2 = 1 hectare)

10. The diagram shows the island of Paula. The scale of the map is 1 : 50 000.

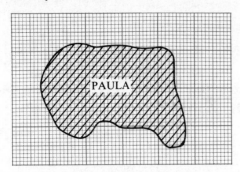

(a) Estimate the area of the map in cm^2.

(b) Estimate the actual area of Paula in km^2.

11. A boy makes a scale drawing of his rectangular bedroom. He uses a scale of 1 : 50.

(a) The dimensions of his drawing are 6 cm by 8 cm. What is the actual area of the bedroom in cm^2?

(b) Copy and complete
Area scale drawing : area bedroom
= 48 : □
= 1 : □

(c) How is the ratio of areas in (b) related to the ratio of lengths (1 : 50)?

In general if the scale giving the ratio of lengths is
$$1 : a$$
then the ratio of areas is
$$1 : a^2$$

12. The sails on a model boat are 20 cm^2 in area. The boat is built on a scale of 1 : 100. What is the area in m^2 of the boat's actual sails?

13. The area of a football pitch is 8000 m^2. On a map the pitch's area is 0.8 cm^2.

(a) What is the area of the pitch in cm^2?

(b) What is the ratio of the areas?

(c) What is the scale of the map?

14. A cylindrical water tank has a diameter of 4 m and a height of 3 m. A model of the tank is made using a scale of 1 : 100.

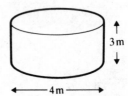

(a) What is the diameter of the base of the model?

(b) What is the area of the base of the model?

(c) What is the ratio of the area of the base of the model to that of the tank?

(d) What is the volume of the model?

(e) What is the ratio of the volume of the model to that of the tank?

15. Copy and complete

(a) $1 \, \text{cm}^2 = \square \, \text{mm}^2$ (b) $1 \, \text{m}^2 = \square \, \text{cm}^2$

(c) $1 \, \text{km}^2 = \square \, \text{m}^2$ (d) $1 \, \text{km}^2 = \square \, \text{cm}^2$

(e) $1 \, \text{cm}^3 = \square \, \text{mm}^3$ (f) $1 \, \text{m}^3 = \square \, \text{cm}^3$

(g) $1 \, \text{km}^3 = \square \, \text{m}^3$ (h) $1 \, \text{km}^3 = \square \, \text{cm}^3$

16. The scale of a model is 5 cm : 200 m.

(a) What distance is represented by 1 cm?

(b) What area is represented by 1 cm^2?

(c) What volume is represented by 1 cm^3?

Summary

By the end of this chapter these are the things you should know.

5.1 Area revision (pages 49–50)

How to find the area of a shape by counting squares.
$1\,m^2 = 10\,000\,cm^2$
$1\,cm^2 = 100\,mm^2$

5.2 Circles (page 51)

Revision of circumference and area

$$A = \pi r^2$$
$$C = 2\pi r$$

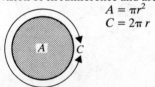

5.3 Areas and sectors (page 52)

Part of the circumference of a circle is called an **arc**.
How to find the length of an arc.
How to find the area of a sector.

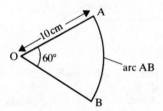

Length of arc $= \dfrac{60}{360} \times 2\pi \times 10 = 10.8\,cm$

Area of sector $= \dfrac{60}{360} \times \pi \times 10^2 = 52.4\,cm^2$

5.4 Triangles and quadrilaterals (pages 53–54)

Revision of how to find area of:

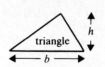

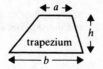

5.5 Solids (pages 55–56)

How to find the curved surface area of some regular solids.

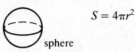

$$S = 4\pi r^2$$

sphere

5.6 Volumes (pages 56–58)

How to find the volume of cuboids, cylinders, prisms, spheres and cones.

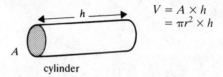

$$V = A \times h$$
$$= \pi r^2 \times h$$

cylinder

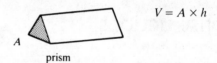

$$V = A \times h$$

prism

$$V = \tfrac{4}{3}\pi r^3$$

sphere

$$V = \tfrac{1}{3}\pi r^2 h$$

cone

5.7 Measurement and scales (pages 59–60)

How to change a map distance to an actual distance given the scale of the map.

Scale 1 : 25 000
A distance of 3 cm on map represents
$3\,cm \times 25\,000 = 75\,000\,cm = 750\,m$
on the ground.

If scale of a map is $1 : a$ then ratio of areas is $1^2 : a^2$.

6 Geometry

6.1 Constructions

Constructing a triangle

Construct a triangle ABC with AB = 8cm, BC = 6cm and AC = 4cm, using a ruler and compasses only.

[1] Draw AB.

A —————————————— B

[2] Centre B, with your compasses, draw an arc radius 6cm.

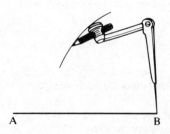

[3] Centre A, draw an arc radius 4cm.

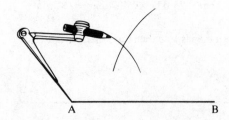

[4] The two arcs intersect at C.

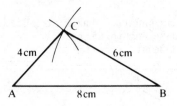

1. Draw triangles which have side lengths.
   (a) 6cm, 4cm, and 5cm
   (b) 5cm, 4cm, and 4cm
   (c) 5cm, 12cm, and 13cm
   Name each type of triangle you have drawn.

2. Use your protractor to draw a triangle with two sides and an included angle of:
   (a) 6cm, 6cm, and 30°
   (b) 3cm, 4cm, and 90°
   (c) 5cm, 4cm, and 135°
   For each triangle measure the length of the third side.

3. Use your protractor to draw a triangle with two angles and the side between them of:
   (a) 40°, 70°, and 5cm
   (b) 55°, 55°, and 4cm
   (c) 30°, 120°, and 3cm
   For each triangle measure the lengths of the other two sides.

Using a set square

4. (a) Draw a straight line, XY, with a ruler. Leave the ruler along XY.
(b) Place your set square ABC against the ruler, as in the diagram above. Use side AB to draw a straight line at an angle to your line XY.

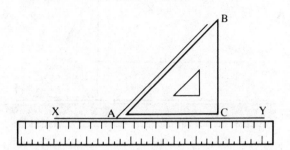

(c) Slide side AC along the ruler, about 5 cm. Use side AB to draw another straight line, as in the diagram below.

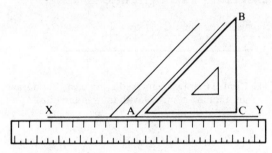

(d) Repeat (c) to give two more lines.
(e) Using a coloured pencil, mark in the corresponding angles.
(f) Measure the corresponding angles with a protractor. Are they equal? What can you say about the lines?
(g) Use a coloured pencil to mark in the alternate angles. (Hint: What must you first do to the parallel lines?)

5. Repeat Question 4, but this time use side BC of the set square to draw the parallel lines. What is the size of each corresponding angle?

6. Can you use a set square to draw a line at right angles to another line? How?

7. Write down the sizes of the three angles of your set square.

8. Here is how to draw a line through a point, so that it is parallel to another line:
(a) Draw a straight line FG. Mark a point P about 8 cm from FG.

(b) Place one edge of the set square on FG. Place a ruler against the second edge of the set square, as in the drawing below (the shaded set square),

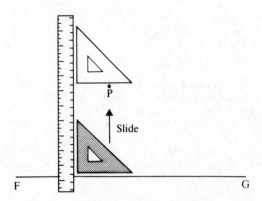

(c) Slide the set square along the ruler until the edge that was along FG now reaches P. This is shown by the white set square in the drawing above.
(d) Draw a line through P.

9. Repeat Question 8, with the point P:
(a) 6 cm from FG (b) 10 cm from FG

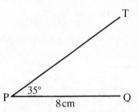

10. Draw a line PQ, 8 cm long. Now use your protractor to draw PT so that TP̂Q is 35°, as shown above.
Use your compasses to construct triangle PQR where QR is 6 cm. What do you notice?

11. Repeat Question 10 but this time make PQ = 8.4 cm, TP̂Q = 30°, and QR = 4.2 cm. What size is PR̂Q?

12. Using only your compasses, and a ruler, draw an exact copy of the shape.

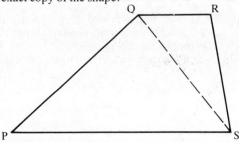

13. (a) Draw triangle PQS with the measurements given below.

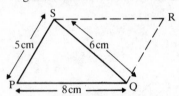

(b) Use your compasses to find a point R, such that SR = 8cm and QR = 5cm.
(c) What can you say about:
   (i) shape PQRS?   (ii) lines PQ and SR?

14. Use the idea in Question 13 to draw a parallelogram with sides 7cm and 4cm long and one diagonal 5.5cm long.

15. (a) Draw a line PQ 6cm long. Use your compasses to find a point 4.5cm from both P and Q.
(b) Now use only compasses and a ruler to draw a line through this point, parallel to PQ.

16. Using only your ruler and compasses, make an exact copy of the angle shown below.
(*Hint:* you will need to draw a triangle.)

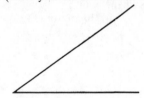

17. (a) Make an exact copy of the line PQ and the three points X, Y and Z shown below.

(b) Using two set squares only, draw a line parallel to PQ through each of the points X, Y and Z, as in the diagram below.
(c) Draw a line through each point, at right angles to PQ.

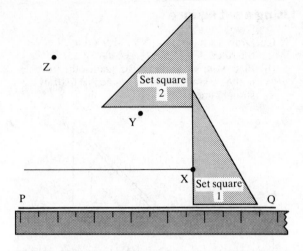

6.2 Bisecting

Bisecting a straight line

To bisect the line PQ.

[1] Centre P draw an arc, radius at least $\frac{1}{2}$PQ. Draw another arc centre Q with the same radius.

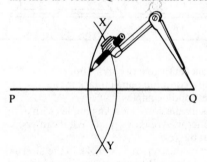

[2] The arcs meet at X and Y. Join XY.

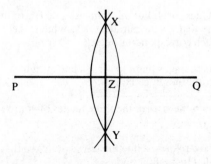

[3] XY is perpendicular to PQ and bisects PQ at Z.
PZ = QZ

1. Draw the line AB = 7cm.
Bisect the line.

2. Repeat Question 1 for AB = 9cm.

3. (a) Construct triangle ABC with AB = 9cm,
BC = 6cm and AC = 5cm.
(b) Bisect each of the sides of the triangle AB, BC
and AC.
(c) What do you notice?

4. The construction below is one way to draw a line
from X to RS, at right angles to RS. Write a flow
chart for the construction.

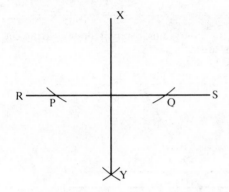

5. Draw a line LM, 5cm long. Mark a point X above
the line. Construct a line from X to LM which is at
right angles to LM.

6. Draw a line PQ, 6cm long. Construct a line
through Q, at right angles to PQ. Mark a point R
on this line so that QR is 8cm. Join PR and
measure its length.

7. Using your drawing from Question 6, construct a
line from Q to PR, which is at right angles to PR.
This line intersects PR at N. Measure the lengths of
PN, NR and NQ.

8. Draw triangle XYZ with the dimensions given
below.

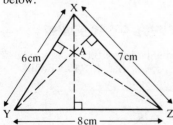

From X construct a line at right angles to YZ.
From Y construct a line at right angles to XZ.
From Z construct a line at right angles to XY.
What do you notice about your three lines?

9. Repeat Question 8 for another triangle.

Bisecting an angle

To bisect the angle ABC.

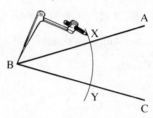

[1] Centre B, draw an arc to cut AB at X and BC at Y.

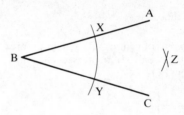

[2] Centre X draw an arc. Centre Y draw an arc with
the **same** radius to meet the first arc at Z.

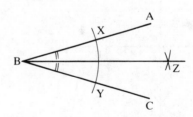

[3] Join BZ. This line bisects AB̂C.

10. With your protractor draw an angle of 50°. Bisect
this angle. Use your protractor to check the
accuracy of your construction.

11. Repeat Question 10 for angles of:
(a) 90°   (b) 60°   (c) 45°
(d) 120°   (e) 230°   (f) 330°

12. (a) Draw a triangle LMN
with dimensions as shown
on the right.
(b) Use the above
construction to bisect
LMN.
(c) What can you say about
this line and the line LN?

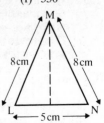

6.3 Constructing angles

In section 6.2 you saw how to construct a line at right angles to another line, and how to bisect any angle. In this section we will use these ideas to construct angles of 90°, 60°, 45°, 30°, 22½°, and 15°, without a protractor.

90° angle

To construct an angle of 90° at a point X on a line.

[1] Centre X, draw two arcs with your compasses to cut the line at A and B.

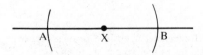

[2] Increase the radius of your compasses. Draw arcs centre A and then centre B to intersect each other at P and Q. Join PQ.

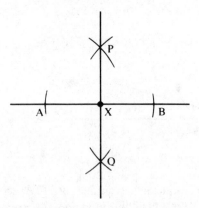

[3] AX̂P = 90°

1. Construct an angle of 90° for yourself.

2. (a) How many right angles are there in a rectangle?
   (b) Construct the rectangle ABCD with
      AB = 8 cm and BC = 6 cm.
      (Make sure you construct each right angle with your compasses)

3. Construct a square of side 5 cm.

4. (a) Construct an angle of 90°.
   (b) Bisect this angle to get an angle of 45°.

60° angle

To construct an angle of 60° at a point X on a line.

[1] Centre X draw a large arc to cut the line at P.

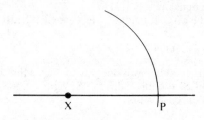

[2] Using the **same** radius, centre P, draw an arc to cut the first arc at Q.
Join XQ.

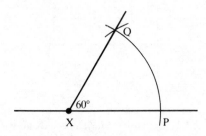

[3] The angle QX̂P = 60°.

5. Construct an angle of 60° for yourself.

6. Construct an equilateral triangle of side 5 cm.

7. Using only a straight edge and compasses draw an angle of 60°. Draw the bisector of this angle. Measure the size of each part.

8. Construct an angle of 15°. (Hint: bisect an angle of 60° twice)

Shapes containing these angles

9. Use only a straight edge and compasses to construct an isosceles triangle RST with the dimensions given below.

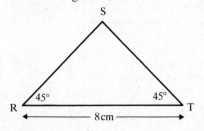

10. (a) Use only a straight edge and compasses to construct triangle ABC, with the dimensions shown on the right.

(b) Measure BC and hence calculate the area of triangle ABC and the length of AB.

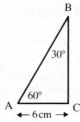

11. Construct the following triangles ABC, with AB = 7 cm and
(a) $\hat{A} = 90°$, $\hat{B} = 45°$
(b) $\hat{A} = 90°$, $\hat{B} = 30°$
(c) $\hat{A} = 45°$, $\hat{B} = 30°$
(d) $\hat{A} = 15°$, $\hat{B} = 75°$

12. Construct the rhombus ABCD with side 6 cm and $A\hat{B}C = 60°$.

13. Construct the parallelogram WXYZ, with WX = 8 cm, XY = 6 cm and $W\hat{X}Y = 135°$.

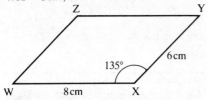

14. (a) Use only a straight edge and compasses to construct triangle PQR with the dimensions given on the right.

(b) Do you agree that QR is the height of the triangle? What is the area of triangle PQR?

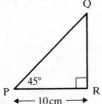

(c) Now construct triangle PSR, on the same base PR, and with $R\hat{P}S = 22\frac{1}{2}°$. Locate point S so that triangle PSR *has the same area* as triangle PQR.
(*Hint:* Would it help to draw a line through Q parallel to PR? Why?)

15. Use only a straight edge and compasses to construct the quadrilateral ABCD, with dimensions given on the right.

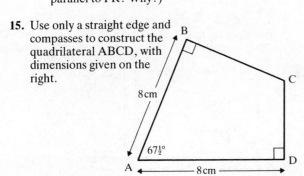

6.4 Ratios and similar triangles

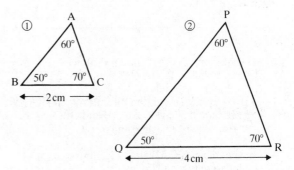

1. Angle $\hat{A}$ of triangle ① corresponds to $\hat{P}$ of triangle ②. Side AB of triangle ① corresponds to PQ of triangle ②.
(a) Find an angle which corresponds to:
   (i) $\hat{C}$ (ii) $\hat{Q}$ (iii) $\hat{R}$
(b) Are the corresponding angles equal?
(c) Find a side which corresponds to:
   (i) QR   (ii) PR   (iii) CB
(d) Are the corresponding sides equal?

Triangles ① and ② are different sizes, but their corresponding angles are equal.
They are called **similar** triangles.

2. Are the triangles in each pair similar?

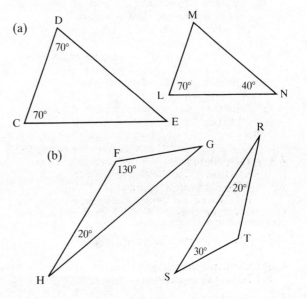

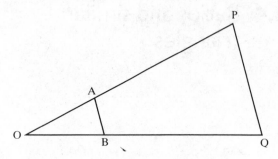

3. Look at triangles OAB and OPQ above.
   Â corresponds to P̂. OA corresponds to OP.
   (a) What corresponds to:
        (i) B̂   (ii) Ô?   (iii) PQ?   (iv) OQ?
   (b) Measure the angles of OAB and OPQ.
       Are the two triangles similar? Why?

4. For the triangles OAB and OPQ above:
   (a) measure OA and OP.
   (b) measure OB and OQ.
   (c) measure AB and PQ.
   What do you notice about your results?

5. Use your answers to Question 4 to write down the
   ratios of the corresponding edges.
   (a) OA:OP   (b) OB:OQ   (c) AB:PQ
   What do you notice about the three ratios?

6. Measure the sides of triangles ① and ② above.
   Now find these ratios in their simplest form.
   (a) AB:PQ   (b) AC:PR   (c) BC:QR
   What do you notice about the three ratios?

7. (a) Look at the similar triangles in Question 2. For
       each pair of triangles write down the three
       pairs of corresponding sides.
   (b) Measure each pair of corresponding sides, and
       write the measurements as a ratio.
       What do you notice?

8. (a) Construct two different triangles with angles
       60°, 30° and 90°.
   (b) Measure each side of the triangles.
   (c) For the corresponding sides, write the
       measurements as a ratio in simplest form.
       What do you notice?

Look again at triangles ① and ② at the top of page 67.
AB corresponds to PQ.   AB : PQ = 1 : 2
BC corresponds to QR.   BC : QR = 1 : 2
AC corresponds to PR.   AC : PR = 1 : 2

**For two similar triangles, the ratios of the
corresponding edges are equal.**

These equal ratios can be written as fractions.

i.e $\dfrac{AB}{PQ} = \dfrac{BC}{QR} = \dfrac{CA}{RP}$

Using ratios to find side lengths

Example

Triangles LMN and SRT are similar. (They are
not drawn to scale.)
Find the value of x.

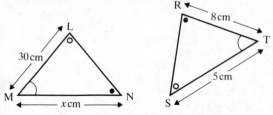

MN corresponds to RT. LM corresponds to SR.

$\dfrac{MN}{RT} = \dfrac{LM}{SR}$

$\dfrac{x}{8} = \dfrac{30}{5}$

Multiplying both fractions by 8 gives:

$x = 48$

9. Use the method shown above on these similar
   triangles to find the unknown length. (Not to
   scale.)

(a)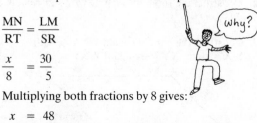

(b)

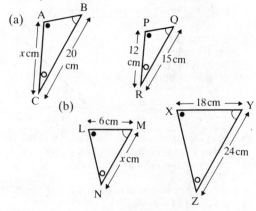

10. Use ratios to find first x and then y.

(a)

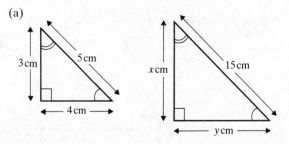

(b)

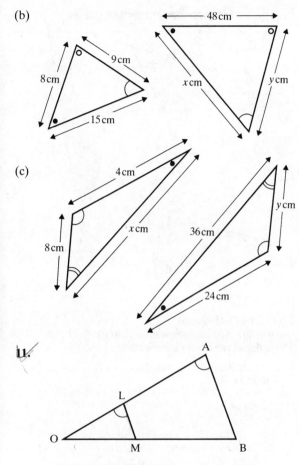

6.5 Congruency

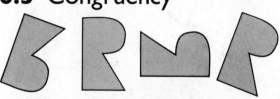

Are the four shapes above identical? How could you be sure? One way would be to use a tracing of one of the shapes and see if it fitted exactly on top of each of the others. Try it.

Shapes that are equal so that if you cut out a copy of one it could be made to fit exactly on top of the other are said to be **congruent**.

The four shapes above are congruent.

1. In the diagram below, are the two shapes congruent?

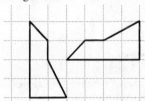

Make a copy of the shapes on squared paper and draw a third shape that is congruent to them.

2. (a) Are all squares congruent to themselves?
   (b) Are all 10cm squares congruent to themselves?
   (c) Are these two squares congruent?

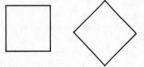

3. (a) Are these two shapes congruent?

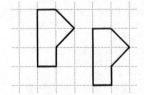

(b) Are these two shapes congruent?

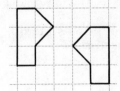

Note that, as in Question 3, two shapes are congruent if one will fit exactly on to the other. It does not matter if you have to imagine turning the shape over to fit.

11.

Explain why OLM and OAB are similar. Write down the three pairs of corresponding edges.
(a) If LM = 5cm, AB = 35cm and OM = 7cm find the length of OB.
(b) If LM = 4cm, AB = 6cm and OA = 27cm find the length of OL.
(c) If OM = 3cm, MB = 4cm and AB = 14cm find the length of LM.
(d) If OM = LM = MB = xcm, find AB.

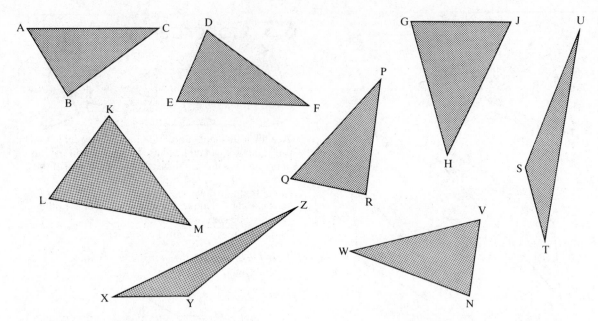

Congruent triangles

4. (a) There are four pairs of congruent triangles
     drawn above. Pick out the pairs.
   (b) Use tracing paper to check if you were right.
   (c) For which pairs did you need to turn your
       tracing over, to make the triangles fit exactly?

5. (a) If you trace triangle ABC and fit it onto
       triangle PQR, angle A fits onto angle Q.
       Do you agree?
   (b) We say Â **maps** to Q̂, or Â → Q̂.
       Complete the mapping:
       Â → Q̂
       B̂ →
       Ĉ →

6. Write down the mappings for the angles in each of
   the other pairs of congruent triangles above.

7. (a) If you fit the tracing of triangle ABC onto
       triangle PQR, side AB fits onto side QR.
       Do you agree?
   (b) Complete the mapping:
       AB → QR
       BC →
       CA →

8. Write down the mappings for the sides in each of
   the other pairs of congruent triangles.

The sign for *triangle* is Δ.
The sign for *is congruent to* is ≡.

ΔABC ≡ ΔQRP means
triangle ABC is congruent to triangle QRP
The order of the letters is important.

From the order, you can tell that Â → Q̂.
B̂ → R̂ and Ĉ → P̂.
You can also tell that AB → QR, BC → RP and
CA → PQ.

9. Look at these two triangles. All the measurements
   of their sides and angles are given.

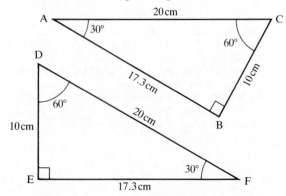

(a) Are the triangles congruent?
    Trace ΔABC to find out. Did you have to turn
    your tracing over ?
(b) Could you tell that the triangles were
    congruent without tracing them? How?
(c) Complete the mapping of angles:
    Â →   , B̂ →   , Ĉ →
(d) Complete the mapping of sides:
    AB →   , BC →   , CA →
(e) Explain why it is correct to write
    ΔABC ≡ ΔFED

10. (a) Are these two triangles congruent?

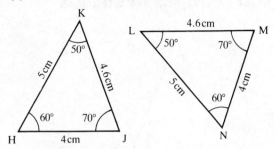

(b) Complete the mapping:
$\hat{H} \rightarrow$ HJ $\rightarrow$
$\hat{J} \rightarrow$ JK $\rightarrow$
$\hat{K} \rightarrow$ KH $\rightarrow$

(c) Complete the statement: $\triangle$HJK $\equiv$

11. Look at the two congruent triangles below.

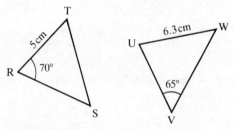

$\triangle$RST $\equiv$ $\triangle$UWV

Use the information given in the diagram to answer these questions.

(a) What are the lengths of RS and UV?
(b) What are the sizes of RŜT and VÛW?
(c) Which angle of $\triangle$UWV is the same size as RŜT? What size is it?
(d) Find a side which is the same length as WV.

12. Look at these two congruent triangles:

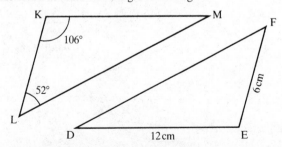

Using the information given in the diagram, answer these questions.

(a) What is the size of KM̂L?
(b) Write down the size of each angle of $\triangle$DEF.
(c) Write down the lengths of the sides of $\triangle$KLM if you can.

13. You are told the following information about two triangles:
$\triangle$XYZ $\equiv$ $\triangle$ABC
XY = 7 cm, XZ = 5 cm
YX̂Z = 100°
Draw a sketch of both triangles and write down all you know about the sides and angles of $\triangle$ABC.

More about triangles

Two triangles will be congruent if:
[1] three sides of one equal three sides of the other (S.S.S.), or
[2] two sides and the included angle of each are equal (S.A.S.), or
[3] two angles and a corresponding side of each are equal (A.A.S.), or
[4] both have a right angle, and the hypotenuse and a corresponding side of each are equal (R.H.S.).

14 (a) Which pairs of triangles below are congruent? Say which test you have used.
(b) For each pair, write down the equal angles and equal sides.

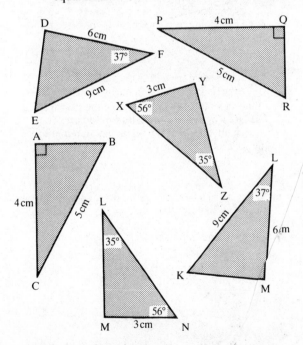

15. In Question 14, the triangles ABC and QRP are congruent. The **congruency statement** for them is:
$\triangle$ABC $\equiv$ $\triangle$QRP
Copy and complete the congruency statements for the other triangles:
$\triangle$LMN $\equiv$ . . . .
$\triangle$DEF $\equiv$ . . . .

16. Draw the triangle ABC when:
  (a) AB = 3 cm, BC = 4 cm, CA = 2 cm
  (b) AB = 4 cm, BC = 5 cm, B̂ = 30°
  (c) Â = 50°, B̂ = 70°, BC = 5 cm
  (d) AB = 5 cm, BC = 4 cm, Ĉ = 90°

17. (a) Try using the measurements in Question 16(a)
         to draw another triangle with a *different* shape.
         Can you do it? Will all triangles drawn to these
         measurements be congruent?
   (b) Repeat for the other parts of Question 16.

18. Draw two *different* triangles ABC, with
    AB = 6 cm, B̂ = 30° and AC = 4 cm. Explain why
    these triangles are not congruent.

19. The three triangles shown below are congruent.
    Write down the sizes of all the unmarked angles
    and sides.

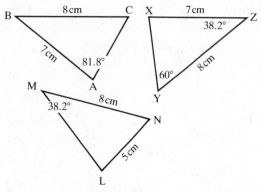

20. Draw a rectangle PQRS. Mark in the diagonal PR.
    Explain why the two triangles formed are
    congruent, and write a congruency statement for
    them.

6.6 Angles in circles

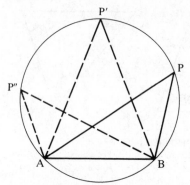

1. (a) Draw a circle, and mark a chord AB on it, as
         shown above.
   (b) Mark a point P on the larger arc.
         Join PA, then PB.
   (c) Measure AP̂B.
   (d) Repeat for at least four others points P. What
         do you notice about the sizes of the angles
         AP̂B, AP̂′B, AP̂″B, etc?

2. (a) Now mark a point Q on the smaller arc, in your
         drawing for Question 1.
         Join QA and QB.
   (b) Measure AQ̂B.
   (c) Repeat for at least four other points Q. What
         do you notice about the sizes of angles AQ̂B?

3. Add your measurements for one angle APB and
    one angle AQB. What is their sum?

4. (a) Draw a circle, with a dotted chord LM.
   (b) Choose a point X on the major arc, and Y on
         the minor arc, Join XL, XM, YL, and YM as
         shown in the diagram.

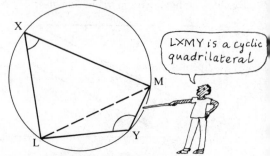

LXMY is a cyclic quadrilateral

   (c) Measure LX̂M and LŶM. Add the
         measurements. What do you notice?

5. (a) On your drawing for Question 4, join XY with
         a dotted line, to form a new chord.
   (b) Do you agree that angles XM̂Y and XL̂Y stand
         on this chord?
   (c) Measure XM̂Y and XL̂Y. Add the
         measurements. What do you notice?

6. Repeat Questions 4 and 5 for two more circles, using different positions of L and M.
Each time find:
(a) the sum of LX̂M and LŶM
(b) the sum of XL̂Y and XM̂Y
What do you notice?

7. (a) In the drawing for Question 4, do you agree that shape LXMY is a quadrilateral? Because it is in a circle, it is called a **cyclic quadrilateral**.
(b) Do you agree that LX̂M and LŶM are opposite angles in a cyclic quadrilateral?
(c) Is the same true for XL̂Y and XM̂Y?
(d) Using what you learned in Questions 4–6, copy and complete: *The sum of the opposite angles in a cyclic quadrilateral is . . . .*

8. (a) Draw a circle with centre O. Mark two points A and B on it, as shown below. Join OA and OB, and measure AÔB.

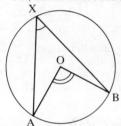

(b) Mark any point X on the major arc. Join AX and BX. Measure AX̂B.
(c) What do you notice about the sizes of AÔB and AX̂B?

9. Repeat Question 8 for at least two different positions of A and B.

From the questions on page 72, you should have found:
[1] All angles at the circumference, standing on the same chord and in the same segment of a circle, are equal.
[2] The sum of the opposite angles in a cyclic quadrilateral is 180°.
[3] An angle at the centre of a circle is twice the size of the corresponding angle at the circumference.

10. Without measuring, find the value of the letter in each circle. Each time, say which of the above properties you are using.
Note. A dot represents the centre of the circle.

(a)   (b)

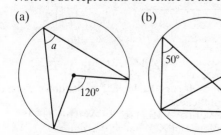

(c)   (d)

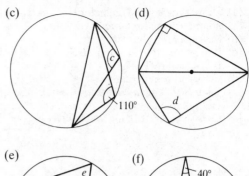

(e)   (f)

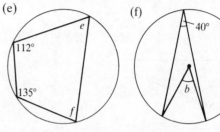

11. Without measuring, find the value of the letter. The dot represents the centre of the circle.

(a)   (b)

(c)   (d)

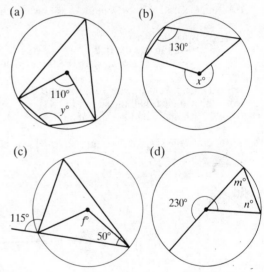

12. In the drawing below, AB is a diameter of the circle.

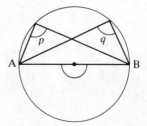

(a) What shape is each segment?
(b) What size is the marked angle at the centre?
(c) What size would you expect angles p and q to be?
(d) Measure p and q. Were you correct?

13. (a) Draw a circle and a diameter HJ. Mark any
point K on the circumference. Join HK and JK.
(b) Measure HKJ. Is it 90°?
(c) Repeat for other positions of K.
Is HKJ always 90°?
(d) Copy and complete:
An angle in a semi-circle is a . . . . angle.

14. In the circle below, LM is a diameter.

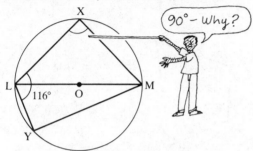

(a) Copy the drawing. Without measuring, mark
on it the sizes of LXM, LYM and XMY.
(b) Join OX and OY. Now mark the angle which
is:
(i) twice the size of XMY
(ii) twice the size of XLY.
Write the size on each of the three angles.

15. Look again at your drawing for Question 14.
(a) Which angle is half the size of LOX?
(b) Which angle is half the size of YOL?

16. Write down the sizes of the angles marked with a
letter.

(a)   (b)

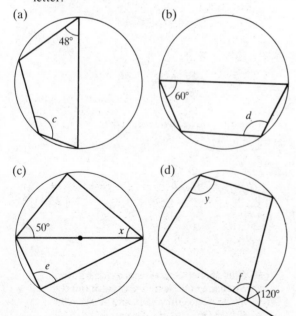

(c)   (d)

(e)   (f)

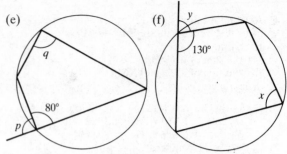

17. In Question 16(d), the angle marked 120° is an
exterior angle of the cyclic quadrilateral.
(a) Which is the exterior angle in drawings (e) and
(f)?
(b) For drawings (d), (e) and (f) is any interior
angle of the quadrilateral the same as the
exterior angle?

The ideas in Questions 16 and 17 lead to another
important result about angles in circles:
An exterior angle of a cyclic quadrilateral is equal to
the interior opposite angle.

18. In drawing 16 (e), $\hat{p}$ is the exterior angle, and $\hat{q}$ is
the interior opposite angle. $\hat{p} = \hat{q} = 100°$.
In drawing 16 (f), which is the exterior angle?
Which is the interior opposite angle? What size is
each?

19. Copy the diagram below, and find the marked
angles. Give reasons for your answers.

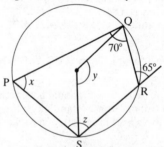

20. Draw a circle with diameter LM. Mark two points,
P and Q, on the circumference, as shown below.
Join PQ, PM, PL, QM and QL. Mark point X.

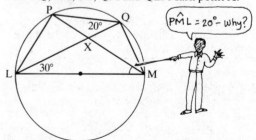

If QLM = 30°, and POL = 20°, write down, with
reasons, the sizes of:
(a) QPM (b) PML (c) LOM (d) QMP
(e) MPL (f) PXQ

6.7 Quadrilaterals

The angle sum of any quadrilateral is 360°.

Quadrilaterals may be classified according to the properties of their sides, angles, or diagonals.

Quadrilateral		Sides	Angles	Diagonals
Trapezium		One pair parallel.	—	—
Kite		Two pairs of adjacent sides are equal.	One pair of opposite angles equal.	One diagonal bisects the other at right angles.
Parallelogram		Opposite sides parallel and equal.	Opposite angles equal.	Bisect each other.
Rhombus		All sides equal; opposite sides parallel.	Opposite angles equal.	Bisect each other at right angles.
Rectangle		Opposite sides parallel and equal.	All angles equal 90°.	Bisect each other.
Square		All sides equal; opposite sides parallel and equal.	All angles equal 90°.	Bisect each other at right angles.

By examining the list you see that some shapes possess all the properties of another shape. Thus, a square is a rectangle because the square satisfies all the conditions required of a rectangle. In set language, the set of squares is a subset of the set of rectangles. For example, examine the following Venn diagram.
$R \cap S$ = set of squares

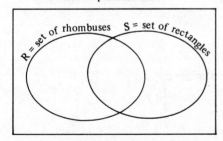

set of quadrilaterals

1. Draw a Venn diagram to show the subsets:
$P = \{x|x \text{ is a parallelogram}\}$,
$R = \{x|x \text{ is a rhombus}\}$,
$S = \{x|x \text{ is a square}\}$, of the set $Q = \{x|x \text{ is a quadrilateral}\}$.

2. Draw a Venn diagram to show the sets of quadrilaterals that are trapeziums, parallelograms, and squares.

3. ABCD is a square, ABXY is a rhombus with the side AB common to both figures. Describe the triangle DAY, giving reasons for your answer.

4. ABCD is a rectangle, ABXY is a parallelogram with the side AB common to both figures. Which of the following statements is true?
(a) CDYX is a parellelogram
(b) CDYX cannot be a rhombus
(c) CDYX must be a rectangle
(d) If CDYX is a rectangle, then so is ABXY.

5. A pair of congruent isosceles triangles are joined along an equal side. Draw diagrams to show that the resulting quadrilateral can be:
(a) a parallelogram
(b) a rhombus
(c) a kite.

6. ABC is a right-angled isosceles triangle with $\hat{B} = 90°$. ACX is an isosceles triangle drawn on the side AC. Describe the triangle ACX if:
(a) ABCX is a square
(b) ABCX is a kite
(c) ACX = 105°.

7. AOC, BOD are diagonals of a quadrilateral, intersecting at O. Name the quadrilateral if:
(a) OA = OC, OB > OD, and $A\hat{O}B = 90°$
(b) OA = OC, OB = OD, and $A\hat{O}C > 90°$
(c) OA = OB = OC = OD.

8. AOC, BOD are two rods that are pivoted at their centre point O. Name the quadrilateral ABCD if:
   (a) AC = BD   (b) AÔB = 90°
   (c) AO = OB and AÔB = 90°.

9. ABCD is a square, BCXY is a parallelogram drawn on the side BC outside the square and in the same plane. For each of the following statements, state whether:
   (A) it must be true
   (B) it may be true
   (C) it must be false
   (a) BCXY is a rectangle
   (b) ADXY is a parallelogram
   (c) ADXY is a square
   (d) ADXY is a rectangle
   (e) ABY is equilateral.

10. PQRS is a square, RSTU is a rhombus with RŜT ≠ 90°. The figures are cut out of card and hinged along the common side RS. For each of the following statements, state whether:
    (A) it must be true
    (B) it may be true
    (C) it must be false
    (a) PST is an isosceles triangle
    (b) PST is an equilateral triangle
    (c) PQUT is a rectangle
    (d) PQUT is a parallelogram
    (e) PQUT is a rhombus.

11. If one angle of a parallelogram is 35°, find the other three angles.

12. If one angle of a rhombus is 70°, find the other three angles.

13. If two adjacent angles of a kite are 130° and 57°, find the size of the other two angles.

6.8 Plans and elevations

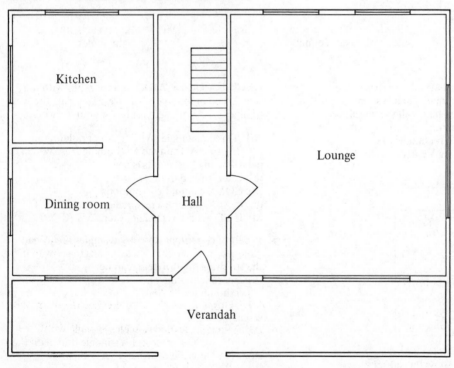

Scale 1 : 100

Plans

1. Above is the **plan** of the ground floor of a modern house.
   (a) What symbol is used to represent a door?
   (b) What symbol represents a window?
   (c) How many doors and windows are there, on the ground floor?

2. Do you agree that 1 cm on the plan above represents 1 metre?

3. Measure the diagram, and write down the length, width and area of the ground floor (excluding the verandah).

4. Is a **plan** a view from directly above or from one side?

5. How long is the verandah?

6. How many square metres of floor covering would be needed for the lounge floor?

7. About how thick are the walls of the bungalow?

8. On squared paper, draw a plan of your classroom floor. Use a scale of 1 : 100. Carefully mark in the doors and windows.

9. Look at the diagram below. It shows the homes of three families who live in a remote country area. A water pump is to be installed, at a position which is the same distance from each home. Where should it be put?

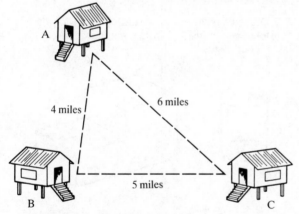

4 miles
6 miles
5 miles

Solve the above problem in this way:
(a) Draw a scale plan of the homes, using 1 cm to represent 1 mile.
(b) Draw a line, such that each point on the line is the same distance from B and C.
(c) Draw a line, such that each point on the line is the same distance from A and B.
(d) The two lines intersect at a point. Call the point L.
(e) Explain why L is the required position for the pump.

10. Two towns are 4 miles apart. A school is built 2 miles from one town and 3 miles from the other. There is a straight road joining the two towns. Where should a bus stop be placed on this road, so that the students at the school have the shortest walk?

Elevations

11. Here is a drawing of a box.
Below are three diagrams of the box, made by looking at it from three different directions.

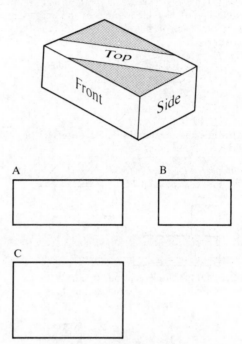

A

B

C

Compare the diagrams with the drawing above.
Which diagram shows the box:
    (i) from directly above?
    (ii) from directly in front?
    (iii) directly from one side?

12. The **plan** is the view from directly above. Which diagram above is the plan?

13. A view directly from one side is called a **side elevation**.
Which diagram is a side elevation?

14. A view from directly in front is called the **front elevation**.
Which diagram is the front elevation?

Example

Four equal cubes are placed on a table with three in a row and one behind as in this diagram.

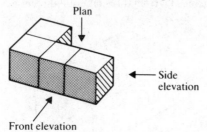

Draw the plan, front and side elevations of the solid.

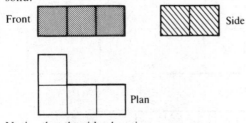

Notice that the side elevation appears as two squares together. The second square does *not* appear behind the first.

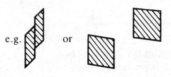

A number of wooden or cardboard cubes will help in the following question.

15. Draw the plan, front and side elevations for these arrangements of cubes.

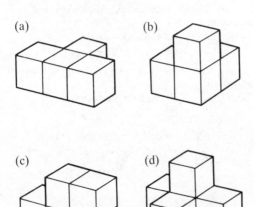

16. Here is a photograph of a brick, which has three holes through it. The sketches show the front and side elevations (not to scale).

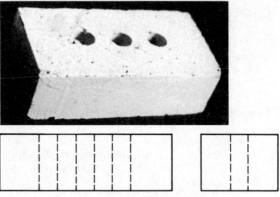

(a) What do the dotted lines represent?
(b) Why is there only one pair of dotted lines on the side elevation?
(c) Make a rough sketch of the plan of the brick.

In Question 16 the dotted lines in the elevations represent the hidden parts of the solid.

17. Draw the plan, front and side elevations for the following solids. Use dotted lines to represent hidden edges.

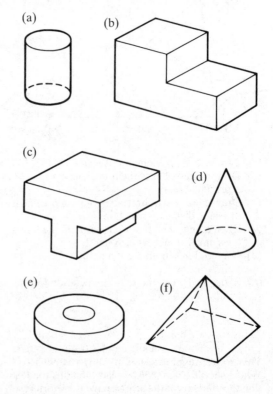

18. Draw a rough plan, front elevation and side elevation for the mug and the sugar container in the photograph above. (Take each one separately, and don't forget the hidden edges.)

19. The dimensions of the brick in Question 16 are: length 22 cm, width 10 cm, height 6.5 cm. The holes each have diameter 2.5 cm and are 2.5 cm apart. On a large sheet of squared paper, draw accurately the plan, front elevation and side elevation of the brick.

20. The sketch on the right shows a short plastic tube. It is 12 cm long, with an inside radius of 3 cm and an outside radius of 4 cm. On squared paper, draw a full-scale plan and two elevations for the tube.

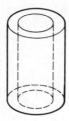

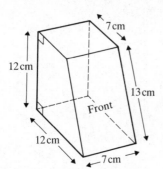

21. (a) Do you agree that the diagram below is a rough plan of the shape above? (The top of the shape is a square. The front, back and base are rectangular.)

(b) Why is the line across the centre not dotted?
(c) Draw accurately the plan, front elevation and side elevation for the shape. Write down the scale you have used.

22. Draw accurately on squared paper the plan and two elevations for the shape.

(a)

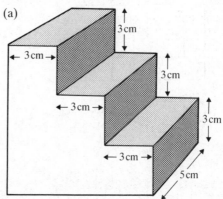

(b)

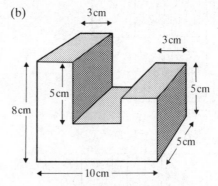

23. The plan, front elevation and side elevation are usually arranged as shown below. The light lines are called **projection lines**. They show how the different views are connected to each other. Note the distances that are marked equal.

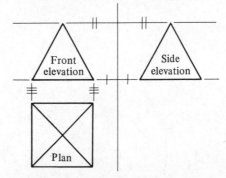

(a) Sketch the solid which has the plan and elevations shown above.
(b) What is it called?

24. Sketch these solids.

(a)

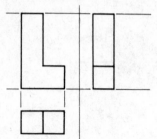

(b)

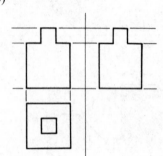

(c)

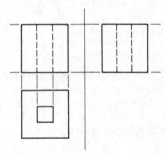

(d)

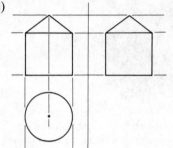

(e)

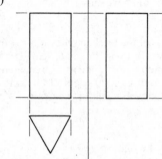

(f)

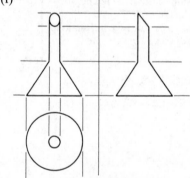

Summary

By the end of this chapter, these are the things you should know about.

6.1 Constructions (pages 62–64)

Using ruler and set square to draw parallel lines.

6.2 Bisecting (pages 64–65)

Using compasses to bisect a line.
Using compasses to bisect an angle.

6.3 Constructing angles (pages 66–67)

How to use a ruler and compasses to construct angles of 90° and 60°.
Using bisecting to construct other angles.

6.4 Ratios and similar triangles (pages 67–68)

The meaning of **similar triangles**.

 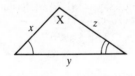

$$\frac{a}{x} = \frac{b}{y} = \frac{c}{z}$$

6.5 Congruency (pages 69–72)

Two shapes are **congruent** if they are identically equal.
How to label congruent triangles.
How to recognise when triangles are congruent by the cases (S.S.S), (S.A.S.), (A.A.S.), (R.H.S)

6.6 Angles in circles (pages 72–74)

Angles on the same chord are equal.

The angle at the centre of a circle is twice the angle at the circumference standing on the same arc.

6.7 Quadrilaterals (page 75–76)

Revision of properties of:

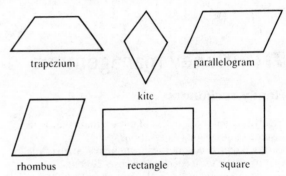

trapezium   parallelogram

kite

rhombus   rectangle   square

Using a Venn diagram to show how these shapes are related.

6.8 Plans and elevations (page 76–80)

What a **plan, front elevation** and **side elevation** are.

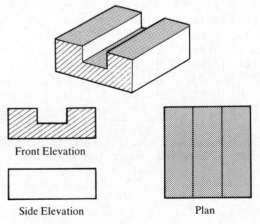

Front Elevation

Side Elevation   Plan

You should also be able to sketch a solid, given its plan, front elevation and side elevation.

7 Consumer arithmetic

7.1 Money management

Ready reckoners

Ready reckoners are books of tables, that you can use instead of doing long calculations.

Part of a ready reckoner is shown below. It gives the cost of *n* articles, if each article costs 29 cents. The complete table shows the cost of up to 1000 articles. But even using just this part of the table, you can work out a great many costs quickly.

Ready reckoner for a unit cost of 29 cents								
No.	$	No.	$	No.	$	No.	$
1	0.29	11	3.19	21	6.09	31	8.99
2	0.58	12	3.48	22	6.38	32	9.28
3	0.87	13	3.77	23	6.67	33	9.57
4	1.16	14	4.06	24	6.96	34	9.86
5	1.45	15	4.35	25	7.25	35	10.15
6	1.74	16	4.64	26	7.54	36	10.44
7	2.03	17	4.93	27	7.83	37	10.73
8	2.32	18	5.22	28	8.12	38	11.02
9	2.61	19	5.51	29	8.41	39	11.31
10	2.90	20	5.80	30	8.70	40	11.60

1. Do you agree that 12 biros at 29 cents each cost $3.48? If the unit is 29 cents, write down the cost of:
   (a) 17 stamps   (b) 37 mangoes
   (c) 29 rulers   (d) 6m of cotton
   (e) 16 kg of rice   (f) 22 spools of thread

2. 9 ice lollies at 29 cents each cost $2.61. Do you agree? Write down the cost of:

(a) 90 ice lollies   (b) 900 ice lollies
What is the quick way to work these out?

3. If a notebook costs 29 cents, write down the cost of:
   (a) 70 notebooks   (b) 180 notebooks
   (c) 1800 notebooks   (d) 3700 notebooks

4. How would you use the table to find the cost of 49 notebooks at 29 cents each?

Example 1

Find the cost of 284 candles at 29 cents each.

280 candles cost $81.20   (28 candles × 10)
  4 candles cost $1.16
     Total $82.36

---

5. If each item costs 29 cents, find the cost of:
   (a) 43 items   (b) 46 items   (c) 48 items
   (d) 430 items   (e) 439 items   (f) 409 items

6. For a unit cost of 29 cents, find the cost of:
   (a) 56 items   (b) 64 items   (c) 99 items
   (d) 334 items   (e) 276 items   (f) 154 items
   (g) 1000 items   (h) 3004 items   (i) 1750 items

Bills

In many types of bill the unit cost depends on the number of units bought or used.
For example, in the electricity bill shown below, the cost of units is as follows:
   First 50 units cost 30 cents per unit
   Further units cost 20 cents per unit

ELECTRICITY BILL		89–03–31

METER READING		UNITS USED
Previous	Present	
1642	1732	90

Rate
50 units at 30¢   = $15.00
40 units at 20¢   = $8.00

TOTAL DUE $23.00

7. Using the rates shown above, find the electricity bill for a man who uses:
(a) 30 units   (b) 50 units
(c) 51 units   (d) 85 units

8. The electricity rates for government buildings are:
First 100 units cost 40 cents each,
next 100 units cost 35 cents each,
next 200 units cost 30 cents each,
remaining units cost 25 cents each.
(a) What is the cost of the 101st unit?
(b) What is the cost of the 220th unit?
(c) What is the cost of the 401st unit?

9. Using the rates in Question 8 work out the bill for a building which uses:
(a) 60 units   (b) 160 units
(c) 200 units   (d) 201 units
(e) 375 units   (f) 430 units
(g) 1000 units   (h) 2000 units

10. On 1st January a meter reads 2432 units. Two months later it reads 2546 units. What is the electricity bill if units cost 32 cents each and there is a fuel surcharge of 15 cents per unit?

11. A.J. Singh's electricity bill is $49.88. How many units does he use if the cost per unit is 43 cents?

Example 2

Electricity rates on a certain island are:
First 60 units cost 50 cents each
next 100 units cost 45 cents each
remaining units cost 40 cents each.
Find the number of units used by a man whose electricity bill is $77.40

First 60 units cost 60 × 50¢   = $30.00
Next 100 units cost 100 × 45¢ = $45.00

160 units cost $75.00

The man used $77.40–$75.00 = $2.40 of electricity at 40 cents per unit.

Number of 40¢ units used = $\dfrac{2.40}{0.40}$ = 6

Total number of units used = 160 + 6 = 166.

12. Use the rates as shown in Example 2 to find the number of units used if a man's electricity bill is:
(a) $25.00   (b) $30.45
(c) $62.40   (d) $85.40
(e) $99.80   (f) $106.60

13. A monthly telephone bill is made up of a $25 rental, while calls cost 35 cents each.
How many calls were made if the monthly bill is:
(a) $25.00   (b) $28.50
(c) $37.60   (d) $66.65?

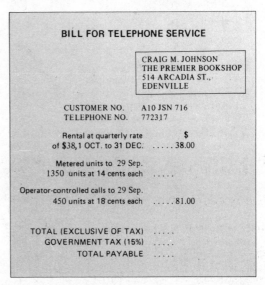

BILL FOR TELEPHONE SERVICE

CRAIG M. JOHNSON
THE PREMIER BOOKSHOP
514 ARCADIA ST.,
EDENVILLE

CUSTOMER NO.   A10 JSN 716
TELEPHONE NO.   772317

Rental at quarterly rate $
of $38,1 OCT. to 31 DEC. 38.00

Metered units to 29 Sep.
1350 units at 14 cents each   . . . . .

Operator-controlled calls to 29 Sep.
450 units at 18 cents each 81.00

TOTAL (EXCLUSIVE OF TAX)   . . . . .
GOVERNMENT TAX (15%)   . . . . .
TOTAL PAYABLE   . . . . .

14. The telephone bills on a certain island look like the one shown above.
Operator-controlled calls are where the operator connects you to the number you want. What do you think metered units are?

15. Copy the telephone bill above from *rental at quarterly rate*. Fill in the missing costs and find the total payable.

16. Find the total payable by Ellie Lin. She uses 4380 metered units and 369 operator-controlled units, and the government tax is 15%.

17. Find the total payable by John Gonzales. He uses 5837 metered units and 962 operator-controlled units, and the government tax is 15%.

18. Jason Soper rents a car for a business trip.
The rates are:
$120 for the first 24 hours
$100 for the next 24 hours
$90 for each subsequent 24 hours
plus 10 cents per mile driven.
Find the rental cost to Jason if he rents the car at midday on Monday and returns it at midday the following Saturday, having driven 503 miles.

19. Using the rates for a car rental as in Question 18, find how long Jason kept the car if his bill was $579.10 and he drove the car a total of 891 miles.

20. A printer makes the following charges for personal stationery.

	Cost in cents for each	
	Sheet of notepaper	Envelope
First 100	8	10
Next 200	7	9
Next 300	6	8
Remainder	5	7

Find the cost if you buy:
(a) 100 sheets and 100 envelopes
(b) 250 sheets and 100 envelopes
(c) 800 sheets and 300 envelopes
(d) 1000 sheets and 800 envelopes
(e) 1850 sheets and 1850 envelopes

21. Copy and complete the table below, for the weekly bills of the Edmondson family, over 4 weeks.

Week	Food ($)	Clothing ($)	Rent ($)	Sundries ($)	Totals ($)
1	26.10	14.25	35.00		85.75
2			35.00	18.00	104.27
3	19.90	3.95			
4	21.75		35.00	8.70	75.20
Totals ($)	89.07	57.90	140.00		338.67

22. John Edmondson is the only wage-earner.
(a) Calculate the average (mean) spending of the Edmondson family per week, and hence calculate what they might spend in a year.
(b) What is the least amount of money that John Edmondson needs to take home in a year, if an annual electricity bill of $640 is added to their year's spending?

Foreign exchange

In Barbados the unit of currency is the Barbados dollar, Bds $. In St Lucia the Eastern Caribbean dollar, EC$, is used. To buy goods in St Lucia a man from Barbados must change his Bds $ to EC$. The current rate of exchange is:
    Bds $1.00 = EC $1.35

Example 3

Change Bds $80 to EC$

Bds $80 = EC$ 1.35 × 80
        = EC$ 108
---

23. Change the following to EC$:
(a) Bds $60   (b) Bds $25
(c) Bds $16.25   (d) Bds $481.96

Example 4

Change EC $80 to Bds $

EC $80 = Bds $80 ÷ 1.35

    = Bds $ $\frac{8000}{135}$

    = Bds $ $\frac{1600}{27}$

    = Bds $ 59.26

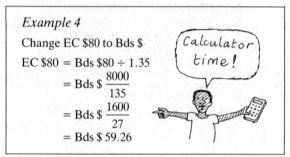
---

24. Change the following to Bds $:
(a) EC $135   (b) EC $675
(c) EC $900   (d) EC $84

Other exchange rates with the Bds $ are shown in the table below.

Trinidad and Tobago   TT $1.00 = Bds $0.55
Jamaica   J $1.00 = Bds $0.34
United States   US$1.00 = Bds $2.00
United Kingdom   UK £1.00 = Bds $2.95
Guyana   G$1.00 = Bds $0.27

25. Use the table above to calculate the value of Bds $1.00 in:
(a) TT $ (b) J $ (c) US $ (d) G $

26. Change the following to Bds $:
(a) TT $200   (b) US $50   (c) UK £25
(d) G $3000   (e) J $684   (f) US $78.25

27. Change:
(a) Bds $30 to J $ (b) Bds $100 to US $
(c) Bds $265 to G $ (d) Bds $4000 to UK £
(e) Bds $65.50 to TT $

28. A bottle of rum costs Bds $10.00 in Barbados. The same bottle is sold for US $6.50 in the United States.
In which country is it cheaper and by how much?

29. Caricom travellers cheques are issued in TT $. How much will you receive in Bds $ if you cash:
  (a) TT $600   (b) TT $820?

30. If in Question 29, a 1% commission is charged on travellers cheques, how much will you receive in Bds $ if you cash:
  (a) TT $500   (b) TT $1030?

Example 5

If Bds $1.00 = EC $1.35 and Bds $1.00 = TT $1.80 change EC $90 to TT $.

EC $1.00 $\quad = $ Bds $ \dfrac{1.00}{1.35}$

So EC $90 $\quad = $ Bds $ \dfrac{1.00}{1.35} \times 90$

$\qquad\qquad = $ Bds $ \dfrac{9000}{135}$

$\qquad\qquad = $ TT $ \dfrac{9000}{135} \times 1.8$

$\qquad\qquad = $ TT $120

---

31. Using the exchange rates on page 84, change:
  (a) EC $270 to TT $ (b) US $150 to EC $
  (c) G $4000 to US $ (d) UK £250 to US $
  (e) TT $710 to EC $

32. Mrs Cummings takes TT $1000 in travellers cheques to Jamaica. In Jamaica she spends J $700. How much money, in TT $, does she return with?

33. John Smith flies from London with £450 to Barbados. There he spends Bds $620 before going onto Antigua where he spends EC $450. How much money does he have left, in UK £, on his return to London?

Conversion graphs

Simple currency exchanges can be read from conversion graphs.

Example 6

Given that Bds $1.00 = EC $1.35, draw a graph to convert:
(a) Bds $4.00 to EC $ (b) EC $5.00 to Bds $

Using a suitable scale draw a horizontal axis to represent Bds $ and a vertical axis to represent EC $.
Join with a straight line the two points which can be plotted, (0, 0) and (1.00, 1.35)

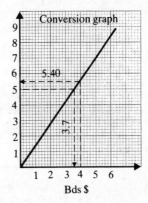

From the graph you can see that:
(a) Bds $4.00 = EC $5.40
(b) EC $5.00 = Bds $3.70

---

34. Given that US $10 = EC $27, draw a graph to convert:
  (a) EC $54 to US $ (b) EC $90 to US $
  (c) US $35 to EC $ (d) US $8.50 to EC $
  Use a horizontal scale of 1 cm to US $4 and a vertical scale of 1 cm to EC $10.

35. Given that £2.00 = J $17.00 draw a graph to convert:
  (a) J $30.00 to £   (b) J $75.00 to £
  (c) £12 to J $ (d) £6.30 to J $
  Use a horizontal scale of 1 cm to £1 and a vertical scale of 1 cm to J $10.

36. Given that UK £10 = US $14.90 draw a graph to convert:
  (a) US $20 to £   (b) US $46 to £
  (c) £24 to US $ (d) £50 to US $
  Use a horizontal scale of 1 cm to £5 and a vertical scale of 1 cm to US $5.

7.2 Profit and loss

Mrs Walcott bought a radio for $50 and sold it for $60.
Her profit was $60–$50 = $10.
We can write:

profit = selling price − cost price

Mrs Walcott's profit as a fraction of the cost price $= \dfrac{10}{50}$

Her percentage profit $= \dfrac{10}{50} \times 100\%$

$$= 20\%$$

Generally we write:

percentage profit $= \dfrac{\text{selling price–cost price}}{\text{cost price}} \times 100\%$

1. Jason made a table for $80. He sold it for $100.
   (a) What was his profit?
   (b) What was his percentage profit?

2. Mr Fowler buys chickens for $15 and sells them for
   $20 each.
   (a) What is his profit?
   (b) What is his percentage profit?

Example 1

Ann Felix bought a car for $20 000 and sold it for
$15 000. What was her percentage loss?

Ann's loss = $20 000 – $15 000
           = $5000

Ann's percentage loss $= \dfrac{\$5000}{\$20\ 000} \times 100\%$
                       $= 25\%$

---

3. Jason bought his bicycle for $450. He sold it for
   $300.
   (a) What was his loss?
   (b) What was his percentage loss?

4. A storekeeper buys 500 pens for $100. He sells
   each pen for 30 cents.
   (a) What is his profit per pen?
   (b) What is his percentage profit?

5. A farmer grows 800 kg of tomatoes at a cost of
   $2500. He sells them at $3 per kilogram. Find his
   percentage profit or loss.

6. Paul buys six dozen eggs for $28.80 and sells them
   for $3 per half dozen. Find his percentage profit or
   loss.

7. Copy and complete the table below.

Item	Cost price ($)	Selling Price ($)	Percentage Profit
Calculator	120	140	
Pencil	0.35	0.40	
T.V.	850	1020	
Bed	600	480	
Book	6.75	10.25	

If the cost price of an item and the percentage profit/loss is
known, it is a simple matter to find the selling price.

Example 2

Find the selling price of a stove bought for $1200
and sold at a 15% profit.

Profit   = 15% of $1200

$$= \dfrac{15}{100} \times \dfrac{\$1200}{1}$$

$$= \$180$$

Selling price = cost price + profit
             = $1200 + $180
             = $1380

---

8. A suit costs $300 to make. What is:
   (a) the profit
   (b) the selling price
   if it is sold for a 12% profit?

9. Andrew Prescot buys his car for $26 750 and sells it
   at a 20% loss.
   (a) What was his loss?
   (b) What did he sell the car for?

10. A cassette recorder is priced at $720. It is sold in a
    sale at a 7% discount.
    (a) What is the discount?
    (b) What is the sale price?

11. A shirt is sold at a $12\frac{1}{2}\%$ discount. What is the
    selling price if it cost $50?

12. Janette buys an electric iron for $120. She sells it
    for a $33\frac{1}{3}\%$ profit. What is the selling price?

13. Import duty on cosmetics is 45%. What will be the
    sale price of a face cream costing $5.60 before
    duty?

14. A sales tax of 3% is levied on all purchases in a
    certain country. What will be the cash price of a
    pair of scissors costing $19.00?

15. Copy and complete the table below.

Item	Cost Price ($)	Selling Price ($)	Percent Profit
Table	260		$37\frac{1}{2}$
Dress	95		6
Carpet	1060		13
Umbrella	26		$4\frac{1}{2}$
Ruler	0.80		$57\frac{1}{2}$

16. From which of these would a government get a larger income?
(a) A purchase tax of 10% on 200 articles at a cost price of $350 each
(b) A purchase tax of 15% on 60 articles at a cost price of $800 each
(c) A purchase tax of 20% on 25 articles at a cost price of $1500 each

It is possible to work out the cost price of an item if the selling price and the percentage profit/loss is known. This calculation is a little more difficult than the method used in the questions above.

Example 3

Find the cost price of a glass sold for $6.50 at a profit of 30%.

Write C.P. for cost price
Then profit = 30% of C.P.
and C.P. + 30% of C.P. = selling price
$$130\% \text{ of C.P.} = \$6.50$$
$$\frac{130}{100} \times \text{C.P.} = \$6.50$$
$$\text{C.P.} = \frac{100}{130} \times \$6.50$$
$$\text{C.P.} = \$5.00$$

Study Example 3 carefully. Notice you cannot work out the profit directly as you do not know the cost price.

17. A vase is sold for $12 at a 20% profit. What is the cost price?

18. The selling price of a chair is $98. What is its cost price if a 40% profit is made?

19. An electric blender has a price of $240 after import duty is added to the cost price. What is the cost price of the blender if import duty is 20%?

20. Mr. Lockhart's salary after a 15% pay increase was $23 000. What was his salary before the increase?

21. A dressmaker sells a skirt for $75. If she makes a 25% profit, how much did it cost her to make it?

22. After a 5% price increase, the cost of a telephone rental went up to $45 per month. What was the rental before the increase?

The cost price can be found in a similar manner if the percentage loss or discount is given.

Example 4

Find the cost price of a car sold for $18 000 at a loss of 10%.

Loss = 10% of C.P.
C.P. – 10% of C.P. = selling price
$$90\% \text{ of C.P.} = \$18\,000$$
$$\frac{90}{100} \times \text{C.P.} = \$18\,000$$
$$\text{C.P.} = \frac{100}{90} \times \$18\,000 = \$20\,000$$

---

23. A watch is sold for $16 at a loss of 20%. What is the cost price?

24. Irvin Ramsaran sold his motor bike for $7700 at a loss of 30%. What did he pay for the bike?

25. A pair of jeans was sold for $53.82 after a discount of 22%. What was the price before discount?

26. The cost of an item is $33.30 after a $7\frac{1}{2}$% discount. What is the price of the item before discount?

27. A loss of 15% is incurred when a radio is sold for $68. At what price must the radio be sold to make a 15% profit?

28. Copy and complete the table below.

Item	Cost Price	Selling Price	Percent Profit	Percent Loss
Curtains	$120	$130		
Mat		$25	25%	
Tiles	$180			4%
Sofa		$980		2%
Bookcase	$620	$530		
Cabinet	$900		$6\frac{3}{4}$%	
Centre table		$168.30		$17\frac{1}{2}$%

29. A 20% profit is made on the sale of a fridge for $1800. What would be its sale price if it was sold for a loss of 25%?

30. Mrs Henderson's weekly wage was $130 after a 20% wage increase. What would be her wage if instead she received a 50% increase?

31. Alfred's salary after paying tax at 25% is $14 000. What is his salary before tax?

32. The price of a pair of shoes was reduced by $18 after a 20% discount. What was
(a) the original price of the shoes
(b) the discounted price of the shoes?

7.3 Interest and investment

Revision – simple interest

Interest is the payment or fee made to a bank for the use of a loan of money.
The borrower has to pay back:
  (a) the original loan
  (b) the interest on the loan
in the same way a bank will pay you interest on any money you lend to (deposit in) the bank.

Simple interest is calculated as a percentage per year of the loan. This percentage is called the **rate** of interest.

Example 1

Find (a) the interest (b) the total repayment on a loan of $10 000 for 3 years if the rate of interest is 16% per annum.

$$\text{Interest after 1 year} = 16\% \text{ of } \$10\ 000$$
$$= \frac{16}{100} \times \frac{\$10\ 000}{1}$$
$$= \$1600$$
$$\text{Interest after 3 years} = 3 \times \$1600$$
$$= \$4800$$
$$\text{Total repayment} = \text{loan} + \text{interest}$$
$$= \$10\ 000 + \$4800$$
$$= \$14\ 800$$

---

1. Find the simple interest on:
   (a) $600 for 2 years at 7%
   (b) $8000 for 4 years at 5%
   (c) $4300 for 3 years at 14%
   (d) $800 for 6 months at 10%
   (e) $1800 for $3\frac{1}{2}$ years at 12%

2. David puts $900 in his credit union. How much money does he have altogether in two years if the interest rate is 4% per annum?

3. Susan borrows $2000 from her bank whose interest rate on loans is 13%. Find:
   (a) the interest she pays if she keeps the money for 4 years.
   (b) her total repayment.

In Book 3 we used the simple interest formula
$$I = \frac{P \times R \times T}{100}$$
to calculate interest, where I = interest, P = principal, R = rate and T = time in years.
Substituting into this formula shortens the working of many simple interest problems.

Example 2

Find the simple interest on $800 for $4\frac{1}{2}$ years at 6%.

$P = 800$, $R = 6$, $T = 4\frac{1}{2}$
So
$$I = \frac{800 \times 6 \times 4\frac{1}{2}}{100}$$
$$= \frac{800 \times 6 \times 9}{100 \times 2}$$
$$= 4 \times 6 \times 9$$
$$= 216$$
So interest is $216

---

4. Use the formula to find the simple interest on a loan of:
   (a) $1000 for 2 years at 15% p.a.
   (b) $800 for 3 years at 16% p.a.
   (c) $2400 for $1\frac{1}{2}$ years at 12% p.a.
   (d) $6000 for $3\frac{1}{2}$ years at $12\frac{1}{2}$% p.a.

5. Find the simple interest paid on a loan of $5000:
   (a) in 4 years, at 15% p.a.
   (b) in $4\frac{1}{2}$ years, at 10% p.a.
   (c) in $5\frac{1}{4}$ years, at $8\frac{3}{4}$% p.a.
   (d) in $2\frac{1}{3}$ years, at $16\frac{1}{2}$% p.a.

The formula for simple interest can be rearranged as:

$$P = \frac{100\,I}{RT} \qquad T = \frac{100\,I}{PR} \qquad R = \frac{100\,I}{PT}$$

You should be able to arrive at each of these formulas for yourself.

6. Use the formula to find P, given:
   (a) $I = \$90$, $T = 4$ years, $R = 9\%$
   (b) $I = \$60$, $T = 2$ years, $R = 6\%$
   (c) $I = \$180$, $T = 3$ years, $R = 12\frac{1}{2}\%$

7. Use the formula to find T, given:
   (a) $I = \$225$, $P = \$750$, $R = 10\%$
   (b) $I = \$120$, $P = \$300$, $R = 16\%$
   (c) $I = \$364$, $P = \$800$, $R = 13\%$

8. $10 000 is borrowed at 15% p.a.
   After what length of time is the amount of simple interest equal to the loan?

9. Use the formula to find R, given:
    (a) $I = \$126$, $\quad P = \$700$, $\quad T = 2$ years
    (b) $I = \$171$, $\quad P = \$600$, $\quad T = 3$ years
    (c) $I = \$675$, $\quad P = \$1250$, $\quad T = 4$ years

10. Start with the formula $I = \dfrac{PTR}{100}$. Set out the steps to show how it can be rearranged to give each formula above.

Compound interest

Banks do not usually use simple interest to calculate interest payments. Instead the interest after each year is added to the principal and the following year's interest is found from that new principal. This method of computing interest is called **compound interest.**

Example 3

Find the compound interest on $600 for 2 years at 12%

$$\text{Interest for first year} = 12\% \text{ of } \$600$$
$$= \frac{12}{100} \times \$600$$
$$= \$72$$
$$\text{Principal after first year} = \$600 + \$72 = \$672$$
$$\text{Interest for second year} = 12\% \text{ of } \$672$$

new principal

$$= \frac{12}{100} \times \$672$$
$$= 12 \times \$6.72$$
$$= \$80.64$$
$$\text{Total compound interest} = \$72 + \$80.64$$
$$= \$152.64$$
$$(\text{Total amount after 2 years} = \$672 + \$80.64$$
$$= \$752.64)$$

Notice, in Example 3 that, because the interest is compounded, the interest in the second year is $80.64 and not $72 as under simple interest.

11. Find the compound interest on:
    (a) $500 for 2 years at 10%
    (b) $600 for 2 years at 20%
    (c) $1000 for 2 years at 5%
    (d) $900 for 3 years at 10%
    (e) $4000 for 3 years at 15%

12. In Question 11 find the total amount in each case.

13. Alvin Haynes deposits $2000 in his bank. What is the amount in the bank after 3 years compound interest at 4%?

14. Peter Gabriel takes a loan of $20 000 to buy a new car. How much must he repay if he borrows the amount for 3 years at 15% per annum compound interest?

15. Which is the better investment?
    (a) $600 at 7% simple interest for 3 years.
    (b) $600 at 6% compound interest for 3 years.

16. An apartment built for $50 000 increases in value by 6% each year. How much is it worth after three years?

Unlike the apartment in Question 16, some goods decrease (depreciate) in value. In such cases the annual depreciation is subtracted.

Example 4

Find the value of a car costing $30 000 after 2 years if it depreciates at a rate of 8%.

$$\text{Decrease in value in 1st year} = 8\% \text{ of } \$30\ 000$$
$$= \frac{8}{100} \times \$30\ 000$$
$$= \$2400$$
$$\text{Value at end of the 1st year} = \$30\ 000 - \$2400$$
$$= \$27\ 600$$
$$\text{Decrease in value in 2nd year} = 8\% \text{ of } \$27\ 600$$
$$= \frac{8}{100} \times \$27\ 600$$
$$= \$2208$$
$$\text{Value at end of 2nd year} = \$27\ 600 - \$2208$$
$$= \$25\ 392$$

---

17. A pick-up truck depreciates in value at a rate of 10% per annum. What will be the value of the truck in two years' time, if it is now worth $35 000?

18. For insurance purposes a food processor is valued at $60 000. The insurers assume a 20% annual depreciation. What will be the insurance value of the processor in three years' time?

19. Owing to migration the population of a small island decreases annually by 2%. If the population is 4000 at present, what will be the population in two years' time?

20. The mass of a radioactive lump of matter decreases by 50% every week. What will be the mass of the lump in three weeks, time if its mass is 200 g at present?

Ready reckoners for interest payments

The calculation of compound interest for periods longer than three years is greatly simplified using ready reckoners. The tables usually show the amount that $1 becomes after a given number of years at a particular rate of interest.

Years	\$1 at yearly compound interest				
	10%	11%	12%	13%	14%
1	1.10	1.11	1.12	1.13	1.14
2	1.21	1.23	1.25	1.28	1.30
3	1.33	1.37	1.40	1.45	1.48
4	1.46	1.52	1.57	1.64	1.69
5	1.61	1.69	1.76	1.85	1.93
6	1.77	1.88	1.97	2.11	2.20
7	1.95	2.09	2.21	2.38	2.51
8	2.15	2.32	2.48	2.69	2.86
9	2.37	2.58	2.78	3.04	3.26
10	2.61	2.86	3.11	3.44	3.72

You might find a table like the one above in a ready reckoner. It shows that if you borrow \$1 at 11% compound interest, you owe \$2.09 altogether, after 7 years. The interest has been calculated at the end of each year, and added to the loan.

21. How much do you owe at the end of the time, if you borrow \$1 for:
  (a) 3 years at 13% compound interest
  (b) 7 years at 14% compound interest
  (c) 9 years at 11% compound interest
  (d) 6 years at 10% compound interest?

Example 5

Find the final value of an investment of \$7000 at 12% for 5 years.

From the table above:
\$1 at 12% for 5 years amounts to \$1.76
So \$7000 amounts to 7000 × \$1.76 = \$12 320

---

22. Use the compound interest table at the top of the column to find the final value of an investment of:
  (a) \$10 at 12% for 10 years
  (b) \$100 at 13% for 8 years
  (c) \$1000 at 14% for 7 years
  (d) \$200 at 14% for 6 years
  (e) \$700 at 12% for 10 years

23. A house is priced at \$60 000. A man wishing to buy it takes a loan for this amount at 14% compound interest. If he is to repay the loan over 10 years find:
  (a) his total repayment
  (b) the amount he repays each month, if he pays equal monthly installments over ten years.

7.4 Hire Purchase and mortgages

Hire Purchase – revision

Many goods, because of their price, cannot be bought easily by cash. These goods may also be offered on **hire purchase**. That is, the purchaser pays an initial deposit and pays the balance in a series of monthly or weekly installments.

The hire purchase price is more expensive than the cash price. The difference is really the **interest** payable on the loan of the goods.

Example 1

A television can be purchased for \$1800 cash or on H.P. for a deposit of 20% and 18 monthly payments of \$90. Find:
(a) H.P. price
(b) interest charged
(c) percent interest charged

(a) Deposit $= 20\%$ of \$1800

$$= \frac{20}{100} \times \frac{\$1800}{1}$$

$$= \$360$$

Total monthly payments $= 18 \times \$90$
$\qquad\qquad\qquad\qquad = \$1620$
    H.P. price $=$ deposit $+$ total monthly payment
$\qquad\qquad\qquad = \$360 + \$1620$
$\qquad\qquad\qquad = \$1980$

(b) Interest $\quad = $ H.P. price $-$ cash price
$\qquad\qquad\qquad = \$1980 - \$1800$
$\qquad\qquad\qquad = \$180$

(c) Interest rate $\quad = \dfrac{\text{interest}}{\text{cash price}} \times 100\%$

$$= \frac{180}{1800} \times 100\% = 10\%$$

---

1. A video recorder has a cash price of \$2500. Find the H.P. price if it may also be bought for a deposit of 10% and 24 monthly payments of \$95.

2. An armchair priced at \$940 can be bought in two ways.
  A: for cash with a 5% discount
  B: By hire purchase with a 15% deposit and 12 monthly payments of \$75
  Find:
  (a) the amount payable by each method
  (b) the interest charged.

3. The cash price of a refrigerator is $3020. It can be bought on hire purchase for a deposit of 20% and 24 monthly payments of $110. Find:
   (a) the H.P. price
   (b) the interest charged
   (c) the per cent interest charged.

4. A diamond ring has a cash price of $8400. It can be bought on hire purchase for a deposit of 25% and 36 monthly payments of $200. Find:
   (a) the H.P. price
   (b) the interest charged
   (c) the per cent interest charged.

5. A gas stove has a cash price of $1500. It can be bought also for an H.P. price of $1800. If the deposit for hire purchase is 10%, find:
   (a) the total monthly installments
   (b) the monthly installment if 12 monthly payments are made.

6. The cash price of an electric drill is $240. When purchased on hire purchase an interest of 20% of the cash price is added. Find:
   (a) the H.P. price
   (b) the total monthly payment if the deposit is $60
   (c) the monthly payment if 12 payments are made.

Mortgages

Houses are expensive things to buy. These are usually bought on a type of hire purchase agreement made with a bank.
The purchaser first pays a deposit and the bank gives him a loan or **mortgage** to cover the balance. The mortgage is repayable monthly over a long period of time. The interest payments on such loans cost a lot of money.

> *Example 2*
>
> A house costing $80 000 can be bought with a 10% deposit and a bank mortgage.
> Find: (a) the mortgage
>   (b) the total repaid to the bank if monthly payments of $720 are made over 25 years.
>
> (a) Deposit = 10% of $80 000 = $\dfrac{10}{100}$ × $80 000
>   = $8000
>   Mortgage = $80 000 − $8000
>   = $72 000
>
> (b) Total mortgage repayments
>   = 25 × 12 × $720
>   = $216 000

Notice in the example above that the interest on the mortgage amounted to $216 000 − $72 000 = $144 000. This is more than the cost of the house.
Why do you think the interest charged is so large?

The mortgage in Example 2 is called a **90% mortgage** as the purchaser has made a deposit of 10% and only needs to borrow 90% of the cost of the house.

7. A house for sale costs $70 000. What is the mortgage if the deposit is:
   (a) 10% of the cash price
   (b) 15% of the cash price
   (c) $7\frac{1}{2}$% of the cash price
   (d) $37\frac{1}{2}$% of the cash price?

8. A core house has a cash price of $30000. The People's Bank offer you a 90% mortgage over 20 years.
   Find:
   (a) the deposit payable
   (b) the total monthly payments if $315 is to be paid each month
   (c) the amount you will pay for your house altogether.

9. A luxury apartment is priced at $250 000. An 80% mortgage can be obtained over 15 years.
   Find:
   (a) the deposit payable
   (b) the total monthly repayment if $2200 is to be paid each month
   (c) the amount payable altogether for the house.

A table for mortgages

The table below is one sort of **ready reckoner**. (You met another on page 82).
This table allows you to work out mortgage repayments quickly.

Mortgage	Monthly repayments ($) over:		
	15 years	20 years	25 years
$500	5.50	5.25	5
$1000	11	10.50	10
$5000	55	52.50	50
$10 000	110	105	100
$20 000	220	210	200
$30 000	330	315	300
$40 000	440	420	400
$50 000	550	525	500
$100 000	1100	1050	1000

If your mortgage is $35 000, and you are repaying it over 20 years, you will pay $367.50 a month.
Do you agree?
Where does the figure $367.50 come from?

Use the table to answer the questions that follow.

10. If your mortgage is $45 000, how much will you repay each month, over:
(a) 15 years   (b) 20 years   (c) 25 years?

11. You have a 20-year mortgage. How much will you repay each month, if the mortgage is:
(a) $55 000   (b) $53 000
(c) $42 000   (d) $42 500
(e) $120 000   (f) $130 500?

12. You are buying a house that costs $100 000. You get an 85% mortgage, for 25 years.
(a) How much will your deposit be?
(b) How much is your mortgage (in $)?
(c) How much will you repay monthly?
(d) How much will you pay for the house, altogether?

13. Suppose you are buying a Sweet Home costing $125 000. You get a 90% mortgage for 25 years.
(a) How much will your deposit be?
(b) How much will your mortgage be?
(c) How much will you repay monthly?
(d) How much will you pay in total?

14. The way to get a mortgage varies from place to place. Find out how to get a mortgage in your area. From the bank? From a housing society?

7.5 Rates and taxes

Who pays:
for new roads?   for the airport?
for new schools?   for the fire brigade?
for your teachers?   for the police?

The answer is: *We all pay!*
We pay:
    income tax if we earn more than a certain amount;
    rates if we own land or buildings;
    import taxes if we import goods from overseas.

We pay:
income tax and import tax to the **government**;
rates to the **local council** or government.

1. Write down each word or phrase, and its meaning:
government   income tax
local council   imports
or district council   salary
tax   wage

2. (a) Where is the headquarters of the government, in your country?
(b) Where are your local council offices?
(c) Find out whether your government has a tax on car owners (a road tax).

Income tax

Brinsey works in a large store.
He earns a good wage each week. But he cannot keep all of it for himself. The government takes some of it as income tax.
The government charges income tax to help pay for all the things listed above.

Working people do not pay tax on all their income. Part of their earnings are not taxed. This part is called **tax-free income**.

The amount of income that is tax-free depends on the number of **dependents** a worker has to look after.

Some examples of dependents are:
    a wife
    a young son or daughter
    an old father who does not work
A tax-free allowance is made for each dependent.

Example 1

On a certain island, the tax-free allowances are:

	$
Personal tax-free allowances	2000
Additional allowances:	
Wife	1500
Each child	500
Any other dependent relative	400

A man earns $10 000 a year.
He has a wife and two children.
(a) How much of his income is tax-free?
(b) How much of his income is taxable?

(a) His tax-free income is:
    $2000 + $1500 + $1000 = $4500
(b) His taxable income is therefore:
    $10 000 − $4500 = $5500

---

3. Brinsey has a wife and 3 children. He earns $13 500 a year. Use the list in Example 1 to find:
    (a) his tax-free income   (b) his taxable income

4. (a) What is the total tax-free allowance of a man with a wife and 6 children?
    (b) If he earns $6500, how much tax does he pay?

Example 2

The rate of income tax on Brinsey's island is:

Taxable income	Tax rate
First $1000	5%
Next $1000	10%
Next $3000	15%
Next $5000	20%
Next $5000	25%
Next $10 000	30%

Brinsey's taxable income is $6500.
So he pays the following tax:
    5% of $1000 = $50
+ 10% of $1000 = $100
+ 15% of $3000 = $450
+ 20% of $1500 = $300
                     —————
        Total = $900

The amount of money left in Brinsey's pocket after paying tax
i.e. $6500 − $900 = $5600
is called his **net income.**
His salary before tax, $6500, is called his **gross income.**

5. Where does the $1500 come from, in Example 2?

6. Use the tax rates shown in Example 2 to calculate the amount of tax that Brinsey pays, if his taxable income is:
    (a) $4500   (b) $8750   (c) $13 500
    Set out your working as in Example 2.

7. Selwyn earns $20 000 taxable income. The tax rates are those in Example 2.
    (a) How much of his income is taxed at 30%?
    (b) Find the total tax he pays.

8. Abdool earns $20 000 a year. He has a wife, 4 children, a sister and his old father to support. Use the lists in Examples 1 and 2 to help you answer these questions.
    (a) How much of his income is tax-free?
    (b) How much income tax does he pay?
    (c) What is his net income?

9. Vincent earns $6200 a year. He has a wife and one child to support.
    (a) How much income tax does he pay?
        (Use the lists in Example 1 and 2.)
    (b) What is his net income?

Use the following table of tax rates and allowances to answer Questions 10 to 15.

Tax free allowances	Tax rates	
$1500 Personal allowance	First $4000	10%
$1000 Spouse	Next $6000	20%
$500 Child	Next $10 000	30%
$100 per month National Insurance contribution	over $20 000	40%

10. Jerome Chambers is a single man earning $6700. Find:
    (a) his tax free allowance
    (b) his taxable income
    (c) the tax he pays
    (d) his net income.

11. Jerome's brother Isaac is married with three children. He earns $8200. Find:
    (a) his tax free allowance
    (b) his taxable income
    (c) the tax he pays
    (d) his net income.

12. Mary Beaupierre is an unmarried mother of four children. She earns $4200. Find:
    (a) her tax free allowance
    (b) her net income.

13. Lawrence Largepocket earns $31 700.
    He has no dependent relatives. Find:
    (a) his taxable income
    (b) his net income.

14. Darius David pays $400 in income tax. If he is a
    married man with one child, what is his gross
    income?

15. Find who pays most tax:
    A: a married man with two children earning
       $15 000
    B: a single man earning $13 000
    C: a single woman with one child earning $14 000.

Rates

Rates are taxes on land and buildings.
They are levied by the local council.

The local council decides the **rateable value** of each
building and piece of land in the council's area.
Each owner is charged rates which are a percentage of
the rateable value of his property.

Samson has a house and garden in Toptown.
The real value of this property is $45 000.
The *rateable value* is always much lower than the *real
value*.
The rateable value is $1950.
Samson is charged a per cent of this rateable value.

16. Samson gets a **rate demand** from the council, as
    shown below.

    ┌───┐
    │   │
    │ From: Mayor and councillors of the city of Toptown │
    │   │
    │   Date: 6/1/1990   │
    │   │
    │ General rate demand   │
    │   │
    │   ⎧ Lot .....20.   │
    │ Address of   ⎨ Street ...Thirty-Second Street │
    │ property   ⎩ Division Topville   │
    │   │
    │ Owner ....Sampson Osn   │
    │ Assessed valuation ......$.1950   │
    │ Rate percentage.........22%   │
    │ Amount of demand ....$.429   │
    │   │
    │ Payable in four equal instalments on the │
    │ undermentioned due date: │
    │   │
    │ 1 February 1990   │
    │ 1 April 1990   │
    │ 1 July 1990   │
    │ 1 October 1990   │
    │   │
    └───┘

    (a) Write down two other words that mean the
        same as 'Assessed valuation'.
    (b) Calculate 22% of $1950.
    (c) Is the amount of the demand correct?
    (d) How much should Samson pay per instalment?

17. The rate for all properties in Subryanville is 22%.
    How much is paid in rates for a property, if its
    rateable value is:
    (a) $2500   (b) $1450   (c) $3600?

18. Calculate the rateable value of a property, if the
    rates are 22%, and the amount paid is:
    (a) $440   (b) $550   (c) $715

19. The council always tells its ratepayers how it spends
    the rates.
    The total spending by a certain city council one
    year was $10 000 000. Some of it was as follows:

	$
City Police	70 000
Sanitation	500 000
Drains	1 100 000
Refuse	1 800 000
Road lighting	2 700 000

    Find what per cent of the total rates was spent on:
    (a) the police   (b) refuse.

20. The total rateable value (= assessed valuation) of
    the property in a city is $50 000 000.
    (a) How much money would be obtained from a
        rate of 1%?
    (b) What rate is needed, to give $10 000 000?
    (c) The city wants to spend $2 000 000 on a new
        swimming pool. What extra per cent has to be
        added to the rate, in order to raise enough
        money for the pool?

21. In the Greenfield district the assessed valuation of
    property is:
        Land $5 300 000
        Buildings $26 700 000
    The Greenfield district council plans to spend
    $9 280 000 next year.
    (a) What is the total rateable value of the
        property?
    (b) What rate should the council charge, to cover
        its spending?

22. The Bay Tree district council charges a rate of
    24%. The total rateable value of property in the
    district is $18 000 000. Next year the council plans
    to spend $3 500 000. How much will be left over for
    building a new road?

Summary

By the end of this chapter, these are the things you should know about:

7.1 Money management (pages 82–85)

How to use ready reckoners.

No.	$	No.	$	No.	$
⋮		⋮		⋮	
6	2.22	16	5.92	26	9.62
7	2.59	17	6.29	27	9.99
8	2.96	18	6.66	28	10.36
⋮		⋮		⋮	

Ready reckoner for a unit cost of 37 cents

The cost of 34 items at 37 cents each

$$28 \text{ items cost } \$10.36$$
$$6 \text{ items cost } \ \$2.22$$
$$\overline{34 \text{ items cost } \$12.58}$$

How to calculate electricity bills
  e.g. A man uses 110 units of electricity. What is his bill if the first 50 units cost 40 cents each and remaining units 30 cents each?
    First 50 units cost $50 \times 40¢ = \$20$
    Next 60 units cost $60 \times 30¢ \quad \$18$

    Total bill $= \$38$

How to work out foreign exchange.
  e.g. Given UK £1 = EC $4.15, find: EC $80 in UK £.
  EC $1.00 $=$ UK £1 ÷ 4.15

  $$\text{EC } \$80.00 = \text{UK } £\frac{1}{4.15} \times 80$$

  $$= \text{UK } £\frac{8000}{415}$$

  $$= \text{UK } £19.28$$

How to draw conversion graphs and read them.

7.2 Profit and loss (pages 86–87)

How to find percentage profit, given cost price and selling price.
  e.g. What is percent profit on a radio bought for $80 and sold for $90?
    Profit $= \$90 - \$80 = \$10$

  $$\text{Percent profit} = \frac{\$10}{\$80} \times 100\%$$

  $$= 12\frac{1}{2}\%$$

How to find selling price given percent profit and cost price.
  e.g. What is selling price of a radio bought for $80 and sold for a $12\frac{1}{2}\%$ profit?

    Profit $= 12\frac{1}{2}\%$ of cost price
       $= 12\frac{1}{2}\%$ of $80

  $$= \frac{25}{200} \times \frac{\$80}{1}$$

  $$= \$10$$
  Selling price $= \$80 + \$10 = \$90$

How to find the cost price given the selling price and percent profit.
  e.g. What is the cost price of a radio sold for $90 at a $12\frac{1}{2}$ profit?
    Write C.P. for cost price

    Profit $= 12\frac{1}{2}\%$ of C.P.
  Profit + C.P. = selling price
  $12\frac{1}{2}\%$ of CP + CP = $90
    $112\frac{1}{2}\%$ of CP = $90

  $$\frac{112\frac{1}{2}}{100} \times \text{CP} = \$90$$

  $$\text{CP} = \frac{100}{112\frac{1}{2}} \times \$90$$

  $$= \frac{8}{9} \times \$90 = \$80$$

7.3 Interest and Investment (pages 88–90)

How to find simple interest using the formula

$$I = \frac{PRT}{100}$$

The meaning of compound interest. How to find compound interest.
  e.g. Find the compound interest on $500 at 6% for 2 years.

  Interest for 1st year = 6% of $500

  $$= \frac{6}{100} \times \$500$$

  $$= \$30$$

  Principal after 1st year $= \$500 + \$30 = \$530$
  Interest for 2nd year = 6% of $530

  $$= \frac{6}{100} \times \$530$$

  $$= 6 \times \$5.30$$
  $$= \$31.80$$
  Total interest $= \$30 + \$31.80 = \$61.80$

How to use ready reckoners to find interest.

7.4 Hire purchase and mortgages (pages 90–92)

The meaning of hire purchase.
How to calculate the hire purchase price.

  e.g. A dining room set has a cash price of $1050.
    What is the HP price if a deposit of 10% and
    12 payments of $90 are needed?

$$\text{Deposit} = 10\% \text{ of } \$1050$$

$$= \frac{10}{100} \times \$1050$$

$$= \$105$$
$$\text{Total payments} = 12 \times \$90 = \$1080$$
$$\text{H.P. price} = \$105 + \$1080$$
$$= \$1185$$

How to **take out a mortgage**.
What **mortgage repayments** are.
What an **80% mortgage** is.
How to calculate the cost of a house paid for on a
mortgage.

7.5 Rates and taxes (pages 92–94)

What **income tax, tax-free income, tax-free allowances,
dependents, gross income** and **net income** are.
How to calculate income tax, given the tax rates.

  e.g. Daniel Murphy has a wife and two children.
    His annual salary is $20 000, find his net salary
    given the information below.

Tax-free allowances	Income Tax rates
$2000 personal allowance	20% on first $4000
$1000 spouse	
$500 each child	25% on remainder

$$\text{Tax free income} = \$2000 + \$1000 + 2 \times \$500$$
$$= \$4000$$
$$\text{Taxable income} = \$20\ 000 - \$4000$$
$$= \$16\ 000$$

Tax paid:
 20% of $4000 = $800
 25% of $12 000 = $3000
Total income tax = $3800
Net salary = $20 000 − $3800
    = $16 200

The meaning of **rates, rateable value,** and **assessed
valuation**.
How to calculate rates, when you know the rateable
value and the % rates.

8 Statistics 1

8.1 Bar and pie charts – revision

1. (a) Draw a bar chart to show the following information.

Number of ice creams sold	23	35	20	44	15
Day	Monday	Tuesday	Wednesday	Thursday	Friday

(b) What was the mean sale?

2. The table below shows the number of goals scored in 30 football matches.

Goals scored	0	1	2	3	4	5	6
Number of matches	1	5	9	9	2	3	1

(a) Draw a bar chart to display this information.
(b) How many goals were scored altogether in the 30 matches?
(c) What was the mean number of goals scored in each match?

3. The block graph shows the number and sizes of shoes sold in a store in a single day.

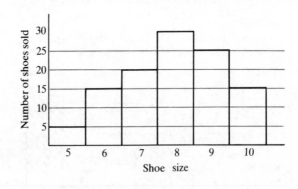

(a) How many shoes were sold that day?
(b) What is the mean shoe size?
(c) What is the modal size?

4. The block graph shows the number of children per
family, for the families in Donovan.

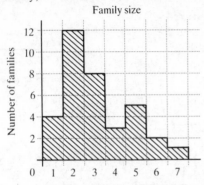

Family size

(a) How many families are there in Donovan?
(b) How many children are there in Donovan?
(c) What is the mean number of children per family?
(d) What is the mode?

5. The scores of 20 students in a French test were as
follows:

    5 7 7 6 4 8   9 7 7 6
    8 7 6 7 8 9 10 4 6 8

(a) Set up a frequency table for the scores.
(b) Draw a bar chart to illustrate the information.
(c) What was the mean score?
(d) What was the median score?
(e) What was the modal score?
(f) What fraction of the students scored less than 7?

6. The number of cars sold by a garage on each day in
September is shown below.

    2 4 2 1 0 5 1 2 2 1 3 4 4 5 3
    2 1 2 3 6 0 1 3 3 2 4 2 1 1 3

(a) Set up a frequency table for the data.
(b) Draw a bar chart to show the information.
(c) What was the mean number of cars sold each day?
(d) Find the median and mode.

7. The bar chart shows the amount of money spent by
a small business over a four-year period.

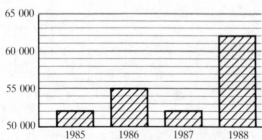

(a) Find the mean amount spent between 1985 and
1988.
(b) How much was spent in 1989 if the mean
amount of money spent between 1985 and 1989
was $60 000?

Another way of illustrating data is with a pie chart.

Example

David won $100 at a lottery. He spent it as
follows.
    Shirt $30   Record $20
    Cap $10   Savings $30
    Cinema $10

Angle representing money spent on shirt

$$= \frac{30}{100} \times 360°$$

$$= 108°$$

Pie chart showing
David's expenditure.

8. In the village of Atwater there are 240 people on
the voting list.
At one election they voted as follows:
    150 Labour   10 Radical
     60 Independent   20 Did not vote
Draw a pie chart to show this.

9. The 300 students at Marigot High School travel to
school as follows:
    110 bus   160 walk
     20 car   10 cycle
Draw a pie chart to show this information.

10. The 32 students of class 1B voted for their favourite
subjects. The results were as follows:
    English 4   French 2
    Maths 12   Social Studies 6
    Science 8
(a) Display this data on a pie chart.
(b) What percent like English as their favourite
subject?

11. The council in the town of St. Peter's spent money
from rates as follows:
        45% on public services
        25% on road maintenance
        10% on transportation
        10% on sewage improvements
         5% on landscaping
         5% on investments
(a) Display this data on a pie chart.
(b) If $3000 was spent on landscaping, what was
their total budget?

12. The pie chart shows the
results of a survey of
favourite sports among
1000 people.

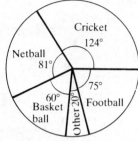

(a) What fraction of the people surveyed have
basketball as their favourite sport?
(b) How many people indicated cricket as their
favourite sport?

13. The pie chart shows the
budget of a certain
island.

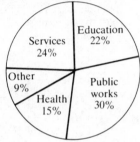

(a) Draw the pie chart again indicating clearly the
angle in each sector.
(b) If $5 million is spent on health, what is the total
budget?
(c) Work out how much is spent on each area and
draw a bar chart to illustrate this data.

14. The pie chart illustrates
the sales of different makes
of the motor oil.

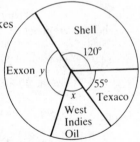

(a) What percentage of the sales does Texaco
have?
(b) If West Indies Oil accounts for 15% of the total
oil sales, calculate the angles x and y.

15. A fruit importer checks the number of bad oranges
in 100 boxes. This is what he found.

Number of bad oranges	0	1	2	3	4 or more
Number of boxes	55	32	10	3	0

(a) Draw a pie chart to show this data.
(b) Calculate the mean number of bad oranges in a
box.

8.2 Histograms

In Question 15 on this page a block graph could have
been drawn instead.

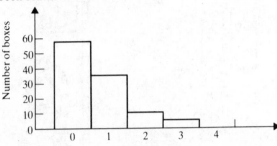

Such a graph of a frequency distribution is usually
called a **histogram**.
It is different from a bar graph in that
(1) there are no spaces between the bars
(2) the **area** of each rectangle and not the height
represents the frequency
If the width of each bar is the same, then the height
represents the frequency.

1. In a rifle competition, marksmen fire at a target.
Each man has five shots. Here are the results
showing the number of bulls scored:

Number of bulls	0	1	2	3	4	5
Frequency	9	7	10	42	72	10

(a) Draw a histogram to show the data.
(b) What is the mode?

2. A dust meter collects and counts particles of dust
from samples of air. The following results were
obtained from 200 samples:

Number of particles	0	1	2	3	4	5	6	7	8
Frequency	12	28	44	48	36	20	9	2	1

(a) Draw a histogram to show the data.
(b) Calculate the mean number of particles in the
sample.

3. The shoe sizes of 25 students in class are
6 6 5 7 4 5 4 3 4 6
2 7 6 5 5 5 4 6 4 7
3 5 6 4 2
(a) Draw a frequency table for the sizes.
(b) Draw a histogram representing the data.
(c) What is the median size?

Histograms may be drawn for grouped frequency
distributions but care must be taken with class
intervals.

Interval boundaries

A group of 25 children measure each other's heights and record the answers by putting a tick on a chart:

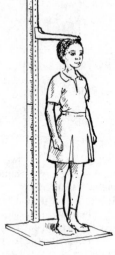

Height (cm)	
135–139	
140–144	✓
145–149	
150–154	✓✓✓
155–159	
160–164	✓
165–169	✓

4. Suppose the heights are rounded off to the nearest cm. At which interval would you put a tick for a child whose height is:
   (a) 140.4 cm   (b) 149.2 cm   (c) 149.9 cm
   (d) 161.3 cm   (e) 164.8 cm   (f) 139.6 cm?

5. Into which interval would you put a height of:
   (a) 159.5 cm   (b) 139.5 cm   (c) 144.5 cm?

6. What is the greatest height that belongs to the interval 155–159 cm? What is the least height belonging to this interval?

7. What does the word 'boundary' mean?

8. The interval 155–159 cm will contain all heights from 154.5 cm *up to* 159.5 cm. Do you agree? The **interval boundaries** are 154.5 and 159.5 cm.

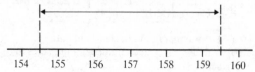

If heights are measured to the nearest cm, write down the interval boundaries for the intervals:
   (a) 135–139 cm   (b) 140–144 cm
   (c) 145–149 cm   (d) 150–154 cm

9. This is the completed frequency table for the 25 children.

Height (cm)	Frequency
135–139	1
140–144	3
145–149	4
150–154	7
155–159	5
160–164	4
165–169	1

The histogram for this table must show the interval boundaries, at 134.5 cm, 139.5 cm, etc. Below is part of the graph. Copy and complete it. Write a title for it.

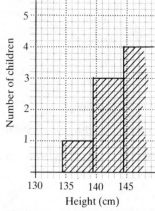

10. The histogram below shows the results of weighing 100 apples to the nearest gram.
    (a) How many apples are in the interval 110–119 grams?
    (b) Why are the boundaries of this interval drawn at 109.5 and 119.5?

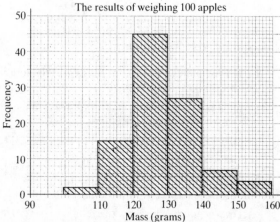

The results of weighing 100 apples

11. Draw up a frequency table using the information in the graph. Use intervals 100–109, 110–119 etc.

12. In a biology experiment, the leaves of a plant are measured and recorded to the nearest mm, as shown on the right.

Length (mm)	Frequency
20–24	1
25–29	4
30–34	8
35–39	18
40–44	25
45–49	24
50–54	17
55–59	2
60–64	1

(a) Write down the interval boundaries, starting at 19.5 mm.

(b) Draw a histogram of the results. Use one small division to represent one unit, as in the graph in Question 10.

13. The heights of 154 boys, to the nearest cm, are:

Height (cm)	160	161	162	163	164	165	166
Frequency	4	5	6	9	16	22	27

Height (cm)	167	168	169	170	171	172
Frequency	25	18	11	6	3	2

(a) Redraw the frequency table, using intervals 160–161, 162–163, 164–165, etc.

(b) What are the boundaries of the interval 164–165 cm?

(c) What is the boundary between the intervals 166–167 cm and 168–169 cm?

(d) Draw a histogram using the intervals in (a).

14. The percentage marks of 100 students in a test were:

Marks %	0–	20–	30–	40–	50–	60–	70–	80–
No. of students	5	6	13	22	24	16	8	6

(a) Draw up another frequency table using equal intervals of 20 marks.

(b) Write down the boundaries for each interval.

(c) Illustrate the information by a histogram.

Frequency polygons

Frequency distributions can also be illustrated by a **frequency polygon**. Frequencies are represented by single points, at the centre of each interval (mid-interval value). The points are joined by straight lines.

Example

The mass in kg of 20 children are as follows.

Mass (kg)	10–19	20–29	30–39	40–49	50–59
No. of children	1	2	6	12	3

Draw a frequency polygon to show this.

The interval 10–19 goes from 9.5 up to 19.5. The centre of the interval is at

$$\frac{9.5 + 19.5}{2} = \frac{29}{2} = 14.5$$

So frequency polygon is:

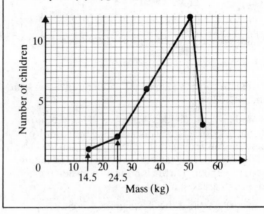

15. Draw frequency polygons to illustrate the data in Questions 2, 3, 9 and 12.

16. Here are the weights of cattle sold at a livestock market:

Mass (kg)	Frequency
450–	16
500–	130
550–	42
600–649	12

The interval 500– means 500–549.

(a) What is the mid-interval value of the range 500–549?

(b) Draw a frequency polygon to show this information.

17. The lengths of insect larvae are measured to the nearest mm.

Length (mm)	Frequency
20–	15
25–	33
30–	58
35–	50
40–44	4

(a) How many insect larvae were measured?

(b) Explain why the mid-interval value of the first interval is 22 mm.

(c) Draw a frequency polygon of the information.

8.3 Medians and quartiles

The heights of eleven boys, in cm, are 150, 146, 158, 165, 168, 170, 158, 154, 162, 180, 181.
Written in ascending order they are:
146, 150, 154, 158, 158, 162, 165, 168, 170, 180, 181.

The **median** height is the height of the middle boy – the sixth, i.e. 162 cm.

The median value divides this group of heights into two. The group can be further divided into four by finding the **lower quartile** and the **upper quartile**. The lower quartile is midway between the first and median height, the upper quartile is midway between the median and greatest height.

The lower quartile is the 3rd height = 154 cm
The upper quartile is the 9th height = 170 cm

The **interquartile range**
= Upper quartile – lower quartile
= 170 cm – 154 cm
= 16 m

146, 150, | 154 |, 158, 158, (162) , 165, 168, | 170 | , 180, 181
　　　　　L.Q.　　　　Median　　　　U.Q.

1. Find the median of the numbers:
   (a) 2, 3, 5, 7, 8
   (b) 6, 1, 4, 3, 9
   (c) 4, 4, 1, 4, 6, 2

2. Find the median, upper and lower quartiles of the following numbers:
   (a) 2, 5, 7, 9, 10, 11, 13
   (b) 4, 3, 6, 2, 1, 8, 4
   (c) 7, 2, 1, 7, 6, 9, 15, 13, 4, 9, 1

3. In Question 2 state the interquartile ranges.

4. The masses of five people are 70 kg, 64 kg, 58 kg, 80 kg, 78 kg:
   (a) What is the median mass?
   (b) What is the lower and upper quartile?
   (c) Write down the interquartile range.

5. The shoe size of 20 students are given in the table below

Shoe Size	4	5	6	7	8	9
No. of students	1	1	4	6	6	2

   (a) What is the median size?
   (b) Find the lower and upper quartiles.

6. The ages of a class of 30 boys are given below.

Age	13	14	15	16
No. of Boys	2	6	18	4

   (a) What is the median age?
   (b) Find the lower and upper quartiles.
   (c) Write down the interquartile range.

7. The marks of 40 students in a mathematics test were as follows.

Mark	3	4	5	6	7	8	9	10
No. of students	3	8	6	10	6	4	2	1

   (a) Find the median mark.
   (b) Calculate the interquartile range.

8. The histogram below shows the number of brothers and sisters a class of 25 children has.

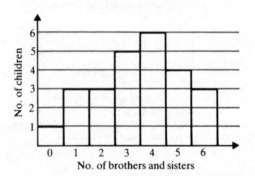

   (a) What is the median number of brothers and sisters?
   (b) Find the upper and lower quartiles.

8.4 Cumulative frequency

Running totals

The prefect of Form IVA keeps a record of those students arriving late for classes. To see how well or badly they are doing, she keeps a **running total** as well.

Day	Number late	Running total
Monday	1	1
Tuesday	2	3
Wednesday	1	4
Thursday	1	5
Friday	2	7

A block graph to show class lateness could look like this:

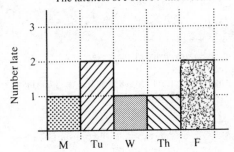

The lateness of Form IV this week

Or the block graph show the running totals:

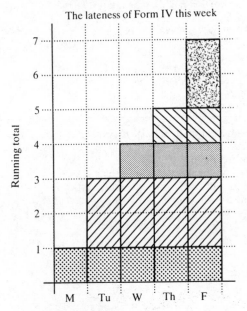

The lateness of Form IV this week

1. Explain how:
   (a) the running total has been worked out, in the table above.
   (b) the second block graph has been drawn up.

2. Jamsit keeps a few hens in his yard. His daily egg collection for a week, starting with Sunday, was 9, 10, 12, 7, 8, 11, 10.
   Draw up a table to show the daily egg collection and a running total column.
   (a) What was his week's total?
   (b) By which day had he got 36 eggs?

3. Lily also has a few hens, but she only records the running totals of eggs. Here they are for a week:

Day	Running total
Sunday	8
Monday	15
Tuesday	21
Wednesday	29
Thursday	36
Friday	42
Saturday	53

   (a) Lily reckons she has covered the costs of keeping the hens, if she gets at least 40 eggs per week.
   By which day will she have done that?
   (b) Draw a table to show the daily total of eggs collected.

4. Draw two block graphs to show the egg production of Lily's hens, one for the daily totals and one for the running totals.

5. Draw up a 'Running total' table for the leaf measurements in Question 12 on page 101. Start your table like this.

Length (mm)	Number of leaves	Running total
20–24	1	1
25–29	4	5
30–34	8	13

   (a) How many leaves have a length of less than 45 mm?
   (b) A scientist wants to take 20 of the longest leaves for further tests. What might be the length of the shortest of these leaves?

Cumulative frequency

The heights of 25 children are shown in a frequency table in Question 9 on page 100.
The number of children in each interval is called the frequency. Another name for a running total is **cumulative frequency** or C.F.

Here is the beginning of the cumulative frequency table for the children's heights. The right-hand column shows the height corresponding to each number in the C.F. column.

Height (cm)	C.F.	Heights of children represented by C.F.
135–139	1	less than 139.5 cm
140–144	4	less than 144.5 cm
145–149	8	less than 149.5 cm

6. Copy and complete the table, using the information in Question 9 on page 100.

7. Using your completed table, write down:
   (a) the number of children below 159.5 cm
   (b) the height that describes the smallest 8 children
   (c) the height that describes the tallest 5 children.

8. Below is part of a graph of cumulative frequency, for the heights of the 25 children.

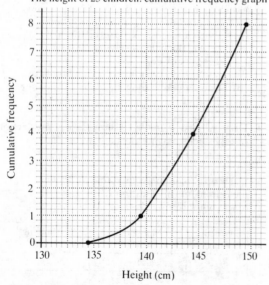

The height of 25 children: cumulative frequency graph

The cumulative frequency is always plotted at the upper end of each interval.

For example, the dot for heights *less than* 144.5 is plotted *at* 144.5.
(a) Why has the point (134.5, 0) been plotted?
(b) Copy and complete the graph, using your table from Question 6.
(c) From your graph, read off the height corresponding to a C.F. of 13.
(d) Does a C.F. of 13 out of 25 give the mean, the median or the mode?

9. The lengths of 100 mice, measured to the nearest mm, were:

Length (mm)	Frequency
125–129	3
130–134	12
135–139	20
140–144	34
145–149	25
150–154	4
155–159	1
160–164	1

I'm really an average sort of mouse

(a) Draw up a cumulative frequency table for this information.
(b) What is the greatest length that belongs to the interval 130–134 mm?
(c) Draw a cumulative frequency graph of the information.
(d) Using a C.F. of 50, estimate the median length of the mice from your graph.

10. 100 pigs were weighed to the nearest kg:

Mass (kg)	Number of pigs
70–74	6
75–79	13
80–84	24
85–89	30
90–94	16
95–99	11

Draw up a cumulative frequency table and use it to draw a cumulative frequency graph. Use your graph to estimate:
(a) the number of pigs lighter than 82 kg
(b) the number of pigs heavier than 88 kg
(c) the median mass.

8.5 Using cumulative frequency graphs

Here is the cumulative frequency table and graph, for the 100 apples of Question 10, page 100.

Mass (grams)	100–109	110–119	120–129	130–139	140–149	150–159
Frequency	2	15	45	27	7	4
Cumulative frequency	2	17	62	89	96	100

The results of weighing 100 apples: cumulative frequency graph

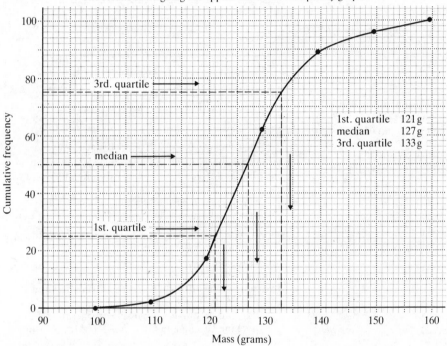

If you arrange 100 apples in order of mass, the median falls between the 50th and 51st apples. When using a cumulative frequency graph, it is accurate enough to read off the 50th value as the median.
The graph shows that the median mass of the apples is 127 g.

The median measures the half-way value of numbers placed in order.

The quarter and three-quarter values are **quartiles**.

For the 100 apples:
The median = the mass at C.F. 50
The first quartile = the mass at C.F. 25
The third quartile = the mass at C.F. 75

The graph shows that the values of the quartiles are 121 g and 133 g.

On a C.F. curve:
The first quartile is sometimes called the **25th percentile**
The median is the **50th percentile**.
The third quartile is the **75th percentile**.
Can you explain why?

1. From the graph above, find the value of:
   (a) the 60th percentile
   (b) the 40th percentile
   (c) the 85th percentile

2. The lengths of 80 sticks, measured to the nearest cm, are:

Length (cm)	30	31	32	33	34	35	36
Frequency	2	8	16	25	17	9	3

(a) Draw up a cumulative frequency table.
(b) Draw a cumulative frequency graph, starting at $(29.5, 0)$.
(c) Read off the median length.
(d) Use a C.F. of 20 to read off the first quartile.
(e) What is the value of the third quartile?

3. In an aptitude test, the scores were:

```
22  44  49  33  38  33  37  16   7  27
38  17  43  28  27  22  31  23  14  25
37  13  17  22  23  28  20  27  36  25
19  36  26  28  16  27  29  36  41  17
16  31  41   6  35  22  28  14  43  36
```

(a) Draw up a frequency table using intervals 0.5 to 10.5, 10.5 to 20.5, etc.
(b) Draw a cumulative frequency graph of the scores.
(c) Use the graph to obtain an estimate of the median score and the values of the quartiles.

4. The marks of 100 candidates in a test were:

Mark	Frequency
0–19	5
20–29	6
30–39	13
40–49	22
50–59	24
60–69	16
70–79	8
80–100	6

(a) Draw up a cumulative frequency table using the limits *less than 19.5, less than 29.5*, etc. Be careful, because the intervals are not equal.
(b) Use the table to plot a cumulative frequency graph.
(c) Read off the values of the quartiles and the median from your graph.
(d) What pass mark allows 60% of the candidates to pass?
(e) What per cent of the candidates pass, if the pass mark is 41?

The range

Two machines A and B are used to fill 1-litre tins of paint. 20 tins are taken from each machine's output. The contents of each tin are measured, to see how accurately the machines fill the tins.

Here are the results:

Volume of paint (ml)	Frequency	
	Machine A	Machine B
996	1	0
997	2	0
998	2	2
999	3	8
1000	3	5
1001	4	3
1002	2	2
1003	2	0
1004	1	0

From the table you can see that the accuracy of the machines is different. If you work out the mean you will find –

    Machine A: mean 1000.5 ml
    Machine B: mean 999.75 ml

So, on average, machine A puts more paint into the tins than machine B does. But that is only one way of comparing them.
You can also use the range.
The range is the difference between the highest and lowest possible values in a set.
    Machine A: range = $(1004.5 - 995.5)$ ml = 9 ml
    Machine B: range = $(1002.5 - 997.5)$ ml = 5 ml

5. Which machine above do you think is more satisfactory? Explain why. Give two reasons if possible.

The interquartile range and semi-interquartile range

The results of weighing two groups of students.

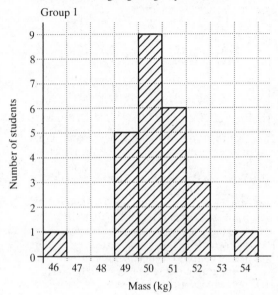

Group 1

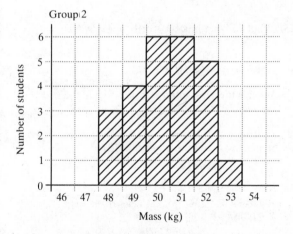

Group 2

6. Two groups of 25 students are weighed. The block graphs above record the result.
   (a) In group 1, which two masses are not typical of the group?
   (b) What is the range for each group?
   (c) Look at the ranges you wrote down in (b). In which group would you expect the results to be more spread out?
   (d) Now look at the centre part of each block graph. In which group are the results more spread out?
   (e) Do you think the range gives a good idea of the shape of the graph?

In Question 6, the range alone does not give a good idea of the shapes of the graphs.
You would get a better idea of their shapes if you also found the interquartile range.

The interquartile range is the difference in value between the first and third quartiles.

7. Below is the cumulative frequency graph for the students in Group 1.

Group 1. Cumulative frequency graph

(a) Out of 25 students, which one is the median?
(b) Half of 13 is $6\frac{1}{2}$. Do you agree that the first quartile should be at C.F. $6\frac{1}{2}$?
(c) Explain why the third quartile is at C.F. $19\frac{1}{2}$.
(d) Write down the mass that corresponds to:
   (i) the first quartile   (ii) the third quartile
(e) Do you agree that the interquartile range is 1.6 kg? Explain.

8. For Group 1 in Question 6, the range is 9 kg while the interquartile range is 1.6 kg. Does the interquartile range give a better idea of the shape of the block graph? Explain why.

9. Draw a cumulative frequency graph for Group 2. From your graph find:
   (a) the quartiles   (b) the interquartile range

10. (a) Compare the ranges and interquartile ranges of Groups 1 and 2. What do these tell you about the shapes of the two block graphs?
   (b) Now compare the block graphs. Are they the shapes you would expect? Explain.

11. What is the range and interquartile range for the graph on page 105?

12. A lab technician checks the accuracy of two balances A and B, using a standard 100 g mass. He weighs the mass a hundred times on each balance, and records the readings. The frequency table for the results is shown below.

Reading (g)	Frequency for A	for B
99.97	12	3
99.98	48	8
99.99	29	19
100.00	11	28
100.01	0	23
100.02	0	10
100.03	0	7
100.04	0	2

(a) Construct a cumulative frequency table for each balance.
(b) Draw a cumulative frequency graph for each balance.
(c) For each, find:
    (i) the median   (ii) the range
    (iii) the interquartile range
(d) Which machine is more accurate? Explain your choice.

13. Use a graph to estimate the median mass of 300 ten-week old rats, given these results:

Mass (g)	38–	40–	42–	44–	46–
Frequency	139	89	52	20	0

14. The table shows the marks obtained by 100 candidates on two mathematics papers.

Number of marks	Number of candidates	
	Paper A	Paper B
0–20	0	0
21–30	5	0
31–40	10	0
41–50	15	0
51–60	18	20
61–70	18	20
71–80	11	36
81–90	10	16
91–100	13	8

(a) Plot the cumulative frequency curves of the marks for each paper. What is the range, for each?
(b) What pass mark would allow 70% of the candidates to pass paper A?
(c) What pass mark would allow 70% of the candidates to pass paper B?
(d) Use the graph to estimate the median and the interquartile range in each case.
(e) Using your results in (d), describe how the block graphs of the results should differ.
(f) Draw block graphs of the results, for papers A and B. Compare them. Are they the shapes you expected?

15. What do you think the word *semi-interquartile* means?

16. The semi-interquartile range
$$= \tfrac{1}{2} \times \text{interquartile range}$$
What is the semi-interquartile range of the graph on page 105?

17. Calculate the semi-interquartile ranges for machines A and B in Question 12.

18. This table gives the masses of 500 men to the nearest kilogram.

Mass (kg)	Frequency
Under 55	60
55–	124
65–	147
75–	86
85–	55
95 and over	28

From a graph of cumulative frequency, estimate the median and the interquartile range. Then calculate the semi-interquartile range.

Summary

By the end of this chapter, these are the things you should know about.

8.1 Revision – bar and pie charts (pages 97–99)

How to draw a bar chart.
How to draw a pie chart.
How to read a bar or pie chart.

8.2 Histograms (pages 99–101)

A block graph of a frequency distribution is usually called a **histogram**.
In a histogram there are no spaces between the bars and the area of each rectangle represents the frequency.

How to work out interval boundaries.
    For the interval 100–104 cm, the interval boundaries are at 99.5 cm and 104.5 cm.
How to draw a histogram that properly shows the interval boundaries.

The middle value of an interval is called the **mid-interval value**.
    If the interval boundaries are at 99.5 cm and 104.5 cm,

$$\text{the mid-interval value} = \frac{99.5\,\text{cm} + 104.5\,\text{cm}}{2}$$
$$= 102\,\text{cm}$$

How to draw a frequency polygon.

e.g.

Height (cm)	120–129	130–139	140–149	150–159
No. of children	3	1	7	4

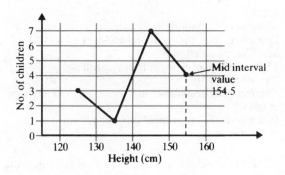

8.3 Median and quartiles (page 102)

How to find the **median** of a set of numbers,
    e.g. 4, 1, 6, 5, 1 in order is 1, 1, <u>4</u>, 5, 6
    The middle number or median is 4.
How to find the **lower quartile, upper quartile** and interquartile range of a set of numbers.

    e.g. 1, 3, 4, 7, 7, 9, 10, 14, 16, 16, 18

    Interquartile range is 16 − 4 = 12

8.4 Cumulative (pages 103–104)

Cumulative frequency is a running total of the frequency.
How to draw up a cumulative frequency table.
e.g.

Mass (kg)	40–49	50–59	60–69	70–79	80–89
Frequency	4	13	20	10	3
Cumulative frequency	4	17	37	47	50

How to draw a graph of cumulative frequency and use it to find the median.

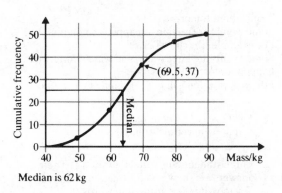

Median is 62 kg

8.5 Using cumulative frequency graphs (pages 105–108)

The meaning of **median, first quartile, third quartile, interquartile range** and **semi-interquartile range**.
How to find each of these from a cumulative frequency graph.
By comparing the range and the interquartile range, you can tell how spread out a set of results is.

9 Probability I

9.1 The idea of probability

Is it certain?

Think about tomorrow.
Some events are **certain** to happen tomorrow.
For example, the sun will rise.
Some events are **impossible**, and will definitely not happen tomorrow.
For example, you will not run a mile in 5 seconds.

1. *I will live to be a hundred.*
   Is this event certain or impossible?

2. Three students answered Question 1. Their answers are shown on the diagram below. Try to write their answers in words.

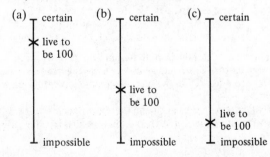

3. Draw a diagram like those in Question 2. Mark a cross on it to show whether you think the event is nearly certain, nearly impossible, or whether you are not sure.
   (a) I will get married.
   (b) If I buy a new pen it will write.
   (c) It will rain tomorrow.
   (d) I will reach school in time tomorrow.
   (e) I will take 20 catches in a cricket match.

4. Are some of the events in Question 3 more likely to happen than others? Pick out the most likely event.

What is probability?

Some events are more likely to happen than others.
In mathematics, the word **probability** is used to describe this situation.
There is a **high probability** that you will put on shoes or sandals tomorrow.
There is a **low probability** that you will win a large sum of money tomorrow.
In mathematics, the probability of an event is given a number from 0 to 1.

5. Try to decide for yourself how certain or impossible an event is, if its probability is described as:
   (a) 0   (b) 1   (c) $\frac{1}{2}$ (d) $\frac{9}{10}$ (e) $\frac{2}{10}$

The diagram below shows the meaning of different probabilities. You can see that:
the probability of a **certain** event is **1**;
the probability of an **impossible** event is **0**;
if an event is **as likely to happen as not**, its probability is 0.5.

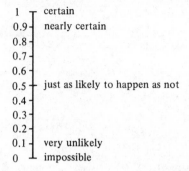

1 — certain
0.9 — nearly certain
0.8 —
0.7 —
0.6 —
0.5 — just as likely to happen as not
0.4 —
0.3 —
0.2 —
0.1 — very unlikely
0 — impossible

6. Look again at Question 3. Give each event a probability between 0 and 1.

9.2 Experimental probability

You will need . . .
In this section you will need:
a one-cent coin and a plastic cup.

1. Call the face of the coin with a 1 written on it *face one*. Call the other face *face two*.
Put the coin in the plastic cup, shake it, and tip it onto your desk top. Repeat this 100 times.
Keep a record of which face turns up each time, in a table like the one below.

Face one	Face two
̶H̶H̶ ̶ //	̶H̶H̶ ̶H̶H̶

For what fraction of the total number of throws was the outcome (i.e. the result):
(a) face one   (b) face two?

2. Now collect the results from nine of your friends and record them in a table like the one below.

	Face one	Face two
My result	48	52
Friend 1		
2		
.		
.		
.		
.		
9		
Totals		

For what fraction of the total number of throws was the outcome:
(a) face one   (b) face two?

3. Look at your results for Questions 1 and 2.
When you throw a coin are you:
(a) more likely to get face one? *or*
(b) more likely to get face two? *or*
(c) equally likely to get either?

4. (a) What probability would you assign to one of two events which were equally likely? Explain why.
(b) Look at your results for Question 2. Can you see a way to calculate the probability of getting face one? Explain it.

We define the probability that an event occurs, i.e. a **"success"**, Pr(S), as

$$\mathbf{Pr(S)} = \frac{\textbf{number of successful outcomes}}{\textbf{total number of outcomes}}$$

You should have found that in Question 1

$$Pr(\text{face 1}) = \frac{\text{number of times face 1 occurred}}{\text{total number of throws}}$$

$$= \frac{\text{about 50}}{100} \text{ or nearly } \tfrac{1}{2}, \text{ or } 0.5$$

and in Question 2

$$Pr(\text{face 1}) = \frac{\text{about 500}}{1000} \text{ or nearly } \tfrac{1}{2}, \text{ or } 0.5.$$

5. Suppose that the coin is bent and that this affects the outcome. If face one turns up 700 times out of 1000 throws:
   (a) what is the probability of this event?
   (b) what is the probability that face two turns up?
   (c) what is the sum of the probabilities?

The probability of many events that occur can be found either by experiment or survey.

Example

Fifty people were asked their favourite sport. The results are shown in the table

Sport	Cricket	Basketball	Netball	Football
No. of people	17	8	20	5

Calculate the probability that
(a) a person's favourite sport is football
(b) a person's favourite sport is *not* netball

(a) Pr (favourite sport is football) =

$$\frac{\text{number of people liking football}}{\text{total number of people}} = \frac{5}{50} = \frac{1}{10}$$

(b) Pr (favourite sport is not netball)

$$= \frac{\text{number people who like sports other than netball}}{\text{total number of people}}$$

$$= \frac{17 + 8 + 5}{50} = \frac{30}{50} = \frac{3}{5}$$

---

6. In a class of 25 students, 6 wear glasses. What is the probability that a student picked at random:
   (a) wears glasses   (b) does not wear glasses?

7. Packets of flower seeds are checked for purity, in case any weed seeds have been included. Here is a **frequency table** showing the results of checking 100 packets:

Number of weed seeds	0	1	2	3	4	5	6	7	8
Number of packets	5	16	26	19	13	12	5	2	2

What is the probability that a packet contains:
(a) 6 weed seeds   (b) 1 weed seed
(c) more than 6 weed seeds?

8. A scientist weighs kittens at birth with the following results:

Mass (g)	190	200	210	220	230	240	250
Frequency	13	34	57	50	29	12	5

(a) How many kittens did the scientist weigh?
(b) Find the probability that a kitten weighs:
   (i) 250g   (ii) less than 250g

9. The histogram shows the number and size of shoes sold in a store on one working day.
   (a) How many shoes were sold that day?
   (b) What is the probability that a customer on that day bought:
      (i) a size 6 shoe   (ii) a size 9 or 10?

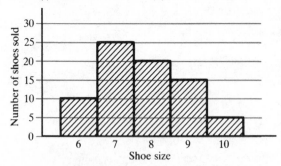

10. A test report on 32 cars gives these maximum speeds:

Maximum speed (km/h)	Number of cars
100–119	3
120–139	9
140–159	5
160–179	5
180–199	5
200–219	3
220–239	1
240–259	1

Find the probability that a car picked at random has a maximum speed of:
(a) 120–139 km/h   (b) less than 120 km/h.

11. These are the marks of 50 men who took a skills test. The maximum mark was 240.

Marks	Number of candidates
0–29	2
30–59	5
60–89	9
90–119	16
120–149	8
150–179	7
180–209	2
over 210	1

What is the probability that a man chosen at random scored:
(a) 120–149   (b) less than 30
(c) 120–179   (d) over 180?

12. Throw a die 100 times.
(a) Copy and complete the table

Score	1	2	3	4	5	6
Frequency						

(b) What is the probability of throwing:
    (i) a 2   (ii) an even number?

9.3 Theoretical probability

Often it is impractical or too time consuming to carry out an experiment. In these cases we can still calculate the theoretical probability of an event. It is defined in the same way as experimental probability, that is:

$$Pr(success) = \frac{number\ of\ successes}{total\ number\ of\ outcomes}$$

Example

One card is chosen from a pack of 52 playing cards. What is the probability that the card is:
(a) a King   (b) a black card?

(a) $Pr(King)$ $= \dfrac{number\ of\ Kings}{total\ number\ of\ cards}$

$= \dfrac{4}{52} = \dfrac{1}{13}$

(b) $Pr(Black\ card)$ $= \dfrac{number\ of\ black\ cards}{total\ number\ of\ cards}$

$= \dfrac{26}{52} = \dfrac{1}{2}$

---

1. A die is thrown.
(a) In how many different ways could it land?
(b) What is the probability that a 3 is thrown?

2. What is the probability of picking an ace from a pack of cards?

3. A bag contains two white beads and three black beads. One bead is chosen at random.

What is the probability that the bead is
(a) white   (b) black?

4. A letter is chosen at random from the word MATHEMATICS. What is the probability that the letter is:
(a) an A   (b) an M?

5. One card is chosen from the set of picture cards in a pack.
If K = {kings} and R = {red cards}, write down:
(a) $n(K)$ (b) $Pr(K)$ (c) $n(R)$ (d) $Pr(R)$

6. One card is chosen from the set of non-picture cards in a pack.
   If A = {aces} and B = {black cards}, write down:
   (a) $n(A)$ (b) $Pr(A)$ (c) $n(B)$ (d) $Pr(B)$

7. A bag contains 3 blue beads, 5 green beads, and 2 red beads. One is picked out. Which colour is:
   (a) most likely   (b) least likely
   to be chosen?

8. A box contains 30 buttons made up as follows: 5 blue, 6 green, 8 red, 4 yellow, 7 whites. One button is picked from the box.
   (a) How many buttons are there altogether?
   (b) Calculate: (i) $Pr(R)$ (ii) $Pr(B)$ (iii) $Pr(G)$ (iv) $Pr(Y)$

9. A bag contains the following currency notes: ten $1, twenty $5, forty $10, thirty $20.
   The notes are shaken up and one is chosen.
   (a) How many notes are there altogether?
   (b) Calculate: (i) $Pr(\$1)$ (ii) $Pr(\$5)$ (iii) $Pr(\$10)$ (iv) $Pr(\$20)$

10. A box contains 20 biros. 3 of them are faulty. One biro is chosen from the box. What is the probability that it is:

    (a) faulty   (b) not faulty?

11. A die is rolled once. Calculate:
    (a) $Pr(5)$ (b) $Pr(6)$ (c) Pr (even number)
    (d) Pr (odd number)   (e) Pr (number < 5)
    (f) Pr (number > 2)   (g) Pr (multiple of 3)
    (h) Pr (number not divisible by 3)

12. A class has 15 boys and 30 girls. The teacher chooses the class monitor as follows:
         the students' names are written on slips of paper, which are folded and put in a bag;
         the bag is shaken and one name drawn out.
    This person will be the monitor.
    What is the probability that the monitor will be:
    (a) a boy   (b) a girl?

13. Look at your answers for Question 12.
    (a) Is it more likely that the monitor will be a boy or a girl?
    (b) What can you say about the sum of the two probabilities?
    (c) What does a probability of 1 mean?

9.4 Using your knowledge

Probability and insurance

Insurance companies use ideas of probability to calculate the premiums people must pay for life insurance.
The table below shows the probability of a person of a given age dying before next birthday. It is not complete.

Age	Number of persons	Number of deaths before next birthday	Probability of dying before next birthday
16	20 000	400	$\dfrac{400}{20\,000} = \dfrac{20}{1000}$
17	40 000	600	
18	40 000	500	$\dfrac{500}{40\,000} = \dfrac{12.5}{1000}$
19	30 000	270	
20	40 000	320	
21	40 000	120	$\dfrac{120}{40\,000} = \dfrac{3}{1000}$

1. Look at the table above. What is the probability of choosing one of the 600 17 year-olds who will die before next birthday? Give your answer as a fraction with denominator 1000.

2. (a) Find the other two missing probabilities in the table.
   (b) Which age group has the highest probability of death before next birthday?
   (c) Which age group has the lowest probability of death before next birthday?

3. Long Life Insurance Company decide to insure 6000 people aged 21, for 1 year.
   They agree to pay $25 000 to the dependents of any of them who die before next birthday.
   (a) Out of 1000 21 year-olds, how many are likely to die before next birthday?
   (b) Out of 6000 21 year-olds, how many are likely to die before next birthday?
   (c) How much will the insurance company have to pay out to the dependents, on these deaths?

4. In Question 3, 6000 people are being insured. The insurance company wants to collect enough money in premiums from these people, to do two things:
        (i) to pay out $25 000 to the dependents of each person who dies before next birthday,
        (ii) to make $90 000 for itself (to cover expenses and to give some profit).

(a) How much money is the company likely to pay out to dependents?
(b) How much money should it collect in premiums, for the year?
(c) How much will each person pay in premiums, for the year?
(d) How much will each person pay per month?

5. Use the ideas in Questions 3 and 4 to find the monthly premium which must be paid by each of 6000 people for each age group in the table. Remember, the insurance company must:
   (i) pay out $25 000 to the dependents of each person who dies before next birthday,
   (ii) make $90 000 for itself, from each group.

6. (a) Which age group in Question 5 pays
   (i) the highest premium?
   (ii) the lowest premium?
   (b) Explain why different age groups pay different insurance premiums.

Probability and gambling

Many people gamble because they feel they will make money in the end. But this is not likely to happen, as you will see below.

7. (a) What is the probability of obtaining a 3 when throwing a die?
   (b) In what fraction of a large number of throws would you expect to get a 3?
   (c) On average would you agree that 3 is likely to occur once every six throws?

8. In a gambling game you throw a die for 2¢ a go. You win 10¢ if you get a 3.
   (a) How much money would you expect to win in six throws?
   (b) How much money would you expect to win in one throw?
   (c) How much money would you expect to win if you have one hundred throws?
   (d) How much money would you pay out, in (c)?
   (e) Would you make a net gain or a loss?

9. A very simple 'one-armed bandit' is shown below. Inside there are two discs, each with five pictures on. When you put in money and pull a lever, 10 cents a play, the discs spin round separately.

   (a) What is the probability of:
      (i) event A   (ii) event B   (iii) event C?
   (b) Why does event C have the biggest prize?
   (c) Suppose you decide to have 25 plays on the machine. How much will that cost you?
   (d) How much are you likely to win, in 25 plays?
   (e) Are you likely to make a profit or a loss? How much?

Disc one   Disc two

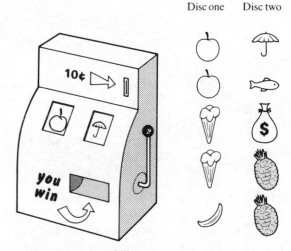

The prizes are as follows

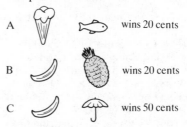

A   wins 20 cents

B   wins 20 cents

C   wins 50 cents

10. Two cards are to be drawn from a pack of 52 playing cards. To join in, you pay $1. If you choose one queen you win $5. If you choose two queens you win $10. Find the probability that:
    (a) the first card only is a queen
    (b) both cards are queens
    (c) either card, but not both, is a queen
    (d) neither card is a queen
    (e) you win $5
    (f) you win $10

A survey

11. Suppose you were to pick out any number, of all the 5-digit numbers. What is the probability that it would end with:
(a) a 5?   (b) a 2?

12. Lee carried out a survey on a telephone directory. He picked out a set of numbers at random, and recorded the last digit of each number. The results are shown in this bar chart.

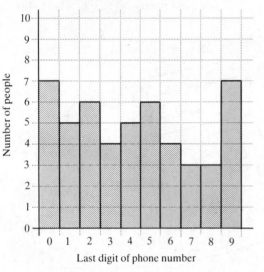

Last digit of phone number

(a) How many telephone numbers did Lee pick out?
(b) Using the results, estimate the probability that the final digit is:
   (i) a 6   (ii) a 6 or higher   (iii) a 3 or lower
(c) Estimate the probability that the phone number is: (i) 1   (ii) 3   (iii) 8
(d) Now think about phone numbers. Do you think the telephone company assigns them in order? e.g. 50575, 50576, 50577 . . .
   Should the probability for each final digit be the same?
(e) Do you think there was something wrong with Lee's survey? What was it?
(f) Work with four of your friends, and do a survey like Lee's. Each person should survey 100 phone numbers (total 1000). Calculate the probability for each final digit.

Summary

By the end of this chapter these are the things you should know about.

9.1 The idea of probability (pages 110–111)

Some events are more likely to happen than others. In mathematics, the likelihood of an event happening is described by a number between 0 and 1.
This number is the **probability** of the event.
The probability of a certain event happening is 1.
The probability of an impossible event happening is 0.

9.2 Experimental probability (pages 111–113)

How to find the probability of an event by performing an experiment.
The occurrence of a particular event is called a **success**.

$$Pr(\text{success}) = \frac{\text{number of successful outcomes}}{\text{total number of outcomes.}}$$

For example:
A coin is thrown 100 times, 52 heads occurred.

$$Pr(\text{head}) = \frac{52}{100}.$$

9.3 Theoretical probability (pages 113–114)

How to find the probability of simple events (without performing experiments).
   For example:
   What is the probability of throwing a head?

$$Pr(\text{head}) = \frac{\text{number of successes}}{\text{total number of outcomes}}$$
$$= \frac{1}{2}$$

9.4 Using your knowledge (pages 114–116)

Using probability to show that you are not likely to make a profit in gambling.
How insurance companies use probability to calculate monthly premiums.

10 Algebra 1

10.1 Revision

We often use letters to stand for numbers, and we can manipulate the letters in a similar way.

$$3 + 3 + 3 + 3 = 4 \times 3 = 12$$
$$a + a + a + a = 4 \times a = 4a$$

$$3 \times 3 \times 3 \times 3 = 3^4 = 81$$
$$a \times a \times a \times a = a^4$$

1. Write down, using the letters, the perimeter of each shape.

(a)   (b)   (c)

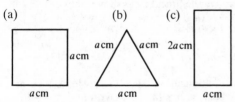

2. Find the perimeter of each shape in Question 1, when:
   (a) $a = 5$ (b) $a = 7$ (c) $a = 12$

3. Write down the perimeter of each rectangle.

   (a)   (b)

   b cm [rectangle] $2y$ cm [rectangle]
       l cm $3x$ cm

4. Do you agree that the perimeter of the first rectangle in Question 3 can be written as:
   (a) $(l + b + l + b)$ cm
   (b) $(2l + 2b)$ cm
   (c) $2(l + b)$ cm?

5. Find the perimeter of the rectangle in Question 3(a), when:
   (a) $l = 6, b = 3$ (b) $l = 12, b = 5$

6. Find the perimeter of the rectangle in Question 3(b), when:
   (a) $x = 5, y = 2$ (b) $x = 10, y = 7$

Additions can be written in a shorter way.
$$3a + 2a + 7a = 12a$$
$$5b + 3b + 8b = 16b$$

7. Write in a shorter way:
   (a) $3x + 2x$ (b) $7y + 9y$ (c) $5z + 7z + 8z$
   (d) $9x - 3x$ (e) $12y - 7y$ (f) $9z - 6z - 2z$

8. Find the value of each expression in Question 7, when $x = 3, y = 8, z = 12$.

Multiplications can be written in a shorter way
$$2 \times 3 \times p \times r = 6pr$$
$$2 \times 5m \times 10n = 100mn$$
$$\tfrac{1}{3} \times 5x \times (-9z) = -15xz$$

9. Write in a shorter way:
   (a) $m \times n \times 2 \times 5$ (b) $p \times x \times y^2$
   (c) $a \times 2b \times c^2$ (d) $(-a) \times (-2b) \times (-3c)$

10. Simplify:
  (a) $2 \times 3a$
  (b) $5b \times 4$
  (c) $4a \times 3b$
  (d) $7a \times 2a$
  (e) $3 \times 2b \times 4c$
  (f) $2a \times 5b \times 3c$
  (g) $-3 \times 7y$
  (h) $(-6p) \times (-5)$
  (i) $(-3q) \times 4p$
  (j) $(-5y) \times (-3y)$
  (k) $3a \times 2a \times a$
  (l) $(-2x) \times (5x) \times (-4x)$

11. Simplify:
  (a) $6a \div 2$
  (b) $8b \div 4b$
  (c) $5a \div 2a$
  (d) $4pq \div q$
  (e) $6ab \div 2ab$
  (f) $8pq \div 2q$
  (g) $10 \div 2x$
  (h) $3 \div 6y$
  (i) $a^2b \div ab$
  (j) $a^2b^2 \div ab^2$
  (k) $7ab^4 \div 3a^3b$
  (l) $4x^2y^2z^2 \div xy^3z^2$

The value of an expression can be found if you know the values of the letters.
  If $a = 3$ and $b = 2$ then
  $5a + 7b = 15 + 14 = 29$
  $ab + a + b = 6 + 3 + 2 = 1$

12. Find the value of the expression when $m = 2, n = 3$ and $p = 4$.
  (a) $5m + 7n + 2p$
  (b) $2m \times 3n \times p$
  (c) $5mnp$
  (d) m^2n
  (e) pm^3
  (f) $p^2 + n^2$
  (g) $mn + 2p$
  (h) $p^3n \div 6$

Simplifying expressions

Expressions with several terms are simplified by collecting like terms together.

i.e. $3a + 4b - 2a + 5b$
  $= (3a - 2a) + (4b + 5b)$
  $= \quad a \quad + \quad 9b$

or $x + 3y + 7x - 12x$
  $= 3y + (x + 7x - 12x)$
  $= 3y - 4x$

13. Simplify:
  (a) $3x + 5x$
  (b) $8a + 2a$
  (c) $14b - 2b$
  (d) $-7y + 4y$
  (e) $8a + 3a - 2a$
  (f) $7b - 3b - b$
  (g) $4p - 7p - 5p$
  (h) $3ab + 5ab + 9ab$
  (i) $2a^2 + 7a^2$
  (j) $9b^2 - 2b^2$
  (k) $x^2 + 3x^2 + 7x^2$
  (l) $8y^3 - 2y^3 - 4y^3$

14. Collect like terms together and simplify:
  (a) $4a + 3a + 7b + 5b$
  (b) $7a + 3b + 4a + 2b$
  (c) $4a + 9b - 2a - 3b$
  (d) $6x - 3y - 2x + 7y$
  (e) $x - y - 8x - 9y$
  (f) $5xy + 2z - 3xy - 5z$
  (g) $3ab + pq - ab + 5pq$
  (h) $a^2 + b^2 + 6a^2 - 3b^2$
  (i) $4a^3 - a - a^3 + 5a$

More complicated expressions can be simplified by adding and subtracting like terms in the same way.

  (a) $3pq - 8pq + 4pq = -pq$
  (b) $xy + 2ab - 5xy + 10ab$
      $= (xy - 5xy) + (2ab + 10ab)$
      $= -4xy + 12ab$

15. Simplify the expression:
  (a) $4a + 3a + 7b + 5b$
  (b) $4p + 9q - 2p - 3q$
  (c) $6z^3 - z - 7z^3 + 4z$
  (d) $a^2 + b^2 + 6a^2 - 3b^2$
  (e) $p^2 + 2pq + 6pq - 4p^2$

16. Simplify the expression:
  (a) $mn + 4xy + 17xy - mn + xy$
  (b) $3p^2q + lm + 14p^2q + 6lm$
  (c) $pqr + abx + mny + 5abx$
  (d) $15ab - 29ab + 4pq + ab$
  (e) $x^2y^2 - 4xy + 13xy + 3x^2y^2$

17. Simplify:
  (a) $4x^2 + 7x^2$
  (b) $2mn + 5mn - 3mn$
  (c) $4l^2m^2 - 7l^2m^2$
  (d) $8pqr - 9pqr - 15pqr$
  (e) $-3 \times 5m$
  (f) $6a \times 11b$
  (g) $7a^2 \times 3a^3$
  (h) $(-4pq) \times (-2p^2q^3)$
  (i) $10m^2 \div 2$
  (j) $7a^2b^3 \div 2ab$
  (k) $4x^5 \div 7x^8$
  (l) $2lm^2n^3 \div 3l^3m^2n$

Removing brackets

$3 \times (x + 5y + 4z)$ can be written as $3x + 15y + 12z$
Each term inside the brackets is multiplied by the term outside.
  $-4p \times (p^2 - 6q + r) = -4p^3 + 24pq - 4pr$
This uses the rules for multiplying negative numbers. Make sure you understand it.

18. Remove the brackets, as shown above.
  (a) $5 \times (a + b)$
  (b) $4 \times (p + 2q)$
  (c) $3 \times (m^2 + 2n)$
  (d) $10 \times (p + q^2 + 2r)$
  (e) $-2 \times (a - 2b)$
  (f) $-3 \times (-3a + 4b^2)$
  (g) $-m \times (n + m)$
  (h) $-4y \times (3x - 2)$

19. The multiplication sign is usually left out before brackets. So $5 \times (a + b)$ is written as $5(a + b)$. In the same way, write these without the multiplication sign.
  (a) $3 \times (x + y)$
  (b) $-1 \times (x - y)$
  (c) $5 \times (l + 2m)$
  (d) $p^2 \times (q - p)$
  (e) $r^2 \times (p + q)$
  (f) $m \times (m^2 - m)$

Example 1

Remove the brackets.
  (a) $3(a + 2b + 5c)$
      $= 3a + 6b + 15c$

  (b) $2x(y + 4z) - 3y(z - 2w)$
      $= 2xy + 8xz - 3yz + 6yw$

why is this positive?

20. Remove the brackets:
(a) $2(a + b)$
(b) $3(x + 2y)$
(c) $4(3p - 5q)$
(d) $5a(b + c)$
(e) $3p(q - 2r)$
(f) $5(a - 2b + 3c)$
(g) $2x(y - 2 + 3w)$
(h) $-3(2l + m)$
(i) $-2l(m - 5n)$
(j) $p(p + 3q - 5r)$
(k) $-4y(3x - 2)$
(l) $4x(x^2 - x + 1)$

21. Remove the brackets and simplify:
(a) $3(x + y) + 2(x - y)$
(b) $5(l + 2m) - (m - 2l)$
(c) $6(p - q) + 4(r - q - p)$
(d) $4a(b + c - a) + 2c(3a + b)$
(e) $-(m - 5) + 4m(m + 2)$
(f) $-3(mn + m) + 4n(2 - m)$

22. Remove the brackets and simplify:
(a) $m(2 + n) + n(m - 3) - (mn - m)$
(b) $-(x^2 - 1) - x^2(4 - x) + 5(6 - x^3)$
(c) $pq(p^2 + 1) + pq(1 + p^{-2})$
(d) $xy(x^{-3} + x) + 5xy(3 + y^{-3})$
(e) $p^{-2}(p^3 - p^4) + p^{-1}(pq + p^2q)$
(f) $\frac{1}{3}p^2(p - p^{-1}) + \frac{5}{3}p(p^2 + p^{-2})$

23. Remove the brackets and simplify:
(a) $3(x + y) + 2(x - y)$
(b) $4(x + y) + 3(2x + 5y)$
(c) $8(a - b) - 3(2a - b)$
(d) $6(x - 3) + 5(x + 2)$
(e) $x(x^2 + 1) + 2x(x^2 + 5)$
(f) $7a - 4a(b + 3)$

24. Remove the brackets and simplify:
(a) $2(x - 3y) + 3(y - 2z) + 4(z - 5x)$
(b) $3m(2 + n) + 5n(1 - 3m) + 12mn$
(c) $x(x^2 - 1) + x^2(x + 2) - x(5 - x^2)$

Factorizing expressions

3 is common to each of the terms $3l$, $6m$ and $9n$
So $3l + 6m + 9n = 3(l + 2m + 3n)$

x is common to each of the terms ax and bx
So $ax + bx = (a + b)x$

25. Copy and complete:
(a) $3x + 3y = 3(\quad)$
(b) $5a - 5b = 5(\quad)$
(c) $4x + 4y + 4z = 4(\quad)$
(d) $6a - 6b + 6c = 6(\quad)$
(e) $2x + 6y = 2(\quad)$
(f) $8a - 4b = 4(\quad)$
(g) $3x + 6y + 9z = 3(\quad)$
(h) $25a - 10b - 5c = 5(\quad)$

26. Copy and complete:
(a) $ax + ay = a(\quad)$
(b) $pa - pb = p(\quad)$
(c) $px + py + pz = p(\quad)$
(d) $ra - rb + rc = r(\quad)$

(e) $qx + 3qy = q(\quad)$
(f) $5sa - sb = s(\quad)$
(g) $2tx + 5ty + tz = t(\quad)$
(h) $7la - 4lb - lc = l(\quad)$

27. Copy and complete:
(a) $px + qx = (\quad)x$
(b) $as - bs = (\quad)s$
(c) $px + qx + rx = (\quad)x$
(d) $ra - sa + ta = (\quad)a$
(e) $3ly + 2my = (\quad)y$
(f) $6fh - 5gh = (\quad)h$
(g) $4xt + 9yt + zt = (\quad)t$
(h) $2lg - 7mg - 3ng = (\quad)g$

28. Factorize:
(a) $2a + 2b$
(b) $3a - 3b$
(c) $4x + 12y$
(d) $9p - 6q$
(e) $px + py$
(f) $ra - rb$
(g) $7sx + 4sy$
(h) $2ta - 7tb$
(i) $xa + xb + xc$
(j) $la - lb - lc$
(k) $4rx + 5ry + rz$
(l) $pa - 6pb + 8pc$

29. Factorize:
(a) $lx + mx$
(b) $an - bn$
(c) $7py + 2qy$
(d) $rt - 5st$
(e) $pt + qt + rt$
(f) $an + bn - cn$
(g) $5lx + mx + 2nx$
(h) $4kg - 2lg - mg$

$2m$ is common to each of the terms $2lm$, $6mn$ and $10mp$
so $2lm + 6mn + 10mp$ can be written
as $2m(l + 3n + 5p)$.

$2m$ is one factor of $2lm + 6mn + 10mp$,
$(l + 3n + 5p)$ is the other factor.

x is common to each of the terms x^2 and $3x$
So $x^2 + 3x = (x + 3)x$
$(x + 3)$ and x are the factors of $x^2 + 3x$

30. Copy and complete, as shown above.
(a) $3m + 5mn + m^2 = m(\quad)$
(b) $2p + 3pr + p^2 = p(\quad)$
(c) $6l + 2lm + 2l^2 = 2l(\quad)$
(d) $5rs + 50rs^2 + 15r^2s = 5rs(\quad)$

31. Factorize, as in Question 30.
(a) $4p + 2pr + 6pz$
(b) $5m + 15mp + 25mg$
(c) $9sr + 3s + 6s^2$
(d) $4lm + 2mn + 8pmn$
(e) $ab^2 + 6ab^3 + 2a^2b^2$
(f) $2x^2y^2 + 3xy^2 + x^2y^2$

32. Factorize:
(a) $x^2 + 3x$
(b) $y^2 - 5y$
(c) $2z^2 + 3z$
(d) $4m^2 - m$
(e) $x^3 + 2xy$
(f) $4y^2z - y^3$
(g) $ab^2 + a^2b$
(h) $x^2yz^2 - xyz^3$
(i) $\pi r^2 + 2\pi rh$
(j) $2lm^2 + 8l^2m$
(k) $x^4 + x^3 + x^2$
(l) $32y + 16y^3 + 8y^5$

33. Factorize:
  (a) $abc^2 + ab^2 + a^2b$
  (b) $p^3q^2r + p^2q^2r^2 + pq^2r^3$
  (c) $7axy + 14bxy + 21cxy$
  (d) $8x^6 + 16x^4 + 48x^3$
  (e) $2lmp - lm + 5lm^2$
  (f) $f^4g^2 - 6f^2g^3 + 2fg^4$
  (g) $5abcd + 35bcde$
  (h) $24k^2lm^2n - 32kl^2m^2n^3$
  (i) $16abcx - 28bcdx - 20cdex$

34. Factorize:

  (a) $\dfrac{p}{4} - \dfrac{q}{8} + \dfrac{r}{12}$

  (b) $\dfrac{12a}{x} - \dfrac{6b}{x} - \dfrac{24c}{x}$

  (c) $\dfrac{l^2m}{n} + \dfrac{lm^2}{n^2} + \dfrac{l^2m^2}{n^3}$

35. Remove the brackets and factorize:
  (a) $3(x - 5) + 4(x - 2) - 5$
  (b) $x(y + 3) + 2x(4 - y) - 10xy$
  (c) $a(b + c) + b(c - a) + 3c$
  (d) $lm(5l + m) + 2l^2(m - 3) + 6l(m^2 + l)$

36. Factorize the expression.
  (a) $x^2y + 3xy + 4xy^2$
  (b) $2rs + 18rst + 8r^2s^2 + 10rst^2$
  (c) $14mn^2 + 2mn + 8m^2n + 8m^2n^2$
  (d) $\frac{1}{8}g^2h + \frac{5}{8}g^3h + 2g^3h^3$
  (e) $\frac{1}{2}x^2y + 2xy^2 + x^2y^3 + \frac{3}{4}x^4y^4$

Example 2

Factorize:
$$ax + bx + ay + by = x(a + b) + y(a + b)$$
$$= (x + y)(a + b)$$

---

37. Copy and complete, as shown in Example 2.
  (a) $px + qx + py + qy = x(\quad) + y(\quad)$
                   $= (x + y)(\quad)$
  (b) $ax - bx + ay - by = x(\quad) + y(\quad)$
                   $= (x + y)(\quad)$
  (c) $ut^2 + us + vt^2 + vs = u(\quad) + v(\quad)$
                   $= (u + v)(\quad)$
  (d) $2lx + mx - my - 2ly = x(\quad) - y(\quad)$
                   $= (x - y)(\quad)$

38. Collect like terms together, then factorize:
  (a) $rx + sy + sx + ry$
  (b) $sy + 2ry + 2rx + sx$
  (c) $by + 3ay + bx + 3ax$
  (d) $2ap + 2bp + 2qb + 2qa$
  (e) $8ap + 2bq + 2pb + 8aq$

39. Factorize:
  (a) $6t^2y + xz + 3t^2x + 2yz$
  (b) $2ax - 3by + 3bx - 2ay$
  (c) $mp^2 - 2mq - 2nq + np^2$

  (d) $gx - 4hy + 2gy - 2hx$
  (e) $a^2l - b^2m + b^2l - a^2m$

40. Factorize:
  (a) $px + qx - rx + py + qy - ry$
  (b) $ax^2 - ay - az^3 + bx^2 - by - bz^3$
  (c) $2fx + gy - 3fz + 2gx + fy - 3gz$
  (d) $8mx - 10nx + 10ny - 8my$
  (e) $3m^2x - 4n^3y^2 - 3m^2y^2 + 4n^3x$

Fractions in algebra

(a) $\dfrac{1}{3} + \dfrac{2}{7} = \dfrac{7}{21} + \dfrac{6}{21} = \dfrac{13}{21}$

The factors are given a common denominator.
e.g. $\frac{1}{3}$ and $\frac{7}{21}$ mean the same thing
– they are equivalent fractions.

(b) $\dfrac{a}{3} + \dfrac{a}{2} = \dfrac{2a}{6} + \dfrac{3a}{6} = \dfrac{5a}{6}$

Again, both fractions are given a common denominator.

$\dfrac{a}{3}$ and $\dfrac{2a}{6}$ mean the same thing

– they are equivalent fractions, just like $\frac{1}{3}$ and $\frac{7}{21}$.

(c) $\dfrac{x}{2} + \dfrac{y}{4} = \dfrac{2x + y}{4}$

41. Simplify, as shown above.

  (a) $\dfrac{3}{4} + \dfrac{1}{8}$ (b) $\dfrac{2}{3} + \dfrac{1}{4}$

  (c) $\dfrac{5}{6} - \dfrac{1}{3}$ (d) $\dfrac{5}{7} - \dfrac{2}{3} + \dfrac{1}{4}$

42. Simplify, as shown above.

  (a) $\dfrac{a}{5} + \dfrac{a}{3}$ (b) $\dfrac{2a}{9} + \dfrac{a}{5}$

  (c) $3a + \dfrac{2a}{3}$ (d) $\dfrac{3a}{4} - \dfrac{a}{6} + \dfrac{a}{3}$

  (e) $\dfrac{a}{7} - \dfrac{2a}{3}$ (f) $\dfrac{5a}{11} + \dfrac{a}{7} + \dfrac{a}{3}$

43. Simplify, as shown in (c) above.

  (a) $\dfrac{2x}{3} + \dfrac{y}{6}$ (b) $\dfrac{3y}{11} + \dfrac{x}{3}$

  (c) $\dfrac{y}{2} + \dfrac{2x}{5} + \dfrac{z}{2}$ (d) $\dfrac{x}{4} + \dfrac{y^2}{2}$

  (e) $\dfrac{3x}{2} + \dfrac{5y^2}{2} + \dfrac{y}{4}$ (f) $\dfrac{x^2}{9} + \dfrac{2y}{7}$

44. If $x = 2$, $y = 3$ and $z = 4$ find the value of each answer for Question 43.

Example 3

(a) $\dfrac{2}{b} + \dfrac{b}{7} = \dfrac{14}{7b} + \dfrac{b^2}{7b} = \dfrac{14 + b^2}{7b}$

Again, the fractions are given a common denominator.

Note that $\dfrac{2}{b}$ and $\dfrac{14}{7b}$ are equivalent.

(b) $\dfrac{x}{5} + \dfrac{4}{y} = \dfrac{xy}{5y} + \dfrac{20}{5y} = \dfrac{xy + 20}{5y}$

---

45. Simplify:

(a) $\dfrac{p}{3q} + \dfrac{2q}{p}$ (b) $\dfrac{5}{m} + \dfrac{4l}{3m}$

(c) $\dfrac{5}{4} + \dfrac{3z}{x}$ (d) $\dfrac{1}{pq} + \dfrac{3}{r}$

(e) $\dfrac{xy}{z} + \dfrac{az}{y}$ (f) $\dfrac{ab}{5c} + \dfrac{bc}{4a}$

Example 4

Simplify.

$\dfrac{2}{(x - 1)} + \dfrac{3}{(x - 2)}$

$= \dfrac{2(x - 2)}{(x - 1)(x - 2)} + \dfrac{3(x - 1)}{(x - 1)(x - 2)}$

$= \dfrac{2(x - 2) + 3(x - 1)}{(x - 1)(x - 2)}$

---

46. Show that the result in Example 4 can be

written as $\dfrac{(5x - 7)}{(x - 1)(x - 2)}$

47. Write the answer as a single fraction, as in Question 46.

(a) $\dfrac{5}{(x + 3)} + \dfrac{3}{(x - 1)}$ (b) $\dfrac{6}{(x + 1)} - \dfrac{4}{(x - 3)}$

(c) $\dfrac{1}{(x - 1)} + \dfrac{1}{(x + 1)}$ (d) $\dfrac{(x + 3)}{4} + \dfrac{(x - 1)}{5}$

(e) $\dfrac{(x - 2)}{5} - \dfrac{(2x - 1)}{7}$ (f) $\dfrac{4}{(x + 1)} + \dfrac{3}{(x + 2)}$

48. Simplify:

(a) $xy\left(\dfrac{1}{x} + \dfrac{1}{y} \right)$ (b) $mn\left(\dfrac{2}{m} - \dfrac{3}{n} \right)$

(c) $2xyz\left(\dfrac{1}{xy} - \dfrac{2}{yz} \right)$ (d) $p^2q\left(\dfrac{1}{pq} + \dfrac{2}{p^2q} \right)$

(e) $a^3b^3\left(\dfrac{1}{a^2b} + \dfrac{a^2}{b^3} \right)$

(f) $gh^2(g^{-1}h^{-1} + g^{-1}h^{-2})$

$g^{-1} = \dfrac{1}{g}$

49. The mean of p numbers is 48. The mean of another q numbers is 51. Express, as a single fraction, the mean of $p + q$ numbers.

50. Avril cycles 10 km at x km/h and then 14 km at y km/h. Express the time for the journey as a single fraction.

51. b bananas cost \$1.45 and a apples cost \$2.35.
  (a) How much does one banana cost?
  (b) How much does one apple cost?
  (c) Write as a single fraction the cost of one banana and one apple.

10.2 Binary operations

Example 1

An operation $*$ is defined by $\boxed{a * b = 2a + b}$

$3 * 5 = 2 \times 3 + 5 = 11$ but $5 * 3 = 2 \times 5 + 3 = 13$, so $*$ is *not commutative*.

$(3 * 5) * 6 = 11 * 6 = 2 \times 11 + 6 = 28$
$3 * (5 * 6) = 3 * 16 = 2 \times 3 + 16 = 22$ so $*$ is *not associative*.

Example 2

An operation $\square$ is defined by $\boxed{a \,\square\, b = 2ab}$

$3 \,\square\, 5 = 2 \times 3 \times 5 = 30$ and $5 \,\square\, 3 = 2 \times 5 \times 3 = 30$
also $a \,\square\, b = b \,\square\, a = 2ab$, for all a and b,
so $\square$ is *commutative*.

$(3 \,\square\, 5) \,\square\, 6 = 30 \,\square\, 6 = 2 \times 30 \times 6 = 360$ and
$3 \,\square\, (5 \,\square\, 6) = 3 \,\square\, 60 = 2 \times 3 \times 60 = 360$
also $(a \,\square\, b) \,\square\, c = a \,\square\, (b \,\square\, c) = 4abc$,
for all a, b and c,
so $\square$ is *associative*.

1. An operation $*$ is defined by $a * b = 3a + b$. Find:
   (a) $4 * 6$ (b) $6 * 4$ (c) $6 * 2$
   (d) $(4 * 6) * 2$ (e) $4 * (6 * 2)$
   Is $*$ commutative? Is $*$ associative?

2. An operation $\square$ is defined by $a \square b = 3ab$. Find:
   (a) $4 \square 6$ (b) $6 \square 4$ (c) $6 \square 2$
   (d) $(4 \square 6) \square 2$ (e) $4 \square (6 \square 2)$
   Explain why $\square$ is commutative.
   Find $(a \square b) \square c$ and $a \square (b \square c)$ and hence show that $\square$ is associative.

3. An operation $*$ is defined by $p * q = p^2 + q^2$. Find:
   (a) $2 * 3$ (b) $3 * 2$ (c) $3 * 4$
   (d) $(2 * 3) * 4$ (e) $2 * (3 * 4)$
   Is $*$ commutative? Is $*$ associative?
   Explain your answers.

4. An operation $\square$ is defined by $p \square q = p^2q^2$. Find:
   (a) $2 \square 3$ (b) $3 \square 2$ (c) $3 \square 4$
   (d) $(2 \square 3) \square 4$ (e) $2 \square (3 \square 4)$
   Is $\square$ commutative? Is $\square$ associative?
   Explain your answers.

5. An operation $*$ is defined by $x * y = x$.
   (a) By finding $3 * 4$ and $4 * 3$ show that $*$ is not commutative.
   (b) By finding $(x * y) * z$ and $x * (y * z)$ show that $*$ is associative.

6. The operation $\circ$ is defined by $a \circ b = \sqrt{a^2 + b^2}$.
   (a) Find $5 \circ 12$ and $12 \circ 5$ and explain why $\circ$ is commutative.
   (b) Find $(3 \circ 4) \circ 12$ and $3 \circ (4 \circ 12)$. Do you think $\circ$ is associative? Justify your answer by finding $(a \circ b) \circ c$ and $a \circ (b \circ c)$.

7. Repeat Question 6 if $\circ$ is defined by $(a + b)^{-1}$.

8. The operation $*$ is defined by $p * q = pq + p + q$.
   (a) Find $2 * 3$ and $3 * 2$ and explain why $*$ is commutative.
   (b) Find $(2 * 3) * 4$ and $2 * (3 * 4)$. Do you think $*$ is associative?
   Justify your answer by finding $(p * q) * r$ and $p * (q * r)$.

9. The operation $\circ$ is defined by $x \circ y = x^2 + y^2 - xy$.
   (a) Find $4 \circ 5$ and $5 \circ 4$. Is $\circ$ commutative?
   (b) Find $(3 \circ 4) \circ 5$ and $3 \circ (4 \circ 5)$. Is $\circ$ associative?

I thought only surgeons made operations.

10.3 Linear equations

Example 1

Use the **function machine** idea to solve
$2(3x + 1) - 5 = 21$

We can show the left-hand side of the equations as:

$$x \rightarrow \boxed{\times 3} \rightarrow \boxed{+ 1} \rightarrow \boxed{\times 2} \rightarrow \boxed{- 5} \rightarrow 2(3x + 1) - 5$$

We can then use the machine in reverse with 21:

$$4 \leftarrow \boxed{\div 3} \leftarrow \boxed{- 1} \leftarrow \boxed{\div 2} \leftarrow \boxed{+ 5} \leftarrow 21$$

So $x = 4$.

Check: $2(3 \times 4 + 1) - 5 = 2 \times 13 - 5 = 21$

1. Show the expression as a function machine:
   (a) $2x + 3$ (b) $3(x - 4)$ (c) $4(2x + 1)$
   For each, also show the reverse machine.

2. Using the reverse machines in Question 1, solve:
   (a) $2x + 3 = 19$ (b) $3(x - 4) = 24$
   (c) $4(2x + 1) = 76$

3. Using the function machine idea solve:
   (a) $3x + 2 = 50$ (b) $2(x - 9) = 14$
   (c) $5(3x - 1) = 100$
   Check your answers by substitution.

4. Solve the equation.
   (a) $2(3x + 5) = 52$ (b) $5(4x + 1) = 185$
   (c) $7(2x - 3) = 133$ (d) $3(9x - 4) = 15$
   (e) $3(2x + 9) = 15$ (f) $6(5x + 11) = 36$
   (g) $4(2x + 1) = 24$ (h) $8(5x - 2) = 32$

5. Solve the equation.
   (a) $5x + 2 = 37$ (b) $6(x - 4) = 96$
   (c) $3(2x + 7) = 51$ (d) $\dfrac{x}{3} + 5 = 9$
   (e) $\dfrac{(x - 7)}{4} = 15$ (f) $4\left(\dfrac{x}{5} + 3\right) = 28$

6. Find the value of x which makes the statement true.
   (a) $3(2x + 1) - 7 = 50$
   (b) $5(3x + 2) + 4 = 134$
   (c) $7(4x - 3) + 9 = 156$
   (d) $4(5x - 3) - 1 = 107$

7. Solve the equation.
   (a) $2\left(\dfrac{x}{5} - 1\right) + 3 = 7$ (b) $\dfrac{3x - 4}{7} + 2 = 7$

8. 9 is added to five times a number and the result is then doubled. The answer is 188.
Show this information as an equation.
Solve the equation to find the number.

An alternative way of solving a linear equation is to use the **balance idea**. Any process applied to one side of the equation must also be applied to the other side, if the equation is to remain in balance. This is shown in Example 2 below.

Example 2

(a) $\quad x + 5 = 11$
$\quad x + 5 - 5 = 11 - 5$
$\quad\quad x = 6$

(b) $\quad 3x = 39$
$\quad \frac{1}{3} \times 3x = \frac{1}{3} \times 39$
$\quad\quad x = 13$

(c) $\quad 7x - 6 = 50$
$\quad 7x - 6 + 6 = 50 + 6$
$\quad\quad 7x = 56$
$\quad \frac{1}{7} \times 7x = \frac{1}{7} \times 56$
$\quad\quad x = 8$

---

9. Solve:
(a) $x + 5 = 19$ (b) $x + 4 = 12$ (c) $x + 73 = 95$
(d) $x + 7 = 3$ (e) $x + 23 = -4$

10. Solve:
(a) $x - 5 = 19$ (b) $x - 4 = 12$ (c) $x - 67 = 82$
(d) $x - 4 = -9$ (e) $x - 6 = -5$

11. Solve:
(a) $3x = 12$ (b) $5x = 60$ (c) $13x = 117$
(d) $8x = 4$ (e) $15x = 3$

12. Solve:
(a) $\dfrac{x}{2} = 5$ (b) $\dfrac{x}{7} = 6$ (c) $\dfrac{x}{19} = 2$

(d) $\dfrac{x}{3} = -4$ (e) $\dfrac{x}{22} = -3$

13. Solve:
(a) $2x + 5 = 11$ (b) $3x + 8 = 29$
(c) $7x + 15 = 92$ (d) $4x - 3 = 29$
(e) $12x - 23 = 25$

14. Solve:
(a) $\dfrac{x}{2} + 5 = 11$ (b) $\dfrac{x}{3} + 8 = 29$

(c) $\dfrac{x}{6} + 11 = 29$ (d) $\dfrac{x}{8} - 5 = 15$

(e) $\dfrac{x}{11} - 8 = 3$

Example 3

Use the balance idea to solve $5x - 7 = 3x + 19$.

Collect the x terms on the left-hand side of the equation by subtracting $3x$ from each side, then adding 7 to each side.
$(-3x)$ $\quad\quad\quad\quad\quad\quad\quad\quad 2x - 7 = 19$
$(+7)$ $\quad\quad\quad\quad\quad\quad\quad\quad\quad 2x = 26$
$(\div 2)$ $\quad\quad\quad\quad\quad\quad\quad\quad\quad\quad x = 13$

---

15. By using the method in Example 3, solve:
(a) $7x + 9 = 2x + 49$ (b) $8x - 15 = 3x + 20$
Check your answers by substitution.

16. Solve the equation.
(a) $9x - 5 = 6x + 34$ (b) $5x - 7 = 25 - 3x$
(c) $8x + 3 = 5x - 21$ (d) $4 + 7x = 19 - 2x$

17. Solve:
(a) $2x + 1 = x + 7$ (b) $9x + 4 = 6x + 10$
(c) $5x - 7 = 3x + 11$ (d) $12x - 23 = 8x - 3$
(e) $4x + 3 = 2x - 9$ (f) $8x - 1 = 5x - 22$
(g) $7x + 4 = 2x + 7$ (h) $6x - 13 = 4x - 19$

18. Solve:
(a) $7x + 5 = 11x + 1$ (b) $5x + 14 = 7x + 4$
(c) $4x - 3 = 9x - 23$ (d) $2x - 15 = 11x + 12$
(e) $4x + 3 = 38 - x$ (f) $7x - 5 = 43 - 3x$
(g) $19 - 3x = 41 - 4x$ (h) $43 - 2x = 7 - 9x$

Example 4

Solve the equation by first removing the brackets:
$$5(x + 3) = 2(x + 9)$$
$$5x + 15 = 2x + 18$$
$(-2x)$ $\quad\quad\quad 3x + 15 = 18$
(-15) $\quad\quad\quad\quad\quad 3x = 3$
$(\div 3)$ $\quad\quad\quad\quad\quad\quad x = 1$

---

19. Solve:
(a) $2(x + 1) = 8$ (b) $3(x - 2) = 6$
(c) $2(x + 1) = x + 9$ (d) $3(x - 2) = 2x - 5$

20. Solve:
(a) $3(x + 1) = 2(x + 5)$ (b) $4(x - 1) = 3(x + 2)$
(c) $5(x + 3) = 4(x + 7)$ (d) $5(x - 2) = 3(x + 2)$

21. Solve:
(a) $4(x + 3) = 2(x + 7)$ (b) $7(x + 1) = 5(x + 3)$
(c) $5(x - 2) = 2(x + 4)$ (d) $6(x - 3) = 2(x + 3)$

Example 5

Solve $\dfrac{x-1}{3} - 5 = \dfrac{2x}{7} - 4$

First remove the two denominators. You can do this by multiplying each side of the equation by 21 (the L.C.M. of 3 and 7):

$7(x-1) - 5 \times 21 = 6x - 4 \times 21$

Next remove brackets:

$7x - 7 - 105 = 6x - 84$

Then collect x terms:

$7x - 6x = -84 + 105 + 7$

so $x = 28$

22. Solve the equation by the method shown in Example 5.

(a) $\dfrac{x}{2} + \dfrac{x}{4} = 15$ (b) $\dfrac{2x}{3} + \dfrac{x}{9} = 42$

(c) $\dfrac{x}{5} - 3 = \dfrac{x}{10} + 4$ (d) $\dfrac{4x}{7} - 5 = 1 - \dfrac{3x}{14}$

23. Solve:

(a) $\dfrac{x}{3} + 6 = \dfrac{3x}{7} + 4$

(b) $\dfrac{x-5}{4} - 7 = \dfrac{x}{5}$

(c) $\dfrac{(2x-3)}{5} + \dfrac{x}{4} = 2$

(d) $\dfrac{2(x-1)}{3} = \dfrac{(3x+1)}{5} + 9$

24. Find the value of x which makes the statement true. Check your answer by substitution.

(a) $\dfrac{2x}{5} - 4 = \dfrac{x}{7} + 5$ (b) $\dfrac{5x}{3} + 4 = 97 - \dfrac{2x}{5}$

(c) $\dfrac{x+4}{3} + \dfrac{x-1}{2} = 20$ (d) $\dfrac{36}{x} - 5 = \dfrac{17}{2x}$

25. Solve:

(a) $\dfrac{x-5}{3} + \dfrac{x-2}{2} = 4$

(b) $\dfrac{2x+1}{7} - \dfrac{3x+2}{16} = 1$

multiply both sides by 2x

26. The same number is added to both the numerator and the denominator of the fraction $\frac{17}{25}$. The result is $\frac{3}{4}$. What number was added?

27. Repeat Question 26, for the result $\frac{9}{10}$.

28. Solve:

(a) $2(3(4x+5) + 6) = 18$

(b) $5(3x+4) - 16 = 2(7x-5) + 43$

10.4 Linear inequalities

If x is less than 4, we write $x < 4$.
$x \leqslant 4$ means x is less than or equal to 4.

If x is a positive whole number and if $x < 4$ then $x \in \{1, 2, 3\}$.
If x is any number, and $x < 4$ then x could be $^-1, 1\frac{1}{2}, 0.1$ etc. (i.e. all numbers less than 4).
The statement $4 > x$ is equivalent to $x < 4$.

The number line

A number line is a useful way of showing a result and also of finding which numbers satisfy inequalities such as $x < {}^-5$. For example:

$x < {}^-5$

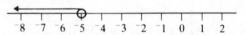

$x \geqslant {}^-2$

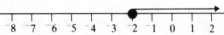

Note: The filled-in circle ● for $x \geqslant {}^-2$ is used to show that x can equal $^-2$.
The empty circle ○ for $x < {}^-5$ is used to show that x is less than $^-5$ but not equal to $^-5$.

Inequalities can be solved in a similar way to equations, except that multiplying or dividing by a negative number involves a change in the inequality sign (see Example 2).

Example 1

$5x - 4 > 3x - 16$
$2x - 4 > -16$ subtracting $3x$ from each side
$2x > -12$ adding 4 to each side
$x > -6$ dividing both sides by 2

Example 2

$16 - 5x \geqslant 1 - 2x$
$16 - 3x \geqslant 1$ adding $2x$ to each side
$-3x \geqslant -15$ subtracting 16 from each side
$x \leqslant 5$ dividing by -3, so reverse the inequality sign.

1. Solve the inequality:

(a) $x + 2 < 6$ (b) $x - 5 \geqslant 12$
(c) $x + 7 < 2$ (d) $x - 5 > 8$
(e) $2x < 12$ (f) $3x > 15$
(g) $5x \leqslant 20$ (h) $7x > 49$

2. For each part of Question 1, write down the whole numbers for $0 < x < 10$ which satisfy the inequality.

3. Solve the inequality:
(a) $3x + 2 > 14$
(b) $2x - 5 \leqslant 7$
(c) $5x + 3 < 18$
(d) $2x - 5 > 3$
(e) $2x - 3 \geqslant 6$
(f) $3x + 8 < 2$
(g) $4x - 5 \leqslant 11$
(h) $3x + 7 > 1$

4. For each part of Question 3 write down the whole numbers for $^-6 < x < 6$ which satisfy the inequality.

5. Solve the inequality:
(a) $2x + 2 \geqslant x + 8$
(b) $5x - 2 < x + 6$
(c) $3x - 5 > 2x + 7$
(d) $4x - 3 < 2x + 5$
(e) $3x + 7 \leqslant x + 1$
(f) $5x + 8 > 3x - 2$

6. For each part of Question 5 show your solution on a number line.

7. Solve the inequality:
(a) $3x + 2 \geqslant 17 - 2x$
(b) $7x - 3 \leqslant 5 - x$
(c) $5x + 33 > 5 - 2x$
(d) $8x + 3 < 48 - x$
(e) $2x - 5 > 10 - 3x$
(f) $6 - x \leqslant 2 - 3x$

8. For each part of Question 7 show your solution on a number line.

9. Solve the inequality:
(a) $3x - 8 \geqslant x + 4$
(b) $4x - 6 \leqslant x - 2$
(c) $8x - 3 > 5 + 6x$
(d) $2x - 3 \leqslant 15 - x$
(e) $12 + x < 8 + 3x$
(f) $1 + x \geqslant 7 + 4x$
(g) $x + 1 > 13 - 5x$
(h) $7 + 2x \leqslant 4 - 7x$
(i) $16 - 9x > 1 - 6x$

Remember: in the following questions if you multiply or divide by a negative number you must reverse the inequality sign.

10. Solve the inequality:
(a) $-3x < -12$
(b) $-3x \leqslant 12$
(c) $-4x > -20$
(d) $-4x \geqslant 20$

11. Solve the inequality:
(a) $1 - 3x < -11$
(b) $4 - 3x \leqslant 16$
(c) $5 - 4x > -15$
(d) $7 - 4x > 27$

12. Solve the inequality:
(a) $4 - 3x > 1$
(b) $3 - 2x \leqslant 15$
(c) $5 - x \geqslant 2$
(d) $17 - 3x < 2$

13. For each part of Question 12, write down the whole numbers for $^-5 < x < 5$ which satisfy the inequality.

14. Solve the inequality and show your results on a number line:
(a) $8 - 3x > 4 + x$
(b) $15 - 7x < 5 + 3x$
(c) $14 + x \geqslant 2 + 3x$
(d) $2 + 3x \leqslant 18 + 7x$
(e) $2 - x > 8 - 3x$
(f) $5x - 1 \leqslant 7x + 9$

15. Solve the inequality and show your results on a number line:
(a) $5 - 2x < x - 19$
(b) $3x + 2 \geqslant 17 - 7x$
(c) $2x - 9 \leqslant 17 + 15x$
(d) $2(5 + 3x) > 52$
(e) $13 \leqslant 5(x - 2)$
(f) $4 > 3(1 - 2x) + 13$

16. Solve the inequality and show your results on a number line:
(a) $\dfrac{10}{x} > 2$
(b) $\dfrac{8}{x} < 16$
(c) $\dfrac{3}{x} \geqslant 12$
(d) $\dfrac{18}{x} < 3$

17. A rectangle is 9 cm long. Its area is greater than 63 cm^2. What can you say about the width of the rectangle?

18. A rectangle has a perimeter of 24 cm and its length is greater than 8 cm. What can you say about its width?

Inequalities and mappings

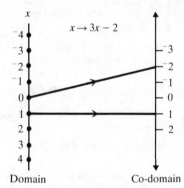

Domain   Co-domain

19. Copy and complete the mapping diagram above, so that an arrow goes from each element of the domain. For what values of x in the domain is:
(a) $3x - 2 = 1$
(b) $3x - 2 > 4$?
(c) $3x - 2 < -2$?

20. Using the same domain as in Question 19, draw a mapping diagram to show $x \to 3 - 2x$.
For what values of x is:
(a) $3 - 2x = 3$
(b) $3 - 2x > 3$
(c) $3 - 2x < 3$?

21. Use your diagrams in Questions 19 and 20 to say for what values of x in the domain:
(a) $3x - 2 > 0$
(b) $3 - 2x < 0$

Here is another way to solve the inequality $3 - 2x < 0$.
(i) Draw a number line, and put a circle above the value of x for which $3 - 2x = 0$ (that is, $x = 1\frac{1}{2}$).
(ii) Now indicate the values of x for which $3 - 2x$ is greater or less than 0.

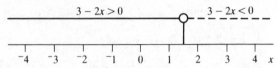

The diagram above shows $3 - 2x > 0$ by a solid line, and $3 - 2x < 0$ by a dotted line.
The ○ shows where $3 - 2x = 0$.

22. Use a number line like the one above to show when the expression is positive (> 0), negative (< 0) or zero ($= 0$).
(a) $x - 3$ (b) $5x - 3$ (c) $2x + 1$
(d) $4 - x$ (e) $4 - 3x$ (f) $1 - 2x$

23. Look again at your diagrams in Question 22. Write down the values of x for which:
(a) $x - 3 > 0$ and $2x + 1 < 0$
(b) $5x - 3 < 0$ and $4 - 3x > 0$
(c) $4 - x > 0$ and $1 - 2x < 0$

Solution sets for inequalities

The solution set for $x + 3 \leqslant 7$ is
   $\{1, 2, 3, 4\}$ if x is a positive whole number,
or $\{x : x \leqslant 4\}$ if x is any real number.

$\{x : 2 \leqslant x < 7\}$ is a shorthand way of writing:
'the set of values of x between 2 and 7, including 2 but excluding 7'.

This set can be represented on the number line as:

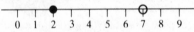

The black circle means *including*; the white circle means *excluding*.

Example 3

If U = {all real numbers from 0 to 10 inclusive},
A = $\{x : 1 < x < 5\}$, and B = $\{x : 3 \leqslant x \leqslant 7\}$
find A ∩ B and A ∪ B.

Using a number line:

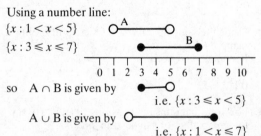

---

24. Assuming that you can use any whole number from 0 to 10 write down the solution set for:
(a) $x < 5$ (b) $x > 3$
(c) $x + 5 < 9$ (d) $x - 3 \geqslant 4$

25. Assuming that you can use any whole number from 0 to 20 find the solution set for:
(a) $x + 8 < 19$ (b) $x - 12 \geqslant 3$
(c) $2x + 5 \leqslant 17$ (d) $3x - 5 > 16$

26. Writing your answer as $\{x : x \quad \}$ find the solution set for:
(a) $x + 9 > 15$ (b) $x - 5 < 17$
(c) $5x + 4 > 39$ (d) $4x - 13 < 19$
(e) $14 - x > 9$

27. Writing your answer as $\{x : x \quad \}$ find the solution set for:
(a) $3x + 7 < 22$ (b) $6x - 5 > 19$
(c) $18 - 3x < 6$ (d) $2(3x + 5) > 52$
(e) $5 - x < 68 - 8x$

28. Using a number line, find the solution set for:
(a) $\{x : 1 < x < 9\} \cap \{x : 5 \leqslant x < 13\}$
(b) $\{x : 5 \leqslant x < 12\} \cup \{x : 2 < x \leqslant 11\}$
(c) $\{x : 4 < x < 17\} \cap \{x : 6 \leqslant x \leqslant 14\}$
(d) $\{x : 2 \leqslant x < 19\} \cup \{x : 7 < x \leqslant 19\}$

29. Describe each of A, B, C and D below as: $\{x : \quad x \quad \}$

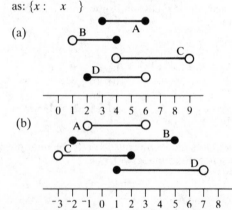

30. Using the information in Question 29, write down for each diagram:
(a) A ∩ B   (b) B ∩ C   (c) C ∩ D
(d) A ∪ B   (e) B ∪ C   (f) C ∪ D
(g) C ∩ D'

31. Writing your answer as $\{x : \quad \}$ find the solution set for:
(a) $\{x : 2x + 3 > 15\} \cap \{x : 4x - 7 < 41\}$
(b) $\{x : 5x - 1 < 19\} \cup \{x : 2x - 9 < 11\}$
(c) $\{x : 2 \leqslant x < 13\} \cap \{x : 4x - 3 > 21\}$
(d) $\{x : 4 < x \leqslant 9\} \cup \{x : 3x + 5 < 23\}$
(e) $\{x : 12 < x < 5\} \cap \{x : 17 - x > 8\}$
(f) $\{x : 6 - x > 1\} \cup \{x : 4 - x \leqslant 1\}$
(g) $\{x : 2x + 1 \leqslant 5x - 8\} \cap \{x : 4x - 1 > 11 - 2x\}$

10.5 Simultaneous equations

Using graphs

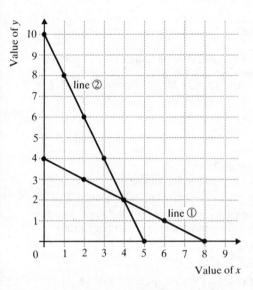

1. Look at the graph above. Write down the co-ordinates of each point:
   (a) on line ①   (b) on line ②
   What are the co-ordinates of the point which lies on both lines?

2. Say which set of points in Question 1 makes this equation a true statement:
   (a) $2x + y = 10$ (b) $x + 2y = 8$

3. Write down the ordered pair which makes both $2x + y = 10$ and $x + 2y = 8$ true statements at the same time.

Each of the equations $2x + y = 10$ and $x + 2y = 8$ can be represented by a set of points (or line) on a graph. The point where the two lines intersect (that is, the common ordered pair) makes both equations true at the same time.
This ordered pair $(4, 2)$ is the **solution** of the simultaneous equations.

4. (a) Write down some of the ordered pairs which make $y = x + 1$ a true statement.
   (b) On a copy of the graph in Question 1 draw the line $y = x + 1$.
   (c) Write down the co-ordinates of the point where $y = x + 1$ intersects (i) line ① (ii) line ②

5. Check your answers for Question 4 by showing that:
   (a) $(2, 3)$ is the solution of $y = x + 1$ *and* $x + 2y = 8$
   (b) $(3, 4)$ is the solution of $y = x + 1$ *and* $2x + y = 10$

6. Copy and complete the table of values:

   (a)

x	0	1	2	3	4
$y = 2x + 1$	1				

   (b)

x	0	1	2	3	4
$y = 3x - 2$	−2				

   (c) Which ordered pair makes both $y = 2x + 1$ *and* $y = 3x - 2$ true at the same time?

7. Check your answer for Question 6 (c) by showing on a graph the lines $y = 2x + 1$ and $y = 3x - 2$, and finding their point of intersection.

8. First complete a table of values like the ones in Question 6 and then show the lines on a graph, to solve the simultaneous equations:
   (a) $y = 3x + 1$ *and* $y = 2x + 3$
   (b) $x + y = 8$ *and* $y = 2x - 1$
   (c) $y = 4x - 5$ *and* $x + 2y = 8$

9. Look again at the equations in Question 7. Do you agree that, at the point of intersection, $3x - 2 = 2x + 1$? Explain why. Then solve this equation to check your answer for Question 7.

10. Look again at the equations in Question 8 (b). Do you agree that at the point of intersection, $x + (2x - 1) = 8$? Explain why, then solve this equation.

11. Solve the equations in Question 8 (a) by equating the two expressions for y.

12. Solve the equations in Question 8 (c) by substituting $4x - 5$ for y in the second equation.

13. Solve the two simultaneous equations by substituting $3x + 2$ for y in the second equation.
    (a) $y = 3x + 2$ *and* $2x + y = 7$
    (b) $y = 3x + 2$ *and* $4x - y = 5$
    (c) $y = 3x + 2$ *and* $y = 5x - 4$
    (d) $y = 3x + 2$ *and* $2x + 3y = 17$

Elimination method

$$\left.\begin{array}{l} 3x + 2y = 16 \\ x + 2y = 12 \end{array}\right\} \text{ are a pair of simultaneous equations}$$

We are trying to find values for x and y which make both equations true at the same time.
We can do this by eliminating either the x-terms or the y-terms.
In this example we can eliminate the y-terms by subtracting the second equation from the first.

$$\begin{array}{l} 3x + 2y = 16 \ldots [1] \\ \underline{x + 2y = 12 \ldots [2]} \\ 2x + 0 = 4 \ldots [1] - [2] \end{array}$$

So $2x = 4$ i.e. $x = 2$
Substituting $x = 2$ into equation [1] gives
      $6 + 2y = 16$
So $2y = 10$ i.e. $y = 5$

$x = 2, y = 5$ are the required values of x and y.
You can check this by substituting into [3] :
      $2 + 10 = 12$

14. Solve the simultaneous equations by adding or subtracting:
   (a) $2x + 3y = 13$ (b) $4x + y = 15$
       $x - 3y = 2$ $2x + y = 11$

15. Solve the simultaneous equations. Check your results by substitution.
   (a) $4x + y = 8$ (b) $7x + 2y = 26$
       $3x + y = 10$ $3x - 2y = 14$
   (c) $5x + 3y = 12$
       $8x + 3y = 9$

Example 1
$$\begin{array}{l} 3x + 2y = 8 \ldots [1] \\ 5x + y = 11 \ldots [2] \end{array}$$

To make the coefficients of y the same in each equation, multiply [2] by 2.

$[2] \times 2$ $10x + 2y = 22 \ldots [3]$

To eliminate the y terms, subtract equation [1] from equation [3].

$[3] - [1]$ $7x + 0 = 14$ i.e. $x = 2$

Substituting $x = 2$ into equation [2] gives
$$10 + y = 11 \qquad \text{i.e. } y = 1$$

---

16. Solve the simultaneous equations by multiplying one equation by an appropriate number.
   (a) $5x + 6y = 37$ (b) $8x + 7y = 6$
       $2x - 3y = 4$ $4x + 3y = 2$

17. Solve the simultaneous equations. Check your results by substitution.
   (a) $x + 5y = 26$ (b) $5x + 7y = 18$
       $x + 2y = 14$ $3y - 5x = 22$
   (c) $4x - 7y = 41$
       $4x - 3y = 29$

18. Solve the simultaneous equations. Check your results by substitution.
   (a) $5x + 3y = 27$ (b) $7x + 4y = 2$
       $2x + y = 10$ $3x - y = 9$
   (c) $6x + 5y = 35$
       $x - 2y = 3$

Example 2
$$\begin{array}{l} 2x + 5y = 16 \ldots [1] \\ 3x - 4y = 1 \ldots [2] \end{array}$$

To make the coefficients of y the same in each equation we have to change both equations.

$\begin{array}{l} [1] \times 4 \quad 8x + 20y = 64 \ldots [3] \\ [2] \times 5 \quad 15x - 20y = 5 \ldots [4] \end{array}$

To eliminate the y terms, add equation [3] to equation [4]

$[3] + [4]$ $23x = 69$ i.e. $x = 3$

Substituting $x = 3$ into equation [1] gives
$$6 + 5y = 16 \text{ or } 5y = 10 \text{ i.e. } y = 2$$

---

19. Solve the simultaneous equations by multiplying each equation by an appropriate number.
   (a) $3x + 2y = 20$ (b) $2x + 7y = 31$
       $7x - 5y = 37$ $3x + 4y = 27$

20. Solve the simultaneous equations. Check your results by substitution.
   (a) $4x + 3y = 23$ (b) $2x + 3y = 28$
       $2x + 5y = 29$ $3x + 2y = 27$
   (c) $7x - 4y = 37$ (d) $2x + 7y = 25$
       $2x + 3y = -6$ $7x + 2y = 20$
   (e) $4a + 3b = 22$ (f) $3p + 3q = 15$
       $5a - 4b = 43$ $2p + 5q = 14$

Substitution method

> *Example 3*
>
> An alternative way of solving simultaneous equations is by the direct substitution of one of the variables.
>
> $$3x + 5y = 21 \ldots [1]$$
> $$2x + y = 7 \ldots [2]$$
>
> We can rewrite equation [2] as $y = 7 - 2x$ and then substitute this value of y into equation [1] giving:
>
> $$3x + 5(7 - 2x) = 21$$
> i.e. $\quad 3x + 35 - 10x = 21,$
> $$\text{or } 14 = 7x, \qquad \text{so } x = 2.$$
> Substituting $x = 2$ gives $y = 7 - 2 \times 2,$ so $y = 3.$

21. Solve the simultaneous equations by substituting one of the variables:
  (a) $3x - 4y = 23$
      $y = 2x + 3$
  (b) $5x - 2y = 1$
      $y = 3x - 2$
  (c) $2x + 3y = 8$
      $x + 4y = 9$

22. Solve the simultaneous equations by substituting one of the variables:
  (a) $7x - 2y = 8$
      $3x + y = 9$
  (b) $4x + 3y = 31$
      $2y = x - 5$
  (c) $5x + 6y = 8$
      $2x + 3y = 5$

23. Check your results for Questions 21 and 22 by using the elimination method instead.

24. Solve the simultaneous equations by whichever method you prefer:
  (a) $8x - 2y = 26$
      $3x + y = 15$
  (b) $7x + 3y = 15$
      $x - 2y = 7$
  (c) $9x - 5y = 47$
      $3x + 2y = 1$
  (d) $5x - 6y = 2$
      $2x + 3y = 17$
  (e) $4x + 5y = 16$
      $6x + 2y = 13$
  (f) $5 + 3x = 2y$
      $3y + 7 = 2x$
  (g) $x + y = 3 = 2x - y$
  (h) $3x - 7 = y = 3 - 2x$

25. Solve the simultaneous equations:
  (a) $4x + 3y = 22$
      $x + 3y = 1$
  (b) $3x + 7y = 32$
      $x - 2y = 7$
  (c) $2x + 5y = 24$
      $5x - 2y = 31$
  (d) $3y = 7x + 1$
      $2y = 5x - 1$

26. Find the ordered pair which makes both equations true at the same time:
  (a) $7x - 3y = 68$
      $2x + 5y = 37$
  (b) $4x + 5y = 27$
      $6x + 7y = 38$

10.6 Word problems

Linear equations

> *Example 1*
>
> The perimeter of a rectangle is 78 cm. One side is 5 cm longer than the other. Find the length of each side.
>
>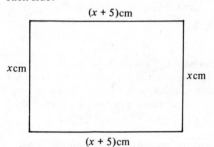
>
> $(x + 5)$cm
>
> $x$cm $x$cm
>
> $(x + 5)$cm
>
> Let the length of one side be x cm. Then the length of the other side is $(x + 5)$ cm.
>
> So $x + x + (x + 5) + (x + 5) = 78.$
> $$\text{i.e. } 4x + 10 = 78;$$
> $$4x = 68;$$
> $$x = 17.$$
>
> The lengths of the sides of the rectangle are 17 cm and 22 cm.

> *Example 2*
>
> Find three consecutive numbers so that their sum is 96.
>
> Let the first number be n, then the second is $(n + 1)$ and the third is $(n + 2)$.
>
> So $n + (n + 1) + (n + 2) = 96.$
> $$\text{i.e. } 3n + 3 = 96;$$
> $$3n = 93;$$
> $$n = 31.$$
>
> The numbers are 31, 32, and 33.

1. The perimeter of a rectangle is 98 cm. One side is 7 cm longer than the other. Form an equation and hence find the length of each side.

2. The perimeter of a rectangle is 72 cm. One side is three times the length of the other. Form an equation and hence find the length of each side.

3. Find the three consecutive numbers so that their sum is 78.

4. Find three consecutive even numbers so that their sum is 108.

5. A rectangular room is 2.3 m longer than it is wide. Its perimeter is 17 m. Form an equation and hence find the length of each wall.

6. A rectangular room is 3.1 m longer than it is wide. It has one doorway, 1.1 m wide and 25.5 m of skirting board are required. By forming an equation, find the length of each wall.
   Does the position of the doorway affect your answer?

7. Two boys have $33 in cash between them. One gives $6 to the other and finds he now has twice as much money as his friend. Form an equation by letting x be the amount one boy had at the start. Hence find how much each has then.

8. Two girls have 72 photos of pop stars between them. One gives 11 to the other and finds she now has half the number her friend has. Form an equation by letting n be the number of photos one girl had at the start. Hence find how many each has now.

Example 3

The same number is added to both the numerator and denominator of the fraction $\frac{13}{24}$. The resulting fraction is $\frac{3}{4}$.

Find the number added.

This problem can be represented by the equation

$$\frac{13 + x}{24 + x} = \frac{3}{4}.$$

The equation can be re-written as
$4(13 + x) = 3(24 + x)$ so $x = 20$.

---

9. The same number is added to both the numerator and denominator of the fraction $\frac{13}{31}$.
   If the resulting fraction is $\frac{5}{8}$, find the number.

10. A number is added to the numerator of the fraction $\frac{3}{8}$ and double this number is added to the denominator. If the resulting fraction is $\frac{7}{15}$, find the number.

11. One week a man buys 20 litres of gas. Each week for the next three weeks he buys the same amount but each week he pays 2 cents more per litre than in the previous week. If his total bill at the end of the four weeks is $18.40, find the price per litre of gas in the last week.

12. A householder can pay for his electricity in one of two ways:
    (i) a fixed charge of $13.65 plus 11 cents per unit, or
    (ii) a fixed charge of $6.75 plus 17 cents per unit.
    Find how many units are used if it makes no difference which method is used. Which method is more advantageous if more than this number of units is used?

13. A man can choose to pay cash for a car in which case he gets a discount of 5%. Alternatively he can pay in instalments over one year, in which case he has to pay an extra 7% for hire purchase charges. If the difference between the two methods is $900, find the quoted price of the car.

14. During a particular month a salesman lunches at three different restaurants. The cost of the set meal in the second is $4.50 more than in the first. In the third the set meal is half what it costs in the second restaurant. If during the month he has 7 set meals in the first restaurant, 3 in the second, and 8 in the third, and the total bill is $150.50, find the cost of a meal in each restaurant.

Simultaneous equations

Example 4

3 oranges and 2 bananas weigh 610 grams.
5 oranges and 4 bananas weigh 1070 grams.
How much do 1 orange and 1 banana weigh?

Let r represent the mass of an orange and b represent the mass of a banana. The information above can be shown as:
$$3r + 2b \quad 610 \ \ldots [1]$$
$$5r + 4b = 1070 \ldots [2]$$
Multiply [1] by 2:
$$6r + 4b = 1220 \ldots [3]$$
Subtract [2] from [3]:
$$r + 0 = 150 \qquad\qquad \text{so } r = 150$$
Substituting in [1]:
$$3 \times 150 + 2b = 610 \qquad \text{so } b = 80$$
So 1 orange and 1 banana weigh 230 grams.

---

15. 7 pencils and 2 rulers weigh 93 grams. 5 pencils and 6 rulers weigh 135 grams. By forming a pair of simultaneous equations find how much:
    (a) a pencil weighs   (b) a ruler weighs

16. A car and a van cost $16 500. Two cars and three vans of the same type cost $40 500.
    Find the cost of:
    (a) one car   (b) one van

17. The perimeter of a rectangle is 58 cm. If the length were doubled and the width trebled the perimeter would be 140 cm. Find:
(a) the length   (b) the width

18. The wages of 5 men and 6 boys amount to $114 per day. The wages of 7 men and 8 boys amount to $157 per day. Find the daily wages of:
(a) a man   (b) a boy

19. The top and bottom marks in a maths test and a physics test were the same.
In the maths test 3 boys got the top mark and 5 boys got the bottom mark. Together their total marks came to 331.
In the physics test 7 boys got the top mark and 4 boys got the bottom mark. Together their total marks came to 665.
Find the top and bottom mark in each test.

20. Three times the first number plus seven times the second number equals 95. Four times the first number minus eleven times the second number equals 25. Find the two numbers.

21. Find two numbers such that their sum is 77 and their difference is 25.

22. If 7 pencils and 5 rubbers cost $1.16, whereas 5 pencils and 3 rubbers cost 76 cents, find the cost of each.

23. If 2 adult's tickets and 5 children's tickets at the circus cost $10.50, whereas 3 adult's tickets and 4 children's tickets cost $11.55, find the cost of each type of ticket.

Example 5

A ferry with a vehicle deck 112.5 m long can carry 17 cars and 6 minibuses end on. Another ferry with a vehicle deck 264 m long can carry 40 cars and 14 minibuses end on. Use this information to find the average car length and average minibus length for the vehicles carried.

If c metres is the average length of a car, and m metres that of a minibus then:

$$17c + 6m = 112.5 \ldots [1]$$
$$40c + 14m = 264 \ldots [2]$$

$[1] \times 14 \qquad 238c + 84m = 1575 \ldots [3]$
$[2] \times 6 \qquad 240c + 84m = 1584 \ldots [4]$
$[4] - [3] \qquad\qquad 2c = 9$

so $c = 4.5$ and hence $m = 6$.
i.e. The average length of a car is 4.5 m and that of a minibus 6 m.

---

24. A man takes 4 hours to cover a two-stage journey. On one occasion he averages 60 km/h and 80 km/h for the two stages whereas on another occasion he averages 45 km/h and 100 km/h. Find the length of each stage.

25. A car park at the airport can hold a maximum of 400 cars, or cars and coaches. A coach occupies a space equivalent to 5 cars. The charges per day are $1.20 for a car and $2.25 for a coach. When the car park was full the takings on a particular day came to $450. Assuming the vehicles stayed all day, find the number of cars and number of coaches in the car park.

26. A women bought 180 stamps. Some of these cost 7 cents and others 9 cents. The total cost of the stamps was $13.78. Find the number of each type bought. How would your answer be altered if for the same amount of money only 178 stamps had been bought?

27. The total area of four sides of a rectangular box of height 3 cm is 72 cm^2. If the length were to be increased by 10% and the breadth decreased by 20%, this area would remain unchanged. Find the length and breadth of the box.

28. A sum of money is made up of an equal number of 10c and 50c pieces. When the number of 50c pieces is increased by 12 and the number of 10c pieces is halved, the sum of money is increased by $4.50. Find the original sum of money.

29. The wages of 12 men and 5 boys come to $446.40 per day. At a similar rate 10 men and 3 boys would earn $348.48 per day.
Assuming each man and boy work an 8 hour day, find the hourly rate each is paid.
If the hourly rate for men was increased by 10% whilst that of the boys was only increased by 5%, find the cost of employing each group above for one day.

30. Find two numbers such that their sum is 15 and their product 56.

Summary

By the end of this chapter, these are the things you should know about.

10.1 Revision (pages 117–121)

How to simplify expressions such as:
$3a - 2a + 5a$ and $(3a) \times (-2a) \times (5a)$

How to evaluate expressions such as $2ab + 5b$ when a and b are known.

How to simplify more complicated expressions by collecting like terms:

$$xy + 2ab - 5xy + 10ab = (2ab + 10ab) + (xy - 5xy)$$
$$= 12ab - 4xy$$

How to remove brackets in expressions:

$$3(x + y) = 3x + 3y$$
$$\text{or } 6a(2b - 5c) = 12ab - 30ac$$

How to factorize expressions:

$$3a + 6b = 3(a + 2b)$$
$$2lm + 4ln + 8lp = 2l(m + 2n + 4p)$$

How to use fractions in algebra:

$$\frac{2a}{3} + \frac{4a}{3} = \frac{6a}{3} = 2a$$

Common Denominator = 2b

$$\frac{a}{b} + \frac{c}{2b} = \frac{2a + c}{2b}$$

10.2 Binary operations (pages 121–122)

How to use operations such as $*$ defined by
$a * b$

$$= 2ab + b$$
When $a = 5, b = 7$
$$5 * 7 = 2.5.7 + 7 = 70 + 7 = 77$$

How to identify whether $*$ is
commutative $a * b = b * a$
or associative $(a * b) * c = a * (b * c)$

10.3 Linear equations (pages 122–124)

How to solve linear equations using the function machine method:

$$3x + 2 = 17$$

$$x \to \boxed{\times 3} \to \boxed{+2} \to 17$$

$$5 \leftarrow \boxed{\div 3} \leftarrow \boxed{-2} \leftarrow 17 \quad \text{so } x = 5$$

How to solve linear equations using the balance idea:

$$3x + 2 = 2x + 7$$
$$(-2x) \qquad x + 2 = 7$$
$$(-2) \qquad \qquad x = 5$$

10.4 Linear inequalities (pages 124–126)

How to solve linear inequalities using the balance idea:

$$3x + 2 > 2x + 7$$
$$(-2x) \qquad x + 2 > 7$$
$$(-2) \qquad \qquad x > 5$$

How to represent the solutions on a number line.

How to represent the solution set for an inequality
i.e. $\{x : x > 5\}$
or $\{x : 1 \leqslant x \leqslant 5\}$

10.5 Simultaneous equations (pages 127–129)

How to solve simultaneous equations using:
 (i) a graph and the intersection of the two lines.
 (ii) the elimination method, multiplying one or both equations by a suitable number and then adding or subtracting.
(iii) the substitution of one of the variables.

10.6 Word problems (pages 129–131)

How to form linear equations to represent word problems.
How to form a pair of simultaneous equations to represent word problems.
Hence how to solve the problems.

11 Graphs 2

Instructions for drawing the graph of:
$y = 2x^2 - 3x - 2$ for $x = {}^-3$ to $x = 3$.

First, draw up a table of values.

x	$^-3$	$^-2$	$^-1$	0	1	2	3
$2x^2$	18	8	2	0	2	8	18
$-3x$	9	6	3	0	$^-3$	$^-6$	$^-9$
-2	-2	-2	-2	-2	-2	-2	-2
y	25	12	3	$^-2$	$^-3$	0	7

Then draw the x, y axes, choose a suitable scale for each axis and plot the points.

Finally draw a smooth curve through the points. Do not use your ruler.

11.1 Quadratic graphs

Equations like $y = 3x + 2$ give linear graphs. They are **linear equations**.

Equations like $y = 3x^2 + 5$ or $y = 2x^2 - 3x - 2$ give non-linear graphs.

Each equation contains the term x^2. They are called **quadratic equations**.

1. (a) What sort of equation is $y = x^2 + 1$?
   (b) Will its graph be linear or non-linear?
   (c) To draw the graph of $y = x^2 + 1$, make a table of values for $x = {}^-3$ to $x = 3$.
   (d) The graph of $y = x^2 + 1$ has been started below. Copy the drawing and complete it.

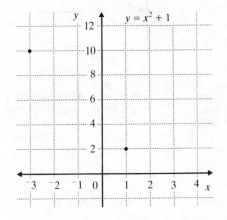

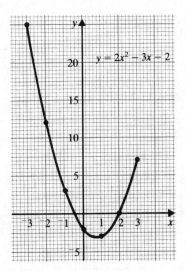

Note It is often easier to work out the positive values of x first. Look at the patterns in the table. Notice also that the values of x^2 are always positive.

2. (a) A different scale has been used for the x and y axes on the graph. Why is this?
   (b) Do the points on your graph lie on a straight line?
   (c) Do they lie on a curve? Join them up smoothly.

3. Draw a graph of $y = x^2 + 3$. Start by making a table of values for x from $^-3$ to 3. Choose the scale for each axis carefully. Can you draw a smooth curve through your points?

4. Draw a graph of $y = x^2 - 4$. First make a table of values for x from $^-3$ to 3. You will notice that your y-axis needs to be marked from $^-4$ to 6.

5. Draw the graph of $y = 6 - x^2$ for values of x from $^-2$ to 4. The table of values is started for you:

x	$^-2$	$^-1$	0	1	2
x^2	4	1	0	1	4
$y = 6 - x^2$	2	5	6		

In what way is the graph different from the others you have drawn?

6. Draw the graph of $y = 10 - x^2$ for values of x from $^-3$ to 3.

7. (a) Copy and complete the table for the relation
$y = x^2 + x - 2$

x	$^-3$	$^-2$	$^-1$	0	1	2	3
x^2	9				1	4	
$+x$	$^-3$		$^-1$			2	
-2	$^-2$	$^-2$		$^-2$			
y	4	0		$^-2$		4	

(b) Using a suitable scale, plot this graph.

8. (a) Complete the table below for $y = x^2 + 5x - 6$

x	$^-2$	$^-1$	0	1	2	3	4
x^2		1			4	9	16
$+5x$		-5					
-6	$^-6$	$^-6$				$^-6$	
y		$^-10$	$^-6$				30

(b) Draw the graph of $y = x^2 + 5x - 6$

9. Draw up tables of values for $x = {}^-3$ to $x = {}^+3$ for these equations.
(a) $y = x^2 - 5x + 6$ (b) $y = 6 + x - x^2$
(c) $y = 2x^2 - x - 3$ (d) $y = 5 - 2x - 3x^2$

10. Use the tables of values in Question 10 to draw graphs of these relations.

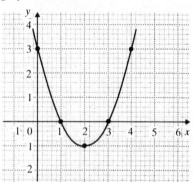

11. Look at the quadratic graph above.
(a) Write down the x co-ordinates of the two points where the curve crosses the x-axis.
(b) Do you agree that $y = 0$ at these points?

12. Complete the table of values below for each of the given equations, and draw their graph.

x	$^-3$	$^-2$	$^-1$	0	1	2	3	4	5	6
y										

(a) $y = x^2 + 2x - 8$ (b) $y = x^2 + x - 6$
(c) $y = x^2 + 3x - 10$ (d) $y = x^2 - 2x - 3$

For each graph find the values of x for which $y = 0$.

11.2 Solving quadratic equations graphically

Equations with the term x^2 in them are called **quadratic equations**. $x^2 = 4$ is a quadratic equation.
Solving it gives $x = \pm \sqrt{4}$, so, $x = 2$ or $x = -2$.

In general, all quadratic equations have two solutions. A simple graphical way to solve

$$x^2 = 4$$

is to plot the graphs of $y = x^2$ and $y = 4$ and find where they meet.

The tables of values are:

x	$^-3$	$^-2$	$^-1$	0	1	2	3
$y = x^2$	9	4	1	0	1	4	9

and

x	$^-3$	$^-2$	$^-1$	0	1	2	3
$y = 4$	4	4	4	4	4	4	4

The graphs are:

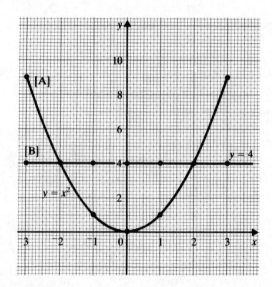

The set of points that lie on the curve [A] are solutions to the equation $y = x^2$. The set of points that lie on the line [B] are solutions to the equation $y = 4$.
So the set of points that lie on both lines are solutions to both equations.

There are two points of intersection:
$(^-2, 4)$ and $(2, 4)$.
Hence the solution to $x^2 = 4$ is $x = {}^-2$ or $x = 2$.

1. (a) Plot graphs of $y = x^2$ and $y = 6$
for $^-3 \leqslant x \leqslant 3$ (that is $x = ^-3$ to $x = 3$).
   (b) Write down the points of intersection of the
two graphs.
   (c) Hence write down the solution to $x^2 = 6$.

2.

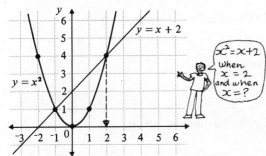

(a) The graphs above meet at two points. Do you
agree that $x^2 = x + 2$ at these points?
   (b) Write down the co-ordinates of the two points,
and hence find the solution of the simultaneous
equations $y = x^2$ and $y = x + 2$.

3. (a) Plot graphs of $y = x^2$ and $y = 3x - 2$
for $^-3 \leqslant x \leqslant 3$.
   (b) Write down the co-ordinates of the points of
intersection of the two graphs.
   (c) Do you agree that $x^2 = 3x - 2$ at these points?
   (d) Hence find the solution of $x^2 = 3x - 2$

4.

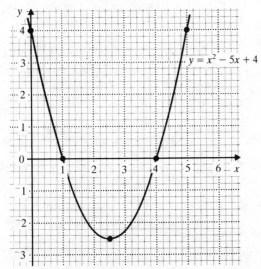

(a) The graph above shows the set of points that
are solutions to the equation $y = x^2 - 5x + 4$.
Where does the line $y = 0$ meet this curve?
   (b) Hence find the solution to $x^2 - 5x + 4 = 0$.

   (c) Where does the line $y = 4$ meet the curve?
Hence find the solution to $x^2 - 5x + 4 = 4$.

5. (a) Draw a table of values for
$y = x^2 - 3x + 2$, for $^-3 \leqslant x \leqslant 3$
   (b) Plot the graph of this relation.
   (c) Use your graph to find the solution to:
      (i) $x^2 - 3x + 2 = 0$
      (ii) $x^2 - 3x + 2 = 2$
      (iii) $x^2 - 3x + 2 = 4$

6. (a) Draw a table of values for $y = x^2 - 2x + 1$ for
$^-2 \leqslant x \leqslant 4$
   (b) Draw the graph and find the values of x for
which:
      (i) $x^2 - 2x + 1 = 4$
      (ii) $x^2 - 2x + 1 = 9$
      (iii) $x^2 - 2x + 1 = 0$

7. (a) Draw the graph of $y = x^2 - 5x + 6$
for $^-2 \leqslant x \leqslant 4$
   (b) Use your graph to find the solution to
$x^2 - 5x + 6 = 0$
   (c) On the same axes plot $y = 2x$
   (d) Hence find the solution to
$$x^2 - 5x + 6 = 2x$$
How do you find the two values of x?

8. Look through the graphs you have drawn in the last
two sections. Describe the shape of those graphs
which have:
   (a) a positive x^2 term
   (b) a negative x^2 term

The graphs of all quadratic relations have the same
basic shape either

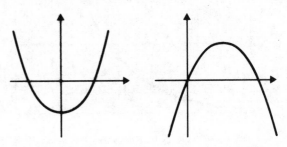

This type of curve is called a parabola.

Quadratic curves or parabolas have important uses in
the modern world. For example car headlights use
parabolic mirrors to throw a straight beam of light.

Television "dishes" are also
parabolic in shape.

9. Find out more about parabolas and their use.

11.3 Non-linear relations

The quadratic relation gives rise to a non-linear graph. Another type of non-linear graph encountered frequently in nature is the exponential curve. Exponential curves show the growth of population with time, the growth of invested money at compound interest rates, etc.

Example 1

A cancer cell divides into two every 5 seconds.

Plot a graph to show this growth over the first 30 seconds.

The table of values is:

Time t (seconds)	0	5	10	15	20	25	30
Number of cancer cells n	1	2	4	8	16	32	64

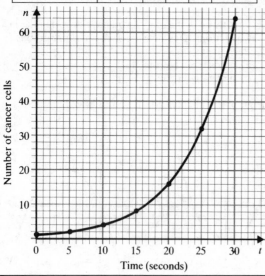

The graph in Example 1 is a typical exponential curve. By inspection it can be seen that n and t are related by the equation.

$$n = 2^{t/5}$$

In general exponential curves have equations of the form

$$y \propto a^x \text{ or } y = ka^x$$

1. Mary Quan is a biologist who studies liver diseases. She measured the growth of diseased cells in a liver sample by counting the number at the end of each minute. The results are shown in the table below, where y is the total number of diseased cells.

t (min)	1	2	3	4	5
y	3	9	27	81	243

Plot a graph of y against t. Let 1 cm on the vertical axis represent 10 cells, and 3 cm on the horizontal axis represent 1 minute. Is $y \propto 3^t$?

2. The population of a colony of insects increases as follows:

Week (w)	1	2	3	4	5	6
No. of insects (n)	4	16	64	256	1024	4096

(a) Plot the graph, using a scale of 2 cm to represent 1 week on the horizontal axis and 1 cm to represent 400 insects on the vertical axis.
(b) Estimate the number of insects after $4\frac{1}{2}$ weeks.
(c) After how many weeks are there 100 insects?
(d) Do you agree that the equation of the curve is $n = 4^w$?

3. (a) Copy and complete the table for $y = 2^x$

x	0	1	2	3	4	5	6
$y = 2^x$	1			8		32	

(b) Use a scale of 2 cm to represent 1 unit on the x axis and 2 cm to represent 10 units of the y axis and plot the graph.
(c) Estimate the value of x for which $y = 40$.
(d) Estimate the value of $2^{2.5}$.

4. The population of an island increases as follows:

Year	1979	1980	1981	1982	1983	1984
Population (thousands)	20	21	22.05	23.15	24.3	25.5

(a) Use 1 cm to represent 1 year on the horizontal axis and 1 cm to represents 500 people on the vertical axis, and plot the graph.
(b) When did the island's population reach 23 000?
(c) Estimate the population in 1985.

5. $100 is invested at 10% compound interest. The total amount after each year is given by the table below.

Year	0	1	2	3	4	5
Amount ($)	100	110	121	133	146	161

(a) Use a scale of 2 cm to represent 1 year on the horizontal axis and 1 cm to represent $10 on the vertical axis and plot the graph.
(b) When does the amount reach $150?
(c) Estimate the amount after 6 years.

6. (a) Find out all you can about Robert Malthus. Ask your social studies or science teachers.

(b) Find out the population of your country in 1900, 1910, 1920 etc.

(c) Plot a graph of population against time for your country.

(d) Is this graph an exponential curve?

(e) Do you think your country will have too many people to feed in the year 2050?

7. (a) A piece of paper is folded in half, then folded in half again and again. Copy and complete the table.

Number of Folds	0	1	2	3	4	5	6
Number of sheets	1	2	4	8			

(b) Plot a graph of this.

(c) If the thickness of 100 sheets of paper is 1 cm, find the thickness of the paper after 9 folds.

(d) How thick do you think the paper will be after 30 folds?
The answer may surprise you!

8. (a) Copy and complete the table.

x	$\frac{1}{4}$	$\frac{1}{2}$	1	2	4	8	16	32
$y = \dfrac{1}{x}$								

(b) Plot the graph of $y = 1/x$ for the above values of x.

(c) Do the points on your graph lie on a smooth curve?

(d) Describe the shape of this curve; in particular, what happens when x gets very large?

11.4 Variation

Revision: ratio

1. Part of a pattern of squares is shown on the right.
(a) What fraction of the squares is shaded?
(b) What fraction of the squares is white?

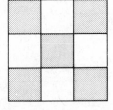

2. Look again at the squares in Question 1. What is the ratio of white squares to shaded squares? Explain what you mean by *ratio*.

3. Write the ratio in its simplest form.
(a) 2 : 18   (b) 3 : 9   (c) 16 : 24
(d) 14 : 30   (e) 3 : 11   (f) 15 : 9

4. 5 miles are equivalent to 8 kilometres. So the ratio *number of miles : number of kilometres* for a given distance is therefore 5 : 8. How many kilometres are equivalent to:
(a) 1 mile   (b) 10 miles
(c) 20 miles   (d) 48 miles?

5. How many miles are equivalent to:
(a) 1 km   (b) 10 km   (c) 56 km
(d) 72 km   (e) 92 km   (f) 193 km?

6. Errol's hens lay brown eggs and white eggs in the ratio 15 : 7. How many of each would you expect in a batch of 286 eggs?

7. Find the value of x if:
(a) $x : 8 = 3 : 2$ (b) $7 : x = 42 : 60$

8. If $p : q = x : y$, complete:
(a) $\dfrac{p}{q} = —$ (b) $\dfrac{p}{x} = —$ (c) $py =$

9. A car travels for one hour at a steady 90 km/h. Make a table showing the total distance travelled after each 10-minute period. Do you agree that the time and distance are always in the ratio 2 : 3?

10. Repeat Question 9 for a car travelling at a steady 72 km/h. In what ratio are the time and distance now?

11. Taking π as 3.14, write down the circumference of a circle of radius:
(a) 2 cm   (b) 5 cm   (c) 10 cm   (d) 20 cm
For each circle write down the ratio length of radius : length of circumference. What do you notice about the ratios?

Varies directly as

In Question 9, the time taken and distance travelled by the car are always in the same ratio, 2 : 3.
As the time increases, the distance increases.
We say **the distance varies directly as the time**.

Using D = distance, T = time, we can write this in symbols as $D \propto T$

The symbol $\propto$ means *varies as*.

12. From the values that are filled in, say whether $D \propto T$ for the car journey described in each table.

(i)
D	12	28	32		48	60		100
T	3	7	8	10		15	21	

(ii)
D	3	15		24	30	33		141
T	2	10	12	16			22	78

(iii)

D	4	25	81	100	256	324		900
T	2	5	9		16		21	30

(iv)

D	6.4	16		32	38.4	48		96
T	2	5	6	10		15	20	

13. (a) For which tables above is it possible to find a constant k, such that $D = kT$?
   (b) Use these values of k to find the missing numbers for these tables.

14. For each table in Question 12 draw a graph of D against T, using each pair of values as the co-ordinates of a point.

15. (a) Do you agree that for tables (i), (ii) and (iv) in Question 12, the points on the graphs lie on straight lines?
   (b) Did you find that the points for table (iii) lie on a smooth curve?
   (c) Do you agree that when $D \propto T$ the points on the graph lie on a straight line?

16. Write down the total surface area of each cube shown on the right.
Does the surface area vary directly as the length of the edge of the cube?

2 cm

1 cm

3 cm

17. (a) Look again at the cubes in Question 16. Complete the table for a set of cubes:

Length of edge (cm)	1	2	3	4	5
Square of length (cm^2)	1	4	9		
Surface area (cm^2)	6	24			

   (b) What is the relationship between the surface area s, and l^2, the square of the length of an edge?
   (c) Is $s \propto l^2$?
   Is $s = 6l^2$?

The constant of variation

If $y \propto x$, then you can find a constant k, so that $y = kx$.

In the same way, if $y \propto x^2$, you can find a constant k, so that $y = kx^2$.

The constant k is called the **constant of variation**. Sometimes it is called the **constant of proportionality**. Other letters of the alphabet may be used for this constant. For example, $y = ax^2$ or $y = cx$.

18. $y \propto x$ so we can write $y = cx$. Find the value of the constant of variation if:
   (a) $y = 15$ when $x = 3$ **(b)** $y = 30$ when $x = 10$
   (c) $y = 3$ when $x = 6$ **(d)** $y = 7$ when $x = 21$

19. $y \propto x^2$ so $y = kx^2$. Find the value of k if:
   (a) $y = 9$ when $x = 3$ **(b)** $y = 100$ when $x = 10$
   (c) $y = 48$ when $x = 4$ **(d)** $y = 16$ when $x = 64$

20. The circumference of a circle varies directly as its diameter. What is the constant of variation?

21. The area of a circle, A, varies directly as the square of its radius r, so $A \propto r^2$.
Complete the statement $A = \square r^2$.
What is the value of this constant of variation?

Direct and inverse variation

If $y \propto x$, we say that y varies directly as x.

If $y \propto x^2$, we say that y varies directly as x^2.

Example 1

If $y \propto x^2$ and $y = 12$ when $x = 2$, find y when $x = 5$.

$$y = kx^2, \text{ so } 12 = k \times 2^2,$$
$$\text{and } k = 3$$

When $x = 5, y = 3 \times 5^2$,
$$\text{so } y = 75$$

If $y \propto \dfrac{1}{x}$, we say that y varies inversely as x.

If $y \propto \dfrac{1}{x^2}$, we say that y varies inversely as x^2.

Example 2

If $y \propto \dfrac{1}{x^2}$ and $y = 4$ when $x = 3$, find y when $x = 2$.

$$y = \frac{k}{x^2}, \text{ so } 4 = \frac{k}{3^2}$$
$$\text{and } k = 4.3^2 = 36$$

When $x = 2, y = \dfrac{36}{2^2}$
$$\text{so } y = 9$$

---

22. If $y \propto x$ and $y = 8$ when $x = 3$, find y when $x = 18$.

23. If $p \propto q$ and $p = 7$ when $q = 5$, find q when $p = 2$.

24. The distance travelled by a car varies directly as the time taken for the journey. Find how far the car travels in $2\frac{1}{2}$ hours if it travels $75\,km$ in $1\frac{1}{2}$ hours.

25. If $y \propto x^2$ and $y = 96$ when $x = 4$, find y when $x = 5$.

26. If $p \propto q^2$ and $p = 45$ when $q = 3$, find q when $p = 80$.

27. The surface area of a cube varies directly as the square of the length of each edge of the cube. Write this statement as an equation and find the constant of variation. Hence write down the surface area for an edge length of $4\,cm$.

28. If $V \propto r^3$ and $V = 6.4$ when $r = 4$, find V when $r = 3$.

29. If $y \propto \sqrt{x}$ and $y = 20$ when $x = 25$, find y when $x = 9$.

30. The time of swing of a pendulum varies directly as the square root of its length. Find the time for a length of $100\,cm$ if the time for a length of $16\,cm$ is 0.8 seconds.

31. If y varies inversely as x and $y = 8$ when $x = 3$ find:
(a) y when $x = 4$ (b) x when $y = 10$.

32. If p varies inversely as q^2 and $p = 15$ when $q = 2$ find:
(a) p when $q = 10$ (b) q when $p = 0.15$.

33. The current in a circuit is inversely proportional to the resistance. Find the current when the resistance is 48 ohms, if the current is 12 amps when the resistance is 20 ohms.

34. If x varies inversely as y, and y varies inversely as z^2, show that x varies directly as z^2.

35. In Question 34, if $x = 5$ when $y = 7$, and $y = 3$ when $z = 2$, find x when $z = 6$.

36. The two ends of a magnet are called its north pole and its south pole.

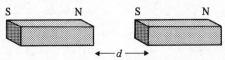

If you put the north pole of one magnet near the south pole of another magnet, they are attracted to each other.
The force of attraction, F, varies inversely as the square of d, their distance apart.
(a) If c is the constant of variation, write down the equation which represents this information.
(b) If $F = 0.2$ when $d = 6$, find the value of c.
(c) Use this value to find F when $d = 1.2$.

11.5 Variation and graphs

1. The volume V of a cylinder of radius r and height h is given by the formula:

$$V = \pi r^2 h$$

Using $\pi = 3.14$ and $h = 10$, complete the table:

r	1	2	3	4	5	6	7	8	9
r^2	1	4	9						
V	31.4	125.6							

Is $V \propto r$?   Is $V \propto r^2$?
What is the constant of variation?

2. Draw a graph to show your results from Question 1, using as co-ordinates:
(a) the values of r and V (the second point is $(2, 125.6)$)
(b) the values of r^2 and V (the second point is $(4, 125.6)$)
In which of your two graphs do the points lie on a straight line?

You should have found in Questions 1 and 2 that V varies as r^2 but does not vary as r.
$V = kr^2$ so the second graph is a straight line.
$V \neq kr$ so the first graph is not a straight line; it is a curve.

3. (a) Using the formula $V = \pi r^2$ write down the values of V when $r = 2\,cm$ and h is $1\,cm$, $2\,cm$, $3\,cm$, $4\,cm$, $5\,cm$, and $6\,cm$.
(b) Draw a graph using the values of h and V as co-ordinates of the points. Do the points lie on a straight line?
(c) Is $V \propto h$? What is the constant of variation?

4. If $V \propto x^3$ and $V = 16$ when $x = 2$ find:
(a) the constant of variation
(b) the value of V when $x = 3$.

5. Complete the table for the cube shown on the right.

x	1	2	3	4	5	6
x^2	1	4				
x^3	1	8				
V	1	8				

x cm

x cm

x cm

6. Draw a graph to show your results from Question 5, using as co-ordinates:
   (a) the values of x and V
   (b) the values of x^2 and V
   (c) the values of x^3 and V
   In which of the three graphs do the points lie in a straight line?
   (d) Copy and complete: $V = \square\, x^{\square}$

The graph of $y = kx^n$ – direct variation

In Questions 4 and 5 you should have found:
$V \propto x^3$, but V does not vary as x or x^2.
So only the graph of V against x^3 is a straight line.

If $y \propto x^n$, where n is any number, we can write $y = kx^n$, where k is a constant.

If $y = kx^n$, the graph of y against x^n will be a straight line.

7. If $y = 32$ when $x = 4$, find the constant of variation for:
   (a) $y \propto x$ (b) $y \propto x^2$ (c) $y \propto x^3$ (d) $y \propto \sqrt{x}$

8. For each part of Question 7, find:
   (a) the value of y when $x = 9$
   (b) the value of x when $y = \frac{1}{2}$.

9. If $y \propto \sqrt{x}$ and $y = 6$ when $x = 9$, find the constant of variation. Use this to find the value of y when $x = 2.25$.

10. The time t of the swing of a pendulum varies directly as the square root of the length l of the pendulum. That is, $t \propto \sqrt{l}$
    (a) If the time of swing is 1 second for a pendulum of length 25 cm, find the constant of variation.
    (b) Find the time of swing of a pendulum of length 289 cm.

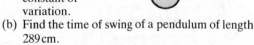

The graph of $y = k\dfrac{1}{x^n}$

– inverse variation

11. The graph below shows the time t taken for a journey, when travelling at different average speeds v.
    (a) Is t proportional to v?
    (b) How long is the journey?

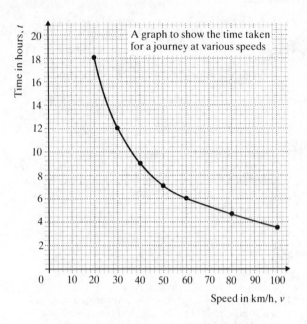

A graph to show the time taken for a journey at various speeds

(vertical axis: Time in hours, t; horizontal axis: Speed in km/h, v)

12. (a) Use the graph above to complete the table.

Speed v (km/h)	20	30	40	50	60	70	80	90	100
Time t (h)	18			7.2					3.6

   (b) For each value of v find the corresponding value of $\dfrac{1}{v}$.

   Make another table showing $\dfrac{1}{v}$ and t.

   (c) Now draw another graph using the values $\dfrac{1}{v}$ and t as the co-ordinates.

13. Do the points on your graph in Question 12 lie in a straight line?
    (a) Does t vary as $\dfrac{1}{v}$? Is $t = k \times \dfrac{1}{v}$?
    (b) Find the value of k.

You should have found in Question 13 that t varies as $\frac{1}{v}$. So $t \propto \frac{1}{v}$.

We say t **varies inversely as** v.

Therefore $t = k \times \frac{1}{v}$ or $t = k \cdot \frac{1}{v}$

(A dot is often used instead of a multiply sign).

14. In an experiment in electricity, the voltage V is kept constant, while the resistance R is changed. The values for R and the current I are listed in the table.

Resistance, R (ohms)	20	40	50	80	100	200
Current, I (amps)	10	5	4	2.5	2	1

(a) Show that these values satisfy Ohm's Law $V = IR$.
(b) For each value of R find the corresponding value of $\frac{1}{R}$. Make a table showing $\frac{1}{R}$ and I.
(c) Now draw a graph using the values of $\frac{1}{R}$ and I as co-ordinates.
     Does I vary inversely as R?
(d) Find the constant of variation.

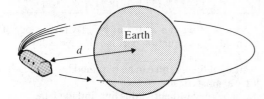

15. When a satellite orbits the earth, it is attracted towards the earth with a force F. This force gets weaker as the satellite gets further from the earth. In fact F varies inversely as the square of the satellite's distance d from the earth.

That is, $F \propto \frac{1}{d^2}$

Explain how you could prove by drawing a graph that F varies inversely as d^2.

16. Using the values $\frac{1}{d^2}$ and F as co-ordinates, draw a graph to show that $F \propto \frac{1}{d^2}$ for:

d	2	3	4	5	6	7	8	9
F	7.5	3.33	1.875	1.2	0.83	0.61	0.47	0.37

17. In Question 16, $F = k \cdot \frac{1}{d^2}$. Use one pair of values from the table to find k, the constant of variation.

If $y \propto \frac{1}{x^n}$ where n is any number, we say that y varies inversely as x^n.

Therefore $y = k \cdot \frac{1}{x^n}$ and a graph of y against $\frac{1}{x^n}$ will be a straight line.

Using graphs and variation

18. A car does a journey in three parts. In each part it travels at a steady speed. The three steady speeds are 60 km/h, 40 km/h and 120 km/h.
    (a) Suppose D = distance and T = time.
        If the speed is steady, $D \propto T$ for each part. Work out the constant of variation for each part.

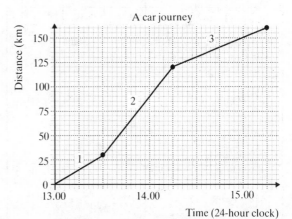

A car journey

(b) The three parts of the journey are shown on the graph above. Which speed has been used for which part?
(c) The horizontal axis shows the time in 24-hour time. So 13.00 is 1 o'clock in the afternoon, for example. How long did each part of the journey take? How long did the whole journey take?
(d) How many kilometres was the whole journey?

The graph of $y = mx + c$

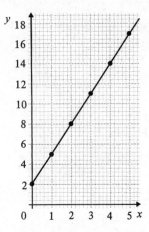

19. Look at the graph above.
    Its equation is of the type $y = mx + c$.
    (a) What information does the c give? Find the
        value of c for this graph.
    (b) Now choose one point. Use its co-ordinates to
        find the value of m.

Example 1

The relationship between s and t is given by
$s = at^2 + b$ where a and b are constants.

Experimental results for s and t are:

t	0.25	0.5	0.75	1.0	1.25
s	3.13	3.53	4.18	5.10	6.28

By plotting s against t^2 as shown, a straight line
can be drawn.

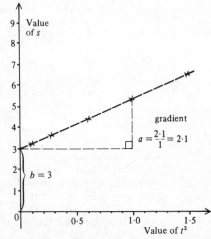

The values of a and b can be found from the
gradient and y-intercept. So $s = 2.1t^2 + 3$.

---

20. S is proportional to T^2. Experimental results are
    recorded as follows:

T	1	2	3	4	5
S	3.17	12.81	28.75	51.16	80.41

Draw a graph of S against T^2 and use the gradient
of this straight line to find the constant of variation.

21. The relationship between x and y is given by
    $y = k\left(\dfrac{1}{x^2}\right) + c$. Experimental results are found
    to be:

x	0.3	0.4	0.5	0.6	0.7	0.8
y	63.2	36.9	24.7	18.0	14.2	11.5

Draw a graph of y against $1/x^2$. Do these points lie
on a straight line? Use this line to find the values of
k and c.

22. Two quantities v and p are believed to be related,
    with v varying directly as a power of p, i.e. $v \propto p^n$.
    Experimental data is collected and shown in the
    table below.

p	1.1	1.3	1.4	1.7	1.9
v	4.61	5.93	6.63	8.87	10.48

p	2.2	2.5	2.8	3.2	4.0
v	13.05	15.81	18.74	22.90	32

Since $v \propto p^n$ we can write $v = kp^n$. By taking logs of
each side, this equation becomes $\log v = n \log p + \log k$.
A straight line graph can be obtained by plotting
$\log v$ against $\log p$.
n will be the gradient of this line and $\log k$ the
y-intercept.
Find $\log p$ and $\log v$ for each pair of results in the
table. By plotting $\log v$ against $\log p$, find the value
of n and also the constant of variation. Hence find v
when $p = 2$.

Summary

By the end of this chapter, you should know about these things:

11.1 Quadratic graphs (pages 133–134)

That a quadratic graph is a curve looking like this:

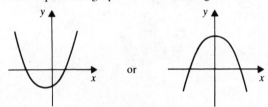

or

The equation always has an x^2 term

e.g. $y = x^2 + 4x - 6$

or $y = 5 - 2x - 6x^2$

To plot a graph like this,
(a) complete a table of values
(b) choose a suitable scale
(c) plot the points
(d) join them with a smooth curve – do not use a ruler.

11.2 Solving quadratic equations graphically (pages 134–135)

You can solve a quadratic equation like $x^2 = x + 2$ by plotting
$y = x^2$
and $y = x + 2$ and finding where they meet.

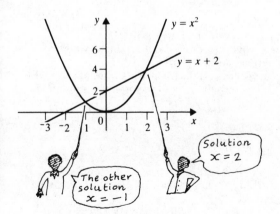

11.3 Non-linear relations (pages 136–137)

The exponential curve typically illustrates population growth or the growth of monetary investments.

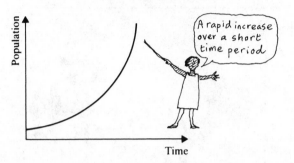

11.4 Variation (pages 137–139)

The statement $D \propto T$ means D *varies directly as T.*
This means D gets larger as T gets larger.
If $D \propto T$ then we can write
$D = kT$ where k is the constant of variation.

If $y \propto x$ or $y \propto x^2$ we say y varies directly as x or x^2
If $y \propto \dfrac{1}{x}$ or $y \propto \dfrac{1}{x^2}$ we say y varies inversely as x or x^2

11.5 Variation and graphs (pages 139–142)

If $y \propto x$, then we can write $y = kx$.
The graph of y against x will be a straight line.
If $y \propto x^2$, then we can write $y = kx^2$.
The graph of y plotted against the values for x^2 will be a straight line.

In general, if $y = kx^n$, the graph of y against x^n will be a straight line.

Suppose y gets smaller as x gets larger.

If $y \propto \dfrac{1}{x}$, then we say y *varies inversely as x.*

If $y = 3^t$ then we say y varies *exponentially* as t, since t is the exponent of the equation.

If $y = 3^t$, then the graph of y against 3^t is a straight line, but the graph of y against t is an exponential curve that rises steeply.
(Graphs of population growth against time, and compound interest against time, are exponential curves.)
Using the graph of $y = mx + c$ to find relationships between quantities.

12 Transformations 1

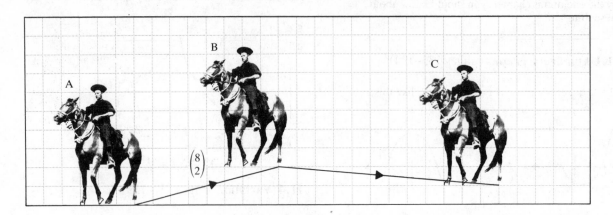

12.1 Translations

A translation maps a shape to another position by a movement that is equivalent to sliding without turning.

In the picture above the horseman is shown in three positions. The horseman at A can be mapped to the **image** at B by a translation that moves 8 spaces to the right and 2 spaces up.

We can write this as a **column vector.**

$A \rightarrow B = \begin{pmatrix} 8 \\ 2 \end{pmatrix}$ and $B \rightarrow A = \begin{pmatrix} {}^-8 \\ {}^-2 \end{pmatrix}$

1. Write as a column vector:
   (a) $B \rightarrow C$ (b) $A \rightarrow C$ (c) $C \rightarrow A$

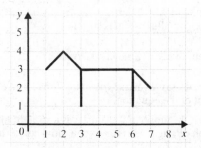

2. The diagram shows a horse.
   (a) Draw a copy of the diagram.
   (b) Draw the image of the horse using the translation $\begin{pmatrix} 2 \\ 3 \end{pmatrix}$
   (c) The end of the tail is the point $(7, 2)$. What is the image of this point after the translation?

3. The diagram shows a triangle ABC.

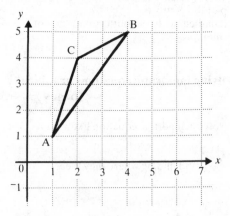

Draw a copy of this diagram.
On your copy draw also the triangles whose vertices are as follows.
In each case, if the triangle is a translation of ABC, write down the column vector of the translation.

   (a) $(4, {}^-1), (7, 3), (5, 2)$ (b) $(2, 1), (4, 2), (5, 5)$
   (c) $(0, 0), (0, 3), (2, 4)$ (d) $(0, 1), (1, 4), (3, 5)$
   (e) $(2, 0), (3, 3), (5, 4)$

4. (a) Are all the triangles in Question 3 congruent to ABC?
   (b) Does a translation always produce a congruent image?
   (c) If two triangles are congruent must one be a translation of the other?

5. The vector $\begin{pmatrix} 4 \\ 3 \end{pmatrix}$ maps the triangle ABC

to its image PQR. Point A maps to P, as shown in the diagram below.

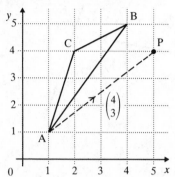

(a) What are the co-ordinates of A?
(b) What are the co-ordinates of P?
(c) Given the vector and the co-ordinates of A, explain how to find the co-ordinates of P without a diagram.

6. (a) For Question 5, complete the statement:

$$\begin{pmatrix} 4 \\ 3 \end{pmatrix}$$

A $\longrightarrow$ P

(1, 1) $\longrightarrow$ (   )

(b) Write a similar statement for the mapping B → Q and C → R.
(c) On squared paper, draw a pair of axes marked from ⁻1 to 10. Now mark in triangles ABC and PQR.
(d) Do you agree that a translation maps all points the same distance and in the same direction?
(e) Do you agree that shape ABC and its image PQR are congruent?

7. Another translation maps the triangle PQR to STU.

The vector for the translation is $\begin{pmatrix} 1 \\ -1 \end{pmatrix}$.

(a) Show STU on your diagram for Question 6.
(b) Write down the co-ordinates of S, T and U.

8. What is the translation vector that maps ABC to STU?

Complete: $\begin{pmatrix} 4 \\ 3 \end{pmatrix} + \begin{pmatrix} 1 \\ -1 \end{pmatrix} = \begin{pmatrix} \\ \end{pmatrix}$.

9. X, Y and Z are three points. The vector

$\begin{pmatrix} 2 \\ 7 \end{pmatrix}$ maps X to Y and $\begin{pmatrix} 1 \\ -6 \end{pmatrix}$ maps Y to Z.

(a) What single vector maps X to Z?
(b) What vector would map Z to X?

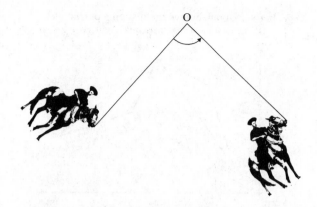

12.2 Rotations

The picture above shows a horseman and its image under a **rotation**.
A rotation has a **centre** and an **angle**. The angle is measured in an anticlockwise direction.
The rotation is 90°, centre O.

1. The diagrams show a triangle ABC and its image following a rotation. In each case write down the angle and centre of rotation.

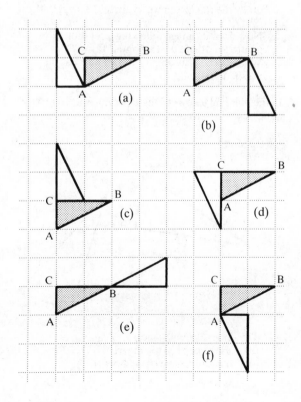

2. In the diagram below, the mapping of triangle ABC to RBQ is a rotation of 90°, with centre B.

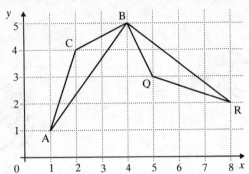

Draw a copy of triangle ABC using squared paper. Now draw its image after a rotation of:
(a) 180°, centre B   (b) 90°, centre C
(c) 90°, centre A
Each time, write down the co-ordinates of the images of A, B and C.

3. Repeat Question 2 for a rotation of:
(a) 90°, centre (5, 4)
(b) 180°, centre (6, 5)
Use tracing paper to help you.

4. Draw the trapezium with vertices (0, 0), (3, 0), (2, 1), (1, 1).
Now draw its image following a rotation, centre (0, 0), of 90°, 180° and 270°.
What can you say about the symmetry of the finished drawing?

In the diagram below, triangle XYZ has been rotated anticlockwise to triangle X'Y'Z'.

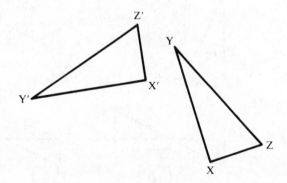

Let the line XY be rotated to X'Y'.
To find the centre of rotation, you need to join two points to their images.

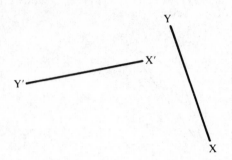

Now find the perpendicular bisectors of XX' and YY'.

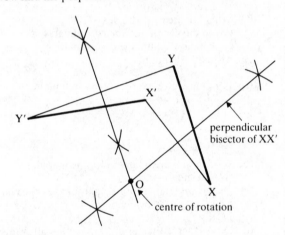

perpendicular bisector of XX'

centre of rotation

The perpendicular bisectors meet at the centre of rotation.
You can check by drawing arcs XX' and YY' using O as a centre.

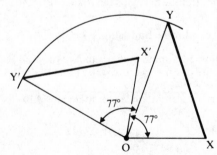

To find the angle of rotation measure the angle XOX' (or YOY').
When shapes are drawn on squared paper, it is often easy to draw the perpendicular bisectors without using compasses.

5. Draw two equal lines XY and X′Y′ anywhere on your page and find the centre and angle of rotation that maps XY → X′Y′.

6. Draw these triangles and find the centre and angle of rotation for each mapping.
  (a) $(5, 0), (5, 2), (4, 2) \rightarrow (2, 3), (0, 3), (0, 2)$
  (b) $(5, 0), (5, 2), (4, 2) \rightarrow (1, 0), (1, ^-2), (2, ^-2)$
  (c) $(0, 1), (2, 2), (1, 2) \rightarrow (3, 2), (4, 0), (4, 2)$
  (d) $(0, 0), (0, 2), (0, 2) \rightarrow (2, 4), (4, 0), (4, 4)$

7. Two squares are $(1, ^-1), (3, ^-1), (3, 1), (1, 1)$ and $(^-1, ^-1), (^-3, ^-1), (^-3, 1), (^-1, 1)$.
Show on a diagram that one square may be mapped to the other by a rotation centre $(0, ^-2)$.
Find two other possible centres of rotation.

Rotations and rotational symmetry

8. The triangle ABC is equilateral. Its centre is G. Trace the triangle and place your tracing over it. Place the point of your pencil at G, and rotate the tracing in an anticlockwise direction.

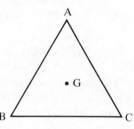

  (a) What angle of rotation about G maps the triangle onto itself?
  (b) How many times does the triangle map onto itself, in one complete turn?
  (c) What is the order of rotational symmetry of the triangle?

9. (a) What rotation about its centre maps the shape onto itself?
  (b) Write down its order of rotational symmetry.

  (i)

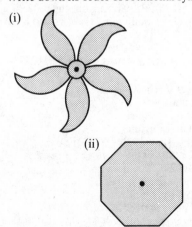

  (ii)

10. What is the order of rotational symmetry of:
  (a) a square (b) a parallelogram
  (c) an isosceles triangle (d) a rhombus?

12.3 Reflections

The image of a boat reflected in the water looks identical but upside down.

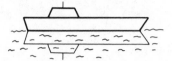

In mathematics, the idea of a real reflection is used.

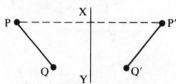

P′Q′ is the **reflection** of PQ in the line XY.
XY is called the **mirror line.**
P and P′ are the same distance from XY so PX = XP′ and PP′ is perpendicular to XY.
P′Q′ is the same length as PQ.

1. On your own paper draw a line and mark two points P, Q anywhere on one side of the line (as in the diagram above.) Use compasses or a set square to draw lines from P and Q perpendicular to the mirror line and so find P′ and Q′ by measurement. Measure the lengths PQ and P′Q′. Should they be the same?

2. Repeat Question 1 for P, Q on opposite sides of a mirror line.
Where do the lines PQ and P′Q′ meet?

3. What is the mirror line for the reflection of a horseman?

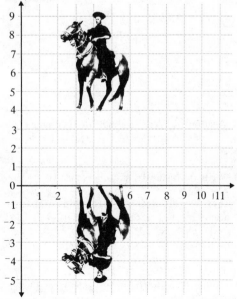

It is often easy to see where a mirror line is when shapes are drawn on squared paper. But you can always find the mirror line by using the properties of reflections.

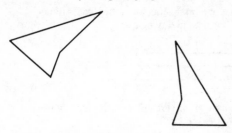

To find the mirror line, join corresponding points and find the centres of these lines.

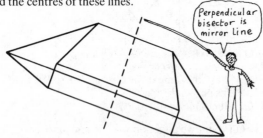

> Perpendicular bisector is mirror Line

4. On squared paper plot these two triangles:
$(1.5, ^-2), (7, ^-1), (0.5, ^-9)$
$(^-1.5, 2), (1, 7), (^-8.5, 3)$
Show that one is a reflection of the other by finding the mirror line.

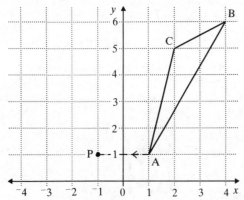

5. A reflection maps triangle ABC to its image PQR.
  (a) The position of A is $(1, 1)$. What is the position of P?
  (b) Complete: $A (1, 1) \rightarrow P(\quad)$.
  (c) Write down similar statements for $B \rightarrow Q$ and $C \rightarrow R$.
  (d) If (x, y) is any point, complete this statement for a reflection in the y-axis: $(x, y) \rightarrow (\quad)$.

6. Copy triangle ABC above and show its image after reflection in the line:
  (a) $x = 3$ (b) $y = 3$ (c) $y = 5 - x$
  Each time, write down the vertices of the image triangle.

7. Under a reflection, are a shape and its image congruent? Write *Yes* or *No*.

8. Copy triangle ABC above. Show its image XYZ, with vertices at $(^-4, 6), (1, 9)$ and $(0, 7)$. Find the equation of the mirror line.

9. A reflection maps the following points:
$(5, 2) \rightarrow (5, 2)$
$(2, 5) \rightarrow (2, ^-1)$
$(0, 0) \rightarrow (0, 4)$
What is the equation of the mirror line of the reflection?

10. Draw a copy of the triangle ABC, from Question 5. Next, draw its image after a reflection in the line $x = 4$.
Now reflect the image in the line $x = 6$.
  (a) What type of transformation maps the original triangle to its final image?
  (b) What vector represents this transformation?
  (c) Explain briefly how two reflections may produce a translation.

11. Now draw triangle ABC (from Question 5) and its image after a reflection in $x = 5$, followed by a reflection in $x = 6$.
  (a) Could ABC map to its final image by a translation?
  (b) What vector represents this translation?
  (c) What is the connection between this vector and the distance between the lines $x = 5$ and $x = 6$?

12. (a) What vector represents the translation that is equivalent to a reflection in $x = 1$ followed by a reflection in $x = 5$?
  (b) Draw a triangle with vertices at $(1, 1), (0, 3)$ and $(1, 5)$. By carrying out the reflections in (a), check that your answer for (a) is correct.

Reflections and lines of symmetry

13. The diagram shows a square and one of its diagonals.
  (a) What is the image of the square after reflection in this diagonal?
  (b) In how many ways can a square be mapped to itself using reflections?
  (c) How many lines of symmetry does a square possess?
  (d) Copy the square, and mark in all its lines of symmetry.

14. (a) What is the image of the isosceles triangle, after reflection in the dashed line?

(b) In how many ways can an isosceles triangle be mapped to itself using reflections?

(c) How many lines of symmetry does an isosceles triangle possess?

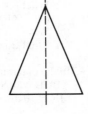

15. Write down the number of lines of symmetry for the shape on the right.

16. Write down the number of lines of symmetry of:
(a) an equilateral triangle   (b) a kite
(c) a regular pentagon   (d) a rhombus

17. Reflections can be used to produce patterns.

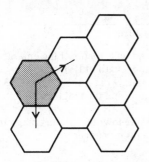

The shaded hexagon can be reflected to the other hexagons.
Show on your own sketch how to get to the other hexagons using reflections.
Can you show how to do the same using:
(a) translations
(b) rotations?

12.4 Enlargements

An enlargement changes *the size and position of* an object. An enlargement has a **centre** and a **scale factor**. The centre of the enlargement above is O.

Measure the height of each photograph.
The larger photograph is an enlargement of the smaller one by a scale factor 3.
The smaller one is also called an enlargement of the larger one (even though it is smaller): the scale factor is $\frac{1}{3}$.

1. In the diagram below, a rectangle has been enlarged by a scale factor 2, using O as centre.

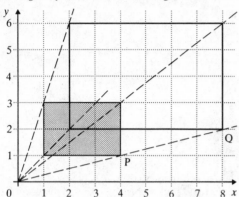

(a) In the enlargement, the image of P is Q. What can you say about the lengths of OP and OQ?
(b) What are the lengths of the sides of the small rectangle? What are the lengths of the sides of the large rectangle?
(c) How does an enlargement scale factor 2 change the lengths of the sides?

2. For Question 1, describe the enlargement that maps the large rectangle to the small one.

3. In this diagram, triangle ABC is mapped to triangle DEF by an enlargement, centre S.
SD = 3SA and SE = 3SB

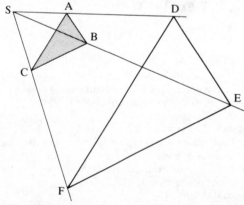

(a) What is the scale factor of the enlargement?
(b) Complete: SF = ...
(c) If AB = 3 units, what is the length of DE?
(d) If DF = 12 units, what is the length of AC?

4. On squared paper, draw the triangles ABC and PQR with:
A (1, 1), B(4, 5), C(2, 4)
P (2, 0), Q(8, 8), R(4, 6)
(a) Is △PQR an enlargement of △ABC?
(b) Draw lines through AP, BQ and CR to find the centre of enlargement.
(c) What is the scale factor of the enlargement?

5. On the same drawing as Question 4 draw the triangle KLM with K(5, 1), L(8, 5), M(6, 4).
(a) What is the centre of the enlargement that maps KLM to PQR?
(b) What transformation maps KLM to ABC?
(c) What transformation maps ABC to KLM?

6. In the diagram, KLMN is an enlargement of ABCD with S as centre.
MN = 10cm, CD = 4cm, and BC = 3cm.

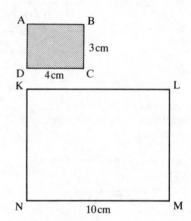

(a) What is the scale factor of the enlargement?
(b) What is the length of LM?
(c) If SA = 3cm, what is the length of SK?
(d) AC = 5cm. Find the length of KM.

7. In the diagram below, PQR is an enlargement of ABC, using a point S as centre.

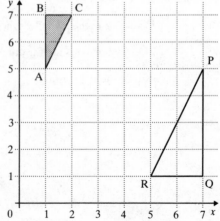

(a) Make your own copy of the diagram.
(b) Join AP, BQ and CR to find the position of S.

8. Look again at the diagram in Question 7. ABC is an enlargement of PQR. What is the ratio of the scale factor?

Negative enlargements

In Question 7, the image of each point appears on the opposite side of the centre of enlargement. We say that the scale factor is negative.
In this diagram, P'Q'R' is the image of PQR under an enlargement centre S, scale factor $^-1\frac{1}{2}$.

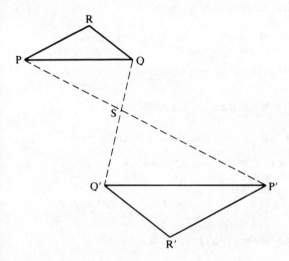

Note that P'Q' is parallel to PQ but in the opposite sense. The *length* SP' $= 1\frac{1}{2} \times$ the *length* SP but because SP' and SP are in opposite directions the scale factor is $^-1\frac{1}{2}$.

9. In the diagram above
(a) if SP = 3 cm, what is the length of SP' and PP'?
(b) if SQ = 2 cm, find SQ' and QQ'.
(c) if PR = 2.8 cm, what is P'R'?

10. On squared paper draw the shape with vertices $(1, 1), (3, 1), (3, 3), (2, 3)$ and its image following the enlargement:
(a) centre O, scale factor $^-2$
(b) centre $(0, 2)$, scale factor $^-2$
Describe the transformation that maps image (a) to image (b).

11. On squared paper draw the shape with vertices $(1, 1), (3, 1), (2, 2), (2, 3), (1, 3)$.
Now draw its image using an enlargement centre O, scale factor $^-1$.
What other transformation describes this mapping?

Scale factors and area

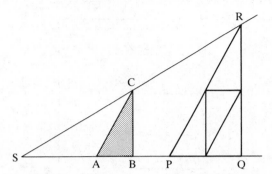

$\triangle$PQR is an enlargement of $\triangle$ABC by a scale factor 2.
$\triangle$PQR contains 4 smaller triangles, each the same size as $\triangle$ABC.
When the scale factor is 2, the area increases by 4.

When the scale factor is k, the area increases by k^2.

12. A square of side 2 cm is enlarged to a square of side 3 cm.
(a) What is the scale factor of the enlargement?
(b) What are the areas of each square?
(c) What is the area scale factor?

13. In the diagram, ABCDE is mapped to KLMNR by an enlargement, scale factor 3.

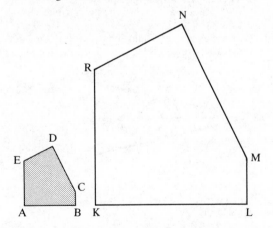

Which of the following statements are true?
(a) KL = 3 AB
(b) DC = 3 NM
(c) Area KLMNR = 3 × area ABCDE
(d) Area KLMNR = 9 × area ABCDE
(e) RL = 9 × EB

14. A square of side 2 cm is enlarged by a scale factor 3 using its centre as the centre of enlargement.

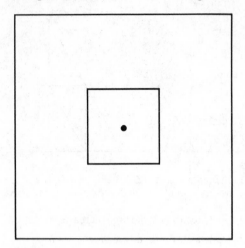

Which of the following are true?
(a) Area of the large square = $3 \times 4 \, \text{cm}^2$
(b) Area of the large square = $9 \times 4 \, \text{cm}^2$
(c) Area of the large square
   = area of small square + $2 \times 4 \, \text{cm}^2$.
(d) Area of the small square
   = $\frac{1}{9} \times$ area of the large square.
(e) Perimeter of the large square
   = $9 \times$ the perimeter of the small square.

15. Two circles centres A and B have radius 2 cm and 3 cm respectively. S is the centre of enlargement.

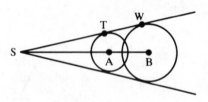

Which of the following are true?
(a) $SB = 1\frac{1}{2} SA$
(b) $SA = AB$
(c) $TW = \frac{1}{2} ST$
(d) circumference of circle centre A
   = $\frac{2}{3} \times$ circumference of circle centre B.
(e) ratio of areas of circles is 2 : 3
(f) ratio of areas of circles is 4 : 9

16. Rectangle XYZW is enlarged by a scale factor 5 to rectangle XPQR.
(a) Draw a sketch of the two rectangles.
(b) What is the centre of enlargement?
(c) If $XY = 4$ cm, what is the length of YP?
(d) If the area of XPQR = $100 \, \text{cm}^2$, what is the area of XYZW?

Summary

By the end of this chapter, these are the things you should know about:

12.1 Translations (pages 144–145)

A **translation** changes position without turning.
You can describe a translation by a column vector.
$\begin{pmatrix} 4 \\ -3 \end{pmatrix}$ means 4 units to *right* and 3 units *down*.

12.2 Rotations (pages 145–147)

A **rotation** is described by a **centre** and an **angle**, measured *anticlockwise*.
How to find the centre of a rotation.
   A shape that maps on to itself more than once has rotational symmetry.
   A square has rotational symmetry of **order 4**.

12.3 Reflections (pages 147–149)

A **reflection** is defined by a **mirror line.** An object and its image are equal distances from the mirror line. The line joining a point to its image is perpendicular to the mirror line.
How to find the mirror line given an object and its image.
A shape that can be reflected on to itself by a reflection is said to have reflective symmetry.
A square possesses 4 lines of symmetry.

12.4 Enlargements (pages 149–152)

An **enlargement** is defined by a **centre** and a **scale factor.**

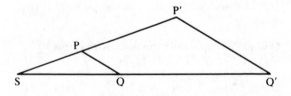

If $P \rightarrow P'$ and $Q \rightarrow Q'$ then
$$\frac{SP'}{SP} = \frac{SQ'}{SQ} = \text{scale of the enlargement.}$$

   A line PQ and its image P'Q' will be parallel.
A **negative scale factor** produces an image on the opposite side of the centre of enlargement.
If the scale factor is k then the **area scale factor** is k^2.

13 Trigonometry 1

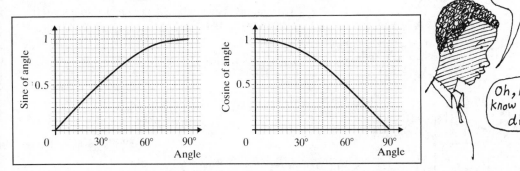

Have you ever seen a sine wave?

Oh, I didn't know they did!

13.1 Sine and cosine

The **sine** of an angle in a right-angled triangle is the ratio of two of the sides.

$$\sin \theta = \frac{2}{10} = 0.2$$

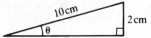

From the graph above you can see that $\sin \theta = 0.2$ if θ is approximately 12°. Tables or a calculator give a more accurate value of 11.54°

The **cosine** of an angle in a right-angled triangle is the ratio of two of the sides.

$$\cos \theta = \frac{17}{20} = 0.85$$

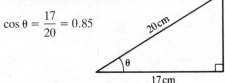

From the graph above, you can see that $\cos \theta = 0.85$ if θ is approximately 30°. Tables or a calculator give a more accurate value of 31.8°.

For one of the acute angles in a right-angled triangle, the sides are **opposite** the angle, **adjacent** (next to) the angle and the **hypotenuse**. You should learn the ratios.

$$\sin \theta = \frac{\text{opposite}}{\text{hypotenuse}}$$

$$\cos \theta = \frac{\text{adjacent}}{\text{hypotenuse}}$$

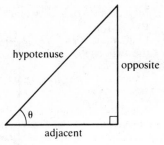

Example 1

Find the angle θ.

You know the hypotenuse and the side opposite θ. Use sine:

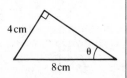

$$\sin \theta = \frac{\text{opposite}}{\text{hypotenuse}} = \tfrac{4}{8} = 0.5$$

From tables or a calculator, $\theta = 30°$.

1. Use 3-figure tables or a calculator to find the size of the unknown angle, given:
   (a) $\sin a = 0.309$ (b) $\sin b = 0.521$
   (c) $\cos c = 0.809$ (d) $\cos d = 0.319$
   (e) $\sin e = 1.0$ (f) $\cos f = 1.0$

2. Use the triangle on the right to write down:
   (a) $\sin 36.9°$
   (b) $\cos 53.1°$
   (c) $\sin 53.1°$
   (d) $\cos 36.9°$

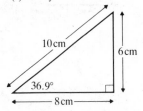

3. Find the size of the marked angle.

   (a)   (b)

   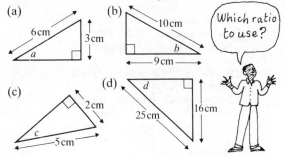

   Which ratio to use?

   (c)   (d)

4. Find the size of the marked angle.

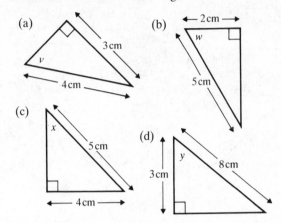

(a)

(b) ← 2cm →

(c)

(d)

5. Find the length of the marked edge.

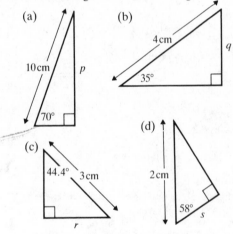

(a)

(b)

(c)

(d)

6. Find the length of the marked edge.

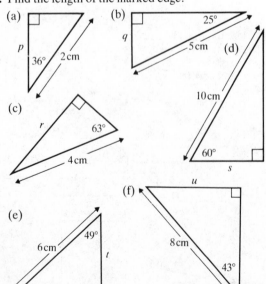

(a)

(b)

(c)

(d)

(e)

(f)

13.2 Tangent

The **tangent** of an angle in a right-angled triangle is the ratio of two of the sides.

$$\tan \theta = \frac{\text{opposite}}{\text{adjacent}}$$

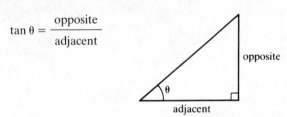

opposite

θ

adjacent

Example 1

Find the unknown angles.

$\tan a = \frac{5}{8} = 0.625$

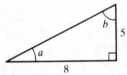

From tables or a calculator, $a = 32°$
So $b = 90° - 32° = 58°$

---

1. Find the unknown angles:

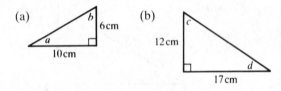

(a)   (b)

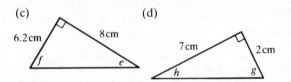

(c)   (d)

2. In a square ABCD, the point M is the mid-point of BC.
Find the size of the angle x.

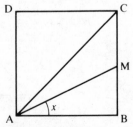

3. A foot of a ladder is 2m from a vertical wall. Find the angle the ladder makes with the horizontal if the height of the top of the ladder is
(a) 5.5m   (b) 7.5m

The word **tangent** is used because it refers to the length of the tangent to a circle of radius 1.

The length AT = tan θ.

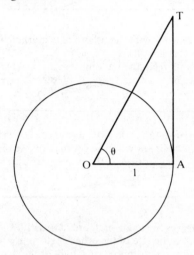

You can see from the diagram that tan 0° = 0 and tan 45° = 1.
You can also see that as θ increases towards 90°, the length AT becomes larger without limit.
Here is a graph of tan θ.

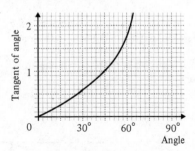

4. Use tables or a calculator to write down the value of the tangent of 10°, 20°, 30°, 40°, 50°, 60° and 65°. Use these values to draw your own graph of tan θ for 0° ≤ θ ≤ 65°.

5. The values of tan θ increase very rapidly after 65°. Find the tangent of:
(a) 70°   (b) 80°   (c) 85°   (d) 87°
(e) 88°   (f) 88.5°   (g) 89°   (h) 89.5°

6. What is the length of the tangent AT in the diagram above if θ = 89.9°?

Example 2

Find the length t.

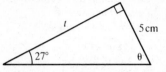

Using tangents, it is easier to use the angle opposite the unknown side.
θ = 90° − 27° = 63°

$$\tan 63° = \frac{\text{opposite}}{\text{adjacent}} = \frac{t}{5}$$

$$\frac{t}{5} = \tan 63° = 1.96$$

$$t = 5 \times 1.96 = 9.8 \text{cm}$$

7. Find the length t:

(a)   (b)

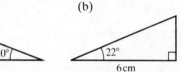

(c)   (d)

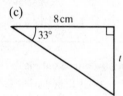
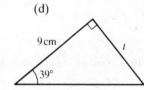

8. Find the length t:

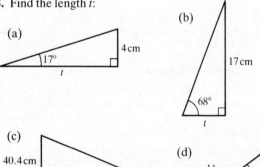

(a)   (b)

(c)   (d)

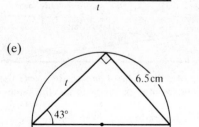
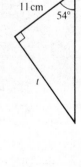

(e)

9. You can find the height of
a tree by measuring a
distance and an angle.

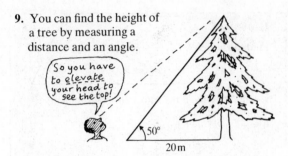

What is the height of the tree?

In Question 9, the angle 50° is called the angle of
elevation of the tree.

Example 3

A tower has an angle of elevation of 70°
measured from a point 15 m from the foot of the
tower.

The diagram looks like this.

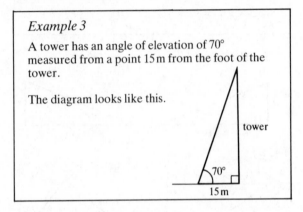

---

10. Calculate the height of the tower in Example 3.

11. The angle of elevation of a tree at 10 m distance
from the foot of the tree is 43°. Find the height of
the tree.

12. A tower is known to be 30 m high. How far is an
observer from the foot of the tower if the angle of
elevation is:
(a) 45°   (b) 30°   (c) 10°?
(Ignore the height of the observer.)

13. A sailor sights the top of a cliff at an angle of
elevation of 8°. He knows that the height of the cliff
is about 100 m above sea level. Find his distance
from the cliff to the nearest 100 m.

A surveyor can use a theodolite to measure the angle of
elevation of a landmark. If the angle he measures is
below the horizontal, it is called the angle of
depression.

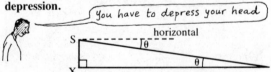

In the diagram, θ is the angle of depression. Note that,
because LX is horizontal, the angle at L is the same
as θ.
So, the angle of depression of L from S is θ,
and the angle of elevation of S from L is θ.

Example 4

The angle of depression of a point on the ground
from the top of a 50 m building is 28°.

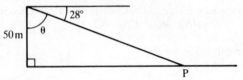

It is best to work with the other angle marked θ.
θ = 90° − 28° = 62°
Distance of P from the building
= 50 × tan 62°
= 94 m

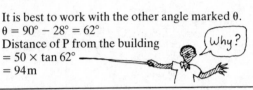

---

14. A surveyor standing at 340 m above sea level sights
the top of a hill known to be 280 m above sea level.

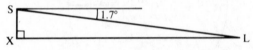

He measures the angle of depression as 1.7°.
(a) What is the size of the other angle at S?
(b) What is the difference in height of the two
hills?
(c) Calculate the horizontal distance XL.

15. For another landmark, the difference in height is
80 m and the angle of depression is 2°. How far
distant is it?

16. From a coastal lookout point A, 80 m above the
sea, a man sights two boats B and C in the same
direction.
The angles of depression of the two boats are 13°
and 24° respectively.
Find the distances of B and C from a point below A
and so find the distance between the boats.

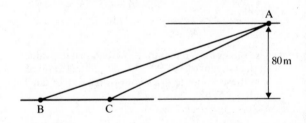

13.3 Bearings

The position of an object relative to another object is called its **bearing**.
The bearing is given as an angle. It is measured *in a clockwise direction from North*.

Example

A tanker travels from Trinidad on a bearing of 147°, for a distance of 100 km. Show this in a diagram and find how far the tanker has travelled east and south.

The distance the tanker has travelled east and south of its starting point can be found from the diagram.
You can see that:
$PQ = 100 \sin 33°$
$TQ = 100 \cos 33°$

---

1. By drawing a diagram like the one above find the distance travelled east and south by a ship sailing on a bearing of:
   (a) 132° for 100 km   (b) 151° for 50 km
   (c) 165° for 20 km

2. By drawing a diagram like the one above, find the distance travelled west and south by a ship sailing on a bearing of:
   (a) 210° for 100 km   (b) 236° for 50 km
   (c) 261° for 20 km

3. By drawing a diagram like the one above, find the distance travelled west and north by a ship sailing on a bearing of:
   (a) 293° for 100 km   (b) 311° for 50 km
   (c) 347° for 22 km

4. A ship sails on a course made up of three stages:
   (i) 10 km on a bearing of 130°
   (ii) 20 km on a bearing of 215°
   (iii) 40 km on a bearing of 330°
   Find for each stage the distance travelled:
   (a) in the east-west direction
   (b) in the north–south direction
   Find also the total distance travelled to the north and west of the ship's starting point.

5. After sailing from port, a ship finishes 10 km east and 20 km south of its starting point. Find the bearing on which the ship sailed.

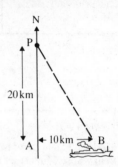

6. Use Pythagoras' result to find how far the ship in Question 5 finished from port.

7. Find the bearing on which a ship sails from port if it finishes:
   (a) 20 km east and 10 km south
   (b) 20 km west and 30 km south
   (c) 10 km west and 40 km north
   (d) 30 km west and 20 km north
   (e) 40 km east and 20 km south

8. Find, by using the appropriate sine or cosine, the distances travelled east-west and north-south by a ship sailing on a bearing of:
   (a) 66° for 10 km   (b) 126° for 20 km
   (c) 256° for 40 km   (d) 296° for 50 km
   (e) 320° for 25 km   (f) 335° for 17 km
   Each time, give the direction of the distance (east or west, north or south).

9. A submarine starts at point A, and makes a journey in three stages:
   (i) 40.00 km on a bearing of 130°, to B
   (ii) from B, 40.00 km on a bearing of 240°, to C
   (iii) from C, 42.64 km on a bearing of 30°, to D
   (a) For each stage, find the distance travelled in the east-west and north-south directions.
   (b) Find how far D is north or south and east or west of A.
   (c) Make a careful sketch of the submarine's journey. Remember, the bearing is always measured from the north.

13.4 Pythagoras' Theorem

In a right-angled triangle, the square of the hypotenuse is equal to the sum of the squares of the other two sides.

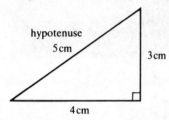

In this triangle,
$$3^2 + 4^2 = 9 + 16 = 25 = 5^2$$

Example 1

Find the height of an isosceles triangle of base 8 cm whose equal sides are of length 10 cm.

In the diagram, triangle AMC is right-angled.

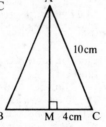

$$AM^2 + MC^2 = AC^2$$
$$AM^2 + 4^2 = 10^2$$
$$AM^2 + 16 = 100$$
$$AM^2 = 84$$

$$AM = 9.1 \text{ cm}$$

---

1. Calculate the length of the hypotenuse of a right-angled triangle whose other two sides are of length:
   (a) 6 cm, 8 cm   (b) 10 cm, 24 cm   (c) 7 cm, 24 cm

2. Calculate the length of the shortest side of a right-angled triangle whose other two sides are of length:
   (a) 60 cm, 61 cm   (b) 4 cm, 4.1 cm
   (c) 2.9 cm, 2.1 cm

3. Find, to three significant figures, the length of the diagonal of a square of side:
   (a) 1 cm   (b) 10 cm   (c) 100 cm

4. Find the length of the diagonal of a rectangle of sides 7 cm and 8 cm.

5. The lengths of the sides of an isosceles triangle are 12 cm, 12 cm and 10 cm. Find the height of the triangle and its area.

6. Find the height of an equilateral triangle of side 10 cm.

Example 2

Find the length of the longest straight rod that will just fit inside a box of dimensions 60 cm × 30 cm × 20 cm.

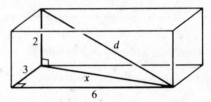

To simplify the working, let the dimensions be 6 × 3 × 2 units.
In the diagram,
$$x^2 = 3^2 + 6^2 = 45$$
$$d^2 = x^2 + 2^2 = 45 + 4 = 49$$
So, $d = 7$ units
The longest rod is of length 70 cm.

---

7. Find the longest rod that can fit inside a box with dimensions:
   (a) 1 cm, 4 cm, 8 cm   (b) 50 cm, 60 cm, 80 cm

8. Is it possible to fit a rod of length 32 cm inside a cube of side 10 cm?

9. Find the length of a diagonal of a cube of side:
   (a) 5 cm   (b) 20 cm   (c) 8 cm

10. A rod of length 7 cm will almost fit inside a cube of side x cm, when x is a whole number. What is x?

11. Two triangles ABC and XYZ have the following dimensions.
    $AB = 12, BC = 5, \hat{B} = 90°$
    $XY = 12, YZ = 13, \hat{X} = 90°$
    (a) For each, calculate the length of the third side.
    (b) Are the triangles congruent?

12. Two sides of a right-angled triangle are 3 cm and 4 cm. What is the length of the third side if it is not the hypotenuse?

13.5 Angles in solids

Example

A pyramid of vertical height 8 cm has a square base of side 5 cm. Find the angle between a sloping face and the base, and the angle between a sloping edge and the base.

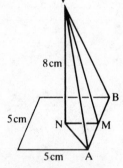

Part of the pyramid is shown in the diagram. M is the mid-point of AB. N is the centre of the square.

It is best to draw the right-angled triangles you want.

The angle made by the face VAB with the base is VM̂N.

$$\tan \theta = \frac{8}{2.5} = 3.2$$
$$\theta = 72.6°$$

The angle made by the edge VA with the base is VÂN.

By Pythagoras, the diagonal of the square is √50 cm
so AN = ½ √50 = 3.54

$$\tan x = \frac{8}{3.54} = 2.26$$
$$x = 66°$$

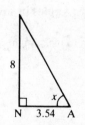

1. A square based pyramid of vertical height 10 cm sits on a square of side 12 cm.
   (a) What is the length of the diagonal of the square?
   (b) Draw triangles like VNM and VNA above.
   (c) Calculate the angles θ and x as in the example.

2. A cube has side 10 cm.
   (a) Use Pythagoras to find the length BC.
   (b) Draw a copy of the right-angled triangle ABC.
   (c) Find angles x and θ.

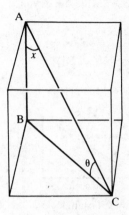

3. A cuboid has dimensions 1 cm × 1½ cm × 2 cm.

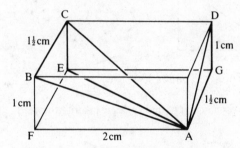

   (a) Draw separately the triangles ABF and ADG.
   (b) Find the angles BÂF and DÂG.
   (c) Use Pythagoras to find the length AE.
   (d) Draw the triangle CAE.
   (e) Calculate the angle CÂE.

4. A flag pole is 10 m high. The angles of elevation of the top of the pole from two points, south and east of the pole are 10° and 20° respectively.

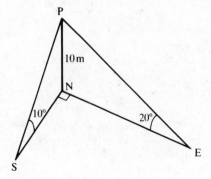

   (a) Calculate SN.
   (b) Calculate EN.
   (c) Hence find the distance ES.

Summary

By the end of this chapter, these are the things you should know about:

13.1 Sine and cosine (pages 153–154)

How to use sine and cosine to find an angle in a right-angled triangle.

$$\sin \theta = \frac{\text{opposite}}{\text{hypotenuse}}$$

$$\cos \theta = \frac{\text{adjacent}}{\text{hypotenuse}}$$

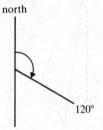

How to find a side of a right-angled triangle.

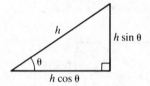

13.2 Tangent (pages 154–156)

How to use tangent to find an angle in a right-angled triangle.

$$\tan \theta = \frac{\text{opposite}}{\text{adjacent}}$$

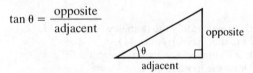

How to find a side of a right-angled triangle.

13.3 Bearings (page 157)

What bearings are and how to use them.
Bearings are always measured clockwise from the north.

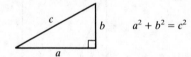

13.4 Pythagoras' theorem (page 158)

In a right-angled triangle

$$a^2 + b^2 = c^2$$

How to use Pythagoras in solids.

13.5 Angles in solids (page 159)

How to pick a right-angled triangle in a solid.

Practice Papers for
Basic CXC examination

Practice Paper A

Multiple choice
Time allowed 90 minutes

1. Which number is nearest in size to 0.18?
   (a) 0.1   (b) 0.2   (c) 1   (d) 2

2. The arrow diagram shows a map which is:

   (a) one-to-one
   (b) one-to-many
   (c) many-to-many
   (d) many-to-one

3. Given $x = 2$ and $y = 4$, then x^3y is:
   (a) 8   (b) 24   (c) 32   (d) 100

4. The scores of ten boys in a test were:
   3, 8, 2, 7, 5, 3, 6, 6, 9, 1
   The median score is:
   (a) 3   (b) 5   (c) $5\frac{1}{2}$ (d) 6

5. The H.C.F. of 15, 10 and 25 is:
   (a) 5   (b) 10   (c) 25   (d) 150

6. The number of corners a cuboid has is:
   (a) 4   (b) 6   (c) 8   (d) 12

7. The value of $0.0045 \div 0.09$ is:
   (a) 0.0005   (b) 0.05   (c) 0.5   (d) 5

8. In the relation $x \to x^2$, 3 is mapped onto:
   (a) 3   (b) 6   (c) 9   (d) 10

9. Simplify $3a - b + a$:
   (a) $4ab$ (b) 3   (c) $4a - b$ (d) $2a - b$

10. The number of prime numbers between 85 and 100 is:
    (a) 1   (b) 2   (c) 3   (d) 4

11. The number of different ways that three books can be placed on a shelf is:
    (a) 1   (b) 2   (c) 3   (d) 6

12. In the triangle ABC, AB = BC and angle BAC = 50°.
    Angle ABC is:
    (a) 50°   (b) 80°   (c) 90°   (d) 100°

13. A piece of string is 19.25 cm long. A piece 3.599 cm is cut from it.
    The remaining length is:
    (a) 15.349 cm   (b) 15.651 cm
    (c) 16.349 cm   (d) 16.651 cm

14. Given $f : x \to 3x - 5$, the value of $f(4)$ is:
    (a) $^-3$ (b) 2   (c) 7   (d) 17

15. Simplify $4(n + 5)$:
    (a) $4n + 5$ (b) $4n + 20$
    (c) $n + 20$ (d) 24

16. Six green beads and two red beads are placed in a bag. One bead is picked at random.
    The probability that the bead chosen is red is:
    (a) $\frac{1}{8}$ (b) $\frac{1}{4}$ (c) $\frac{1}{3}$ (d) $\frac{1}{2}$

17. The L.C.M. of 6, 12 and 18 is:
    (a) 6   (b) 12   (c) 18   (d) 36

18. In the diagram the line CD is
    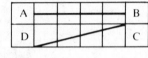
    (a) shorter than AB
    (b) the same length as AB
    (c) longer than AB
    (d) you cannot tell.

19. Which is the smallest number?
    (a) $\frac{2}{3}$ (b) 0.7   (c) 0.623   (d) 66%

20. Given $f : x \to 3x - 1$, the value of x when $f(x) = 8$ is:
    (a) $^-3$ (b) $^-2\frac{2}{3}$ (c) $2\frac{1}{3}$ (d) 3

21. If $3x + 2 = 11$, then x is:
    (a) $2\frac{1}{5}$ (b) 3   (c) $4\frac{1}{3}$ (d) 6

22. The mass in kilograms of seven bunches of bananas was 12, 12, 14, 15, 16, 18 and 19.
    The interquartile range of the masses is:
    (a) 2   (b) 4   (c) 6   (d) 7

23. The value of $40 \div 10\frac{1}{2}$ is:
    (a) $\frac{21}{80}$ (b) $3\frac{17}{21}$ (c) $10\frac{1}{2}$ (d) 420

24. The smallest whole number solution of $5x + 2 > 17$ is:
    (a) 2   (b) 3   (c) 4   (d) 6

25. The number $\sqrt{2}$ is a member of the set of:
    (a) integers   (b) rationals
    (c) irrationals   (d) whole numbers

26. A tin of milk costs $1.25 and is sold for $1.30.
    What is the percentage profit?
    (a) 3.84%   (b) 4%   (c) 38.4%   (d) 40%

27. The area of the triangle is:

    (a) $6\,\text{cm}^2$ (b) $10\,\text{cm}^2$
    (c) $12\,\text{cm}^2$ (d) $60\,\text{cm}^2$

28. The relation *double and subtract five* can be written as:
    (a) $x \to 2(x - 5)$ (b) $x \to 2x - 5$
    (c) $x \to \frac{1}{2}(x + 5)$ (d) $x \to \frac{1}{2}x + 5$

29. In the diagram, O is the
centre of a circle and
the angle ACB = 40°.
The smaller angle
AOB is:
(a) 20°   (b) 40°
(c) 80°   (d) 140°

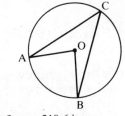

30. Written to three significant figures 219.6 is:
(a) 200   (b) 210   (c) 219   (d) 220

31. If A ⊂ B, then A ∩ B is equal to:
(a) { }   (b) A   (c) B   (d) A'

32. A radio can be bought on hire purchase for a
deposit of $60.00 and nine monthly payments of
$17.50.
What is the total hire purchase price?
(a) $158   (b) $163.50   (c) $217.50
(d) $1575.00

33. If $7x + 3 = 3x + 11$ then x is:
(a) $\frac{4}{5}$ (b) $1\frac{2}{5}$ (c) 2   (d) $3\frac{1}{2}$

34. In the figure, AB is
parallel to CD, then:
(a) $x = y$
(b) $x = 180°$
(c) $x + y = 180°$
(d) $x = y - 180°$

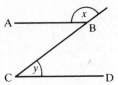

35. The point (4, 2) when reflected in the line $x = 1$
becomes:
(a) $(^-2, 2)$ (b) $(3, 2)$ (c) $(4, 0)$ (d) $(4, 1)$

36. In a pie chart an angle of 60° represents $150. What
does an angle of 150° represent?
(a) $60   (b) $150   (c) $325   (d) $375

37. The area of a circle of radius 5 cm is approximately:
(a) $15\,cm^2$ (b) $25\,cm^2$ (c) $30\,cm^2$ (d) $75\,cm^2$

38. When a watch is sold for $100, a profit of 25% is
made on the cost price. What is the cost price?
(a) $25   (b) $75   (c) $80   (d) $125

39. If $n - 17 = 64$, then $n - 18$ is equal to:
(a) 63   (b) 64   (c) 65   (d) another value

40. Rum punch is sometimes made using 1 part lime
juice to 2 parts sugar to 3 parts rum. If two bottles
of rum are available, how much lime juice is
required?
(a) $\frac{1}{3}$ bottle   (b) $\frac{2}{3}$ bottle   (c) $1\frac{1}{2}$ bottles
(d) 3 bottles

41. The area of the
figure is:
(a) 7 squares
(b) 8 squares
(c) $8\frac{1}{2}$ squares
(d) 9 squares

42. The point (3, 2) is rotated anticlockwise about the
origin through 90°. Its image is:
(a) $(^-2, 3)$ (b) $(2, ^-3)$ (c) $(^-2, ^-3)$ (d) $(3, 2)$

43. In the Venn diagram, A = {tall boys},
B = {fat boys} and U = {boys}.

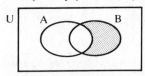

The shaded portion represents:
(a) {fat boys}   (b) {fat, short boys}
(c) {short boys}   (d) {tall, fat boys}

44. The interest on $600 invested for 5 years is $210.
The interest rate is:
(a) 3%   (b) 5%   (c) 7%   (d) 90%

45. Give $e + f = 8$, then $e + f + g$ is equal to:
(a) $8 + g$ (b) 9   (c) 12   (d) $8g$

46. Four blue marbles and three white marbles are
placed in a hat. One marble is taken out at random
and found to be white.
What is the probability that the next marble chosen
is also white?
(a) $\frac{1}{7}$ (b) $\frac{1}{6}$ (c) $\frac{1}{3}$ (d) $\frac{1}{2}$

47. The number 0.042 written in standard form is:
(a) 0.042×10^{-2} (b) 0.42×10^{-1}
(c) 4.2×10^{-2} (d) 4.2×10^{2}

48. In triangle ABC,
AC = 8 cm, BC = 6 cm.
Then AB is:
(a) 7 cm   (b) 10 cm
(c) 14 cm   (d) 24 cm

49. If US $1.00 = EC $2.70, then EC$540 is:
(a) US $50.00   (b) US $145.80
(c) US $200.00   (d) US $ 1458.00

50. D = {doctors} and A = {artists}.
Then the Venn diagram shows that:

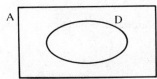

(a) all doctors are artists
(b) some doctors are artists
(c) some artists are doctors
(d) all artists are doctors.

51. The complete solution of $x^2 + 5x + 6 = 0$ is:
(a) $x = ^-3, x = ^-2$ (b) $x = 3, x = 2$
(c) $x = ^-6, x = 1$ (d) $x = 6, x = ^-1$

52. How many different numbers could you write down which lie between 0.41 and 0.42?
(a) 0   (b) 1   (c) 8, 9 or 10
(d) more than you can count.

53.

Tax Allowance	Tax Rate
Single man $1000	First $3000: no tax
Married man $2000	next $5000: 20%
Each child $500	over $8000: 30%

What is the total tax allowance for a married man with three children?
(a) $1500 (b) $2500   (c) $3500   (d) $4500

54. Use the information in Question 53. A single man's income is $10 000. How much tax does he pay?
(a) $1200   (b) $1300   (c) $1800   (d) $2700

55. The formula $s = \frac{1}{2}at^2$ can be written to give t in terms of s and a. So t is:

(a) as (b) $\frac{2s - a}{2}$ (c) $\sqrt{\frac{s}{2a}}$ (d) $\sqrt{\frac{2s}{a}}$

56. Triangle ABC is reflected in the line AC. Which one of these statements is false?

(a) The image of C is C.
(b) DB is perpendicular to AC.
(c) DB bisects the angle ABC.
(d) angle DAC = angle CAB.

57. In a certain country the electricity charges are:
Fixed charge $5
First 100 units: 11c per unit.
More than 100 units: 7c per unit.
How much does 320 units cost?
(a) $26.40   (b) $31.40   (c) $57.60   (d) $62.60

58. To the nearest centimetre, the length and width of a piece of paper are 30 cm and 24 cm respectively. What is the largest possible area of the paper?
(a) 720 cm^2 (b) 744.20 cm^2 (c) 747.25 cm^2
(d) 775 cm^2

59. How many cubes of side 1 cm would fit into a cube of side 2 cm?
(a) 2   (b) 4   (c) 6   (d) 8

60. A successful banana farmer manages to make a profit of 5c on each pound of bananas he sells. Approximately how many pounds must he sell each year if he has been ordered to support each of his six children to the value of $20 per week?
(a) up to 1000 lb
(b) 1000–10 000 lb
(c) 10 000–100 000 lb
(d) more than 100 000 lb.

Practice Paper B

Multiple choice
Time allowed 90 minutes

1. A man buys a car for $15 000 and sells it for $12 000. His percentage loss is:
(a) 20%   (b) 25%   (c) 80%   (d) 125%

2. The value of $640.5 \div 0.021$ is:
(a) 3050   (b) 3500   (c) 30 500 (d) 305 000

3. The Venn diagram shows that:

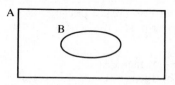

(a) A ⊂ B   (b) A ⊃ B
(c) A ∩ B = φ   (d) A = B

4. The number 384 645 correct to two significant figures is:
(a) 38   (b) 39
(c) 380 000   (d) 390 000

5. The map $x \to x^2 - 1$ which has a domain $\{ ^-2, ^-1, 0, 1, 2 \}$ is a:
(a) one-to-one mapping
(b) many-to-one mapping
(c) one-to-many mapping
(d) many-to-many mapping.

6. The number of prime numbers between 185 and 200 is:
(a) 2   (b) 3   (c) 4   (d) 5

7. In the rhombus ABCD, angle BAD is 50°. The angle BDC is:
(a) 50°   (b) 65°
(c) 90°   (d) 130°
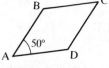

8. The expression $\frac{a}{b} + \frac{b}{c}$ is the same as:

(a) $\frac{ac + b^2}{bc}$ (b) $\frac{a + b}{b + c}$

(c) $\frac{ac + b}{bc}$ (d) $\frac{ab + bc}{bc}$

9. Sales tax of $7\frac{1}{2}$% has to be paid on a radio worth $400. The selling price is:
(a) $30   (b) $370
(c) $430   (d) $453.33

10. The radius of a circle whose circumference is 77 cm is:
(a) $12\frac{1}{4}$ cm   (b) $37\frac{1}{2}$ cm
(c) 49 cm   (d) 484 cm

11. The point $(3, ^-4)$ is mapped to $(4, ^-1)$ under a translation. The image of $(2, ^-1)$ under the same translation is:
(a) $(1, ^-6)$ (b) $(1, 4)$
(c) $(3, ^-6)$ (d) $(3, 2)$

12. In a state lottery prizes of $5000, $2000, $1000, and eight prizes of $50 are awarded. If lottery tickets cost $1 each, how many must be sold if the lottery is to realize a profit of $10 000?
(a) 8400   (b) 10 000
(c) 18 040   (d) 18 400

13. The mean of 7 numbers is 13. What will be the new mean if the number 5 is added to these numbers?
(a) $11\frac{3}{8}$ (b) 12   (c) $13\frac{5}{7}$ (d) 18

14. From the formula $PV = RT$, find the value of V if $P = 3, R = 2$ and $T = 6$.
(a) $\frac{1}{4}$ (b) 4   (c) $8\frac{2}{3}$ (d) 9

15. The H.C.F. of 16, 8 and 12 is:
(a) 4   (b) 8   (c) 16   (d) 48

16. The number of subsets of $\{a, b, c\}$ is:
(a) 6   (b) 7   (c) 8   (d) 9

17. If $f : x \rightarrow 6 - 2x$ then $f(^-2)$ is equal to:
(a) $^-8$ (b) 2   (c) 8   (d) 10

18. The area of triangle ABC is:
(a) $1.098 \, \text{cm}^2$
(b) $10.98 \, \text{cm}^2$
(c) $21.96 \, \text{cm}^2$
(d) $219.6 \, \text{cm}^2$

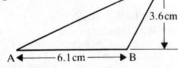

19. The median of the marks 5, 3, 8, 6, 2, 2, 8, 8, 3, 9, is:
(a) 2   (b) $5\frac{2}{5}$ (c) $5\frac{1}{2}$ (d) 8

20. If A = {pigs } and B = {animals with wings} then A ∩ B is:
(a) {pigs with wings}   (b) {flying pigs}
(c) {pigs or winged animals}
(d) {pigs and winged animals}

21. The graph below is described by the equation:

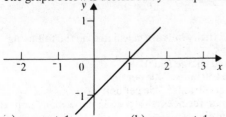

(a) $y = x + 1$ (b) $y = -x + 1$
(c) $y = x - 1$ (d) $y = -x - 1$

22. If EC $5.20 = £1, then £1.30 is the same as:
(a) $0.40   (b) $4.00   (c) $6.76   (d) $67.60

23. The next number in the sequence 1, 4, 13, 40, 121 is:
(a) 202   (b) 310   (c) 360   (d) 364

24. In the sector AOB, the angle AOB = 60° and OA = 21 cm. The arc length AB is:
(a) 21 cm   (b) 22 cm
(c) 44 cm   (d) 231 cm

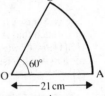

25. The pie chart illustrates how a man earning $200 per week spends his money:

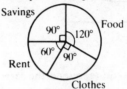

On food the man spends:
(a) $16.67   (b) $33.33   (c) $50   (d) $66.67

26. Use the pie chart in Question 25. The percentage of his weekly wage spent on rent is:
(a) $7\frac{1}{2}$%   (b) $8\frac{1}{3}$%   (c) 15%   (d) $16\frac{2}{3}$%

27. Use the pie chart in Question 25. If the man decides to save $10 more each week, what will be the new angle on the pie chart representing his savings?
(a) $65\frac{5}{8}$°   (b) 70°   (c) 78°   (d) 108°

28. The point $(3, ^-2)$ is reflected in the line $y = 1$. Its image is:
(a) $(3, 4)$ (b) $(3, ^-1)$ (c) $(1, ^-2)$ (d) $(2, ^-2)$

29. If x is an integer and $^-3 < 1 + x \leqslant 1$, the solution set for these inequalities is:
(a) $\{^-3, ^-2, ^-1, 0, 1\}$ (b) $\{^-4, ^-3, ^-2, ^-1, 0\}$
(c) $\{^-3, ^-2, ^-1, 0\}$ (d) $\{^-3, ^-2, ^-1\}$

30. A man invests $500 at 6% simple interest. What is his total saving after 4 years?
(a) $120   (b) $380   (c) $512   (d) $620

31. A man sells a table at a profit of 5%. If he sold the table for $420, what is its cost price?
(a) $399   (b) $400   (c) $440   (d) $441

32. A plane leaves Melville Hall Airport at 1725 hours and arrives in Antigua at 1805 hours. If the average speed of the plane is 330 km/h, the distance travelled by the plane is:
(a) 220 km   (b) $247\frac{1}{2}$ km
(c) 440 km   (d) 495 km

33. If x pounds of dasheen costs p dollars, then y pounds of dasheen cost

(a) $\dfrac{y}{px}$ dollars   (b) $\dfrac{x}{py}$ dollars

(c) $\dfrac{px}{y}$ dollars   (d) $\dfrac{py}{x}$ dollars

34. The two sets A and B intersect and are both subsets of U, such that $A \cup B = U$.
If $n(U) = 40$, $n(A) = 18$ and $n(B) = 25$ then $n(A \cap B)$ is:

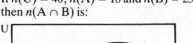

(a) 3   (b) 7
(c) 12   (d) 15

35. Which of the following best represents the curve $y = \dfrac{1}{x}$ for $x > 0$?

(a)   (b)   (c)   (d)

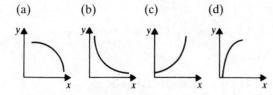

36. The number 0.000 0489 when written in standard form is:
(a) 48.9×10^{-6} (b) 4.89×10^{5}
(c) 4.89×10^{-4} (d) 4.89×10^{-5}

37. If $A = \{$factors of 24$\}$ then $n(A)$ equals:
(a) 4   (b) 6   (c) 7   (d) 8

38. A fraction is a member of the set of:
(a) rational numbers   (b) integers
(c) whole numbers   (d) natural numbers

39. The unit square OABC is mapped to OA'B'C' under the transformation **T**.
T is:

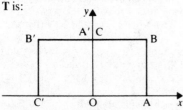

(a) a rotation of 90°
(b) a reflection in the y-axis
(c) a translation of $\begin{pmatrix} -1 \\ 0 \end{pmatrix}$
(d) a rotation of 180°

40. The value of $(x^2 - 2yz)/x$ where $x = 4$, $y = 3$ and $z = 5$ is:
(a) $^-5\frac{1}{2}$ (b) $^-3\frac{1}{2}$ (c) $9\frac{1}{2}$ (d) $11\frac{1}{2}$

41. A sewing machine worth $650 is bought on hire purchase by paying a 10% deposit and making twelve monthly payments.
How much money must be paid each month?
(a) \$48.75   (b) \$51.25
(c) \$54.17   (d) \$59.58

42. Two variables x and y are related as in the tables below:

x	2	4	6	8
y	5	11	17	23

x and y are related by the equation:
(a) $y = 2x + 1$ (b) $\frac{1}{2}y = x + 1$
(c) $y = 3(x - 1)$ (d) $y + 1 = 3x$

43. How many cubes of side 2 cm can fit in a cube of side 8 cm?
(a) 4   (b) 16   (c) 27   (d) 64

44. A bag contains 3 green, 5 white and 1 orange ball. What is the probability that a green ball is selected?
(a) $\frac{1}{9}$ (b) $\frac{1}{3}$ (c) $\frac{1}{2}$ (d) $\frac{2}{3}$

45. If $a * b = 2a + b + 6$, then $^-1 * 2$ is:
(a) 6   (b) 8   (c) 9   (d) 10

46. In the diagram AB is the diameter of the circle. $AC = 8$ cm, $BC = 6$ cm.
What is the radius of the circle?
(a) 4 cm   (b) 5 cm
(c) 7 cm   (d) 10 cm

47. If x is inversely proportional to the square of r and is proportional to m, and k is a constant, then x equals:
(a) $\dfrac{km}{r^2}$ (b) $\dfrac{kr^2}{m}$ (c) $\dfrac{km^2}{r}$ (d) $\dfrac{k}{r^2} + m$

48. Electricity bills are calculated on the following basis.
Fixed charge \$8.00
First 50 units   40c per unit
Over 50 units   35c per unit
A man receives a bill for \$35. How many units did he use?
(a) 20   (b) 68   (c) 70   (d) 100

49. In the Venn diagram the shaded region is represented by.

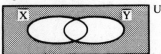

(a) $X \cup Y$ (b) $X' \cap Y'$ (c) $(X \cap Y)'$ (d) $X' \cup Y'$

50. The function f is defined by $f(x) = 3 - 3x$.
The value of x for which $f(x) = 6$ is:
(a) $^-15$ (b) $^-1$ (c) 1   (d) 15

51. A certain number is written as 400 correct to two significant figures.
The smallest possible value of the number is:
(a) 350   (b) 390   (c) 395   (d) 399

52. The L.C.M. of 3, 12 and 9 is:
(a) 3   (b) 18   (c) 36   (d) 54

53. In the diagram
angle BAC = 25° and
angle ACD = 60°.
Angle AOD is:
(a) 35°   (b) 85°
(c) 90°   (d) 95°

54. The formula $A = \pi r(2c + r)$ when written in terms of c is:
(a) $\dfrac{A}{\pi r} - r$ (b) $\dfrac{A - \pi r^2}{2\pi r}$ (c) $\dfrac{\pi r^2 - A}{2\pi r}$
(d) $\dfrac{A - r - \pi r}{2}$

55. What is the cost of 9 eggs if a dozen are sold for $5.60?
(a) $3.50   (b) $4.15   (c) $4.20   (d) $4.90

56. The value of $\dfrac{8237 \times 69 \times 0.096}{0.0047}$ correct to
one significant figure is:
(a) 1 000 000   (b) 9 000 000   (c) 10 000 000
(d) 90 000 000

57. A trapezium has an area of $36\,\text{cm}^2$, with the lengths of the two parallel sides 4 cm and 5 cm.
The perpendicular height is:
(a) 4 cm   (b) 8 cm   (c) 13 cm   (d) 16 cm

58. If $f : x \rightarrow 3 - 2x - x^2$, then $f(^-4)$ is:
(a) $^-21$ (b) $^-5$ (c) 11   (d) 27

59. A man pays tax at the rate of 30% on income over $3500. How much tax does he pay each month if he receives an annual income of $10 700?
(a) $180   (b) $200   (c) $600   (d) $2160

60. If $3x - 9 = 6 - 2(3 - x)$ then x is:
(a) 1   (b) $1\frac{4}{5}$ (c) $4\frac{1}{2}$ (d) 9

Practice Paper 1

Longer questions
Time allowed: $2\frac{1}{2}$ hours

1. (a) Without using tables or a calculator, find the
exact value of: $\dfrac{3.24 \times 0.6}{0.04}$

   (b) A cricketer's batting average after eight
completed innings is 30 runs. If the cricketer's
score in his next innings is 40, what is his new
average?

2. A fence to a rectangular enclosure has a width w,
which is 5 m shorter than its length.
   (a) Write down an expression for the perimeter of
the enclosure.
   (b) If the perimeter is not to exceed 150 m, find the
maximum possible width of the enclosure.

3. Using ruler and compass only, construct a triangle
ABC with angle ABC = 90°, AB = 8 cm and
BC = 6 cm.
   (a) Find by measurement, the length of AC in
centimetres.
   (b) Bisect the angle ACB and measure AX where
X is the point at which this angle bisector
meets AB.

4. (a) The point ($^-2$, 1) is reflected in the line $y = 2$.
Find its image.
   (b) The translation $\begin{pmatrix} 2 \\ 3 \end{pmatrix}$ takes the point (x, y) to the
point $(2, 1)$. Find x and y.
   (c) What is the image of the point $(1, 2)$ after a
rotation about the origin of:
      (i) 90°   (ii) 180°?

5. (a) A man receives $80 simple interest on a sum of
money invested in a bank after 5 years. If the
interest rate is 6% find the sum of money he
originally invested.
   (b) Find the cost price of a washing machine which
is sold for $1500, if the manufacturer makes a
profit of 15%.

6. Two dice are thrown. Find:
   (a) the probability that the sum of the two
up-turned faces is 7
   (b) the probability of throwing a double six.

7. (a) The scale of a map is 1 : 25 000.
      (i) What does a distance of 12 cm represent
on the ground?
      (ii) A rectangular field has a length of 120 m
and a width of 80 m. What is its area on
the map?

   (b) (i) A bunch of bananas weighs 15 kg to the
nearest kilogram. What is its maximum
possible weight?
      (ii) A cube has an edge of 8 cm correct to the
nearest cm. What could be the cube's
smallest possible volume?

8. A certain Caribbean island's budget was as follows:

Ministry	Education and Health	Agriculture	Commerce and Works	Home affairs	Finance
Amounts in millions of EC $	15	25	23	12	5

   (a) What was the total amount budgeted?
   (b) Draw a pie chart to show the amount spent by
each Ministry, working out each angle to the
nearest degree.
   (c) What percentage of the budget is spent on
agriculture?

9. Shade on a graph the region defined by the
inequalities:
$x \geq 0, y \geq 0, x + y \leq 8, x \leq 3$
Write down the co-ordinates of the corners of the
region formed. Hence or otherwise find the largest
value of y in this region.

10. Solve the equations:
   (a) $3x + 2 = x + 10$ (b) $3(x + 2) = x + 10$

Practice Paper 2

Longer questions
Time allowed $2\frac{1}{2}$ hours

1. (a) Work out: $2\frac{3}{4} + 1\frac{3}{7}$
   (b) Calculate to two decimal places:
   $1.82 \times 91.3 - 62$

2. (a) The volume of a sphere is given by the formula $\frac{4}{3}\pi r^3$ where $\pi = \frac{22}{7}$ and r is the radius of the sphere.
   Find the volume of a sphere of radius 7 cm.
   (b) If the operation $*$ is defined by
   $a * b = 2a + 5b - 3$ find:
   (i) $3 * 4$ (ii) $4 * 3$ (iii) $(3 * 4) * 5$.

3. (a) A man wishes to buy a refrigerator priced at $1800 for cash. Instead he makes a Hire Purchase agreement.
   He pays a deposit of $300 and then makes 24 monthly payments of $75.
   How much would he save if he bought the refrigerator directly?
   (b) A consumption tax of 25% is charged on imported cloth. Find the cost of a piece of cloth which retails at $40.
   (c) If £1 = EC$3.75, find:
   (i) the value of EC$1 in pounds
   (ii) the values of £450 in EC dollars.

4. An athletics track is formed by joining two semi-circles of diameter 80 m, to a square of side 80 m.

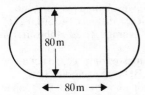

   (a) Find the perimeter of the track.
   (b) If an athlete runs around the track in one minute, find his average speed in km/hr.

5. Construct a rectangle ABCD, with AB = 8 cm and BC = 5 cm.
   Measure the length of the diagonal AC.
   Check your result by *calculating* its length.

6. The figure shows the number of goals scored by a team in football matches over a season.

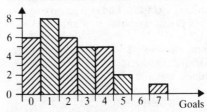

   (a) How many matches did the team play?
   (b) How many goals did the team score over the season?
   (c) What was the probability that the team scored 3 goals in a game?
   (d) What was the probability that the team scored 1 goal or fewer in a game?

7. Solve the equations:
   (a) $3x - 2 = 7 - x$
   (b) $6x + y = 4, 3x - 2y = -3$

8. Copy and complete the table for
   $y = \dfrac{4}{x}$.

x	$^-2$	$^-1$	$^-\frac{1}{2}$	$^-\frac{1}{4}$	$\frac{1}{4}$	$\frac{1}{2}$	1	2
y	$^-2$							

   Using 2 cm to represent one unit on the x-axis and 1 cm to represent one unit on the y-axis, draw the graph of
   $y = \dfrac{4}{x}$ for $^-2 \le x \le 2$

   Using the same axes draw the graph of $y = 2x - 1$
   From your graphs write down the
   values of x for which $\dfrac{4}{x} = 2x - 1$

9. Use tables to calculate $\dfrac{3.61^2 - 3.61}{7.63^3 - 3.61^3}$

10. The angles of an irregular pentagon are $x°, 2x°, 3x°, x° + 40°$ and $x° + 20°$.
   Find the size of each angle and comment.

Practice Paper 3

Longer questions
Time allowed $2\frac{1}{2}$ hours

1. (a) Estimate $2382 \times 0.000\,467$ to one significant figure. Write your answer in standard form.
   (b) If 1 mile = 1.609 km, find correct to two decimal places the number of miles in 3.8 km.

2. (a) Find the cost in EC$ of a shirt which sells for US$15 in America, if it is imported into Dominica and a 35% consumption tax is levied.
   Assume US $1.00 = EC $2.71
   (b) Tax free allowances and rates of income tax are shown below.

Allowances ($)		Rate of Taxation	
Single person	1000	First $1000	20%
Children under 12	500	Next $2000	30%
Married man	2000	Remainder	40%
Children 12–16	800		

   A married man with two children aged 5 and 13 earns $10 000 a year. Find:
   (i) his taxable income if National Insurance of 5% of his salary must be paid before taxes are deducted,
   (ii) the total tax paid for the whole year.

3. (a) Two magazines and three maths text books cost $17. Find the cost of one magazine, if also four text books and three magazines cost $24.
   (b) If x is an integer, find the solution set for the inequality $3 < 3x - 5 < 8$.

4. A metal girder of length 8 m has a cross section as shown below.

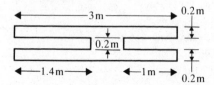

   (a) Find the area of cross section of the girder.
   (b) Find the volume of the girder.

5. The marks of twenty children in a test were:
   4 3 6 6 8 2 0 5 9 1
   1 3 7 3 5 4 9 5 6 6
   (a) Find the mean, mode and median marks.
   (b) Write down the range and interquartile range.
   (c) What is the probability that a child picked at random scores 8 or more?

6. The diagram shows the plan of a house drawn to a scale of 1 : 500.

   (a) How many doors and windows are shown?
   (b) What are the dimensions of the bedroom?
   (c) What is the area of the house?

7. The number of micro-organisms in a laboratory tank at any time are given by the table below.

Number	5	10	20	40	80	160
Time (hours)	0	1	2	3	4	5

   (a) Using a suitable scale draw a graph for the above relation.
   (b) How many organisms are there in the tank after $2\frac{1}{2}$ hours?
   (c) Write down a mathematical relation or rule for this mapping.

8. (a) A shopkeeper buys 250 tins of milk for $300. He sells them for $1.50 each. Calculate his percentage profit.
   (b) A small aircraft leaves Antigua at 0650 and arrives in Dominica, a distance of 180 km, at 0735. What is the average speed of the aircraft?

9. Using a ruler and compasses only, construct an equilateral triangle ABC with each side 8 cm. Construct the perpendicular from A to BC to meet BC at X. Measure AX.

10. In the figure below, AB = 12 cm, DC = 5 cm and $B\hat{A}C = 30°$. Angle BDA is a right angle.

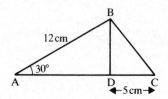

    Calculate:
    (a) the length BD,   (b) the angle BCA.

Practice Paper 4

Longer questions
Time allowed 2½ hours

1. (a) A boy shares $15 between himself and two friends in the ratio 5 : 3 : 1. How much does each friend get?
   (b) A man buys a house for $25 000 and sells it for $29 000. Calculate his percentage profit. Give your answer correct to two significant figures.

2. (a) Three times a certain number when subtracted from fifteen and then divided by two is equal to four. Find the number.
   (b) If the surface area of a sphere is given by the formula $S = 4\pi r^2$, find the radius of a spherical balloon whose surface area is 176cm². Take $\pi = \frac{22}{7}$.

3. Telephone bills are worked out as follows:

Rental of telephone	$15
First 40 calls	15¢ per call
Remaining calls	10 ¢ per call

   (a) A consumer makes 80 calls. Calculate the bill.
   (b) A consumer's bill was $28.10. How many calls did he make?
   (c) If a 5% discount is given for bills of over $25, find the sum the consumer in (b) actually paid.

4. The figure shows part of a stairway. The height and length of each stair is 35cm.

   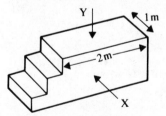

   (a) Using a scale of 4cm to 1m draw the plan and side elevation of the stairway in the direction of the arrows X and Y.
   (b) If the stairway is solid, find the volume of wood needed to make it.

5. The mass of 30 rats kept in a laboratory is shown in the table below.

Mass (g)	300–349	350–399	400–449	450–499	500–549
No. of rats	2	7	12	6	3

   (a) Draw a frequency polygon to show this data.
   (b) What is the probability that a rat chosen at random weighs more than 450g?

6. (a) A man wishes to invest $2000 for a period of 3 years. How much will each of the following investments give him?
      (i) a bank which gives 5% compound interest,
      (ii) a trust which pays 6% simple interest,
   (b) An American tourist changes US $100 into Jamaican dollars at US $1 = JA $3.45. He spends JA $70 before changing the remainder back into US currency. How much US currency does he receive?

7. In the figure AB is the arc of a circle of radius 20cm. Angle AOB = 30°.

   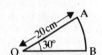

   (a) Find the length of the arc AB ($\pi = 3.14$).
   (b) The edge OA is stuck to the edge OB so that a cone is formed. Find the radius of the circle forming the base of the cone.

8. 6 pens and 3 pencils cost $8.40, while $6.80 can buy 4 pens and 5 pencils.
   (a) Write $x for the cost of a pen and $y for the cost of pencil, and form two equations.
   (b) Solve your equations to find the cost of a pen and a pencil.

9. The table below shows the printing cost per book, C dollars, of producing n copies of a book.

Number of copies, (n)	20	40	60	80	100
Cost per copy, C($)	14.00	9.00	7.33	5.50	5.00
Number of copies, (n)	120	140	160	180	200
Cost per copy, C($)	4.60	4.43	4.23	4.11	4.00

   (a) Using a scale of 1cm to represent 20 units on the n-axis and 1cm to 1 unit on the C-axis draw a graph of C against n.
   (b) From your graph determine the cost per book of making 105 copies.

10. (a) A map is made using the scale 1 : 50 000. Find the actual area of a field whose map area is 4cm².
    (b) An athlete runs 100m in 10.4 seconds, correct to the nearest tenth of a second. Find his average speed in km/hr. What is his greatest possible average speed in km/hr?

Practice Paper 5

Longer questions
Time allowed $2\frac{1}{2}$ hours

1. (a) Work out $\dfrac{1\frac{3}{4} + 2\frac{2}{3}}{3\frac{5}{8}}$

   (b) Work out correct to 2 decimal places:

   $$\frac{68.10 - 49.02}{0.04}$$

2. (a) If an account is paid before the end of the month, a discount of $2\frac{1}{2}\%$ is allowed. Find what amount should be paid to settle a bill of $38 before the end of the month.
   (b) A consumer uses 150 units of electricity at 35.2 cents per unit with a standing charge of $4.80. Calculate the electricity bill.

3. Construct, using a ruler and compasses only, a parallelogram ABCD with AB = 8 cm, BC = 6 cm and angle ABC = 45°.
   Measure the length of AD and AC.

4. A man earning $11 000 a year has tax free allowances of $900 for himself, $800 for his wife and $400 for his son. The remainder of his income is taxable. The rate of tax is 33% on the first $6000 of taxable income and 75% on the rest. Calculate:
   (a) his taxable income
   (b) the tax due for the year
   (c) his net annual income.

5. The length and breadth of a rectangle are measured to the nearest tenth of a metre as 6.4 m and 3.1 m.
   (a) Find the largest possible value for:
      (i) the perimeter of the rectangle
      (ii) the area of the rectangle.
   (b) On the plan of a house 1 cm represents 10 m. Find the area of a room which is represented on the plan by an area of 80 cm².

6. The masses of 30 men, correct to the nearest kilogram are as follows:
   61 64 67 52 59 64 74 68 51 76 70 66 55
   56 72 55 66 88 69 74 62 71 64 71 84 54
   68 59 70 63
   (a) Draw a tally chart and a frequency table for the groups 50–54, 55–59, etc.
   (b) Draw a histogram for this data and state the modal class.
   (c) Estimate the mean mass of the men.

7. The rectangle A(2, 4), B(2, 6), C(4, 6) and D(4, 4) is rotated through 90° clockwise about the origin.
   (a) Write down the co-ordinates of its image A'B'C'D'.
   (b) If A'B'C'D' is reflected in the y-axis, write down the co-ordinates of its image A"B"C"D".

8. Complete the table for the relation $y = 3^x + 1$

x	0	1	2	3	4	5
y			10		82	

   Using a scale of 2 cm for 1 unit on the x-axis and 1 cm for 20 units on the y-axis, plot the graph of this relation.
   For the same values of x plot the graph of $y = 20x$ and hence estimate solutions to the equation $3^x + 1 = 20x$.

9. A rectangular field is 70 m long and 30 m wide. A path joining two diagonally-opposite corners runs across the field.
   (a) Find the length of the path. Give your answer correct to two significant figures.
   (b) A man standing at one end of the path sees a tree with an angle of elevation of 12° at the far end. Calculate the height of the tree. Give your answer correct to two significant figures.

10. Solve the equations:
   (a) $2x + 19 = 3x - 7$
   (b) $4(x - 7) = 6(x + 3)$
   (c) $x + 2y = 11; 3x + 4y = 25$

Practice Paper 6

Longer questions
Time allowed $2\frac{1}{2}$ hours

1. On graph paper, where O is the origin and X is the point (2, 3) show by careful drawing the sets
   A = {P : OP ≤ 5 cm}, B = {Q : XQ < 2 cm}.
   (a) Indicate clearly the region A ∪ B.
   (b) List three members of the set A ∩ B.

2. (a) Draw an arrow graph for the mapping
   $x \rightarrow 2 - x^2$ using {⁻3, ⁻2, ⁻1, 0, 2, 3} as
   the domain. Is this mapping a function?
   (b) Give an example of a one-to-one mapping and a one-to-many mapping.
   (c) If $f : x \rightarrow 3x + 2$ find the value of x for which $f(x) = 14$.

3. In the figure BE is parallel to CD, AB = 6 cm, BC = 4 cm and BE = 5 cm.

   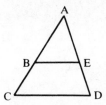

   (a) Calculate the length of CD.
   (b) Find the ratio AE : ED.
   (c) Find the ratio
   area of triangle ABE : area of triangle ACD.

4. (a) Death duties of 15% are paid on a legacy of
   $9500. The eldest son takes 45%, the second
   son takes 35% and the third son the remainder.
   What percentage of the original legacy does the
   third son receive after payment of the death
   duties on his share?
   (b) Find the total annual insurance premium
   payable on a house valued at $30 000 with
   contents valued at $5000 when the premium for
   the building is 0.15% and the premium for the
   contents is 1.25%.

5. Construct a rhombus ABCD with side 7 cm and
   angle ABC = 76°. Draw the reflection of ABCD in
   the line BC and measure the length of AC.

6. (a) Calculate the average speed in km/h for the
   journey of 3300 m in 2 min 56 sec.
   (b) 60 kg of sugar is divided up among three people
   in the ratio 2 : 3 : 4. How much does the person
   receiving the greatest amount receive?
   (c) Calculate to three decimal places:
   $(0.242 \times 16.1) \div 0.4$.

7. (a) The expenditure of a company during the year
   was divided as follows:
   wages and salaries 55%, power 5%,
   materials 10%, plant maintenance 15%,
   profit $7\frac{1}{2}$% and miscellaneous expenditure $7\frac{1}{2}$%.
   Show this data on a pie chart indicating the
   angle for each sector.
   (b) A box contains 3 red, 2 white and 4 black
   beads. A bead is drawn from the box at
   random.
   What is the probability that the bead is:
   (i) red   (ii) not red
   (iii) either red or black?

8. (a) Six boxes of matches and four bars of soap cost
   $6.50, while three bars of soap and two boxes
   of matches cost $4.25. Find the cost of one bar
   of soap. What is the cost of a box of matches?
   (b) Solve the inequality $3 + 6x < 4x - 4$.

9. Using a suitable scale and axes, plot the graph of
   $y = 3x^2 - 2x - 4$ for $⁻3 \leqslant x \leqslant 3$.
   From your graph estimate the solutions
   of $3x^2 - 2x - 4 = 0$.

10. Find the area of each shape giving your answers
    correct to two significant figures.
    (a)   (b)

    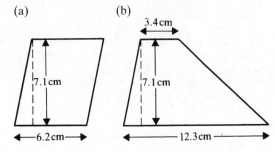

PART 2
General CXC syllabus (compulsory)

❙ Sets 2

1.1 More about sets

Example

In a class of 22 students, 10 studied Maths only, 4 studied Spanish only, whilst 8 studied both subjects.
This information can be shown on a Venn diagram.

Students in class (22)

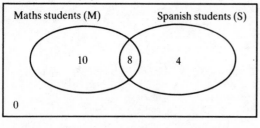

---

1. Look at the diagram in the example above.
   (a) Do you agree that, of the 22 students:
     (i) $n(M) = 18$ (ii) $n(S) = 12$
     (iii) $n(M \cap S) = 8$ (iv) $n(M \cup S) = 22$
     (v) all 22 students studied at least one of the two subjects.
   (b) Do you agree that:
     $n(M \cup S) = n(M) + n(S) - n(M \cap S)$?

2. Show the following information on a Venn diagram.
   100 people were interviewed
   50 said they preferred tea
   25 said they preferred coffee
   10 said they liked both
   15 said they liked neither

3. (a) In Question 2 how many of the 100 people liked:
     (i) tea (T)   (ii) coffee (C)
     (iii) tea *and* coffee (T ∩ C)
     (iv) *either* tea *or* coffee (T ∪ C)?
   (b) Do you agree that:
     $n(T \cup C) = n(T) + n(C) - n(T \cap C)$?

The results in Questions 1 and 3 are important. They say that the number of elements in the union of two sets can be found by adding the number of elements in each set and then subtracting the number of elements in the intersection of the two sets.

$$n(A \cup B) = n(A) + n(B) - n(A \cap B)$$

4. Use the above result to find:
   (a) $n(A \cup B)$ when:
     $n(A) = 10, n(B) = 12$ and $n(A \cap B) = 6$
   (b) $n(P \cap Q)$ when:
     $n(P \cup Q) = 20, n(P) = 10$ and $n(Q) = 15$

5. Show the information in each part of Question 4 on a Venn diagram.

6. All pupils in a class of 35 have to take French or History. If 17 take French and 24 take History, how many take both?

7. (a) Make six copies of the diagram below.

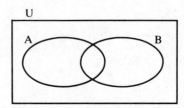

   (b) On your copies of the diagram above shade in:
     (i) the complement of A, i.e. A′

(ii) the complement of B, i.e. B'
(iii) the complement of A ∩ B, i.e. (A ∩ B)'
(iv) the complement of A ∪ B, i.e. (A ∪ B)'
(v) the intersection of A' and B', i.e. A' ∩ B'
(vi) the union of A' and B', i.e. A' ∪ B'
(c) Do you agree that:
(i) (A ∩ B)' = A' ∪ B'
(ii) (A ∪ B)' = A' ∩ B'

8. U = {whole numbers from 1 to 10}
M = {multiples of 3}
S = {square numbers}
(a) Write down the elements in:
(i) M   (ii) S   (iii) M ∩ S
(iv) M'   (v) S'   (vi) M ∪ S
(b) Use your results from:
(i) M' ∩ S' and (M ∪ S)'
(ii) M' ∪ S' and (M ∩ S)'
(c) Do you agree that your results for each part of (b) are the same?

9. (a) Draw a Venn diagram to show the sets U, M and S in Question 8.
(b) On a copy of the diagram shade in M' ∩ S' and check that this is (M ∪ S)'
(c) On a copy of the diagram shade in M' ∪ S' and check that this is (M ∩ S)'.

The two results in Questions 7 and 8 are important. They are known as De Morgan's Laws.

(i) (A ∩ B)' = A' ∪ B'
(ii) (A ∪ B)' = A' ∩ B'

The first says that the complement of the intersection of two sets is found from the union of their complements.

In the second, the complement of the union of two sets is found from the intersection of their complements.

10. (a) Make a copy of the Venn diagram below, and shade in the regions which represent:
(i) P ∩ R   (ii) Q ∩ R

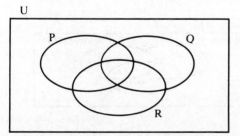

(b) Use these two results to shade the region representing (P ∩ R) ∪ (Q ∩ R).

11. (a) On another copy of the Venn diagram above, shade in the regions which represent:
(i) P ∪ Q   (ii) (P ∪ Q) ∩ R
(b) Does this suggest, from Questions 10 and 11 that (P ∩ R) ∪ (Q ∩ R) = (P ∪ Q) ∩ R?

12. If U = {1, 2, 3, 4, 5, 6, 7, 8, 9, 10}.
P = {1, 3, 6, 10},
Q = {2, 4, 6, 8, 10}, and
R = {3, 6, 9}, find
(a) P ∩ R   (b) Q ∩ R
(c) (P ∩ R) ∪ (Q ∩ R)
(d) P ∪ Q   (e) (P ∪ Q) ∩ R

13. In Question 12, were your answers for parts (c) and (e) the same? If not, check your working.

14. Draw two copies of the Venn diagram given in Question 10.
(a) On the first copy, shade P ∪ R and Q ∪ R. Then shade (P ∪ R) ∩ (Q ∪ R).
(b) On the second copy, shade P ∩ Q. Then shade (P ∩ Q) ∪ R.
(c) Compare your two diagrams. Is it true that: (P ∪ R) ∩ (Q ∪ R) = (P ∩ R) ∪ R?
(d) Check this result using the sets given in Question 12.

15. Draw four copies of the universal set and three intersecting subsets X, Y and Z. By shading show that:
(a) (X ∩ Z) ∪ (Y ∩ Z) = (X ∪ Y) ∩ Z
(b) (X ∪ Z) ∩ (Y ∪ Z) = (X ∩ Y) ∪ Z

1.2 Problems using three sets

Example 1

There are 43 members in a youth club. 25 play badminton, 16 play chess and 20 play tennis.
5 play all three games, 2 play chess and tennis but not badminton, 12 play tennis and badminton, and 10 play only badminton.
How many do not play any of these games?

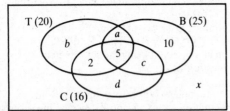

Certain information in this problem can be entered directly onto the diagram namely the 2, 5 and 10.

The number playing tennis and badminton only, denoted by a, can be found by subtracting the 5 who play all three games from 12.

$$a = 12 - 5 = 7$$

Since the total number playing each of tennis and badminton is known, b and c can now be found. In the same way d can be found.

$$b = 20 - 2 - 5 - 7 = 6$$
$$c = 25 - 5 - 10 - 7 = 3$$
$$d = 16 - 2 - 5 - 3 = 6$$

The number not playing any game, x, is finally found by subtracting from 43 the total numbers within the three loops.

$$x = 43 - 39 = 4$$

---

1. During the long vacation 24 boys could choose to work on a farm or on a school building project. 8 chose to go to both, 12 worked on the farm and 17 worked on the building project. How many boys did not go to either?

2. 30 fifth-formers had the opportunity of doing a diving course and a first-aid course. 3 decided to do both, 18 chose the first-aid course and 7 did neither. How many chose:
   (a) diving   (b) diving only?

3. Of 53 fishermen, 17 caught only snapper, 25 caught only cavalli, and 9 were unlucky and caught neither. Find how many caught both.

4. There are 56 sixth-formers who are taking English, History or Geography; 32 take English, 24 take History and 29 take Geography; 7 take all three subjects.
   If 12 take History and Geography only, and 8 take Geography only, show that 22 must be taking only English.

5. When 92 housewives shop in the market, 41 buy tomatoes, carrots and beans, 14 buy tomatoes and carrots only, and 9 buy beans only.
   If 58 buy tomatoes and beans, 75 buy some tomatoes and 68 buy some beans, find how many buy only carrots.
   (Assume all buy at least one of these vegetables.)

6. A group of people book holiday flights at a Trinidad travel agency. 72 of them will need American currency, 53 will need English currency and 29 will need Bajan currency. 19 will need American and Bajan currency, 14 will need American and English currency, while 7 will need English and Bajan currency.
   If 44 of them need only American currency, find out how many need all three currencies, and how many need at least one of the three currencies.

7. In a survey of 50 houses, 35 had a garden, 25 had two floors, 15 had showers and 10 had none of these. 5 of the houses had all three. 10 were two-storey and had a shower. 20 were two-storey and had a garden.
   Find how many of the houses had a garden and a shower.

Example 2

The diagram below shows the number of students in Form Four who belong to the cricket team (T), the debating society (S) and the chess club (C).

Students in Form Four

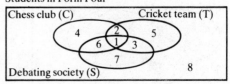

There are eleven students in the cricket team.

One of the cricket team also belongs to the chess club and the debating society.

Two of the cricket team are in the chess club but not in the debating society.

8. Look at the Venn diagram in Example 2.
   How many students from Form Four belong to:
   (a) the chess club
   (b) the debating society
   (c) either the chess club *or* the debating society
   (d) the chess club *and* the debating society *but not* the cricket club
   (e) the debating society *but not* the chess club or the cricket team?

9. Using the sets C, S, and T from Example 2, write down:
   (a) $n(T)$ (b) $n(S)$
   (c) $n(C)$ (d) $n(C \cap S)$
   (e) $n(C \cup T)$ (f) $n(C \cup T) \cap S$
   (g) $n((C \cap T)$ *but not* S)   (h) $n((C \cup T) \cap S')$
   (i) $n(C \cap (T \cup S)')$ (j) $n(C \cup T \cup S)$

10. How many students are in Form Four altogether?

11. Draw a Venn diagram, taking your own class as the universal set. On it show these three intersecting subsets:
    B = {boys}
    A = {students whose first name contains the letter 'a'}
    G = {students who wear glasses}
    In each region of your Venn diagram, write down the number of students who belong there. (Your diagram should look a bit like the one in Example 2.)

12. In the Venn diagram below, $n((G \cap S) \cap B') = 3$.
    Copy the diagram and mark this information on it:
    (i) $n(G \cap B \cap S) = 2$
    (ii) $n((G \cap B) \cap S') = 1$
    (iii) $n(G \cap (S \cap B)') = 4$

Teenagers in Sesame Street

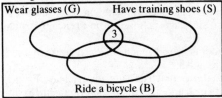

From your completed diagram, write down:
(a) the number of teenagers who have training shoes and glasses, and ride a bike
(b) $n(G \cap S)$
(c) $n(G \cap B)$
(d) $n(G \cap (S \cap B))$

13. Mark this information on your diagram for Question 12:
    (i) $n((S \cap B) \cap G') = 5$
    (ii) $n((S \cap (G \cup B)') = 6$
    (iii) $n((B \cap (G \cup S)') = 7$
    From your completed diagram, write down:
    (a) $n(S)$ (b) $n(B)$
    (c) $n(S \cap B)$ (d) $n(G \cup S \cup B)$

14. n(universal set) = 30, $n(A \cap B) = 7$, $n(A \cap B') = 4$ and $n(B \cap A') = 6$.
    Draw a Venn diagram, with subsets A and B, to show this information. Use your diagram to find:
    (a) $n(A)$ (b) $n(B)$ (c) $n(A \cup B)'$

15. If $n(P) = 16$, $n(Q) = 8$ and $n(P \cap Q) = 3$, find $n(P \cup Q)$.

16. If $n(U) = 42$, $n(X) = 16$, $n(X \cap Y) = 11$ and $n(X \cup Y)' = 6$, find:
    (a) $n(X \cup Y)$ (b) $n(Y)$ (c) $n(X')$
    (d) $n(Y')$ (e) $n(X \cap Y)'$ (f) $n(X \cap Y')$

Example 3

There are 86 students taking languages; 25 take French and German, 17 take French and Spanish, and 5 take German and Spanish; 57 take French, 31 take Spanish and 42 take German. Find how many students take all three languages.

Number of students (86)

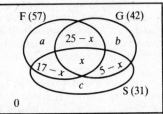

In this problem it is necessary to denote the number in the required region by a letter, say x. The numbers in the other regions may be found in terms of x.
For example, 25 take French and German, so if x take all three languages, $(25 - x)$ take French and German only.
Similarly $(17 - x)$ take French and Spanish only, and $(5 - x)$ take German and Spanish only.
The numbers taking one language only may then be found as is shown.

$$a = 57 - (25 - x) - x - (17 - x) = 15 + x$$
$$b = 42 - (25 - x) - x - (5 - x) = 12 + x$$
$$c = 31 - (17 - x) - x - (5 - x) = 9 + x$$

Since the total number of students within the three loops is 86, an equation may be formed.
i.e. $86 = 57 + (5 - x) + (12 + x) + (9 + x)$.

---

17. Solve the equation in Example 3, and find the numbers of students taking all three languages. Check that the total numbers within the 7 regions of the diagram come to 86 as is required.

18. There are 89 students taking sciences; 18 take Physics and Chemistry, 9 take Physics and Biology and 26 take Chemistry and Biology; 43 take Biology, 56 take Chemistry and 35 take Physics. How many students take all three subjects?

19. 47 gardeners grow ochroes, pumpkins or beans, and sell them in the market. On one Saturday, 25 bring ochroes to the market, 18 bring pumpkins and 21 bring beans; 12 bring only ochroes, 3 bring only pumpkins and 4 bring only beans; 5 bring all three vegetables. How many bring ochroes and pumpkins but not beans? How many bring none of these vegetables?

20. In a popularity poll three T.V. programmes A, B, and C were being compared. Of 100 viewers, 13 liked none of the three programmes; 56 liked A, 47 liked B, and 45 liked C. 18 liked A and B only, 12 liked B and C only, and 15 liked A and C only. Find how many of the 100 viewers liked all three programmes.

21. In one hour, 79 people bought Sunday newspapers at the corner of Cascade Street. 27 bought the *Sunday Voice,* 58 the *Sunday Event* and 35 the *West Indies News*. 16 bought the *Sunday Voice* and *Sunday Event* only, 18 bought the *Sunday Event* and *West Indies News* only, while 1 person bought the *Sunday Voice* and *West Indies News* only. If all 79 people bought at least one of these papers, find how many bought the *Sunday Voice* only.

22. In a survey of 250 workers, 78 went to work by taxi or car, 63 by bus or car, and 51 by taxi or bus. 16 used only their car, 25 used only taxi and 8 used only bus. 5 used all three forms of transport. How many of the workers used none of these forms of transport?

23. Use a Venn diagram to find the H.C.F. of 576, 720 and 1260.

24. Look at the Venn diagram below.

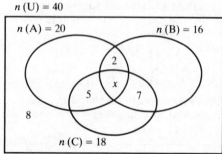

$n\,(U) = 40$

$n\,(A) = 20$ $n\,(B) = 16$

2

x

5   7

8

$n\,(C) = 18$

(a) Do you agree that the number of elements in A *but not* B or C is:
$20 - 2 - x - 5$ or $13 - x$?
(b) Write down, in terms of x, the number of elements in:
   (i) B *but not* C or A
   (ii) C *but not* B or A
(c) The total number of elements in the universal set is 40. Use this fact to solve the equation for x, and then write down $n(A \cap B \cap C)$.

25. There are 40 students in the sixth form. 20 of them study maths, 16 study physics and 18 study chemistry.
2 of the students take maths and physics but not chemistry, 7 take physics and chemistry but not maths, and 5 take chemistry and maths but not physics. 8 take none of these three subjects.
(a) Draw a Venn diagram to show this information.
(b) Let x be the number of students who take maths, physics and chemistry.
In terms of x, write down the number of students in each of the remaining three regions of the Venn diagram.
(c) Use the information to form an equation. Solve the equation to find the number of students who take all three subjects.

26. Using your diagram for Question 25, write down the number of students who take:
(a) maths and physics
(b) chemistry *but not* maths or physics.

27. 50 adult students enroll in a home economics course. They can take cookery, dressmaking, and home care.
7 take cookery *and* dressmaking *but not* home care.
10 take dressmaking *and* home care *but not* cookery.
9 take home care *and* cookery *but not* dressmaking.
Altogether 25 students take cookery, 23 take dressmaking and 34 take home care.
Use a Venn diagram like the one in Question 24 to find how many students take all three subjects.

28. In a class of 26, each student learns one or more foreign languages, chosen from French, German and Spanish.
20 students learn French, 12 learn German and 10 learn Spanish.
7 learn both French *and* German, 5 learn French *and* Spanish and 6 learn both German *and* Spanish.
(a) Draw a Venn diagram to show this information.
(b) By letting $n(F \cap G \cap S) = x$, find how many learn all three languages.

29. Draw a Venn diagram to show the following information, for three sets P, Q and R:
$n(P) = 24, n(Q) = 28, n(R) = 21, n(P \cap Q) = 11,$
$n(Q \cap R) = 14, n(R \cap P) = 9$ and
$n(P \cup Q \cup R) = 45$
Use your diagram to find:
(a) $n(P \cap Q \cap R)$
(b) $n((P \cap Q)$ *but not* R)
(c) $n(P$ *but not* Q or R)
(d) $n((P \cup Q)$ *but not* R)

30. A safe in a store on Florida Street was blown open one night, and all the contents stolen. Next day, the police found evidence that the thief was an expert safe-blower who used plastic explosive. A nightwatchman claimed that the thief was over 1.90 metres tall.

(a) On the police files, there are:
20 people over 1.90m tall, who use plastic explosive but are not expert safe-blowers;
10 people over 1.90m tall, who are expert safe-blowers but do not use plastic explosive;
30 people who are expert safe-blowers and use plastic explosive, but are not over 1.90m tall.
If S = {expert safe-blowers},
T = {people over 1.90m tall}, and
P = {people who use plastic explosive},
show this information on a Venn diagram.

(b) Only 5 people on the police files use plastic explosive but are not expert safe-blowers and are not over 1.90m tall. Altogether, the police know of 58 criminals who use plastic explosive.
Using this extra information, find out how many of the people on the police files could have committed the robbery.

(c) If the nightwatchman had not seen the thief, how many people on the police files would have been suspected of the robbery?

1.3 Sets and logic

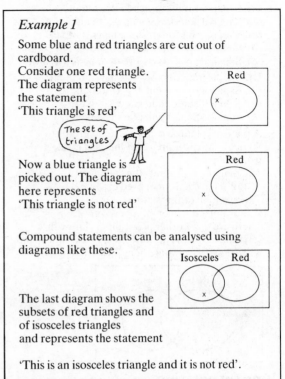

Example 1

Some blue and red triangles are cut out of cardboard.
Consider one red triangle.
The diagram represents the statement
'This triangle is red'

The set of triangles

Now a blue triangle is picked out. The diagram here represents
'This triangle is not red'

Compound statements can be analysed using diagrams like these.

The last diagram shows the subsets of red triangles and of isosceles triangles and represents the statement

'This is an isosceles triangle and it is not red'.

1. For each of the following, draw a diagram to represent the statements:
   (a) This triangle is blue.
   (b) This triangle is not isosceles.
   (c) This triangle is red and isosceles.
   (d) This red triangle is not isosceles.
   (e) This triangle is neither red nor isosceles.
   (f) This blue triangle is not isosceles.

2. Sam attends a boys' school. The boys at the school are either Seniors or Juniors.
   All the boys must play football or cricket. Which of the following are represented by the diagram?
   (The × represents Sam.)

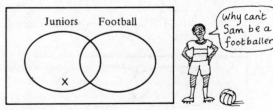

   (a) Sam is a Senior who plays cricket.
   (b) Sam is a Junior who does not play football.
   (c) Sam plays cricket and is not a Senior.
   (d) Sam is a Junior who plays football.
   (e) Sam is a Junior who plays cricket.

3. For the diagram in Question 2, which of the following are true statements?
   (a) Sam is a Junior or he plays football.
   (b) Sam is a Senior or he plays cricket.
   (c) Sam is not a Junior or he plays football.
   (d) Sam does not play football and he is a Senior.
   (e) Sam does not play football or he is a Senior.

4. Draw a diagram to represent the statement:
   (a) Sam is a Junior and plays football.
   (b) Sam is a Senior and plays football.
   (c) Sam is a Senior and plays volleyball.

5. A pack of coloured cards are numbered 1 to 10. Some of the cards are red. One card is selected from the pack.
   The diagram represents the statement:
   'It is a red even-numbered card.'
   The negation of this statement is
   'It is not a red even-numbered card.'
   There are three other possibilities. Draw three separate diagrams to show these possibilities, and write down a true statement for each diagram.

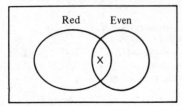

Using set notation

Example 2

Sam is a boy. The set T of tall boys is shown in this diagram and × represents Sam.

Boys

In set language you can write:
Sam ε T
Or you can simply make the statement:
Sam is a tall boy.

6. In this diagram, F is the set of boys in the football team and × represents Sam.
   Boys

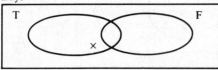

Write a statement in words for each case, and say whether it is true:
   (a) Sam ε F   (b) Sam ε T
   (c) Sam ε F ∩ T   (d) Sam ε F ∩ T

7. The diagram shows the numbers from 1 to 20 and the subsets
   E = {even numbers},
   T = {multiples of 3}.
   The letter *n* represents a number:

Numbers from 1 to 20

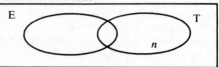

For each of the following, rewrite the statement in set language and say whether it is true:
   (a) *n* is even
   (b) *n* is not even
   (c) *n* is not a multiple of 3
   (d) *n* is a multiple of 6.

8. Use the information in the diagram of Question 7 to say whether the statement is certainly true, may be true or is certainly false:
   (a) $n = 10$ (b) $n = 12$ (c) $n = 9$
   (d) $n \neq 17$ (e) $n \neq 15$ (f) *n* is 3, 9 or 15.

9. Here are five statements that could be true about Sam:
   (a) Sam is not in the football team.
   (b) Sam is not a tall boy.
   (c) Sam is not a tall boy and he is not in the football team.
   (d) Sam is either a tall boy or he is in the football team.
   (e) Sam is a tall boy but he is not in the football team.
   Here are another five statements about Sam in set language:
   (i) Sam ε T′   (ii) Sam ε T ∪ F
   (iii) Sam ε F′   (iv) Sam ε T ∩ F′
   (v) Sam ε T′ ∩ F′
   Match each of the first five statements with the equivalent statement from the second group.

10. A pack of ten cards is numbered 1 to 10. Some of the cards are red.

Ten cards numbered 1 to 10

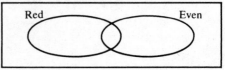

On separate diagrams, mark a × to show the position of a card that is:
   (a) red but not even   (b) even and red
   (c) odd and not red   (d) not red and not odd.

11. Let the sets of cards in Question 10 be R and E.
A card *c* has the number 3, but you do not know its
colour. What can you say about the truth of these?
(a) $c \notin E$ (b) $c \in R$
(c) $c \in R \cup E$ (d) $c \in (R \cup E)'$
(e) $c \notin R \cap E$ (f) $c \in R' \cup E'$

All, some and none

The words **all, some** and **none** often occur in arguments,
and special care has to be taken in using them. Their
meaning is clear from these diagrams:

Example 3

People

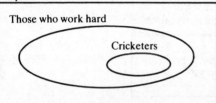

All cricketers work hard.

People

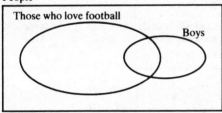

Some boys love football.

Things

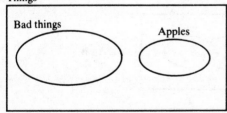

None of the apples are bad.

Care must also be taken when negating
statements like these.
The negation of *All cricketers work hard* is *NOT
all cricketers work hard*. Another way to say this
is *Some cricketers do not work hard*.

In the same way, the negation of *None of the
apples are bad* is *Some of the apples are bad.*

---

12. Draw a Venn diagram to illustrate the premises:
All mongrels are dogs.
Scruff is not a dog.
Is the conclusion *Scruff is not a mongrel* valid?

13. Draw a Venn diagram to illustrate the premises:
All mongrels are dogs.
Scruff is not a mongrel.
Is the conclusion *Scruff is not a dog* valid?

14. Draw a diagram to illustrate:
Some men are mechanics.
All mechanics are tidy.
Is the conclusion *Some men are tidy* a valid
conclusion?

15. Consider these two premises about sets of animals:
Some tree climbers are meat-eaters.
All meat-eaters like fish.
By drawing a Venn diagram, decide whether each
of the following must be correct, may be correct or
must be wrong:
(a) Some tree climbers like fish.
(b) All tree climbers like fish.
(c) None of the tree climbers like fish.
(d) Some fish lovers climb trees.

16. Draw a Venn diagram to test the reasoning:
All students hate homework.
No gardener is a student.
Therefore no gardener hates homework.

17. Draw a Venn diagram to test the reasoning:
All footballers are athletes.
Cricketers are athletes.
Therefore some cricketers are footballers.

18. Write down the negation of:
(a) All men are wise.
(b) All cats love milk.
(c) No cat sleeps at night.
(d) Some parrots are blue.

19. Draw a valid conclusion from:
All tall men have loud voices.
No mice have loud voices.

20. Draw a valid conclusion from:
Some snakes are venomous
All venomous creatures should be avoided.

21. Consider the following:
Some music lovers like dancing.
No-one who dances is unhappy.
Which, if either, is a valid conclusion?
(a) Some music lovers are happy.
(b) All music lovers are happy.

Summary

By the end of this chapter these are the things you
should know about.

1.1 More about sets (pages 176–177)

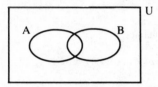

That for any Venn diagram:
$$n(A \cup B) = n(A) + n(B) - n(A \cap B)$$
De Morgan's Laws

$$(A \cap B)' = A' \cup B'$$
$$(A \cup B)' = A' \cap B'$$

How to find regions such as
$(P \cup Q) \cap R$ as a three-loop Venn diagram.

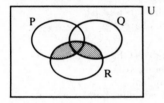

1.2 Problems using three sets (pages 178–181)

How to show information on a three-loop Venn
diagram.
How to solve everyday problems involving three
subsets using a Venn diagram.
The difference between the terms/sets

    A
    A only
    A and B
    A and B only
    A and B but not C
in relation to everyday problems.
How to find the number of elements in specified regions
of a Venn diagram.

1.3 Sets and logic (pages 181–183)

The idea of representing statements such as
this triangle is red with a Venn diagram,

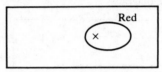

and also *this triangle is isosceles and not red.*

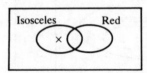

Using set notation to represent statements like the ones
above.

i.e. $T \in R$
or $T \in I \cap R'$

The idea of using Venn diagrams to represent the
words *all, some* or *none.*

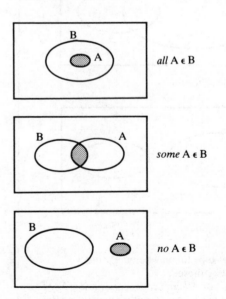

The idea of using diagrams like these to draw
conclusions about information, and to decide whether
the conclusions are valid or not.

2 Relations and functions I

2.1 Facts about functions

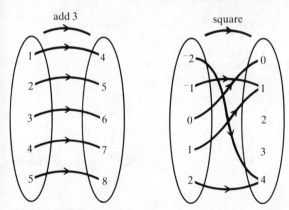

A **function** is a mapping in which each element of the
first set is mapped to only one element of the second set
– that is, to a **unique** element of the second set.
The first set is called the **domain** of the function.
The second set is called the **co-domain** of the function.

Only 1–1 mappings (like the first example above) or
M–1 mappings (like the second example) are functions.

For a mapping to be a function, *every* element in the
domain must be mapped to only one element in the
co-domain.

Those elements of the co-domain which are images are
called the **range** or **image set** of the function.

1. The domain of the first function above is
    $\{1, 2, 3, 4, 5\}$.
    What is the domain of the second function?

2. The co-domain of the second function is
    $\{0, 1, 2, 3, 4\}$.
    Do you agree that the image set is $\{0, 1, 4\}$?

3. (a) Write down the elements in the co-domain of
        the first function.
    (b) What can you say about the image set of this
        function?

The rule for a function

There are two ways to describe the **rule** for a particular
function, using symbols.
Look again at the two functions at the start of the page.
We can call the first function f, and write:

$$f : x \rightarrow x + 3$$

which is read as
f is a function such that x maps to x + 3
or we can write:

$$f(x) = x + 3$$

which is read as
the image of x when using function f is x + 3.

In the first function $2 \rightarrow 5$ and $f(1) = 4$.

4. If the second function at the start of the page is
    called g, copy and complete:
    (a) $g : x \rightarrow \square$ (b) $g(x) = \square$

5. Using the functions f and g, write down:
    (a) $f(2)$ (b) $g(2)$ (c) $f(5)$ (d) $g(^-2)$

Defining a function

A function can be defined in any of these ways –
 (i) by drawing a mapping diagram, like those on page 185
 (ii) by writing down its rule (in either form) and its domain, e.g.
   $f : x \to x + 3$ where $x \in \{1, 2, 3, 4, 5\}$
 (iii) by showing its ordered pairs as a list:
   $\{(1, 4), (2, 5), (3, 6), (4, 7), (5, 8)\}$
   or in a table:

x	1	2	3	4	5
$f(x)$	4	5	6	7	8

 (iv) by showing the function as a graph:

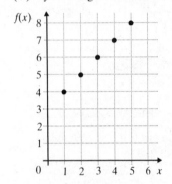

Note: If the domain of the function above were *all the numbers from 1 to 5* then the graph would be a straight line, instead of a set of points.

6. Function g is defined by the second mapping diagram on page 185. Now show it using methods (ii), (iii) and (iv) above.

7. The rule for function g is $g(x) = x^2$. If its domain is $\{^-2, ^-1\tfrac{1}{2}, ^-1, ^-\tfrac{1}{2}, 0, \tfrac{1}{2}, 1, 1\tfrac{1}{2}, 2\}$, copy and complete the table below:

x	$^-2$	$^-1\tfrac{1}{2}$	$^-1$	$^-\tfrac{1}{2}$	0	$\tfrac{1}{2}$	1	$1\tfrac{1}{2}$	2
$g(x)$	4		1		0		1		4

Show the four new points on the graph you drew for Question 6.

8. If the domain for function g had been $\{$all the numbers from $^-2$ to $2\}$, what could you say about the shape of the graph?

9. Using the domain in Question 7, complete:
 (a) $g : \tfrac{1}{2} \to \square$ (b) $g : ^-1\tfrac{1}{2} \to \square$
 (c) $g(^-\tfrac{1}{2}) = \square$ (d) $g(1\tfrac{1}{2}) = \square$

10. $k : x \to 2x + 1$ where $x \in \{1, 2, 3, 4, 5\}$.
 Do you agree that the image of 3 is 7?
 What number has 5 as its image?

11. Using function k from Question 10, find:
 (a) $k(1)$ (b) $k(4)$ (c) $k(5)$
 (d) p if $k(p) = 5$ (e) q if $k(q) = 7$

12. $h : x \to 3x - 2$ where $x \in \{1, 2, 3, 4, 5\}$.
 Write down the ordered pairs which describe this function.

13. (a) Show function h from Question 12 as a graph.
 (b) What can you say about this set of points?
 (c) How would your graph differ if the domain of h were $\{$all the numbers from 1 to 5$\}$?

14. Function l is defined by the set of ordered pairs:
   $\{(0, 0), (1, 3), (2, 6), (3, 9), (4, 12), (5, 15)\}$
 (a) What is the domain of l?
 (b) What is the range of l?
 (c) What is the image of 2?
 (d) What number has 12 as its image?
 (e) Copy and complete for l:
       (i) $l : x \to \square$ (ii) $l(x) = \square$

15. Show function l from Question 14 as a graph.

16. The graph of function m is shown below:

 (a) List the ordered pairs for the graph.
 (b) Write down the rule for function m.
 (c) What is the domain of m?
 (d) What is the image of (i) 5?   (ii) 3?
 (e) What number has $^-2$ as its image?

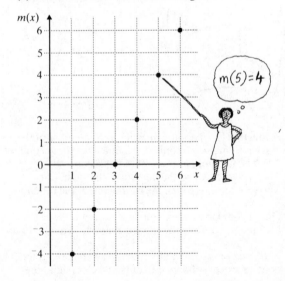

2.2 Some special functions

1. Which of the following represent functions?
Give reasons for your answers.

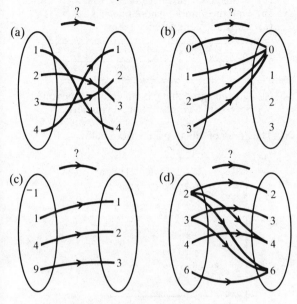

(a) (b) (c) (d)

2. (a) Can you say what the arrow stands for, in each
of the mapping diagrams above?
(b) What can you say about all the elements in the
domain in Question 1(b)?
(c) Why is there no arrow from ⁻1
in Question 1(c)?
(d) Why is there only one arrow from the 4 and 6,
in Question 1(d)?

Reminder A mapping represents a function only where
each element of the domain maps to just one element of
the co-domain. In other words, there is just *one* arrow
from each element of the domain.

3. Draw a mapping diagram for each of the
1–1 functions which have {p, q, r} as the domain
and co-domain. One of them is shown below:

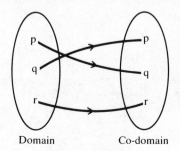

Domain   Co-domain

4. How many of your functions in Question 3 do not
have *any* element as its own image?

A 1–1 function which maps a set onto itself is an
example of a **permutation**.

5. Do you agree that READ is a rearrangement of
DEAR? Show this as a 1–1 function.

6. Find all the possible 1–1 functions which map the
set {D, E, A, R} onto itself, but where no letter is
its own image. One of them is shown below:

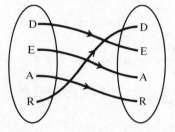

7. How many different functions are there which map
the set {p, q, r} into the set {0, 1}?
Show each of these as a mapping diagram.

8. In how many of your functions in Question 7 does
every element of the domain have *the same image?*

The constant function

If every element of the domain maps onto the same
image, the function is called a **constant function.**

The mapping diagram in Question 1(b) shows a
constant function. The element 0 in the co-domain is
assigned to every element in the domain. The rule for
this function is $f : x \rightarrow 0$.

9. Using the same domain and co-domain as in
Question 1(b), show a constant function where
every element of the domain maps to:
(a) 1   (b) 2   (c) 3

10. Show as $f : x \rightarrow \square$ the rule for each function in
Question 9.

11. (a) Write down the ordered pairs for the graph.

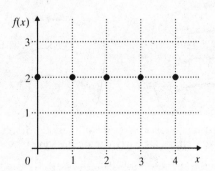

(b) Does this graph represent a 1–1 or a M–1 function?
(c) What is the domain of the function?
(d) What number is the image of every element in the domain?
(e) Write down the rule for this function.

12. In Question 11 how would the graph differ, if the domain were { all numbers from 0 to 3}?

13. Using as domain {all numbers from 0 to 4} draw a graph like the one above to show:
(a) the constant function $g : x \rightarrow 1$
(b) the constant function $h : x \rightarrow 3$

14. What would the graph of the constant function $k : x \rightarrow 0$ look like, with domain:
(a) {0, 1, 2, 3, 4}
(b) {all the numbers from 0 to 4}?

15. A maths test is given to a class of 30 students. The test is marked out of 100. What can you say about the test if the graph of the results is:
(a) the constant function $f : x \rightarrow 100$
(b) the constant function $z : x \rightarrow 0$?

16. Each of 30 students was asked to choose one of cricket, badminton or swimming. Under what circumstances would a graph of their choices be a constant function?

17. Look at your answers for Question 3. Did you have one function in which every element was its own image? Write down the set of ordered pairs for this function. What do you notice?

18. Draw the mapping diagram in which each element of {D, E, A, R} is its own image. How would you describe this function?

The identity function

If every element of the domain maps onto itself, we say the function is an **identity function**.
Two examples are shown below:

(i) 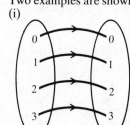   (ii)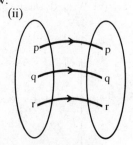

When an identity function is shown as a set of ordered pairs, the two elements in each pair are the same:

$\{(0, 0), (1, 1), (2, 2), (3, 3)\}$ or $\{(p, p), (q, q), (r, r)\}$

In other words every element maps onto itself.
The rule for an identity function is written either as $f : x \rightarrow x$ or $f(x) = x$.

19. $g : x \rightarrow x$ where $x \in \{1, 2, 3, 4, 5\}$.
(a) Write down the image of 3.
(b) Find the number whose image is 5.
(c) Copy and complete the table:

x	1	2	3	4	5
$g(x)$	1				

(d) Do you agree that g is an identity function?
(e) Show g as a graph. What do you notice?

20. The graph of function h is shown below:

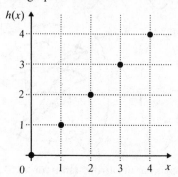

(a) Write down the ordered pairs for the graph.
(b) What is the image of 4?
(c) Which number has 1 as its image?
(d) Does this graph show an identity function?
(e) What is the rule for this function?

2.3 The inverse of a function

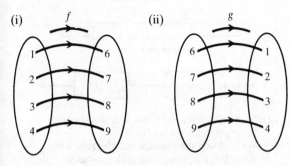

(i) f (ii) g

1. Look at the two mapping diagrams above.
   (a) Does each represent a function?
   (b) How could you obtain the second diagram from the first one?
   (c) What does the arrow mean in:
       (i) the first diagram
       (ii) the second diagram?
   (d) What is the connection between your answers in (c)?
   (e) Write down the rule for each function.

The second diagram above could have been obtained from the first one, simply by reversing each arrow. The new mapping formed in this way is called the **inverse** of the first mapping.
The rule for the second mapping is *subtract 5*. This is the **inverse** of the rule for the first mapping, *add 5*.

2. Draw the inverse of each function shown below. For each say whether the inverse is also a function.

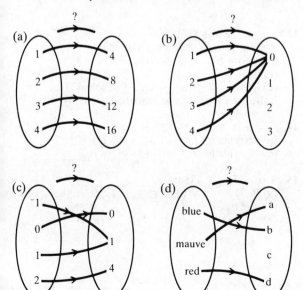

3. Write down, where possible, the inverse of:
   (a) *add 3*   (b) *multiply by 4*
   (c) *multiply by 0*   (d) *square*

4. Look again at your answers for Question 2. Do you agree that:
   (a) if the function is M–1, then its inverse is *not* a function?
   (b) if not all the elements in the co-domain are images, then the inverse cannot be a function?
   (c) only 1–1 functions can have inverses which are also functions?
   (d) the square root of a number can be positive or negative?

Inverse functions

The inverse of a M–1 function is a 1–M mapping – it is not a function.
Only functions which are 1–1 can have inverses that are also functions.
A 1–1 function will have an inverse which is also a function, *only if there is an arrow to each element of its co-domain.*
In other words, its image set must be the same as the co-domain.
Otherwise there would be an element without an image in the domain of the inverse.

Look at mapping (i) for Question 1.
The function $f : x \rightarrow x + 5$ has the domain $\{1, 2, 3, 4\}$.
The inverse of f is another function, $g : x \rightarrow x - 5$, with domain $\{6, 7, 8, 9\}$.
The domain of g was the co-domain of f.

5. Draw a mapping diagram for the function. Then write down (i) the domain and (ii) the rule, for the inverse function.
   (a) $f : x \rightarrow x + 4$ where $x \in \{0, 1, 2, 3\}$
   (b) $g : x \rightarrow 3x$ where $x \in \{1, 2, 3, 4\}$
   (c) $h : x \rightarrow x - 3$ where $x \in \{6, 7, 8, 9\}$
   (d) $k : x \rightarrow \dfrac{x}{5}$ where $x \in \{5, 10, 15, 20\}$

6. A function f is defined by:
   $\{(1, 4), (2, 7), (3, 10), (4, 13), (5, 16)\}$
   (a) Find the rule for f.
   (b) Find the rule for the inverse function and write down its domain.

7. (a) Write down the ordered pairs for the function shown below.

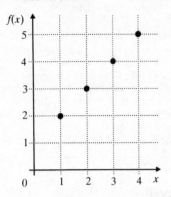

(b) What is the rule for this function?
(c) Does this function have an inverse which is also a function?
(d) Write down the domain and the rule for the inverse function.

8. The graph below shows a *constant* function:

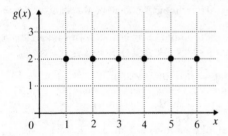

(a) Write down the rule for the function.
(b) Is this function 1–1 or M–1?
(c) Write down the ordered pairs for the inverse of the function.
(d) Is the inverse a function or not?

9. The graph below shows an *identity* function.

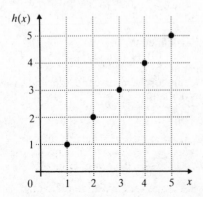

What can you say about the inverse of an identity function?

10. Put each of the numbers 0, 1, 2, 3, 4, 5 into the function machine in turn. Write down the output.

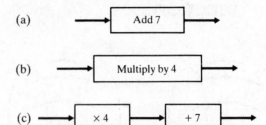

11. (a) Write down the rule which describes each function in Question 10.
(b) Write down the domain and the rule which describes the inverse of each function.

12. Draw a function machine for each rule below. Then draw the inverse function machine and use this to write down the inverse rule.
(a) $f : x \rightarrow x - 4$
(b) $g : x \rightarrow 5x$
(c) $h : x \rightarrow 5x - 4$

Naming an inverse function

In Question 12 (a), the rule for the inverse of function f was $x \rightarrow x + 4$.
If the inverse of f is also a function, it is called f^{-1}.

In the same way, for Questions 12 (b) and (c):

$$g^{-1} : x \rightarrow \frac{x}{5}$$

$$h^{-1} : x \rightarrow \frac{(x + 4)}{5}$$

13. $f : x \rightarrow x + 3$ and $f^{-1} : x \rightarrow x - 3$.
Write *true* or *false* for each statement.
(a) $f(5) = 8$ (b) $f^{-1}(5) = 2$
(c) $f(8) = 6$ (d) $f^{-1}(8) = 5$
(e) $f(17) = 20$ (f) $f^{-1}(20) = 23$
If the statement is false, rewrite it correctly.

14. $f : x \rightarrow 7x$ and $g : x \rightarrow x - 8$. Find:
(a) the rule for f^{-1} (b) $f^{-1}(21)$
(c) the rule for g^{-1} (d) $g^{-1}(17)$

15. $h : x \rightarrow 7x - 8$. Find:
(a) $h(3)$ (b) $h(7)$ (c) $h(8)$
(d) the rule for h^{-1}
(e) $h^{-1}(13)$ (f) $h^{-1}(41)$ (g) $h^{-1}(48)$

2.4 The composition of functions

Look at the diagram below.

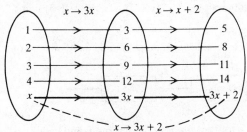

It shows what happens when you use $x \to 3x$ first and then $x \to x + 2$.
This combination is equivalent to using
$x \to 3x + 2$
$x \to 3x + 2$ is called the *composite* of
$x \to 3x$ followed by $x \to x + 2$

1. Draw an arrow graph, using $\{1, 2, 3, 4, 5\}$ as domain, to show:
   (a) $x \to x + 2$ followed by $x \to 3x$
   (b) $x \to 5x$ followed by $x \to x - 3$
   (c) $x \to x - 4$ followed by $x \to 7x$
   For each part write down the composite as $x \to$

2. Draw an arrow graph, using $\{0, 1, 2, 3, 4\}$ as domain, to show:
   (a) $x \to x^2$ followed by $x \to x + 4$
   (b) $x \to x + 4$ followed by $x \to x^2$
   (c) $x \to x + 1$ followed by $x \to 1/x$
   For each part write down the composite as $x \to$.

3. Write down the composite of:
   (a) $x \to x - 3$ followed by $x \to 5x$
   (b) $x \to 2x$ followed by $x \to x + 5$
   (c) $x \to x - 2$ followed by $x \to x^2$
   (d) $x \to x + 3$ followed by $x \to 1/x$

4. Using $\{^-2, ^-1, 0, 1, 2\}$ as domain, find the image set for each composite function in Question 3.

5. Write down the composite of:
   (a) $x \to 3x + 4$ followed by $x \to 2x + 1$
   (b) $x \to 2x - 7$ followed by $x \to 3x + 5$
   (c) $x \to 5x + 1$ followed by $x \to 4x - 3$
   (d) $x \to 4x - 1$ followed by $x \to x^2 + 2$

6. Using $\{0, 1, 2, 3, 4, 5\}$ as domain, find the image set for each composite function in Question 5.

7. Which is the composite of $x \to 3x + 1$ followed by $x \to 2x + 5$?
   (a) $x \to 6x + 6$ (b) $x \to 6x + 5$
   (c) $x \to 6x + 16$ (d) $x \to 6x + 7$

8. Is the composite of $x \to 2x + 5$ followed by $x \to 3x + 1$ given in Question 7?

9. Which is the composite of $x \to 5x - 2$ followed by $x \to 3x - 1$?
   (a) $x \to 15x - 3$ (b) $x \to 15x + 7$
   (c) $x \to 15x - 7$ (d) $x \to 15x + 2$

10. Is the composite of $x \to 3x - 1$ followed by $x \to 5x - 2$ given in Question 9?

11. Is $x \to 4x + 3$ followed by $x \to 3x + 2$ the same as $x \to 3x + 2$ followed by $x \to 4x + 3$?
    For each composite find the image of $\{1, 2, 3, 4, 5\}$.

Example 1

In the diagram f is the function where $x \to 4x$, with domain $\{0, 1, 2, 3, 4, 5\}$.
g is the function $x \to x + 7$, with the image set of f as its domain.

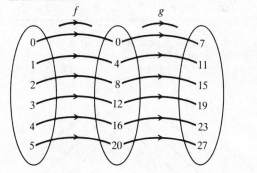

---

12. Use the diagram of Example 1 to write down:
    (a) $f(2)$ and then $g(8)$
    (b) $f(5)$ and then $g(20)$
    (c) $f(0)$ and then $g(0)$

13. Use the diagram of Example 1 to find:
    (a) the image of 2 using f followed by g
    (b) the image of 5 using f followed by g
    (c) the image of 0 using f followed by g

14. Use your answers for Questions 12 and 13 to help you write down:
    (a) $g[f(2)]$ (b) $g[f(5)]$ (c) $g[f(0)]$

15. Do you agree that the mapping in Example 1 from the first set $\{0, 1, 2, 3, 4, 5\}$ to the last set $\{7, 11, 15, 19, 23, 27\}$ is a function?
    Copy and complete the rule for this function:
    $$x \to$$

When we combine two functions f and g in the way shown above, the single function which maps the first set onto the last set is called the **composition** of f and g.

16. In Question 15 you should have found that the rule for the *composition* of f and g was $x \to 4x + 7$.
    Can you suggest a label for this function?

Example 2

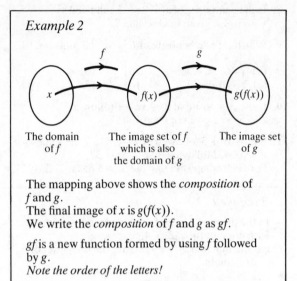

The domain   The image set of *f*   The image set
of *f*   which is also   of *g*
                  the domain of *g*

The mapping above shows the *composition* of
f and *g*.
The final image of *x* is *g(f(x))*.
We write the *composition* of *f* and *g* as *gf*.

gf is a new function formed by using *f* followed
by *g*.
Note the order of the letters!

17. Look at the diagram below. It shows the
composition of *f* and *g*. Write down the rule for:
  (a) *f*   (b) *g*   (c) *gf*

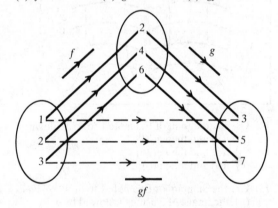

18. Look at the diagram below. It shows the
composition of *g* and *f*. Write down the rule for:
  (a) *g*   (b) *f*   (c) *fg*

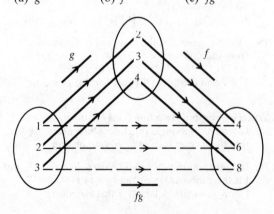

19. Look at your answers for Questions 17 and 18. Do
you agree that *gf* and *fg* are different functions?

You should have found in Question 17 that the
composition of *f* and *g* was $x \rightarrow 2x + 1$, where $\{1, 2, 3\}$
maps onto $\{3, 5, 7\}$.
In Question 18 the *composition* of *g* and *f* was a
different function, $x \rightarrow 2(x + 1)$, where $\{1, 2, 3\}$ maps
onto $\{4, 6, 8\}$.

gf stands for the *composition* of *f* and *g*, and means you
use *f* first, then *g*. i.e.

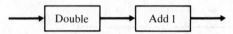

fg stands for the *composition* of *g* and *f*, and means you
use *g* first, then *f*. i.e.

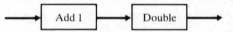

gf and *fg* are called **composite functions.**

Example 3

If $h : x \rightarrow x^2$ and $k : x \rightarrow x + 3$
find $kh(4)$, $hk(5)$, kh and hk.

$h(4) = 16$ so $kh(4) = 16 + 3 = 19$
$k(5) = 8$ so $hk(5) = (8)^2 = 64$

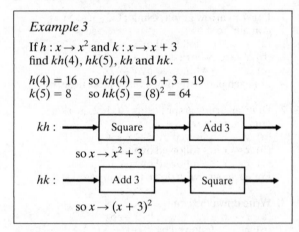

kh :
so $x \rightarrow x^2 + 3$

hk :
so $x \rightarrow (x + 3)^2$

20. If $f : x \rightarrow 2x$ and $g : x \rightarrow x - 3$ find:
  (a) $f(3)$ (b) $g(6)$ (c) $gf(3)$
  (d) $g(8)$ (e) $f(5)$ (f) $fg(8)$
  Write the rules for *gf* and *fg* as $x \rightarrow$

21. If $h : x \rightarrow x^2$ and $k : x \rightarrow x - 1$ find:
  (a) $h(5)$ (b) $k(25)$ (c) $kh(5)$
  (d) $k(4)$ (e) $h(3)$ (f) $hk(4)$
  Write the rules for *kh* and *hk* as $x \rightarrow$

22. If $p : x \rightarrow 3x$ and $q : x \rightarrow x + 2$, write the rules for
  qp and *pq* as $x \rightarrow$. Use these to find:
  (a) $qp(2)$ (b) $qp(7)$ (c) $qp(11)$
  (d) $pq(2)$ (e) $pq(7)$ (f) $pq(11)$

23. If $l : x \rightarrow 4x$ and $m : x \rightarrow x^2$, write the rules for *lm*
  and *ml* as $x \rightarrow$. Use these to find:
  (a) $lm(3)$ (b) $ml(5)$ (c) $lml(1)$

24. f is a function defined by the ordered pairs
$\{(1, 5), (2, 6), (3, 7), (4, 8), (5, 9)\}$.
g is another function defined by the ordered pairs
$\{(5, 15), (6, 18), (7, 21), (8, 24), (9, 27)\}$.
(a) Draw a mapping diagram to show the
composition of f and g.
(b) Write down the domain of f.
(c) Write down the domain of g.
(d) Write down the image set of gf.
(e) Write as $x \to$ the rules for:
     (i) f (ii) g (iii) gf
(f) Find: (i) $f(3)$ (ii) $g(6)$ (iii) $gf(5)$

25. g is defined as in Question 24 and h is another
function defined by the ordered pairs
$\{(15, 11), (18, 14), (21, 17), (24, 20), (27, 23)\}$.
(a) Draw a mapping diagram to show the
composition of g and h.
(b) Write down the domain of hg.
(c) Write down the image set of hg.
(d) Write the rules for h and hg as $x \to$
(e) Find: (i) $h(21)$ (ii) $hg(6)$

26. The function machine below shows the three
functions f, g and h as defined in Questions 24 and
25.

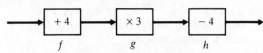

Use the machine to find the image of:
(a) 1   (b) 2   (c) 3   (d) 4   (e) 5
Do you agree that this machine represents a
composite function of f, g and h?
What is: (i) $hgf(2)$?   (ii) $hgf(5)$?

27. If $f : x \to x + 3$, $g : x \to 4x$ and $h : x \to x - 3$, show
as a function machine:
(a) fg (b) gf (c) hg (d) gh
Use your machines to write down:
(e) $fg(5)$ (f) $gf(2)$ (g) $hg(7)$ (h) $gh(4)$
Write as $x \to$, the rule for:
(i) fg (j) gf (k) hg (l) gh

28. Using f, g and h from Question 27, show as a
function machine:
(a) hgf (b) fgh (c) fh (d) hf
Write the rule for each machine as $x \to$.
What do you notice about your last two answers?
What is the special name for this function?

Summary of ideas

$gf(x)$ is the image of x using f first and then g.

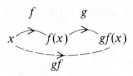

For example: if $f : x \to 3x + 1$
          and $g : x \to x^2$
          then $gf(x) = g(3x + 1) = (3x + 1)^2$

$fg(x)$ is the image of x using g first and then f.

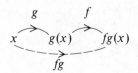

So in the above example:

$$fg(x) = f(x^2) = 3x^2 + 1$$

gf (or $g \circ f$) is called the composite of g on f.
fg (or $f \circ g$) is the composite of f on g.

Notice $fg \neq gf$.
Composition of functions is not commutative.

29. If $f : x \to 2x + 1$ and $g : x \to x^2$, find:
(a) $f(3)$ (b) $g(7)$ (c) $gf(3)$
(d) $fg(7)$ (e) $gf(7)$ (f) $fg(3)$
Write down $gf(x)$ and $fg(x)$.

30. If $f : x \to 5x - 2$ and $g : x \to x^2$, find:
(a) $f(2)$ (b) $g(8)$ (c) $gf(2)$
(d) $fg(8)$ (e) $gf(8)$ (f) $fg(2)$
Write down $gf(x)$ and $fg(x)$.

31. If $f : x \to 3x - 7$ and $g : x \to 2x + 5$, find gf and fg.
Hence write down:
(a) $gf(2)$ (b) $fg(2)$
(c) $gf(^-3)$ (d) $fg(^-3)$

32. If $f : x \to 2x - 7$ and $g : x \to 3x + 5$, find gf and fg.
Hence write down:
(a) $gf(4)$ (b) $fg(1)$
(c) $gf(0)$ (d) $fg(^-2)$

33. If $f : x \to 3x - 1$ and $g : x \to x^2$, find:
(a) $gf(x)$ (b) $fg(x)$
(c) $gg(x)$ (d) $ff(x)$

34. If $f : x \to x^2$ and $g : x \to 4x + 1$, find:
(a) $fg(x)$ (b) $gf(x)$
(c) $ff(x)$ (d) $gg(x)$

35. If $h : x \to 2x - 1$ and $k : x \to x^3$, find:
(a) kh (b) hk
(c) kk (d) hh

36. If $h : x \to x^3$ and $k : x \to 1 - x$, find:
   (a) hk (b) kh
   (c) hh (d) kk

37. If $f : x \to x + 1$ and $g : x \to x^2$, express in terms of f and g:
   (a) $x \to (x + 1)^2$ (b) $x \to x^2 + 1$
   (c) $x \to x^4$ (d) $x \to x + 2$

38. If $h : x \to x^2$ and $k : x \to x - 1$, express in terms of h and k:
   (a) $x \to (x - 1)^2$ (b) $x \to x^2 - 1$
   (c) $x \to x - 3$ (d) $x \to (x^2 - 1)^2$

39. For which pair is $fg = gf$?
   (a) $f : x \to 3x$ (b) $f : x \to x + 5$
       $g : x \to 2x$ $g : x \to x - 2$
   (c) $f : x \to 3x$ (d) $f : x \to 3x - 2$
       $g : x \to x - 2$ $g : x \to 4x - 3$
   (e) $f : x \to 5x + 3$
       $g : x \to 2x - 1$

40. Show in each case that ff is the identity, i.e. $x \to x$.
   (a) $f : x \to - x$ (b) $f : x \to 4 - x$
   (c) $f : x \to 1/x$

41. Show in each case that gf is the identity. Show also that $fg = gf$.
   (a) $f : x \to x + 7$ (b) $f : x \to 5x$
       $g : x \to x - 7$ $g : x \to \frac{1}{5}x$
   (c) $f : x \to 2x + 5$
       $g : x \to \frac{1}{2}(x - 5)$

42. If $f : x \to 2x + 1$, find:
   (a) ff (b) fff (c) $ffff$

43. If $h : x \to x + 3$, and $k : x \to 4x$, show that:
   (a) $h^4 : x \to x + 12$ (b) $k^3 : x \to 64x$

2.5 Composition and inverses

1. Describe each flow chart as $x \to$

   (a) $\to \boxed{\times 3} \to \boxed{+ 2} \to$ (b) $\to \boxed{\times 4} \to \boxed{- 3} \to$

Draw the inverse of each flow chart and write down the rule for the inverse.

2. Describe each flow chart as $x \to$.

   (a) $\to \boxed{- 5} \to \boxed{\times 4} \to$ (b) $\to \boxed{+ 2} \to \boxed{\div 3} \to$

Draw the inverse of each flow chart and write down the rule for the inverse.

3. Draw a flow chart to show:
   (a) $x \to 4x + 7$ (b) $x \to 3x - 5$
   (c) $x \to 5(x + 2)$ (d) $x \to 7(x - 5)$
Use your flow charts to help you write down the inverse of each rule.

4. Draw a flow chart to show:
   (a) $x \to 6x - 1$ (b) $x \to (x + 3) \div 2$
   (c) $x \to x^2 + 3$ (d) $x \to (x + 1)^2$
Use your flow charts to help you write down the inverse of each rule.

5. Write down the inverse of each rule:
   (a) $x \to 3x - 7$ (b) $x \to 2(x + 5)$
   (c) $x \to \frac{1}{3}x + \frac{2}{3}$ (d) $x \to (x - 4) \div 3$

Example 1

Find the inverse of $f : x \to 3(x + 2) - 1$

First show $x \to 3(x + 2) - 1$ as a function machine.

$x \to \boxed{+ 2} \to \boxed{\times 3} \to \boxed{- 1} \to 3(x + 2) - 1$

To find the inverse, reverse the machine.

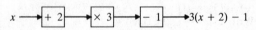

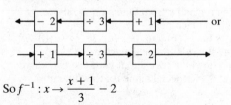

So $f^{-1} : x \to \dfrac{x + 1}{3} - 2$

---

6. Use the method shown in Example 1 above to find the inverse of:
   (a) $g : x \to 2x + 3$ (b) $h : x \to 4(x - 5)$
   (c) $k : x \to 4(x + 3) - 2$ (d) $l : x \to 3(2x + 1)$
   (e) $m : x \to \dfrac{(x + 1)}{3} - 2$

7. Using function f in Example 1, find:
(a) $f(5)$ (b) $f^{-1}(20)$

8. Use the functions given in Question 6 and your answers to the exercise to write down:
(a) $g(5)$ (b) $h(7)$ (c) $k(3)$
(d) $l(4)$ (e) $g^{-1}(13)$ (f) $h^{-1}(8)$
(g) $k^{-1}(22)$ (h) $l^{-1}(27)$

9. $f : x \rightarrow 4x + 1$. Find:
(a) f^{-1} (b) $f(2)$ (c) $f^{-1}(9)$ (d) $f^{-1}(2)$

10. $g : x \rightarrow 2(x + 5)$. Find:
(a) g^{-1} (b) $g(1)$ (c) $g^{-1}(12)$ (d) $g^{-1}(1)$

11. $h : x \rightarrow (x - 3) \div 2$. Find:
(a) h^{-1} (b) $h(3)$ (c) $h^{-1}(0)$ (d) $h^{-1}(3)$

12. $k : x \rightarrow x^2 - 4$. Find:
(a) k^{-1} (b) $k(5)$ (c) $k^{-1}(21)$ (d) $k^{-1}(5)$

13. $f : x \rightarrow 3(2x + 1) + 4$. Find:
(a) f^{-1} (b) $f(3)$ (c) $f^{-1}(25)$ (d) $f^{-1}(4)$

Inverse of a composite function

> *Example 2*
>
> Given $f : x \rightarrow 2x$ and $g : x \rightarrow x + 3$ find the inverse of gf.
>
> $gf(x) = g(2x) = 2x + 3$
>
>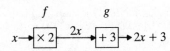
>
> The inverse of gf is written as $(gf)^{-1}$.
>
> So $(gf)^{-1} : x \rightarrow \dfrac{x - 3}{2}$
>
> Notice $(gf)^{-1} = f^{-1}g^{-1}$

14. $f : x \rightarrow 3x,\ g : x \rightarrow x + 2$. Find:
(a) gf (b) f^{-1} (c) g^{-1} (d) $(gf)^{-1}$
Find also fg and show that $(fg)^{-1} = g^{-1}f^{-1}$.

15. $f : x \rightarrow 4x,\ g : x \rightarrow x - 3$. Find:
(a) fg (b) f^{-1} (c) g^{-1} (d) $(fg)^{-1}$
Find also gf and show that $(gf)^{-1} = f^{-1}g^{-1}$.

16. $f : x \rightarrow 3x + 2,\ g : x \rightarrow 4x$. Find:
(a) gf (b) $(gf)^{-1}$ (c) fg (d) $(fg)^{-1}$

17. $h : x \rightarrow x + 5,\ k : x \rightarrow 2x - 1$. Find:
(a) hk (b) $(hk)^{-1}$ (c) kh (d) $(kh)^{-1}$

18. $f(x) = 3x + 1,\ g(x) = x + 2$. Find:
(a) $fg(4)$ (b) $f^{-1}(19)$ (c) $g^{-1}(6)$
Show also that $(gf)^{-1}(15) = 4$.

19. $f(x) = 2x + 1,\ g(x) = 3x - 2$.
Find x when:
(a) $gf(x) = 19$ (b) $fg(x) = 21$

Inverse functions and equations

> *Example 3*
>
> A function $f : x \rightarrow 2x + 3$ can be shown as
>
>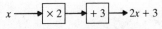
>
> Its *inverse*, denoted by f^{-1}, can be found by using the flow chart backwards.
>
>
>
> i.e. $f^{-1} : x \rightarrow \dfrac{(x - 3)}{2}$, or $f^{-1}(x) = \dfrac{(x - 3)}{2}$
>
> We can use the idea of the inverse process to solve the equation $2x + 3 = 13$.
>
> $5 \leftarrow \boxed{\div 2} \leftarrow \boxed{-3} \leftarrow 13$
>
> By using 13 as the right-hand side, the solution is $x = 5$.

20. Draw a flow chart to show $x \rightarrow 3x + 4$ and hence solve $3x + 4 = 19$.

21. Draw a flow chart to show $x \rightarrow 5x - 2$ and hence solve $5x - 2 = 13$.

22. Use a flow chart and its inverse to solve:
(a) $5x + 3 = 38$ (b) $7x - 2 = 47$
(c) $4x + 7 = 3$ (d) $6x - 15 = 6$

23. Use a flow chart and its inverse to solve:
(a) $3(2x + 5) = 57$ (b) $4(5x - 9) = 184$
(c) $2(x + 3) + 5 = 9$ (d) $5(x - 2) + 4 = -21$

24. If $f(x) = 4x - 7$, find x when:
(a) $f(x) = 9$ (b) $f(x) = 21$ (c) $f(x) = -15$

25. If $g(x) = 6(x + 2) - 5$, find x when:
   (a) $g(x) = 25$ (b) $g(x) = 73$ (c) $g(x) = -17$

26. Solve:
   (a) $7(2x + 3) + 5 = 33$
   (b) $2(9x - 4) - 3 = -47$
   (c) $\frac{1}{4}(x - 5) + \frac{3}{4} = 15$

27. Draw a flow chart to show
   $f : x \rightarrow [7(2x - 3) + 5] \div 2$.
   Find f^{-1}. Hence find x when $f(x) = 20$.
   Find also $f^{-1}(6)$.

28. Draw a flow chart to show
   $g : x \rightarrow 3[2(4x - 1) + 2] - 5$.
   Find g^{-1}. Hence find x when $g(x) = 163$.

Composites and inverses

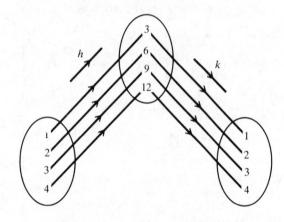

29. Look at the mapping diagram below.
   (a) Write the rules for h and k as $x \rightarrow$
   (b) What is
       (i) the domain
       (ii) the image set
       of the composition of h and k?
   (c) Write the rule for kh as $x \rightarrow$
   (d) What special function is kh?

30. (a) Draw a mapping diagram to show the function
       $f : x \rightarrow 4x$ with domain $\{1, 2, 3, 4, 5\}$.
   (b) Draw a second mapping diagram to show the
       inverse function f^{-1}.
   (c) Use your diagrams for (a) and (b) to say what
       special function is the *composition* of f and f^{-1}.

In Question 29, k is the inverse of h. You should have
found that the *composition* of h and k was an identity
function with $x \rightarrow x$.

The *composition* of a function and its inverse is always
an identity function.
If i is an identity function then $f^{-1}f = i$.

31. $f : x \rightarrow x + 7$ and f^{-1} is its inverse.
   Copy and complete the function machine below
   which shows the *composition* of f and f^{-1}.

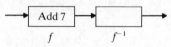

$\qquad f \qquad\qquad f^{-1}$

   Use your completed diagram to explain why $f^{-1}f$ is
   an identity function.

32. $f^{-1} : x \rightarrow x - 6$. Draw a function machine to show
   the *composition* of f^{-1} and f.
   What can you say about ff^{-1}?

33. $g : x \rightarrow 4x + 5$ and $h : x \rightarrow \dfrac{(x - 5)}{4}$
   (a) Draw function machines for g and h.
   (b) What is the connection between g and h?
   (c) Copy and complete the function machine
       below to show the *composition* of g and h.

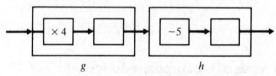

$\qquad\quad g \qquad\qquad\qquad h$

   (d) Use your completed diagram to explain
       (i) why h is the inverse of g and
       (ii) why the *composition* of g and h is an
            identity function.

34. Use your diagram in Question 33 (c) to explain why
   gh is also an identity function.

35. Look at the diagram for Question 29. Find:
   (a) $kh(4)$ (b) $hk(6)$ (c) $h^{-1}(9)$ (d) $h^{-1}h(1)$

36. Look at the diagram for Question 32. Find:
   (a) $f(2)$ (b) $f^{-1}(15)$ (c) $f^{-1}f(2)$ (d) $ff^{-1}(8)$

37. Using g and h as defined in Question 33 find:
   (a) $g(3)$ (b) $g^{-1}(13)$ (c) $g^{-1}g(1)$
   (d) $gg^{-1}(9)$ (e) $h(21)$ (f) $h^{-1}(5)$
   (g) $h^{-1}h(17)$ (h) $hh^{-1}(4)$
   Write as $x \rightarrow$, the rule for:
   (i) g^{-1} (j) h^{-1} (k) $g^{-1}g$ (l) hh^{-1}

38. $l : x \rightarrow 2x$, $m : x \rightarrow x + 1$, $n : x \rightarrow x^2$.
   Write as $x \rightarrow$, the rule for:
   (a) lm (b) ml (c) nm (d) mn
   (a) ln (f) nl (g) ll (h) mm

39. Using l, m and n as in Question 38.
   (a) find $mmm(7)$ and write down the rule for
       mmm.
   (b) show that: (i) $lm = mml$ (ii) $nl = lln$

40. Look at the function machines below.

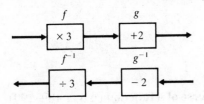

Write as $x \to$ the rule for:
(a) f (b) g (c) f^{-1} (d) g^{-1}
(e) the *composition* of f and g (i.e. gf)
(f) the *composition* of g^{-1} and f^{-1} (i.e. $f^{-1}g^{-1}$)
Do you agree that the inverse of gf is $f^{-1}g^{-1}$?

41. If $h : x \to 5x$ and $k : x \to x - 2$ find:
(a) kh and the inverse of kh
(b) k^{-1}, h^{-1} and the *composition* of k^{-1} and h^{-1}
   (i.e. $h^{-1}k^{-1}$)
Use function machines to show that the inverse of kh is $h^{-1}k^{-1}$.
Show also that the inverse of hk is the *composition* of h^{-1} and k^{-1} (i.e. $k^{-1}h^{-1}$).

In Question 41, kh is:

$x \to$ [h] $\longrightarrow$ [k] $\mapsto$ $hk(x)$

so the inverse of kh is

$h^{-1}k^{-1}(x)$ $\longleftarrow$ [h^{-1}] $\longleftarrow$ [k^{-1}] $\leftarrow x$

So $(kh)^{-1}$ is the same as $k^{-1}h^{-1}$

Self-inverse functions

42. Copy and complete the mapping diagram below for $f : x \to 4 - x$.

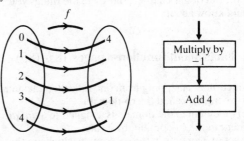

(a) Draw the mapping diagram for f^{-1} and write the rule for the inverse as $x \to$.
(b) Write down the rule for the machine shown above, and also for the reverse machine.
(c) Do the machine and mapping show the same function? Do you agree that $f^{-1} = f$?

In Question 42 you should have found that the rule for f^{-1} was $x \to 4 - x$. In this case the inverse is the same as the original function.
We call f a **self-inverse function.**

43. $g : x \to 6 - x$ and $h : x \to \dfrac{1}{x}$. Find:

(a) $g(5)$ and then $gg(5)$
(b) $g(2)$ and then $gg(2)$
(c) $h(3)$ and then $hh(3)$
(d) $h(4)$ and then $hh(4)$
What can you say about the function described by gg and hh? What is special about the functions g and h?

Summary

By the end of this chapter, these are the things you should know about:

2.1 Facts about functions (pages 185–186)

A function is a mapping from one set called the **domain** to a second set called the **co-domain**.

Every element in the domain is assigned to a *unique* element in the co-domain, by a rule.

The set of elements in the co-domain which are the images of elements in the domain is called the **range** or **image set.**

Only M–1 or 1–1 mappings are functions.

The rule for a function f may be given as:
$$f : x \rightarrow 2x + 3$$
or as $f(x) = 2x + 3$
but the function is not fully defined until the domain is stated.

You can show a function in any of these ways:
  (i) by drawing a mapping diagram
  (ii) by stating its rule and its domain
  (iii) by listing the ordered pairs
  (iv) by showing the ordered pairs as a graph.

2.2 Some special functions (pages 187–188)

You should be able to tell whether a mapping is a function.

Only 1–1 or M–1 mappings are functions.

One arrow must go from *each* member of the domain.

A 1–1 mapping of a set onto itself is a rearrangement or **permutation** of the elements of the set.

In a **constant function**, every element maps to the same single element,
  e.g. $f : x \rightarrow k$ where k is a constant.

The graph of a constant function is a horizontal line or set of points.

In an **identity function,** every element maps to itself,
  e.g. $f : x \rightarrow x$.

The graph of an identity function is a line or set of points at 45° to the horizontal.

2.3 The inverse of a function (pages 189–190)

The **inverse** of a function is obtained by reversing the arrows in a mapping diagram.

The inverse is a function only if the original function was 1–1 with an arrow to each element of the co-domain.

The inverse of function f is called f^{-1}.

You can find the rule for the inverse of a function by drawing the function machine and then the reverse function machine.

2.4 The composition of functions
(pages 191–194)

The **composition** of functions f and g means:
do f first, then g. It is written as gf.

If you do g first, then f, the composite function is fg.

You should be able to write down the rule for gf given the rule for f and for g.
$$\text{e.g. } f : x \rightarrow 2x + 1, g : x \rightarrow 3x - 2$$
$$fg(x) = f(3x - 2) = 2(3x - 2) + 1$$
$$= 6x - 3$$

2.5 Composition and inverse (pages 194–197)

You should be able to draw function machines and their reverse machines to find the inverse of more complicated functions.

You should be able to use the idea of a composite function and its inverse to help you solve linear equations.

You should know that the composition of a function and its inverse is an identity function, i.e. $f^{-1}f = i$, and that the inverse of the composite function (fg) is $g^{-1}f^{-1}$.

You should understand the idea of a *self-inverse* function, e.g. $f : x \rightarrow \dfrac{1}{x}$

3 Graphs 3

3.1 Revision

Straight line graphs

The graph below shows part of the line $y = 2x + 1$.

A table of values for this graph is

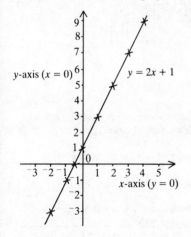

A table of values for this graph is

x	$^-2$	$^-1$	0	1	2	3	4
y	$^-3$	$^-1$	1	3	5	7	9

Each pair of values in the table are the co-ordinates of a point on the line.
i.e. the points are:
$(^-2, ^-3), (^-1, ^-1), (0, 1), (1, 3), (2, 5), (3, 7), (4, 9)$

The equation $y = 2x + 1$ describes this set of ordered pairs.

1. Represent each set of ordered pairs as a graph:
   (a) $(0, 2), (1, 3), (2, 4), (3, 5), (4, 6), (5, 7), (6, 8)$
   (b) $(^-2, ^-4), (^-1, ^-2), (0, 0), (1, 2), (2, 4), (3, 6), (4, 8)$
   (c) $(0, ^-1), (1, 2), (2, 5), (3, 8), (4, 11), (5, 14), (6, 17)$
   (d) $(^-1, 7), (0, 6), (1, 5), (2, 4), (3, 3), (4, 2), (5, 1), (6, 0)$

2. For each part of Question 1 write down the (x, y) equation which describes the set of ordered pairs.

3. Copy and complete the table of values for each equation:

x	$^-2$	$^-1$	0	1	2	3	4	5	6
y									

   (a) $y = x + 3$ (b) $y = 3x$
   (c) $y = 2x + 3$ (d) $y = 7 - x$

4. For each part of Question 3 show the information as a graph. In what ways are these four graphs similar to those you drew in Question 1?

5. Write down the (x, y) equation which describes the set of ordered pairs:
   (a) $(^-2, 3), (^-1, 4), (0, 5), (1, 6), (2, 7), (3, 8), (4, 9), (5, 10), (6, 11)$
   (b) $(^-3, ^-12), (^-2, ^-8), (^-1, ^-4), (0, 0), (1, 4), (2, 8), (3, 12), (4, 16), (5, 20)$
   (c) $(^-1, 6), (0, 5), (1, 4), (2, 3), (3, 2), (4, 1), (5, 0), (6, ^-1)$
   (d) $(0, ^-2), (1, 1), (2, 4), (3, 7), (4, 10), (5, 13), (6, 16)$
   (e) $(^-3, 16), (^-2, 14), (^-1, 12), (0, 10), (1, 8), (2, 6), (3, 4), (4, 2), (5, 0)$
   (f) $(^-2, 2), (0, 3), (2, 4), (4, 5), (6, 6), (8, 7)$

6. Complete a table of values as in Question 3 for each equation:
(a) $y = 5x - 3$ (b) $y = 4 - 3x$
(c) $y = \frac{1}{2}x + \frac{1}{2}$ (d) $y = 3(x - 2)$

7. For each part of Questions 5 and 6 draw the corresponding graph. Which graphs are similar?

8. What point is common to the graphs in Question 6 (b) and 6 (c)?

Quadratic graphs

9. (a) Complete the table of values below.

x	$^-2$	$^-1$	0	1	2	3
x^2	4					9
$x^2 - 2$	2					7

(b) Use your table to plot the graph of $y = x^2 - 2$ for values of x from $^-2$ to 3. Join these points with a smooth curve.
(c) For what values of x does your curve cross the x-axis?

10. (a) Plot a graph of $y = x^2$ for values of x from $^-4$ to $^+4$. Join the points with a smooth curve.
(b) Now plot the image of this graph, after a translation described by the vector $\begin{pmatrix} 0 \\ 4 \end{pmatrix}$.
(c) By looking at the co-ordinates of its points, work out the equation of the image graph.

11. Complete the table of values below for each of the given equations.

x	$^-5$	$^-4$	$^-3$	$^-2$	$^-1$	0	1	2	3	4	5
y											

(a) $y = x^2 - 1$ (b) $y = x^2 - 4$
(c) $y = x^2 - 7$

12. (a) For each function in Question 11 draw the quadratic graph. Label the graphs [1], [2] and [3].
(b) For each graph, find where $y = 0$.
(c) Use your answers to find a value for $\sqrt{7}$.

13. (a) In what ways are your curves in Question 12 similar?
(b) How would you move the first curve to obtain the other two? Is the movement a translation?
(c) Write a vector to describe the translation of curve [1] to curve [3].
(d) Write a vector to describe the translation of curve [3] to curve [2].

14. (a) Complete the table below for $y = 4 - x^2$.

x	$^-5$	$^-4$	$^-3$	$^-2$	$^-1$	0	1	2	3	4	5
y											

(b) Now draw the graph for $y = 4 - x^2$. For what values of x is $y = 0$?
(c) What is the connection between this graph and the graph for $y = x^2 - 4$, from Question 11 (b)?

The shapes of quadratic graphs

In general:
the curve for a quadratic expression with a *positive* x^2 term is ∪-shaped;
the curve for a quadratic expression with a *negative* x^2 term is ∩-shaped.

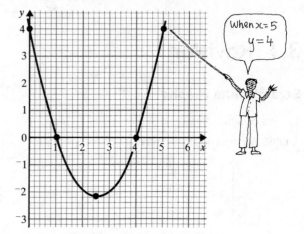

When $x = 5$
$y = 4$

15. Look at the graph above.
(a) Write down the co-ordinates of the five points. Check that they satisfy the equation $y = x^2 - 5x + 4$.
(b) What is the value of y, at each point on the x-axis?
(c) For what values of x is $x^2 - 5x + 4 = 0$?

16. Complete the table below for $y = 6 + x - x^2$

x	$^-5$	$^-4$	$^-3$	$^-2$	$^-1$	0	1	2	3	4	5
y											

(a) Now draw the graph for $y = 6 + x - x^2$
(b) For what values of x is $6 + x - x^2 = 0$?

17. Complete the table of values below for each of the given equations.

x	$^-3$	$^-2$	$^-1$	0	1	2	3	4	5	6
y										

(a) $y = x^2 + 2x - 8$ (e) $y = 2x^2 + 3x - 2$
(b) $y = x^2 + x - 6$ (f) $y = 3x^2 - 10x - 8$
(c) $y = x^2 + 3x - 10$ (g) $y = 6 - x - 2x^2$
(d) $y = x^2 - 2x - 3$ (h) $y = 21 + 5x - 6x^2$

18. (a) Draw the graph for each quadratic equation in Question 17.
(b) For each graph find the values of x for which $y = 0$.

3.2 Graphs of functions

1. Copy and complete the table for $f : x \rightarrow 2x + 3$.

x	0	1	2	3	4	5
$f(x)$						

Draw a graph of this function with the domain {all numbers from 0 to 5}.

Your graph in Question 1 should be a straight line. This is called a **linear function**.

2. Is the function in Question 1 a 1–1 function? Is its inverse also a function? What is:
(a) the rule for f^{-1} (b) $f^{-1}(11)$?

3. Look at the graph and use it to complete the table below.

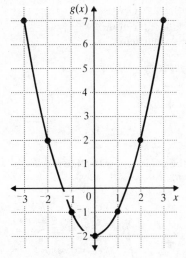

x	$^-3$	$^-2$	$^-1$	0	1	2	3
$g(x)$					$^-1$		

Show that the graph and your table of values fit the rule $g : x \rightarrow x^2 - 2$.

4. (a) Do you agree that the graph in Question 3 represents a function?
(b) What is the domain of g?
(c) What is the image set of g?
(d) What can you say about $g\,(^-3)$ and $g(3)$?
(e) Is g a 1–1 or a M–1 function?
(f) For what x is $g(x) = 2$?
(g) Explain why the inverse of g is not a function.

The rule for the function in Question 3 includes an x^2 term. The graph is a ∪-shaped curve.
This is called a **quadratic function.**

5. Copy and complete the table for $h : x \to x^3$.

x	$^-3$	$^-2$	$^-1$	0	1	2	3
$h(x)$		$^-8$			1		27

Draw a graph of this function taking as the domain {all numbers from $^-3$ to 3}.

6. Is your graph in Question 5:
   (a) a straight line   (b) a ∪-shaped curve
   (c) neither of the above?

7. (a) What is the range for h in Question 5?
   (b) Is h a 1–1 or a M–1 function?
   (c) Do you agree that the inverse of h is a
      function?
   (d) What is the domain of h^{-1}?
   (e) Can you suggest the rule for h^{-1}?

You should have found that the graph in Question 5
was   -shaped.

The rule for h includes an x^3 term.
This is called a **cubic function.**

cubics make better slides too!

8. (a) Look at the graph. Show that the marked
     points fit the rule $x \to 2^x$.

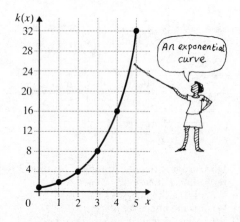
An exponential curve

   (b) What is the domain of k?
   (c) What is the image set of k?
   (d) Find (i) $k(3)$ (ii) $k(4)$
   (e) Is the inverse of k also a function?

The rule for k has x as an index (or exponent).
This is called an **exponential function.**

3.3 Graphs of inequalities

Lines and regions

1. Look at the graph below. Do you agree that each of
the points shown on the line make the statement
$x + y = 8$ true?

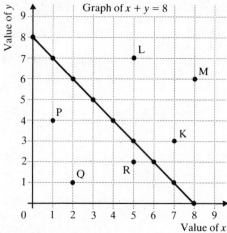
Graph of $x + y = 8$

   (a) Write down the values of $x + y$ at each of the
     points P, Q, and R.
   (b) Write down the values of $x + y$ at each of the
     points K, L and M.
   (c) How do your values in (a) and (b) differ from
     those on the line?

2. (a) Choose two more points below the line in
     Question 1. Find $x + y$. Do you agree that at
     each of these points $x + y < 8$?
   (b) Choose two more points above the line in
     Question 1. Find $x + y$. Do you agree that at
     each of these points $x + y > 8$?

3. (a) Do you agree that the points on the grid below
     show all the ways that a total score of 7 can be
     made, when rolling two dice?

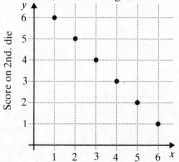

   (b) Copy this grid and mark on it all the points
     representing: (i) a total score less than 7
                 (ii) a total score greater than 7.
   What do you notice?

You should have found in Question 3 that the points representing *a total score less than 7* all lie below the line of marked dots, and that the points representing *a total score greater than 7* all lie above the line.

Only the points on the line make $x + y = 7$. For the points below the line $x + y < 7$ while for the points above the line $x + y > 7$.

In Question 1, the line $x + y = 8$ divides the grid into two regions. In the region below the line, $x + y < 8$ at all points. In the region above the line, $x + y > 8$ at all points.

4. Look at the graph below. Write down the co-ordinates of the points P, Q, R, S, T, U, and V.

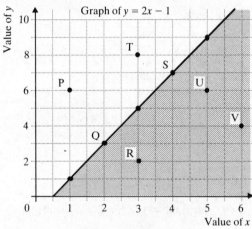

(a) For each of the seven points say whether $y > 2x - 1$ or $y < 2x - 1$ or $y = 2x - 1$
(b) Which of the three statements in (a) would you use to describe all the points:
   (i) in the shaded region?
   (ii) in the other region?
(c) Do you agree that $y = 2x + 1$ for all the points on the line that separates the two regions?

5. For which of the points P $(4, 3)$, Q$(4, 5)$, R$(6, 7)$, S$(0, 3)$, T$(2, 1)$, U$(4, 1)$, V$(5, 2)$ and W$(0, 1)$ is:
   (a) $y = x + 1$ (b) $y < x + 1$ (c) $y > x + 1$?

6. Use your answers for Question 5 to say which of the points:
   (a) lie on the line $y = x + 1$
   (b) lie on the same side of the line $y = x + 1$

7. Draw a graph of the line and shade in one side to show the required region:
   (a) line $x + y = 5$, region $x + y > 5$
   (b) line $y = 3x + 1$, region $y < 3x + 1$

Intersecting regions

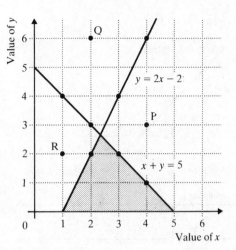

In the diagram above, the point P $(4, 3)$ lies between the lines $y = 2x - 2$ and $x + y = 5$. It lies in the region $y < 2x - 2$, since $3 < 2 \times 4 - 2$. It also lies in the region $x + y > 5$, since $4 + 3 > 5$.
So P lies in the region where

$$x + y > 5 \text{ and } y < 2x - 2$$

8. (a) Show that Q$(2, 6)$ lies in the region where $x + y > 5$ *and* $y > 2x - 2$.
   (b) Show that R $(1, 2)$ lies in the region where $x + y < 5$ *and* $y > 2x - 2$.
   (c) Use a pair of inequalities to describe the shaded region on the graph above.

9. Write down the co-ordinates of two points on the graph above which lie in the region where $x + y < 5$ *and* $y < 2x - 2$.

10. Look at the graph below. Do you agree that the shaded region is where $y < 4$?

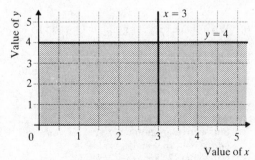

(a) Which part of the graph is the intersection of the regions where $y < 4$ and $x < 3$?
(b) Write down the co-ordinates of three points in the region where $y < 4$ *and* $x > 3$.

11. The shaded region below is the intersection of the regions to the right of line ①, above line ② and under line ③.

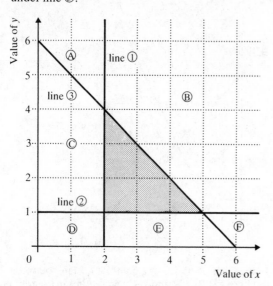

(a) Write down the equations of the three lines.
(b) Use three inequalities to describe the shaded region.

12. Each region of the graph above has a letter. Which letter represents the region where:
(a) $y < 1$ *and* $x < 2$
(b) $x < 2$ *and* $x + y > 5$
(c) $x > 2$ *and* $y > 1$ *and* $x + y > 5$
(d) $x < 2$ *anx* $y > 1$ *and* $x + y < 5$?

13. (a) Draw the line $x + y = 6$ on a graph. Shade the region where $x + y > 6$.
(b) On the same graph the line $y = 3x$.
Shade the region where $y > 3x$.
(c) On the same graph draw the line $y = x + 1$.
Shade the region where $y < x + 1$.

14. (a) What shape on your graph in Question 13 is left unshaded?
(b) Use three inequalities to describe this region.
(c) Does the point $(2, 3\frac{1}{2})$ lie within the region?

15. (a) On one graph draw the three lines $y = 4x$, $y = x + 2$ and $x + y = 8$.
(b) Shade in the region where $y < 4x$ *and* $y > x + 2$ *and* $x + y < 8$.
(c) Show that $(2, 5)$ lies within this region.

16. Find whole number values for x and y when $x + y > 2$ *and* $y < x + 1$ *and* $y > 2x - 3$.

Regions and inequalities

The graph of $y = x^2 - 4$ is shown

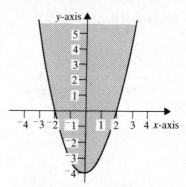

The points in the shaded region are where $y > x^2 - 4$.
The points on the curved line are where $y = x^2 - 4$.
The points in the unshaded region are where $y < x^2 - 4$.

17. Draw a sketch of the graph above and shade the region where:
(a) $y > x^2 - 4$ and $y < 0$
(b) $y > x^2 - 4$ and $y > 2$
(c) $y < x^2 - 4$ and $y > 0$
(d) $y < x^2 - 4$ and $y - 2$

18. Sketch the graph of $y = 3 - x^2$ and shade in the region where:
(a) $y < 3 - x^2$ and $y > 0$
(b) $y < 3 - x^2$ and $y < -1$
(c) $y > 3 - x^2$ and $y < 0$
(d) $y > 3 - x^2$ and $y > 1$

19. Sketch the graphs of $y = x^2 - 2$ and $y = x$ on the same piece of paper. Shade the region where:
(a) $y > x^2 - 2$ and $y < x$
(b) $y \leqslant x^2 - 2$ and $y > x$

20. Sketch the graphs of $y = x^2$ and $x + y = 4$ on the same piece of paper. Shade the region where:
(a) $y < x^2$ and $x + y > 4$
(b) $y \geqslant x^2$ and $x + y \leqslant 4$

21. The graphs of $y = 6/x$ and $x + y = 7$ are shown below.

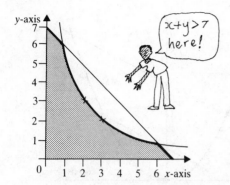

Copy the graph and shade the region where:
(a) $y > 6/x$ and $x + y < 7$
(b) $y < 6/x$ and $x + y \geq 7$
Describe the region shaded on the graph, including the heavy lines.

22. The graphs of $y = (x - 1)^2$ and $y = 4 - x^2$ are shown below.

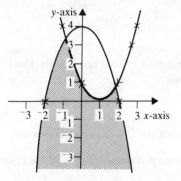

Copy the graph and shade the region where:
(a) $y \leq 4 - x^2$ and $y > (x - 1)^2$
(b) $y > 4 - x^2$ and $y < (x - 1)^2$
Describe the region shaded on the graph, including the heavy line.

23. Sketch the graphs of $y = 4 - x^2$ and $y = \dfrac{6}{x}$, for

$0 < x < 5$. Shade the region where:

(a) $y \leq 4 - x^2$ and $y \geq \dfrac{6}{x}$

(b) $y \geq 4 - x^2$ and $y < \dfrac{6}{x}$

3.4 Finding roots using graphs

1. Look at the graph below. Check that the co-ordinates of each of the seven marked points fit the equation $y = x^2 - 6x + 8$.

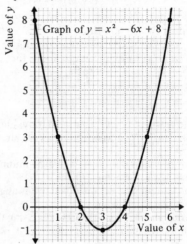

For what values of x is:
(a) $y = 3$ (b) $y = 8$ (c) $y = 0$ (d) $y = {}^-1$?

2. Use your answers to Question 1 to write down the solutions of:
(a) $x^2 - 6x + 8 = 0$ (b) $x^2 - 6x + 8 = 3$
(c) $x^2 - 6x + 8 = -1$ (d) $x^2 - 6x = 0$

3. (a) Copy and complete the table below.

x	0	1	2	3	4	5	6
x^2	0			9			36
$6x$	0		12	18			
$x^2 - 6x + 5$	5			$^-4$			

(b) Use your table above to draw the graph of $y = x^2 - 6x + 5$ for values of x from 0 to 6.
(c) On your graph draw the lines $y = 5, y = 0, y = {}^-3$ and $y = {}^-4$.
(d) Write down the co-ordinates of the points where the lines in (c) meet the curve $y = x^2 - 6x + 5$.

4. Use your answers to Question 3 to write down the solutions for:
(a) $x^2 - 6x + 5 = 0$ (b) $x^2 - 6x + 5 = -3$
(c) $x^2 - 6x + 5 = -4$ (d) $x^2 - 6x = 0$

5. (a) Explain how you used the graphs in Question 3 and 4 to solve the equation $x^2 - 6x = 0$.
(b) How could you use these graphs to solve the equation $x^2 - 6x + 3 = 0$?

Example 1

Use a graphical method to solve the equations:
(i) $x^2 - 7x + 10 = 0$
(ii) $x^2 - 7x + 6 = 0$

You could solve the first equation by drawing the graph of $y = x^2 - 7x + 10 = 0$ and then finding the values of x for which $y = 0$ (i.e. where the graph crosses the x-axis).

The second equation can be written as $x^2 - 7x + 10 = 4$. You could solve this equation by finding the values of x on the graph above for which $y = 4$ (i.e. by finding where the line $y = 4$ meets the curve $y = x^2 - 7x + 10$).

6. (a) Draw the graph of $y = x^2 - 7x + 10$ for values of x from 0 to 7. (You will need to show values of y from $^-3$ to 10).
  (b) Solve the equation $x^2 - 7x + 10 = 0$ by finding the values of x for which $y = 0$.
  (c) Solve the equation $x^2 - 7x + 6 = 0$ by finding the values of x for which $y = 4$.
  (d) Check your answers for (b) and (c) by using the factorization method.

7. (a) Copy and complete the table below.

x	0	1	2	3	4	5	6
$4x^2$							
$8x$							
$4x^2 - 8x + 3$							

  (b) Use your table above to draw the graph of $y = 4x^2 - 8x + 3$ for values of x from 0 to 6.
  (c) Use your completed graph to solve the equation $4x^2 - 8x + 3 = 0$.
  (d) Check your answers for (c) by using the factorization method.

8. (a) Make a table of values for $y = x^2 - 2x$ for values of x from $^-3$ to 5.
  (b) Draw the graph of $y = x^2 - 2x$.
  (c) Use your graph to solve:
  (i) $x^2 - 2x = 3$ (ii) $x^2 - 2x - 8 = 0$
  (iii) $x^2 - 2x - 15 = 0$ (iv) $x^2 - 2x = 0$
  (v) $x^2 - 2x + 1 = 0$ (vi) $x^2 - 2x = -2$
  Which of these equations have just one solution?
  Which of them have no solution?

I thought all quadratics had two solutions

Are you talking about real solutions?

The graphs of $y = x^2$, $y = x + 6$ and $y = x + 2$ are shown below.

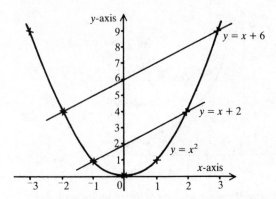

The solutions of the equation $x^2 = x + 6$ are given by the x co-ordinates of the points where the graphs of $y = x^2$ and $y = x + 6$ meet, i.e. when $x = ^-2$ or when $x = 3$.

9. Draw your copy of the graph above, and use it to write down the solutions of:
  (a) $x^2 = x + 2$ (b) $x^2 = 6$
  (c) $x^2 = 2$ (d) $x + 6 = 7$.

10. Show the lines $y = x$, $y = 6 - x$ and $y = 2 - x$ on your graph in Question 9, and hence write down the solutions of:
  (a) $x^2 = x$ (b) $x^2 = 6 - x$
  (c) $x^2 = 2 - x$ (d) $6 - x = x + 2$.

11. Draw the graph of $y = x^2 - 2x$ with the domain $^-3 \leqslant x \leqslant 5$.
  Draw on the same graph the lines $y = 8$, $y = x$, and $y = x + 4$.
  Hence write down the solutions of:
  (a) $x^2 - 2x = 8$
  (b) $x^2 - 2x = x$
  (c) $x^2 - 2x = x + 4$.

12. Draw the graph of $y = x^2 - 4x + 3$ with the domain $^-1 \leqslant x \leqslant 5$. Draw on the same graph the lines $y = 8$, $y = x - 1$, and $y = 7 - x$.
  Hence write down the solutions of:
  (a) $x^2 - 4x + 3 = 8$ (b) $x^2 - 4x + 3 = x - 1$
  (c) $x^2 - 4x + 3 = 7 - x$.

13. By drawing the graph of one curve and three lines solve:
  (a) $x^2 - 3x - 4 = 6$ (b) $x^2 - 3x - 4 = x + 1$
  (c) $x^2 - 3x - 4 = 4 - x$.

14. Use a graphical method to find the solution set for:
  (a) $8 - x^2 = 4$ (b) $8 - x^2 = x - 4$
  (c) $8 - x^2 = 6 - x$.

15. Draw your own copy of the graph shown below.

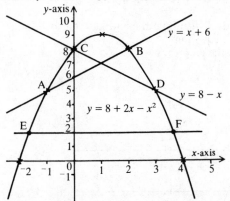

Use your graph to write down an equation which has as its solutions:
(a) $x = {}^-1$ and $x = 2$ (use the points A and B)
(b) $x = 0$ and $x = 3$ (use the points C and D)
(c) the x co-ordinates of the points E and F.

16. Use your graph in Question 15 to solve:
$8 + 2x - x^2 = 4 - x$.

17. By drawing two graphs, solve the simultaneous equations:
$y = x^2 + 3$ and $y = 4x$.

Example 2

Use a graphical method to solve $\dfrac{3}{x} = x - 2$

Hence write down the solution set for $x^2 - 2x - 3 = 0$.

The graph of $y = \dfrac{3}{x}$ meets $y = x - 2$

at the points where $x = 3$ and $x = {}^-1$.

$\dfrac{3}{x} = x - 2$ can be re-written as:

$x^2 - 2x - 3 = 0$. Its solution set is $\{{}^-1, 3\}$.

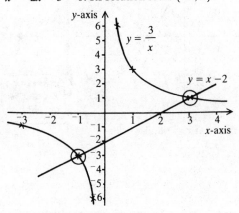

---

18. Draw the graphs of $y = \dfrac{9}{x}$, $y = x$, and $y = 3x$.

Hence find the solution set for:
(a) $\dfrac{9}{x} = 3$ (b) $\dfrac{9}{x} = x$ (c) $\dfrac{9}{x} = 3x$.

19. Draw the graphs of $y = \dfrac{10}{x}$, $y = x + 3$, and

$y = x - 3$. Hence find the solution set for:
(a) $\dfrac{10}{x} = x + 3$ (b) $\dfrac{10}{x} = x - 3$.

20. Show that your results for Question 19 can be used to find the solution sets for:
(a) $x^2 + 3x - 10 = 0$ (b) $x^2 - 3x - 10 = 0$

21. Draw the graphs of $y = x^2 - 1$ and $y = 2x - x^2$ using a scale of 5 cm to 1 unit on the x-axis. Hence find, as accurately as you can, the solution set for $2x^2 - 2x - 1 = 0$.

22. Make an accurate graph of the curve $y = x^3$ shown below.

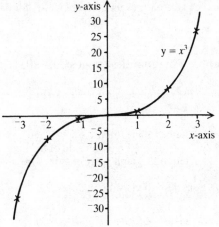

Use your graph to find the solution set for:
(a) $x^3 = x$ (b) $x^3 = 4x$ (c) $x^3 = 9x$

23. Use your graph in Question 22 to find the solution set for:

$$x^3 = 7x - 6$$

Show that this equation can also be written as:

$$(x - 1)(x^2 + x - 6) = 0$$

Hence find the solution set for $x^2 + x - 6 = 0$.

Summary

By the end of this chapter these are the things you should know about.

3.1 Revision (pages 199–201)

How to complete a table of values for equations such as $y = 2x + 3$ or $y = x^2 - 2$
How to draw straight line and quadratic graphs.
How to find values of x when $y = 0$.
The idea that a positive x^2 quadratic is $\cup$ shaped and a negative x^2 quadratic is $\cap$ shaped.

3.2 Graphs of functions (pages 201–202)

A **linear function** has a rule such as $x \to 2x + 3$.
A **quadratic function** has a rule with an x^2 term.
A **cubic function** has a rule with an x^3 term.
An **exponential function** has a rule such as $x \to 2^x$.
You should be able to draw up tables of values for each type of function, and plot their graphs.

3.3 Graphs of inequalities (pages 202–205)

How to show the region on a graph defined by an inequality e.g. $x + y < 8$

If $x + y = 8$ describes a line, then $x + y < 8$ and $x + y > 8$ describe regions on either side of the line.
Describing regions on a graph using one or more inequalities.
Shading regions described by inequalities.

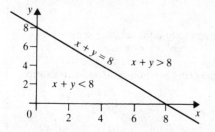

3.4 Finding roots using graphs (pages 205–207)

How to use a quadratic graph to solve the associated quadratic equation.
e.g. Plot the graph of $y = x^2 - 4$
Hence solve:
(a) $x^2 - 4 = 0$ (b) $x^2 - 4 = 2$

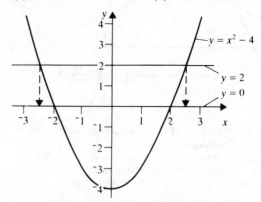

Solutions of $x^2 - 4 = 0$ occur where $y = x^2 - 4$ and $y = 0$ meet.

i.e. $x = {}^-2$ and $x = 2$

Solutions of $x^2 - 4 = 2$ occur where $y = x^2 - 4$ and $y = 2$ meet.

i.e. $x = {}^-2.4$ and $x = 2.4$

How to solve simultaneous equations such as

$y = x^2 - 3x + 2$ and $y = x - 1$

using the intersection of two graphs.

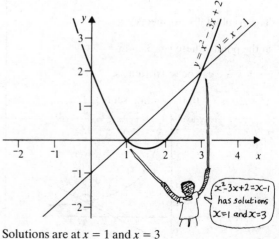

$x^2 - 3x + 2 = x - 1$
has solutions
$x = 1$ and $x = 3$

Solutions are at $x = 1$ and $x = 3$

4 Gradients

4.1 Gradients of straight lines

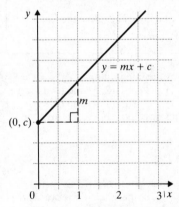

Any line whose equation is in the form

$$y = mx + c$$

crosses the y-axis at the point $(0, c)$.

This point is called the y-**intercept**.
The value of m tells you how steep the line is.
This value of m is called the **gradient** of the line.

1. On a graph like the one above draw the lines with equations:
   (a) $y = 2x + 1$; $y = 2x + 4$; $y = 2x - 1$
   (b) $y = x - 3$; $y = 3x - 3$; $y = \frac{1}{2}x - 3$

2. Do you agree that each of the lines:
   (a) in Question 1 (a) has a gradient of 2
   (b) in Question 1 (b) has a y-intercept of ⁻3?

3. Which line in Question 1(b) is the steepest?

4. For each line in Question 1 (a) write down the co-ordinates of the y-intercept.

5. For each line in Question 1 (b) write down the value of the gradient.

6. The equation of the third line in Question 1 (b) can also be written as $2y = x - 6$.
What must you do with the equation $2y = x - 6$ before you can find the y-intercept and the gradient of the line?

Example 1

Find the y-intercept and the gradient of:
   (i) the line $2y = x - 6$
   (ii) the line $3x + 2y = 6$

To do this each equation must be rewritten in the form $y = \square x + \square$.

   (i) For $2y = x - 6$, this can be done by dividing each side of the equation by 2.
   This gives $y = \frac{1}{2}x - 3$. Therefore the y-intercept is $(0, -3)$ and the gradient is $\frac{1}{2}$.

   (ii) $3x + 2y = 6$ must first be rewritten as $2y = -3x + 6$.
   Each side is then divided by 2, which gives $y = -\frac{3}{2}x + 3$.
   The y-intercept is $(0, 3)$. The gradient is $-\frac{3}{2}$.

---

7. By rewriting the equation in the form of $y = \square x + \square$, find the y-intercept and gradient.
   (a) $2y = 4x + 6$ (b) $2y = 6x - 4$
   (c) $3y = 4x + 1$ (d) $4x + 2y = 8$
   (e) $3x + 6y = 2$ (f) $2y - 4x = -5$

Finding gradients

The gradient of a line tells us how steep it is.
In other words it tells how the value of y increases when
the value of x increases.

The **gradient of a line** is defined as:

$$\frac{\text{the increase in the value of } y}{\text{the corresponding increase in the value of } x}$$

Example 2

Find the gradient of the line joining the points
$(1, 3)$ and $(5, 11)$.

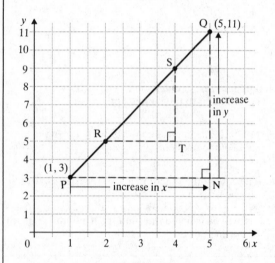

You can find the gradient of this line by first
drawing the right-angled triangle PQN and then
finding:

$$\frac{\text{the increase in } y}{\text{the increase in } x} = \frac{11 - 3}{5 - 1} = \frac{8}{4} = 2$$

Since line PQ is straight, each part of it has the
same gradient. So you could find its gradient
using *any* right-angled triangle on the line. For
example, using triangle RST above:

$$\frac{\text{the increase in } y}{\text{the increase in } x} = \frac{ST}{TR} = \frac{9 - 5}{4 - 2} = 2$$

---

8. By first drawing a diagram like the one above, find
the gradient of the line joining:
(a) $(1, 2)$ and $(3, 6)$ (b) $(1, 4)$ and $(3, 10)$
(c) $(4, 1)$ and $(5, 3)$ (d) $(3, 1)$ and $(5, 2)$

9. Use a diagram like the one above to show that the
gradient of the line joining the points (x_1, y_1) and

(x_2, y_2) is $\dfrac{y_2 - y_1}{x_2 - x_1}$.

Example 3

Find the gradient of the line joining the points
$(1, 5)$ and $(5, 3)$.

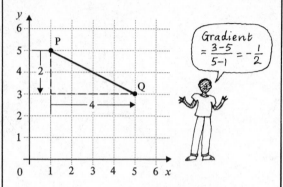

The line PQ above slopes down to the right.
As the value of x increases from 1 to 5 the value
of y *decreases* from 5 to 3. We say the *increase* in
y is -2. The gradient of the line PQ is:

$$\frac{\text{the increase in } y}{\text{the increase in } x} = \frac{-2}{4} = -\frac{1}{2}$$

When the gradient of a line is negative the line
slopes down to the right.

---

10. Find the gradient of the line joining:
(a) $(1, 6)$ and $(3, 2)$ (b) $(2, 5)$ and $(4, 1)$
(c) $(2, 7)$ and $(3, 9)$ (d) $(1, 8)$ and $(3, 7)$
Which of these lines has a positive gradient?

Parallel lines

Parallel lines have the same gradient.
$y = 2x + 3$ and $y = 2x - 1$ are parallel. They both have
a gradient of 2.
$y = 3x + 2$ and $y = -3x + 1$ are *not* parallel. Their
gradients are 3 and -3, which are not the same.

11. Find the gradient of the line joining:
(a) $(1, 2)$ and $(3, 6)$ (b) $(1, 3)$ and $(3, 4)$
(c) $(1, 4)$ and $(2, 2)$ (d) $(1, 4)$ and $(4, 10)$
(e) $(2, 5)$ and $(6, 7)$ (f) $(2, 7)$ and $(5, 1)$

12. Which pairs of lines in Question 11:
(a) are parallel
(b) have the same gradient as $y = -2x + 3$?

13. Which of these lines have the same gradient?
(a) $y = 2x + 3$ (b) $y = 4x + 3$ (c) $y = 2x + 4$
(d) $y = 4x - 3$ (e) $y = 2x - 3$ (f) $y = 4x - 4$

14. Which pairs of lines in Question 13 pass through
the same point on the y-axis?

15. Which of these lines are parallel to $y = 3x - 2$?
(a) $y = 2x - 3$ (b) $y = 3x + 2$ (c) $y = 2x - 2$
(d) $y = 3x - 3$ (e) $y = 2x + 3$ (f) $y = 3x + 3$

16. Which of the lines in Question 15 has the same y-intercept as $y = 3x - 2$?

17. For each table below, write down the equation of the line as $y = \Box\,x + \Box$.

(a)
x	0	1	2	3	4	5	6	7
y	3	4	5	6	7	8	9	10

(b)
x	0	1	2	3	4	5	6	7
y	−1	4	9	14	19	24	29	34

(c)
x	0	1	2	3	4	5	6	7
y	3	8	13	18	23	28	33	38

(d)
x	0	1	2	3	4	5	6	7
y	5	8	11	14	17	20	23	26

18. Which pairs of lines in Question 17:
(a) have the same y-intercept
(b) are parallel?

19. Look at the diagram below. Write down the co-ordinates of:
(a) P   (b) Q   (c) R
What is the gradient of:
(d) PR   (e) PQ   (f) QR?

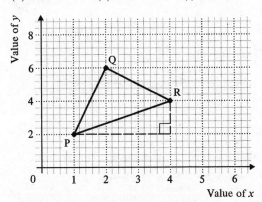

What is the length of each side of $\triangle$PQR?

20. What is (a) the gradient, and   (b) the length, of line PS where P is $(1, 2)$ and S is $(5, 5)$?

Perpendicular lines

21. Look at the diagram below.

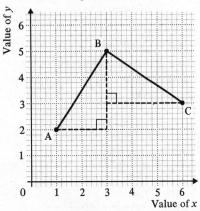

Do you agree that:
(a) the gradient of AB is $\dfrac{5 - 2}{3 - 1} = \dfrac{3}{2}$

(b) the gradient of BC is $\dfrac{3 - 5}{6 - 3} = -\dfrac{2}{3}$?

Find the lengths of AB, BC and AC and show that AB and BC form a right angle.

22. How are the gradients of AB and BC linked?

23. (a) Draw a diagram like the one above to show the points P$(4, 1)$, Q$(5, 4)$ and R$(1, 2)$.
(b) Find the gradients of PQ and PR.
(c) Find the lengths of PQ, PR and RQ and show that RP is at right angles to PQ.
(d) Do you agree that:
(gradient or PR) $\times$ (gradient of PQ) $= -1$?

You should have found in Questions 22 and 23 that if two lines are at right angles, then the product of their gradients is -1.

If $y = mx + c$ and $y = nx + d$ are two perpendicular lines, then $\boldsymbol{m \times n = -1}$.

24. Pick out the pairs of perpendicular lines:
(a) $y = 2x + 3$ (b) $y = 3x + 2$ (c) $y = -\frac{1}{2}x + 1$
(d) $y = \frac{1}{4}x - 1$ (e) $y = -4x + 5$ (f) $y = -\frac{1}{3}x + 4$

25. If P is $(3, 1)$, Q is $(7, 2)$ and R is $(6, 6)$ find the gradients of PQ, QR, and PR. Find which two lines are perpendicular and check your answer using Pythagoras.

4.2 Equations of straight lines

The **gradient of a straight line** is

$$\frac{\text{vertical rise between two points on the line}}{\text{horizontal shift between the same two points}}$$

The graph below shows the line $y = mx + c$.

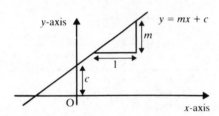

The c refers to the *intercept* on the y-axis, i.e. the line passes through the point $(0, c)$.

The m refers to the *gradient* of the line, i.e. the line rises m units for each unit increase in the direction of the x-axis.

1. Write down the co-ordinates of the marked points on each line in the graph shown below. Use this

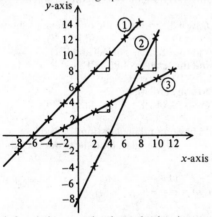

   information to write down the (x, y) equations of each line.

2. For each line in the graph of Question 1, write down:
   (a) the value of c, the intercept
   (b) the value of m, the gradient.

3. Use the information in Question 2 to write down the (x, y) equation of each line. Check your results with Question 1.

4. Use the values of m and c in each equation to *sketch* the graph of:
   (a) $y = 3x + 4$ (b) $y = 5x - 2$
   (c) $y = \frac{1}{2}x + 4$ (d) $y = -x + 3$

5. Write down the (x, y) equation of a line parallel to $y = 2x + 3$ which passes through:
   (a) $(0, 0)$ (b) $(0, 1)$ (c) $(0, 5)$
   (d) $(0, {}^-3)$ (e) $(0, \frac{3}{2})$

6. Write down the (x, y) equation of a line which passes through the point $(0, 2)$ and has a gradient of:
   (a) 3   (b) 5   (c) $\frac{1}{2}$ (d) -2 (e) 0

7. Write down the (x, y) equation of a line which:
   (a) passes through $(0, 5)$ and has a gradient of 3
   (b) passes through $(0, {}^-2)$ and has a gradient of 4
   (c) passes through $(0, 1)$ and has a gradient of -1

8. Find the gradient of a line which passes through:
   (a) $(0, 2)$ and $(1, 5)$ (b) $(0, 4)$ and $(2, 8)$
   (c) $(0, {}^-1)$ and $(1, 3)$ (d) $(0, {}^-3)$ and $(2, 5)$
   Hence write down the (x, y) equation of each line.

9. Find the mid-point of the line joining $(2, 3)$ and $(5, 7)$ and also the distance between the two points.

If you know the gradient of a line and the co-ordinates of any point on the line, then you can find its equation, as shown below.

Example 1

Find the equation of a line of gradient m which passes through the point (h, k).

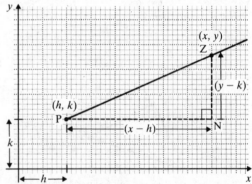

If Z is any point on the line then the gradient of the line ZP is given by: $\dfrac{y - k}{x - h}$

We are told the gradient of the line is m, so we can write the equation of the line as:

$$\frac{y - k}{x - h} = m, \text{ or} \qquad (y - k) = m(x - h)$$

The equation of the line which passes through $(1, 3)$ with a gradient of 2 can be found by substituting the values of h, k and m in the above formula, i.e.

$(y - 3) = 2(x - 1)$ *or* $y = 2x + 1$

10. Use the formula in Example 1 to find the equation of a line which passes through the point $(2, 1)$ and has a gradient of 3.

11. Show that the equation of the line in Question 10 can be written as: $y = 3x - 5$

12. Find the equation of the straight line which:
(a) passes through $(2, 3)$ with a gradient of 4
(b) passes through $(4, 1)$ with a gradient of 3
(c) passes through $(0, 3)$ with a gradient of 2
(d) passes through $(4, 3)$ with a gradient of $\frac{1}{2}$
(e) passes through $(1, 5)$ with a gradient of -2

Example 2

Find the equation of the line which passes through the points $(2, 5)$ and $(3, 9)$.

The gradient of this line is $\dfrac{9 - 5}{3 - 2} = \dfrac{4}{1} = 4$

The line has a gradient of 4 and passes through the point $(2, 5)$, so its equation is:
$(y - 5) = 4(x - 2)$ or $\qquad y = 4x - 3$

---

13. Show that the equation of the line with a gradient of 4 which passes through the point $(3, 9)$ can be written as: $y = 4x - 3$.

14. Find the equation of the line which passes through:
(a) $(4, 1)$ and $(6, 9)$ (b) $(0, 3)$ and $(4, 11)$
(c) $(4, 3)$ and $(8, 5)$ (d) $(1, 5)$ and $(2, 3)$

15. Show that the equation of the line which passes through the points (a, b) and (c, d) is:

$$(y - b) = \frac{(d - b)}{(c - a)}(x - a)$$

Example 3

Find the equation of the line which cuts the x-axis and y-axis at the points $(a, 0)$ and $(0, b)$.

The gradient of this line is $\dfrac{b - 0}{0 - a} = -\dfrac{b}{a}$

The equation is: $(y - 0) = -\dfrac{b}{a}(x - a)$

---

16. Show that the equation in the example above can be rewritten as $\dfrac{x}{a} + \dfrac{y}{b} = 1$. Use this to write down the equation of the line joining:
(a) $(3, 0)$ and $(0, 5)$ (b) $(4, 0)$ and $(0, 7)$
(c) $(2, 0)$ and $(0, {}^-5)$

17. Find the equation of the line passing through:
(a) $(1, 4)$ of gradient -2 (b) $(2, 2)$ and $(5, {}^-4)$
(c) $(3, 0)$ and $(0, 6)$.
What can you say about these lines?

4.3 Gradients of curves

So far you have found the gradients of straight lines. We shall now extend this idea to find the gradients of curves.

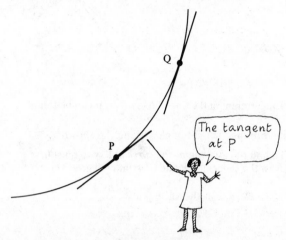

1. Look at the curve drawn above.
(a) Do you think the curve is steeper at point P or at point Q?
(b) Can you suggest a way to measure the gradient of the curve at P and at Q?

2. (a) Make a copy of the diagram above. Join points P and Q with a straight line.
(b) What can you say about the gradient of PQ compared with the gradients of the two straight lines draw at P and Q?
(c) How would you find the gradient of PQ?

A **tangent** to a curve at a point P is the line which just touches the curve at P.
So in the diagram above the lines drawn at P and Q are tangents to the curve at P and Q.

The **gradient** of a curve at any point is defined as the gradient of the tangent to the curve at that point.
So the gradient of the above curve at point P is the same as the gradient of the tangent at P. Its gradient at point Q is the same as the gradient of the tangent at Q.

A straight line joining P and Q on the curve above is called a **chord** of the curve.

You should have found that the gradient of chord PQ is greater than the gradient of the tangent at P but less than the tangent at Q.

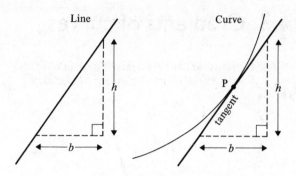

The gradient of the line above is $\dfrac{h}{b}$. It can be found

by forming the right-angled triangle as shown.

To find the gradient of the *curve* at P, you must first draw the tangent at P and then find the gradient

of the tangent as shown. It is also $\dfrac{h}{b}$.

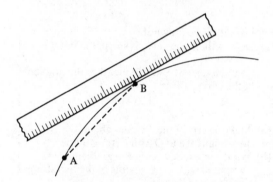

3. (a) Copy the curve above onto squared paper, and find the gradient of the chord AB.
   (b) Use a ruler to find the lines which just touch your curve at A and B. Mark these two tangents on your diagram and then find the gradient of each.
   (c) Do you agree that the gradient of the chord AB is less than the gradient of the tangent at A but greater than the gradient of the tangent at B?

4. (a) Copy and complete the table below for $y = x^2$, and then draw its graph:

x	0	1	2	3	4	5	6
y		1			16		

   (b) Find the gradient of the chord joining the points (1, 1) and (4, 16).
   (c) Use your ruler to draw the tangents to the curve at the points where $x = 1$ and $x = 4$.
   (d) Find the gradient of the two tangents you have drawn.

Distance – time graphs

The top speed of a new car is given as 160 km/h. This means that if the car travels at that speed for 1 hour, it goes a distance of 160 km; in half an hour it goes a distance of 80 km.

If you know how far a car has travelled in a given time, you can calculate its speed from the formula:

$$\text{speed} = \frac{\text{distance travelled}}{\text{time taken}}$$

This formula only tells you the *average* speed for the journey. It does not tell you the actual speed of the car at any instant.

Example 1

Find the average speed during the third hour of the car whose journey is shown below.

Graph of a car's journey over 6 hours

During the third hour the car travels 100 km. Therefore its average speed is 100 km/h, which is the gradient of the line BC.

---

5. By finding the gradient of each part of the graph above, find the average speed during:
   (a) the first hour   (b) the second hour
   (c) the fourth hour   (d) the last two hours
   During which hour of the journey was the average speed greatest? How can you tell this from the graph?

4.4 Rates of change

The gradient of a chord joining two points on a curve is the *average rate of change* of y with respect to x over the particular interval.

In the diagram this is $\dfrac{25 - 9}{5 - 3} = \dfrac{16}{2} = 8.$

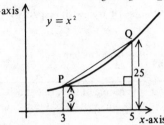

Note. To find the *average* rate of change over a particular interval, you must draw a *chord* and find its gradient, as shown above. However, to find the *actual* rate of change at a particular point you must draw a *tangent* to the curve at that point, and find its gradient.

Example 1

When a car travels 75 m in 3 s,
the *average rate of change* of distance with respect to time (i.e. speed) is $\frac{75}{3} = 25$ m/s.

When the speed of a car increases from 60 km/h to 80 km/h in 1 minute,
the *average rate of change* of speed with respect to time
(i.e. acceleration)

is $\dfrac{80 - 60}{\frac{1}{60}} = 1200$ km per hour per hour.

---

1. Find the gradient of the chord joining the points:
   (a) $(0, 0)$ and $(3, 12)$ (b) $(1, 2)$ and $(5, 10)$
   (c) $(^-3, 1)$ and $(1, 3)$

2. Find the average rate of change of y with respect to x, on the curve $y = x^3$ for the interval $x = 1$ to $x = 4$.

3. Find the gradient of the chord joining the points on $y = x^2 + x$ where:
   (a) $x = 0$ and $x = 3$ (b) $x = 6$ and $x = 7$
   (c) $x = 3$ and $x = 5$.

4. Find the average speed in km/h of a car which travels:
   (a) 150 km in $2\frac{1}{2}$ hours   (b) 12 km in 15 minutes
   (c) 126 m in 3 seconds.

5. Find the average acceleration in km/h² of a car whose speed changes from:
   (a) 72 km/h to 83 km/h in $\frac{1}{4}$ of an hour
   (b) 56 km/h to 59 km/h in 20 seconds.

Example 2

Find the average speed during the third hour and the actual speed at the beginning and end of the third hour for the car whose journey is shown below.

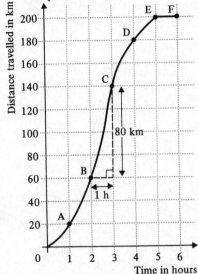

During the third hour the car travels 80 km. Its average speed is therefore 80 km/h. This is given by the gradient of chord BC.
The actual speed of the car at B or C is given by the gradient of the tangent to the curve at B or C.

---

6. (a) Carefully copy the graph above and use your ruler to draw the tangent at B.
   (b) Find the gradient of the tangent at B and the actual speed of the car at B.
   (c) Find the actual speed of the car at C.

7. (a) Find the gradients of chords OA, AB, CD, DE and EF on your copy of the graph.
   (b) Use these results to write down the average speed of the car during the first, second, fourth, fifth and sixth hours.
   (c) During which of the six hours was the average speed greatest? How can you tell from the graph?
   (d) In the last hour the car was stationary. How can you tell this from the gradient of EF?

8. (a) Draw your own graph for a car's journey over six or seven hours.
   (b) Find the average speed of the car during each hour of the journey.
   (c) By drawing tangents, find the actual speed of the car at one or two points.

Example 2

When the radius of a circle changes from 3cm to 3.1cm, the area of the circle increases from $9\pi\,\text{cm}^2$ to $9.61\pi\,\text{cm}^2$.

The *average rate of change* of area with respect to radius is therefore

$$\frac{9.61\pi - 9\pi}{3.1 - 3} = \frac{0.61\pi}{0.1} = 6.1\pi\,\text{cm}^2/\text{cm}.$$

6. Find the average rate of change of the area of a circle with respect to its radius when the radius changes from:
   (a) 5cm to 7cm   (b) 1.2cm to 1.5cm
   (c) 1.9cm to 2.1cm.

7. Find the average rate of change of the volume of a cube with respect to the length of its edge, if the edge length changes from:
   (a) 2cm to 6cm   (b) 1.1cm to 1.3cm
   (c) 0.7cm to 1.2cm

8. Find the average rate of change of the volume of a spherical bubble with respect to its radius when the radius changes from 3cm to 6cm. Find also the average rate of change of the volume with respect to time if the radius changes from 3cm to 6cm over half a second.

Gradients as rates of change

The gradient of the tangent to a curve at a particular point is a measure of *the rate of change* of y with respect to x at that point.

By drawing the tangent to the curve $y = x^2$ at the point $(5, 25)$ and measuring its gradient, we can find the rate of change of y with respect to x at point $(5, 25)$. This is shown in the diagram below.

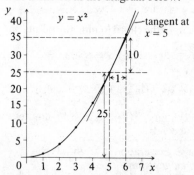

The gradient of the tangent is $\frac{10}{1} = 10$.
So when $x = 5$, the rate of change for $y = x^2$ is 10.

Example 3

The population of bacteria in a colony is given at time t by the formula $p = 3t^2 - 2t + 1$. Find the average rate of increase in the population during the third second. Find also the rate of increase after 3 seconds.

When $t = 2$, $p = 9$. When $t = 3$, $p = 22$. The average rate of increase during the

third second is $\dfrac{22 - 9}{1} = 13$.

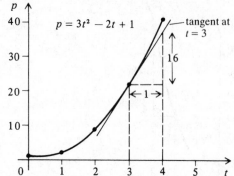

By drawing the curve $p = 3t^2 - 2t + 1$ and the tangent to the curve as shown in the diagram, we find the gradient of the tangent is 16. The rate of increase in the population after 3 seconds is 16.

9. Draw the graph of $y = x^2$, taking values of x from 0 to 8. Find the *average rate of change* of y with respect to x, between the points:
   (a) (2, 4) and (3, 9)   (b) (4, 16) and (5, 25)

10. Using your graph for Question 9, draw the tangent to the curve at the point (3, 9). Find the gradient of the tangent.

11. Draw the graph of $y = x^2 + x$, taking values of x from 0 to 8. By drawing the tangent at the appropriate point, find the rate of increase of y with respect to x at:
    (a) (2, 6)   (b) (3, 12)   (c) (5, 30)   (d) (7, 56)

12. Draw the curve $y = 3x^2 + 1$ for values of x from 0 to 8. Find the gradient of the tangent to the curve at the point:
    (a) (1, 4)   (b) (3, 28)   (c) (4, 49)   (d) (6, 109)

13. By drawing a graph for $A = \pi r^2$, find the rate of change of the area of a circle with respect to its radius when: (a) $r = 3$ (b) $r = 5$ (c) $r = 6$

14. By drawing a graph for $V = \frac{4}{3}\pi r^3$, find the rate of change of the volume of a sphere with respect to its radius, when: (a) $r = 2$ (b) $r = 4$ (c) $r = 5$

Summary

By the end of this chapter, these are the things you should know about:

4.1 Gradients of straight lines (pages 209–211)

When the equation of a straight line is given as $y = mx + c$, then the gradient of the line is m, and the point where it crosses the y-axis is $(0, c)$. This point is called the y-**intercept**.
How to rearrange equations like $2y = x - 6$ as $y = \frac{1}{2}x - 3$, to find the gradient (i.e. $\frac{1}{2}$).
The gradient of a line tells you how steep it is.
It is found from:

$$\frac{\text{the increase in the value of } y}{\text{the corresponding increase in the value of } x}$$

How to find the gradient of a line joining two points whose co-ordinates are given.
    For example if P is $(2, 3)$ and Q is $(5, 8)$, then:

$$\text{the gradient of PQ is } \frac{8 - 3}{5 - 2} = \frac{5}{2}$$

When lines are parallel their gradients are the same.
When two lines are perpendicular the product of their gradients is -1, e.g.
    $y = \frac{5}{2}x - 1$ and $y = -\frac{2}{5}x + 3$ are perpendicular since $-\frac{2}{5} \times \frac{5}{2} = -1$

4.2 Equations of straight lines (pages 212–213)

How to find the equation of a straight line from the y-intercept (c) and the gradient (m) in the form $y = mx + c$

How to find the equation of a line when one point on the line and its gradient are given:

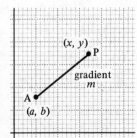

$$\frac{(y - b)}{(x - a)} = m \quad \text{so}$$

$$(y - b) = m(x - a)$$

How to find the equation of a line joining two points:

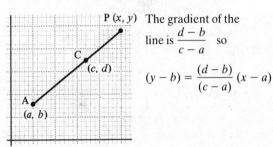

The gradient of the line is $\dfrac{d - b}{c - a}$ so

$$(y - b) = \frac{(d - b)}{(c - a)} (x - a)$$

How to find the equation of a line joining two points $(p, 0)$ and $(0, q)$:

$$\frac{x}{p} + \frac{y}{q} = 1$$

where p and q are the intercepts on the x and y axes.

4.3 Gradients of curves (pages 213–215)

How to find the gradient of the chord which joins two points on a curve.
The idea that the gradient of a curve at a point is the gradient of the tangent to the curve at that point.
How to use a ruler to draw the tangent to a curve at a point and hence find the gradient of the curve at that point.
The formula for finding the average speed of a car:

$$\text{speed} = \frac{\text{distance travelled}}{\text{time taken}}$$

The idea that the gradient of a chord on a distance-time graph gives the average speed for that time interval.
The idea that the gradient of a tangent at a point on a distance-time graph gives the actual speed at that point.

4.4 Rates of change (pages 215–216)

The idea that the gradient of the chord gives the average rate of change over an interval and that the gradient of the tangent at a particular point gives the actual rate of change at that point.
How to find average rates of change and actual rates of change by finding the gradients of chords and the gradients of tangents to curves.
How to apply these ideas to simple situations involving area and volume.

5 Transformations 2

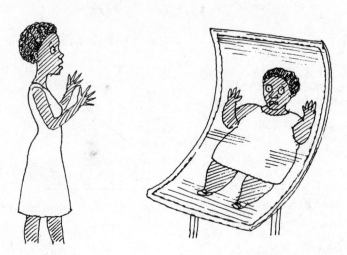

5.1 Revision

Reflections

When a point is reflected in a line, its image is the same perpendicular distance from the mirror line as the original point.

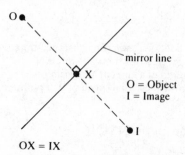

mirror line

O = Object
I = Image

OX = IX

The image of a reflection can be found by folding your paper along the mirror line or by drawing.

1. Find the images of the following points after reflection in the x-axis.
   (a) (2, 3)   (b) (⁻2, 3)   (c) (2, ⁻3)
   (d) (⁻2, ⁻3)   (e) (0, 0)

2. Find the images in Question 1 after reflection in the y-axis.

3. Find the image of the triangle A(2, 1), B(4, 1), C(4, 5) after reflection in:
   (a) the x-axis   (b) the y-axis
   (c) the line $x = 5$ (d) the line $x = 1$
   (e) the line $y = 5$ (f) the line $y = 3$

4. (a) On graph paper draw x- and y- axes for values from ⁻6 to ⁺6.
   (b) Draw the line $y = x$ on these axes.
   (c) Find and plot the image of the points after reflection in the line $y = x$.
       (i) (2, 3)   (ii) (3, 3)   (iii) (⁻1, 4)
       (iv) (4, ⁻1)   (v) (⁻5, ⁻2)   (vi) (2, 5)
   (d) Can you find a quick way of finding images after reflection in $y = x$? What is it?
   (e) What is the image of the point (a, b)?

5. (a) On graph paper draw x- and y- axes for values from ⁻6 to ⁺6.
   (b) Draw the line $y = -x$ on these axes.
   (c) Find and plot the image of the points after reflection in the line $y = x$.
       (i) (3, 4)   (ii) (4, 3)   (iii) (⁻4, ⁻3)
       (iv) (⁻2, ⁻1)   (v) (1, 2)   (vi) (⁻3, 1)
   (d) Can you find a quick way of finding the images after reflection in $y = -x$? What is it?
   (e) What is the image of the point (a, b) after such a reflection?

If the object and image points after a reflection are known, you can find the mirror line by constructing the perpendicular bisector of the two points.

Example 1

The point A (1, 3) is reflected in a line to give an image B(5, 6). Draw accurately the mirror line.

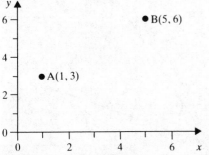

Join the two points. With your compasses construct the perpendicular bisector of the line AB (see page 64 if you have forgotten).

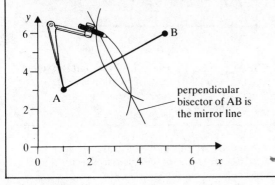

perpendicular bisector of AB is the mirror line

---

6. In each case construct the mirror line.

Object	Image
(a) (2, 3)	(5, 3)
(b) (⁻1, 2)	(4, 4)
(c) (3, 1)	(1, 3)
(d) (⁻3, ⁻2)	(2, 3)
(e) (1, 6)	(⁻3, ⁻1)

7. The triangle X(2, 3), Y(5, 4), Z(6, 1) becomes X'(⁻3, ⁻2), Y'(⁻4, ⁻5), Z'(⁻1, ⁻6) after reflection in a certain line.
(a) Plot the two triangles on graph paper.
(b) Construct the mirror line.
(c) Write down the equation of the mirror line.

In simple cases the equation of the mirror line is easily found either by inspection or by drawing.

8. Find the equation of each of the mirror lines for the following pairs of points.

	Object	Image
(a)	(1, 5)	(1, 3)
(b)	(⁻3, 2)	(7, 2)
(c)	(⁻3, ⁻1)	(⁻3, 4)
(d)	(6, 2)	(2, 6)
(e)	(⁻4, 5)	(⁻5, 4)

9. After reflection in the line *m*, the triangle A(2, ⁻1), B(3, 2), C(4, 1) becomes A'(⁻1, 2), B'(2, 3), C'(1, 4). Find the equation of the line *m*.

10. After reflection in the line *n*, the triangle X(1, 0), Y(1, 2), Z(2, 3) becomes X'(⁻2, 3), Y'(0, 3), Z'(1, 4). By drawing or calculation find the equation of the line *n*.

Rotations

A rotation is completely described by its centre of rotation and its angle of rotation.

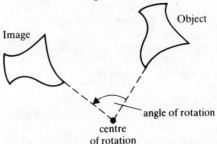

The simplest way to find the image of a shape after a rotation is to use tracing paper or a ruler and protractor.

11. Find the image of the point (3, 1) under these rotations.

	Centre of rotation	Angle of rotation (anticlockwise)
(a)	(0, 0)	90°
(b)	(1, 0)	180°
(c)	(⁻1, 0)	60°
(d)	(3, 4)	200°
(e)	(1, ⁻2)	75°

12. Use a ruler and protractor to find the image of the triangle A(1, 0), B(4, 0), C(4, 2) after a rotation of 90° anticlockwise about:
(a) (0, 2)   (b) (⁻1, 0)
(c) (⁻1, 2)   (d) (3, 1)

13. In the diagram below, triangle ABC is mapped to triangle PQR.

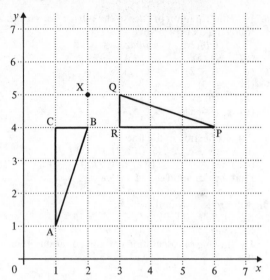

(a) What name is given to this mapping?
(b) What can you say about the distances XA and XP and the distances XB and XQ?
(c) If the whole plane is mapped by this mapping, are any points unchanged?
(d) What is the inverse mapping that maps triangle PQR to triangle ABC?
(e) What can you say about the perpendicular bisectors of AP, BQ and CR?
(f) Are the triangles congruent?

14. Draw a diagram like the one above to show the rotation of triangle PQR about X, through an angle of 90°, to STU.
(a) Describe the mapping that maps triangle ABC to triangle STU.
(b) Are two successive rotations about the same centre always equivalent to a rotation?

If the object and image shapes are known, the centre and angle of rotation can be found by construction as done on page 146.

You draw the perpendicular bisector of each pair of object and image points. The perpendicular bisectors meet at the centre of rotation.

15. Under a rotation, the line $A(7, 1)$, $B(8, 4)$ is mapped onto $A'(4, 6)$, $B'(1, 7)$.
(a) Plot the points on graph paper.
(b) Construct the perpendicular bisectors of AA' and BB'.
(c) What are the co-ordinates of the centre of rotation, C?
(d) With a protractor, measure the angle ACA'.
(e) What is the angle of rotation?

Example 2

Triangle $P(6, 4)$, $Q(5, 1)$, $R(3, 2)$ is rotated onto triangle $P'(0, 8)$, $Q'(3, 7)$, $R'(2, 5)$.
Construct and find the coordinates of the centre of rotation. What is the angle of rotation?

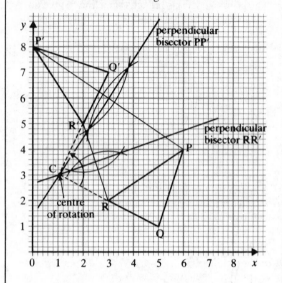

The perpendicular bisectors of PP' and RR' meet at $C(1, 3)$. So the centre of rotation is at $(1, 3)$.
Angle RCR' is the angle of rotation,
i.e. 90° anticlockwise.

16. Copy the above example onto graph paper.
(a) Construct the perpendicular bisector of QQ'. Does it pass through C also?
(b) With your protractor measure the angles:
   (i) $P\hat{C}P'$ (ii) $Q\hat{C}Q'$
   Are they equal to $R\hat{C}R'$?

17. Repeat Question 16 for the lines $A(5, 6)$, $B(3, 8)$ and $A'(6, 3)$, $B'(4, 1)$.

18. Triangle $X(3, 2)$, $Y(7, 2)$, $Z(3, 5)$ is rotated onto the triangle $X'(^-3, 2)$, $Y'(^-3, 6)$, $Z'(^-6, 2)$.
(a) Construct the centre of rotation, C, of the transformation.
(b) Write down the co-ordinates of C.
(c) Find the angle of rotation.

19. Repeat Question 18 for the triangles $X(1, 2)$, $Y(4, 2)$, $Z(1, 3)$ and $X'(^-1, 2)$, $Y'(^-1, 5)$, $Z'(^-2, 2)$.

20. A quadrilateral $P(2, ^-4)$, $Q(4, 1)$, $R(6, ^-8)$, $S(2, ^-6)$ is rotated onto the quadrilateral $P'(4, 0)$, $Q'(^-1, 2)$, $R'(8, 4)$, $S'(6, 0)$.
Find the centre and angle of rotation.

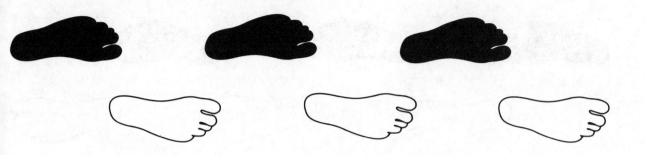

5.2 Glide reflections

Rotations, reflections and translations all preserve distance. That is, under such a transformation both the object and image shape are congruent. There is one further transformation that preserves distance, the **glide reflection.**

A man walking across wet sand leaves the footprints shown above. The left footprints are shaded.

1. Was the man walking in a straight line? Was his pace even?

2. Is the print of a right foot a direct or an opposite image of the print of a left foot?
   Are the footprints congruent to each other?

3. Use a tracing of the footsteps to show how you could map a black footprint to another black footprint using:
   (a) a translation
   (b) two reflections
   (c) two rotations.

4. Would the answers to Question 3 be the same, for mapping a white footprint to a white footprint?

5. Is it possible to map a black footprint to a white footprint using just:
   (a) a reflection
   (b) two successive reflections?

6. Draw a diagram to show how a white footprint can be mapped to a black footprint using a translation followed by a reflection. Show the mirror line on your diagram.

7. For your answer to Question 6, describe the inverse mapping.

In the diagram below, triangle ABC is mapped to triangle PQR by means of a **glide reflection**. The line XY is the **glide axis.**

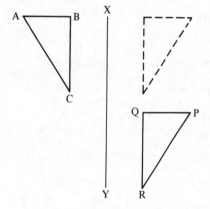

A glide reflection can be thought of as a reflection in the glide axis followed by a translation parallel to the glide axis.

A glide reflection is needed to map a black footprint to a white footprint.

8. Draw a diagram similar to the one above to show that a glide reflection is also equivalent to a translation followed by a reflection.

9. On squared paper draw the triangle A(0, 2), B(2, 0), C(1, 4) and the triangle P(6, 6), Q(4, 4), R(5, 8).
   (a) Are ABC and PQR congruent?
   (b) Find the mid-points of AP, BQ and CR.
   (c) Use your answers to (b) to write down the glide axis.
   (d) Describe the mapping of triangle PQR to triangle ABC.

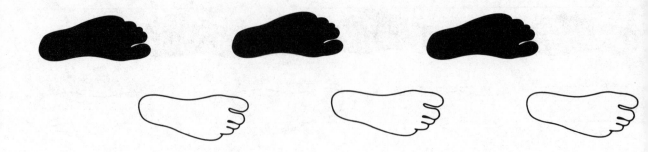

10. In a glide reflection, P maps to P' with the line XY as glide axis. Q is the image of P reflected in XY.

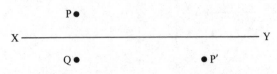

(a) Draw a copy of the diagram and mark N where PQ meets XY and M where PP' meets XY.
(b) Do you agree that PN = NQ and that QP' is parallel to XY? Use these facts to suggest a proof that PM = MP.

11. In a glide reflection, the mapping of a triangle is given by:
$$(^-3, 0) \rightarrow (1, 2) \quad (^-1, 0) \rightarrow (1, 0)$$
$$(^-1, ^-1) \rightarrow (2, 0)$$
Draw a diagram to show the triangle and its image and, by using mid-points, find the glide axis.

12. In the diagram, A and B are two squares:

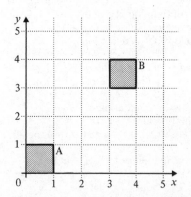

Describe how A can be mapped to B by:
(a) a rotation   (b) a translation
(c) a reflection   (d) a glide reflection

13. A triangle T has vertices $(0, 0), (2, 0), (0, 1)$. T is mapped to T' by a glide reflection of 4 units along the line $y = 0$ as glide axis. T' is mapped to T" by a glide reflection of 3 units along $x = 2$ as glide axis.
(a) Draw a diagram to show T, T' and T".
(b) What single transformation maps T to T"?

14. The glide reflection **U** consists of a translation $\begin{pmatrix} 1 \\ -2 \end{pmatrix}$ and a reflection in the line $y = x$.
(a) Draw the image of triangle A(2, 1), B(4, 1), C(4, 2) under **U**.
(b) If the triangle was first reflected in $y = x$ and then translated through $\begin{pmatrix} 1 \\ -2 \end{pmatrix}$, would the image be the same?

15. Repeat Question 14 for a glide **V** consisting of a reflection in $y = -x$ and a translation $\begin{pmatrix} 2 \\ -1 \end{pmatrix}$.

16. Draw the line AB = 6cm. Mark the point X such that AX is perpendicular to AB and AX = 3cm.
(a) Construct the image X' of X under a glide reflection consisting of the translation $\overrightarrow{AB}$ and a reflection in the line AB.
(b) What is the length of XX'?
(c) What is the angle AX'X?

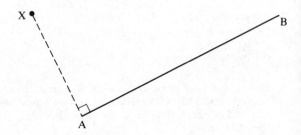

5.3 Shears and stretches

Shears

When a thick book is knocked sideways, as shown in the diagram above, the transformation is called a **shear**. Notice that:
  (i) the bottom cover does not move
  (ii) the book stays the same thickness
  (iii) the top cover moves the greatest distance.

In the diagram below, the rectangle ABCD maps to the parallelogram ABEF by a shear.

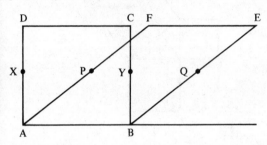

The line AB does not change. It is called the **invariant line** of the shear.
All other points move parallel to AB.
X, the mid-point of AD, moves to P, the mid-point of AF. The line XP is parallel to AB.

1. In the diagram above, if AB = 5 cm and BC = 7 cm, find the area of:
   (a) ABCD   (b) ABEF
   (c) ABC   (d) ABE
   (d) ABX   (f) ABP
   Does a shear change the area of a shape?

2. In the diagram above, Y is the mid-point of BC and Q is the mid-point of BE.
   (a) What is the image of XYCD using the shear?
   (b) The image of DX is FP. Where do these lines meet?
   (c) Given a shape and its image under a shear, describe how you would find the invariant line of the shear.

3. Draw a pair of parallel lines. Let A, B be two points on one line and X, Y, Z be three points on the other.
   (a) What can you say about the areas of triangles ABX, ABY and ABZ?
   (b) What is the invariant line of the shear that relates these three triangles?
   (c) What transformation maps triangle XYA to triangle XYB?
   (d) Write down another pair of triangles in the diagram, that are related by a shear.

4. The diagram shows a rectangle ABCD and a parallelogram PQRS.

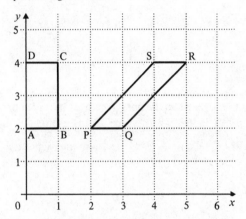

   (a) Make your own copy of the diagram and extend the lines DA to meet SP and CB to meet RQ.
   (b) If a shear of the plane maps ABCD to PQRS, which points remain unchanged?

5. On graph paper, draw the square with vertices (1, 1), (2, 1), (2, 2), (1, 2). A shear with $y = 0$ as invariant line maps (1, 2) to (4, 2). Show on your diagram the images of the other vertices using this shear.

6. In the diagram, triangle ABC is sheared to APQ. The points BCPQ lie on a straight line.

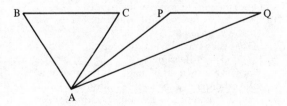

   (a) What can you say about the lengths BP and CQ?
   (b) Describe the invariant line of the shear.

7. In the diagram, X and Y are the mid-points of the
sides of a rectangle. XY is the invariant line of a
shear.

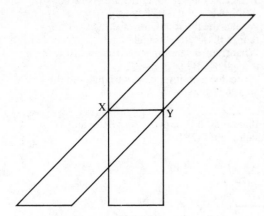

   (a) If points on one side of the invariant line move
       to the right, do the points on the other side also
       move to the right?

   (b) Draw a circle and show a shear of the circle
       using a diameter as the invariant line. Does the
       shape remain a circle?

8. ABCD is a square and BS is any line drawn from B.
A transformation of ABCD has BC lying along BS.
Draw diagrams to show how this transformation
could be:
   (a) a rotation
   (b) a shear.

9. The diagrams on the right show part of a proof of
Pythagoras' Theorem. The square on the
hypotenuse is divided into two parts, by a line. This
line has been drawn from the right angle of the
triangle, parallel to a side of the square.
   (a) Name the type of transformation that each
       arrow represents.
   (b) Does each transformation keep the area of the
       shaded part the same?
   (c) Draw your own set of diagrams to show how
       the other part of the square on the hypotenuse
       could be mapped to the smallest square.
   (d) If the shorter sides of the triangle are 7 cm, and
       11 cm long, what will be the area of the square
       on the hypotenuse? How would you then find
       the length of the hypotenuse?

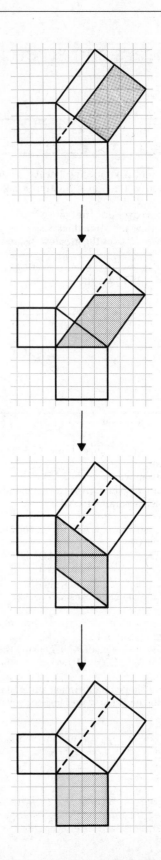

Stretches

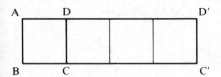

A **one-way stretch** lengthens an object in one direction only. It alters both the size and shape of an object.

In the diagram above the square ABCD has been stretched into the rectangle ABC′D′.

A stretch is completely defined by its **scale factor** and its **invariant line**.

In the above example:
    the scale factor is 4   (BC′ = 4 × BC)
    the invariant line is AB.

10. Describe fully the stretches below.

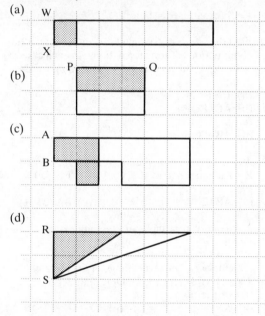

(a)

(b)

(c)

(d)

11. Draw the images of the unit square O(0, 0), A(1, 0), B(1, 1), C(0, 1) under these stretches:

	Scale factor	Invariant line
(a)	2	OC
(b)	3	OA
(c)	2	AB
(d)	$2\frac{1}{2}$	CB

12. The triangle A(2, 3), B(5, 3), C(5, 4) is stretched by a scale factor 2 parallel to the *y*-axis with the *x*-axis invariant. Draw its image.

A **two-way stretch** is really the composition of two one-way stretches.

> *Example*
>
> Find the image of the unit square O(0, 0), A(1, 0), B(1, 1), C(0, 1) after a two-way stretch of scale factor 3 parallel to the *y*-axis and scale factor 2 parallel to the *x*-axis.
>
>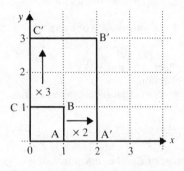

13. Describe fully the stretches below.

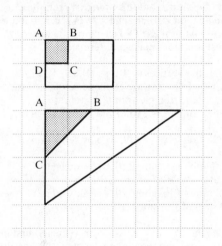

14. The triangle X(2, 1), Y(6, 1), Z(6, 3) is transformed by a two-way stretch **T** onto the triangle X′Y′Z′. Find the image X′Y′Z′ if **T** consists of scale factor 2 parallel to the *x*-axis and scale factor 4 parallel to the *y*-axis. Assume that the axes are the invariant lines.

5.4 Combining transformations

1. Draw a diagram to show the reflection of triangle A(1, 1), B(2, 4), C(1, 4) in the line $x = 2$ and the reflection of the image in the line $x = 4$. Describe the single mapping equivalent to these two.

2. Draw a sketch to show the image of a triangle under the mapping:
   first use a reflection in $x = 1$
   followed by a reflection in $x = -1$
   followed by a reflection in $x = 2$.
   Find the single mapping that is equivalent to these three.

3. (a) On a co-ordinate grid, mark point Z at ($^-3$, 1).
   (b) Show its image, Z′, after reflection in Oy.
   (c) Z″ is the image of Z′, after a rotation of 90°, centre (3, 6). Show Z″, and write down its co-ordinates.

4. Repeat Question 3, but this time carry out the rotation first, on Z, then reflect Z′ in Oy. What are the co-ordinates of Z″? Did changing the order of the transformations make a difference to Z″?

5. A triangle has vertices (0, 0), (2, 0), (0, 4). Find which of the following are equivalent to a half-turn mapping of the triangle about the point (0, 4).
   (a) Reflection in $x = 2$ followed by reflection in $y = 4$.
   (b) Reflection in $y = 4$ followed by reflection in $x = 0$.
   (c) Rotation of 90° about (0, 0) followed by rotation of 90° about ($^-4$, 0).
   (d) Rotation of 10° about (0, 4) followed by rotation of 170° about (0, 4).

6. Triangle A(2, 1), B(5, 1), C(6, 2) is reflected first in the line $y = -1$ and then in the line $y = x$. What are the co-ordinates of its final image?

7. The quadrilateral W(1, 1), X(3, 1), Y(4, 3), Z(1, 5) is reflected first in the line $y = -x$ and then in the y-axis. What are the co-ordinates of its final image?

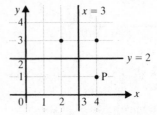
8. Draw the triangle P(2, 2), Q(6, 2), R(6, 4).
   A represents a reflection in the line $x = 3$
   B represents a 180° rotation, centre (1, 1)
   C represents a translation $\begin{pmatrix} 4 \\ -2 \end{pmatrix}$.

   Find the image of triangle PQR under the following combinations of transformations. In each case write down the co-ordinates of the image of the point P.
   (a) **CA** (PQR)
   (b) **AC** (PQR)
   (c) **BC** (PQR)
   (d) **AB** (PQR)

9. **A** is an enlargement, centre (0, 0) scale factor 3;
   B is shear defined by **B** : $(x, y) \rightarrow (x + 3y, y)$.
   Find:
   (a) **AB** (2, 1)   (b) **BA** (2, $^-$1)

10. **X** is a one-way stretch parallel to the x-axis, scale factor 3;
    Y is a rotation about (0, 0) through 90° anticlockwise. Find the image of the rectangle A(1, 1), B(3, 1), C(3, 2), D(1, 2) under the transformations.
    (a) **XY**   (b) **YX**
    For each part, assume that the y-axis is the invariant line.

Summary

By the end of this chapter, these are the things you should know about:

5.1 Revision (pages 218–220)

How to find the image of a point under a reflection.
How to find the mirror line given the object and image point.
    e.g. A → A′ by a reflection.

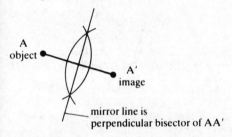

How to find the image of a point under a rotation.
How to find the centre of rotation given the object and image shape.
    e.g. AB → A′B′ by a rotation:

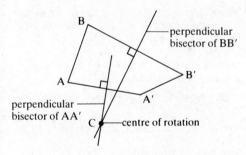

5.2 Glide reflections (pages 221–222)

What a glide reflection is.

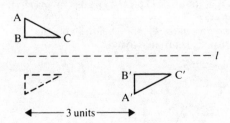

ABC → A′B′C′ by a glide reflection consisting of a reflection in the line *l* and a translation of 3 units parallel to the line *l*.

5.3 Shears and stretches (pages 223–225)

What a **shear** is.

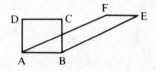

ABCD → ABEF by a shear parallel to the line AB with AB as invariant line.
When a shape undergoes a shear, its area does not change.
How to find the invariant line of a shear.

What a **stretch** is.

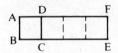

ABCD → ABEF by a stretch factor 4 parallel to the line AB with AB as the invariant line.

5.4 Combining transformations (page 226)

How to find the image of a point under two transformations.
    e.g. M_2 = reflection in $y = 2$
        M_5 = reflection in $y = 5$
What is $M_2M_5 (P)$ where P is the point (1, 1)?
$M_2M_5 (1, 1) = M_2 (1, 3) = (1, 7)$
Note: M_5 is done first, then M_2.

6 Trigonometry 2

6.1 Graphs of trigonometric functions

The tangent curve

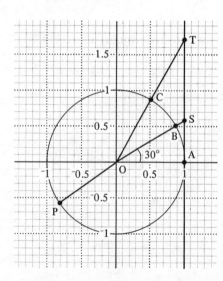

Note: In the exercises that follow, all angles are measured in an anticlockwise direction from OA.

1. Look at the diagram above. OA is 1 unit long and AÔB is 30°.
   (a) Find the length of AS, using the tangent ratio.
   (b) If AÔC is 60°, find the length of AT.

2. In the diagram above, the circle has unit radius and centre O. AT is a tangent to it.
   (a) Look at the angle of 30°. Do you agree that it cuts off length AS on the tangent AT?
   (b) Can you find the length of AS, using the scale on the vertical axis? Do you get the same answer as you did for Question 1 (a)?

3. (a) Make a large copy of the diagram above using cm/mm graph paper.
   (b) Mark on your circle a point P, so that AÔP is 210°. Join PO and extend it to meet AT.
   (c) What distance from A is cut off on AT? (Use the scale on the horizontal axis.)

4. Repeat Question 3 using a point Q on the circle, so that AÔQ is 240°.

5. Using your circle from Question 3, mark a point X so that AÔX is 45°.
   (a) What distance from A is cut off on AT by this angle?
   (b) What difference would it make to your answer if AÔX was 225° instead of 45°?

The tangent of an angle is defined as:
the length that the angle cuts off on a tangent to a circle of unit radius.
You can see this on the diagram below. Note that *tangent* is usually shortened to *tan*.

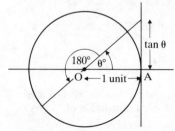

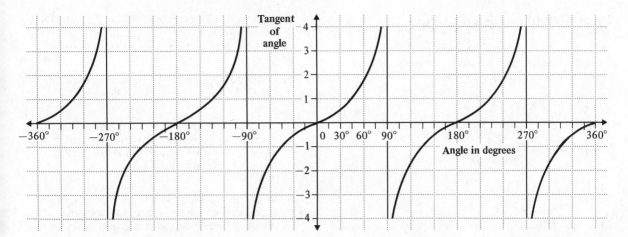

6. What can you say about the tangent of an angle which is nearly 90°?

7. Do you agree that tan (θ + 180°) = tan θ?

8. Look again at your diagram for Question 3. Mark on your circle a point K so that AÔK is 135°. Join KO and extend it to meet TA produced. What distance is cut off on TA produced?

9. Do you agree that the distance from A cut off on the tangent by an angle of 135° is the same as the distance cut off for an angle of 45°, but in the opposite direction?

10. Would it be reasonable to take tan 135° as ⁻1? Explain why.

11. Repeat Question 8, making AÔK:
    (a) 120°   (b) 150°

12. Do you agree that:
    (a) tan 120° = ⁻tan 60°?
    (b) tan 150° = ⁻tan 30°?

13. What can you say about:
    (a) tan 300°   (b) tan 315°   (c) tan 330°?

14. (a) If θ lies between 90° and 180°, explain why tan θ = ⁻tan (180 − θ)°.
    (b) If θ lies between 180° and 270°, explain why tan θ = tan (θ − 180°)°.
    (c) If θ lies between 270° and 360°, explain why tan θ = ⁻tan (360 − θ)°.

15. You will need your diagram from Question 3 again. By taking angles every 15° and measuring the corresponding lengths on AT, copy and complete the table below.

Angle	Tangent
15°	
30°	
45°	1
330°	
345°	
360°	0

16. Now use the graph at the top of the page to find the tangents of the angles listed in Question 15. Compare your two sets of values. Do they agree?

17. Explain why there is a gap in the graph above, for angles near: (a) 90° (b) 270°

18. Use the graph to find another angle which has the same tangent as: (a) 30° (b) 60° (c) 120°

19. Write down another angle which has the same tangent as: (a) 45° (b) 71° (c) 127°

20. Tangents are given in the 3-figure tables at the end of this book. Use these to find:
    (a) tan 45°   (b) tan 225°   (c) tan 315°
    (d) tan 20°   (e) tan 200°   (f) tan 160°
    (g) tan 70°   (h) tan 110°   (i) tan 250°
    (j) tan 35°   (k) tan 145°   (l) tan 325°
    (m) tan 75°   (n) tan 105°   (o) tan 255°

Positive and negative angles

In mathematics, angles measured in an anticlockwise direction are described as **positive**. Angles measured in a clockwise direction are **negative**.

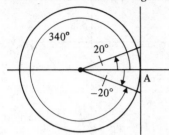

21. Look at the diagram above.
    (a) Do you agree that 340° is the same as ⁻20°?
    (b) Do you agree that tan (−20°) = ⁻tan 20°?

22. Write down the positive angles equivalent to:
    (a) −30°   (b) −50°   (c) −90°   (d) −130°

23. Make a table like the one in Question 15, showing the tangents of negative angles taken at 15° intervals.

24. Compare your answers for Question 23 with the values obtained from the graph at the top of the page. Do they agree?

25. Use the graph to find three other angles which have the same tangent as:
    (a) 20°   (b) 210°   (c) −40°   (d) −200°
    How many angles between −360° and 360° will have the same value for their tangent?

The sine and cosine curves

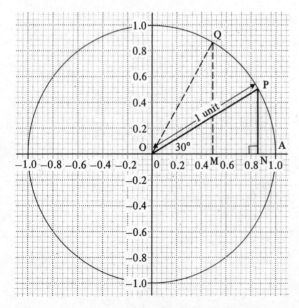

26. Look at the diagram above. Using the scales on the axes, write down the length of: (a) PN (b) ON
    Do you agree that PN = sin 30°, ON = cos 30°?

27. If AÔQ above is 60°, write down the length of:
    (a) QM   (b) OM

28. Suppose that P moves around the circle in an anticlockwise direction. Do you agree that the distance of P from the horizontal axis equals sin AÔP? Explain why.

29. What can you say about the distance ON, as P moves around the circle in an anticlockwise direction? Describe how it changes.

30. Make a larger copy of the diagram below Question 25. On your copy mark a point R on the circle, so that AÔR is 150°
    What is the distance of R from:
    (a) the horizontal axis   (b) the vertical axis?

31. Look at your answers to Questions 28, 29 and 30. What can you say about:
    (a) sin 150° and sin 30°
    (b) cos 150° and cos 30°?

32. Repeat Question 30 using a point S on the circle, so that AÔS is 120°. Do you agree that:
    (a) sin 120° = sin 60°?
    (b) cos 120° = ⁻cos 60°?

The sine of any angle AOP in the diagram on the left is the distance P above or below the horizontal axis.
The cosine of the angle AOP is the distance of P to the right or left of the vertical axis.

Distances above the horizontal axis or to the right of the vertical axis are **positive**.
Distances below the horizontal axis or to the left of the vertical axis are **negative.**

Positive and negative sines and cosines

33. Repeat Question 30 using a point T on the circle so that AÔT is 210°. What can you say about:
    (a) sin 210° compared with sin 150° and sin 30°
    (b) cos 210° and cos 150° compared with cos 30°?

34. Repeat Question 30 using a point U on the circle, so that AÔU is 240°. Do you agree that:
    (a) sin 240° = ⁻sin 60°
    (b) cos 240° = ⁻cos 60°?

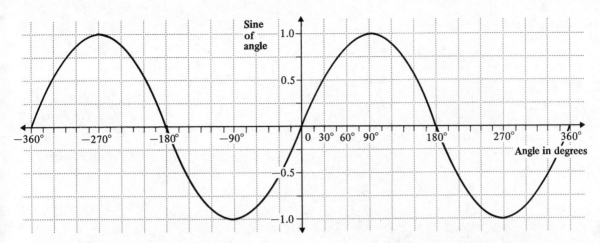

35. Repeat Question 30 using a point V on the circle, so that AÔV is 330°.
(a) Write down the angle whose sine is equal to sin 330°.
(b) Write down two angles whose sines are equal to ⁻sin 330°.
(c) Write down one angle whose cosine is equal to cos 330°.
(d) Write down two angles whose cosines are equal to ⁻cos 330°.

36. Repeat Question 35 using a point W on the circle so that the angle AÔW is 300°.

37. Copy and complete the statement.
(a) For triangles between 0° and 90° both the sine and cosine are . . . .
(b) For the angles between 90° and 180° the sine is positive and the cosine is . . . .
(c) For angles between 180° and 270° both the sine and cosine are . . . .
(d) For angles between 270° and 360° the sine is . . . . and the cosine is . . . .

38. For each part of Question 37 make a similar statement about tangents of angles.

39. You will need your diagram from Question 30 again. By taking angles every 15° and measuring the corresponding lengths PN and ON, copy and complete the table below.

Angle	Sine	Cosine
15°		
30°	0.5	0.867
45°		
⁓	⁓	⁓
330°		
345°		
360°	0	1

40. Now use the graph at the top of the page to find the sines of the angles listed in Question 39. Compare your two sets of values. Do they agree?

41. (a) For what angles does the sine take its largest positive value?
(b) For what angles does the sine take a value of zero?

42. Use the graph to find another angle which has the same sine as:
(a) 30°   (b) 60°   (c) 210°   (d) 240°

43. Write down another angle which has the same sine as:
(a) 45°   (b) 71°   (c) 227°   (d) 280°

44. Use 3-figure tables to write down:
(a) sin 37°   (b) sin 143°   (c) sin 217°

45. Take the diagram you drew for Question 30. Start from OA and work in a clockwise direction, making angles at 15° intervals.
Make a table like the one in Question 39 showing the sines and cosines of these negative angles.

46. Compare your answers for the sines in Question 45 with the values obtained using the graph at the top of the page. Do they agree?

47. Use the graph to find three other angles which have the same sine as:
(a) 20°   (b) 210°   (c) −40°   (d) −200°
How many angles between −360° and 360° will have the same value for their sine?

48. Make a copy of the sine graph at the top of the page. On this copy mark the cosine values that you found in Questions 39 and 45, for angles between −360° and 360°. Join the points with a smooth curve.

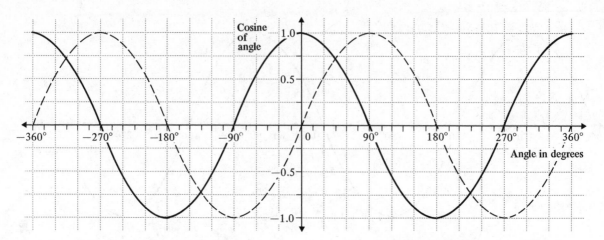

49. What is the connection between the sine and cosine curves? How can the cosine curve be obtained from the sine curve?

50. (a) For what angles between −360° and 360° are the sine and cosine values the same?
(b) For what angles between −360° and 360° is it true that:
sine value = −cosine value?

Your graph in Question 48 should look like the one above. The sine curve is the dotted one.
The cosine curve is the same as the sine curve but translated to the left by 90°.

The two curves cross at 45°, 225°, −135° and −315°. For these angles the values of the sine and cosine are the same (≈ 0.71).

The sine and cosine have the same value (≈ 0.71) but opposite sign when the angles are 135°, 315°, −45° and −225°.

51. Use the graph above to find three other angles which have the same cosine as:
(a) 30°   (b) 240°   (c) −60°   (d) −100°
How many angles between −360° and 360° have the same value for their cosine?

52. Use 3-figure tables to help you write down:
(a) cos 37°   (b) cos 143°   (c) cos 217°

53. (a) For what angles does the cosine take its largest positive value?
(b) For what angles does the cosine take its largest negative value?

54. If θ is an angle between 90° and 180°, do you agree that:
(a) $\cos \theta = \cos (180 - \theta)$?
(b) $\sin \theta = {}^-\sin (180 - \theta)$?

Some important results

55. For what values of θ between −360° and 360° is:
(a) $\sin \theta = 1$ (b) $\sin \theta = 0$?

56. For what values of θ between −360° and 360° is:
(a) $\cos \theta = 1$ (b) $\cos \theta = 0$?

57. Use the graph above to write down the value of:
(a) $\sin 90°$ (b) $\cos 180°$ (c) $\sin 360°$
(d) $\cos 0°$ (e) $\sin 270°$ (f) $\cos 90°$

58. For what values of θ between −360° and 360° is:
(a) $\sin \theta = \frac{1}{2}$ (b) $\sin \theta = {}^-\frac{1}{2}$?

59. For what values of θ between −360° and 360° is:
(a) $\cos \theta = \frac{1}{2}$ (b) $\cos \theta = {}^-\frac{1}{2}$?

60. Use the graph above to write down the value of:
(a) $\sin 30°$ (b) $\cos 300°$ (c) $\sin 210°$
(d) $\cos 60°$ (e) $\sin 330°$ (f) $\cos 240°$

61. Choose an angle between 0° and 90°, and then use the graph to say whether the statement is true or false:
(a) $\cos \theta = \sin (\theta + 90°)$
(b) $\sin \theta = \cos (\theta - 90°)$
(c) $\cos \theta = \sin (90° - \theta)$
(d) $\sin \theta = \cos (90° - \theta)$
Are your answers the same if you choose an angle between 90° and 180°?

6.2 Using tables and calculators

Mathematical tables only give tangent, sine, and cosine values for angles between 0° and 90°.
But from these you can find the values for any angle between −360° and 360°.

For example, to find the sine of an angle greater than 90°, ask yourself these questions:
[1] What angle between 0° and 90° has the same sine as this angle?
[2] Is the value positive or negative?

Example 1

Find sin 146°.

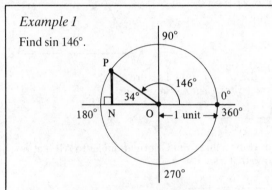

The required sine is the length of PN.
You can see that PÔN = 180° − 146° = 34°.
PN is above the axis and is therefore positive.
Its length is sin 34°.
So sin 146° = sin 34° = 0.559.

Example 2

Find cos 229°.

The required cosine is the length of ON.
You can see that PÔN = 229° − 180° = 49°.
ON is to the left of the axis and is therefore negative.
Its length is cos 49°.
So cos 229° = ⁻cos 49° = ⁻0.651.

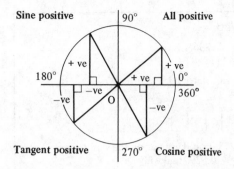

The diagram above shows a quick way of remembering whether the sine, cosine, or tangent of an angle is positive or negative. (It may help to remember the word CAST.)

1. Use 3-figure tables to write down:
   (a) sin 32°   (b) cos 43°   (c) tan 54°

2. With the help of diagrams like those in Examples 1 and 2, use your answers for Question 1 to find:
   (a) sin 148°, sin 212°, sin 328°
   (b) cos 137°, cos 223°, cos 317°
   (c) tan 126°, tan 234°, tan 306°

3. By first finding sin 71° and then using an appropriate diagram, write down:
   (a) sin 289°   (b) sin 109°   (c) sin 251°

4. By first finding cos 22°, and then using an appropriate diagram, write down:
   (a) cos 202°   (b) cos 338°   (c) cos 158°

5. By first finding tan 37° and then using an appropriate diagram, write down:
   (a) tan 143°   (b) tan 323°   (c) tan 217°

6. Use 3-figure tables to write down:
   (a) sin 110°   (b) sin 210°   (c) sin 310°
   (d) cos 121°   (e) cos 221°   (f) cos 331°
   (g) tan 157°   (h) tan 246°   (i) tan 335°

7. Say whether the statement is *true* or *false*:
   (a) $\sin(180° − \theta) = \sin \theta$
   (b) $\cos(360° − \theta) = \cos \theta$
   (c) $\tan(180° + \theta) = \tan \theta$
   Do your answers depend on the size of the angle you choose for θ?

Using a calculator

If you have a **scientific** calculator you can find sines and cosines of angles greater than 90° very easily.
Make sure the calculator is set for degree mode and not radian mode.

Example 3

Find (a) sin 236°

(b) tan 358°

On your calculator:

(a) Press

| 2 | 3 | 6 | sin |

$^-0.8290375$ should appear on the screen so
sin 236° = $^-0.829$ (to 3 s.f.)

(b) Press

| 3 | 5 | 8 | tan |

$^-0.0349207$ should appear on the screen so
tan 358° = $^-0.035$ (to 3 s.f.)

8. Use your calculator to write down correct
to 3 significant figures:
   - (a) sin 46°
   - (b) tan 86°
   - (c) cos 118°
   - (d) sin 125°
   - (e) tan 186°
   - (f) cos 105°
   - (g) cos 243°
   - (h) sin 189°
   - (i) sin 320°
   - (j) tan 343°
   - (k) cos 312°
   - (l) tan 208°

9. Check your answers to Question 6 using your
calculator.

The inverse button, [INV] on your calculator can help

you find one of the values of an angle given its sine or
cosine.

Example 4

Find a value of x such that cos x = $^-0.843$.

Press:

147.45828 appears on the screen
so $x = 147.5°$ (to 1 d.p.)

10. Find a value of x such that:
    - (a) cos x = 0.866
    - (b) sin x = 0.5
    - (c) cos x = $^-0.866$
    - (d) sin x = 0.123
    - (e) cos x = $^-0.314$
    - (f) sin x = $^-0.314$
    - (g) cos x = $^-0.982$
    - (h) sin x = $^-0.042$

6.3 The sine and cosine rules

Even when a triangle does not have a right angle you
can find missing sides or angles using either the **sine** or
cosine rules.

The sine rule

The height XB of ΔBAC
can be found in two ways,
as:
c sin A *or* a sin C
Do you agree?

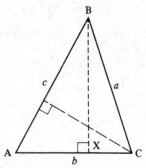

Since these two expressions are equal
we can write: c sin A = a sin C or

$$\frac{c}{\sin C} = \frac{a}{\sin A}$$

By drawing a line from C at right-angles to AB it also
follows that a sin B = b sin A

so $$\frac{a}{\sin A} = \frac{b}{\sin B}$$

Putting these two results together we get:

$$\frac{a}{\sin A} = \frac{b}{\sin B} = \frac{c}{\sin C}$$

This is known as the **sine rule** for triangles.
Note that a is the side *opposite* Â, b is the side opposite
B̂ and c is the side opposite Ĉ.

Example 1

If a = 5cm, b = 4cm and angle B = 35°, find
angles A and C.

We can use the sine rule to find the size
of angle A.

$$\frac{5}{\sin A} = \frac{4}{\sin 35°}$$

$4 \sin A = 5 \sin 35°$

$$\sin A = \frac{5 \sin 35°}{4}$$

$$= 0.717$$

i.e. Â $= 45.8°$

so Ĉ $= 180° - 35° - 45.8° = 99.2°$

Example 2

Use the sine rule again to find c in Example 1.

$$\frac{c}{\sin 99.2°} = \frac{4}{\sin 35°}$$

so $c = \dfrac{4 \sin 99.2°}{\sin 35°} = 6.68\,\text{cm}$

---

1. Copy and complete the statement, for this triangle:

(a) $\dfrac{3}{\sin 40°} = \dfrac{\square}{\sin 65°}$

(b) $\dfrac{3}{\sin 40°} = \dfrac{c}{\square}$

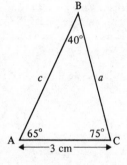

2. Use your results in Question 1 to find the lengths of a and c.

3. Use the sine rule to find angle A.

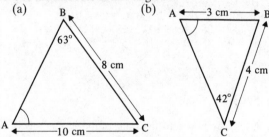

4. Use the sine rule to find the length of b and then c.

(a)

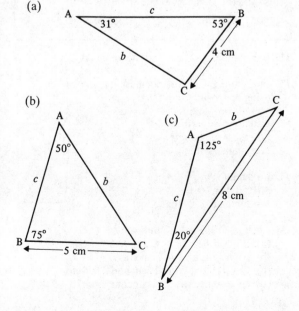

(b)

(c)

5. Use the sine rule to find the other sides and angles in the triangle.

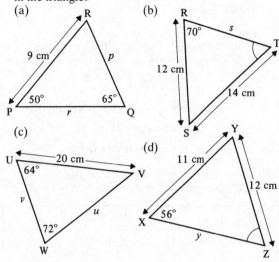

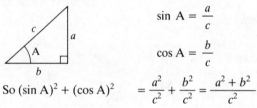

$\sin^2 A + \cos^2 A = 1$

For the triangle below, we can write sin A and cos A in terms of a, b and c.

$$\sin A = \frac{a}{c}$$

$$\cos A = \frac{b}{c}$$

So $(\sin A)^2 + (\cos A)^2 = \dfrac{a^2}{c^2} + \dfrac{b^2}{c^2} = \dfrac{a^2 + b^2}{c^2}$

From Pythagoras' Theorem: $a^2 + b^2 = c^2$

So $(\sin A)^2 + (\cos A)^2 = 1$

This is normally written:

$$\sin^2 A + \cos^2 A = 1$$

The cosine rule

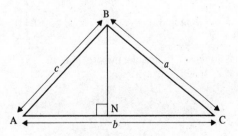

6. For triangle ABC above write down:
(a) the length of BN in terms of angle A
(b) the length of AN in terms of angle A
(c) the length of NC in terms of angle A

7. In triangle BNC above, $a^2 = BN^2 + NC^2$.
Substitute your results from Question 6 to
complete: $a^2 = ($ $)^2 + ($ $)^2$

For Question 7 you should have written:
$a^2 = (c \sin A)^2 + (b - c \cos A)^2$
The right-hand side of this equation can be simplified:
$a^2 = c^2 \sin^2 A + b^2 - 2b \cos A + c^2 \cos^2 A$
$= c^2 (\sin^2 A + \cos^2 A) + b^2 - 2bc \cos A$

Since $\sin^2 A + \cos^2 A = 1$ from above, we can write:

$$a^2 = b^2 + c^2 - 2bc \cos A$$

This is known as the **cosine rule** for triangles.

The cosine rule is only used if two sides and the
included angle (SAS) or all three sides (SSS) are given.

Example 3

In the figure calculate the length AC.

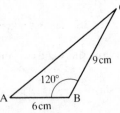

Angle B is the included angle between the given
sides AB and BC. (SAS)
By the cosine rule:
$AC^2 = 6^2 + 9^2 - 2 \times 6 \times 9 \times \cos 120°$
$= 36 + 81 - 108 \times (^-0.500)$
$= 117 + 54$
$AC = \sqrt{171}$
$= 13.1$ (3 s.f.)

---

8. Use the result
$a^2 = b^2 + c^2 - 2bc \cos A$
to find a in the triangle
on the right.

9. Use the cosine rule to
find a if
$b = 7$ cm, $c = 8$ cm and
angle $A = 30°$.

10. Use the cosine rule to find the missing lengths.
(a)   (b)

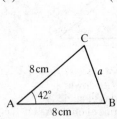 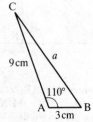

(c)   (d)

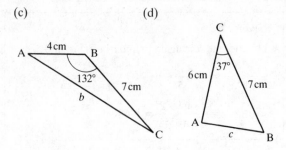

The missing angles in a triangle can be found if you are
given the three sides (SSS) of a triangle.

Example 4

Calculate the angle $A\hat{B}C$.

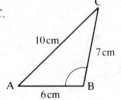

By the cosine rule:
$10^2 = 6^2 + 7^2 - 2 \times 6 \times 7 \times \cos B$
$100 = 36 + 49 - 84 \cos B$
$100 = 85 - 84 \cos B$
$15 = -84 \cos B$
$\cos B = \dfrac{^-15}{84} = ^-0.179$
So $\hat{B} = 100.3°$

Notice that the left-hand side of the equation is
always the square of the side opposite the
required angle.

To find the angle ACB you write

$$6^2 = 10^2 + 7^2 - 2 \times 10 \times 7 \times \cos C$$

---

11. In Example 4 above, find the angle ACB.

12. In Example 4 above, calculate the angle CAB,
using the cosine rule.

13. Use the cosine rule to
find the size of angle A
in triangle ABC.

14. Find angle A in triangle
ABC if $a = 7$ cm,
$b = 5$ cm and $c = 4$ cm.

15. Use the cosine rule to find:
(a) $\hat{B}$ if $a = 8$ cm, $c = 5$ cm and $b = 6$ cm
(b) b if $a = 4$ cm, $c = 7$ cm and $\hat{B} = 45°$
(c) $\hat{C}$ if $a = 9$ cm, $b = 10$ cm and $c = 4$ cm
(d) c if $a = 12$ cm, $b = 20$ cm and $\hat{C} = 70°$

16. Use the cosine rule to find the marked angles.

(a)

(b)

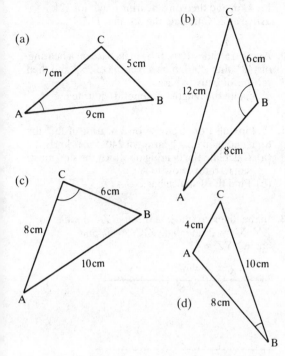

(c)

(d)

Areas of triangles and parallelograms

The area of a triangle
is $\frac{1}{2}$ base $\times$ height.

In $\triangle ABC$ this is
$\frac{1}{2}AC \times BN$

BN = $c \sin \theta$ and
AC = b

so the area of $\triangle ABC$
is $\frac{1}{2}bc \sin \theta$

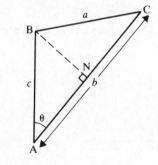

Note that θ is the angle *between* b and c.

17. Use the working above to find the area of $\triangle ABC$ if
AB = 5 cm, AC = 8 cm and the angle B$\hat{A}$C = 30°.

Find the area of the triangle.

(a)   (b)

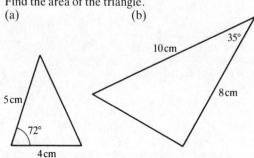

18. Find the area of
parallelogram ABCD
shown on the right.

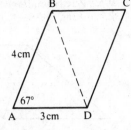

19. Find the area of a
rhombus with one
angle 40° and one side
4 cm.

20. Find the area of a regular hexagon of side 6 cm.

21. Use Hero's formula $A = \sqrt{s(s-a)(s-b)(s-c)}$
where $s = \frac{1}{2}(a + b + c)$ to find the area of a triangle
with sides:
(a) 4 cm, 4 cm, 4 cm
(b) 3 cm, 4 cm, 5 cm.
Check your answers by a second method.

Some harder problems

22. Find all the sides and angles of the triangles below.
(a)

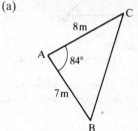

(b)

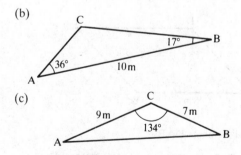

(c)

23. In the figure below, ABCD is a parallelogram.

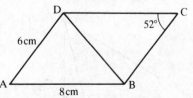

AB = 8 cm, AD = 6 cm and angle DCB = 52°.
(a) What is the angle DAB?
(b) Calculate the length of BD.
(c) Find the angle ABC, hence calculate the length
    of the other diagonal AC.

24. WXYZ is a rhombus with angle ZYX = 40° and ZX = 6 cm.

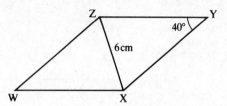

(a) Calculate the length of the side XY.
(b) Find the length of the diagonal WY.

25. In the trapezium PQRS, PS = 8 cm, SR = 5 cm and angle PSR = 115°.

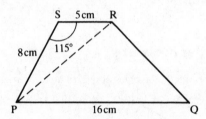

(a) Calculate the length PR.
(b) Calculate the area of the trapezium PQRS.

26. If the area of a triangle is 21 cm² and two of its sides are 12 cm and 7 cm, find the angle between them.

27. ABCD is a parallelogram of area 40 cm², AD = 6 cm and AB = 8 cm.

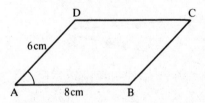

Find the angle DAB.

28. In the figure, RS = 6 cm, angle QRS = 30°, angle QST = 75° and angle QTS = 90°.

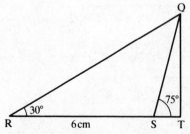

(a) Calculate SQ
(b) Use your result to find QT.

29. A ship sails from a harbour H on a bearing of 280° for 4 km and then on a bearing of 60° for 12 km to arrive at Z. Calculate the distance HZ.

30. An aircraft flies 100 km from its base on a bearing of 148°, then 400 km on a bearing of 250° and then returns directly to base.
Calculate the length of the return journey.

31. A ship sails from a port A on a bearing of 130° for 8 km and then on a bearing of 240° for 14 km.
(a) Calculate the bearing on which the ship must sail to return now to A.
(b) Find the distance back to A.

32. In the diagram, the line through Z is parallel to XY, XY = 20 m, angle ZXY = 60° and angle XYZ = 43°.

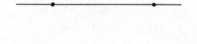

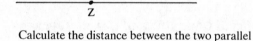

Calculate the distance between the two parallel lines.

33. Find the area of a regular pentagon of side 6 cm.

6.4 Radians

So far, you have measured angles in **degrees**. It is also possible to measure angles in **radians.**

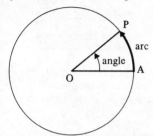

In the circle above, line **OP** can rotate around O. The angle at the centre gets larger as P moves further from A. The length of the arc **AP** also increases as the angle increases. The length of the arc can be used as a measure of the size of the angle at the centre.

If the radius of the circle is 1 cm, the angle is **1 radian** when the arc length is 1 cm.

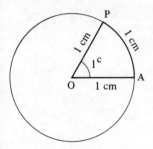

1 radian is written 1^c.
1 radian is about 57°.

The circumference of a circle of radius 1 cm is
$2\pi \times 1 = 2\pi$ cm.
So when OP turns through 360°, the length of the arc is 2π cm. The angle at the centre is therefore 2π radians.

$$360° = 2\pi \text{ radians.}$$

It is useful to remember this table of values:

Radians	Degrees
2π	360
π	180
$\dfrac{\pi}{2}$	90

Example 1

Change (a) $\dfrac{3\pi^c}{5}$ to degrees
  (b) 240° to radians

Remember $\pi^c = 180°$

(a) $\dfrac{3\pi^c}{5} = \dfrac{3 \times 180°}{5} = 108°$

(b) $240° = 240 \times \dfrac{\pi^c}{180°} = \dfrac{4\pi^c}{3}$

1. Change the following to degrees:
   (a) $\dfrac{\pi^c}{4}$ (b) $\dfrac{\pi^c}{6}$ (c) $\dfrac{2\pi^c}{3}$ (d) $\dfrac{3\pi^c}{2}$ (e) $\dfrac{3\pi^c}{4}$

2. Change the following to radians:
   (a) 60° (b) 225° (c) 210° (d) 300° (e) 315°

3. Change these to radians, giving your answers to 2 places of decimals:
   (a) 20° (b) 75° (c) 55° (d) 82° (e) 30°

4. Use your answers for Question 3 to change these to radians:
   (a) 200° (b) 150° (c) 165° (d) 164° (e) 330°

5. Find the following angles in degrees giving your answers to 2 places of decimals:
   (a) 0.5^c (b) 1^c (c) 2^c (d) 1.2^c (e) 2.4^c

6. Use tables to find:
   (a) $\sin \dfrac{\pi}{6}$ (b) $\cos \dfrac{\pi}{6}$ (c) $\tan \dfrac{\pi}{4}$ (d) $\tan \dfrac{\pi}{3}$

7. (a) Copy and complete the table below.

x	0	$\pi/4$	$\pi/2$	$3\pi/4$	π	$5\pi/4$	$3\pi/2$	$7\pi/4$	2π
sin x									

   (b) Hence plot the graph of $x \to \sin x$ for $0 \le x \le 2\pi$.

8. By completing similar tables as in Question 7 plot graphs of:
   (a) $x \to \cos x$ for $0 \le x \le 2\pi$
   (b) $x \to \tan x$ for $0 \le x \le 2\pi$

9. Plot the graphs:
   (a) $y = \sin x + \cos x$
   (b) $y = \sin 2x$
   (c) $y = 2 \sin x - \cos 2x$
   for $0 \le x \le 2\pi$.

Arc measure

For an angle of 1.8^c, the arc length is 1.8 cm if the radius of the circle is 1 cm.
Here is a circle of radius 3 cm:

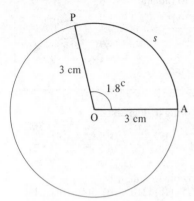

The circle is an enlargement
of a circle of radius 1 cm, by a factor of 3.
Arc length AP = 1.8×3
            = 5.4 cm.

The same method can be used for any circle:

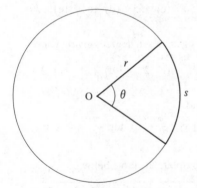

Given: r = radius
          θ = angle at the centre, in radians
          s = arc length
Then $s = r\theta$ where θ is in radians.

10. Find the length of the arc, given:
     (a) $r = 5$ cm, $\theta = 2^c$
     (b) $r = 4$ m, $\theta = 0.1^c$
     (c) $r = 1$ km, $\theta = 0.05^c$

11. Find the size in radians of the angle at the centre of
a circle, given:
     (a) $r = 10$ cm, $s = 5$ cm
     (b) $r = 2$ cm, $s = 0.2$ cm
     (c) $r = 2$ cm, $s = \pi$ cm

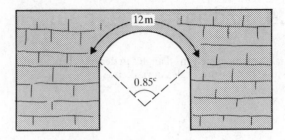

12. The circular arch of the bridge above measures
12 m and the angle at the centre of curvature is
0.85^c. Find the radius of curvature of the arch.

13. A and B are two points on the circumference of a
circle, centre O, radius 10 m. Angle AOB = $5°$.
     (a) Change $5°$ to radians.
     (b) What is the length of arc AB?
     (c) Show that the length of the chord AB is equal
         to $20 \sin 2\frac{1}{2}°$, and evaluate it.
     (d) Is arc length a good approximation to chord
         length, for small angles?

14. A surveyor S sights two hills A and B which are
both 10 km distant. He finds that the angle between
his sights is $4°$, as shown below:

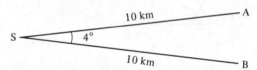

     (a) Change $4°$ to radians.
     (b) Find the arc length AB, to give the
         approximate distance between A and B.

15. In Question 14, arc length is used to find the
approximate straight line distance. This is a good
approximation for small angles.
A boy estimates that the angle
subtended by the moon is $\frac{1}{2}°$, and
he knows that the distance of the
moon from Earth is
approximately 380 000 km.
     (a) Change $\frac{1}{2}°$ to radians.
     (b) Find the approximate
         diameter of the moon.

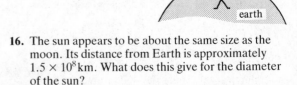

16. The sun appears to be about the same size as the
moon. Its distance from Earth is approximately
1.5×10^8 km. What does this give for the diameter
of the sun?

6.5 Sectors and segments

Sectors

The shaded part of the circle below is called a **sector**.

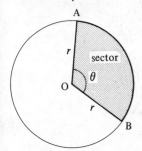

The sector is all that part of the circle enclosed between OA and OB.

The area of the complete circle is πr^2. Suppose $\theta = 120°$. Then the angle of the sector is $\frac{1}{3}$ of a complete turn ($\frac{120}{360} = \frac{1}{3}$) so the area of the sector is $\frac{1}{3}$ of the area of the complete circle, i.e. $\frac{1}{3}\pi r^2$.

For any angle θ:

$$\text{area of sector AOB} = \frac{\theta}{360°} \times \pi r^2$$

If θ is measured in radians, the result is simpler:

$$\text{area of sector AOB} = \frac{\theta}{2\pi} \times \pi r^2 = \frac{1}{2}r^2\theta$$

The area of a sector with angle θ radians is $\frac{1}{2}r^2\theta$.

The unshaded area of the circle is also a sector. It is called the **major sector**; the shaded area is called the **minor sector**. The major sector and minor sector together make up the complete circle.

1. Use the formula to find the area of the sector, if:
   (a) $r = 6\,\text{cm}$, $\theta = \frac{1}{2}^c$
   (b) $r = 2.5\,\text{cm}$, $\theta = 1.2^c$

   (c) $r = 7\,\text{cm}$, $\theta = \dfrac{\pi^c}{4}$

   (d) $r = 12\,\text{cm}$, $\theta = \dfrac{\pi^c}{6}$

2. The pick-up arm of a record player (the arm that carries the stylus or needle) is 25 cm long. In playing a record, it moves through an angle of 0.5 radians.
   (a) What is the distance travelled by the pick-up head?
   (b) What area is swept out by the pick-up arm?

3. A table is in the shape of a sector of a circle, radius 1.2 m, with an angle of 3.5 radians. Draw a diagram of the top of the table and find its area.

4. Part of an athletics field reserved for shot putting is in the shape of a sector of a circle, of angle 0.7 radians and radius 20 m. What area of the field is set aside for shot putting?

5. The diagram below shows a view of a keyhole, in the shape of a rectangle surmounted by part of a circle. The dimensions are shown in the diagram.

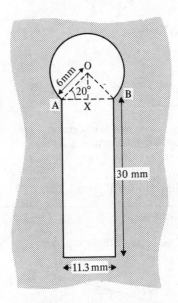

   (a) Find the area of the rectangle.
   (b) Find the area of the triangle AOB.
   (c) What is the size of the reflex angle AOB, in radians?
   (d) Find the size of the major sector AOB.
   (e) What is the total area of the keyhole?

6. The diagram shows a right-angled isosceles triangle ABC with AB = 2 m. BX is the arc of a circle centre A.

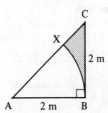

   Which of these gives the area of the shaded portion?

   (a) $4 - \dfrac{\pi}{2}$ (b) $2 - \dfrac{\pi}{4}$ (c) $2 - \dfrac{\pi}{2}$

   (d) 1.57 (e) 0.43 (f) 0.86

Segments

A **segment** of a circle is the part cut off by a chord:

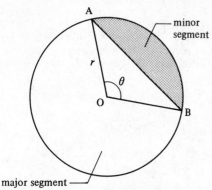

Chord AB divides the circle into two segments, a minor segment (shaded) and a major segment (all the unshaded part).

The area of the minor segment is equal to the area of the sector OAB minus the area of the triangle OAB.

Example 2

Find the area of the segment in the diagram.

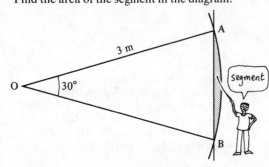

$$\text{Area of sector AOB} = \frac{30°}{360°} \times \pi r^2$$

$$= 2.36 \, \text{m}^2$$

$$\text{Area of triangle AOB} = \tfrac{1}{2} \, ab \sin \theta$$
$$= \tfrac{1}{2} \times 3 \times 3 \times \sin 30°$$
$$= 2.25 \, \text{m}^2$$

$$\text{Area of segment} = 2.36 - 2.25$$
$$= 0.11 \, \text{m}^2$$

In Example 2 you could also write:

Area of sector AOB $= \tfrac{1}{2} r^2 \theta = \tfrac{1}{2} \times 3^2 \times \dfrac{\pi^c}{6} = 2.36 \, \text{m}^2$

since $30° = \dfrac{\pi^c}{6}$.

7. Find the area of the minor segment where:
   (a) $r = 10 \, \text{cm}$, $\theta = 30°$ (b) $r = 5 \, \text{cm}$, $\theta = 45°$
   (c) $r = 4 \, \text{cm}$, $\theta = 1.2^c$ (d) $r = 8.2 \, \text{cm}$, $\theta = 0.7^c$

8. The line XY cuts a circle of radius 8 cm into two segments. XY subtends an angle of 140° at the centre of the circle.

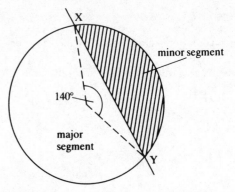

Find:
(a) the area of the circle
(b) sin 140°
(c) the size of 140° in radians
(d) the area of the minor segment cut off by XY
(e) the area of the major segment cut off by XY

9. In the diagram, AB is a chord of a circle of radius 5 cm.

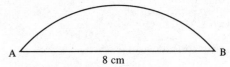

(a) Draw a diagram of the full circle, with centre O.
(b) Find the area of triangle AOB.
(c) Find the size of angle AOB.
(d) Find the area of the segment.

10. Repeat Question 9, with:
   (a) radius = 10 cm, AB = 12 cm
   (b) radius = 10 cm, AB = 10 cm

11. ABC is an equilateral triangle of side 20 cm. An arc AC is drawn with centre B. Calculate the area enclosed between the side AC and the arc AC.

12. A square ABCD has a side of 10 cm. Two arcs are drawn from B to D, one with A as centre and one with C as centre.
   (a) Draw a sketch of ABCD showing the two arcs.
   (b) Calculate the area enclosed between the arcs.

Summary

By the end of this chapter, these are the things you should know about:

6.1 Graphs of trigonometric functions
(pages 228–232)

The tangent of an angle is the length that the angle cuts off on the tangent to a circle of unit radius.

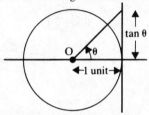

How to use this idea to find the tangents of angles greater than 90° or less than 0°.
You should also remember the general shape of the tangent curve, and these results in particular:
$\tan 0° = 0$, $\tan 45° = 1$, $\tan 90° = \infty$ (infinity)
$\tan \theta = \tan (180 + \theta)$

How to find the sine and cosine of any angle, by drawing the angle in a circle of unit radius.

How to draw the sine and cosine curves.

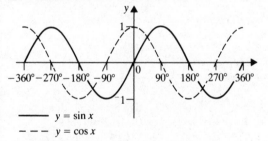

—————— $y = \sin x$
– – – – – $y = \cos x$

Remember these results, in particular:
$\sin 0° = 0$,
$\sin 90° = 1$, $\cos 0° = 1$, $\cos 90° = 0$
$\sin \theta = \sin (180° - \theta)$, $\cos \theta = \cos (360° - \theta)$

6.2 Using tables and calculators
(pages 233–234)

How to use tables to find the sine, cosine and tangent of any angle between 90° and 360°.
Remember the rule for which ones are positive (CAST).

How to use a calculator to find the sine, cosine and tangent of any angle.
How to find the value of an angle given its sine or cosine.

6.3 The sine and cosine rules (pages 234–238)

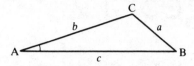

The sine rule: $\dfrac{a}{\sin A} = \dfrac{b}{\sin B} = \dfrac{c}{\sin C}$

The rule: $\sin^2 A + \cos^2 A = 1$
The cosine rule: $a^2 = b^2 + c^2 - 2bc \cos A$

How to use these formulae to find the lengths and angles in any triangles.

How to find the area of a triangle using the formula:

$$\text{Area } \Delta ABC = \tfrac{1}{2}ab \sin \hat{C}$$

6.4 Radians (pages 239–240)

Remember that $360° = 2\pi$ radians.
How to change degrees to radians and vice-versa.

$$\text{e.g. } 40° = 40° \times \frac{\pi}{180°} = \frac{2\pi^c}{9}$$

The formula $s = r\theta$ for arc length where θ is in radians.

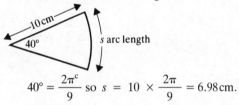

$$40° = \frac{2\pi^c}{9} \text{ so } s = 10 \times \frac{2\pi}{9} = 6.98 \text{ cm.}$$

6.5 Sectors and segments (pages 241–242)

What **sectors** and **segments** are.
The area of a sector $= \tfrac{1}{2}r^2\theta$, where θ is in radians.
How to find the area of a segment.
e.g.

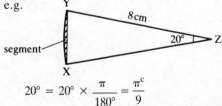

$$20° = 20° \times \frac{\pi}{180°} = \frac{\pi^c}{9}$$

$$\text{Area sector XYZ} = \tfrac{1}{2} \times 8^2 \times \frac{\pi}{9}$$
$$= 11.17 \text{ cm}^2$$

$$\text{Area of triangle XYZ} = \tfrac{1}{2} \times 8 \times 8 \times \sin \frac{\pi}{9}$$
$$= 10.94 \text{ cm}^2$$

$$\text{Area of segment} = 11.17 - 10.94 = 0.23 \text{ cm}^2$$

7 Algebra 2

7.1 Revision

Rules for indices

$$a^m \times a^n = a^{m+n}; \quad a^m \div a^n = a^{m-n}$$
$$a^0 = 1; \quad a^{-n} = \frac{1}{a^n};$$

Example 1

Simplify $\dfrac{a^2bc^3}{a^5b^2} \times \dfrac{ab^3c^2}{bc^4}$

Multiply the two numerators together and the two denominators together, and collect like terms:

$$\frac{a^2bc^3ab^3c^2}{a^5b^2bc^4} \quad \text{or} \quad \frac{a^3b^4c^5}{a^5b^3c^4} \qquad \text{This simplifies to } \frac{bc}{a^2}$$

---

1. Simplify:
   (a) $2x + 3x + 4x$ (b) $2y \times 3y \times 4y$
   (c) $3p - 4q - p + 5q$ (d) $2ab + 3ba - ab$

2. Simplify:
   (a) $x^2 \times x^3 \times x^4$ (b) $p^7 \times p^5 \div p^3$
   (c) $y^4 \times y^{-3} \times y^{-5}$ (d) $q^5 \times q^{-4} \div q^{-2}$

3. Simplify:
   (a) $(x^3)^2$ (b) $(p^{-2})^4$ (c) $(3y^2)^4$

4. Write with positive indices only:
   (a) p^{-5} (b) $x^{-2} \times x^{-5} \times x^4$
   (c) $q^{-3} \div q^4$ (d) $y^2 \times y^{-5} \div y^{-3}$
   (e) $(k^2 \times k^{-3}) \div (k^4 \div k^{-1})$

5. Simplify:
   (a) $lm^3n^2 \div mn^2$ (b) $x^5y^2z^4 \div y^3z^3$

6. Simplify:
   (a) $\dfrac{p^3q}{pq^4}$ (b) $\dfrac{x^4yz^3}{xy^2z^4}$ (c) $\dfrac{k^4l^2m^5}{kl^2m^3}$

Example 2

(a) $-5a(b + c) = -5ab - 5ac$

(b) $-3p(r - 4s) = -3pr + 12ps$

---

7. Remove brackets, collect like terms and simplify:
   (a) $3(x + y) + 4x$ (b) $2(p - q) - 4q$
   (c) $5l - 3(l + m)$ (d) $4k - 2(3n - k)$

8. Simplify by first removing the brackets:
   (a) $2(x - 3) + 3(x + 4) - 5(x - 1)$
   (b) $3(p + q) - 2(p - q) - 4(p + 3q)$
   (c) $4(l - m) + 2(m - 3l) - (5l - 4m)$
   (d) $a(b + c) - b(c - a) - c(a + b)$

9. Simplify:
   (a) $2p(3q + r) + 4p(q - 2r) - p(2q - 3r)$
   (b) $3(2 + mn) + 4(1 - mn) - 5(mn + 2)$
   (c) $3k(2 + l) - 3l(4 - k) + 2(2l - 3k)$

10. Simplify:
    (a) $x[2(y - z) + 3(z - 2y)] + 4xy$
    (b) $2pq(r - 5) + qr(p + 1) - 3pr(2 - q)$

Factorization

$ax + bx = (a + b)x$

$pq - pr = p(q - r)$

11. Factorize:
   (a) $3x + 6y$ (b) $2st - t$
   (c) $kl + km + kn$ (d) $pqr - qrs$
   (e) $2x^2y + xy^2z + xyz^2$

Expressions can often be factorized by first collecting like terms together, and then factorizing each group, before finally finding a bracket which is one of the factors of the original expression.

For example,

$ax + bx + ay + by$ or, $ax + ay + bx + by$
$= (a + b)x + (a + b)y$ $= a(x + y) + b(x + y)$
$= (a + b)(x + y)$ $= (a + b)(x + y)$

12. Copy and complete:
   (a) $ax - bx + ay - by$ $= (\quad)x + (\quad)y$
                           $= (\quad)(x + y)$
   (b) $px - py + qx - qy$ $= p(\quad) + q(\quad)$
                           $= (p + q)(\quad)$
   (c) $ut^2 + vs + us + vt^2$ $= (\quad)t^2 + (\quad)s$
                           $= (\quad)(t^2 + s)$
   (d) $ut^2 - us + vt^2 - vs$ $= u(\quad) + v(\quad)$
                           $= (u + v)(\quad)$
   (e) $2lx + mx - my - 2ly$ $= (\quad)x - (\quad)y$
                           $= (\quad)(x - y)$
   (f) $pr + 3ps - qr - 3qs$ $= p(\quad) - q(\quad)$
                           $= (p - q)(\quad)$

Example 3

Factorize $ap - 3bq - aq + 3bp$.

First collect like terms:
   $ap - aq + 3bp - 3bq$
then take out the common factors:
   $a(p - q) + 3b(p - q)$
   $= (a + 3b)(p - q)$

---

13. Collect like terms together and then factorize:
   (a) $sx + 5tx + sy + 5ty$
   (b) $am - 2al + bm - 2bl$
   (c) $su^2 + 4tv + tu^2 + 4sv$
   (d) $a^2l - b^2m + b^2l - a^2m$
   (e) $2bx + 3cy + 3cx + 2by$
   (f) $3zw^2 - y^2t + 3zt - y^2w^2$

14. Factorize:
   (a) $ax + bx - cx + ay + by - cy$
   (b) $px^2 - py - pz^3 + qx^2 - qy - qz^3$
   (c) $ls + mt + nt + ms + lt + ns$
   (d) $2fx + gy - 3fz + 2gx + fy - 3gz$

15. Factorize:
   (a) $3m^2x - 4n^3y^2 - 3m^2y^2 + 4n^3x$
   (b) $4ax - 5bx + 5by - 4ay$
   (c) $2ac - 4ad + bc - 2bd$
   (d) $10pq - 5pr - 2sq + sr$

16. Factorize:
   (a) $px + qx + py + qy$
   (b) $3lp - 2mq - 2mp + 3lq$
   (c) $2wx - wy + 4xz - 2yz$
   (d) $6xp - 4py + 3xq - 2qy$
   (e) $lx + 2my - lz - 2mz + 2mx + ly$
   (f) $rp - 2rq + sp - 2sq + 2pt - 4tq$
   (g) $2x^2 - 2xm - xn + mn$
   (h) $2lm - m - 6l + 3$

Fractions

$$\frac{a}{b} + \frac{c}{d} = \frac{ad}{bd} + \frac{bc}{bd} = \frac{ad + bc}{bd}$$

Example 4

Simplify $\dfrac{2}{(p + q)} - \dfrac{(p - q)}{3}$

First write with a common denominator:

$$\frac{2 \times 3}{3(p + q)} - \frac{(p - q)(p + q)}{3(p + q)}$$

then write as a single fraction: $\dfrac{6 - (p^2 - q^2)}{3(p + q)}$

---

17. Simplify:
   (a) $\dfrac{x}{3} + \dfrac{x}{2}$ (b) $\dfrac{1}{2p} + \dfrac{1}{3p} + \dfrac{1}{4p}$

   (c) $\dfrac{k}{2} + \dfrac{3}{l}$ (d) $\dfrac{1}{2x} + \dfrac{3}{y} - \dfrac{4}{z}$

18. Simplify:
   (a) $\dfrac{(x - 2)}{4} - \dfrac{(x + 1)}{3}$ (b) $\dfrac{p}{qr} + \dfrac{qr}{pr}$

   (c) $\dfrac{k}{l} \times \dfrac{m}{n} \div \dfrac{kn}{lm}$ (d) $\dfrac{x}{y}\left(\dfrac{2y}{3} - \dfrac{3y}{4}\right)$

19. Simplify:
   (a) $\dfrac{1}{(x - 2)} + \dfrac{1}{(x + 3)}$ (b) $\dfrac{2}{(a + b)} - \dfrac{3}{(a - b)}$

   (c) $\dfrac{(l + m)}{3} - \dfrac{2}{(l - m)}$ (d) $\dfrac{5(p + q)}{r} - \dfrac{3(p - q)}{2r}$

Substitution

Example 5

If $p = 3$, $q = 2$ and $r = {}^-5$ then
$$3pq + qr - 4pr$$
$$= 3 \times 3 \times 2 + 2 \times ({}^-5) - 4 \times 3 \times ({}^-5)$$
$$= 18 - 10 + 60$$
$$= 68$$

---

20. If $x = 4$, $y = {}^-2$ and $z = 7$ find:
(a) $xy + yz$ (b) $2xz - 3xy + z$
(c) $xyz - 3y$ (d) $xy - 3(x - z) + 2y$

21. If $p = 1$, $q = 2$, $r = 3$ and $s = 4$ find:

(a) $\dfrac{pqr}{s}$ (b) $\dfrac{p + q}{r + s}$ (c) $\dfrac{pq + rs}{p + s}$

(d) $\sqrt{qr + s}$ (e) $q(rs)^2$ (f) $q^2 + r^2 - s^2$

7.2 Fractional indices

What do you think $9^{\frac{1}{2}}$ means?
$$9^{\frac{1}{2}} \times 9^{\frac{1}{2}} = 9^{\frac{1}{2}+\frac{1}{2}} = 9^1 = 9$$

But $\sqrt{9} \times \sqrt{9} = 9$,   so $9^{\frac{1}{2}} = \sqrt{9}$

That is, a number to the power $\frac{1}{2}$ is the same as the square root of that number.

In the same way
$$8^{\frac{1}{3}} \times 8^{\frac{1}{3}} \times 8^{\frac{1}{3}} = 8^{\frac{1}{3}+\frac{1}{3}+\frac{1}{3}} = 8$$

So, $8^{\frac{1}{3}} = \sqrt[3]{8} = 2$: $8^{\frac{1}{3}}$ is the cube root of 8.

In general: $a^{\frac{1}{n}} = \sqrt[n]{a}$ i.e. the nth root of a.

Example 1

Find the value of

(a) $27^{\frac{2}{3}}$ (b) $16^{-\frac{3}{4}}$

(a) $27^{\frac{2}{3}} = (27^{\frac{1}{3}})^2 = 3^2 = 9$

(b) $16^{-\frac{3}{4}} = \dfrac{1}{16^{\frac{3}{4}}} = \dfrac{1}{(16^{\frac{1}{4}})^3} = \dfrac{1}{2^3} = \dfrac{1}{8}$

---

1. Find the value of
(a) $16^{\frac{1}{2}}$ (b) $27^{\frac{1}{3}}$ (c) $81^{\frac{1}{4}}$
(d) $1^{\frac{1}{5}}$ (e) $16^{\frac{3}{4}}$ (f) $25^{\frac{3}{2}}$
(g) $4^{-\frac{1}{2}}$ (h) $100^{-\frac{3}{2}}$ (i) $(2\frac{1}{4})^{\frac{1}{2}}$
(j) $125^{-\frac{2}{3}}$ (k) $(\frac{9}{16})^{-\frac{3}{2}}$ (l) $(\frac{25}{36})^{-1.5}$

2. Simplify and hence calculate:
(a) $3^{\frac{1}{2}} \times 3^{\frac{1}{2}}$ (b) $(8^{\frac{1}{3}})^3$
(c) $(2^{-\frac{1}{2}})^4$ (d) $4^{-\frac{2}{3}} \times 4^{\frac{2}{3}}$
(e) $(3^2)^{-\frac{1}{2}}$ (f) $(7^3)^{-\frac{2}{3}}$
(g) $3^{\frac{1}{2}} \div 3^{-\frac{1}{2}}$ (h) $\sqrt{6} \div 6^{-\frac{3}{2}}$
(i) $4^{-\frac{1}{2}} \div 4^{\frac{3}{2}}$ (j) $(\frac{4}{9})^{\frac{1}{2}} \div 3^{\frac{1}{2}}$
(k) $(\frac{9}{16})^{-\frac{3}{2}}$ (l) $(8^{-\frac{2}{3}})^3$

3. Simplify:
(a) $(16a^4)^{\frac{1}{2}}$ (b) $(16a^4)^{-\frac{1}{2}}$
(c) $(x^3y^3)^{\frac{1}{3}}$ (d) $\left(\dfrac{27x^3}{y^3}\right)^{-\frac{1}{3}}$
(e) $(4a^8)^{\frac{3}{2}}$ (f) $(2x^{\frac{3}{2}})^4$
(g) $(\sqrt[3]{4}\,a^{\frac{1}{2}})^6$ (h) $(x^{\frac{1}{3}}y^{-\frac{1}{3}})^3$
(i) $(\frac{25}{4}x^4y^2)^{-\frac{1}{2}}$ (j) $(16x^2y^6)^{-\frac{3}{2}}$
(k) $(x^2y^3z^{-\frac{1}{2}})^2$ (l) $\left(\dfrac{8x^6y^3}{z^{-3}}\right)^{-\frac{2}{3}}$

4. Simplify:
(a) $x^{-2}y^{\frac{1}{3}} \times xy^{\frac{2}{3}}$ (b) $x^{\frac{3}{4}} \div x^{-\frac{1}{4}}$
(c) $(rq)^{\frac{2}{3}} \times r^{\frac{1}{3}}q^{-\frac{1}{3}}$ (d) $r^2s^{-\frac{1}{4}} \div s^{\frac{1}{4}}$
(e) $(x^2y^4)^{\frac{1}{2}} \div y^{-2}$ (f) $(a^4b^2)^{-\frac{3}{4}} \div a^{-1}$
(g) $(a^3b^{-2})^{\frac{1}{4}} \div ab^{\frac{1}{4}}$ (h) $(4a^2)^{-\frac{3}{2}} \div a^{-\frac{1}{2}}$

5. Solve the following equations:
(a) $x^{\frac{1}{3}} = 4$ (b) $x^{-\frac{1}{2}} = 4$
(c) $x^{\frac{2}{3}} = 125$ (d) $x^{-\frac{3}{2}} = \frac{1}{16}$
(e) $2x^{\frac{1}{3}} = 18$ (f) $x\sqrt{x} = 64$
(g) $x^{-\frac{3}{2}} = \frac{1}{64}$ (h) $x^{\frac{1}{3}} = 4$

Example 2

Solve the equation $2 \times 2^{2x} = 128$
$$2 \times 2^{2x} = 128$$
$$\Rightarrow \quad 2^{2x+1} = 128$$
$$= 2^7$$
$$\Rightarrow \quad 2x + 1 = 7 \qquad\qquad \text{so } x = 3$$

---

6. Solve the following equations:
(a) $3^x = 9$ (b) $3^{2x} = 27$
(c) $3^x \times 3^2 = 3^7$ (d) $2 \times 3^x = 54$
(e) $4^{2x} \div 4 = 2^{10}$ (f) $4^{2x+1} = 8 \times 2^x$
(g) $6 \times 6^{2x} = 36 \times 6^x$ (h) $5^{3x-1} = 25 \times 5^{2x}$

7.3 Changing the subject of a formula

The formula for the circumference of a circle is $C = 2\pi r$.

The formula for its area is $A = \pi r^2$.

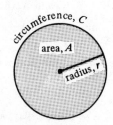

circumference, C

area, A

radius, r

1. Taking π as 3.14, explain how you would find:
   (a) the circumference and
   (b) the area of a circle of radius 5 cm.

2. Taking π as 3.14, find the radius of a circle with:
   (a) a circumference of 62.8 cm
   (b) an area of 78.5 cm^2

You can find the circumference or area of a circle using a function machine:

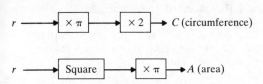

$r \longrightarrow \boxed{\times \pi} \longrightarrow \boxed{\times 2} \longrightarrow C$ (circumference)

$r \longrightarrow \boxed{\text{Square}} \longrightarrow \boxed{\times \pi} \longrightarrow A$ (area)

You can use the reverse machine in each case to find the radius:

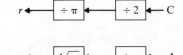

$r \longleftarrow \boxed{\div \pi} \longleftarrow \boxed{\div 2} \longleftarrow C$

and $r \longleftarrow \boxed{\sqrt{}} \longleftarrow \boxed{\div \pi} \longleftarrow A$

So in Question 2 (a) $62.8 \rightarrow 31.4 \rightarrow 10$
and in Question 2 (b) $78.5 \rightarrow 25 \rightarrow 5$

In general, to find r from the circumference:

$$C \rightarrow \frac{C}{2} \rightarrow \frac{C}{2\pi} = r \quad \text{so } r = \frac{C}{2\pi}$$

and to find r from the area:

$$A \rightarrow \frac{A}{\pi} \rightarrow \sqrt{\frac{A}{\pi}} = r \quad \text{so } r = \sqrt{\frac{A}{\pi}}$$

Each formula has been rearranged.
In each the letter r has been made **the subject of the formula.**
The subject of a formula appears on its own on the left-hand side.

The time T for each complete swing of a pendulum of length l is given by the formula:

$$T = 2\pi \sqrt{\frac{l}{g}} \text{, where } g$$

is the acceleration due to gravity.

T is the subject of the formula.

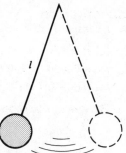

3. The function machine below is for finding T in the formula above, when you start with l. Copy and complete the machine.

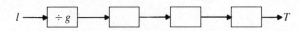

$l \longrightarrow \boxed{\div g} \longrightarrow \boxed{} \longrightarrow \boxed{} \longrightarrow \boxed{} \longrightarrow T$

Taking π as 3.14, use your machine to find T when $l = 20$ and $g = 980$.

4. Now draw the reverse machine for question 3 and show that the formula can be rearranged as

$$l = \left(\frac{T}{2\pi}\right)^2 \times g$$

5. If $T = 1.57$ and $g = 32$, use the formula in Question 4 to find l. (Take π as 3.14).

$x \longrightarrow \boxed{\times m} \longrightarrow \boxed{+ c} \longrightarrow y$

6. (a) Use the machine above to write down a formula with y as its subject (i.e. $y = \quad$).
   (b) Use the reverse machine to rewrite the formula with x as its subject (i.e. $x = \quad$).

7. The formula for converting temperature from Fahrenheit to Centigrade is $C = \dfrac{5}{9}(F - 32)$.
   (a) Draw a function machine to show how you can find C, starting with a value for F.
   (b) Use your machine to find C when F is:
       (i) 41°   (ii) 59°   (iii) 86°   (iv) 212°

8. (a) Draw the reverse machine for Question 7 (a).
   (b) Use this to write down the rearranged formula with F as its subject.
   (c) Find F when C is (i) 50°   (ii) 100°

Example 1

$I = P \times R \times T$

when $P = 300$, $R = 0.05$ and $T = 4$

$I = 300 \times 0.05 \times 4 = 60$

The formula can be shown as a function machine:

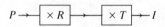

P can be found by using

$P \longleftarrow \boxed{\div R} \longleftarrow \boxed{\div T} \longleftarrow I$

which gives the formula

$$P = \frac{I}{T \times R}$$

---

9. Find the value of the expression for the given data:
   (a) $P \times R \times T$ for $P = 400$, $R = 6$, and $T = 5$
   (b) $l \times b \times h$ for $l = 5$, $b = 7$, and $h = 4$
   (c) $2\pi rh$ for $r = 10$, and $h = 4$, taking $\pi = 3.14$
   (d) $(u + at)$ for $u = 15$, $a = 25$ and $t = 2$
   (e) $\frac{5}{9}(F - 32)$ for $F = 78$

   (f) $2\pi \sqrt{\dfrac{l}{g}}$ for $l = 0.1$ and $g = 10$

10. Draw a function machine as above, to show how to find:
    (a) V using $V = l \times b \times h$, starting with l
    (b) S using $S = 2\pi rh$, starting with r
    (c) v using $v = u + at$, starting with t
    (d) V using $V = \pi r^2 h$, starting with r
    (e) S using $S = \pi r(2h + r)$, starting with h
    (f) C using $C = \frac{5}{9}(F - 32)$, starting with F
    (g) F using $F = \frac{9}{5}C + 32$, starting with C
    (h) s using $s = t(u + \frac{1}{2}at)$, starting with a

11. Use the reverse machine for each part of Question 10 to re-write the formula, making as the subject in each case the letter you originally started with.

12. $V = \pi h(R^2 - r^2)$.
    (a) Find V, when $h = 2$cm, $R = 7.5$cm and $r = 2.5$cm, taking $\pi = 3.14$
    (b) Draw a function machine to show how to find V starting with R
    (c) Use the reverse machine to re-write the formula with R in terms of V, h, r and π.

13. $V = \frac{1}{3}\pi r^2 h$. Draw a function machine to show how to find:
    (a) V, starting with r
    (b) r, starting with V
    (c) r, starting with h
    Find r if $h = 2.1$cm and $V = 100$cm^3.

14. The simple interest formula is $I = \dfrac{P \times R \times T}{100}$
    (a) Copy and complete this function machine for finding I when starting with T.
    (b) Then draw the reverse machine, and complete the equation $T = \dfrac{\square \times \square}{\square \times \square}$

15. (i) Draw a function machine to show how y can be found, starting with x.
        (a) $y = px + q$ (b) $y = k(x - l)$
        (c) $y = r(x - s) + t$ (d) $y = m(nx + l)$
    (ii) Use the reverse machine to rearrange the formula, making x the subject.

16. Use the above ideas to rearrange the formula, making r the subject:
    (a) $A = rh$ (b) $A = 2\pi rh$
    (c) $V = \pi r^2 h$ (d) $S = \pi h(R + r)$
    (e) $V = \dfrac{4}{3}\pi r^3$ (f) $A = P\left(1 + \dfrac{r}{100}\right)$

Example 2

Make R_1 the subject of the formula $V = I(R_1 + R_2)$.
The formula has to be rearranged so that R_1 is by itself on the left-hand side. This time, we will not use a function machine.
Remember that the formula is an equation. It must be kept balanced, so if you carry out an operation on one side of it, you must do the same on the other side.

Step 1: Divide both sides of the equation by I.
$$\frac{V}{I} = (R_1 + R_2)$$

Step 2: Subtract R_2 from both sides.
$$\frac{V}{I} - R_2 = R_1$$

Step 3: Turn the equation around.
$$R_1 = \frac{V}{I} - R_2$$

---

17. Without drawing a function machine, rearrange the formula $V = I(R_1 + R_2)$ so that the subject is:
    (a) R_2 (b) I

18. Without drawing a function machine, rearrange the formula $I = \dfrac{PRT}{100}$ so that the subject is:
    (a) R (b) P

19. If $P = P_0(1 + \alpha t)$, rearrange the formula so that the subject is:
    (a) P_0 (b) α (c) t

Example 3

Make d the subject of the formula $P = \dfrac{k}{d} + mv$

Step 1: Multiply each side by d to remove the fraction

$$P \times d = \left(\dfrac{k}{d} + mv\right) \times d$$

Step 2: Remove the brackets.
$Pd = k + mvd$

Step 3: Collect the d terms on the left.
$Pd - mvd = k$

Step 4: Take d out as a common factor.
$d(P - mv) = k$

Step 5: Divide both sides by $(P - mv)$.

$$d = \dfrac{k}{(P - mv)}$$

---

20. Make sure you understand the working in the above example. Now rearrange the same formula, making the subject: (a) k (b) v

21. $P = \dfrac{mv}{t} - \dfrac{mu}{t}$

Use the method above to rearrange the formula, so that the subject is:
(a) t (b) m (c) v (d) u

22. $\dfrac{x}{p} + \dfrac{y}{q} = 1$.

First multiply each side of the formula by pq and then rearrange it so that the subject is:
(a) x (b) y (c) p (d) q

23. An important formula in physics is $\dfrac{1}{u} + \dfrac{1}{v} = \dfrac{1}{f}$.

(a) By what would you multiply each side of the formula, to remove *all* the fractions?
(b) Rearrange the formula so that the subject is:
(i) u (ii) v (iii) f

24. $P = \dfrac{4K + 3Q}{(K + 5Q)}$.

First multiply each side of the formula by $(K + 5Q)$ and then collect like terms to show that:
(a) $K = \dfrac{Q(3 - 5P)}{(P - 4)}$ (b) $Q = \dfrac{(4 - P)K}{(5P - 3)}$

Example 4

Make F the subject of the formula in
$$C = \tfrac{5}{9}(F - 32)$$

Multiply both sides by 9:
$$9C = 5(F - 32)$$
Remove brackets:
$$9C = 5F - 160$$
Add 160 to both sides:
$$9C + 160 = 5F$$
Divide both sides by 5:
$$\tfrac{9}{5}C + 32 = F$$
So: $F = \tfrac{9}{5}C + 32$

---

25. Rearrange the formula and make as subject the given letter:
(a) l in $A = l \times b$ (b) r in $C = 2\pi r$
(c) I in $V = IR$ (d) L in $S = \pi r L$
(e) f in $v = u + ft$ (f) x in $y = mx + c$

(g) T in $P = \dfrac{RT}{V}$ (h) R in $I = \dfrac{E}{R}$

(i) m in $P = \dfrac{m(v - u)}{t}$ (j) r in $V = \pi r^2 h$

(k) u in $v^2 = u^2 + 2as$ (l) x in $r^2 = (x - a)^2 + y^2$

(m) g in $T = 2\pi\sqrt{\dfrac{l}{g}}$

26. Make r the subject of the formula in:
(a) $S = 4\pi r^2$ (b) $V = 3\pi r h$
(c) $A = \tfrac{1}{2}h(R + r)$ (d) $V = \pi h(R^2 - r^2)$

27. Make t the subject of the formula in:
(a) $s = \dfrac{(u + v)t}{2}$ (b) $u = v - ft$

(c) $R = \dfrac{PV}{mt}$ (d) $T = k(\alpha t + \beta)$

28. Make x the subject of the formula in:
(a) $y = m(x - a)$ (b) $\dfrac{x}{a} + \dfrac{y}{b} = 1$

(c) $(x - a)y = c$ (d) $y = 1 - \dfrac{1}{x}$

29. Make R the subject of the formula in:

(a) $A = P\left(1 + \dfrac{R}{100}\right)$ (b) $Rt = 2R + t$

(c) $V = \dfrac{R}{R - r}$ (d) $K = \dfrac{R + 1}{R + 2}$

For Questions 30 to 34 write down the correct result
(or results) from those given:

30. If $a = \dfrac{b}{x}$ then x is:

    (a) ab (b) $\dfrac{a}{b}$ (c) $\dfrac{b}{a}$ (d) $a + b$

31. If $P = \dfrac{mv^2}{2g}$ then v is:

    (a) $\sqrt{2Pg - m}$ (b) $\sqrt{\dfrac{2gP}{m}}$

    (c) $\dfrac{2g}{m}\sqrt{P}$ (d) $\dfrac{\sqrt{2gP}}{m}$

32. If $A = 2\pi r(r + h)$ then h is:

    (a) $A - 2\pi r^2$ (b) $\dfrac{A - 2\pi r^2}{2\pi r}$

    (c) $\dfrac{A - 2\pi r}{r}$ (d) $\dfrac{A}{2\pi r} - r$

33. If $y = \dfrac{3x + 1}{x + 2}$ then x is:

    (a) $\dfrac{3y + 1}{y + 2}$ (b) $\dfrac{1 - 2y}{3 + y}$

    (c) $\dfrac{2y - 1}{3 - y}$ (d) $\dfrac{y - 3}{1 - 2y}$

34. If $\dfrac{1}{u} + \dfrac{1}{v} = \dfrac{1}{f}$, then u is:

    (a) $f - v$ (b) $\dfrac{v + f}{vf}$

    (c) $\dfrac{vf}{v - f}$ (d) $\dfrac{v - f}{v + f}$

7.4 The product of two brackets

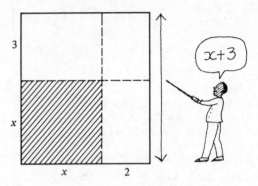

1. Look at the diagram above.
    (a) What shape is the shaded part? What is its area?
    (b) Write down the area of each of the three small rectangles.
    (c) Use (a) and (b) to write down the area of the complete rectangle.
    (d) Write down the area of the complete rectangle as the product of its length and breadth.

The area of the rectangle above can be written as
$$(x + 3) \times (x + 2)$$
$$= x \times (x + 2) + 3 \times (x + 2)$$
$$= x^2 + 2x + 3x + 6$$
$$= x^2 + 5x + 6$$

An alternative way of simplifying the two brackets is shown on the right.

$$(x + 3) \times (x + 2)$$
$$= x^2 + 2x + 3x + 6$$
$$= x^2 + 5x + 6$$

2. Simplify the expression as shown above:
    (a) $(x + 3) \times (x + 4)$ (b) $(x + 6) \times (x + 2)$
    (c) $(x + 3) \times (x + 5)$ (d) $(x + 7) \times (x + 2)$
    (e) $(x + 3) \times (x + 1)$ (f) $(x + 1) \times (x + 2)$

Your answer to Question 2 (a) should be:
$$x^2 + 7x + 12$$
This is a **quadratic expression**, because it contains x to the power 2 and no higher. That is, it contains a term in x^2 but not in x^3, x^4 etc.

3. Look carefully at your answers to Question 2. Is each a quadratic expression?

4. For Question 2, write down a quick way of finding:
    (a) the term with x
    (b) the term with just a number.

5. Use your answer to Question 4 to explain why
$(x + a) \times (x + b) = x^2 + (a + b)x + ab$

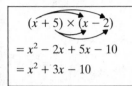

$(x + 5) \times (x - 2)$
$= x^2 - 2x + 5x - 10$
$= x^2 + 3x - 10$

$(x - 3) \times (x - 2)$
$= x^2 - 2x - 3x + 6$
$= x^2 - 5x + 6$

6. Look at the two sets of working above and make sure you understand them.
Do you agree that in each result:
(a) the number in the x term is obtained by adding the numbers in the two brackets?
   e.g. $5 + (-2)$ and $(-3) + (-2)$

(b) the number term is obtained by multiplying the numbers in the two brackets?
   e.g. $5 \times (-2)$ and $(-3) \times (-2)$

7. Simplify the expression as shown above.
(a) $(x + 7) \times (x - 2)$ (b) $(x + 5) \times (x - 3)$
(c) $(x + 2) \times (x - 5)$ (d) $(x + 8) \times (x - 7)$
(e) $(x + 3) \times (x - 7)$ (f) $(x - 3) \times (x + 2)$

8. $(x - 3) \times (x - 4)$ can be written as $(x - 3)(x - 4)$.
The $\times$ sign is left out.
Simplify the expression, as in Question 7.
(a) $(x - 3)(x - 4)$ (b) $(x - 2)(x - 5)$
(c) $(x - 7)(x - 3)$ (d) $(x - 9)(x - 7)$
(e) $(x - 2)(x - 2)$ (f) $(x - 1)(x - 1)$

9. Simplify the expression, as above:
(a) $(x + 3)(x + 9)$ (b) $(x + 4)(x - 5)$
(c) $(x - 6)(x + 7)$ (d) $(x - 4)(x - 7)$
(e) $(x - 4)(x - 11)$ (f) $(x + 3)(x - 10)$

10. Check that your answers for Question 9 are correct, by letting $x = 2$.

11. Use the above ideas to write the product $(a + b)(c + d)$ without brackets.

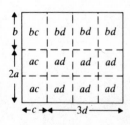

$(2a + b \times (c + 3d)$
$= 2a \times c + 2a \times 3d$
$\quad + b \times c + b \times 3d$
$= 2ac + 6ad + bc + 3bd$

12. (a) The rectangle above has sides of length $(2a + b)$ and $(c + 3d)$. Do you agree that its area is $(2a + b)(c + 3d)$?
(b) Do you agree that both methods above show that $(2a + b)(c + 3d)$ can be written as:
$2ac + 6ad + bc + 3bd$?

13. Use the ideas in Question 12 to write the product without brackets.
(a) $(2p + q)(r + 3s)$ (b) $(a + 3b)(2c + d)$
(c) $(3x + y)(6 + 5m)$ (d) $(2p + 5q)(l + m)$
(e) $(5a + b)(4c + d)$ (f) $(x + 3y)(p + 7q)$

14. Simplify.
(a) $\left(\dfrac{1}{a} + \dfrac{b}{6} \right)\left(\dfrac{c}{3} + \dfrac{d}{2} \right)$

(b) $\left(\dfrac{3x}{4} + \dfrac{y}{z} \right)\left(\dfrac{1}{z} + \dfrac{xz}{5} \right)$

(c) $\left(4 + \dfrac{5}{b} \right)\left(\dfrac{3}{a} + \dfrac{b}{a} \right)$

(d) $\left(\dfrac{x}{3} + \dfrac{y}{3} \right)\left(\dfrac{4}{a} + \dfrac{b}{3} \right)$

(e) $\left(\dfrac{6}{x} - \dfrac{5}{y} \right)\left(\dfrac{a}{5} + \dfrac{1}{ab} \right)$

Simplifying $(a + b)^2$

15. Look at the working shown on the right.
Do you agree that $(a + b)^2 = a^2 + 2ab + b^2$?
Check this result by first drawing a square of side $(a + b)$. Mark in it two smaller squares of sides a and b. Then find its area.

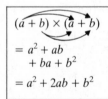

$(a + b) \times (a + b)$
$= a^2 + ab$
$\quad + ba + b^2$
$= a^2 + 2ab + b^2$

16. Show that $(a + b)^2 = a^2 + 2ab + b^2$ when:
(a) $a = 3, b = 4$ (b) $a = 9, b = 11$

(c) $a = 20, b = 1$ (d) $a = \dfrac{1}{3}, b = \dfrac{1}{2}$

17. Do you agree that:
$31^2 = (30 + 1)^2 = 30^2 + 2 \times 30 \times 1 + 1^2$
$\qquad\qquad\qquad\qquad = 900 + 60 + 1$?

Use this method to find:
(a) 41^2 (b) 51^2 (c) 23^2 (d) 72^2

Simplifying $(a - b)^2$

18. Use the diagram on the right to show that:
$(a - b)^2 = a^2 - 2ab + b^2$

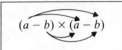

$(a - b) \times (a - b)$

19. Show that $(a - b)^2 = a^2 - 2ab + b^2$ when:
(a) $a = 5, b = 3$ (b) $a = 15, b = 5$
(c) $a = 20, b = 1$ (d) $a = 1.4, b = 1.7$

20. Do you agree that:
$29^2 = (30 - 1)^2 = 30^2 - 2 \times 30 \times 1 + 1^2$
$= 900 - 60 + 1?$
Use this method to find:
(a) 39^2 (b) 49^2 (c) 27^2 (d) 68^2

Simplifying $(a + b)(a - b)$

21. Use the diagram on the right to show that:
$(a + b)(a - b) = a^2 - b^2$

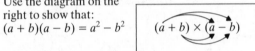

$(a + b) \times (a - b)$

22. Show that $a^2 - b^2 = (a + b)(a - b)$ when:
(a) $a = 5, b = 4$ (b) $a = 7, b = 3$
(c) $a = 21, b = 20$

23. Copy and complete the statement:
(a) $8^2 - 3^2 = (\quad + \quad) \times (\quad - \quad) =$
(b) $37^2 - 27^2 = (\quad + \quad) \times (\quad - \quad) =$

24. Find:
(a) $61^2 - 60^2$ (b) $55^2 - 45^2$

25. Write as the product of two brackets:
(a) $x^2 - y^2$ (b) $p^2 - q^2$ (c) $m^2 - 9$
(d) $4p^2 - q^2$ (e) $x^2 - 9y^2$ (f) $4d^2 - 9m^2$

26. Write as the product of two brackets:
(a) $\dfrac{1}{x^2} - \dfrac{9}{a^2}$ (b) $\dfrac{a^2}{x^2} - 4y^2$

(c) $\dfrac{m^2 n^2}{4} - 1$ (d) $25 - \dfrac{a^2 b^2}{16c^4}$

7.5 Completing the square

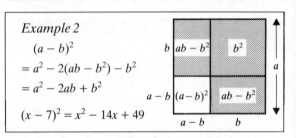

Example 1
$(a + b)^2$
$= a^2 + ab + ab + b^2$
$= a^2 + 2ab + b^2$

$(x + 5)^2 = x^2 + 10x + 25$

Example 2
$(a - b)^2$
$= a^2 - 2(ab - b^2) - b^2$
$= a^2 - 2ab + b^2$

$(x - 7)^2 = x^2 - 14x + 49$

$(a + b)^2 = a^2 + 2ab + b^2$
and $(a - b)^2 = a^2 - 2ab + b^2$
are two important results and should be learnt.

1. Copy and complete:
(a) $(7 + 8)^2 = 7^2 + \quad + \quad$
(b) $(5 + 9)^2 = \quad + \quad + \quad$
(c) $(8 - 3)^2 = 8^2 - \quad + \quad$
(d) $(11 - 7)^2 = \quad - \quad + \quad$

2. Copy and complete:
(a) $21^2 = (20 + 1)^2 = \quad = $
(b) $52^2 = (50 + 2)^2 = \quad = $
(c) $29^2 = (30 - 1)^2 = \quad = $
(d) $77^2 = (80 - 3)^2 = \quad = $

3. Copy and complete:
(a) $(9.1)^2 = (9 + 0.1)^2 = \quad = $
(b) $(12.3)^2 = (12 + 0.3)^2 = \quad = $
(c) $(4.9)^2 = (5 - 0.1)^2 = \quad = $
(d) $(19.8)^2 = (20 - 0.2)^2 = \quad = $

4. Write without brackets:
(a) $(l + m)^2$ (b) $(x - y)^2$ (c) $(2p + q)^2$
(d) $(a - 3b)^2$ (e) $(4m + 3n)^2$

5. Write without brackets:
(a) $(x + 6)^2$ (b) $(x + 11)^2$ (c) $(x - 5)^2$
(d) $(x - 13)^2$ (e) $(2x + 1)^2$ (f) $(5x + 1)^2$
(g) $(3x - 1)^2$ (h) $(7x - 1)^2$ (i) $(3x + 5)^2$
(j) $(4x - 7)^2$

6. Copy and complete:
   (a) $7^2 + 2 \times 7 \times 5 + 5^2 = ($ $+$ $)^2 =$
   (b) $8^2 + 2 \times 8 \times 3 + 3^2 = ($ $+$ $)^2 =$
   (c) $6^2 - 2 \times 6 \times 4 + 4^2 = ($ $-$ $)^2 =$
   (d) $9^2 - 2 \times 9 \times 6 + 6^2 = ($ $-$ $)^2 =$

7. Copy and complete:
   (a) $p^2 + 2pq + q^2 = ($ $+$ $)^2$
   (b) $l^2 - 2lm + m^2 = ($ $-$ $)^2$
   (c) $x^2 + 12x + 36 = ($ $+$ $)^2$
   (d) $y^2 - 18y + 81 = ($ $-$ $)^2$

8. Write as a square:
   (a) $x^2 + 8x + 16$ (b) $x^2 + 20x + 100$
   (c) $x^2 - 14x + 49$ (d) $x^2 - x + \frac{1}{4}$
   (e) $9x^2 + 6x + 1$ (f) $25x^2 + 10x + 1$
   (g) $16x^2 - 8x + 1$ (h) $36x^2 - 12x + 1$

9. Write as a square:
   (a) $x^2 + 6xy + 9y^2$ (b) $4l^2 + 4lm + m^2$
   (c) $a^2 + 10ab + 25b^2$ (d) $p^2 - 8pq + 16q^2$
   (e) $64x^2 - 16xy + y^2$ (f) $100l^2 - 20lm + m^2$
   (g) $4a^2 + 12ab + 9b^2$ (h) $16p^2 - 24pq + 9q^2$

10. Show that:
   (a) $(m - n)^2 + (m + n)^2 = 2(m^2 + n^2)$
   (b) $(m - n)^2 + 4mn = (m + n)^2$

11. Show that $(m^2 - n^2)^2 + (2mn)^2 = (m^2 + n^2)^2$.
   Hence write down in terms of m and n the lengths
   of the sides of a right-angled triangle.
   By putting $m = 2$ and $n = 1$, find the dimensions of
   one such triangle.

12. Simplify:
   (a) $(x + 1)^2 + (x + 2)^2 + (x + 3)^2$
   (b) $(x - 3)^2 + (x - 1)^2 + (x + 1)^2 + (x + 3)^2$
   (c) $(x + y)^2 + (y + z)^2 + (z + x)^2$
   (d) $(2x + y)^2 - (3x - 2y)^2 + (x + 2y)^2$

To make a perfect square from $x^2 + 6x$, it is necessary
to add $(\frac{1}{2}$ coefficient of $x)^2$, i.e. 9.

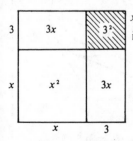

$x^2 + 6x + (3)^2 = (x + 3)^2$
i.e.

$$x^2 + 6x = x^2 + (3x + 3x)$$
$$= (x + 3)^2 - 3^2$$

13. Copy and complete:
   (a) $x^2 + 4x = (x + $ $)^2 -$
   (b) $x^2 + 8x = (x + $ $)^2 -$
   (c) $x^2 + 12x = (x + $ $)^2 -$
   (d) $x^2 + 20x = (x + $ $)^2 -$
   (e) $x^2 - 6x = (x - $ $)^2 -$
   (f) $x^2 - 10x = (x - $ $)^2 -$
   (g) $x^2 - 4x = (x - $ $)^2 -$
   (h) $x^2 - 14x = (x - $ $)^2 -$

Example 3

$x^2 + 10x + 28 = (x + 5)^2 + 28 - 5^2$
$\qquad\qquad\qquad = (x + 5)^2 + 3$

---

14. Copy and complete:
   (a) $x^2 + 2x + 5 = (x + 1)^2 +$
   (b) $x^2 + 6x + 12 = (x + 3)^2 +$
   (c) $x^2 + 16x + 100 = (x + $ $)^2 +$
   (d) $x^2 + 18x + 100 = (x + $ $)^2 +$
   (e) $x^2 + 10x + 3 = (x + $ $)^2 -$
   (f) $x^2 - 8x + 25 = (x - $ $)^2 +$
   (g) $x^2 - 12x + 40 = (x - $ $)^2 +$
   (h) $x^2 - 16x + 10 = (x - $ $)^2 -$

15. Write in the form $(x + a)^2 + b$:
   (a) $x^2 + 14x$ (b) $x^2 + 22x$
   (c) $x^2 - 18x$ (d) $x^2 - 20x$
   (e) $x^2 + 3x$ (f) $x^2 + x$
   (g) $x^2 - 3x$ (h) $x^2 - 5x$

16. Write in the form $(x + p)^2 + q$:
   (a) $x^2 + 6x + 17$ (b) $x^2 + 10x + 20$
   (c) $x^2 - 8x + 21$ (d) $x^2 - 24x - 100$
   (e) $x^2 + 3x + 5$ (f) $x^2 + 5x + 3$
   (g) $x^2 - 3x + 7$ (h) $x^2 - x + 4$

Example 4

Write $9x^2 + 6x - 2$ in the form $(ax + b)^2 + c$

$(3x + 1)^2 = (3x + 1)(3x + 1)$
$\qquad\qquad = 9x^2 + 6x + 1$
So $9x^2 + 6x - 2 = 9x^2 + 6x + 1 - 3$
$\qquad\qquad\qquad = (3x + 1)^2 - 3$

---

17. Write in the form $(ax + b)^2 + c$
   (a) $4x^2 + 4x + 3$ (b) $9x^2 + 12x - 3$
   (c) $4x^2 - 12x + 8$ (d) $16x^2 - 24x - 14$
   (e) $25x^2 - 20x - 6$ (f) $9x^2 - 12x + 17$

Example 5

Write $6x^2 - 10x - 3$ in the form $a(x + b)^2 + c$

$6x^2 - 10x - 3 = 6[x^2 - \frac{10}{6}x - \frac{3}{6}]$
$\qquad\qquad\qquad = 6[x^2 - \frac{5}{3}x - \frac{1}{2}]$
$\qquad\qquad\qquad = 6[(x - \frac{5}{6})^2 - (\frac{5}{6})^2 - \frac{1}{2}]$
$\qquad\qquad\qquad = 6[x - \frac{5}{6})^2 - \frac{43}{36}]$
$\qquad\qquad\qquad = 6(x - \frac{5}{6})^2 - 7\frac{1}{6}$

---

18. Write in the form $a(x + b)^2 + c$
   (a) $2x^2 + 6x + 2$ (b) $4x^2 - 4x - 17$
   (c) $6x^2 - 4x + 6$ (d) $5x^2 - 12x + 8$
   (e) $5x^2 - 3x + 2$ (f) $3x^2 - 14x + 3$

7.6 The difference between two squares

Look at the two diagrams below.

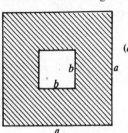 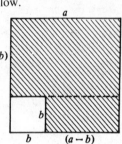

$$a^2 - b^2 = (a - b)a + (a - b)b$$
$$= (a - b)(a + b)$$
$$(7.6)^2 - (2.4)^2 = (7.6 - 2.4)(7.6 + 2.4)$$
$$= 5.2 \times 10$$
$$= 52$$

$$a^2 - b^2 = (a - b)(a + b)$$

This is an important result and should be learnt.

1. Copy and complete:
   (a) $7^2 - 3^2 = (7 - 3)(\quad) =$
   (b) $14^2 - 6^2 = (14 - 6)(\quad) =$
   (c) $89^2 - 11^2 = (89 - 11)(\quad) =$
   (d) $28^2 - 18^2 = (28 - 18)(\quad) =$
   (e) $53^2 - 33^2 = (\quad)(53 + 33) =$
   (f) $72^2 - 42^2 = (\quad)(72 + 42) =$

2. Copy and complete:
   (a) $(8.6)^2 - (1.4)^2 = (8.6 - 1.4)(\quad) =$
   (b) $(5.9)^2 - (4.1)^2 = (5.9 - 4.1)(\quad) =$
   (c) $(6.2)^2 - (3.8)^2 = (6.2 - 3.8)(\quad) =$
   (d) $(4.7)^2 - (2.7)^2 = (4.7 - 2.7)(\quad) =$
   (e) $(5.9)^2 - (3.9)^2 = (\quad)(5.9 + 3.9) =$
   (f) $(7.5)^2 - (3.5)^2 = (\quad)(7.5 + 3.5) =$

3. First write your answers as a product and then find:
   (a) $8^2 - 2^2$ (b) $12^2 - 8^2$ (c) $53^2 - 47^2$
   (d) $91^2 - 71^2$ (e) $127^2 - 73^2$ (f) $259^2 - 59^2$
   (g) $381^2 - 119^2$ (h) $276^2 - 226^2$

4. First write your answers as a product and then find:
   (a) $(5.7)^2 - (4.3)^2$ (b) $(8.1)^2 - (1.9)^2$
   (c) $(2.6)^2 - (1.4)^2$ (d) $(5.7)^2 - (3.7)^2$
   (e) $(6.8)^2 - (4.2)^2$ (f) $(7.9)^2 - (2.9)^2$
   (g) $(5.16)^2 - (4.84)^2$ (h) $(8.29)^2 - (1.71)^2$

5. Copy and complete:
   (a) $p^2 - q^2 = (p - q)(\quad)$
   (b) $(l^2 - m^2) = (\quad)(l + m)$
   (c) $p^2 - 4q^2 = (p - 2q)(\quad)$
   (d) $(9l^2 - m^2) = (\quad)(3l + m)$
   (e) $9p^2 - 4q^2 = (3p - 2q)(\quad)$
   (f) $(16l^2 - 9m^2) = (\quad)(4l + 3m)$

6. Write as the product of two brackets:
   (a) $x^2 - y^2$ (b) $s^2 - t^2$
   (c) $4a^2 - b^2$ (d) $l^2 - 9m^2$
   (e) $16a^2 - b^2$ (f) $p^2 - 25q^2$
   (g) $16a^2 - 25b^2$ (h) $49p^2 - 16q^2$

7. Write as the product of two brackets:
   (a) $b^2 - c^2$ (b) $81x^2 - y^2$
   (c) $p^2 - 100q^2$ (d) $100a^2 - 81b^2$
   (e) $(xy)^2 - z^2$ (f) $a^2 - b^2c^2$
   (g) $4p^2 - q^2r^2$ (h) $9l^2m^2 - n^4$

8. Write as the product of two brackets:
   (a) $a^2b^2 - c^2d^2$ (b) $x^2y^2z^2 - w^2$
   (c) $16p^2q^2 - 81r^2$ (d) $l^4 - n^4$
   (e) $(a + b)^2 - c^2$ (f) $p^2 - (q + r)^2$
   (g) $(x + y)^2 - (y + z)^2$ (h) $(l + m)^2 - (l - m)^2$

9. Find the length of the third side of a right-angled triangle ABC where:
   (a) AC = 13 cm, AB = 12 cm
   (b) AC = 25 cm, AB = 7 cm
   (c) AC = 41 cm, BC = 9 cm

10. PR is the hypotenuse of a right-angled triangle PQR. Find QR when:
    (a) PR = 61 cm, PQ = 11 cm
    (b) PR = 85 cm, PQ = 13 cm
    (c) PR = 3.9 cm, PQ = 1.5 cm
    (d) PR = 3.2 cm, PQ = 1.2 cm

Example

Find the volume of concrete in a pipe 6.3 m long with an external diameter of 1.7 m and an internal diameter of 1.5 m.

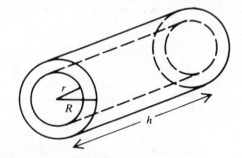

$$V = \pi R^2 h - \pi r^2 h = \pi h(R^2 - r^2)$$

i.e. $V = \pi h(R - r)(R + r)$

so $V = \pi \times 6.3 \times (1.7 - 1.5) \times (1.7 + 1.5)$

$$V = \pi \times 6.3 \times 0.2 \times 3.2$$

$$V = 4.03\pi$$

Taking π as 3.14, the volume of concrete is 12.66 m³.

11. Look at the diagram.

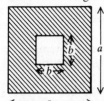

Find the area of the shaded part of the diagram where:
(a) $a = 5.7$ cm, and $b = 4.3$ cm
(b) $a = 13.2$ cm, and $b = 6.8$ cm
(c) $a = 7.9$ cm, and $b = 4.7$ cm

12. Look at the diagram.
Find in terms of π the area of the shaded part of the diagram where:
(a) $R = 25$ cm, and $r = 5$ cm
(b) $R = 16.8$ cm, and $r = 3.2$ cm
(c) $R = 5.9$ cm, and $r = 3.7$ cm

13. A plastic duct has a square cross section like that in Question 11. Find the volume of plastic where the length of the duct is:
(a) 18.3 cm, and $a = 3.1$ cm, $b = 2.1$ cm
(b) 6.5 m, and $a = 1.8$ m, $b = 1.3$ m
(c) 51 cm, and $a = 2.6$ cm, $b = 1.1$ cm

14. Find the volume of concrete in a pipe, like that in the example where:
(a) $R = 1.8$ m, $r = 1.4$ m, and $h = 7.2$ m
(b) $R = 57$ cm, $r = 43$ cm and $h = 276$ cm
(c) $R = 8.3$ cm, $r = 6.9$ cm, and $h = 45$ cm

15. The volume of a cone is given by $V = \frac{1}{3}\pi r^2 h$.
A conical container is made by removing a cone of radius r from a cone of radius R as shown in the diagram.

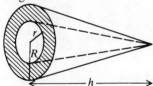

Find the volume of material in the container where:
(a) $R = 13.2$ cm, $r = 9.4$ cm, and $h = 24.1$ cm
(b) $R = 47$ cm, $r = 36$ cm, and $h = 215$ cm

16. In the diagram below $A\hat{B}C = B\hat{D}C = 90°$,
$AC = 15.3$ cm, $AB = 11.8$ cm and $BD = 6.5$ cm.

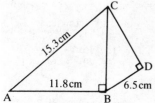

Use the Theorem of Pythagoras to find the length of BC and hence find the length of DC.

7.7 Factorising quadratic expressions

On page 250, you learned that a quadratic expression is one which contains a term in x^2, but no higher power of x. Examples are: $x^2 + 2x - 3$
$$x^2 - 1$$

Example 1

Write $x^2 + 5x + 4$ as the product of two brackets.

We can write the brackets as:
$(x + 4)(x + \square)$
The product of the number terms must be 4
i.e. $4 \times \square = 4$
so $\square = 1$

Check: $(x + 4)(x + 1) = x^2 + x + 4x + 4$
$$= x^2 + 5x + 4$$

---

1. Use the ideas in Example 1 to complete:
(a) $x^2 + 7x + 6 = (x + 6)(x + \square)$
(b) $x^2 + 16x + 15 = (x + 1)(x + \square)$
(c) $x^2 + 8x + 15 = (x + 5)(x + \square)$
(d) $x^2 + 9x + 20 = (x + 5)(x + \square)$
(e) $x^2 + 5x + 6 = (x + 3)(x + \square)$

2. Use the ideas in Example 1 to complete:
(a) $x^2 + 6x + 5 = (x + \square)(x + \square)$
(b) $x^2 + 12x + 11 = (x + \square)(x + \square)$
(c) $x^2 + 10x + 21 = (x + \square)(x + \square)$
(d) $x^2 + 7x + 10 = (x + \square)(x + \square)$
(e) $x^2 + 10x + 16 = (x + \square)(x + \square)$
(f) $x^2 + 9x + 18 = (x + \square)(x + \square)$

Example 2

(a) $\quad x^2 - 3x + 2 = (x - 2)(x - 1)$
$$= x^2 - x - 2x + 2$$

(b) $x^2 - 4x + 3 = (x - 3)(x - 3)$
$$= x^2 - x - 3x + 3$$

---

3. Copy and complete:
When two negative numbers are multiplied together the answer is a . . . . number.

4. Use the idea above to complete:
(a) $x^2 - 6x + 8 = (x - 2)(x - \square)$
(b) $x^2 - 8x + 15 = (x - 3)(x - \square)$
(c) $x^2 - 5x + 4 = (x - 1)(x - \square)$
(d) $x^2 - 9x + 8 = (x - 8)(x - \square)$
(e) $x^2 - 6x + 9 = (x - 3)(x - \square)$
(f) $x^2 - 5x + 6 = (x - 2)(x - \square$

5. Factorise, and check that your answer is correct.
   (a) $x^2 - 8x + 7 = (x - \square)(x - \square)$
   (b) $x^2 - 6x + 5 = (x - \square)(x - \square)$
   (c) $x^2 - 7x + 10 = (x - \square)(x - \square)$
   (d) $x^2 - 11x + 18 = (x - \square)(x - \square)$
   (e) $x^2 - 8x + 16 = (x - \square)(x - \square)$
   (f) $x^2 - 6x + 9 = (x - \square)(x - \square)$

Example 3

(a) $x^2 + 2x - 3 = (x + 3)(x - 1)$
$$= x^2 - x + 3x - 3$$

(b) $x^2 + 3x - 10 = (x + 5)(x - 2)$
$$= x^2 - 2x + 5x - 10$$

---

6. Copy and complete:
When a negative number and a positive number are multiplied together, the answer is a . . . . number.

7. Use the above ideas to complete.
   (a) $x^2 + 7x - 8 = (x + 8)(x - \square)$
   (b) $x^2 - 5x - 6 = (x + 1)(x - \square)$
   (c) $x^2 + 4x - 12 = (x + 6)(x - \square)$
   (d) $x^2 - 5x - 14 = (x - 7)(x + \square)$
   (e) $x^2 + 5x - 14 = (x - 2)(x + \square)$

8. Factorise, and check that your answer is correct.
   (a) $x^2 + 10x - 11 = (x + \square)(x - \square)$
   (b) $x^2 + 4x - 21 = (x + \square)(x - \square)$
   (c) $x^2 - 2x - 35 = (x - \square)(x - \square)$
   (d) $x^2 - 4x - 21 = (x + \square)(x - \square)$
   (e) $x^2 + 32x + 60 = (x + \square)(x + \square)$
   (f) $x^2 - x - 2 = (x + \square)(x - \square)$

Example 4

Factorise $x^2 + 10x + 24$

The expression has to be written in the form
$(x + a)(x + b)$
24 is the product of a and b.
10 is the sum of a and b.
We must find the factors of 24 whose sum is 10.
$$\begin{aligned} 24 &= 24 \times 1 & 24 + 1 &= 25 \\ &= 12 \times 2 & 12 + 2 &= 14 \\ &= 8 \times 3 & 8 + 3 &= 11 \\ &= 6 \times 4 & 6 + 4 &= 10 \end{aligned}$$
So $x^2 + 10x + 24 = (x + 6)(x + 4)$
Check the answer by removing the brackets.

---

9. Use the ideas in Example 4 to factorise:
   (a) $x^2 + 16x + 55$ (b) $x^2 + 18x + 32$
   (c) $x^2 + 19x + 18$ (d) $x^2 + 13x + 36$
   (e) $x^2 + 21x + 90$ (f) $x^2 + 10x + 25$

Example 5

Factorise $x^2 - 6x + 8$

The product is positive, but the middle term is negative. This means that both factors must be negative.
$8 = (-4) \times (-2)$ and $-6 = (-4) + (-2)$
So $x^2 - 6x + 8 = (x - 4)(x - 2)$ (Check it.)

---

10. Use the ideas in Example 5 to factorise:
   (a) $x^2 - 12x + 35$ (b) $x^2 - 19x + 48$
   (c) $x^2 - 9x + 8$ (d) $x^2 - 16x + 60$
   (e) $x^2 - 22x + 96$ (f) $x^2 - 12x + 36$
   (g) $z^2 - 10z + 16$ (h) $x^2 + 6x - 27$
   (i) $y^2 - 15y - 54$ (j) $z^2 - 12z + 20$

Example 6

Factorise $x^2 - 3x - 18$

The product of the factors is -18. Since it is negative, one factor must be negative and one positive.
$$\begin{aligned} 18 &= 18 \times 1 & 18 - 1 &= 17 & 1 - 18 &= -17 \\ &= 9 \times 2 & 9 - 2 &= 7 & 2 - 9 &= -7 \\ &= 6 \times 3 & 6 - 3 &= 3 & 3 - 6 &= -3 \end{aligned}$$
So $x^2 - 3x - 18 = (x + 3)(x - 6)$ (Check it.)

---

11. Use the ideas in Example 6 to factorise:
   (a) $x^2 + 9x - 22$ (b) $x^2 + 4x - 12$
   (c) $x^2 + 16x - 17$ (d) $x^2 - 8x - 33$
   (e) $x^2 - 5x - 24$ (f) $x^2 + 0x - 49$

12. Factorise, and check that your answer is correct.
   (a) $x^2 + 2x + 1$ (b) $x^2 - 1$
   (c) $x^2 - 2x + 1$ (d) $x^2 - 4x + 3$
   (e) $x^2 + 2x - 8$ (f) $x^2 + 4x - 21$
   (g) $x^2 - 100$ (h) $x^2 - 64$
   (i) $x^2 - x - 42$ (j) $x^2 + 15x + 26$

Example 7

Factorise $12x^2 + 8x + 1$

This time the factors will be of the form
$(ax + 1)(bx + 1)$ and you have to try the different factors of 12, i.e. $12 \times 1, 6 \times 2, 4 \times 3$
$12x^2 + 8x + 1 = (6x + 1)(2x + 1)$
Check by removing the brackets.

---

13. Use the ideas in Example 7 to factorise:
   (a) $15x^2 + 8x + 1$ (b) $11x^2 + 12x + 1$
   (c) $24x^2 + 10x - 1$ (d) $16x^2 + 6x - 1$
   (e) $30x^2 - x - 1$ (f) $49x^2 - 14x + 1$

14. Factorise:
   (a) $18x^2 + 9x + 1$ (b) $33x^2 + 8x - 1$
   (c) $40x^2 - 6x - 1$ (d) $72x^2 - x - 1$
   (e) $36x^2 + 0x - 1$ (f) $121x^2 + 22x + 1$

Example 8

Factorise $15x^2 - 38x + 11$

This time the factors will be of the form
$(ax + b)(cx + d)$ where $ac = 15$ and $bd = 11$.

It helps to start with the number which has only
two factors, i.e. $(\Box x - 11)(\Box x - 1)$. The factors
for 15 must fit in the $\Box$'s. They could be 15 and 1,
1 and 15, 5 and 3 or 3 and 5. You can only find
which of these is the correct pair by trying each
and checking.

$15x^2 - 38x + 11 = (5x - 11)(3x - 1)$

15. Use the ideas in Example 8 to factorise these.
(*Hint:* start if possible with the number which has
only two factors.)
(a) $5x^2 + 12x + 7$ (b) $8x^2 + 14x + 5$
(c) $11x^2 + 25x + 6$ (d) $7x^2 - 22x + 15$
(e) $10x^2 + 29x - 3$ (f) $4x^2 - 51x - 13$
(g) $7x^2 + 59x + 24$ (h) $5x^2 + 13x - 18$
(i) $25x^2 + 20x + 4$ (j) $9x^2 - 42x + 49$

16. Factorise:
(a) $3x^2 + 23x + 14$ (b) $6x^2 + 31x + 5$
(c) $8x^2 - 23x + 15$ (d) $7x^2 - 27x + 18$
(e) $4x^2 + 5x - 6$ (f) $25x^2 + 40x - 9$
(g) $5x^2 - 37x - 24$ (h) $12x^2 - 4x - 21$
(i) $36x^2 + 60x + 25$ (j) $49x^2 - 56x + 16$
(k) $15x^2 + 11x - 14$ (l) $15x^2 - 34x - 13$

7.8 Solving quadratic equations

Using factors

1. p and q are two different numbers. If $pq = 0$, do
you agree that *either $p = 0$ or $q = 0$*?

2. If $(x - 2)(x - 3) = 0$, do you agree that
either $x - 2 = 0$ or $x - 3 = 0$?

3. If $(x - 3)(x + 1) = 0$, do you agree that
either $x = 3$ or $x = -1$? Give reasons.

Any equation of the form $ax^2 + bx + c = 0$ is called a
quadratic equation.
To solve an equation like this you must factorise the
left-hand side.

Example 1

Solve $x^2 - 5x + 6 = 0$

This can be written as: $(x - 2)(x - 3) = 0$
Since the right-hand side is zero, one bracket
must be zero.
i.e. *either* $(x - 2) = 0$ so $x = 2$
    or $(x - 3) = 0$ so $x = 3$
The solutions of this equation are 2 and 3.
The solution set is $\{2, 3\}$.

4. For what values of x is:
(a) $(x - 3)(x - 4) = 0$
(b) $(x - 5)(x - 6) = 0$
(c) $(x - 5)(x + 2) = 0$
(d) $(x - 2)(x + 5) = 0$
(e) $(x + 4)(x - 7) = 0$
(f) $(x + 6)(x - 3) = 0$?

5. Write down the two solutions of the quadratic
equation:
(a) $(x - 3)(x - 4) = 0$
(b) $(x + 5)(x - 2) = 0$
(c) $(x + 2)(x + 9) = 0$
(d) $(2x - 1)(x - 3) = 0$
(e) $(4x - 1)(5x - 1) = 0$
(f) $x(x - 3) = 0$
(g) $(7x + 1)(4x + 1) = 0$
(h) $(2x - 3)(3x - 2) = 0$

6. Find the solutions of the equation by first
factorising the left-hand side.
(a) $x^2 - 6x + 5 = 0$ (b) $x^2 - 10x + 24 = 0$
(c) $x^2 - 15x + 56 = 0$ (d) $x^2 - 6x + 8 = 0$
(e) $x^2 - 12x + 32 = 0$ (f) $x^2 - 9x + 20 = 0$

7. First factorise the L.H.S. of the equation and hence
solve:
(a) $x^2 - 6x + 5 = 0$ (b) $x^2 - 5x + 6 = 0$
(c) $x^2 - 7x + 10 = 0$ (d) $x^2 + 8x + 12 = 0$
(e) $x^2 + 4x + 3 = 0$ (f) $x^2 + 10x + 16 = 0$
(g) $x^2 + 6x - 7 = 0$ (h) $x^2 + 5x - 14 = 0$
(i) $x^2 + 3x - 28 = 0$ (j) $x^2 - 5x - 6 = 0$
(k) $x^2 - 6x - 16 = 0$ (l) $x^2 - 10x - 39 = 0$

8. Find the solution set for the equations.
(a) $x^2 - 7x + 10 = 0$ (b) $x^2 - 7x + 12 = 0$
(c) $x^2 - 10x + 21 = 0$ (d) $x^2 - 13x + 42 = 0$
(e) $x^2 - 13x + 36 = 0$ (f) $x^2 - 4x + 4 = 0$

9. Write down the two solutions of the quadratic
equation:
(a) $(x + 3)(x - 7) = 0$ (b) $(3x - 1)(x + 4) = 0$
(c) $x(3x + 1) = 0$ (d) $(7x - 2)(3x + 4) = 0$
(e) $(5 - x)(2 - x) = 0$ (f) $(4 + x)(3 - x) = 0$

Example 2

Solve $6x^2 - x - 15 = 0$.

This can be written as: $(3x - 5)(2x + 3) = 0$
either $3x - 5 = 0$ so $x = \frac{5}{3}$
or $2x + 3 = 0$ so $x = -\frac{3}{2}$

The solution set for this equation is $\{-\frac{3}{2}, \frac{5}{3}\}$.

10. Factorise the left-hand side of the equation and then find the solution set.
(a) $x^2 - 7x - 8 = 0$ (b) $x^2 + 2x - 15 = 0$
(c) $6x^2 - 5x + 1 = 0$ (d) $5x^2 - 6x + 1 = 0$
(e) $3x^2 - 8x + 5 = 0$ (f) $5x^2 - 12x + 7 = 0$
(g) $2x^2 + 3x - 9 = 0$ (h) $7x^2 - 10x - 8 = 0$
(i) $4x^2 - 51x - 13 = 0$ (j) $5x^2 + 13x - 18 = 0$
(k) $9x^2 - 6x + 1 = 0$ (l) $25x^2 + 20x + 4 = 0$
(m) $9x^2 - 8x - 1 = 0$ (n) $4x^2 - 20x + 25 = 0$

11. First factorise the L.H.S. of the equation and hence solve:
(a) $2x^2 - 3x + 1 = 0$ (b) $6x^2 - 5x + 1 = 0$
(c) $8x^2 - 6x + 1 = 0$ (d) $7x^2 + 8x + 1 = 0$
(e) $10x^2 - 7x + 1 = 0$ (f) $12x^2 - 7x + 1 = 0$
(g) $2x^2 - 9x + 4 = 0$ (h) $3x^2 - 16x + 5 = 0$
(i) $4x^2 - 7x + 3 = 0$ (j) $2x^2 - 5x - 3 = 0$
(k) $3x^2 - x - 2 = 0$ (l) $4x^2 + 5x - 6 = 0$

12. First factorise the L.H.S. of the equation and hence solve:
(a) $12 - 7x + x^2 = 0$ (b) $12 - x - x^2 = 0$
(c) $10 - 3x - x^2 = 0$ (d) $2 - 5x - 3x^2 = 0$
(e) $3 + 5x - 2x^2 = 0$ (f) $3 + 10x - 8x^2 = 0$

Example 3

Solve the equation $x^2 + 5x = -4$.

(i) Rearrange the equation to give zero on the right:
$x^2 + 5x + 4 = 0$

(ii) Factorise the expression on the left.
$x^2 + 5x + 4 = 0$
$(x + 4)(x + 1) = 0$

(iii) If $(x + 4)(x + 1) = 0$, then
either $x + 4 = 0$, so $x = -4$
or $x + 1 = 0$, so $x = -1$

So both $x = -4$ and $x = -1$ are solutions for the equation.

13. Rewrite the quadratic equation to give zero on the right of $=$, as shown above, and then solve.
(a) $x^2 + 7x = -12$ (b) $x^2 + 5x = 14$
(c) $x^2 + 5x = -6$ (d) $x^2 - 8x = 9$
(e) $x^2 + 7x = -6$ (f) $x^2 - 2x = 24$

14. Collect the like terms together, and solve the quadratic equation.
(a) $10 + 4x - x + x^2 = 28$
(b) $3x^2 + 40 + 8x = 2x^2 + 89 + 8x$
(c) $2x^2 - 60 + 4x + 2x^2 = 3x^2 + 3x - 40$
(d) $-x^2 = 8x - 11x - 88$
(e) $92 - x^2 = 11x + 32$
(f) $500 + 13x = 34x + x^2 + 610$

15. $2x^2 + 6x + 4 = 0$ $x^2 + 3x + 2 = 0$
(a) Do you agree that both equations say the same?
(b) Solve each. Which one is the easier to solve? Are your answers the same?

16. First divide the numbers by a common factor. Then solve the equation.
(a) $2x^2 - 14x - 36 = 0$ (b) $5x^2 - 5 = 0$
(c) $6x^2 - 54 = 0$ (d) $4x^2 - 40x + 64 = 0$
(e) $9x^2 - 63x = -54$ (f) $13x^2 - 65x = 182$

17. Do you agree that $x^2 - 4 = (x - 2)(x + 2)$?
Use this to solve:
(a) $x^2 - 4 = 0$ (b) $x^2 = 4$

18. (a) Do you agree that the solution set for $x^2 = 9$ is $\{-3, 3\}$?
(b) Write down the solution set for:
(i) $x^2 = 16$ (ii) $x^2 - 25 = 0$ (iii) $x^2 = 81$

19. Find the solution set for:
(a) $(x - 1)^2 = 4$ (b) $(x - 3)^2 = 25$

20. (a) Explain why the solutions of $(x - 1)^2 = 3$ are $1 + \sqrt{3}$ or $1 - \sqrt{3}$.
(b) Show that $(x - 1)^2 = 3$ can be written as $x^2 - 2x - 2 = 0$.
(c) Try to factorise $x^2 - 2x - 2$.
(d) Are there any solutions for $x^2 - 2x - 2 = 0$?

21. Where possible, write down the solutions for:
(a) $x^2 = 36$ (b) $x^2 = 5$ (c) $x^2 = -4$

22. Solve the quadratic equation by first factorising the left-hand side.
(a) $x^2 - 4x + 4 = 0$ (b) $x^2 - 2x + 1 = 0$
(c) $x^2 - 6x + 9 = 0$ (d) $x^2 - 10x + 25 = 0$
(e) $x^2 + 8x + 16 = 0$ (f) $x^2 + 12x + 36 = 0$
(g) $x^2 + 4x + 4 = 0$ (h) $x^2 + 6x + 9 = 0$
(i) $4x^2 - 4x + 1 = 0$ (j) $9x^2 + 6x + 1 = 0$

You should have found in Question 22 that each of the equations has a *single* solution, since both factors are the same.
In most of the other exercises on this page each of the equations has *two* solutions.
However in Question 21 (c), the equation $x^2 = -4$ has *no* solution since it is not possible to find the square root of a negative number.
In general a quadratic equation can have either *one* or *two* or *no* solutions.

You probably found that you were not able to factorise the equation $x^2 - 2x - 2$ in Question 20 (c). However, the equation $x^2 - 2x - 2 = 0$ does have two solutions, $1 + \sqrt{3}$ and $1 - \sqrt{3}$.

In the next examples, you will learn how to solve quadratic equations even if you cannot factorise the expression.

Completing the square

Example 4

Write $x^2 + 6x + 19$ as $(x + p)^2 + q$.

We can write $x^2 + 6x$ as $(x + 3)^2 - 9$
Now $x^2 + 6x + 19$
$= (x + 3)^2 - 9 + 19$
$= (x + 3)^2 + 10$ so $p = 3$ and $q = 10$
Note: the number within the brackets above, i.e. 3, is half the coefficient of the x-term (6).

---

23. Write in the form $(x + p)^2 + q$:
    (a) $x^2 + 6x + 10$ (b) $x^2 + 4x + 10$
    (c) $x^2 + 8x + 18$ (d) $x^2 + 10x + 27$
    (e) $x^2 + 2x + 5$ (f) $x^2 + 12x - 5$
    (g) $x^2 + 18x + 100$ (h) $x^2 + 16x + 40$

24. Write in the form $(x - p)^2 + q$:
    (a) $x^2 - 6x + 10$ (b) $x^2 - 4x + 10$
    (c) $x^2 - 10x + 30$ (d) $x^2 - 8x - 1$
    (e) $x^2 - 2x + 3$ (f) $x^2 - 12x + 36$
    (g) $x^2 - x + \frac{1}{4}$ (h) $x^2 - 8x - 10$

Example 5

Solve $x^2 + 6x - 7 = 0$

$x^2 + 6x - 7$ can be written as
$(x + 3)^2 - 16 = 0$ or $(x + 3)^2 = 16$

If $(x + 3)^2 = 16$ then $(x + 3) = 4$ or $(x + 3) = -4$
so $x = 1$ or $x = {}^-7$

This method of solving the equation is known as **completing the square.**

---

25. Solve the equation by first taking the square root of each side:
    (a) $(x - 2)^2 = 25$ (b) $(x - 5)^2 = 64$
    (c) $(x - 3)^2 = 16$ (d) $(x + 4)^2 = 1$
    (e) $(x + 6)^2 = 49$ (f) $(x + 2)^2 = 4$

26. Complete the square, to solve:
    (a) $x^2 + 6x - 16 = 0$ (b) $x^2 + 10x - 11 = 0$
    (c) $x^2 + 8x - 20 = 0$ (d) $x^2 + 12x - 45 = 0$
    (e) $x^2 - 6x + 5 = 0$ (f) $x^2 - 10x + 16 = 0$
    Check your answers by factorisation.

27. Solve the equation by first completing the square:
    (a) $x^2 - 6x + 8 = 0$ (b) $x^2 - 12x + 11 = 0$
    (c) $x^2 - 14x + 24 = 0$ (d) $x^2 + 8x + 12 = 0$
    (e) $x^2 + 10x - 39 = 0$ (f) $x^2 + 2x - 63 = 0$

28. Solve the equation by first taking the square root of each side:
    (a) $(x - 1)^2 = 5$ (b) $(x - 4)^2 = 7$
    (c) $(x - 6)^2 = 11$ (d) $(x + 2)^2 = 3$
    (e) $(x + 5)^2 = 2$ (f) $(x + 1)^2 = 13$

29. Solve the equation by first completing the square:
    (a) $x^2 - 6x + 1 = 0$ (b) $x^2 - 16x + 3 = 0$
    (c) $x^2 - 4x + 1 = 0$ (d) $x^2 + 2x - 7 = 0$
    (e) $x^2 + 6x - 12 = 0$ (f) $x^2 + 14x - 3 = 0$

30. Solve the equations:
    (a) $(x + 5)^2 = 40$ (b) $x^2 + 10x - 15 = 0$
    (c) $x^2 + 8x - 24 = 0$ (d) $x^2 - 6x - 31 = 0$
    (e) $x^2 + 6x - 11 = 0$ (f) $x^2 - 12x + 16 = 0$
    (You may leave your answers in square-root form.)

Example 6

Solve $2x^2 - 5x + 2 = 0$

First divide each term by the coefficient of x^2:

$$x^2 - \frac{5}{2}x + 1 = 0$$

Now complete the square:

$$\left(x - \frac{5}{4}\right)^2 - \frac{25}{16} + 1 = 0$$

We can write this as:

$$\left(x - \frac{5}{4}\right)^2 = \frac{25}{16} - 1 = \frac{9}{16}$$

Taking the square root:

$$\left(x - \frac{5}{4}\right) = \frac{3}{4} \text{ or } - \frac{3}{4}$$

So $x = \frac{5}{4} + \frac{3}{4} = 2$ or $x = \frac{5}{4} - \frac{3}{4} = \frac{1}{2}$

---

31. First divide each term in the equation by the co-efficient of x^2, and then complete the square to solve:
    (a) $2x^2 - 6x + 4 = 0$ (b) $2x^2 - 3x + 1 = 0$
    (c) $4x^2 - 8x - 12 = 0$ (d) $4x^2 - 5x + 1 = 0$
    (e) $2x^2 - 7x + 3 = 0$ (f) $4x^2 - 13x + 3 = 0$
    (g) $5x^2 - 10x - 75 = 0$ (h) $5x^2 + 11x + 2 = 0$
    (i) $3x^2 - 10x + 3 = 0$ (j) $2x^2 + 5x + 2 = 0$
    (k) $3x^2 - 8x + 5 = 0$ (l) $2x^2 + 9x + 7 = 0$

Using the formula

You can use the idea of completing the square to solve any quadratic equation of the form $ax^2 + bx + c = 0$

First divide each term by a: $x^2 + \dfrac{bx}{a} + \dfrac{c}{a} = 0$

This can be written as:

$$\left(x + \frac{b}{2a}\right)^2 - \frac{b^2}{4a^2} + \frac{c}{a} = 0$$

$$\text{or } \left(x + \frac{b}{2a}\right)^2 = \frac{b^2}{4a^2} - \frac{c}{a} = \frac{b^2 - 4ac}{4a^2}$$

Taking the square root of each side:

$$x + \frac{b}{2a} = \pm\sqrt{\frac{b^2 - 4ac}{4a^2}} = \pm\frac{\sqrt{b^2 - 4ac}}{2a}$$

So there are two possible values for x:

$$x = \frac{-b + \sqrt{b^2 - 4ac}}{2a} \text{ or } x = \frac{-b - \sqrt{b^2 - 4ac}}{2a}$$

These formulae give the solution for any quadratic equation of the form $ax^2 + bx + c = 0$.

Example 7

Using the formula, solve $x^2 + 6x - 7 = 0$

In this equation $a = 1$, $b = 6$ and $c = -7$.
Substituting these values into the formula we get:

$$x = \frac{-6 + \sqrt{6^2 - 4 \times 1 \times (^-7)}}{2 \times 1}$$

$$\text{or } x = \frac{-6 - \sqrt{6^2 - 4 \times 1 \times (^-7)}}{2 \times 1}$$

$$\text{i.e. } x = \frac{-6 + \sqrt{36 + 28}}{2} \text{ or } x = \frac{-6 - \sqrt{36 + 28}}{2}$$

$$\text{i.e. } x = \frac{-6 + 8}{2} = 1 \text{ or } x = \frac{-6 - 8}{2} = {^-7}$$

The solution set for $x^2 + 6x - 7 = 0$ is $\{1, {^-7}\}$.

---

32. Evaluate the formula $\dfrac{-b \pm \sqrt{b^2 - 4ac}}{2a}$ when:

    (a) $a = 3$, $b = {^-7}$ and $c = 2$
    (b) $a = 5$, $b = {^-8}$ and $c = 3$
    (c) $a = 3$, $b = 4$ and $c = {^-2}$
    (d) $a = 7$, $b = 11$ and $c = 2$

33. First write down the values of a, b and c, and then use the formula to solve:
    (a) $x^2 + 6x - 16 = 0$ (b) $x^2 - 6x + 5 = 0$
    (c) $x^2 + 8x - 20 = 0$ (d) $x^2 - 10x + 16 = 0$
    (e) $x^2 + 10x - 11 = 0$ (f) $x^2 + 12x - 45 = 0$

34. Solve the equation by using the above formula:
    (a) $x^2 + 4x + 3 = 0$ (b) $x^2 - 9x + 14 = 0$
    (c) $2x^2 - 7x + 3 = 0$ (d) $x^2 + 7x + 10 = 0$
    (e) $x^2 + 8x - 20 = 0$ (f) $4x^2 + 11x - 3 = 0$

35. Solve the equation by using the above formula:
    (a) $x^2 - 5x + 1 = 0$ (b) $x^2 - 7x + 3 = 0$
    (c) $x^2 + 4x - 9 = 0$ (d) $x^2 + 6x + 2 = 0$
    (e) $3x^2 - 2x - 6 = 0$ (f) $5x^2 - 9x + 1 = 0$

36. Use the formula to solve:
    (a) $x^2 + 10x - 24 = 0$ (b) $2x^2 + 13x - 7 = 0$
    (c) $4x^2 - 16x + 15 = 0$ (d) $2x^2 + 5x + 2 = 0$

37. Use the formula to solve:
    (a) $10x^2 - 11x + 1 = 0$ (b) $x^2 + 8x + 16 = 0$
    (c) $4x^2 + 0x - 9 = 0$ (d) $x^2 + x + 1 = 0$

38. For each equation in Question 37, write down the value of $b^2 - 4ac$.
Do you agree that the equation has:
    (a) two solutions when $b^2 - 4ac > 0$
    (b) one solution when $b^2 - 4ac = 0$
    (c) no solutions when $b^2 - 4ac < 0$?

In the formula $x = \dfrac{-b \pm \sqrt{b^2 - 4ac}}{2a}$

The value of $b^2 - 4ac$ determines how many solutions an equation has.
[1] When $b^2 - 4ac < 0$ there are no real solutions, since you cannot find the square root of a negative number.
[2] When $b^2 = 4ac$ there is only one solution.
[3] When $b^2 - 4ac > 0$ there are two solutions.

39. For each equation write down the value of $b^2 - 4ac$ and state whether the equation has two, one, or no solutions.
    (a) $x^2 + 2x + 3 = 0$ (b) $x^2 + 9x + 1 = 0$
    (c) $25x^2 + 10x + 1 = 0$ (d) $5x^2 + 2x + 1 = 0$

what's an "unreal" situation?

Ever tried solving $x^2 + 4 = 0$?

7.9 Word problems

$x^2 + px + q$ is called a **quadratic expression** since it contains an x^2 term but no term in x^3 or higher powers of x.

If $x^2 + px + q = (x + a)(x + b)$
then we can write:
$$x^2 + px + q = x^2 + (a + b)x + ab$$
so $p = (a + b)$ and $q = ab$
p is the sum of a and b, q is the product of a and b

1. If $x^2 + px + q = (x + a)(x + b)$ write down the values of p and q when:
   (a) $a = 6, b = 11$ (b) $a = 5, b = {}^-12$
   (c) $a = {}^-7, b = 8$ (d) $a = {}^-2, b = {}^-9$

2. If $x^2 + px + q = (x + A)(x + B)$ write down the values of A and B when:
   (a) $p = 12, q = 35$ (b) $p = 6, q = 5$
   (c) $p = 2, q = {}^-15$ (d) $p = {}^-10, q = 21$

Example 1

Write down two numbers whose sum is 8 and whose product is 15.

$a + b = 8, ab = 15$ so $p = 8, q = 15$
We can show this as the quadratic equation
$$x^2 + 8x + 15 = 0$$
or $(x + 3)(x + 5) = 0$
so $a = 3$ and $b = 5$

---

3. Write down the two numbers:
   (a) whose sum is 7 and whose product is 12
   (b) whose sum is 5 and whose product is 6
   (c) whose sum is 4 and whose product is 3

4. Write down the two numbers:
   (a) whose sum is 3 and whose product is -10
   (b) whose sum is 4 and whose product is -77
   (c) whose sum is -1 and whose product is -30

5. Write down the two numbers:
   (a) whose sum is -9 and whose product is 20
   (b) whose sum is -7 and whose product is 10
   (c) whose sum is -5 and whose product is 4

6. One side of a rectangle is 10 cm longer than the other. If the area of the rectangle is $56\,\text{cm}^2$, show this information as a quadratic equation and hence find the length of each side.

7. One side of a rectangle is 5 cm longer than the other. The area of the rectangle is $84\,\text{cm}^2$. If x cm is the length of one side, show this information as a quadratic equation and then solve it.

Example 2

If the length of a rectangle is 5 cm more than its width and the area is $24\,\text{cm}^2$ find the length and the width of the rectangle.

If we call the width of the rectangle w cm, then its length is $(w + 5)$ cm. Its area is $24\,\text{cm}^2$, so
$$w(w + 5) = 24$$
i.e. $w^2 + 5w = 24$
and $w^2 + 5w - 24 = 0$
so $(w - 5)(w + 8) = 0$
so $w = 5$ or $w = {}^-8$
The width of the rectangle is 5 cm (we cannot have a width of $^-8$ cm)

---

8. The length of a room is 4 metres longer than its width. The height of the room is 3 metres and its volume is $1000\,\text{m}^3$.
   Find the length and width of the room.

9. The three sides of a right-angled triangle are as shown in the diagram below.

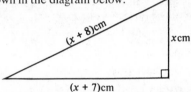

$(x + 7)$cm

Use Pythagoras' Theorem to form a quadratic equation and then by factorising, find the length of the three sides.

10. The hypotenuse of a right-angled triangle is 1 cm longer than the second side of the triangle and 2 cm longer than the third side. Using x cm as the length of the shortest side, write down a quadratic equation to describe the triangle. (Use Pythagoras' Theorem.)
    Solve the equation to find the length of the sides.

11. The hypotenuse of a right-angled triangle is 1 cm longer than one side and 8 cm longer than the other. Find the length of each side.

Example 3

Find two consecutive numbers whose squares add up to 85.

Let x be the first number so $(x + 1)$ is the other
so $x^2 + (x + 1)^2 = 85$
$$x^2 + x^2 + 2x + 1 = 85$$
$$2x^2 + 2x - 84 = 0$$
$x^2 + x - 42 = 0$ i.e. $(x + 7)(x - 6) = 0$
so $x = 6$ or $^-7$
The two numbers are 6 and 7 or $^-7$ and $^-6$

12. The squares of two consecutive odd numbers add up to 74. Show this information as a quadratic equation and hence find the numbers.

13. The sum of the squares of three consecutive numbers is 77. If x is the smallest number, show this information as a quadratic equation. Solve the equation to find the numbers.

14. The sum of the squares of three consecutive numbers is 110. Show this information as a quadratic equation and hence find the numbers.

Example 4

A man makes a daily journey of 40 km. When he increases his normal speed by 5 km/h, he finds that he takes 2 minutes less time than usual. Find his normal speed.

Let x km/h be the man's normal speed.

The time taken for a journey of 40 km is $\dfrac{40}{x}$ h.

When his speed is increased by 5 km/h, an equation can be formed.

$$\frac{40}{x} - \frac{40}{x+5} = \frac{2}{60} = \frac{1}{30}$$

This can be rewritten as

$$30 \times 40\,(x + 5 - x) = x(x + 5)$$

or $x^2 + 5x - 6000 = 0$

Factorising this equation gives

$$(x - 75)(x + 80) = 0 \quad \text{i.e. } x = 75 \text{ or } x = {}^-80$$

The man's normal speed is 75 km/h.
(A negative speed is not realistic.)

---

15. A man makes a daily journey of 50 km. When he increases his normal speed by 10 km/h he finds he takes 10 minutes less than usual.
Find his normal speed.

16. A man makes a trip of 180 km. On his return journey his average speed is reduced by 10 km/h and he takes 15 minutes longer.
Find his average speed on the outward journey.

17. If one edge of a cube is increased in length by 3 cm, and a second edge is decreased in length by 2 cm, the volume of the cuboid formed is 55 cm^3 more than the volume of the cube.
Find the length of each edge of the original cube.

7.10 Simultaneous equations

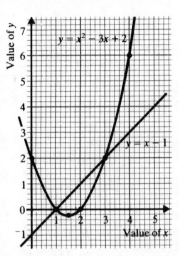

You can solve a pair of simultaneous equations *either* by drawing their graphs and finding the points of intersection, *or* by substituting one expression for x or y into the other equation.

Example

Solve the simultaneous equations $2x^2 - y^2 = 14$ and $y = x - 1$.
Substituting $y = x - 1$ into the first equation:
$$2x^2 - (x - 1)^2 = 14$$
so $\quad 2x^2 - (x^2 - 2x + 1) = 14$
i.e. $\qquad x^2 + 2x - 15 = 0$
$$(x - 3)(x + 5) = 0$$
so $x = 3$ or $x = {}^-5$.
When $x = 3$, $y = 2$. When $x = {}^-5$, $y = {}^-6$.

---

1. Look at the graphs of $y = x^2 - 3x + 2$ and $y = x - 1$, above. Write down the co-ordinates of the two points where the graphs intersect. Do you agree that each of these points makes the statements
$y = x^2 - 3x + 2$ and $y = x - 1$ both true at the same time?

2. (a) Solve the equation $x^2 - 3x + 2 = x - 1$.
    (b) For each value of x write down the corresponding values of $x^2 - 3x + 2$ and $x - 1$.
    (c) What is the connection between your answers in (a) and (b), and the co-ordinates you wrote for Question 1?

3. (a) On a copy of the graph above draw the line $y = x + 2$. Find the co-ordinates of the points where this line intersects $y = x^2 - 3x + 2$.
    (b) Check the x co-ordinates in (a), by solving the equation $x^2 - 3x + 2 = x + 2$.

4. Explain how you would solve the simultaneous equations $y = 2x - 2$ and $y = x^2 - 3x + 2$.
(a) graphically   (b) by substitution
Solve the equations using each method.

5. Use each method in Question 4 to solve the equations $y = 3x - 6$ and $y = x^2 - 3x + 2$.

6. (a) Draw the graphs of $y = x^2 - 4x + 3$ and $y = 2x - 5$ for values of x from 0 to 6.
    (b) Find the points of intersection of your two graphs.
    (c) Check your answers for (b) by first solving $x^2 - 4x + 3 = 2x - 5$, and then finding the corresponding y values.

7. Use the method shown in the example to solve:
    (a) $x^2 + y^2 = 25$ *and* $y = x - 1$
    (b) $xy = 15$ *and* $y = x - 2$
    (c) $x^2 + xy + y^2 = 3$ *and* $y = x$
    (d) $x^2 + y^2 = 5$ *and* $x - 2y = 3$

8. Solve the simultaneous equations by first substituting a y expression in the place of x^2, and solving for y.
    (a) $x^2 + y^2 = 6$ *and* $y = x^2$
    (b) $x^2 + y^2 = 15$ *and* $y = x^2 - 3$

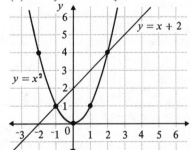

9. (a) The graphs above meet at two points. Do you agree that $x^2 = x + 2$ at these points?
    (b) Write down the co-ordinates of the two points, and hence find the solution of the simultaneous equations $y = x^2$ and $y = x + 2$.
    (c) Check your answer to (b) by solving the quadratic equation in (a).

10. Draw graphs to solve these simultaneous equations, and check your answers by substitution.
    (a) $y = 5x - 3$ (b) $y = 3 - 5x$
        $y = x^2 + x$ $y = x^2 - 2x + 5$

11. (a) Solve the simultaneous equations $y = x^2 - 4x + 3$ *and* $y = 2x^2 - 5x + 1$ by first drawing the graph of each using values of x from $^-2$ to 5, and then finding where the two graphs intersect.
    (b) Check your answers for (a) by substitution.

Summary

By the end of this chapter, these are the things you should know about:

7.1 Revision (pages 244–246)

Indices: $a^m \times a^n = a^{m+n}$, $a^m \div a^n = a^{m-n}$

$$a^0 = 1, a^{-n} = \frac{1}{a^n},$$

How to simplify expressions using these rules.

Brackets: removing brackets from expressions like
$(2a + b)(3x - 4a)$

Factorisation: $ax + 3by - 3bx - ay$
$= a(x - y) - 3b(x - y)$
$= (a - 3b)(x - y)$

Fractions: simplifying expressions with fractions
like $\dfrac{(a + 3)}{2} - \dfrac{4}{(b - 1)}$

Substitution: evaluating expressions such as
$xy + yz - 3zx$ when given the values of
x, y and z.

7.2 Fractional indices (page 247)

That $a^{\frac{1}{n}} = \sqrt[n]{a}$

How to simplify expressions involving fractional indices:

$$64^{-\frac{2}{3}} = \frac{1}{64^{\frac{2}{3}}} = \frac{1}{4^2} = \frac{1}{16} \quad \boxed{\sqrt[3]{64} = 4}$$

7.3 Changing the subject of a formula
(pages 247–250)

How to use a function machine and its reverse to rearrange a formula such as $V = \pi r^2 h$ so that its subject is either r or h.
How to change the subject of a formula which
involves fractions $\left(\text{such as } \dfrac{1}{u} + \dfrac{1}{v} = \dfrac{1}{f} \right)$ by first
removing all the fractions.

7.4 The product of two brackets
(pages 250–252)

Remember these results:
$(x - 4)(x + 5) = x^2 + 5x - 4x - 20$
$\qquad\qquad\quad = x^2 + x - 20$
$(a + b)^2 = a^2 + 2ab + b^2$
$(a - b)^2 = a^2 - 2ab + b^2$
$(a + b)(a - b) = a^2 - b^2$

7.5 Completing the square (pages 252–253)

How to write a quadratic expression such as
$x^2 + 6x + 19$ in the form $(x + p)^2 + q$,
i.e. as $(x + 3)^2 + 10$.
This is called completing the square.

7.6 The difference between two squares
(pages 254–255)

How to use $a^2 - b^2 = (a + b)(a - b)$
to evaluate $6.9^2 - 3.1^2 = 10 \times 3.8 = 38$
and in everyday problems.

7.7 Factorising quadratic expressions
(pages 255–257)

How to factorise a quadratic expression,
e.g. $x^2 + 3x + 2 = (x + 2)(x + 1)$
$\qquad 15x^2 - 38x + 11 = (5x - 11)(3x - 1)$

7.8 Solving quadratic equations
(pages 257–260)

A quadratic equation may have two, one, or no solutions.
How to solve quadratic equations using factors:

(a) If $x^2 + 3x + 2 = 0$, then $(x + 2)(x + 1) = 0$
So *either* $(x + 2) = 0$, giving $x = {}^-2$
$\qquad$ *or* $(x + 1) = 0$, giving $x = {}^-1$.
The solutions of the equation are
$x = {}^-2$ and $x = {}^-1$.

(b) $6x^2 - x - 15 = 0$ is $(3x - 5)(2x + 3) = 0$
so $x = \frac{5}{3}$ or $-\frac{3}{2}$.

How to solve a quadratic equation by completing the square.
The formula for the solutions of $ax^2 + bx + c = 0$
i.e. $\ x = \dfrac{-b + \sqrt{b^2 - 4ac}}{2a}$

or $\quad x = \dfrac{-b - \sqrt{b^2 - 4ac}}{2a}$

How to use this formula to solve quadratic equations.
How to use a graph to solve quadratic equations.

7.9 Word problems (pages 261–262)

How to solve simple word problems which can be described by a quadratic equation.

7.10 Simultaneous equations (page 263)

How to solve simultaneous equations
such as $y = x^2 - 3x + 2$ and $y = x - 1$ using:
$\qquad$ The intersection of the two graphs
$\qquad$ The method of substitution which involves solving a quadratic equation.

8 Statistics 2

8.1 Revision

Statistical information is called **data**. The data in this table give the scores of 50 students in a general knowledge quiz. The maximum possible score is 30:

Score	Frequency
1–5	2
6–10	6
11–15	10
16–20	14
21–25	12
26–30	6

The data has been **grouped** into **frequency classes** of width 5 marks.
The frequency interval 16–20 has the greatest number of students: it is the **modal interval**.
The **range** is 30 marks.
The same data can be shown in a **cumulative frequency table**:

Score	Cumulative frequency
⩽ 5	2
⩽ 10	8
⩽ 15	18
⩽ 20	32
⩽ 25	44
⩽ 30	50

The **median** is the mark of the middle student in order of scores. There is no middle student out of 50 so we use half-way between the 25th and 26th student. The table shows that the median lies in the interval 16–20.

Cumulative frequency can be displayed in a graph:

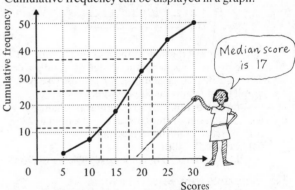

The cumulative frequencies is always plotted at the right-hand end of each class interval. For example, for the interval 1–5, the cumulative frequency is plotted at 5.
The graph can be used to read off approximations to the median and the **quartiles**. The graph gives these values:

Measure	Cumulative frequency	Score
Median	25	17
1st. quartile	$12\frac{1}{2}$	12
3rd. quartile	$37\frac{1}{2}$	22

The approximations give a measure of the **spread** of the data.
The **interquartile range** (i.q.r.) is 22–12 = 10.
The **semi-interquartile range** (s.i.q.r.) is half the i.q.r., or 10 ÷ 2 = 5.

The median is called the **50th. percentile**.
The first and third quartiles are the **25th.** and **75th. percentiles**.

1. For each cumulative frequency curve, draw the histogram (block graph) using the same intervals:

(a)

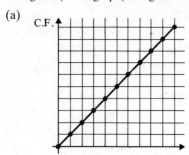

(b)

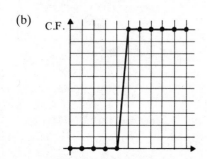

2. Draw a copy of the cumulative frequency curve of the scores in the general knowledge quiz, on page 265. Use 2-cm squares marked in tenths. Use your graph to find approximate answers to:
   (a) the number of students scoring less than 18
   (b) the number of students scoring more than 22
   (c) the score of the 60th. percentile
   (d) the score of 40th. percentile
   (e) the pass mark, if only the best 20% are to pass.

3. The marks of 25 children in a school test were:

Mark	1	2	3	4	5	6	7	8	9	10
Frequency	1	2	3	4	5	3	3	2	1	1

   (a) Draw up a cumulative frequency table using intervals ≤ 2, ≤ 4, ... , ≤ 10.
   (b) Draw a cumulative frequency graph.
   (c) Read off the values of the median and the first and third quartiles.
   (d) Find the i.q.r. and the s.i.q.r.

4. This table gives the heights of 110 plants:

Height (cm)	16	17	18	19	20	21	22	23	24	25
Frequency	3	5	10	16	24	21	15	9	5	2

Draw up a table of cumulative frequency and use it to read off the median height to the nearest centimetre.

5. A survey of a sample of 100 car owners gives the following data:

Engine size (c.c.)	Number of cars
≤ 600	6
601–800	13
801–1000	25
1001–1200	26
1201–1400	14
1401–1600	16

   (a) Draw up a cumulative frequency table for the data.
   (b) Draw a cumulative frequency graph.
   (c) Use your graph to find approximate values for the median and the quartiles.
   (d) Calculate the s.i.q.r.
   (e) In order to conserve petrol, drivers are encouraged to buy cars with smaller engines. If the 16 who own the larger cars in the 1401–1600 c.c. range replace their cars with cars in the next smallest range, what would be the effect on the median and on the interquartile range?

6. The table shows the heights of 31 men who apply for jobs in a police department.

Height (cm)	Number of applicants
Under 170	4
– 175	10
– 180	7
– 185	5
– 190	5

   (a) If the 31 applicants stand in order of height, which ones represent the median and the first and third quartiles?
   (b) Use a cumulative frequency graph to find approximations to the median height and the interquartile range.
   (c) On the horizontal scale of your graph show the median and the interquartile range. How does this show that the police department's encouragement of taller applicants is having effect?

7. The scores of 65 candidates are shown by the table:

20 or less	3	60 or less	55
30 or less	10	70 or less	60
40 or less	20	80 or less	64
50 or less	46	90 or less	65

Find, to the nearest whole number:
(a) the median score
(b) the 1st. and 3rd. quartiles

8.2 The mean

The mean is an average value for a set of data. It can be used for comparison. For example, a chicken farmer can find the total number of eggs laid in one year by his hens, and divide by the number of hens, to obtain the mean number of eggs laid per bird. If the mean is higher one year then it tells him that the hens are more productive.

Calculating the mean is best done using an **assumed mean.**

Example 1

A farmer keeps a careful record of the eggs laid by each of ten hens in a year, and obtains the values:
217, 212, 233, 210, 208, 224, 219, 220, 221, 228.

The mean appears to be near 220 so use this as an assumed mean. Then write down the difference between each number, and the assumed mean:

$-3, -8, 13, -10, -12, 4, -1, 0, 1, 8.$

The sum of these differences is $26 - 34 = -12$

The mean of the differences is $-\dfrac{12}{10} = -1.2$

So the mean $= 220 - 1.2 =$ **218.8**

This is the same answer as you would get if you added up all the eggs and divided by 10.

Example 2

A chicken-breeding co-operative keeps a record of the eggs laid in 1 year by a sample of 100 hens.

Eggs laid	Number of hens
278	2
279	4
280	7
281	12
282	14
283	18
284	15
285	12
286	8
287	4
288	2
289	2

The mean is calculated from the frequency table. An assumed mean of 283 eggs looks best.

Eggs laid x	Frequency f	Difference d	$f \times d$
278	2	-5	-10
279	4	-4	-16
280	7	-3	-21
281	12	-2	-24
282	14	-1	-14
283	18	0	0
284	15	1	15
285	12	2	24
286	8	3	24
287	4	4	16
288	2	5	10
289	2	6	12
Totals	$\Sigma f = 100$		$\Sigma fd = 16$

Mean of differences $= \dfrac{16}{100} = 0.16$

Mean number of eggs $= 283 + 0.16$
$= 283.16$

Using Σ (sigma)

If the number of eggs each hen lays is x, then the total is found by adding up all the x's. This is written as:

$$\Sigma x$$

This is read as *sigma x* and means simply 'add up all the *x* values'.
If there are n hens, then the mean is found by dividing by n:

$$\text{Mean} = \frac{\Sigma x}{n}$$

This formula means 'add up all the *x* values and divide by *n*'.

Using Σ, you can write:

$$\text{Mean} = \text{Assumed mean} + \frac{\Sigma fd}{\Sigma f}$$

1. Repeat Example 1 using an assumed mean of 215.

2. Use an assumed mean of 15 to find the mean of the following twenty numbers: 12, 14, 11, 17, 18, 10, 20, 19, 13, 14, 15, 16, 15, 13, 17, 16, 13, 12, 19, 20.

3. Use an assumed mean of 20 to find the mean of the following thirty numbers:
19, 17, 22, 20, 21, 18, 16, 25, 19, 19, 18, 23, 24, 20, 17, 17, 25, 18, 17, 23, 22, 25, 16, 11, 23, 23, 25, 19, 21, 18.

4. Here are the total scores of two dice, thrown together twenty times: 9, 2, 8, 6, 10, 7, 7, 4, 5, 8, 9, 12, 3, 10, 8, 11, 7, 4, 6, 9.
Calculate the mean score.

5. A biologist takes a sample of 10 grasses and measures the stem length. His results are: 30, 28, 32, 29, 25, 27, 31, 39, 33, 26 cm.
(a) If x cm is the stem length, find Σx.
(b) Calculate the mean stem length.

6. Recalculate the mean of the data in Question 5, using an assumed mean of 30 cm.

7. Two dice are thrown together 100 times. The following table is used to record the results and to calculate the mean:

Score x	Frequency f	Difference d	$f \times d$
2	1	−5	−5
3	4	−4	−16
4	7	−3	
5	8	−2	
6	12	−1	
7	15	0	
8	16	1	
9	16	2	
10	12	3	
11	7	4	
12	2	5	

(a) What score has been used for an assumed mean?
(b) Complete the table.
(c) Find the values of Σf and Σfd.
(d) What is the mean score?

8. Recalculate the mean of the data in Question 7, using an assumed mean of 8.

9. A biologist takes a sample of 200 grasses to measure stem length, and obtains the following data:

Length x cm	Frequency f	Length x cm	Frequency f
25	1	33	15
26	3	34	19
27	4	35	22
28	6	36	26
29	8	37	30
30	10	38	20
31	12	39	8
32	14	40	2

(a) Check that $\Sigma f = 200$.
(b) Draw up a table to calculate the mean, using an assumed mean of 36 cm.
(c) Use your answer for the mean to find the value of Σx.

10. Recalculate the mean of the data in Question 9, using an assumed mean of 34 cm.

11. Recalculate the mean of the data in Example 2, using an assumed mean of 284.

12. A sample of 50 electric light bulbs was tested for length of life, and the results were:

Hours	80	81	82	83	84	85	86
No. of bulbs	1	5	11	18	8	4	3

Calculate the mean length of life.

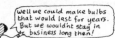

13. In a game, a machine shows the numbers 0, 1, 2 or 3. An analysis of 100 games produces the results:

Number	0	1	2	3
Frequency	25	55	15	5

Calculate the mean of the numbers displayed.

14. Calculate the mean of the number x, from the following data:

x	99.6	99.7	99.8	99.9	100.0	100.1
f	3	8	17	32	22	8

15. The table shows the length of 100 rods:

Length (mm)	196	197	198	199	200
Frequency	9	18	31	22	20

(a) Calculate the mean length.
(b) Calculate the mean length of the 80 rods that measure less than 200 mm.

8.3 Grouped frequencies

A frequency table recording the heights of 25 children is shown below:

Height (cm)	Frequency
140–144	1
145–149	3
150–154	11
155–159	7
160–164	2
165–169	0
170–174	1

The table shows that 7 children had heights in the **class interval** 155–159 cm. This interval includes all heights between 154.5 cm and 159.5 cm.
154.5 cm and 159.5 cm are the **interval boundaries.**
The **mid-interval value** is 157 cm.
The mean height of the children can be calculated using the mid-interval value. This will give an *approximation* to the mean because it assumes that all 7 children have a height of 157 cm.
The approximation will usually be sufficiently near the mean.

Using the mid-interval value

Here is how to calculate the mean height for the children, using an assumed mean of 157 cm:

Mid-interval value (cm)	Frequency f	Difference d	f × d
142	1	−15	−15
147	3	−10	−30
152	11	−5	−55
157	7	0	0
162	2	5	10
167	0	10	0
172	1	15	15

$$\Sigma f = 25$$
$$\Sigma fd = -75$$
$$\text{Mean} = 157 + \frac{-75}{25} = 154 \text{ cm}$$

1. Repeat the calculation shown on the left, using an assumed mean of 154 cm.

2. A quality test of 20 metre rods showed that they ranged from 995 mm to 1004 mm in length. Measured to the nearest mm the results were:

Length (mm)	Frequency	Length (mm)	Frequency
995	1	1000	2
996	3	1001	1
997	4	1002	1
998	2	1003	0
999	5	1004	1

(a) 4 rods are recorded as 997 mm. What is the longest possible length they could be? What is the shortest possible length they could be? State the class interval in which they lie.
(b) Calculate the mean length.

3. A group of students record the distances of their homes from school:

Distance (km)	Number of students
Under 1	10
1–2	15
2–3	7
3–4	2
4–5	1

(a) What is the mid-interval value of the class interval 2–3 km?
(b) Use mid-interval values to calculate the mean distance from school.

4. A census gives the following data for the ages of the population of a small village:

Age (years)	0–9	10–19	20–29	30–39
Number	92	88	85	68
Age (years)	40–49	50–59	60–69	70+
Number	55	52	42	18

(a) The interval 10–19 years contains all those from just 10 years old to almost 20 years old. What is the mid-interval value?
(b) Calculate the mean age. Use 75 years for the mid-interval value of the 70+ class.

Example

The distribution of marks in a test for a certain class of students is given in this table:

Marks	Frequency	Marks	Frequency
1–10	0	51–60	10
11–20	0	61–70	4
21–30	0	71–80	3
31–40	1	81–90	1
41–50	6	91–100	0

Six students obtained marks in the 41–50 interval. That means they scored more than 40 and less than 51. The class boundaries of the interval are 40.5 and 50.5, so the mid-interval value of the class is 45.5, even though such a mark was not given to any student.
To calculate the mean, the table is drawn up like this, using an assumed mean of 55.5:

Mid-interval value	Frequency	Difference d	$f \times d$
35.5	1	−20	−20
45.5	6	−10	−60

5. Complete the table above and calculate the mean mark.

6. The table shows the marks obtained by 100 candidates in two mathematics papers.

Number of marks	Number of candidates	
	Paper A	Paper B
0–20	0	0
21–30	5	0
31–40	10	0
41–50	15	0
51–60	18	20
61–70	19	20
71–80	11	40
81–90	10	12
91–100	12	8

(a) What is the mid-interval value of the interval 21–30?
(b) Draw separate tables to calculate the mean mark obtained in each paper.

8.4 Standard deviation

Ungrouped data – no assumed mean

Each of these diagrams shows ten rods which have a mean length of 20 cm:

Set 1

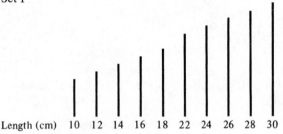

Length (cm) 10 12 14 16 18 22 24 26 28 30

Set 2

Length (cm) 15 16 17 18 19 21 22 23 24 25

It is clear that the rods of Set 2 lie closer to the mean than those of Set 1. This table for Set 1 shows the difference of each rod from the mean. This difference is called the **deviation** from the mean.

Set 1

Length (cm)	Deviation d
10	−10
12	−8
14	−6
16	−4
18	−2
22	2
24	4
26	6
28	8
30	10

As you can see from the table, the sum of the deviations is zero. So the spread cannot be measured by the mean of these deviations. Instead, use the **squares** of the deviations, which gives positive values.

The squares of the deviations are shown below:

Set 1

Length (cm)	Deviation d	d^2
10	−10	100
12	−8	64
14	−6	36
16	−4	16
18	−2	4
22	2	4
24	4	16
26	6	36
28	8	64
30	10	100
		$\Sigma d^2 = 440$

Mean of $d^2 = \dfrac{440}{10} = 44$

This value is calculated from the squares of the deviations. Its square root will therefore give a measure of the deviations.
This measure is called the **standard deviation (s.d.).**

For Set 1, the s.d. $= \sqrt{44} \approx 6.63$

In symbols, the formula is:
$$\textbf{s.d.} = \sqrt{\dfrac{\Sigma d^2}{n}}$$

1. Draw up a table for Set 2 and calculate the s.d.

2. How do the values of the s.d. for Set 1 and Set 2 show that the rods of Set 1 are spread further from the mean?

3. Calculate the mean and standard deviation of the eight numbers: 0, 5, 6, 6, 7, 8, 10, 14.

4. Use the results of Question 3 to find the mean and standard deviation of the eight numbers: 10, 15, 16, 16, 17, 18, 20, 24.

5. Find the mean and standard deviation of the five scores: 6, 7, 9, 13, 15.

6. Find the mean and standard deviation of the six scores: 15, 12, 11, 7, 13, 14.

The larger the s.d. the bigger the spread of scores from the mean.

Example 1

The test scores of a group of students are given in this table:

Score	1	2	3	4	5	6	7	8	9
Frequency	1	2	4	7	10	7	4	2	1

By symmetry, the mean score is 5. The standard deviation is calculated like this:

Score x	Frequency f	Deviation d	d^2	$f \times d^2$
1	1	−4	16	16
2	2	−3	9	18
3	4	−2	4	16
4	7	−1	1	7
5	10	0	0	0
6	7	1	1	7
7	4	2	4	16
8	2	3	9	18
9	1	4	16	16
	$\Sigma f = 38$			$\Sigma fd^2 = 114$

$\dfrac{114}{38} = 3$ so s.d. $= \sqrt{3} \approx 1.73$

Σf is the total of students.

Σfd^2 is the total of the squares of the deviations from the mean.
Note that 14 students have scores that differ by more than one standard deviation (i.e. by more than 1.73) from the mean. These are the students that score 1, 2, 3, 7, 8, or 9.

In general, for ungrouped data,
$$\textbf{s.d.} = \sqrt{\dfrac{\Sigma fd^2}{n}}$$

7. The test scores in English for a class of students were:

Score	1	2	3	4	5	6	7	8	9	10
Frequency	0	0	1	1	2	5	9	8	4	0

(a) Show that the mean score is 7.
(b) Draw up a table like the one in Example 1 to calculate the standard deviation.
(c) How many students have scores that differ by more than one s.d. from the mean?

8. The scores in mathematics for the same class were:

Score	1	2	3	4	5	6	7	8	9	10
Frequency	1	1	1	1	3	4	4	6	5	4

(a) Calculate the mean score.
(b) Calculate the standard deviation.

9. These are the scores for 20 throws of a die:

Score	x	1	2	3	4	5	6
Frequency	f	3	5	6	3	1	2

(a) What is the value of Σf?

(b) Calculate the value of $\dfrac{\Sigma fx}{\Sigma f}$.

What name is given to this measure?
(c) Find the standard deviation.
(d) What percentage of the scores lies within one standard deviation of the mean?

10. Calculate the mean and standard deviation of the variable X from the following data:

X	12	13	14	15	16	17	18	19
f	1	2	2	4	4	7	4	1

11. Calculate the mean and standard deviation for these lengths:

Length (cm)	80	81	82	83	84	85	86	87
Frequency	1	2	1	3	4	4	4	1

12. The frequency table gives the scores of a pair of dice, obtained in 100 throws:

Score	Frequency	Score	Frequency
2	0	8	15
3	3	9	21
4	7	10	11
5	8	11	8
6	8	12	7
7	12		

(a) Show that the mean score is an integer.
(b) Calculate the standard deviation of the scores.
(c) Show that approximately two-thirds of the scores lie within one standard deviation of the mean.

Grouped data – using an assumed mean

So far you have used the formulas

$$\text{s.d.} = \sqrt{\frac{\Sigma d^2}{n}} \quad \text{or} \quad \text{s.d.} = \sqrt{\frac{\Sigma fd^2}{n}}$$

These formulas are easy to use only if the mean is a convenient number. Otherwise, the deviations and their squares become complicated and the arithmetic is difficult.

For grouped data, it is usual to work with an assumed mean. The formula then becomes

$$\text{s.d.} = \sqrt{\frac{\Sigma fd^2}{n} - \left(\frac{\Sigma fd}{n}\right)^2}$$

where $d = x - x_a$, that is the difference between the mid-point of the class interval x and the assumed mean x_a.
This formula is, in fact, equivalent to those above.

Example 2

The marks in an exam of 50 students were:

Mark	1–10	11–20	21–30	31–40	41–50	51–60
Frequency	2	5	21	13	6	3

Find the mean and standard deviation.

Assume the mean to be 25.5.

Mark	Frequency f	Mid mark x	$x - x_a = d$	fd	fd^2
1–10	2	5.5	−20	−40	800
11–20	5	15.5	−10	−50	500
21–30	21	25.5	0	0	0
31–40	13	35.5	10	130	1300
41–50	6	45.5	20	120	2400
51–60	3	55.5	30	90	2700
	$\Sigma f = 50$			$\Sigma fd = 250$	$\Sigma fd^2 = 7700$

$$\text{Mean} = 25.5 + \frac{\Sigma fd}{\Sigma f}$$

$$= 25.5 + \frac{250}{50} = 30.5$$

Using the formula:

$$\text{s.d.} = \sqrt{\frac{7700}{50} - \left(\frac{250}{50}\right)^2}$$

$$= \sqrt{154 - 5^2}$$

$$= 11.4$$

---

13. The age in years of 40 people in a certain village are:

Age (years)	0–9	10–19	20–29	30–39
Frequency	8	13	6	6
Age (years)	40–49	50–59	60–69	70–79
Frequency	3	1	2	1

(a) Use an assumed mean of 24.5 to estimate the mean age.
(b) Estimate the standard deviation.

14. The heights of 60 children in a school were:

Height (cm)	100–109	110–119	120–129	130–139
Frequency	3	7	13	20
Height (cm)	140–149	150–159	160–169	170–179
Frequency	7	6	2	2

Use an assumed mean of 134.5 cm to estimate the mean and standard deviation.

15. (a) In Question 14, use an assumed mean of 114.5 cm to calculate the mean and standard deviation.
   (b) Do you get the same answer as in Question 14?
   (c) Which assumed mean made the calculation simpler?

16. The marks in a test of 70 students were:

Marks	0–9	10–19	20–29	30–39	40–49
Frequency	2	5	10	13	21
Marks	50–59	60–69	70–79	80–89	90–99
Frequency	6	6	3	2	2

Estimate the mean and the s.d.

17. The masses of 100 school children were:

Mass (kg)	31–35	36–40	41–45	46–50
Frequency	6	8	22	31
Mass (kg)	51–55	56–60	61–65	66–70
Frequency	12	11	5	5

(a) Estimate the mean and s.d.
(b) How many children have masses that differ by more than one s.d. from the mean?

18. A biologist measures the lengths of 190 leaves:

Length (cm)	0–1.9	2–3.9	4–5.9
Frequency	3	33	62
Length (cm)	6–7.9	8–9.9	10–11.9
Frequency	49	36	7

(a) Estimate the mean and s.d.
(b) How many leaves have lengths that differ by more than one s.d. from the mean?

The same formula s.d. $= \sqrt{\dfrac{\Sigma fd^2}{\Sigma f} - \left(\dfrac{\Sigma fd}{\Sigma f}\right)^2}$

can also be used for ungrouped data when working with an assumed mean, x_a.

In these cases, $d = x - x_a$

where x is simply the value for each item.

19. A bus company recorded the number of bus breakdowns that occurred over a 50-week period. Calculate the mean and s.d., using the formula.

Breakdowns per week	0	1	2	3	4	5
Frequency	2	7	20	15	4	2

20. The numbers of errors made by a typist in typing 100 pages were as follows:

Errors per page	0	1	2	3	4	5
Number of pages	3	5	6	11	15	16
Errors per page	6	7	8	9	10	
Number of pages	15	12	8	6	3	

Use the formula to calculate the mean and s.d.

Not again! This typewriter can't type.

8.5 Using standard deviation

A group of 50 students took two different tests. The mean values and standard deviations for each test were different. These histograms show, for each test, how the standard deviation measures the way in which the marks were spread from the mean:

Test 1

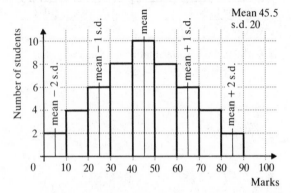

Mean 45.5
s.d. 20

Test 2

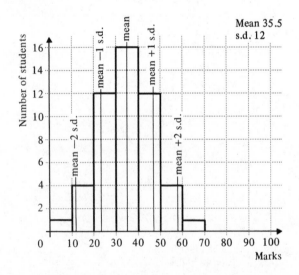

Mean 35.5
s.d. 12

In both tests, about two-thirds of the students lie within one s.d. of the mean and almost all of them lie within two s.d. of the mean.

Looking at the graphs you can see that it must have been harder to obtain a high mark on Test 2 than on Test 1, because the mean for Test 2 is lower by ten marks than the mean for Test 1, and because the marks for Test 2 are closer to the mean than the marks for Test 1.

For example, a mark of 65 on Test 1 would be equivalent to a mark of 47 on Test 2, because both are about 1 s.d. above the mean.

Questions 1 to 5 refer to these tests:

1. George obtained a mark of 25 for Test 1. If he got an equivalent mark for Test 2, what mark would you expect him to have received?

2. Ivy scored 59 on Test 2. If she did equally well on Test 1, what mark did she obtain?

3. Clem got 50 marks on both tests. Did he perform better in one test than in the other? Which one?

4. Rahab scored 60 in Test 1 and 50 in Test 2. She thought she had done better in Test 1. What do you think?

5. Don scored 85 on Test 1. Should he be pleased to have scored 60 on Test 2?

6. A woodwork examination had two parts, one practical and one written. The marks of the practical had a mean of 50 and s.d. of 10. The written part had a mean of 45 and s.d. of 20.
   (a) What marks on the practical are 1 s.d. above and 1 s.d. below the mean?
   (b) What marks on the written part are 1 s.d. and 2 s.d. above the mean?
   (c) Express a mark of 25 on the written paper in terms of its mean and standard deviation.
   (d) Which is the better mark relative to the other candidates: 70 on the written part or 70 on the practical?

7. A craft examination consists of a practical session and a written paper. The marks of the practical had a mean of 60 and s.d. of 10. The marks of the written paper had a mean of 50 and s.d. of 15.
   (a) What marks are 1 s.d. above the mean, in each part of the examination?
   (b) 80% of the candidates' marks are within 2 s.d. of the mean, in each paper. Give this as a range of marks for each paper.
   (c) Express a mark of 65 in the practical in terms of the mean and s.d.
   (d) What mark in the written paper would be equivalent to a mark of 65 in the practical?

How can I fail my exam with 70%?

But everyone else scored over 80%!

Comparing sets of data

Two sets of data are easier to compare if they have the same mean and standard deviations.

Example

The marks of eight students in a road safety test were 5, 7, 9, 9, 11, 11, 13, 15. Change the marks so that they have a mean of 50 and a standard deviation of 24.

First, find the mean and s.d. of the marks.
Then express the deviation of each mark in terms of the s.d. All the working is shown in this table:

Mark x	Deviation d	d^2	$\dfrac{d}{s.d}$
5	-5	25	$-\frac{5}{3}$
7	-3	9	-1
9	-1	1	$-\frac{1}{3}$
9	-1	1	$-\frac{1}{3}$
11	1	1	$\frac{1}{3}$
11	1	1	$\frac{1}{3}$
13	3	9	1
15	5	25	$\frac{5}{3}$
$\Sigma x = 80$		$\Sigma d^2 = 72$	

$$\text{Mean} = \frac{\Sigma x}{8} = 10$$

$$\text{Standard deviation} = \sqrt{\frac{\Sigma d^2}{8}} = \sqrt{9} = 3$$

The table cannot all be completed at once. Σx and the mean have to be found first, before the d column can be completed.
Then Σd^2 and the standard deviation have to be found, before the last column is completed.

Look at the first mark, 5. It represents a deviation of -5 from the mean. Since the standard deviation is 3, this deviation is $-\frac{5}{3}$ times the standard deviation.

When the first mark is changed to fit the new mean, it will still differ by $-\frac{5}{3}$ times the standard deviation from the new mean.

Old mark = (mean -5) = (mean $-\frac{5}{3}$ s.d.)
New mark = (mean $-\frac{5}{3}$ s.d.) = $(50 - \frac{5}{3} \times 24) = 10$
So the mark 5 is changed to 10.

---

8. For the example opposite, show that the other marks become, in order, 26, 42, 42, 58, 58, 74 and 90, when the marks are changed to have a mean of 50 and a standard deviation of 24.

9. The marks of ten students in a road safety test were 5, 6, 8, 10, 10, 10, 10, 12, 14, 15.
   (a) Find the mean and the standard deviation of these marks.
   (b) Find the new marks if these are changed to have a mean of 40 and standard deviation of 12.

10. The table shows the distribution of marks in an examination:

Mark	1–10	11–20	21–30	31–40
Frequency	1	2	3	5
Mark	41–50	51–60	61–70	71–80
Frequency	7	6	3	3

   (a) Use mid-interval values of 5, 15, 25, etc. to calculate the mean and standard deviation to 2 significant figures.
   (b) If the marks are changed so that they have a mean of 50 and standard deviation of 20, find the new mark for a candidate who scored 72.
   (c) What was the original mark of a candidate whose new mark is 40?

11. Two boys compare their marks in two tests. Michael claims he has done better than Vishnu because his total marks are higher.

	History	Geography
Vishnu	32	60
Michael	64	50

   In history the mean was 40 with s.d. 24.
   In geography the mean was 55 with s.d. 5.
   (a) Re-scale both sets of marks to a mean of 50 with s.d. 15.
   (b) Does Michael have the better total score now?

12. The half-yearly tests for 4 boys had these results:

Boy	Anab	Ben	Caleb	Daniel
Test 1	50	70	60	30
Test 2	40	40	50	35

   The marks had a mean of 50 with s.d. 20 for Test 1, and a mean of 40 with s.d. 10 for Test 2.
   (a) Re-scale the marks of Test 2 to have the same mean and s.d. as for Test 1.
   (b) Find the total of the re-scaled marks, for each boy, and arrange the four boys in order of merit.

8.6 Extending your knowledge

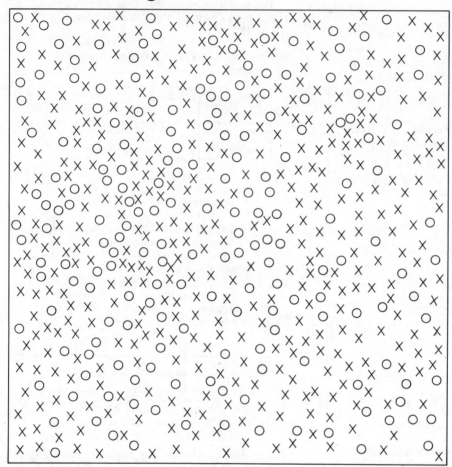

Sampling

You can use **sampling** when you want to estimate the
total number of objects in a set, *without* counting each
one.
The following questions will show you how.

1. The diagram above was drawn from a coloured
   photograph of fish on a coral reef. An × represents
   a green fish and an ○ represents a gold one. Can
   you think of a way to find the number of fish in the
   photograph, without counting?

2. (a) Take a piece of tracing paper, and carefully
       draw a square 2 cm × 2 cm on it.
   (b) Choose the most crowded part of the diagram.
       Place your square on this part and count the
       number of ×'s and ○'s in it.
   (c) Now repeat (b) for the least crowded part of
       the diagram.

   (d) Next choose a part of the diagram which is
       mediumly crowded. Count the number of ×'s
       and ○'s in it.
   (e) Find the mean of your three results.
   (f) What is the area of:
       (i) the small square?
       (ii) the diagram?
   (g) Using your answers for (e) and (f) estimate the
       number of fish in the photograph.

3. Repeat Question 2, but choose different positions
   for your squares. Do you get nearly the same
   answers?

4. Using the method in Question 2, estimate:
   (a) the number of green fish
   (b) the number of gold fish

Summary

By the end of this chapter these are the things you should know about:

8.1 Revision (pages 265–266)

The meaning of **data, frequency classes, range, mode.**
Using a **cumulative frequency** graph to find an approximation to the **median** and the **quartiles.**
The **interquartile range (i.q.r)** and **semi-interquartile range (s.i.q.r.)** are measures of spread.
The meaning of **percentile.**

8.2 The mean (pages 267–268)

How to calculate the mean using an **assumed mean.**
Using Σ (**sigma**) to express a sum:

$$\text{Mean} = \frac{\Sigma x}{n}$$

where x is the value for each item and there are n items; also

$$\text{mean} = \text{assumed mean} + \frac{\Sigma d}{n}$$

where d is the difference between each value and the mean (the **deviation**).
How to use a frequency table to calculate the mean:

$$\text{mean} = \frac{\Sigma fx}{\Sigma f} \text{ and mean} = \text{assumed mean} + \frac{\Sigma fd}{\Sigma f}$$

where f is the frequency for each value.

8.3 Grouped frequencies (pages 269–270)

Revision of **class interval.**
How to use **mid-interval** values to calculate the mean.

8.4 Standard deviation (pages 270–273)

How to measure the **deviation** of a value from the mean value.
The meaning of **standard deviation (s.d.)**

How to calculate s.d. for ungrouped data without using an assumed mean.

$$\text{s.d.} = \sqrt{\frac{\Sigma fd^2}{n}}$$

where d is the difference between each value and the mean.

How to calculate s.d. for grouped data using an assumed mean.

$$\text{s.d.} = \sqrt{\frac{\Sigma fd^2}{\Sigma f} - \left(\frac{\Sigma fd}{\Sigma f}\right)^2}$$

where d is the difference between each mid-interval value and the assumed mean.

8.5 Using standard deviation (pages 274–275)

Comparing two sets of data.
How to change a set of values to a new mean and s.d.

8.6 Extending your knowledge (page 276)

How to estimate size of a population by taking a **sample**.

It is often very difficult to count a number of small objects lying randomly in a large area. For example:
  $\times$'s and $\bigcirc$'s in the diagram opposite
  shells on a beach
  plants in a field
Here is a way to get a good estimate for the number of $\times$'s in the diagram opposite, without counting them all.
  (i) Draw a small square on tracing paper. Place your tracing on the most crowded part of the diagram. Count the number of objects within the small square.
  (ii) Repeat for the least crowded part of the diagram, and then for a mediumly crowded part.
  (iii) Take the mean of your three results.
  (iv) Using the idea:

$$\frac{\text{area of small square}}{\text{area of diagram}} = \frac{\text{no. of } \times \text{'s in small square}}{\text{no. of } \times \text{'s in diagram}}$$

you can estimate the number of $\times$'s in the diagram.

9 Probability 2

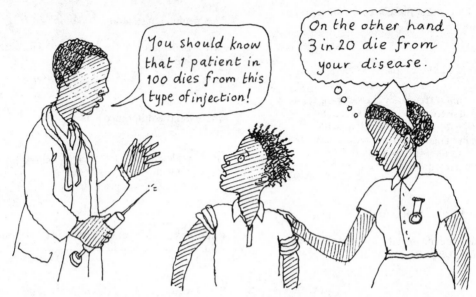

9.1 Revision

Outcomes and probability

The probability of an event tells us how likely it is to
happen. A scale from 0 to 1 is used. A probability of 1
means that the event is certain to happen, whereas 0
means that is it impossible.
The closer the probability is to 1, the more likely the
event will happen.

You can find the probability of a particular event in two
ways:
either by carrying out a large number of experiments,
and calculating the fraction of them in which the event
happens;
or without doing any experiments, by writing down the
total number of possible events, and finding the
fraction of these that is the required event.

Example 1

It is found that for every 100 beans planted, on
average 90 germinate into plants. The probability
that a particular bean will produce a plant is
therefore $\frac{90}{100}$ or 0.9.

Note
The probability of 0.9 above tells what is *likely* to
happen. It does not tell what definitely *will*
happen.

Example 2

When a die is rolled there are six possible
outcomes, 1, 2, 3, 4, 5, and 6. Two of these
numbers are multiples of 3. The probability of
obtaining a multiple of 3 is therefore $\frac{2}{6}$ or $\frac{1}{3}$.

---

1. Assign a probability of 0 or 1 to the event.
   (a) One day I shall die.
   (b) Tomorrow it will snow.
   (c) I will get 100% in my maths exam.
   (d) If I put ice in the sun it will melt.
   (e) I shall grow 2 cm taller today.

2. Choose a decimal between 0 and 1 to describe the
   probability of the event:
   (a) The next baby born will be a boy.
   (b) A card drawn from a pack will be:
       (i) red   (ii) a heart   (iii) a King.
   (c) A throw of a die will give a 5.
   (d) A number chosen from 1 to 10 will have a name
       that begins with f.

3. (a) One month of the year has to be chosen. List
       the possible outcomes.
   (b) How many of the outcomes in (a) begin with
       the letter J?
   (c) What is the probability that the chosen month
       will begin with the letter:
       (i) J   (ii) M   (iii) D   (iv) P?

4. (a) One day of the week has to be chosen. List the possible outcomes.
   (b) What is the probability that a day is chosen which begins with the letter:
       (i) T   (ii) S   (iii) F   (iv) B?

5. Drop five drawing pins onto the table and record how many have their points facing up, like this, ⊥ and how many have their points facing down, like this ⦨. Repeat the experiment 20 times. What is the probability that a drawing pin will fall point up?

Sample space

When a die is rolled there are six possible outcomes or events, $\{1, 2, 3, 4, 5, 6\}$.
The set of possible events is called the **sample space** and is denoted by **S**.
A particular event will be a subset of S.
For example *multiples of three* is the subset $\{3, 6\}$ of S.
Call this subset E.

The probability of an event is written as $Pr(E)$.

$$Pr(E) = \frac{\text{number of events in the required space}}{\text{total number in sample space}}$$

For the event *multiples of three*, then

$$Pr(E) = \frac{n(E)}{n(S)} = \frac{2}{6} = \frac{1}{3}$$

The probability of any event can be found in this way, *as long as all the outcomes are equally likely.*

Example 3

When tossing three coins find the probability of obtaining two heads.
(Take a head to be the side with the number on, and the tail to be the other side.)

Each coin could fall as a head (H) or a tail (T).

10c	H	H	H	T	H	T	T	T
5c	H	H	T	H	T	H	T	T
1c	H	T	H	H	T	T	H	T

There are eight possible outcomes so $n(S) = 8$.
In three of these there are 2 heads so $n(E) = 3$.
The probability of obtaining 2 heads is $\frac{3}{8}$.

---

6. For the three coins and sample space in the above example, find the probability of obtaining:
   (a) one tail   (b) one head
   (c) two tails   (d) three heads

7. Show the sample space for the possible outcomes when two coins are tossed. Use this to find the probability of obtaining:
   (a) one head   (b) two heads
   (c) one tail   (d) no tails

8. What is the probability of obtaining no tails, when tossing three coins?

9. Look at the sample space in example 3. List those events in which *at least* one tail occurs.
   (a) What is the probability of obtaining *at least* one tail?
   (b) How is your answer for (a) connected to your answer for Question 8?

10. What is the probability of obtaining *at least* one tail when tossing two coins?

11. The Venn diagram below shows a sample space S and a subset for the event E.

Sample space S

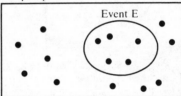

If E' represents the event not taking place, explain why $Pr(E') = 1 - Pr(E)$.

12. Use the above diagram to explain why the probability of not getting a multiple of 3 when rolling a die is $(1 - \frac{2}{6})$.

13. What is the probability of obtaining a score of at least 3, when rolling a die?

14. What is the probability of not getting two heads, when tossing three coins?

15. A bag contains four coins: a 1-cent piece (P), a 5-cent piece (F), a 10-cent piece (T) and a 20-cent piece (Q). Write down the sample space for the possible outcomes if just two coins are picked out. What is the probability of picking:
   (a) a 5-cent piece
   (b) a 5-cent piece and a 10-cent piece
   (c) a sum of at least 26 cents
   (d) a sum of less than 30 cents?

16. A card is drawn from an ordinary pack. What is the probability that it is:
   (a) an ace   (b) a black card
   (c) a Jack, Queen or King
   (d) a number less than seven
   (e) a number which is a multiple of 5
   (f) a number which is a multiple of 3?

9.2 Probability of compound events

Event A *or* event B

So far you have calculated probabilities for single events.
It is also possible to calculate the probability of either event A *or* event B happening. For example you may want to calculate the probability of passing your maths exam *or* your English exam.
For this, the idea of sample space is very important.

Possible results for one roll of a die

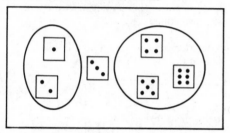

1. The diagram above shows the sample space for one roll of a die. Find the probability of getting:
   (a) a number less than 3
   (b) a number greater than 3
   (c) a number less than 3 *or* a number greater than 3.

2. Is your answer for Question 1 (c) the sum of the probabilities in (a) and (b)?

3. A pack of 52 playing cards is shuffled and one card chosen, without looking.
   The events H, C, R, A, Q and P are:
   H = {obtaining a heart}
   C = {obtaining a club}
   R = {obtaining a red card}
   A = {obtaining an ace}
   Q = {obtaining a queen}
   P = {obtaining a picture card}
   Write down:
   (a) $Pr(H)$ (b) $Pr(R)$ (c) $Pr(A)$ (d) $Pr(P)$
   Now find the probability of obtaining:
   (e) a heart *or* a club   (f) an ace *or* a queen

4. In Question 3 do you agree that:
   (a) $Pr(H\ or\ C) = Pr(H) + Pr(C)$
   (b) $Pr(A\ or\ Q) = Pr(A) + Pr(Q)$?

5. Look again at Question 3. If one card is chosen, what is the probability of obtaining:
   (a) a club *or* a red card
   (b) a heart *or* a red card
   (c) an ace *or* a picture card
   (d) a queen *or* a picture card?

6. Using your answers for Question 5, complete:
   (a) $Pr(C\ or\ R) = Pr(\ \ ) + Pr(\ \ )$
   (b) $Pr(H\ or\ R) = Pr(\ \ )$
   (c) $Pr(A\ or\ P) = Pr(\ \ ) + Pr(\ \ )$
   (d) $Pr(Q\ or\ P) = Pr(\ \ )$

Could you do Questions 5 and 6?
The sample space has 52 elements, because there are 52 cards in the pack.
For Question 5:
(a) There are 13 clubs and 26 red cards in the pack. The clubs are not red cards. So:

$$Pr(C\ or\ R) = \tfrac{13}{52} + \tfrac{26}{52} = \tfrac{39}{52} = \tfrac{3}{4}$$

(b) The probability of obtaining a heart *or* a red card is only $\tfrac{26}{52}$, *or* $\tfrac{1}{2}$, since all the hearts are red cards anyway.
(c) $Pr(A\ or\ P) = \tfrac{4}{52} + \tfrac{12}{52} = \tfrac{16}{52} = \tfrac{4}{13}$
(d) $Pr(Q\ or\ P) = \tfrac{12}{52}$ or $\tfrac{3}{13}$, since all the queens are also picture cards.

7. For the events in Question 3, find how many cards in the sample space are:
   (a) hearts *or* queens   (b) aces *or* red cards
   Now write down:
   (c) $Pr(H\ or\ Q)$ (d) $Pr(A\ or\ R)$

8. For Question 7, do you agree that:
   (a) $Pr(H\ or\ Q) \neq Pr(H) + Pr(Q)$
   (b) $Pr(A\ or\ R) \neq Pr(A) + Pr(R)$?

9. How many cards in the pack are:
   (a) both hearts *and* queens?
   (b) both aces *and* red cards?
   How does this explain your answer for Question 8?

O.K , Heads I win, Tails you lose.

Are there outcomes in common?

Example 1

Suppose you want to find the probability of choosing an ace *or* a queen from a pack of 52 playing cards.

$Pr(A) = \frac{4}{52} = \frac{1}{13}$ $Pr(Q) = \frac{4}{52} = \frac{1}{13}$

$Pr(A \text{ or } Q) = \frac{1}{13} + \frac{1}{13} = \frac{2}{13}$

You simply add the two probabilities. This is only possible *if the events have no outcomes in common*. The events above are shown on the Venn diagram below. The rest of the pack is not shown.

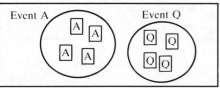

The loops do not intersect, because there are no outcomes in common.
The events form separate or **disjoint** sets.

In general:
$Pr(A \text{ or } Q) = Pr(A) + Pr(Q)$ if the events in the sample space form disjoint sets.

However, two events often have outcomes in common, as shown in Example 1 above.

Example 2

Suppose you want to find the probability of choosing a heart *or* an ace, from the pack of playing cards.
This time, the two events in the sample space overlap.

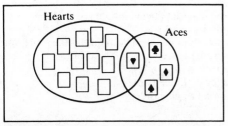

The ace of hearts occurs in both sets, so:

$n(H \text{ or } A) = n(H) + n(A) - 1$
$= 13 + 4 - 1$
$= 16$

$Pr(H \text{ or } A) = \dfrac{16}{52} = \dfrac{4}{13}$

10. For a pack of 52 playing cards, calculate the probability of choosing:
    (a) a red card *or* a spade
    (b) a king *or* a picture card
    (c) a queen *or* a black card
    (d) an ace *or* a red card
    (e) a red card *or* a picture card

11. When a die is rolled, find the probability that the outcome will be:
    (a) a number less than 3 *or* a number greater than 5
    (b) a number less than 5 *or* a number greater than 3
    (c) an even number *or* a number less than 3

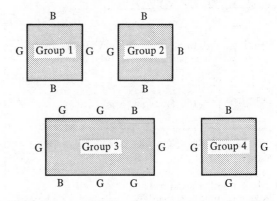

12. The diagram above shows students sitting around four tables in the library. B = boy, G = girl.
    One student is chosen at random.
    Find the probability that the student chosen is:
    (a) a boy   (b) a girl
    (c) from group 1   (d) from group 2
    (e) from group 3   (f) from group 4

13. In Question 12, what can you say about the sum of the probabilities:
    (i) in (a) and (b)   (ii) in (c), (d), (e), and (f)?

14. In Question 12, find the probability of choosing:
    (a) a student from group 1 *or* from group 2
    (b) a student from group 3 *or* from group 4
    (c) a boy from group 1
    (d) a girl from group 4
    (e) a boy *or* a student from group 2
    (f) a girl *or* a student from group 3
    (g) a boy who is not in group 2
    (h) a student who is not in group 3

15. If you roll two dice and add the scores, what is the probability of obtaining:
    (a) a score of 12   (b) a score of 1
    (c) a score of 7   (d) a double?
    Draw a sample space for this situation.

Event A *and* event B

Here you will learn how to calculate the probability of event A *and* event B happening at the same time.

Example 3

A 1-cent coin and a die are put in a shaker.
They are shaken and thrown onto a desk top.
What is the probability of getting a six on the die *and* face one on the coin, at the same time?

First draw a sample space to show all the possible outcomes. Then circle the required outcome.

```
Faces of coin
         Face │ X   X   X   X   X   (X)
         one  │
              │
         Face │ X   X   X   X   X   X
         two  │
              └──────────────────────────
                1   2   3   4   5   6
                    Number on die
```

Each cross above represents a possible outcome.
There are 12 altogether.
The required outcome has been circled.
The probability of the event happening is $\frac{1}{12}$.

---

16. Copy the above diagram. On your copy draw a circle around the event
  'two on the die *and* face one on the coin'.
  What is the probability of this event happening?

17. Make another copy of the diagram. Draw circles around the event:
  'face two on the coin *and* an even number on the die'.
  How many times can this event occur?
  What is the probability of this event happening?

18. Use the diagram above to help you find the probability of obtaining face one on the coin *and* an even number on the die.

19. A black die and a white die are rolled together.
  (a) Write down all the possible pairs of scores that can occur. (You can write them as ordered pairs.)
  (b) How many possible events are there in the sample space?
  (c) How many of these events show the same score on both dice at the same time?
  (d) What is the probability of obtaining the same score on both dice when you roll two together?

```
Number on black die
  6 │ ⊠   X   X   X   X   (X)
  5 │ X   ⊠   X   X   (X)  X
  4 │ X   X   ⊠   (X)  X   X
  3 │ X   X   (X)  ⊠   X   X
  2 │ X   (X)  X   X   ⊠   X
  1 │ (X)  X   X   X   X   ⊠
    └─────────────────────────
      1   2   3   4   5   6
        Number on white die
```

20. The diagram above shows the sample space for two dice rolled at the same time.
  (a) Do you agree that there are 36 possible events?
  (b) Describe the set of circled events.
  (c) What is the probability of getting 'doubles'?
  (d) What can you say about the sums of the scores, for the events marked with □?
  (e) What is the probability of scoring a total of seven, when two dice are rolled together?

21. Make a copy of the diagram above Question 20.
  (a) Write down the different ways of making a total score of nine, when rolling two dice.
  (b) Mark these different ways on the diagram, using a Δ.
  (c) In how many different ways can you make a total score of nine?
  (d) What is the probability of scoring a total of nine, when two dice are rolled together?

22. Use the diagram above to help you find the probability of scoring:
  (a) an even number on both dice at the same time
  (b) a total of three or less
  (c) a total of five or less
  (d) a total of seven or less
  (e) a total of nine or less.

9.3 Using tree diagrams

Often we are interested in the possible outcomes from a series of experiments. When there are several experiments, a **tree diagram** is a useful way to show the sample space.

Example 1

A tree diagram can be used to show the sample space for tossing one coin three times.

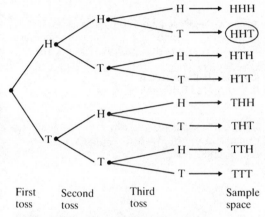

| First toss | Second toss | Third toss | Sample space |

The first toss can give either a head (H) or a tail (T). The second toss can also give a head or a tail, and so can the third. The sample space shows all the possible outcomes. For example HHT indicates head, head and then tail.

---

1. Using the tree diagram above, find the probability of obtaining a tail on the second toss, when tossing a coin three times.

2. What is the probability of not getting the same result on two successive tosses of a coin, when tossing it three times?

3. A tree diagram has been started below, to show the sample space for rolling a die twice. Copy and complete it.

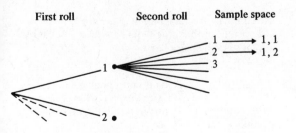

4. Write down the total number of possible outcomes, in Question 3. What is the probability of:
   (a) getting two sixes
   (b) getting just one six
   (c) getting at least one six
   (d) not getting any sixes
   (e) getting a five on the second roll
   (f) getting a three and a four
   (g) getting no ones
   (h) getting a three on the first roll?

5. You should have found in Question 3 that the number of outcomes in the sample space was 36. For each outcome write down the *sum* of the two scores. Find the probability that the sum of two scores is:
   (a) 12   (b) 3   (c) 7   (d) 10

6. Do you agree that each total score in Question 5 is *not equally likely?*

7. (a) For each of the outcomes in Question 3, write down the *product* of the two scores.
   (b) Do you agree that the possible product scores are *not equally likely?*
   (c) Write down the probability that the product of two scores is:
   (i) 36   (ii) 12   (iii) 4   (iv) 21

8. A married couple would like to have three children. Having a boy (B) or having a girl (G) are *equally likely* events.
   Copy and complete the tree diagram below:

| **First baby** | **Second baby** | **Third baby** | **Sample space** |

B •➛ BBB

9. Use your tree diagram in Question 8 to write down the probability of having:
   (a) three boys   (b) only two girls
   (c) no boys   (d) at least one boy
   (e) no more than two boys

10. Repeat Questions 8 and 9 for a couple who would like to have four children.

Tree diagrams showing probabilities

Often we are interested in the probability of an event occurring or not occurring.

Example 2

The tree diagram below shows the probability of *getting a six* or *not getting a six*, when rolling two dice.

Remember, if $Pr(6) = \frac{1}{6}$ and $Pr(\text{not } 6) = \frac{5}{6}$

then $Pr(6, 6) = \frac{1}{6} \times \frac{1}{6} = \frac{1}{36}$

$Pr(6, \text{not } 6) = \frac{1}{6} \times \frac{5}{6} = \frac{5}{36}$, and so on.

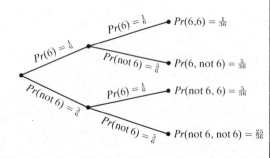

First die   Second die

---

11. The tree diagram above shows the probabilities of getting a six or not getting a six when two dice are rolled.
    Explain why:
    (a) $Pr(6) + Pr(\text{not } 6) = 1$
    (b) $Pr(6, 6) + Pr(\text{not } 6, \text{not } 6) \neq 1$
    (c) the sum of the probabilities of the four possible outcomes $= 1$
    (d) the probability of not getting a six on at least one die is $1 - Pr(6, 6)$.

12. A bag contains 3 red balls and 7 balls of other colours. One ball is picked out, its colour is noted and it is then replaced. This event is repeated three times.
    Copy and complete the tree diagram below.

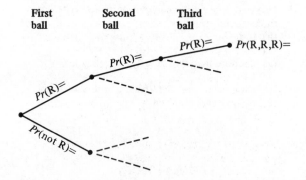

13. Use your tree diagram in Question 12 to write down the probability of picking:
    (a) at least one red ball
    (b) not more than one non-red ball.

In Question 12 the probability of picking a red ball on each occasion is $\frac{3}{10}$, since the selected ball is put back in the bag each time. However, if the selected ball is not put back, there will only be 9 balls to choose from on the second occasion and 8 on the third occasion. In addition if a red ball is picked on the first occasion, then there will be only 2 red balls left in the bag for the second choice.

14. Suppose the chosen ball is not put back in the bag, in Question 12. Find the probability of selecting a red ball on the second occasion, if on the first occasion:
    (a) a red ball is selected
    (b) a non-red ball is selected.

15. Use your answers for Question 14 to complete the tree diagram started below. Here first ball is not replaced in the bag.

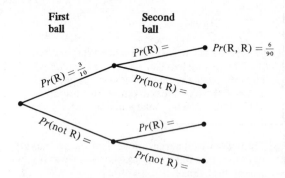

First ball   Second ball

16. For Question 15, check that the sum of the probabilities for the possible outcomes is 1.

17. If neither the first nor the second balls are replaced, in Question 12, what is the probability that all three of the selected balls are red?

18. Re-draw the tree diagram in Question 12 showing the various probabilities when a selected ball is not replaced in the bag.

19. A bag contains 7 red balls and 13 balls of other colours. If three balls are selected, what is the probability that they are all red, if the first and second selected balls are:
    (a) replaced   (b) not replaced?

9.4 Mutually exclusive events

When a coin is tossed once there are two possible outcomes – either a head or a tail. Both events cannot occur together.
We say that these two events are **mutually exclusive.**

In the same way when a is die rolled the six possible scores (1, 2, 3, 4, 5 and 6) are mutually exclusive. No two of these scores can occur at the same time.

Days of the week

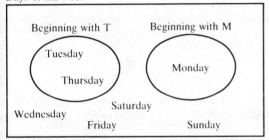

1. Look at the diagram above. If A is the event *picking a day beginning with M,* and B is the event *picking a day beginning with T,* write down:
   (a) $Pr(A)$ (b) $Pr(B)$ (c) $Pr(A \text{ or } B)$

2. For Question 1, do you agree that:
   (a) the events A and B are mutually exclusive?
   (b) $Pr(A \text{ or } B) = Pr(A) + Pr(B)$?

3. (a) Draw a Venn diagram for the days of the week, showing the subsets:
       A = {days of the week beginning with S}
       B = {days of the week with six letters}
   (b) Write down:
       (i) $n(A)$ (ii) $n(B)$ (iii) $n(A \cap B)$

4. For Question 3, if a day of the week is chosen, write down:
   (a) $Pr(A)$ (b) $Pr(B)$ (c) $Pr(A \text{ or } B)$

5. For Question 3, do you agree that:
   (a) the events A and B are *not* mutually exclusive
   (b) $Pr(A \text{ or } B) \neq Pr(A) + Pr(B)$?

6. A = {months of the year beginning with A}
   M = {months of the year beginning with M}
   F = {months of the year with names containing five letters}
   (a) Write down: $n(A), n(M), n(F)$ and hence find:
       (i) $Pr(A)$ (ii) $Pr(M)$ (iii) $Pr(F)$

   (b) Write down: $n(A \cup M)$ and $n(A \cup F)$ and hence find: (i) $Pr(A \text{ or } M)$ (ii) $Pr(A \text{ or } F)$

Sample space S

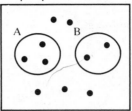

Sample space S

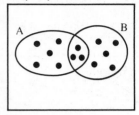

[1]   [2]

In diagram [1] above the subsets A and B do not intersect. They are said to be **disjoint.**
So if A and B represent two events, then they are mutually exclusive.
The probability of either event A *or* event B occurring is the sum of the two separate probabilities.

> If A and B are mutually exclusive events then
> $$Pr(A \text{ or } B) = Pr(A) + Pr(B).$$

In diagram [2] above, the subsets A and B intersect. So if A and B represent two events then they are *not* mutually exclusive.
The probability of either event A *or* event B occurring is no longer $Pr(A) + Pr(B)$.

> If two events are *not* mutually exclusive then
> $$n(A \cup B) = n(A) + n(B) - n(A \cap B)$$
> so $Pr(A \text{ or } B) = Pr(A) + Pr(B) - Pr(A \text{ and } B).$

7. Say whether the events E_1, E_2 etc. are mutually exclusive or not.
   (a) Two coins are tossed. E_1 is getting two heads. E_2 is getting two tails.
   (b) A die is rolled. E_1 is getting an odd number. E_2 is getting a five.
   (c) Two dice are rolled. E_1 is getting a total score of eight. E_2 is getting a total score which is a multiple of four.
   (d) Two dice are rolled. E_1 is getting a total score which is an odd number. E_2 is getting a total score which is divisible by 2.
   (e) Three coins are tossed. E_1 is getting two heads. E_2 is getting two tails. E_3 is getting just one head.
   (f) Three coins are tossed. E_1 is getting one tail, E_2 is getting at least one head.

8. For each of Questions 7 (a), (b), (c) and (d) find:
   (i) $Pr(E_1)$ (ii) $Pr(E_2)$ (iii) $Pr(E_1 \text{ or } E_2)$

9. From your results in Question 8, say for which parts of Question 7 (a) – (d):
   $Pr(E_1 \text{ or } E_2) = Pr(E_1) + Pr(E_2)$.

Rolling a die   **Tossing a coin**

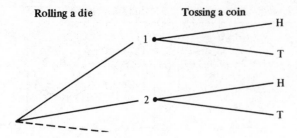

10. Copy and complete the tree diagram to show the possible outcomes, when rolling a die and tossing a coin. Do you agree that:
(a) the outcomes 1, 2, 3, 4, 5 and 6 for the die are mutually exclusive
(b) the outcomes H and T for the coin are mutually exclusive
(c) the twelve branches on the tree represent twelve mutually exclusive events?

11. (a) Write down the probability for each of the twelve possible outcomes in Question 10.
(b) Do you agree that the sum of the twelve probabilities is 1?

12. Copy and complete the tree diagram to show the probability of getting a six when rolling a die and a head or tail when tossing a coin.
Do you agree that:
(a) the outcomes *getting a six* and *not getting a six* are mutually exclusive
(b) the four branches on the tree represent four mutually exclusive events?

13. (a) Write down the probability for each of the four possible outcomes in Question 12.
(b) Explain why the sum of the four probabilities is 1.

14. What is the probability of not getting a six or a tail in Question 12?

15. A pack of 30 cards has 6 cards marked A, 5 cards marked B, 7 cards marked C and 12 cards marked D. The pack is shuffled and one card is drawn. What is the probability that the drawn card is:
(a) marked with an A
(b) not marked with a B
(c) marked with an A or a B
(d) marked with an A or a D
(e) marked with neither a B nor a D?

16. At the end of the year, the students in Form Five are given grades. The probability of obtaining grades A, B, C or D are 0.2, 0.4, 0.3 and 0.1 respectively.
What is the probability of obtaining:
(a) a C or a D   (b) a B or a C
(c) neither an A nor a D   (d) at least a B?

17. Machines X and Y produce bolts. Some of these are perfect, some are slightly defective but still usable, and some are actually rejected. The percentages of each kind of bolt are given in the table below:

	Total number	Perfect	Slightly defective	Rejects
Machine X	450	60%	30%	10%
Machine Y	400	54%	41%	5%

What is the probability that:
(a) a bolt from machine X is rejected
(b) a bolt from machine Y is perfect
(c) a bolt from machine X is either slightly defective or rejected
(d) a bolt from machine Y is not rejected
(e) if both sets of bolts are mixed together then one chosen at random is:
  (i) perfect?
  (ii) slightly defective or rejected?

18. A car manufacturer produces five different types of engine: 1000 cc, 1200 cc, 1600 cc, 2000 cc, and 2500 cc. In a year's production of engines the proportion of each type is 20%, 30%, 25%, 15% and 10% respectively. What is the probability that an engine picked at random is:
(a) 1000 cc or 1200 cc
(b) 2000 cc or 2500 cc
(c) under 2000 cc
(d) over 1200 cc
(e) neither 1600 cc nor 2000 cc
(f) at least 1200 cc
(g) over 1000 cc but under 2000 cc?

9.5 Independent and dependent events

Independent events

When a coin is tossed twice, the outcome of the first toss in no way affects the outcome of the second toss. If a head or tail is obtained on the first toss the probability of getting a head or tail on the second toss remains unchanged.

Two events are said to be **independent** if the occurrence of one of them in no way affects the occurrence of the other.

> When two events A and B are independent, the probability that both will occur is obtained by multiplying their separate probabilities, i.e.
>
> $$Pr(A \ and \ B) = Pr(A) \times Pr(B)$$

Example 1

A coin is tossed and then a die is rolled. What is the probability of obtaining a tail followed by a five?

Method (i)   The sample space for the possible outcomes is:
$\{(H, 1), (H, 2), (H, 3), (H, 4), (H, 5), (H, 6),$
$(T, 1), (T, 2), (T, 3), (T, 4), (T, 5), (T, 6)\}$
It contains twelve elements. One of these represents the event *tail followed by five*.
So $Pr(T, 5) = \frac{1}{12}$

Method (ii) The tree diagram showing the probabilities is:

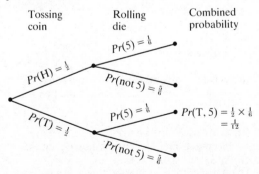

Obtaining a tail on the coin in no way affects the probability of obtaining a five on the die. These events are independent, so:
$Pr(T \ and \ 5) = PR(T) \times Pr(5) = \frac{1}{2} \times \frac{1}{6} = \frac{1}{12}$

1. (a) Use a tree diagram to find the probability of drawing two successive aces from a pack of cards, if the first card is replaced and the pack shuffled before drawing the second card.
   (b) What is the probability of drawing an ace as the first card?
   (c) Explain why the probability of drawing two successive aces is $\frac{16}{2704}$.

2. A die is rolled twice.
   (a) Draw a tree diagram to show the probability of getting two successive fives.
   (b) Do you agree that getting a five on the second roll is independent of the outcome of the first roll?
   (c) Explain why the probability of getting two successive fives is $\frac{1}{36}$.

3. First a red die and then a white die is rolled. Find the probability that the red die shows an even number *and* the white die shows an odd number.

4. A 1-cent piece, a 5-cent piece and a 10-cent piece are tossed in succession.
   (a) Do you agree that the three separate outcomes are independent events?
   (b) What is the probability that:
      (i) each shows a head
      (ii) only the 10-cent piece shows a head?

5. A die is rolled and then a coin is tossed twice. Find the probability of obtaining:
   (a) a two followed by two heads
   (b) a six followed by two tails
   (c) an even number followed by two tails.

6. A die is rolled three times. Find the probability of obtaining:
   (a) a two on all three rolls
   (b) an even number on all three rolls
   (c) a multiple of three on all three rolls
   (d) an even number on the first roll, a six on the second roll *and* a four on the third roll
   (e) an odd number on the first roll, a five on the second roll *and* a multiple of three on the third roll.

7. On a particular day the probability of it not raining is $\frac{5}{12}$, and the probability of a bus arriving on time is $\frac{2}{5}$.
   (a) Do you agree that these are independent events?
   (b) Find the probability that:
      (i) it doesn't rain *and* the bus arrives on time
      (ii) it rains *and* the bus is late.

8. Two packs of cards are shuffled. One card is drawn from each pack. Find the probability that the cards will be in this order:
   (a) heart, heart
   (b) heart, club
   (c) king, king
   (d) spade, ace
   (e) ace, king
   (f) club, picture card

9. If x is selected at random from the set $X = \{1, 2, 3, 4, 5\}$ and y is selected at random from the set $Y = \{2, 4, 6, 8, 10\}$ find the probability:
   (a) $x > 2$ and $y > 2$
   (b) $x > 2$ and $y < 6$
   (c) x is odd and y is a multiple of 4
   (d) x and y are divisible by 5
   (e) x and y are even

10. The probability of a particular football player scoring a goal is $\frac{1}{10}$. The probability that he gets booked in any match is $\frac{2}{9}$. The probability that his team wins is $\frac{3}{5}$.
    (a) Do you agree that these three events are independent?
    (b) Find the probability that:
        (i) all three events take place
        (ii) the player scores a goal, and his team wins, but he does not get booked
        (iii) none of the three events takes place.

11. In a given year, the probability that a man buys a new car is $\frac{1}{5}$, the probability that he visits America is $\frac{1}{3}$ and the probability that he gets injured is $\frac{1}{8}$. Assuming that these are independent events find the probability that:
    (a) he has a new car, goes to America but does not get injured
    (b) he gets injured but does not go to America or have a new car
    (c) none of these three events happens.

12. A restaurant has a 3-course menu which offers several choices for each course.
    The probability that a customer will choose a sea-food starter is $\frac{1}{10}$. The probability that a curry will be chosen as the main course is $\frac{1}{8}$. The probability that fresh fruit will be chosen for the third course is $\frac{3}{5}$.
    Assuming that the choices of courses are independent, find the probability that a customer will choose:
    (a) sea-food, curry and fresh fruit
    (b) curry but neither sea-food nor fresh fruit
    (c) none of the three specified dishes.

Dependent events

Example 2

A bag contains three red balls (R) and five blue balls (B). Two balls are removed without being replaced. Show the various probabilities using a tree diagram.

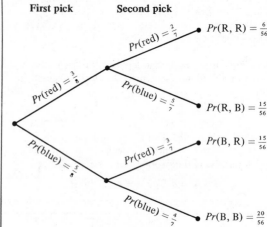

If a red ball is removed first, then two red balls and five blue balls are left.
The probability of picking a second red ball is therefore $\frac{2}{7}$.
However, if a blue ball is removed first, the probability that the second ball will be red is $\frac{3}{7}$.

In this case the probabilities for the second event *depend* on the outcome of the first event. We say the events are **dependent**.

13. A bag contains four red balls and six green balls. Two balls are picked out and not replaced. Find the probability of getting:
    (a) two red balls
    (b) a red ball and then a green ball
    (c) a green ball and then a red ball
    (d) no green balls.

14. What is the probability of picking two aces in succession from a pack of cards, if the first card is not replaced?

15. Three cards are drawn from a pack, without replacement. Find the probability of getting:
    (a) three successive aces
    (b) a three, then an ace and then a king
    (c) no aces.

16. Four cards are drawn from a pack without replacement. Find the probability of getting:
    (a) four successive aces   (b) no aces.

Further problems

17. A box contains ten nuts and their matching bolts.
   (a) If one nut is removed from the box, what is the probability of selecting the matching bolt?
   (b) If a nut and bolt are removed at the same time from the box, what is the probability of their matching?

18. Two cards are drawn from a pack of 52 cards. How many ways are there of choosing:
   (a) any two cards   (b) any two red cards
   (c) any two aces   (d) two red aces?

19. If two cards are drawn from an ordinary pack of cards, use your answers for Question 18 to write down the probability of getting:
   (a) two red aces
   (b) any two aces
   (c) any two red aces.

20. A man has seven pairs of shoes. Two of these pairs are black. If the man wears each pair of shoes only once a week, what is the probability that he wears a black pair of shoes on two successive days during a given week?

21. The table below shows some information about 100 cars in a car park.

	American	Japanese
Front wheel drive	20	8
Rear wheel drive	40	32

If one car is chosen at random what is the probability of it being:
   (a) an American car
   (b) a car with rear wheel drive
   (c) a Japanese car with front wheel drive
   (d) *either* an American car *or* a car with front wheel drive?

22. (a) How many ways are there of selecting two cars at random from 100 cars?
   (b) If in Question 21 two cars are chosen at random, what is the probability that:
      (i) both cars have rear wheel drive
      (ii) both cars are American
      (iii) just one car has front wheel drive
      (iv) at least one of the cars is Japanese
      (v) *either* the cars are both American *or* the cars are both Japanese?

Form 5

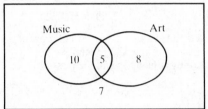

23. The Venn diagram above shows how many pupils in Form 5 study music and art. If two pupils are chosen at random, what is the probability that both do:
   (a) music   (b) art   (c) music and art
   (d) music but not art   (e) neither subject?

Summary

By the end of this chapter these are the things you
should know about:

9.1 Revision: outcomes and sample spaces
(pages 278–279)

Probability is a measure of the likely outcome of some
occurrence.
You can find the probability of a particular event
happening *either* by doing a large number of
experiments *or* by considering all the possible
outcomes.
The **sample space** for an occurrence is the set of all
possible outcomes.
How to use the sample space (S) for finding the
probability of an event (E) occurring:

$$Pr(E) = \frac{n(E)}{n(S)}$$

9.2 Probability of compound events
(pages 280–282)

How to find the probability that either the event A *or*
the event B occurs.
e.g. What is the probability of rolling a 5 or a 6 with a
die?

$$Pr(5 \text{ or } 6) = Pr(5) + Pr(6) = \tfrac{1}{6} + \tfrac{1}{6} = \tfrac{2}{6} = \tfrac{1}{3}$$

How to find the probability that the event A *and* the
event B occurs at the same time.
e.g. What is the probability when rolling two dice of
rolling a 3 on the first dice and a 2 on the second?

$$Pr(3 \text{ and } 2) = Pr(3) \times Pr(2) = \tfrac{1}{6} \times \tfrac{1}{6} = \tfrac{1}{36}$$

9.3 Using tree diagrams (pages 283–284)

How to use a tree diagram to show all the possible
outcomes, and to find probabilities.
e.g. A bag contains three red beads and two green
beads. Two beads are taken from the bag. What is
the probability that both are red?

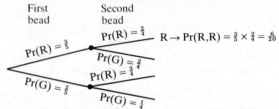

How to use a tree diagram to show the probabilities of
events occurring or not occurring, and how to calculate
probabilities for compound events, i.e. *Pr*(A *and* B),
Pr(A *or* B).

9.4 Mutually exclusive events (pages 285–286)

Two events are **mutually exclusive** if they cannot both
occur at the same time.
Mutually exclusive events are in disjoint subsets in the
sample space. This shows that:
$$Pr(A \text{ or } B) = Pr(A) + Pr(B).$$
The events represented by each branch of a tree
diagram are mutually exclusive.
The sum of the probabilities for the branches is 1.

9.5 Independent and dependent events
(pages 287–289)

Two events are **independent** if the outcome of the first
in no way affects the outcome of the second. When two
events are independent the probability that both will
occur is given by:
$$Pr(A \text{ and } B) = Pr(A) \times Pr(B)$$
When two successive branches on a tree diagram
represent independent events, the probability of those
two events occurring is found by multiplying the
individual probabilities.
Two events are **dependent** if the outcome of the first
affects the outcome of the second. This happens when
the first item selected from a set is *not* replaced before
the second item is selected.

10 Vectors and matrices 1

10.1 Vectors

A **vector** is a quantity that has both **size** (magnitude) and **direction.**

A vector is distinguished from a **scalar** quantity which possesses size only.
For example:

Scalar	Vector
Mass	Weight
Speed	Velocity
Distance	Displacement

The **velocity** of a car is its **speed** in a particular direction.

Vectors are represented geometrically by arrows. The length of the arrow represents the size of the vector and the direction of the arrow is the direction of the vector. Such vectors are usually described in terms of their components as **column vectors**.

Example 1

Write the vectors below as column vectors.

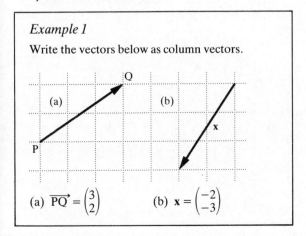

(a) $\overrightarrow{PQ} = \begin{pmatrix} 3 \\ 2 \end{pmatrix}$

(b) $x = \begin{pmatrix} -2 \\ -3 \end{pmatrix}$

1. Write the following vectors as column vectors.

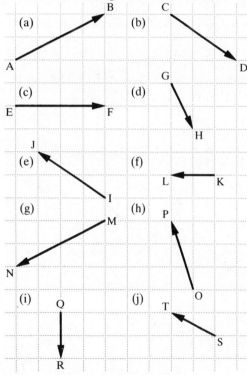

2. Draw the following column vectors

(a) $a = \begin{pmatrix} 1 \\ 2 \end{pmatrix}$

(b) $b = \begin{pmatrix} 1 \\ -2 \end{pmatrix}$

(c) $c = \begin{pmatrix} -1 \\ 2 \end{pmatrix}$

(d) $d = \begin{pmatrix} 2 \\ -4 \end{pmatrix}$

(e) $e = \begin{pmatrix} 2 \\ 4 \end{pmatrix}$

(f) $f = \begin{pmatrix} -1 \\ -2 \end{pmatrix}$

(g) $g = \begin{pmatrix} 3 \\ -6 \end{pmatrix}$

(h) $h = \begin{pmatrix} 3 \\ 0 \end{pmatrix}$

(i) $i = \begin{pmatrix} 0 \\ -2 \end{pmatrix}$

(j) $j = \begin{pmatrix} 0 \\ 1 \end{pmatrix}$

3. In Question 2:
   (a) which pairs of vectors are parallel
   (b) of the parallel pairs, **e** = 2**a**; what other
       relationships can you find?

Example 2

Look at the vectors below.

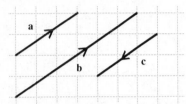

$$\mathbf{a} = \begin{pmatrix} 3 \\ 2 \end{pmatrix}, \qquad \mathbf{b} = \begin{pmatrix} 6 \\ 4 \end{pmatrix}, \qquad \mathbf{c} = \begin{pmatrix} -3 \\ -2 \end{pmatrix}$$

$$\mathbf{b} = \begin{pmatrix} 6 \\ 4 \end{pmatrix} = 2 \times \begin{pmatrix} 3 \\ 2 \end{pmatrix} = 2\mathbf{a}$$

b is parallel to **a** and twice its length.

$$\mathbf{c} = \begin{pmatrix} -3 \\ -2 \end{pmatrix} = -\begin{pmatrix} 3 \\ 2 \end{pmatrix} = -\mathbf{a}$$

c is parallel to **a**, has the same length but goes in
the opposite direction.

---

4. Write the vectors below in terms of **a**.

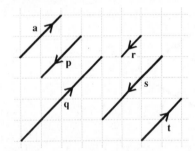

5. If $\mathbf{a} = \begin{pmatrix} 1 \\ 2 \end{pmatrix}$ draw the vectors:
   (a) 2**a**   (b) 3**a**   (c) −**a**
   (d) −4**a**   (e) ½**a**   (f) −2**a**

Vectors as translations

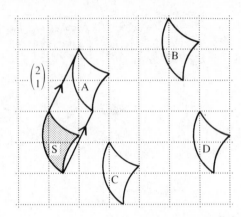

6. Look at the diagram above. The shaded shape is
   mapped onto shape A by a translation described by
   the column vector $\begin{pmatrix} 1 \\ 2 \end{pmatrix}$. This vector means
   move 1 square right and 2 squares up.
   Use a column vector to describe the translation that
   maps the shaded shape onto:
   (a) shape B   (b) shape C   (c) shape D.

7. Use a column vector to describe the translation
   which maps shape A onto:
   (a) shape B   (b) shape C   (c) shape D.

8. Which shape does shape C map onto, if the
   translation is described by:
   (a) $\begin{pmatrix} 3 \\ 1 \end{pmatrix}$ (b) $\begin{pmatrix} 2 \\ 4 \end{pmatrix}$ (c) $\begin{pmatrix} -2 \\ 1 \end{pmatrix}$ (d) $\begin{pmatrix} -1 \\ 3 \end{pmatrix}$?

9. What can you say about the translation which maps
   shape A onto shape B and the translation which
   maps shape C onto shape D?

10. Copy and complete the table below.

	Translation	Vector	Translation	Vector
(a)	A → B	$\begin{pmatrix} \ \\ \ \end{pmatrix}$	B → A	$\begin{pmatrix} \ \\ \ \end{pmatrix}$
(b)	B → D	$\begin{pmatrix} \ \\ \ \end{pmatrix}$	D → B	$\begin{pmatrix} \ \\ \ \end{pmatrix}$
(c)		$\begin{pmatrix} 2 \\ 4 \end{pmatrix}$		$\begin{pmatrix} -2 \\ -4 \end{pmatrix}$

11. What is the connection between the vectors in each
    part of Question 10?

12. Copy and complete the table below.

	Translation	Translation	Translation
(a)	$S \rightarrow A$ $\begin{pmatrix} 1 \\ 2 \end{pmatrix}$	$A \rightarrow B$ $\begin{pmatrix} 3 \\ 1 \end{pmatrix}$	$S \rightarrow B$ $\begin{pmatrix} \\ \end{pmatrix}$
(b)	$C \rightarrow B$ $\begin{pmatrix} \\ \end{pmatrix}$	$B \rightarrow D$ $\begin{pmatrix} \\ \end{pmatrix}$	$C \rightarrow D$ $\begin{pmatrix} \\ \end{pmatrix}$
(c)	$S \rightarrow D$ $\begin{pmatrix} \\ \end{pmatrix}$	$D \rightarrow C$ $\begin{pmatrix} \\ \end{pmatrix}$	$S \rightarrow C$ $\begin{pmatrix} \\ \end{pmatrix}$

13. (a) How can the third vector be obtained from the other two, in each part of Question 12?
(b) Explain the connection between the three translations, in each part of Question 12.

In geometrical applications of vectors, it is useful to think of vectors as representing translations.
The addition of two vectors can then be thought of as the single translation that is equivalent to the two successive translations.

Adding vectors

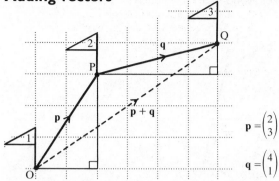

$$\mathbf{p} = \begin{pmatrix} 2 \\ 3 \end{pmatrix}$$

$$\mathbf{q} = \begin{pmatrix} 4 \\ 1 \end{pmatrix}$$

In the diagram above the translation of flag 1 to flag 2 is shown by the arrow from O to P.
The translation of flag 2 to flag 3 is shown by the arrow from P to Q.
The translation of flag 1 to flag 3 could be shown by an arrow from O to Q. It is equivalent to translation

p followed by translation **q**   i.e. $\begin{pmatrix} 2 \\ 3 \end{pmatrix} + \begin{pmatrix} 4 \\ 1 \end{pmatrix} = \begin{pmatrix} 6 \\ 4 \end{pmatrix}$.

14. In the diagram above:
   (a) write **p** and **q** as column vectors,
   (b) write **p** + **q** as a column vector.

Vectors are added by placing the arrows which represent them tip to tail.

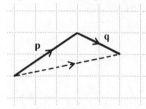

Example 3

If $\mathbf{a} = \begin{pmatrix} -3 \\ -2 \end{pmatrix}$ and $\mathbf{b} = \begin{pmatrix} 2 \\ -1 \end{pmatrix}$, draw a diagram to show **a** + **b**.

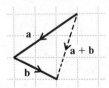

$$\mathbf{a} + \mathbf{b} = \begin{pmatrix} -3 \\ -2 \end{pmatrix} + \begin{pmatrix} 2 \\ -1 \end{pmatrix} = \begin{pmatrix} -1 \\ -3 \end{pmatrix}$$

---

15. If $\mathbf{a} = \begin{pmatrix} 2 \\ -1 \end{pmatrix}$, $\mathbf{b} = \begin{pmatrix} -3 \\ 2 \end{pmatrix}$, $\mathbf{c} = \begin{pmatrix} -1 \\ 4 \end{pmatrix}$

and $\mathbf{d} = \begin{pmatrix} -2 \\ -3 \end{pmatrix}$, draw diagrams to find:

   (a) **a** + **b**   (b) **b** + **a**   (c) **a** + **c**   (d) **c** + **a**
   (e) **b** + **d**   (f) **c** + **d**   (g) **a** + **d**   (h) **a** − **c**

Were you able to do Question 15 (h)?

$$\mathbf{a} - \mathbf{c} = \mathbf{a} + (-\mathbf{c})$$

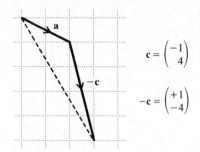

$$\mathbf{c} = \begin{pmatrix} -1 \\ 4 \end{pmatrix}$$

$$-\mathbf{c} = \begin{pmatrix} +1 \\ -4 \end{pmatrix}$$

$$\mathbf{a} - \mathbf{c} = \begin{pmatrix} 2 \\ -1 \end{pmatrix} - \begin{pmatrix} -1 \\ 4 \end{pmatrix} = \begin{pmatrix} 2 \\ -1 \end{pmatrix} + \begin{pmatrix} 1 \\ -4 \end{pmatrix} = \begin{pmatrix} 3 \\ -5 \end{pmatrix}$$

16. Draw diagrams to show $\mathbf{p} - \mathbf{q}$ in the following:

(a) $\mathbf{p} = \begin{pmatrix} 4 \\ 3 \end{pmatrix}, \mathbf{q} = \begin{pmatrix} 1 \\ 2 \end{pmatrix}$ (b) $\mathbf{p} = \begin{pmatrix} 1 \\ 3 \end{pmatrix}, \mathbf{q} = \begin{pmatrix} 2 \\ 1 \end{pmatrix}$

Check your answers by subtracting the column vectors.

17. Draw diagrams to illustrate these vector additions

(a) $\begin{pmatrix} 1 \\ 3 \end{pmatrix} + \begin{pmatrix} 2 \\ 4 \end{pmatrix} = \begin{pmatrix} 3 \\ 7 \end{pmatrix}$ (b) $\begin{pmatrix} 1 \\ 3 \end{pmatrix} + \begin{pmatrix} -2 \\ -4 \end{pmatrix} = \begin{pmatrix} -1 \\ -1 \end{pmatrix}$

(c) $\begin{pmatrix} 2 \\ 0 \end{pmatrix} + \begin{pmatrix} 0 \\ 1 \end{pmatrix} + \begin{pmatrix} -2 \\ -1 \end{pmatrix} = \begin{pmatrix} 0 \\ 0 \end{pmatrix}$

18. Use the diagram on the right to show that:
$$\mathbf{p} + \mathbf{q} = \mathbf{q} + \mathbf{p}$$

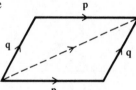

19. Use the diagram on the right to show that:
(a) $\mathbf{p} - \mathbf{q} = \mathbf{p} + (-\mathbf{q})$
(b) $\mathbf{q} + \mathbf{p} + (-\mathbf{q}) = \mathbf{p}$

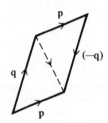

Vector algebra

All vectors have the following properties:

[1] Two vectors $\mathbf{a}$ and $\mathbf{b}$ can be added.

If $\mathbf{a} = \begin{pmatrix} 2 \\ 3 \end{pmatrix}$ and $\mathbf{b} = \begin{pmatrix} 4 \\ 1 \end{pmatrix}$, then $\mathbf{a} + \mathbf{b} = \begin{pmatrix} 6 \\ 4 \end{pmatrix}$.

[2] Vector addition is commutative.

That is, $\mathbf{a} + \mathbf{b} = \mathbf{b} + \mathbf{a}$.

[3] Vector $\mathbf{a}$ can be subtracted from vector $\mathbf{b}$ to give vector $\mathbf{b} - \mathbf{a}$.

If $\mathbf{b} = \begin{pmatrix} 4 \\ 1 \end{pmatrix}$ and $\mathbf{a} = \begin{pmatrix} 2 \\ 3 \end{pmatrix}$ then $\mathbf{b} - \mathbf{a} = \begin{pmatrix} 2 \\ -2 \end{pmatrix}$.

[4] A vector $\mathbf{a}$ can be multipled by a number k. The result is another vector, $k\mathbf{a}$. When the vector is written as a column vector, each component is mutliplied by k.

If $\mathbf{a} = \begin{pmatrix} 2 \\ 3 \end{pmatrix}$ then $5\mathbf{a} = \begin{pmatrix} 5 \times 2 \\ 5 \times 3 \end{pmatrix}$ or $\begin{pmatrix} 10 \\ 15 \end{pmatrix}$

[5] For each vector $\mathbf{a}$ there is the opposite or **inverse vector** $(-\mathbf{a})$, and $\mathbf{a} + (-\mathbf{a}) = \mathbf{0}$.
The result $\mathbf{0}$ is called the **zero vector** or **null vector**.

If $\mathbf{a} = \begin{pmatrix} 3 \\ -2 \end{pmatrix}$ then $-\mathbf{a} = \begin{pmatrix} -3 \\ 2 \end{pmatrix}$ and $\mathbf{a} + (-\mathbf{a}) = \begin{pmatrix} 0 \\ 0 \end{pmatrix}$.

20. $\mathbf{r} = \begin{pmatrix} -1 \\ 5 \end{pmatrix}, \mathbf{s} = \begin{pmatrix} 4 \\ -3 \end{pmatrix}, \mathbf{t} = \begin{pmatrix} 3 \\ -15 \end{pmatrix}$

(a) Write down: (i) $-\mathbf{r}$ (ii) $-\mathbf{s}$ (iii) $-\mathbf{t}$

(b) Show that:
   (i) $\mathbf{r} + \mathbf{s} = \mathbf{s} + \mathbf{r}$ (ii) $\mathbf{t} + (-\mathbf{t}) = \mathbf{0}$
   (iii) $\mathbf{t} = -3\mathbf{r}$ (iv) $\mathbf{t} + \mathbf{r} = -2\mathbf{r}$

(c) Find: (i) $\mathbf{r} + \mathbf{s} + \mathbf{t}$ (ii) $3\mathbf{s} + 2\mathbf{r} + \mathbf{t}$
   (iii) $\frac{1}{3}\mathbf{t}$ (iv) $\frac{2}{3}\mathbf{t}$ (v) $3\mathbf{t} - 2\mathbf{s}$

21. Using the above vectors show that:
$$(\mathbf{r} + \mathbf{s}) + \mathbf{t} = \mathbf{r} + (\mathbf{s} + \mathbf{t})$$
Is vector addition *associative*?

22. If $\mathbf{r} = \begin{pmatrix} 5 \\ 6 \end{pmatrix}$ and $\mathbf{s} = \begin{pmatrix} 3 \\ 4 \end{pmatrix}$, find the values of:

(a) $\mathbf{r} - \mathbf{s}$ (b) $\mathbf{s} - \mathbf{r}$ (c) $2\mathbf{r} - \mathbf{s}$ (d) $3\mathbf{r} - 2\mathbf{s}$
Show also that $3(\mathbf{r} + \mathbf{s}) = 3\mathbf{r} + 3\mathbf{s}$

23. Find the value of each letter:

(a) $\begin{pmatrix} x \\ y \end{pmatrix} + \begin{pmatrix} 2 \\ 3 \end{pmatrix} = \begin{pmatrix} 4 \\ 5 \end{pmatrix}$ (b) $\begin{pmatrix} 3 \\ x \end{pmatrix} + \begin{pmatrix} y \\ 2 \end{pmatrix} = \begin{pmatrix} 6 \\ -3 \end{pmatrix}$

(c) $3\begin{pmatrix} x \\ 2 \end{pmatrix} - 2\begin{pmatrix} 1 \\ y \end{pmatrix} = \begin{pmatrix} 7 \\ 4 \end{pmatrix}$

10.2 Using vectors in geometry

Vectors can be used to prove simple geometrical properties of shapes.
There are two basic ideas

[1]

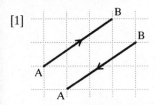

$$\overrightarrow{AB} = -\overrightarrow{BA}$$

[2]

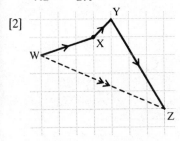

$$\overrightarrow{WX} + \overrightarrow{XY} + \overrightarrow{YZ} = \overrightarrow{WZ}$$

Example 1

Two lines, AC and DB, meet at M. M is the mid-point of AC and DB.

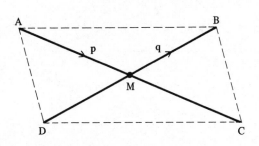

If $\overrightarrow{AM} = \mathbf{p}$ and $\overrightarrow{MB} = \mathbf{q}$, show that:
(i) AB is parallel to DC
(ii) AB = DC.

$$\overrightarrow{AB} = \overrightarrow{AM} + \overrightarrow{MB} = \mathbf{p} + \mathbf{q}$$
$$\overrightarrow{DC} = \overrightarrow{DM} + \overrightarrow{MC} = \mathbf{q} + \mathbf{r}$$
Hence $\overrightarrow{AB} = \overrightarrow{DC}$.

Since the vectors $\overrightarrow{AB}$ and $\overrightarrow{DC}$ are equal, they have the same length (size) and the same direction, i.e. they are parallel.

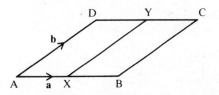

1. In the diagram X and Y are the mid-points of AB and DC of the parallelogram ABCD.
   If $\overrightarrow{AX} = \mathbf{a}$ and $\overrightarrow{AD} = \mathbf{b}$, write in terms of $\mathbf{a}$ and $\mathbf{b}$:
   (a) $\overrightarrow{AB}$ (b) $\overrightarrow{DY}$ (c) $\overrightarrow{AY}$
   (d) $\overrightarrow{AC}$ (e) $\overrightarrow{YB}$ (f) $\overrightarrow{CA}$

2. In the diagram, M and N are the mid-points of AB and AC respectively.
   Complete the following:
   (a) $\overrightarrow{AM} = \frac{1}{2}(\quad)$
   (b) $\overrightarrow{AN} = \frac{1}{2}(\quad)$
   (c) $\overrightarrow{AB} + \quad = \overrightarrow{AC}$
   (d) $\overrightarrow{AM} + \quad = \overrightarrow{AN}$

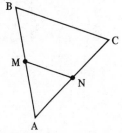

3. In the diagram above, if $\overrightarrow{AB} = \mathbf{p}$ and $\overrightarrow{AC} = \mathbf{q}$, write expressions in terms of $\mathbf{p}$ and $\mathbf{q}$ for:
   (a) $\overrightarrow{AM}$ (b) $\overrightarrow{AN}$ (c) $\overrightarrow{BC}$ (d) $\overrightarrow{MN}$
   Use your answers to show that $\overrightarrow{MN} = \frac{1}{2}\overrightarrow{BC}$.

4. In Question 2, the vector representing MN is half the vector representing BC. Explain why this shows that MN is parallel to BC and why the length of MN is half that of BC.

5. Use the figure on the right to complete:
   (a) $\overrightarrow{AB} + \overrightarrow{BC} =$
   (b) $\overrightarrow{CD} + \overrightarrow{DE} =$
   (c) $\overrightarrow{AC} + \overrightarrow{CE} =$

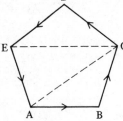

   Now explain why:
   $\overrightarrow{AB} + \overrightarrow{BC} + \overrightarrow{CD} + \overrightarrow{DE} + \overrightarrow{EA}$ is the zero vector.

6. Draw any hexagon ABCDEF. Complete the statement:
   (a) $\overrightarrow{AB} + \overrightarrow{BC} =$ (b) $\overrightarrow{AC} + \overrightarrow{CD} =$
   (c) $\overrightarrow{AD} + \overrightarrow{DE} =$ (d) $\overrightarrow{AE} + \overrightarrow{EF} =$
   Use your results to show that:
   $\overrightarrow{AB} + \overrightarrow{BC} + \overrightarrow{CD} + \overrightarrow{DE} + \overrightarrow{EF} + \overrightarrow{FA} = \mathbf{0}$

7. Look at your answers for Question 5 and 6. Explain why the sum of the vectors representing the sides of any closed polygon, taken in order, is always the zero vector.

8. OABC is a square with
$\overrightarrow{OA} = 2\mathbf{a}$ and
$\overrightarrow{OB} = 3\mathbf{b}$.
M is the mid-point of
BC and N is a point
one-third of the way
along AC.

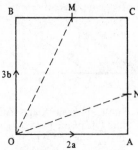

Write down in terms of **a** and **b** the vectors for:
(a) $\overrightarrow{BM}$　(b) $\overrightarrow{MC}$　(c) $\overrightarrow{AN}$　(d) $\overrightarrow{CN}$
Use your results to write down the vectors for:
(e) $\overrightarrow{OM}$　(f) $\overrightarrow{ON}$　(g) $\overrightarrow{BN}$　(h) $\overrightarrow{MN}$
Show that $\overrightarrow{MN}$ is also $\overrightarrow{MB} + \overrightarrow{BO} + \overrightarrow{OA} + \overrightarrow{AN}$.

Example 2

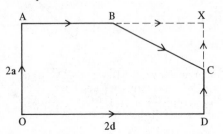

In the diagram above, DC and OA are parallel,
and DC = ½OA.　AB and OD are also parallel,
and AB = ½OD.
$\overrightarrow{OA} = 2\mathbf{a}$ and $\overrightarrow{OD} = 2\mathbf{d}$.
Find a vector representation for $\overrightarrow{BC}$.

$\overrightarrow{AB} = \frac{1}{2}\overrightarrow{OD} = \mathbf{d}$ and $\overrightarrow{DC} = \frac{1}{2}\overrightarrow{OA} = \mathbf{a}$
$\overrightarrow{BC} = \overrightarrow{BA} + \overrightarrow{AO} + \overrightarrow{OD} + \overrightarrow{DC}$
$\qquad = (-\overrightarrow{AB}) + (-\overrightarrow{OA}) + \overrightarrow{OD} + \overrightarrow{DC}$

So BC $= (-\mathbf{d}) + (-2\mathbf{a}) + 2\mathbf{d} + \mathbf{a}$
$\qquad = \mathbf{d} - \mathbf{a}$
This result could also have been obtained from
triangle BXC, since $\overrightarrow{BC} = \overrightarrow{BX} - \overrightarrow{CX} = \mathbf{d} - \mathbf{a}$.

---

9. $\overrightarrow{OA} = \mathbf{a}$ and $\overrightarrow{OB} = \mathbf{b}$.
Write in terms of **a** and **b**:
(a) $\overrightarrow{AO}$
(b) $\overrightarrow{AB}$
(c) $\overrightarrow{BA}$

10. In the parallelogram ABCD,
$\overrightarrow{AB} = \mathbf{u}$ and $\overrightarrow{BC} = \mathbf{v}$. Write in terms of **u** and **v**:
(a) $\overrightarrow{AD}$
(b) $\overrightarrow{CD}$
(c) $\overrightarrow{AC}$

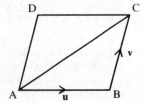

11. Write the vector **x** in terms of **a** and **b** in each of the
following diagrams:
(a)

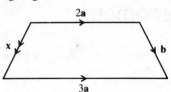

(b)

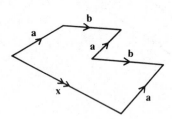

(c)

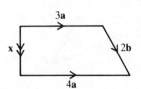

12. ABCD below is a trapezium. Find $\overrightarrow{AC}$ and then
$\overrightarrow{DC}$ in terms of **u** and **v**.

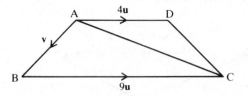

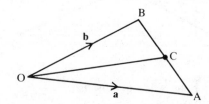

13. In the triangle OAB,
C is the mid-point of
AB and $\overrightarrow{OA} = \mathbf{a}$,
$\overrightarrow{OB} = \mathbf{b}$.
Write in terms of **a** and **b**:
(a) $\overrightarrow{AO}$　　(b) $\overrightarrow{AB}$
(c) $\overrightarrow{AC}$　　(d) $\overrightarrow{OC}$

14. PQRS is any quadrilateral. K, L, M and N are the mid-points of its sides.

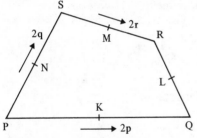

$\overrightarrow{PQ} = 2\mathbf{p}, \overrightarrow{PS} = 2\mathbf{q}$ and $\overrightarrow{SR} = 2\mathbf{r}$.
Find in terms of **p**, **q** and **r**:
- (a) (i) $\overrightarrow{QR}$ (ii) $\overrightarrow{QL}$ (iii) $\overrightarrow{KQ}$ (iv) $\overrightarrow{KL}$
- (b) (i) $\overrightarrow{NS}$ (ii) $\overrightarrow{SM}$ (iii) $\overrightarrow{NM}$
- (c) Do you agree that NM is parallel to KL and that NM = KL?
- (d) Use a similar method to find NK and ML and explain why KLMN is a parallelogram.

Position vectors

In earlier work you used a pair of co-ordinates to describe the position of a point on a graph.
You could also use a **vector.**
Any point P in the plane defines the vector **OP** which joins the origin O to P. **OP** is called the **position vector** of P. The position vector for another point Q is **OQ**.

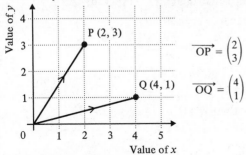

$$\overrightarrow{OP} = \binom{2}{3}$$

$$\overrightarrow{OQ} = \binom{4}{1}$$

The co-ordinates of P are (2, 3)

The position vector of P $= \overrightarrow{OP} = \binom{2}{3}$

A column vector is used for **OP**, to make sure you do not confuse it with the co-ordinate of P.

15. (a) For the diagram above, complete the statement: $\overrightarrow{PQ} = \overrightarrow{PO} + \square = -\overrightarrow{OP} + \square =$
- (b) Find the column vector for PQ.
- (c) If M is the mid-point of PQ write down the column vector for $\overrightarrow{PM}$.
- (d) Complete the statement $\overrightarrow{OM} = \overrightarrow{OP} + \square$.
- (e) Write down the position vector for OM.

16. Compare the column vectors for $\overrightarrow{OP}, \overrightarrow{OQ}$, and $\overrightarrow{OM}$ above.
Can you find the quick way of obtaining $\overrightarrow{OM}$ from $\overrightarrow{OP}$ and $\overrightarrow{OQ}$?

17. In the diagram below, O is the origin. R and S are points with position vectors **r** and **s**. M is the mid-point of RS.

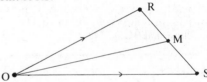

- (a) Write $\overrightarrow{RS}$ in terms of **r** and **s**.
- (b) By first finding $\overrightarrow{RM}$ and then $\overrightarrow{OM}$ write the position vector for $\overrightarrow{OM}$ in terms of **r** and **s**.
- (c) Use this result to check your answer for $\overrightarrow{OM}$ in Question 16.

Example 3

XY is a line with mid-point M, where X is the point (2, 3) and Y is the point (4, −2).
(a) Write down the position vectors of X, Y and M.
(b) If N is the point (6, 4), find the components of $\overrightarrow{MN}$.

(a) $\overrightarrow{OX} = \binom{2}{3}$, $\overrightarrow{OY} = \binom{4}{-2}$

M has co-ordinates $\left(\dfrac{2+4}{2}, \dfrac{3+(-2)}{2} \right)$

$$= (3, 0.5)$$

So $\overrightarrow{OM} = \binom{3}{0.5}$

(b) $\overrightarrow{ON} = \binom{6}{4}$

$\overrightarrow{MN} = \overrightarrow{MO} + \overrightarrow{ON} = -\overrightarrow{OM} + \overrightarrow{ON}$

$$= -\binom{3}{0.5} + \binom{6}{4} = \binom{3}{3.5}$$

---

18. A has co-ordinates (1, 3) and B has co-ordinates (−1, 4). Find the components of:
- (a) the position vector of A
- (b) the position vector of B
- (c) the vector $\overrightarrow{AB}$.

19. Given A(3, −2) and $\overrightarrow{AB} = \binom{2}{4}$, write down:
- (a) the position vector of A
- (b) the position vector of B
- (c) the co-ordinates of B.

20. Given A(4, 1), $\overrightarrow{AB} = \binom{2}{-3}$ and $\overrightarrow{BC} = \binom{2}{1}$, find:
- (a) the position vector of A
- (b) the position vectors of B and C
- (c) the fourth co-ordinate D of the parallelogram ABCD if A, B and C are the first three vertices of the parallelogram.

21. Given A(2, 6), B(3, −1) and C(4, 2) are three vertices of triangle ABC and that M is the mid-point of AB and N is the mid-point of AC:
(a) find the position vectors of A, B and C
(b) find the components of $\overrightarrow{MN}$ and $\overrightarrow{BC}$
(c) show that BC = 2MN.

Example 4

Find the co-ordinates of the point K which divides the line PQ in the ratio 2 : 3.

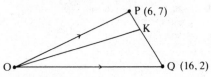

In the diagram PK : KQ = 2 : 3. So if PQ is divided into five parts, PK is two parts and KQ is three parts. In other words PK = $\frac{2}{5}$PQ .

$$\overrightarrow{OP} = \binom{6}{7} \qquad \overrightarrow{OQ} = \binom{16}{2}$$

$$\overrightarrow{PQ} = \overrightarrow{PO} + \overrightarrow{OQ} = -\overrightarrow{OP} + \overrightarrow{OQ}$$

$$= -\binom{6}{7} + \binom{16}{2} = \binom{10}{-5}$$

$$\overrightarrow{OK} = \overrightarrow{OP} + \overrightarrow{PK} = \overrightarrow{OP} + \frac{2}{5}\overrightarrow{PQ}$$

$$\text{So } \overrightarrow{OK} = \binom{6}{7} + \frac{2}{5}\binom{10}{-5}$$

$$= \binom{6}{7} + \binom{4}{-2}$$

$$= \binom{10}{5}$$

The co-ordinates of K are therefore (10, 5).

---

22. R is the point (1, 3) and S is (11, 18). Use the method above to find the co-ordinates of point L which divides the line RS in the ratio 2 : 3. You need to draw a diagram showing O, R, S and L.

23. (a) The points P(6, 7) and Q(16, 12) are joined. Find the co-ordinates of point N which divides PQ in the ratio 1 : 4.
(b) Repeat for other points P(1, 3) and Q(11, 18).

24. P and Q are points with co-ordinates (3, 6) and (12, 8). O is the origin (0, 0). X and Y divide OP and OQ in the ratios 1 : 2 and 1 : 3 respectively. Find the co-ordinates of the point:
(a) X   (b) Y   (c) the mid-point of XY.

25. (a) Show that if X is the mid-point of AB then $\overrightarrow{OX} = \frac{1}{2}\overrightarrow{OA} + \frac{1}{2}\overrightarrow{OB}$.
(b) Use the result in (a) to write down the co-ordinates of the mid-point X of AB, when A and B are the points:
(i) (2, 3), (4, 7)   (ii) (1, 5), (3, 7)
(iii) (1, −1), (5, −3)   (iv) (0, 0), (4, 2)

Lengths of vectors

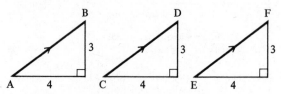

Each of the vectors $\overrightarrow{AB}$, $\overrightarrow{CD}$ and $\overrightarrow{EF}$ can be represented by the column vector $\binom{4}{3}$.

The length (or magnitude) of each vector is $\sqrt{4^2 + 3^2} = 5$ from Pythagoras' Theorem.

If $\mathbf{p} = \binom{a}{b}$ the length of $\mathbf{p}$ is $\sqrt{a^2 + b^2}$

The length (or magnitude) of $\mathbf{p}$ is written as $|\mathbf{p}|$.

Example 5

Find the length of $\overrightarrow{PQ}$ if P is (1, 2) and Q is (4, 6).

First find the vector **PQ**.

$$\overrightarrow{PQ} = \overrightarrow{PO} + \overrightarrow{OQ}$$
$$= -\overrightarrow{OP} + \overrightarrow{OQ}$$

$$= -\binom{1}{2} + \binom{4}{6} = \binom{3}{4}$$

So the length of $\overrightarrow{PQ}$ is $\sqrt{3^2 + 4^2} = 5$

---

26. Find the length of the vector:
(a) $\binom{3}{4}$ (b) $\binom{5}{12}$ (c) $\binom{8}{6}$ (d) $\binom{24}{7}$

27. Find the length of $\overrightarrow{AB}$ when A and B are:
(a) (2, 3), (5, 7)   (b) (5, 6), (13, 12)
(c) (2, 4), (14, 9)   (d) (5, 8), (9, 12)
(e) (1, 6), (9, 21)

28. Find the length of the vector:
(a) $\binom{1}{0}$ (b) $\binom{0}{1}$ (c) $\binom{0}{-1}$ (d) $\binom{-1}{0}$

29. A vector of length one is called a **unit vector**. Find the length of $\overrightarrow{PQ}$ and say whether it is a unit vector, when P and Q are:
(a) (2, 3), (2, 4) (b) (3, 1), (4, 1) (c) (5, 1), (4, 2)
(d) (6, 7), (5, 6) (e) (1, 6), (0, 6) (f) (7, 3), (6, 3)

30. $\begin{pmatrix} 1 \\ 0 \end{pmatrix}$ and $\begin{pmatrix} 0 \\ 1 \end{pmatrix}$ are the unit vectors **i** and **j**.

    (a) Write as a column vector $3\mathbf{i} + 4\mathbf{j}$.
    (b) Complete the statement:

       (i) $\begin{pmatrix} 4 \\ 3 \end{pmatrix} = \square\,\mathbf{i} + \square\,\mathbf{j}$ (ii) $\begin{pmatrix} 3 \\ -2 \end{pmatrix} = \square\,\mathbf{i} + \square\,\mathbf{j}$

10.3 Matrices

Number tables are matrices

The number of runs made by the five best batsmen in High Town School in the first innings of four matches are given in the table. The opposing schools are called P, Q, R, and S:

	P	Q	R	S
Benhoe	8	10	21	9
Lee	10	3	30	15
Singh	7	15	2	23
Marshall	18	6	14	12
Williams	3	12	0	22

The runs made by these same batsmen in their second innings were:

	P	Q	R	S
Benhoe	17	3	1	7
Lee	3	8	5	15
Singh	7	16	21	4
Marshall	0	27	3	6
Williams	18	4	1	16

A **matrix** is an array of numbers arranged in rows and columns. Most numerical tables, like the ones above, can be written as matrices.

A matrix is usually written in brackets. It can also be named using one of the letters of the alphabet: A, B, C, etc. For example, the two matrices above could be written as shown at the top of the next column.

If the two matrices are called A and B, then:

$$A = \begin{pmatrix} 8 & 10 & 21 & 9 \\ 10 & 3 & 30 & 15 \\ 7 & 15 & 2 & 23 \\ 18 & 6 & 14 & 12 \\ 3 & 12 & 0 & 22 \end{pmatrix}$$

$$B = \begin{pmatrix} 17 & 3 & 1 & 7 \\ 3 & 8 & 5 & 15 \\ 7 & 16 & 21 & 4 \\ 0 & 27 & 3 & 6 \\ 18 & 4 & 1 & 16 \end{pmatrix}$$

The first **row** of **A** is (8 10 21 9)

The first **column** of **B** is $\begin{pmatrix} 17 \\ 3 \\ 7 \\ 0 \\ 18 \end{pmatrix}$

A has 5 rows and 4 columns. It is called a 5×4 matrix. (This is read as a *five by four matrix*.)
B is also a 5×4 matrix.

1. Use **A** to find the total number of runs made by Benhoe in the first innings of the four matches.

2. Use **B** to find the total number of runs scored by the five batsmen in the second innings against school Q.

3. Find:
    (a) the total number of runs scored by Benhoe against school P
    (b) the total number of runs scored by Singh against school R.

4. The total scores by the five batsmen for both innings will be given by the matrix $A + B$. Copy and complete the matrix $A + B$, which is started below:

$$A + B = \begin{pmatrix} 25 & 13 & 22 & 16 \\ & & & \\ & & & \\ & & & \\ & & & \end{pmatrix}$$

5. What type of matrix (i.e. how many rows and columns) are the following?

    (a) $(1 \quad 2 \quad 3)$ (b) $\begin{pmatrix} 2 & -1 \\ 1 & 6 \end{pmatrix}$

    (c) $\begin{pmatrix} 2 \\ 3 \end{pmatrix}$ (d) $\begin{pmatrix} 1 & -2 & 4 \\ 2 & 3 & -1 \end{pmatrix}$

    (e) $\begin{pmatrix} 3 & -2 \\ 4 & 1 \\ 2 & 6 \end{pmatrix}$ (f) $\begin{pmatrix} 1 & 2 & 4 \\ 6 & -2 & 3 \\ 1 & 7 & 8 \end{pmatrix}$

In this chapter we will only be concerned with 1×2, 2×2 and 2×1 matrices and their addition, subtraction and multiplication.

In Part 3 of this book we will look at some of the uses of matrices. You will see how matrices can be used to solve simultaneous equations in algebra and can be used to represent transformations in geometry.

Adding matrices

Only matrices of the same type can be added.

Example

Work out

(a) $\begin{pmatrix} 2 & 3 \\ 4 & 1 \end{pmatrix} + \begin{pmatrix} 1 & -2 \\ 3 & -3 \end{pmatrix} = \begin{pmatrix} 2+1 & 3+-2 \\ 4+3 & 1+-3 \end{pmatrix}$

$$= \begin{pmatrix} 3 & 1 \\ 7 & -2 \end{pmatrix}$$

(b) $\begin{pmatrix} 2 & 3 \\ 4 & 1 \end{pmatrix} + \begin{pmatrix} 1 \\ 3 \end{pmatrix}$

    This cannot be done as the first matrix is 2×2 and the second is a 2×1 matrix.

---

6. Below are some matrices:

$$\mathbf{A} = \begin{pmatrix} 2 & 4 \\ 3 & 9 \end{pmatrix} \quad \mathbf{B} = \begin{pmatrix} 3 & -4 \\ 11 & 6 \end{pmatrix} \quad \mathbf{C} = \begin{pmatrix} -3 & 4 \\ -11 & -6 \end{pmatrix}$$

$$\mathbf{D} = \begin{pmatrix} 0 & 0 \\ 0 & 0 \end{pmatrix} \quad \mathbf{E} = \begin{pmatrix} -3 \\ 1 \end{pmatrix} \quad \mathbf{F} = (2 \quad 6)$$

Where possible, work out:
(a) $\mathbf{A} + \mathbf{B}$ (b) $\mathbf{A} + \mathbf{D}$ (c) $\mathbf{B} + \mathbf{A}$
(d) $\mathbf{E} + \mathbf{C}$ (e) $\mathbf{F} + \mathbf{E}$ (f) $\mathbf{B} + \mathbf{C}$

7. (a) Which of the matrices in Question 6 are 2×2?
    (b) What is the effect of adding matrix **D** to another matrix?
    (c) What can you say about **B** and **C**?
    (d) Can you add **A** to **E**? Why not?
    (e) Is matrix addition commutative? Write down any two 2×2 matrices to illustrate your answer.

8. For the matrices in Question 6, work out:
    (a) $(\mathbf{A} + \mathbf{B}) + \mathbf{C}$ (b) $\mathbf{A} + (\mathbf{B} + \mathbf{C})$
Are the results the same?
Is matrix addition associative?

9. **X** and **Y** are matrices:
$$\mathbf{X} = \begin{pmatrix} 2 & -3 \\ -1 & 0 \end{pmatrix}, \mathbf{Y} = \begin{pmatrix} 1 & -2 \\ 2 & 3 \end{pmatrix}$$

The matrix $\mathbf{X} - \mathbf{Y}$ is $\mathbf{X} - \mathbf{Y} = \begin{pmatrix} 1 & -1 \\ -3 & -3 \end{pmatrix}$

(a) Explain the rule for subtracting a matrix.
(b) For the matrices in Question 6, find:
    (i) $\mathbf{A} - \mathbf{B}$ (ii) $\mathbf{D} - \mathbf{A}$ (iii) $\mathbf{E} - \mathbf{F}$
    (iv) $\mathbf{F} - \mathbf{E}$ (v) $\mathbf{A} - \mathbf{D}$ (vi) $\mathbf{C} - \mathbf{B}$

Multiplying by a scalar

A manufacturer of candies produces two flavours (chocolate and rum), and supplies them in two sizes (large and small). The manager of Green Valley Stores finds he has the following stock:

	Size	
	Large	Small
Chocolate	10	22
Rum	15	36

10. The manager wants twice as many of each in stock. Write down the table for this.

11. In matrix form you can show the multiplication by 2 as: $2 \begin{pmatrix} 10 & 22 \\ 15 & 36 \end{pmatrix}$

Write down the answer as a matrix.

12. In the multiplication above, 2 is a **scalar**. Explain how you would multiply a 2×2 matrix by the scalar 3.

13. Let **a** be the vector $\begin{pmatrix} 5 \\ 2 \end{pmatrix}$. Write down the column vector 4**a**. Is the rule for multiplying by a scalar the same for both vectors and matrices?

14. Write as a single matrix:

(a) $2 \begin{pmatrix} 3 & 0 \\ 0 & 1 \end{pmatrix}$ (b) $5 \begin{pmatrix} 3 \\ 4 \end{pmatrix}$

(c) $3 \begin{pmatrix} 2 & 1 \\ -1 & 0 \end{pmatrix} + \frac{1}{2} \begin{pmatrix} 2 & 4 \\ 1 & 6 \end{pmatrix}$ (d) $3 \begin{pmatrix} 1 \\ 2 \end{pmatrix} - 2 \begin{pmatrix} 3 \\ -1 \end{pmatrix}$

15. Find the value of each letter in these matrices

(a) $2 \begin{pmatrix} 1 & 2 \\ 3 & 4 \end{pmatrix} = \begin{pmatrix} a & 4 \\ 6 & b \end{pmatrix}$ (b) $3 \begin{pmatrix} 1 & -2 \\ c & d \end{pmatrix} = \begin{pmatrix} 3 & -6 \\ d & 12 \end{pmatrix}$

(c) $\begin{pmatrix} e & 2 \\ f & -3 \end{pmatrix} + 2 \begin{pmatrix} 3 & -2 \\ f & g \end{pmatrix} = \begin{pmatrix} 10 & -2 \\ -12 & 6 \end{pmatrix}$

(d) $h \begin{pmatrix} 0 & h \\ i & -3 \end{pmatrix} - \begin{pmatrix} 1 & 2 \\ 3 & j \end{pmatrix} = \begin{pmatrix} k & 14 \\ 5 & -12 \end{pmatrix}$

10.4 Multiplying matrices

The number of boys and girls in the first and second forms of Green Trees High School is as follows:

	Boy	Girls
First	10	17
Second	14	9

This can be written as the matrix $\mathbf{X} = \begin{pmatrix} 10 & 17 \\ 14 & 9 \end{pmatrix}$

In the first and second forms, the boys and girls all do woodwork and needlework. During each year, they have to complete pieces of woodwork as follows:

	Woodwork
Boys	3
Girls	1

This can be written as the matrix $\mathbf{Y} = \begin{pmatrix} 3 \\ 1 \end{pmatrix}$

1. What is the total number of pieces of woodwork to be completed by:
   (a) all the boys in year 1 (b) all the boys in year 2
   (c) all the girls in year 1?

2. What is the total number of pieces of woodwork to be completed by:
   (a) in year 1   (b) in year 2?

3. Write the answer to Question 2 in a table:

	Woodwork
First	
Second	

4. Write the answer to Question 3 as a matrix **Z**.

5. The matrix **Z** could be obtained from the matrix multiplication **X** × **Y**, as shown below:

$$\begin{matrix} & B & G \\ F & \\ S & \end{matrix} \begin{pmatrix} 10 & 17 \\ 14 & 9 \end{pmatrix} \times \begin{matrix} & W \\ B \\ G \end{matrix} \begin{pmatrix} 3 \\ 1 \end{pmatrix} = \begin{matrix} & W \\ F \\ S \end{matrix} \begin{pmatrix} 47 \\ 51 \end{pmatrix}$$

6. For the matrix multiplication in Question 5:
   (a) what does the 47 tell you
   (b) what does the 51 tell you?

7. The number of needlework pieces that have to be completed is given by the matrix **D** where:

$$\mathbf{D} = \begin{matrix} & N \\ B \\ G \end{matrix} \begin{pmatrix} 2 \\ 5 \end{pmatrix}$$

What is the total number of needlework pieces that must be completed by:
   (a) all the students in year 1
   (b) all the students in year 2?

8. Set out the multiplication **X** × **D** in the same way as **X** × **Y** in Question 5.

From Questions 1 to 8 you will see that matrix multiplication is more complicated than matrix addition.
To multiply matrices, you have to multiply the **rows of the first matrix** by the **columns of the second matrix.**

Example 1

Work out: $\begin{pmatrix} 1 & 2 \\ 3 & 4 \end{pmatrix}\begin{pmatrix} 5 \\ 6 \end{pmatrix}$

Divide the first matrix into rows, R1 and R2 and the second matrix into columns, C1.

$$\begin{matrix} R1 \\ R2 \end{matrix} \begin{pmatrix} \boxed{1 \quad 2} \\ \boxed{3 \quad 4} \end{pmatrix} \overset{C1}{\begin{pmatrix} \boxed{5} \\ \boxed{6} \end{pmatrix}} = \begin{matrix} R1 \\ R2 \end{matrix} \overset{C1}{\begin{pmatrix} 17 \\ 39 \end{pmatrix}}$$

Notice that the size of the resulting 2×1 matrix is determined by the number of rows in the first matrix, 2 and the number of columns in the second matrix 1.

Now multiply the rows R1, R2 of the first matrix by the columns, C1, of the second matrix.
R1 × C1 = 1 × 5 + 2 × 6 = 17
R2 × C1 = 3 × 5 + 4 × 6 = 39

So $\begin{pmatrix} 1 & 2 \\ 3 & 4 \end{pmatrix}\begin{pmatrix} 5 \\ 6 \end{pmatrix} = \begin{pmatrix} 17 \\ 39 \end{pmatrix}$

---

9. Work out:

   (a) $\begin{pmatrix} 1 & 2 \\ 3 & 4 \end{pmatrix}\begin{pmatrix} 7 \\ 8 \end{pmatrix}$ (b) $\begin{pmatrix} 1 & 3 \\ 4 & 2 \end{pmatrix}\begin{pmatrix} 2 \\ 1 \end{pmatrix}$

   (c) $\begin{pmatrix} 3 & 0 \\ 1 & -4 \end{pmatrix}\begin{pmatrix} 1 \\ -2 \end{pmatrix}$ (d) $\begin{pmatrix} 4 & -1 \\ -3 & 0 \end{pmatrix}\begin{pmatrix} -2 \\ -1 \end{pmatrix}$

   (e) $\begin{pmatrix} 1 & 0 \\ 0 & 1 \end{pmatrix}\begin{pmatrix} 3 \\ 4 \end{pmatrix}$ (f) $\begin{pmatrix} 0 & 1 \\ 1 & 0 \end{pmatrix}\begin{pmatrix} 3 \\ 4 \end{pmatrix}$

The method can be extended to multiply a 2×2 matrix by a 2×2 matrix.

10. At Green Trees High School, the number of pieces of woodwork and needlework to be done by each boy and girl can be written as a single matrix:

$$\mathbf{T} = \begin{matrix} & W & N \\ B \\ G \end{matrix} \begin{pmatrix} 3 & 2 \\ 1 & 5 \end{pmatrix}$$

The product of **T** with the matrix **X** will be:

$$\begin{matrix} & B & G \\ F \\ S \end{matrix} \begin{pmatrix} 10 & 17 \\ 14 & 9 \end{pmatrix} \times \begin{matrix} & W & N \\ B \\ G \end{matrix} \begin{pmatrix} 3 & 2 \\ 1 & 5 \end{pmatrix} = \begin{matrix} & W & N \\ F \\ S \end{matrix} \begin{pmatrix} 47 & - \\ 51 & - \end{pmatrix}$$

Copy and complete the multiplication.

11. Use the same method to complete:

$$\begin{pmatrix} 8 & 1 \\ 2 & 3 \end{pmatrix}\begin{pmatrix} 1 & 4 \\ 2 & 3 \end{pmatrix} = \begin{pmatrix} 10 & \\ & \end{pmatrix}$$

Example 2

This is how to multiply a 2×2 matrix:

$$\begin{array}{cc} & \text{C1} \quad \text{C2} \\ \begin{array}{c} \text{R1} \\ \text{R2} \end{array} & \begin{pmatrix} 4 & 2 \\ 3 & 5 \end{pmatrix} \end{array} \begin{pmatrix} -2 & 1 \\ 3 & 8 \end{pmatrix} = \begin{array}{c} \\ \text{R1} \\ \text{R2} \end{array} \begin{array}{c} \text{C1} \quad \text{C2} \\ \begin{pmatrix} -2 & 20 \\ 9 & 43 \end{pmatrix} \end{array}$$

Use the *rows* of the first matrix and the *columns* of the second matrix.
The first row multiplied by the first column gives the value -2.

The first row multiplied by the second column gives the value 20.

Then move to the second row of the first matrix:

$$\begin{array}{llll} \text{R2} \times \text{C1} & = & 3 \times -2 & + & 5 \times 3 & = 9 \\ \text{R2} \times \text{C2} & = & 3 \times 1 & + & 5 \times 8 = 43 \end{array}$$

---

12. Find the products of these 2×2 matrices:

(a) $\begin{pmatrix} 5 & 2 \\ 4 & 3 \end{pmatrix}\begin{pmatrix} 2 & 8 \\ 7 & 6 \end{pmatrix}$ (b) $\begin{pmatrix} 3 & 8 \\ 2 & -1 \end{pmatrix}\begin{pmatrix} 2 & 6 \\ 5 & -3 \end{pmatrix}$

(c) $\begin{pmatrix} 1 & 0 \\ 0 & 1 \end{pmatrix}\begin{pmatrix} 2 & 3 \\ 4 & 2 \end{pmatrix}$ (d) $\begin{pmatrix} 2 & 3 \\ 4 & 2 \end{pmatrix}\begin{pmatrix} 3 & 0 \\ 0 & 6 \end{pmatrix}$

(e) $\begin{pmatrix} 0 & 1 \\ 1 & 0 \end{pmatrix}\begin{pmatrix} -2 & 1 \\ 3 & 1 \end{pmatrix}$ (f) $\begin{pmatrix} -2 & 0 \\ 1 & 2 \end{pmatrix}\begin{pmatrix} 2 & 3 \\ 4 & 5 \end{pmatrix}$

(g) $\begin{pmatrix} 1 & 1 \\ 2 & -1 \end{pmatrix}\begin{pmatrix} 2 & 4 \\ 0 & 5 \end{pmatrix}$ (h) $\begin{pmatrix} -1 & -1 \\ 0 & 2 \end{pmatrix}\begin{pmatrix} -3 & -1 \\ -2 & -4 \end{pmatrix}$

13. Find the value of each letter in the matrices

(a) $\begin{pmatrix} 1 & 2 \\ 3 & 4 \end{pmatrix}\begin{pmatrix} 2 \\ a \end{pmatrix} = \begin{pmatrix} b \\ 10 \end{pmatrix}$ (b) $\begin{pmatrix} c & -1 \\ 2 & d \end{pmatrix}\begin{pmatrix} 1 \\ 2 \end{pmatrix} = \begin{pmatrix} 4 \\ 6 \end{pmatrix}$

(c) $\begin{pmatrix} 3 & -4 \\ -2 & e \end{pmatrix}\begin{pmatrix} f \\ 2 \end{pmatrix} = \begin{pmatrix} -8 \\ 2 \end{pmatrix}$

(d) $\begin{pmatrix} g & 2 \\ 1 & h \end{pmatrix}\begin{pmatrix} 1 & 2 \\ 3 & 4 \end{pmatrix} = \begin{pmatrix} 9 & i \\ j & 6 \end{pmatrix}$

(e) $2\begin{pmatrix} k & 5 \\ 2 & l \end{pmatrix} + \begin{pmatrix} 3 & m \\ n & -2 \end{pmatrix}\begin{pmatrix} 1 & 3 \\ 2 & 4 \end{pmatrix} = \begin{pmatrix} 3 & 19 \\ 0 & 9 \end{pmatrix}$

(f) $\begin{pmatrix} 4 & 0 \\ 1 & p \end{pmatrix}\begin{pmatrix} q & r \\ -2 & 0 \end{pmatrix} = \begin{pmatrix} 20 & 20 \\ -1 & 5 \end{pmatrix}$

14. If $A = \begin{pmatrix} 2 & 0 \\ 6 & 4 \end{pmatrix}$, $B = \begin{pmatrix} x & 0 \\ 1 & 3 \end{pmatrix}$, and $AB = BA$, find x.

15. If $C = \begin{pmatrix} y & 2 \\ 2 & -y \end{pmatrix}$ and $C^2 = 5\begin{pmatrix} 1 & 0 \\ 0 & 1 \end{pmatrix}$, find y.

Multiplication properties

For Questions 16 to 21, use:

$$A = \begin{pmatrix} 1 & 2 \\ 3 & 4 \end{pmatrix}, B = \begin{pmatrix} 3 & 0 \\ 1 & 4 \end{pmatrix}, C = \begin{pmatrix} -4 & 2 \\ 3 & -1 \end{pmatrix}$$

16. Work out the products:

(a) **AB**   (b) **BA**   (c) **AC**
(d) **CA**   (e) **BC**   (f) **CB**

17. From your answers to Question 16, can you say that matrix multiplication is always commutative?

18. Use your answers to Question 16, to work out:
(a) **(AB)C** (b) **A(BC)** (c) **B(CA)** (d) **(BC)A**

19. Do your answers to Question 18 suggest that matrix multiplication is associative?

20. Work out the products:
(a) **A(AB)** (b) **(AA)B** (c) **B(CC)** (d) **(BC)C**

21. Do the answers to Question 20 suggest that matrix multiplication is always associative?

22. Let $P = \begin{pmatrix} 3 & -1 \\ 0 & 2 \end{pmatrix}, Q = \begin{pmatrix} 2 & 1 \\ 1 & 1 \end{pmatrix}, R = \begin{pmatrix} 0 & 2 \\ 5 & 4 \end{pmatrix}$.

Work out:
(a) **QR**   (b) **P(QR)** (c) **PQ**   (d) **(PQ)R**
Are the answers to (b) and (d) the same?

23. Make up any three 2×2 matrices **X, Y, Z** and find:
(a) **XY**   (b) **(XY)Z**
(c) **YZ**   (d) **X(YZ)**
What do you notice?

24. $I = \begin{pmatrix} 1 & 0 \\ 0 & 1 \end{pmatrix}, A = \begin{pmatrix} 1 & 2 \\ 3 & 4 \end{pmatrix}, B = \begin{pmatrix} 3 & 0 \\ 1 & 4 \end{pmatrix},$

$C = \begin{pmatrix} -4 & 2 \\ 3 & -1 \end{pmatrix}$

Work out:
(a) **IA**   (b) **IB**   (c) **IC**
(d) **AI**   (e) **BI**   (f) **CI**
What do you notice?
Why is **I** called the 2×2 identity matrix?

25. Let $J = \begin{pmatrix} 1 & 0 \\ -1 & 2 \end{pmatrix}$ and $K = \begin{pmatrix} 4 & 5 \\ 4 & 5 \end{pmatrix}$.

(a) Work out the product **JK**.
(b) Make up any 2×2 matrix **M** and work out **JM**. Is the answer **M**?
(c) Is **J** an identity matrix?
(d) Work out the product **KJ**. Does **J** act as an identity?

26. Let $A = \begin{pmatrix} 3 & -1 \\ -12 & 4 \end{pmatrix}$ and $B = \begin{pmatrix} 2 & 0 \\ 3 & 1 \end{pmatrix}$.

(a) Work out the product **AB**.
(b) Is **A** an identity matrix? Check by working out the product **BA**.

27. Let $O = \begin{pmatrix} 0 & 0 \\ 0 & 0 \end{pmatrix}$ and let $A = \begin{pmatrix} 1 & 1 \\ 1 & 1 \end{pmatrix}$.
Find a matrix **B** such that $AB = O$.

Summary

By the end of this chapter these are the things you should know about:

10.1 Vectors (pages 291–294)

How to use **column vectors** to describe a vector.
e.g.

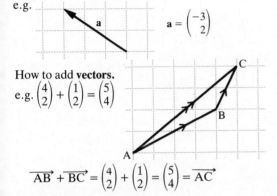

$$a = \begin{pmatrix} -3 \\ 2 \end{pmatrix}$$

How to add **vectors**.

e.g. $\begin{pmatrix} 4 \\ 2 \end{pmatrix} + \begin{pmatrix} 1 \\ 2 \end{pmatrix} = \begin{pmatrix} 5 \\ 4 \end{pmatrix}$

$$\overrightarrow{AB} + \overrightarrow{BC} = \begin{pmatrix} 4 \\ 2 \end{pmatrix} + \begin{pmatrix} 1 \\ 2 \end{pmatrix} = \begin{pmatrix} 5 \\ 4 \end{pmatrix} = \overrightarrow{AC}$$

You should remember that:
(i) $\mathbf{a} + \mathbf{b} = \mathbf{b} + \mathbf{a}$ (commutative)
(ii) $(\mathbf{a} + \mathbf{b}) + \mathbf{c} = \mathbf{a} + (\mathbf{b} + \mathbf{c})$ (associative)
(iii) $\mathbf{a} + (-\mathbf{a}) = \mathbf{0}$
(iv) if $\mathbf{p}$ and $\mathbf{q}$ are shown by arrows of the same length and in the same direction then $\mathbf{p} = \mathbf{q}$
(v) If the two arrows are parallel then one vector is a multiple of the other
(vi) if $\mathbf{q}$ is the same length as $\mathbf{p}$ but in the opposite direction then $\mathbf{q} = -\mathbf{p}$.

10.2 Using vectors in geometry (pages 295–298)

How to use the two ideas:
[1]

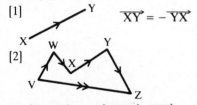

$$\overrightarrow{XY} = -\overrightarrow{YX}$$

[2]

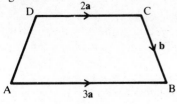

$$\overrightarrow{VW} + \overrightarrow{WX} + \overrightarrow{XY} + \overrightarrow{YZ} = \overrightarrow{VZ}$$

to find vectors which represent lines in geometrical figures.

$$\overrightarrow{AD} = \overrightarrow{AB} + \overrightarrow{BC} + \overrightarrow{CD}$$
$$= 3\mathbf{a} - \mathbf{b} - 2\mathbf{a}$$
$$= \mathbf{a} - \mathbf{b}$$

How to write the position vector of any point.
e.g. If A is the point (2, 3),
the position vector of A is
$$\overrightarrow{OA} = \begin{pmatrix} 2 \\ 3 \end{pmatrix}.$$

How to find the length of a vector.
e.g.

length of $\mathbf{a} = \sqrt{3^2 + 2^2} = \sqrt{13}$.

10.3 Matrices (pages 299–300)

A **matrix** is an array of numbers, arranged in rows and columns.
A **2 × 3 matrix** has **2 rows** and **3 columns**.
How to add matrices

e.g. $\begin{pmatrix} 1 & -2 \\ 3 & 4 \end{pmatrix} + \begin{pmatrix} -1 & 3 \\ 1 & 0 \end{pmatrix} = \begin{pmatrix} 0 & 1 \\ 4 & 4 \end{pmatrix}$

10.4 Multiplying matrices (pages 301–302)

How to multiply matrices, by dividing the first matrix into rows and the second into columns.

e.g.
$$\begin{array}{c} R1 \\ R2 \end{array} \begin{pmatrix} 3 & -1 \\ 4 & 3 \end{pmatrix} \begin{pmatrix} 2 & 0 \\ -1 & 3 \end{pmatrix} = \begin{array}{c} R1 \\ R2 \end{array} \begin{pmatrix} 7 & -3 \\ 5 & 9 \end{pmatrix}$$

$R1 \times C1 = 3 \times 2 + -1 \times -1 = 6 + 1 = 7$
$R1 \times C2 = 3 \times 0 + -1 \times 3 = 0 + -3 = -3$

$R2 \times C1 = 4 \times 2 + 3 \times -1 = 8 - 3 = 5$
$R2 \times C2 = 4 \times 0 + 3 \times 3 = 0 + 9 = 9$

Multiplication of matrices is not commutative:

$$\mathbf{AB} \neq \mathbf{B} \times \mathbf{A}$$

Multiplication of matrices is associative:

$$(\mathbf{AB})\mathbf{C} = \mathbf{A}(\mathbf{BC})$$

The **identity matrix is I.**
For 2 × 2 matrices **I** is
$\begin{pmatrix} 1 & 0 \\ 0 & 1 \end{pmatrix}.$

If **A** is a 2 × 2 matrix, then $\mathbf{AI} = \mathbf{A}$ and $\mathbf{IA} = \mathbf{A}$.

PART 3
General CXC syllabus
(optional)

I Relations and functions 2

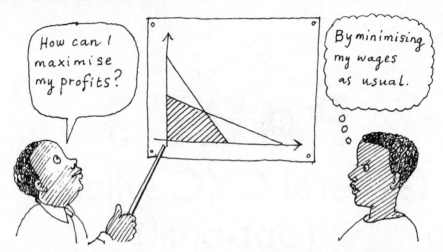

I.I Lines and regions

Earlier in this book we met the idea that inequalities could be used to specify regions on a graph.

Example 1

In the diagram below, points where $2x + 3y = 24$ are on the marked line.

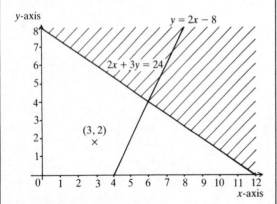

Points where $2x + 3y > 24$ are in the region shaded /////.
i.e. *above* the line $2x + 3y = 24$.

Points where $2x + 3y < 24$ are in the unshaded region.
i.e. *below* the line $2x + 3y = 24$.

In order to find which region in the above diagram corresponds to $y < 2x - 8$ any point such as $(3, 2)$ is used as a check. Substituting gives $2 > 2 \times 3 - 8$ so the point $(3, 2)$ is in the region where $y > 2x - 8$. The region where $y < 2x - 8$ is therefore on the opposite side of the line $y = 2x - 8$, i.e. on the right of this line.

1. Draw the given line and then shade the required region. In each case find whether $(3, 1)$ is in the required region or not.
   (a) line $x + y = 7$, region $x + y < 7$
   (b) line $2x + 3y = 12$, region $2x + 3y > 12$
   (c) line $y = 2x + 1$, region $y > 2x + 1$
   (d) line $y = 3x - 7$, region $y < 3x - 7$

2. Draw the given line and then shade the required region.
   (a) line $3x + 2y = 24$, region $3x + 2y < 24$
   (b) line $y = 2x$, region $y > 2x$
   Shade also the region where both $3x + 2y < 24$ and $y > 2x$. Find whether the points $(2, 5)$ and $(6, 1)$ are in this region or not.

3. Draw the given line and then shade the required region.
   (a) line $y = 3x - 4$, region $y < 3x - 4$
   (b) line $y = x + 2$, region $y < x + 2$
   Shade also the region where both $y < 3x - 4$ and $y < x + 2$. Find whether the points $(3, 4)$ and $(4, 6)$ are in this region or not.

4. Draw the lines $x + 2y = 12$ and $2x + y = 10$. Mark the region where:
 (a) $x + 2y < 12$ and $2x + y > 10$
 (b) $x + 2y > 12$ and $2x + y < 10$
 (c) $x + 2y < 12$ and $2x + y < 10$
 (d) $x + 2y > 12$ and $2x + y > 10$

5. Draw the lines $x + y = 11$, $y = 3x - 1$, and $y = x + 3$.
 Shade the region where $x + y < 11$, $y < 3x - 1$, and $y > x + 3$. Find whether the points $(3, 6)$ and $(2, 7)$ are in this region or not.

Example 2

Shade on a graph the region where $x + 3y \leqslant 24$ and $3x + y < 21$.
Find at what points in this region, with **whole number** values of x and y, $x + y$ is largest.

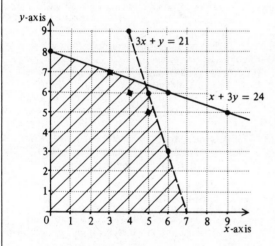

The line $x + 3y = 24$ is shown solid since points *on* the line satisfy $x + 3y \leqslant 24$.
The line $3x + y = 21$ is shown dotted since points on the line do not satisfy $3x + y < 21$.

The points in the shaded region above for which $x + y$ is largest are $(3, 7)$, $(4, 6)$ and $(5, 5)$. The point $(5, 6)$ is excluded since it lies on the dotted line and is therefore not in the region.

---

6. Shade on a graph the region where $2x + y \leqslant 10$ and $x + 2y < 12$. Find at what point in this region, with whole number values of x and y, $x + y$ is largest.

7. Shade on a graph the region where $x + 3y < 18$ and $y \geqslant 2x - 10$. Find at what points in this region with whole number values of x and y, $x + y$ is largest. Explain why $(6, 4)$ is excluded from the region.

8. Using the diagram below say which region is described by:
 (a) $x + y \leqslant 6$, $x + 3y \geqslant 12$ and $y \leqslant 2x + 3$
 (b) $x + y \geqslant 6$, $x + 3y \geqslant 12$ and $y \leqslant 2x + 3$
 (c) $x + 3y \leqslant 12$, and $y \geqslant 2x + 3$.

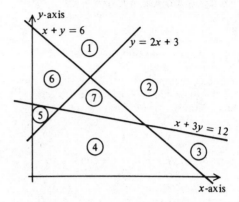

9. Using the diagram above, describe with inequalities the region:
 (a) ⑥   (b) ④   (c) ③

10. Draw the lines $x + y = 7$, $y = 2x + 5$ and $x + 4y = 12$. Mark the region where:
 (a) $x + y \leqslant 7$, $y \leqslant 2x + 5$ and $x + 4y \geqslant 12$
 (b) $x + y \geqslant 7$, $y \leqslant 2x + 5$ and $x + 4y \geqslant 12$
 (c) $x + y \leqslant 7$, $y \geqslant 2x + 5$ and $x + 4y \geqslant 12$

11. Shade on a graph the region where:
 (a) $x + y < 10$, $2x + y > 12$, and $x + 4y \geqslant 16$
 (b) $x + y > 10$, $2x + y > 12$, and $x + 4y \geqslant 16$
 (c) $x + y < 10$, $2x + y < 12$, and $x + 4y \leqslant 16$

1.2 Linear programming

Example 1

A manufacturer makes two types of product, N and L.

Type N requires 12 man-hours to make and $5 worth of raw materials.

Type L requires 9 man-hours to make and $8 worth of raw materials.

The manufacturer has a total of 1080 man-hours and $800 for raw materials available, for these products. Show this information as a pair of inequalities and represent it on a graph.

How many of each type of product can be made?

If N is the number of product N and L is the number of product L, then:
(i) for the time available $12N + 9L \leqslant 1080$
(ii) for the money available $5N + 8L \leqslant 800$

You can show this information on a graph by first drawing the lines $12N + 9L = 1080$ and $5N + 8L = 800$. Then find the region that corresponds to the two inequalities.

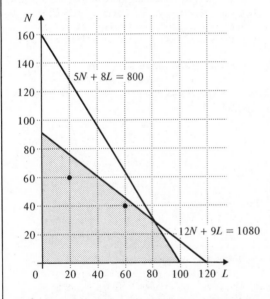

There are many possible solutions which satisfy the two inequalities in the shaded region. Two of these are shown on the graph above. One is 20 of product L and 60 of product N, another is 60 of product L and 40 of product N.

---

1. Show that the inequalities $12N + 9L \leqslant 1080$ and $5N + 8L \leqslant 800$ are satisfied by:
   (a) $L = 20$ and $N = 60$
   (b) $L = 60$ and $N = 40$

2. Use the graph above to find another solution to the problem in Example 1.

3. In a small factory, product X gives a profit of $4 per article and product Y gives a profit of $5 per article. The factory can make no more than 45 articles altogether per week, but must make a profit of at least $200 to stay in business.
   (a) If X is the number of product X made each week and Y is the number of product Y made each week, copy and complete the two inequalities:

   $$X + \square \leqslant 45$$
   $$4X + \square \geqslant 200$$

   (b) Show the information in (a) on a graph and shade the region in which both inequalities are true.
   (c) Use your graph in (b) to say whether, in one week, the factory is able to make:
      (i)   24 of product X and 21 of product Y
      (ii) 16 of product X and 28 of product Y
      (iii) 20 of product X and 23 of product Y

4. A small firm wants to buy a number of new machines of two types.
   Type A costs $2000 and $16 per week to run.
   Type B costs $2400 and $10 per week to run.
   The firm has $18 000 to spend on machines, but wants to keep its weekly running costs to no more than $120.
   (a) If A is the number of machines of type A and B is the number of machines of type B, copy and complete the two inequalities:

   $$2000A + \square \leqslant 18\ 000$$
   $$16A + 10B \leqslant \square$$

   (b) Show the information in (a) on a graph and shade the region in which both inequalities are true.
   (c) Use your graph in (b) to find how many of each type of machine the firm must buy if it needs:
      (i) more than 3 of each type of machine
      (ii) more than 4 machines of type A and more than 2 machines of type B.
   (d) Use your graph in (b) to say whether the firm is able to buy the following machines:
      (i) 3 of type A and 5 of type B
      (ii) 2 of type A and 6 of type B

Example 2

A manufacturer makes two types of sandal.
For a pair of men's sandals the leather costs him
$4, the sewing costs him $5 and his profit is $5.
For a pair of ladies' sandals the leather costs him
$3, the sewing costs $9 and his profit is $6.
$240 is available for leather and $450 is available
for sewing costs.
How many pairs of each type of sandal should he
make, to give the maximum profit?

Let us use L and M to stand for the number of
pairs of ladies' and men's sandals.

For the leather costs we can write:
$3L + 4M \leqslant 240$
For the sewing costs we can write:
$9L + 5M \leqslant 450$
This information is shown on the graph below.

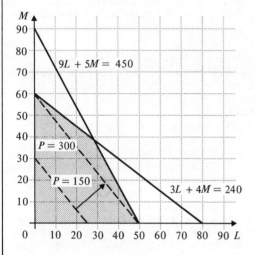

The profit $\$P$ is given by the expression:
$P = 6L + 5M$
For a profit of $150, $6L + 5M = 150$
This line is shown on the graph above. Any point
on this line represents the number of each type of
sandal made, to give a profit of $150. For
example $L = 15$, $M = 12$.

The second line shown is $6L + 5M = 300$. Any
point on this line represents the number of each
type of sandal made, to give a profit of $300.
For example $L = 30$, $M = 24$.

The lines $6L + 5M = 150$ and $6L + 5M = 300$ are
parallel. The maximum profit will be given by the
profit line which can be drawn within the shaded
region, parallel to these lines but as far right as
possible.

5. (a) Make an accurate copy of the graph in
Example 2.
   (b) By moving the edge of your ruler parallel to the
   two profit lines, show that the point where
   $L = 28$ and $M = 39$ lies on the profit line which
   is further to the right, but still within the
   allowed region of the graph.
   (c) Do you agree that $363 is the maximum profit
   that can be made?

6. Look back at Example 1. If the profit on product N
is $5 and the profit on product L is $6, copy and
complete the equation below to show how many of
each product must be made, for a profit of $600.

$$5N + \square = 600$$

On your graph from Question 2, show the line for
this equation.
Show also the line which indicates a profit of $480.
Are these two lines parallel?

7. Use your graph from Question 6 to find how many
of each product must be made, to give a profit of
more than $600.

8. Two kinds of food, F_1 and F_2, are to be mixed
together, so that the vitamin content of the mixture
is at least 8 units of Vitamin B and 12 units of
Vitamin C. The table below shows the vitamin
content of each food in units per kilogram.

Food	Vitamin B	Vitamin C
F_1	1	3
F_2	2	2

   (a) If there are x kg of food F_1 and y kg of food F_2
   in the mixture, write down the two inequalities
   which describe the conditions for the amounts
   of Vitamins B and C.
   (b) Use a graph to show the region where
   $x + 2y \geqslant 8$ and $3x + 2y \geqslant 12$.
   (c) If food F_1 costs $0.60 per kg and food F_2 costs
   $0.50 per kg explain why the equation
   $0.6x + 0.5y \leqslant 3$ represents a mixture of F_1 and
   F_2 which costs less than $3.
   (d) What whole number values of x and y satisfy
   the three inequalities in (b) and (c)?
   (e) Find the least possible cost of the mixture.
   (f) Foods F_1 and F_2 are to be mixed together, to
   give at least 12 units of Vitamin B and 18 units
   of Vitamin C. How much of each food should
   be used, to give a mixture that costs less than
   $4.50? What is the minimum possible cost?

Example 3

An electrical firm has two warehouses, A and B. The cost of using a van to deliver goods to three retail shops, P, Q, and R on the same day is given below:

	P	Q	R
From warehouse A	$12	$4	$8
From warehouse B	$3	$10	$8

Shop P spends at least $72 a week on delivery charges.
Shop Q spends at least $80 a week on delivery charges.
Shop R spends at most $120 a week on delivery charges.

If the number of deliveries each week from warehouses A and B are x and y respectively, we can write inequalities to describe the information.

For P $12x + 3y \geq 72$
For Q $4x + 10y \geq 80$
For R $8x + 8y \leq 120$

---

9. (a) Show on a graph the lines $12x + 3y = 72$, $4x + 10y = 80$ and $8x + 8y = 120$.
(This will be easy once you find where each line crosses the axes, i.e. where $x = 0$ and where $y = 0$.)

(b) Find the region on your graph which corresponds to the three inequalities in Example 3 above.

(c) Find points with whole number values for x and y, which lie within this region. (You may include points *on* the boundary lines since the inequalities include the = sign as well.)

(d) Use your answers for (c) to write down the number of possible deliveries which can be made each week from warehouses A and B.

10. Look again at the points you found in Question 9 (c).
What is the smallest possible value within this region of: (a) x?   (b) y?   (c) $x + y$?

11. (a) Do you agree, in Question 10, that $x + y$ is the total number of deliveries?

(b) What is the smallest number of deliveries which can be made each week from both warehouses together?

12. A manufacturer makes x and y of each of two models X and Y. Each model requires processing by two different machines as shown below:

	Machine 1	Machine 2
Model X	1 hour	3 hours
Model Y	2 hours	1 hour

(a) If neither machine can run for more than 18 hours a day, write down two inequalities.

(b) Show these inequalities on a graph and shade the region which includes the possible values for x and y.

13. (a) If in Question 12 the profit on each model is $1, do you agree that the total profit is $$(x + y)$?

(b) On your graph draw the line which shows a total profit of $5 per day.

(c) Draw also the lines which show a profit per day of: (i) $7   (ii) $9   (iii) $10

(d) Why is it not possible to make a profit of more than $10 per day?

14. Clive wants to buy oranges at 15c each and grapefruits at 25c each. He has only $1.50 to spend. He must buy at least two oranges and one grapefruit and his basket can hold no more than 8 fruits.

(a) If x is the number of oranges and y is the number of grapefruits, write down the four inequalities for x and y which show:
   (i) the maximum capacity of the basket
   (ii) the maximum possible number of oranges
   (iii) the maximum possible number of grapefruit
   (iv) a total cost of less than or equal to $1.50

(b) Show this information on a graph and shade the region in which the values of x and y must lie.

15. (a) If in Question 14 the fruit seller makes a profit of 4c on each orange and 6c on each grapefruit, write down an expression to show her profit.

(b) On your graph, draw the line that shows a profit of: (i) $24   (ii) $36   (iii) $48

(c) Do you agree that your profit lines are parallel? Why is a profit of $48 impossible?

(d) By drawing other profit lines that are parallel to those in (b) and that pass through whole number values of x and y, find the maximum possible profit.

16. A farmer wants to grow two crops, A and B. He needs to plant at least 4 hectares of crop A, which costs $30 a hectare, and at least 2 hectares of crop B, which costs $50 a hectare. He has 8 hectares available, and can spend at most $300. Explain how he might use the 8 hectares.

17. There are 600 passengers and 45 tonnes of cargo that have to be ferried across a river. Two kinds of ferry boat are available: Mariners and Navigators. The Mariner can carry 50 passengers and 6 tonnes of cargo; the Navigator can carry 80 passengers and 3 tonnes of cargo.

(a) If m Mariners and n Navigators are used, write down two inequalities for these conditions.

(b) If only 8 Mariners and 7 Navigators are available, find the smallest number of boats that can be used.

18. For a camp of 72 children, two types of tent are available for hire. The large tent sleeps 8 and costs $32 per week, the small tent sleeps 3 and costs $8 per week. The total number of tents must not exceed 18. Using L for the number of large tents and S for the number of small tents write down inequalities to describe the constraints of:

(a) the number of children

(b) the number of tents

(c) the cost of hiring.

If the cost of hiring is to be kept as small as possible, show the information on a graph and find the number of each type that must be hired. What will be the cost of this for the week?

19. A farmer has 100 hectares of land available for planting cassava and/or potatoes, and he is prepared to outlay at most $5400. The initial outlay on each hectare of cassava is $90, and that on each hectare of potatoes is $36.

Show this information as a pair of inequalities and represent it on a graph.

If the profit on each hectare of cassava is $120 and on each hectare of potatoes $80, find how he should allocate his land to make the maximum profit.

What is the greatest profit that he could make if he was prepared to use 120 hectares?

How many hectares must he be prepared to allocate to make it worth growing only potatoes?

Example 4

A small firm wants to buy a number of new machines of two types.
Type A costs $2000 and $16 per week to run.
Type B costs $2400 and $10 per week to run.
The firm has $18 000 to spend and wishes to keep its running costs to $120 per week. It must buy at least 4 machines of type A and 2 machines of type B.
Find the various possibilities.

Number of machines of type B

The constraints can be summarised as follows:

Purchase costs: $2000A + 2400B \leqslant 18\ 000$
i.e. $5A + 6B \leqslant 45$
Running costs: $16A + 10B \leqslant 120$
i.e. $8A + 5B \leqslant 60$
Also $A \geqslant 4$ and $B \geqslant 2$, where A and B are the number of each machine.
From the graph above, we can see the possibilities are 4 machines of type A and 4 of type B, or 5 of A and 3 of B, or 6 of A and 2 of B.

20. Represent on one graph the set of points (x, y) for which $x \geqslant 2$, $y \geqslant 10$, $4x + y \geqslant 24$ and $3x + 2y \geqslant 36$. Show also the points where $2x + y \leqslant 30$. Hence find the points in this region, with whole number values for x and y, at which $2x + y$ takes its smallest value.

21. A firm with 10 drivers uses vans and lorries to make its deliveries. A van costs $18 per day to run and can carry 600 kg. A lorry costs $45 per day to run and can carry 1100 kg. The firm wants to keep its daily running costs to $270, but be able to deliver at least 6600 kg.
Write down inequalities to describe the constraints of:

(a) drivers

(b) running costs

(c) carrying capacity.

Show this information on a graph and find the various possibilities if the firm decides to use at least five vans.

1.3 Areas under graphs

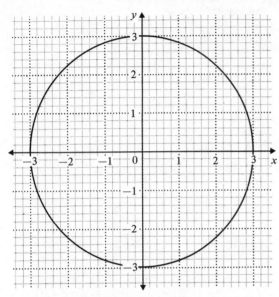

1. (a) Look at the circle drawn above. Do you agree that its area is 9π? Now find its area in cm^2 by counting the squares inside it.
   (Remember, $100\,\text{mm}^2 = 1\,\text{cm}^2$)
   (b) Divide your result in (a) by 9.
   How accurate is:
   (i) your result for π
   (ii) this method for finding the area?

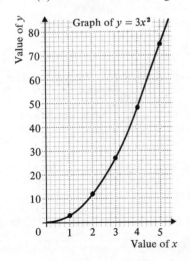

Graph of $y = 3x^2$

2. (a) Make a copy of the above graph on cm/mm graph paper. Take 1 cm for each unit on the x-axis and 1 cm for each ten units on the y-axis.
   (b) Find the area under the graph between $x = 0$ and $x = 5$ by counting squares.
   (c) How close is your area to $125\,\text{cm}^2$?

3. Can you suggest a quicker way to find the area under the curve $y = 3x^2$ between $x = 2$ and $x = 3$, which does not involve counting squares?

4. In Question 3 you may have suggested treating the area as a trapezium – see trapezium ABCD on the right. Find:
   (a) the area of the trapezium ABCD
   (b) the area under the curve DC, by counting squares.

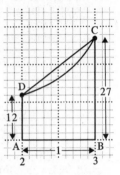

The trapezium rule for finding areas

You can use the ideas in Question 4 (a) to find an approximation for the area under any curve. You do this by dividing the required area into trapeziums, as shown below.

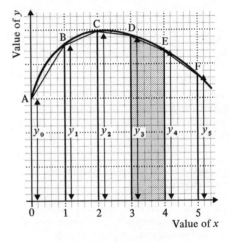

Look at the trapezium D34E shaded above. If y_3 is the height of D and y_4 is the height of E, then its area is:

$$\tfrac{1}{2}(y_3 + y_4) \times 1$$

Using this idea, the total area under the curve from A to F would be:

$$\tfrac{1}{2}(y_0 + y_1) \times 1 + \tfrac{1}{2}(y_1 + y_2) \times 1 + \tfrac{1}{2}(y_2 + y_3) \times 1$$
$$+ \tfrac{1}{2}(y_3 + y_4) \times 1 + \tfrac{1}{2}(y_4 + y_5) \times 1$$

Collecting like terms, this can be written as:

$$\tfrac{1}{2}(y_0 + 2y_1 + 2y_2 + 2y_3 + 2y_4 + y_5) \times 1$$

If you know the y values you can work this out.

5. Look back at the graph for $y = 3x^2$ on page 312. Use it to complete the table of values below:

x	0	1	2	3	4	5
y	0	3				75

Now use the formula:
$\frac{1}{2}(y_0 + 2y_1 + 2y_2 + 2y_3 + 2y_4 + y_5) \times 1$
to show that an approximation to the area under the curve from $x = 0$ to $x = 5$ is $127.5\,\text{cm}^2$.

6. Explain why using trapeziums on the curve $y = 3x^2$ should give an answer larger than $125\,\text{cm}^2$.

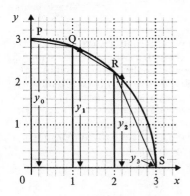

7. The diagram above shows one quarter of the circle from Question 1 on page 312.
   (a) Show that its area can be written as
   $\frac{1}{2}(y_0 + 2y_1 + 2y_2 + y_3) \times 1$
   (b) For the circle $y_0 = 3$, $y_3 = 0$ explain why
   $y_1 = \sqrt{8}$ and $y_2 = \sqrt{5}$.
   (c) Use the above values to find an approximation for the area of the quarter circle.
   (d) Explain why the area you find this way is smaller than the actual area of the quarter circle.

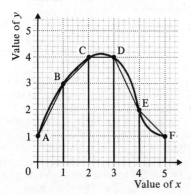

8. Find the area of each of the trapeziums in the graph above, and then find an approximation to the area under the curve.

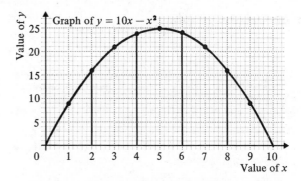

9. Look at the graph above, then complete the table of values below for $y = 10x - x^2$.

x	0	1	2	3	4	5	6	7	8	9	10
y	0	9				25				9	0

   (a) Find the area under the curve by using five trapeziums as shown. (Remember this time the width of each trapezium is 2 units.)
   (b) Find the area under the curve by using ten trapeziums each of width 1 unit.
   (c) Which of your two results would you expect to give a better approximation for the actual area under the curve?
   (d) Suggest a way of getting an even better approximation to the actual area.

If you have a table of values, you can use the trapezium rule to find an approximation to the area under a curve, without actually drawing the graph at all.
A quick way to remember the trapezium rule is:

Add the first and last y value to twice each of the other y values, multiply by the width of each trapezium, and then halve the result.

10. Use the trapezium rule to find the area under the curve, defined by the table of values:

   (a)

x	0	2	4	6	8	10
y	1	2	5	6	4	3

   (b)

x	0	1	2	3	4	5	6
y	6	10	12	11	8	3	1

   (c)

x	1	4	7	10	13	16
y	25	24	20	14	6	4

Speed-time graphs

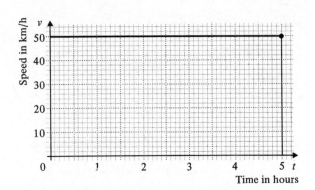

11. The graph above represents a car travelling for five hours at a constant speed of 50 km/h.
    (a) How far did the car travel in the 5 hours?
    (b) How can you find this out from the graph?

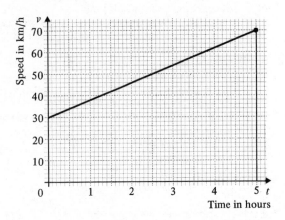

12. The graph above represents a car travelling for five hours at a speed which increases steadily from 30 km/h to 70 km/h.
    (a) What is the car's average speed?
    (b) How far did the car travel in the 5 hours?
    (c) How can you obtain this distance using an area on the graph?

In Question 11 above the car travelled 250 km. This can be found *either* by multiplying the speed by the time (50 × 5) or by using the area under the line, which is the area of a rectangle (50 × 5).

In Question 12 above the distance travelled can be found *either* by assuming the car was travelling for five hours at its average speed ((30 + 70)/2 km/h) *or* as in Question 11 by finding the area under the line. The area under the line in this case is the area of a trapezium ($\frac{1}{2}$(30 + 70) × 5).

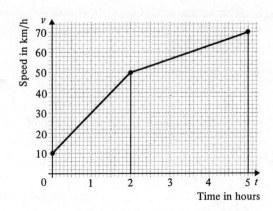

13. The graph above represents a car travelling for two hours at a speed which increases steadily from 10 km/h to 50 km/h and then for three hours at a speed which increases steadily from 50 km/h to 70 km/h. Find how far the car travelled in 5 hours:
    (a) by first finding the average speed for each of the two parts of the journey.
    (b) by finding the area of the two trapeziums shown on the graph.
    Do your answers agree?

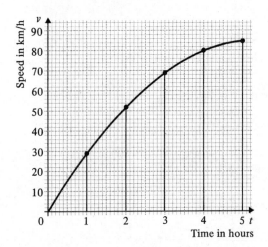

14. The graph above represents a car journey. Its speed is related to the time by the equation $v = 32t - 3t^2$.
    (a) Make a table showing the value of the speed v at the end of each hour.
    (b) For each hour of the journey, find an approximation for the average speed of the car.
    (c) Find how far the car travelled in the 5 hours by:
      (i) using the average speed for each hour
      (ii) finding the area of each of the trapeziums.
    (d) Do you agree that you can find the total distance travelled in the 5 hours by calculating the area under the curve?

1.4 Using tangents and areas

Finding speeds

Distance–time graphs

Example 1

The graph below shows the distance of a particle from its starting point, over an eight-second interval of time.

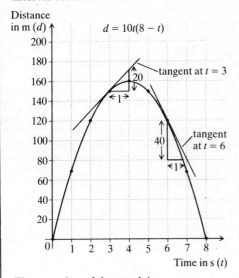

The equation of the graph is:

$$d = 10t(8 - t);$$

The *average* speed during the 2nd second is

$$\frac{(120 - 70)}{1} \text{ m/s}$$

The **actual speed** at any point on a distance-time graph is obtained by finding the **gradient of the tangent** at that point.

The speed after 3 seconds is $\dfrac{170 - 150}{4 - 3} = \dfrac{20}{1}$
$$= 20 \, \text{m/s}^2$$

The speed after 6 seconds is $\dfrac{80 - 120}{7 - 6} = \dfrac{^-40}{1}$
$$= ^-40 \, \text{m/s}^2$$

---

1. Find the average speed of the particle in Example 1 during:
   (a) each one-second time interval
   (b) each two-second time interval.
   Describe how the average speed changes over the eight seconds.

2. Find the speed of the particle in Example 1, at the end of each whole second. Describe how the speed changes over the eight seconds.

3. At what time during the eight seconds is the particle in Example 1:
   (a) at rest   (b) at its starting point?

4. The distance in metres s of a particle from its starting point, at time t, is given by the equation $s = 80t - 8t^2$.
   Draw a graph to show the distance of the particle from its starting point over the first ten seconds.
   Find:
   (a) the average speed of the particle during each of the first five seconds
   (b) the speed of the particle after each of the first five seconds
   (c) at what time the particle is at rest
   (d) at what time the particle returns to its starting point.

5. The distance s moved by a particle in t seconds is given in metres by $s = t^2 + 4t + 3$. By drawing a graph to show the movement of the particle over five seconds, find:
   (a) the distance moved during the first three seconds
   (b) the average speed of the particle during the third second
   (c) the speed of the particle after three seconds
   (d) the initial speed of the particle.

Note:
When the gradient of the tangent at a point is negative, it indicates that the particle is travelling in a direction opposite to its starting direction.

Finding accelerations

Speed–time graphs

Speed is the rate of change of distance with respect to time.

Acceleration is the rate of change of speed with respect to time.

We can find the **acceleration** of a particle at any time by finding the **gradient of the tangent** at that point on a **speed-time graph.**

Example 2

The graph below shows the speed of a particle over the first eight seconds, starting from rest.

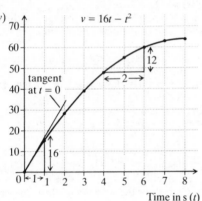

The average acceleration from $t = 4$ to $t = 6$

is $\dfrac{12}{2}$ m/s^2, i.e. 6 m/s^2

The initial acceleration is the gradient of the tangent when $t = 0$, i.e. 16 m/s^2.

Note:

When the speed is increasing, the gradients of the tangents are positive so the acceleration is positive.

When the speed is decreasing, the gradients of the tangents are negative so the acceleration is negative.

If the speed is constant, the gradients of the tangents are zero so the acceleration is zero.

6. Find the average acceleration of the particle in Example 2 during:
   (a) each one-second time interval
   (b) each two-second time interval.

7. Find the acceleration of the particle in Example 2, after each whole second. Describe how the acceleration changes over the eight seconds. At what time during the eight seconds is the acceleration zero?

8. The speed v of a particle, after t seconds, is given in metres per second by $v = 3t^2 + 5$.
   Draw a graph to show the speed of the particle during the first ten seconds.
   Find:
   (a) the average acceleration of the particle during each of the first five seconds
   (b) the acceleration of the particle after each of the first five seconds
   (c) the time at which the acceleration is greatest during the first eight seconds.

9. The speed v of a particle after t seconds is given in metres per second by $v = 15t - 3t^2$.
   By drawing a graph, find the values of t for which the acceleration is:
   (a) positive   (b) negative   (c) zero.

10. Readings are taken every second to record the distance in metres travelled by a particle. The results are shown below.

Time in seconds	1	2	3	4	5	6	7	8
Distance in metres	0.4	7.2	20.4	40	66	98.4	137.2	182.4

   (a) Draw a graph to show this information and find the average speed during each one-second time interval.
   (b) By drawing a tangent to the curve, find the speed after four seconds.
   (c) What can you say about the acceleration during the eight seconds?

Finding distances

Speed–time graphs

Example 3

The graph below shows the speed of a particle over a nine-second interval of time.

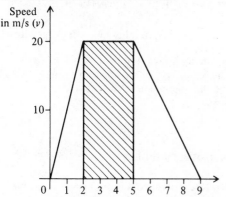

The distance travelled between the second and fifth second is $20 \times 3 = 60$ m. This is shown by the shaded area under the graph.
The distance travelled during the first two seconds is the area under the graph between $t = 0$ and $t = 2$.

$$\text{i.e. } \tfrac{1}{2} \times 2 \times 20 = 20 \text{m}.$$

The distance travelled during any given time-interval can be found from the corresponding area under the speed-time graph.

When the graph is a curve, we can find an approximation for the area under the curve using the trapezium rule.
Using this rule, the areas of the trapeziums formed by the chords to the curve are calculated.

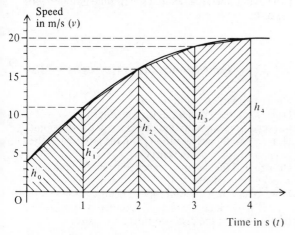

The speed of a particle in metres per second, v, at time t, is given by $v = 4 + 8t - t^2$. We can find an approximate value for the distance travelled in the first four seconds, by finding the area of the four trapeziums under the curve as shown in the diagram above.
The distance travelled
$\approx \tfrac{1}{2}(h_0 + h_1) \times 1 + \tfrac{1}{2}(h_1 + h_2) \times 1 + \tfrac{1}{2}(h_2 + h_3) \times 1 + \tfrac{1}{2}(h_3 + h_4) \times 1.$
$= \tfrac{1}{2}(h_0 + 2h_1 + 2h_2 + 2h_3 + h_4) \times 1$
$= \tfrac{1}{2}(4 + 2 \times 11 + 2 \times 16 + 2 \times 19 + 20) \times 1$
$= 58$ metres.

Example 4

The speed of a particle is given by:

$$v = 8 + 7t - t^2$$

and is shown by the graph below.

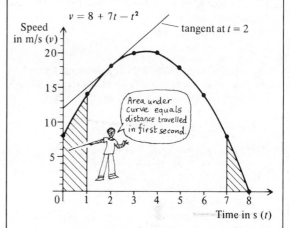

Using the area under the curve, the distance travelled during the first second is approximately:

$$\tfrac{1}{2}(8 + 14) \times 1 = 11 \text{ metres.}$$

Using the area under the curve, the distance travelled during the eighth second is approximately:

$$\tfrac{1}{2}(8 + 0) \times 1 = 4 \text{ metres.}$$

The acceleration when $t = 2$ is given by the gradient of the tangent, i.e. 3m/s^2.

The maximum speed is obtained when $t = 3.5$. At this point, since the gradient of the tangent is zero, the acceleration must be zero.

11. Using the graph of Example 3, find the distance travelled by the particle during the last four seconds.

12. The speed of a car increases from 0 km/h to 60 km/h in twenty seconds. It increases from 60 km/h to 90 km/h in the next fifteen seconds, and finally reduces to 0 km/h over another eighteen seconds. Show this information as a graph and find the distance travelled during each stage.

13. The speed v of a particle in m/s is given by $v = 3t^2 + 5$, where t is the time in seconds. Draw a graph and use the trapezium rule to find the approximate distance travelled by the particle in each of the first four seconds. Find also its average speed during the fifth second.

14. The speed v of a particle in m/s is given by $v = 2 + 3t + t^2$, where t is the time in seconds. Draw a graph and use the trapezium rule to find the total distance travelled during the first five seconds. Find also the average speed over the five seconds.

15. For each of Questions 13 and 14, find the acceleration of the particle after:
(a) 2 seconds (b) 4 seconds (c) 5 seconds.

16. Using the graph of Example 4, find:
(a) the distance travelled during the third second
(b) the distance travelled during the fifth second
(c) the total distance travelled over the eight seconds
(d) the acceleration when: (i) $t = 1$, (ii) $t = 6$.

17. The speed of a particle in m/s is given by $v = t^2 - 5t + 7$. Find by drawing a graph:
(a) the distance travelled during:
   (i) the first second,
   (ii) the next three seconds
(b) the acceleration when: (i) $t = 1$, (ii) $t = 3$
(c) the minimum speed
(d) the greatest speed during the first six seconds
(e) the time when the acceleration is zero.

18. Readings are taken every second to record the speed of a particle in metres per second. The results are shown below:

Time in s	0	1	2	3	4	5	6	7	8
Speed in m/s	24.0	28.3	30.5	30.4	28.0	24.3	18.5	10.1	0

(a) Draw a graph to show this information and find the distance travelled by the particle in each one-second time interval.
(b) Find the average speed over the first eight seconds.
(c) Find the acceleration after 2 seconds.
(d) Find the greatest acceleration.

19. Draw the graph of $y = x^2$ for values of x from 0 to 10. Use the trapezium rule to find an approximation to the area under $y = x^2$ between $x = 2$ and $x = 8$.

Summary

By the end of this chapter these are the things you should know about:

1.1 Lines and regions (pages 306–307)

How to find whether a point lies in a region described by $x + y > 7$ or not.
How to use inequalities $x + y > 7$ or $x + y < 7$ to describe the regions on either side of the line $x + y = 7$.
How to find the region described by two or more inequalities.

1.2 Linear programming (pages 308–311)

How to describe a set of conditions using inequalities.
How to represent these conditions as regions on a graph.
e.g. $x + y \leqslant 8, x \geqslant 0$
$\qquad 2x + y < 10, y \geqslant 0$
How to use the graph to find solutions to everyday problems involving one or more conditions.
How to use a line to show profit and how to find the maximum profit by drawing parallel lines.

1.3 Areas under graphs (pages 312–314)

How to find the area under a graph by counting squares.
How to use trapeziums to find the area under a graph.
How to use a trapezium rule:

$$\text{area} = \tfrac{1}{2}(y_0 + 2y_1 + 2y_2 + 2y_3 + y_4)h$$

How to find the area under a speed-time graph to give the distance travelled.

1.4 Using tangents and areas (pages 315–318)

How to find the tangent to a curve.
How to use the gradient of the tangent to a distance-time curve to find the speed at a given point.
How to find the acceleration from the gradient of the tangent to a speed-time curve.
How to find the distance travelled from the area under a speed-time curve.
How to find the maximum speed from a graph by using the point at which the tangent is horizontal, i.e. when the gradient of the distance-time curve is zero.

2 Graphs 4

2.1 More about graphs

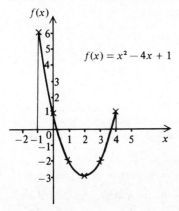

Example 1

Draw the graph of $f(x) = x^2 - 4x + 1$ for the domain $^-1 \leqslant x \leqslant 4$.

x	$^-1$	0	1	2	3	4
x^2	1	0	1	4	9	16
$-4x$	4	0	$^-4$	$^-8$	$^-12$	$^-16$
$x^2 - 4x + 1$	6	1	$^-2$	$^-3$	$^-2$	1

$f(x) = x^2 - 4x + 1$

Note: A graph with a positive x^2 term will be a smooth $\cup$ shaped curve, whilst one with a negative x^2 term will be smooth $\cap$ shaped. The image set (range) above is $^-3 \leqslant f(x) \leqslant 6$.

1. Write down the image set (range) for the graph in Example 1.
   Find $f(\frac{1}{2})$, $f(^-\frac{1}{2})$ and $f(3\frac{1}{2})$.

2. For what values of x in the graph above is:
   (a) $f(x) = 1$ (b) $f(x) = ^-2$
   (c) $f(x) = 6$ (d) $f(x) = 0$?

3. By completing a table as above, draw a graph of:
   (a) $f(x) = x^2 + 2x - 3$ for the domain $^-4 \leqslant x \leqslant 2$
   (b) $f(x) = x^2 - 4x + 4$ for the domain $^-2 \leqslant x \leqslant 4$
   (c) $f(x) = x^2 + 3x + 2$ for the domain $^-3 \leqslant x \leqslant 3$
   (d) $f(x) = x^2 - 5x + 4$ for the domain $^-1 \leqslant x \leqslant 5$

4. For each graph in Question 3, write down the image set (range) and find $f(\frac{1}{2})$.

5. For what values of x in each graph in Question 3 is:
   (a) $f(x) = 0$ (b) $f(x) = 2$
   (c) $f(x) = 4$ (d) $f(x) = ^-3$?

6. By completing a table as in Example 1, draw a graph of:
   (a) $f(x) = 4 - x^2$ for the domain $^-3 \leqslant x \leqslant 3$
   (b) $f(x) = 3x - x^2$ for the domain $^-2 \leqslant x \leqslant 4$
   (c) $f(x) = 3 + 2x - x^2$ for the domain $^-2 \leqslant x \leqslant 4$
   (d) $f(x) = 3 - 2x - x^2$ for the domain $^-4 \leqslant x \leqslant 2$.

7. For each graph in Question 6, write down the image set (range) and find $f(\frac{1}{2})$.

8. For what values of x in each graph in Question 6 is:
   (a) $f(x) = 0$ (b) $f(x) = 1$
   (c) $f(x) = ^-2$ (d) $f(x) = 3$?

9. What can you say about three of the graphs in Question 6? Describe the transformation which would map $f(x) = 4 - x^2$ onto each of the remaining two graphs.

10. Solve the quadratic equation by drawing the associated quadratic graph and find when $f(x) = 0$. In each case, take as the domain $^-5 \leqslant x \leqslant 5$.
    (a) $x^2 - 5x + 6 = 0$ (b) $x^2 + 2x - 8 = 0$
    (c) $x^2 - 5x + 5 = 0$ (d) $x^2 + 2x - 6 = 0$

11. Use your graph in Question 10 to find for what values of x:
    (a) $x^2 - 5x + 6 = 30$ (b) $x^2 + 2x - 8 = 16$

Sketching quadratics

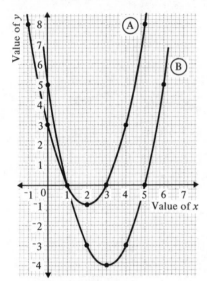

12. Look at the graph above.
    (a) Write down the co-ordinates of the points on curve Ⓐ and show that these fit the equation $y = x^2 - 4x + 3$.
    (b) Write down the co-ordinates of the points on curve Ⓑ and show that these fit the equation $y = x^2 - 6x + 5$.

13. (a) Factorise $x^2 - 4x + 3$. How are the two factors connected to curve Ⓐ above?
    (b) Factorise $x^2 - 6x + 5$. How are the two factors connected to curve Ⓑ above?

A quick way to sketch a quadratic graph such as $y = x^2 - 7x + 10$ is to first write it in factor form:
$y = (x - 2)(x - 5)$.
The graph crosses the x-axis at $y = 0$
– that is, at $x = 2$ and $x = 5$.
You can also find where it crosses the y-axis by putting $x = 0$ in the equation
– it crosses the y-axis at $y = 10$.
You could now draw the axes, mark these three points and sketch the curve.

14. Sketch the curve, by first finding where it crosses the x- and y-axes.
    (a) $y = (x - 2)(x - 3)$ (b) $y = (x - 1)(x - 4)$
    (c) $y = x^2 - 6x + 8$ (d) $y = x^2 - 7x + 12$
    (e) $y = x^2 + x - 2$ (f) $y = x^2 + 4x + 3$

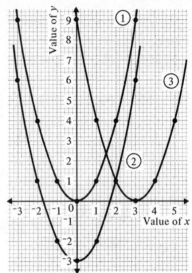

15. Look at the graph above. Which curve is:
    (a) $y = x^2$ (b) $y = x^2 - 3$
    (c) $y = x^2 - 6x + 9$?

16. (a) Trace curve ① above. Does your tracing fit curve ② and curve ③?
    (b) Describe how you would move curve ① to fit onto:
        (i) curve ②   (ii) curve ③.

17. (a) Use your tracing from Question 16. Does this curve fit curve Ⓐ and curve Ⓑ in Question 12?
    (b) Describe how you would move curve ① to fit onto:
        (i) curve Ⓐ   (ii) curve Ⓑ.

18. Rewrite in the form $y = (x - p)^2 - q$.
    (a) $y = x^2 - 4x + 3$ (b) $y = x^2 - 6x + 5$
    (c) $y = x^2$ (d) $y = x^2 - 3$
    (e) $y = x^2 - 6x + 9$

19. The equations in Question 18 correspond to the curves drawn in Questions 12 and 15.
    Look at the p and q values you found for each equation.
    What is the connection between these values and the lowest point of the corresponding curve?

If the equation of a quadratic curve can be written in the form $y = (x - p)^2 - q$, the curve can be drawn by *translating* $y = x^2$.
It is translated p units to the right and q units downwards.
If p is negative then the translation is to the left. If q is negative then the translation is upwards.

20. Use the idea in Question 19 to sketch the curve:
(a) $y = x^2 - 4$ (b) $y = x^2 + 2$
(c) $y = (x - 2)^2$ (d) $y = (x - 5)^2$
(e) $y = (x - 2)^2 - 4$

Maximum and minimum values

Example 2

Find the minimum value of $x^2 - 6x + 10$.

We can write $x^2 - 6x + 10$ as $(x - 3)^2 + 1$.

Since $(x - 3)^2$ is always greater than or equal to 0, the expression $(x - 3)^2 + 1$ is always greater than or equal to 1.
The minimum value of the expression occurs when $x = 3$, since this makes the bracket zero.
Hence, minimum value $= 3^2 - 6 \times 3 + 10 = 1$

21. Write down the minimum value of the expression, and the corresponding value of x:
(a) $(x - 3)^2 + 3$ (b) $(x - 2)^2 + 1$
(c) $(x - 1)^2 + 5$ (d) $(x - 4)^2 - 3$
(e) $(x + 2)^2 + 7$ (f) $(x + 1)^2 - 2$
(g) $x^2 - 6x + 12$ (h) $x^2 - 4x + 5$
(i) $x^2 - 8x + 17$ (j) $x^2 - 10x + 30$

22. (a) Write down the minimum value of each expression in Question 20.
(b) Do you agree that each minimum value for Question 20 is the value of y at the lowest point on the corresponding curve?

23. Look again at the five curves in Questions 12 and 15. For each write down:
(a) the minimum value of y
(b) the value of x at which this occurs
(c) the equation, rewritten in the form $(x - p)^2 - q$
(See your answers for Question 18.)
(d) the connection between your answers for (a) and (b) and the values of p and q.

24. (a) Draw the graph of $y = x^2 - 4x + 7$ for values of x from 0 to 5.
(b) Write down the minimum value of y from your graph.
(c) Write the equation as $y = (x - p)^2 + q$.
(d) Do you agree that the minimum value of y is the value you found for q?
(e) Does this minimum value occur when $x = p$?

25. Look again at your graph for Question 24.
(a) What is the maximum value of y?
(b) For what value of x does this occur?

26. Draw the graph of $y = x^2 - 8x + 7$ for values of x from 0 to 9. Find the minimum and maximum values for y, and the values of x when $y = 0$.

Example 3

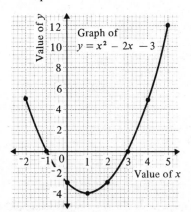

The domain for the graph of $y = x^2 - 2x - 3$ is the set of values of x i.e. $\{x : {}^-2 \leqslant x \leqslant 5\}$.

The minimum value of y is $^-4$ and the maximum value is 12
so the image set for this function is
$\{y : {}^-4 \leqslant y \leqslant 12\}$.

27. Look at the graph in Example 3.
Write down the image set of the function $y = x^2 - 2x - 3$ for a domain which is:
(a) $\{x : 0 \leqslant x \leqslant 5\}$
(b) $\{x : {}^-2 \leqslant x \leqslant 3\}$
(c) $\{x : 2 \leqslant x \leqslant 4\}$

28. For each domain given in Question 27, find the minimum and maximum values of y.

29. (a) Draw the graph of $y = x^2 - 4x - 5$ using as domain $\{x : {}^-2 \leqslant x \leqslant 5\}$.
(b) Find the minimum and maximum values of y and write down the image set.
(c) Write down the image set which would correspond to a domain of $\{x : 1 \leqslant x \leqslant 4\}$.
(d) Find the minimum and maximum values of y for the domain in (c).

30. Look again at the graph of $y = x^2 - 2x - 3$. For which values of x are:
(a) $x^2 - 2x - 3 < 0$ (b) $x^2 - 2x - 3 \geqslant 0$
(c) $x^2 - 2x - 3 < {}^-3$ (d) $x^2 - 2x - 3 \geqslant 5$?

31. (a) Draw the graph of $y = 2x^2 - 5x + 2$ using as domain $\{x : {}^-1 \leqslant x \leqslant 5\}$.
(b) Find the minimum and maximum values of y and write down the image set.
(c) For which values of x in the domain is:
(i) $2x^2 - 5x + 2 > 0$
(ii) $2x^2 - 5x + 2 < 14$?
(d) Write down the image set if the domain had been $\{x : 1 \leqslant x \leqslant 3\}$.

Example 4

Write $4x^2 - 40x + 3$ in the form $(ax + b)^2 + c$, and hence find the minimum value of $4x^2 - 40x + 3$.

$(2x - 10)^2 = (2x - 10)(2x - 10)$
$\qquad\qquad = 4x^2 - 40x + 100$

So $4x^2 - 40x + 3 = (4x^2 - 40x + 100) - 97$
$\qquad\qquad\qquad\quad = (2x - 10)^2 - 97$

The minimum value of $4x^2 - 40x + 3$ occurs when $2x - 10 = 0$
i.e. when $x = 5$.
The minimum value is $^-97$.

---

32. Write in the form $(ax + b)^2 + c$, and hence find the minimum value of:
- (a) $4x^2 + 12x + 11$
- (b) $9x^2 + 12x + 5$
- (c) $16x^2 + 8x + 1$
- (d) $25x^2 + 20x$
- (e) $4x^2 - 16x + 20$
- (f) $49x^2 - 56x + 19$
- (g) $36x^2 - 12x + 1$
- (h) $81x^2 - 18x$

33. Find the maximum value of:
- (a) $9 - 4x - x^2$
- (b) $11 - 6x - x^2$
- (c) $20 + 8x - x^2$
- (d) $24x - 9x^2$

34. For what value of x does the expression take its minimum value?
- (a) $x^2 - 4x + 11$
- (b) $x^2 + 8x + 21$
- (c) $4x^2 + 4x + 3$
- (d) $9x^2 + 12x + 5$

Example 5

Write $3x^2 - 4x + 1$ in the form $a(x + b)^2 + c$ and hence find the minimum value of $3x^2 - 4x + 1$.

$3x^2 - 4x + 1 = 3[x^2 - \tfrac{4}{3}x + \tfrac{1}{3}]$
$\qquad\qquad\quad = 3[(x - \tfrac{4}{6})^2 - (\tfrac{4}{6})^2 + \tfrac{1}{3}]$
$\qquad\qquad\quad = 3[(x - \tfrac{4}{6})^2 - \tfrac{4}{9} + \tfrac{3}{9}]$
$\qquad\qquad\quad = 3(x - \tfrac{2}{3})^2 - \tfrac{1}{3}$

$3(x - \tfrac{2}{3})^2 = 0$ when $x = \tfrac{2}{3}$,
and the minimum value of $3x^2 - 4x + 1$ is $^-\tfrac{1}{3}$.

---

35. Write in the form $a(x + b)^2 + c$, and hence find the minimum value of:
- (a) $3x^2 - 4x + 4$
- (b) $2x^2 - 5x - 2$
- (c) $5x^2 - 6x + 2$
- (d) $7x^2 - 8x - 17$
- (e) $6x^2 + 8x - 3$
- (f) $4x^2 - 7x + 1$

36. Write in the form $a(x + b)^2 + c$, and hence find the maximum value of:
- (a) $6 - 4x - 3x^2$
- (b) $8 + 2x - 3x^2$
- (c) $6 - 7x - 4x^2$
- (d) $3 - 14x - 4x^2$
- (e) $6 + 10x - 5x^2$
- (f) $4 - x - 6x^2$

In general you can write:

$$ax^2 + bx + c = a\left[x^2 + \frac{b}{a}x + \frac{c}{a}\right]$$

$$= a\left[\left(x^2 + \frac{b}{22a}\right)^2 - \left(\frac{b}{2a}\right)^2 + \frac{c}{a}\right]$$

$$= a\left(x + \frac{b}{2a}\right)^2 + \left(c - \frac{b^2}{4a}\right)$$

So the maximum or minimum value of $ax^2 + bx + c$ occurs when:

$$a\left(x + \frac{b}{2a}\right)^2 = 0, \text{ i.e. when } x = -\frac{b}{2a}$$

Example 6

Find the minimum value of $3x^2 - 4x + 1$.

Minimum occurs when $x = -\dfrac{b}{2a}$

$$= -\frac{^-4}{2 \times 3} = \frac{2}{3}$$

Hence minimum value $= 3(\tfrac{2}{3})^2 - 4(\tfrac{2}{3}) + 1$
$\qquad\qquad\qquad\quad = \tfrac{4}{3} - \tfrac{8}{3} + 1 = ^-\tfrac{1}{3}$

---

37. Use the method in Example 6 to check your answers to Questions 34, 35 and 36.

Isn't there some way of doing the maximum amount of work, with the minimum effort?

How about a robot controlled vacuum cleaner?

2.2 Quadratic inequalities

Using factors

Example 1

Find the solution set for $x^2 - 5x + 6 > 0$.

You need to find the values of x for which
$x^2 - 5x + 6$ is positive.
It helps to first factorise the expression,
i.e. $(x - 2)(x - 3)$.

The product of two numbers pq is positive
either if both p and q are positive
or   if both p and q are negative.

So $(x - 2)(x - 3) > 0$
either if $(x - 2) > 0$ and $(x - 3) > 0$ . . . [1]
or   if $(x - 2) < 0$ and $(x - 3) < 0$ . . . [2]

In [1], $x > 2$ and $x > 3$
so x must be greater than 3.
In [2], $x < 2$ and $x < 3$
so x must be less than 2.

So $(x - 2)(x - 3) > 0$ provided $x > 3$ or $x < 2$.

---

1. l and m are two numbers. What can you say about
them if the product $lm < 0$?

2. If $(x - p)(x - q) < 0$, which of the following
statements are true?
  (a) $(x - p) > 0$ and $(x - q) > 0$
  (b) $(x - p) < 0$ and $(x - q) < 0$
  (c) $(x - p) > 0$ and $(x - q) < 0$
  (d) $(x - p) < 0$ and $(x - q) > 0$

3. If $(x - 1)(x - 4) > 0$, use the ideas in Example 1 to
say which statement is true.
  (a) $x < 1$ or $x > 4$.
  (b) x lies between 1 and 4

4. If $(x - 3)(x - 5) < 0$, say which statement is true.
  (a) $x < 3$ or $x > 5$.
  (b) x lies between 3 and 5.

5. Use the above ideas to say for what values of x the
statement is true.
  (a) $(x - 1)(x - 5) > 0$ (b) $(x - 3)(x - 7) < 0$
  (c) $(x - 2)(x - 4) \leqslant 0$ (d) $(x - 4)(x - 7) \geqslant 0$
  (e) $(x^2 - 3x + 2) \leqslant 0$ (f) $(x^2 - 4x + 3) \leqslant 0$

6. For what values of x is the statement true?
  (a) $(x + 1)(x - 5) \geqslant 0$ (b) $(x - 3)(x + 7) \leqslant 0$
  (c) $(x + 2)(x - 4) < 0$ (d) $(x - 4)(x + 7) > 0$
  (e) $(x^2 - 5x + 4) \leqslant 0$ (f) $(x^2 - 9x + 8) \geqslant 0$

Using the number line

The solution set for an inequality such as $2x - 3 > 0$ can
be shown like this:

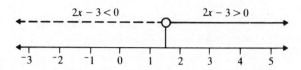

First find where $2x - 3 = 0$. (This is shown above, with
a $\bigcirc$.)
Then use a solid line to show the values of x for which
$2x - 3 > 0$.
The dotted line shows where $2x - 3 < 0$.

Example 2

Find the solution set for $(2x - 3)(x + 2) < 0$.

Use the number line to show where $(2x - 3)$ and
$(x + 2)$ are positive and negative.
The values of x for which $(2x - 3)(x + 2) < 0$ are
then shown beneath the number line.

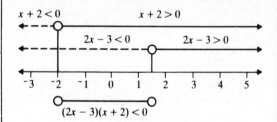

Since in this case the product of the brackets is
negative, one bracket must be positive and the
other negative. This happens where the solid line
and the dotted line overlap (between $^-2$ and $1\frac{1}{2}$).

---

7. Look at the diagram in Example 2 and write down
the values of x for which:
  (a) both $(2x - 3)$ and $(x + 2)$ are positive
  (b) both $(2x - 3)$ and $(x + 2)$ are negative
  (c) $(2x - 3)(x + 2) > 0$

8. Use the ideas of Example 2 to show on a number
line the values of x for which:
  (a) $(2x - 3)(x - 4) < 0$
  (b) $(x + 1)(x - 4) > 0$
  (c) $(x + 3)(x - 2) > 0$
  (d) $(x + 2)(2x - 5) < 0$

9. Use a number line to show the solution set for:
  (a) $(2x - 3)(2x - 7) > 0$
  (b) $(x + 1)(x + 3) < 0$
  (c) $(2x - 1)(x + 2) < 0$
  (d) $(2x + 1)(2x + 3) > 0$

Solution set notation

> *Example 3*
>
> Find the solution set for $(3x - 5)(2x + 3) > 0$.
>
> This is done below, using a quicker method than in Example 2.
>
> *First* find where $(3x - 5)(2x + 3) = 0$
> $(3x - 5)(2x + 3) = 0$ when $3x - 5 = 0$
> or when $\qquad\qquad\qquad 2x + 3 = 0$.
>
> $$3x - 5 = 0 \text{ when } x = \tfrac{5}{3}$$
> $$2x + 3 = 0 \text{ when } x = \tfrac{-3}{2}$$
>
> *Next* mark these values on a number line, using a circle.
>
>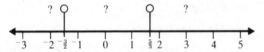
>
> *Then* find the sign of $(3x - 5)(2x + 3)$ in each of the three parts of the number line, by choosing test values for x.
> For example:
> at $x = 0$,
> $(3x - 5)(2x + 3) = {}^-5 \times 3 = {}^-15$ (negative)
> at $x = 3$,
> $(3x - 5)(2x + 3) = 4 \times 9 = 36$ (positive)
> at $x = {}^-2$,
> $(3x - 5)(2x + 3) = {}^-11 \times {}^-1 = 11$ (positive)
>
> So the signs for the different parts of the line are:
>
>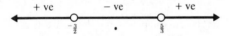
>
> $(3x - 5)(2x + 3) > 0$ when $x < {}^-\tfrac{3}{2}$ or when $x > \tfrac{5}{3}$
> Using set notation, this is written as:
> $\{x : x < {}^-\tfrac{3}{2}\} \cup \{x : x > \tfrac{5}{3}\}$
>
> $(3x - 5)(2x + 3) < 0$ when x lies between ${}^-\tfrac{3}{2}$ and $\tfrac{5}{3}$
> Using set notation, this is written as:
> $$\{x : {}^-\tfrac{3}{2} < x < \tfrac{5}{3}\}$$

10. (a) Write down the values of x for which
$(x - 3)(x - 5) = 0$.
(b) Find whether $(x - 3)(x - 5)$ is positive or negative when:
    (i) $x = 1$ (ii) $x = 4$
    (iii) $x = 7$.
(c) Show this information using a number line.
(d) Use set notation to show when
    (i) $(x - 3)(x - 5) > 0$
    (ii) $(x - 3)(x - 5) < 0$
(e) Repeat (a), (b), (c) and (d), for
$(2x - 3)(3x + 1)$.

11. Use a number line to show the values of x.
(a) $\{x : 1 < x < 4\}$
(b) $\{x : {}^-3 < x < 2\}$
(c) $\{x : x < 3\} \cup \{x : x > 7\}$
(d) $\{x : x < {}^-2\} \cup \{x : x > 1\}$

Using graphs

> *Example 4*
>
> Find the solution set for $x^2 - x - 6 \geqslant 0$
>
> Another way of finding the solutions set is to draw the graph of $y = x^2 - x - 6$ and then to find when y is positive:
>
>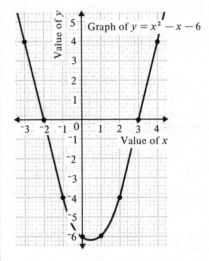
>
> y is positive when the graph is above the x-axis.
> So $x^2 - x - 6 \geqslant 0$ when $x \leqslant {}^-2$ or when $x \geqslant 3$.
>
> The solution set is $\{x : x \leqslant {}^-2\} \cup \{x : x \geqslant 3\}$.

12. Using the graph above, write down the solution set for:
(a) $x^2 - x - 6 \leqslant 0$ (b) $x^2 - x - 6 > 4$
(c) $x^2 - x - 6 < {}^-6$ (d) $x^2 - x - 6 \geqslant {}^-4$

13. (a) Copy and complete the table below.

x	0	1	2	3	4	5	6
$4x^2$	0			36			
$16x$	0			48			
$4x^2 - 16x + 7$	7			${}^-5$			

(b) Draw the graph of $y = 4x^2 - 16x + 7$ for values of x from 0 to 6.
(c) Use your graph to write down the solution set for $4x^2 - 16x + 7 < 0$.

14. Use your graph in Question 13 to write down the solution set for:
(a) $4x^2 - 16x + 7 > 0$ (b) $4x^2 - 16x + 7 \leqslant {}^-5$

15. By drawing a graph find the solution set for:
(a) $x^2 - 5x + 4 \geqslant 0$ (b) $2x^2 - x - 3 < 0$

Example 5

The graph of $f(x) = x^2 - 2x - 3$ is shown below.

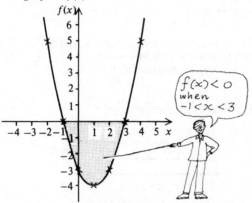

$f(x) < 0$ when $^-1 < x < 3$

$f(x)$ is negative, or below the x-axis, for values of x between $^-1$ and 3.

$f(x)$ is positive, or above the x-axis, when $x > 3$ or when $x < {}^-1$.

So $x^2 - 2x - 3 < 0$ when $^-1 < x < 3$
     $x^2 - 2x - 3 > 0$ when $x < {}^-1$ or when $x > 3$

---

16. Using the graph in Example 5 write down the values of x for which:
(a) $f(x) < {}^-3$ (b) $f(x) > 5$
(c) $f(x > {}^-4$ (d) $f(x) = 0$
Find also the values of x for which $x^2 - 2x - 3 < 2$.

17. Draw the graph of $(f)x) = x^2 + x - 6$ with the domain $^-5 \leqslant x \leqslant 4$.
Find the values of x for which:
(a) $f(x > 0$ (b) $f(x) < 6$
(c) $f(x) > {}^-6$ (d) $f(x) = 14$
Find also the values of x for which $x^2 + x - 6 > {}^-4$.

18. Draw the graph of $f(x) = x^2 - 2x - 8$ with the domain $^-3 \leqslant x \leqslant 5$.
Find the values of x for which:
(a) $f(x) < 0$ (b) $f(x) > {}^-8$
(c) $f(x) \geqslant 7$ (d) $f(x) \leqslant {}^-5$
Find also the values of x for which
$x^2 - 2x - 8 \geqslant {}^-9$.

19. Draw the graph of $f(x) = 9 - x^2$ with the domain $^-4 \leqslant x \leqslant 4$.
Find the values of x for which:
(a) $f(x) > 0$ (b) $f(x) < 8$
(c) $f(x) \geqslant 5$ (d) $f(x) \leqslant {}^-7$
Find also the values of x for which $9 - x^2 = 7$.
Hence find $\sqrt{2}$.

20. Draw the graph of $f(x) = 3 + 2x - x^2$ with the domain $^-2 \leqslant x \leqslant 4$.
Find the values of x for which:
(a) $f(x) < 0$ (b) $f(x) = {}^-5$
(c) $f(x) \geqslant 3$ (d) $f(x) \geqslant 4$
Find also the values of x for which $3 + 2x - x^2 \geqslant \frac{1}{2}$.

21. By drawing a quadratic graph, or otherwise, solve the inequality:
(a) $x^2 - 5x + 6 < 0$ (b) $x^2 + 4x - 5 \geqslant 0$
(c) $5 + 4x - x^2 < 0$ (d) $x^2 - 5x + 6 > 2$
(e) $x^2 + 4x - 5 \leqslant {}^-8$ (f) $5 + 4x - x^2 \geqslant 2$

22. By drawing a suitable graph, or otherwise, solve the inequality:
(a) $x^2 - 4x + 1 < 0$ (b) $1 + 3x - x^2 \geqslant 0$
(c) $x^2 - 5x + 4 < 2$

23. Write down two values of x for which $(x - 2)(x - 4) = 0$.
Hence sketch the graph of $f(x) = (x - 2)(x - 4)$ and write down the solution set for $(x - 2)(x - 4) \leqslant 0$.

24. Write down two values of x for which $(3 - x)(x + 4) = 0$.
Hence sketch the graph of $f(x) = (3 - x)(x + 4)$ and write down the solution set for $(3 - x)(x + 4) < 0$.

25. By sketching the appropriate graphs, write down the solution set for:
(a) $(x - 2)(x - 3) > 0$ (b) $(x - 4)(x + 1) < 0$
(c) $(3 - x)(x - 4) \geqslant 0$

Example 6

Find the solution set for $(x - 1)(x - 2) > 0$.

The solution set may be found either by drawing the graph of $y = (x - 1)(x - 2)$ and finding when $y > 0$ as is shown below, or by considering the sign of each of $(x - 1)$ and $(x - 2)$.

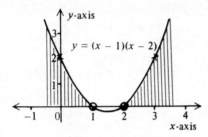

$y > 0$ when $x > 2$ or when $x < 1$

Both $(x - 1)$ and $(x - 2)$ are positive so $x > 2$, *or* both $(x - 1)$ and $(x - 2)$ are negative so $x < 1$.

The solution set is $\{x : x < 1\} \cup \{x : x > 2\}$

---

26. By drawing a graph of $y = (x - 2)(x - 3)$ find the solution set for $(x - 2)(x - 3) > 0$.

27. By drawing a graph of $y = (x - 1)(x - 4)$ find the solution set for $(x - 1)(x - 4) < 0$.

28. By drawing a graph of $y = (x + 2)(x - 3)$ find the solution set for $(x + 2)(x - 3) < 0$.

29. By drawing a graph of $y = (x + 4)(x + 3)$ find the solution set for $(x + 4)(x + 3) > 0$.

30. For what values of x is:
  (a) $(x - 2) > 0$ (b) $(x - 5) > 0$
  (c) $(x - 2) > 0 \text{ and } (x - 5) > 0$
  (d) $(x - 2) < 0$ (e) $(x - 5) < 0$
  (f) $(x - 2) < 0 \text{ and } (x - 5) < 0$?
  Use your results for (c) and (f) to write down the solution set for $(x - 2)(x - 5) > 0$.

31. For what values of x is:
  (a) $(x - 3) > 0$ (b) $(x - 4) < 0$
  (c) $(x - 3) > 0 \text{ and } (x - 4) < 0$
  (d) $(x - 3) < 0$ (e) $(x - 4) > 0$
  (f) $(x - 3) < 0 \text{ and } (x - 4) > 0$?
  Use your results for (c) and (f) to write down the solution set for $(x - 3)(x - 4) < 0$.

32. Find the solution set for $(x + 3)(x - 4) > 0$ by using the fact that *either* the value of each bracket is positive, *or* the value of each bracket is negative.

33. Find the solution set for $(x + 4)(x + 5) < 0$ by using the fact that *either* the value of the first bracket is positive whilst the second is negative, *or* the value of the first bracket is negative whilst the second is positive.

34. Look at the diagram below.

$(x - 5) < 0 \qquad (x - 5) > 0$
$(x - 3) < 0 \qquad (x - 3) > 0$

0 1 2 3 4 5 6 7 8 9 10

  (a) When is $(x - 5) > 0 \text{ and } (x - 3) > 0$?
  (b) When is $(x - 5) < 0 \text{ and } (x - 3) < 0$?
  (c) Write down the solution set for:
$$(x - 5)(x - 3) > 0$$

35. Look at the diagram below.

$(x + 4) < 0 \qquad (x + 4) > 0$
$(1 - x) > 0 \qquad (1 - x) < 0$

$^-6$ $^-5$ $^-4$ $^-3$ $^-2$ $^-1$ 0 1 2 3 4

  (a) When is $(x + 4) > 0 \text{ and } (1 - x) > 0$?
  (b) When is $(x + 4) < 0 \text{ and } (1 - x) < 0$?
  (c) Write down the solution set for:
$$(x + 4)(1 - x) > 0$$

36. Use a number line as in Question 35 to show when $(x - 4)$ and $(x + 2)$ are each positive or negative. Hence find the solution set for $(x - 4)(x + 2) > 0$.

37. Use a number line as in Question 36 to show when $(3 - x)$ and $(3 + x)$ are each positive or negative. Hence find the solution set for $(3 - x)(3 + x) > 0$.

38. Find the solution set for:
  (a) $(x - 1)(x - 6) > 0$ (b) $(x - 3)(x + 2) < 0$
  (c) $(x + 5)(4 - x) > 0$ (d) $(x + 1)(x + 2) < 0$
  (e) $(3 - x)(2 - x) > 0$ (f) $(2x - 1)(x - 4) > 0$
  (g) $(x + 3)(4x - 1) < 0$ (h) $(2x + 1)(1 - 5x) > 0$

Summary

By the end of this chapter, these are the things you should know about:

2.1 More about graphs (pages 319–322)

You should be able to draw a quadratic curve for a given domain and find values of x which have particular images.

How to sketch a graph when the equation is given in the form $y = (x - a)(x - b)$.
It crosses the x-axis when $x = a$ and $x = b$ and it crosses the y-axis when $y = ab$. So you can first mark in the points $(a, 0), (b, 0)$ and $(0, ab)$, and then sketch the graph.

How to sketch a graph when the equation is given in the form $y = (x - p)^2 - q$.
This graph is a translation of $y = x^2$, p units to the right and q units downwards.

How to find the minimum value of a quadratic expression either by drawing a graph or by writing the expression in the form $(x - p)^2 + q$. The minimum value is q and this occurs when $x = p$.

How to find the maximum value of a quadratic expression by drawing a graph.

How to find the image set corresponding to a particular domain for a quadratic function, by using the graph and the minimum and maximum values of y.

2.2 Quadratic inequalities (pages 323–326)

How to find the solution set for a quadratic inequality such as $(x - 2)(x - 3) < 0$ by:
  (a) using the factors
  (b) using a number line

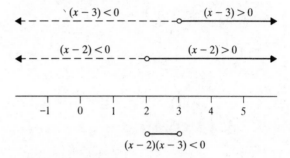

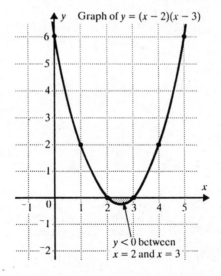

  (c) using a graph

How to use the solution set notation $\{x : 2 < x < 3\}$ etc.

Graph of $y = (x - 2)(x - 3)$

$y < 0$ between $x = 2$ and $x = 3$

3 Trigonometry 3

$d = \frac{x}{360} \times 2\pi R \cos \lambda$
So much for the shortest distance between two points being a straight line!

3.1 Lengths and angles in 3–D shapes

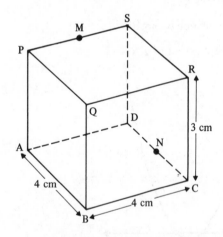

1. The 3–D shape above is a cuboid. M and N are the mid-points of PS and CD. Look at triangle ABC in the cuboid.
Do you agree that the length of AC is $\sqrt{32}$ cm?
Use Pythagoras' Theorem to find the following lengths:
(a) AN in △ADN   (b) AS in △APS
(c) AM in △APM

2. If you can identify the right-angled triangles in a 3-D shape, then you can find various lengths. But first you must know which angles are right angles.
Say whether the angle is a right angle or not:
(a) AĈR   (b) PÂN   (c) BÂS   (d) BÂM

3. Use Pythagoras' Theorem and your answers for Question 2 to find the following lengths. Leave your answers in square-root form.
(a) AR in △ACR   (b) PN in △PAN
(c) BS in △BAS   (d) BM in △BAM

4. Another way of finding BM in Question 3 (d) would be to use △BPM.
(a) Do you agree that BP̂M is a right angle?
(b) Find the length of BP.
(c) Now use Pythagoras' Theorem to find BM.

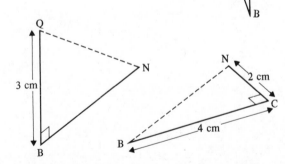

5. Look again at the cuboid opposite and the two triangles above.
(a) Do you agree that QB̂N and BĈN are both right angles?
(b) By first finding BN in △BCN and then using △QBN, find the length of QN.

6. (a) Do you agree that MŜN in the cuboid is a
    right angle?
    (b) Find the length of SN using ΔSDN.
    (c) Show by using ΔMSN that the length of
    MN is √17cm.

7. Look at the wedge above. ABCD is a rectangle on
the ground. PCDQ is another rectangle in a vertical
plane. M is the mid-point of AD.

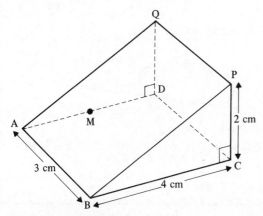

Find the length of:
(a) AC and then AP.
(b) PD and then PM
Check your result for PM by finding the length of
QM and then using ΔPQM.

8. Use the diagram in Question 7 and the 3-figure
table at the end of the book to find:
(a) PB̂C (b) PÂC (c) PM̂C (d) PD̂C
Are these four angles all different?

9. The 3-D shape VABCD is a pyramid. Its vertex V
is directly above N, the centre of its base. M is the
mid-point of BC.

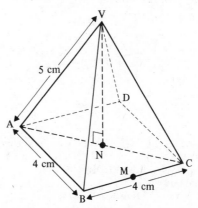

(a) Use ΔABC to find the length of AC.
(b) Write down the length of AN.
(c) Use ΔVAN to find the length of VN and then
    the angle between VA and ABCD.
(d) Write down the length of NM.
(e) Use ΔVMN to find the length of VM and then
    the angle between VM and ABCD.
(f) Explain why VÂN and VM̂N are different in
    size.

10. Look back at the cuboid for Question 1.
(a) Find the angle between the plane ABCD and
    the line:
    (i) AP   (ii) AQ   (iii) AR
    (iv) AS   (v) AM
(b) Find the angle between BM and the plane
    APSD.

The angle between a line and a plane

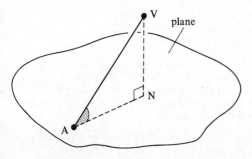

In the diagram above, A is a point in the plane and V is
a point above the plane.
A line VN is drawn at right angles to the plane, meeting
it at N. VÂN is defined as the angle between the line
VA and the plane.

The angle between two planes

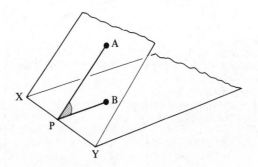

In the diagram above, the two planes have a common
line XY. P is a point on XY. Lines AP and BP are
drawn in each plane at right-angles to the line XY.
AP̂B is defined as the angle between the two planes.

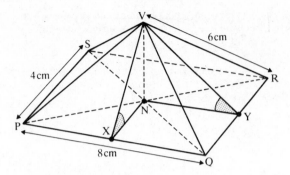

11. The 3-D shape VPQRS is a pyramid with its vertex V directly above N, the centre of its base. X and Y are the mid-points of PQ and QR.
Do you agree that:
(a) NY and VY are at right angles to QR
(b) VŶN is the angle between the plane VQR and the base of the pyramid PQRS
(c) NX and VX are at right angles to PQ
(d) VX̂N is the angle between the plane VPQ and the plane PQRS?
Find:
(e) PR, NR and then VN from ΔVNR
(f) NY and then VŶN from ΔVYN
(g) NX and then VX̂N from ΔVXN.
Explain why VŶN ≠ VX̂N.

12. (a) Use the diagram in Question 9 to find the angle between the face VBC and the plane ABCD.
(b) Which of your answers in Question 8 is the angle between the planes ABPQ and ABCD?

Some harder problems

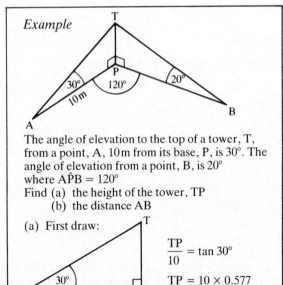

Example

The angle of elevation to the top of a tower, T, from a point, A, 10 m from its base, P, is 30°. The angle of elevation from a point, B, is 20° where AP̂B = 120°
Find (a) the height of the tower, TP
(b) the distance AB

(a) First draw:

$$\frac{TP}{10} = \tan 30°$$

$$TP = 10 \times 0.577$$
$$= 5.77 \text{ m}$$

(b) To find AB, you need to find PB.
Draw:

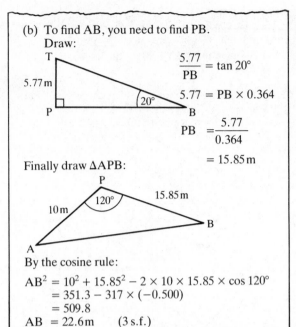

$$\frac{5.77}{PB} = \tan 20°$$

$$5.77 = PB \times 0.364$$

$$PB = \frac{5.77}{0.364}$$

$$= 15.85 \text{ m}$$

Finally draw ΔAPB:

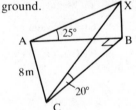

By the cosine rule:
$$AB^2 = 10^2 + 15.85^2 - 2 \times 10 \times 15.85 \times \cos 120°$$
$$= 351.3 - 317 \times (-0.500)$$
$$= 509.8$$
$$AB = 22.6 \text{ m} \qquad (3 \text{ s.f.})$$

13. An observer at the top of a tower of height 7 m sees a man due west of him at an angle of depression of 25°. He sees another man due north of him at an angle of depression of 30°.
Find the distance between the two men on the ground.

14. In the diagram A, B and C are points in a horizontal plane and B is vertically below X.
XÂB = 25°, XĈB = 20° and AC = 8 m.
Find:
(a) the length AB in terms of XB
(b) the length BC in terms of XB
(c) the length of XB.

15. The angle of elevation of the top of a tower is 28° from a point X due south of it. The angle of elevation of the top of the tower from another point Y due west of it is 34°. Find the height of the tower if the distance XY is 40 m.

16. The angle of elevation of the top of a lighthouse is 42° from a point P on a bearing of 280° from it. The angle of elevation of the top of the lighthouse from another point Q on a bearing of 120° from the front of the lighthouse is 29°. If the distance from P to the foot of the lighthouse is 35 m, find:
(a) the height of the lighthouse
(b) the distance PQ.

3.2 Vectors and the real world

Velocity vectors

Two cars that pass each other on the highway could be travelling in the same direction or in opposite directions. We use the word **velocity**, rather than **speed**, when we want to include the idea of direction.

An arrow can be used to represent both the direction and the speed of the car.

Velocity of car A $\xrightarrow{\text{60 km/h}}$ v_a

Velocity of car B $\xrightarrow{\text{80 km/h}}$ v_b

The length of the arrow represents the size of the speed. The direction of the arrow shows which way the car is going.

1. Look at the diagram above. Car B is moving with a velocity represented by the vector v_b. It passes car A which is moving with a velocity of v_a. Find $v_b - v_a$.

2. If car B was moving at 80 km/h in the *opposite* direction to car A, explain why $v_b - v_a = 140$ km/h.

In Questions 1 and 2 the vector represented by $v_b - v_a$ is called the velocity of car B *relative to* car A. It is the velocity with which car B appears to be moving if you are sitting in car A.

In Question 1 the velocity of car B relative to car A is 20 km/h $\xrightarrow{\hspace{1cm}}$ **whereas in Question 2 the velocity of car B relative to car A is 140 km/h.** $\xrightarrow{\hspace{2cm}}$

A similar situation occurs when an aeroplane is flying in a wind. If the wind is behind the aeroplane it will make it fly faster whereas if the aeroplane is flying into the wind its speed will be reduced.

3. An aeroplane can fly at 600 km/h when there is no wind. At what speed will it actually travel if it is flying:
    (a) directly into a wind of 50 km/h
    (b) with a wind of 50 km/h coming from directly behind it?

4. If the aeroplane in Question 3 was travelling due west at 600 km/h and it met at wind of 50 km/h coming from the north, in which direction would it move?
    What difference would it make if the wind had come from the south?

In Question 3 the aeroplane would fly either at 550 km/h or at 650 km/h, depending on whether it was going into the wind or had the wind behind it.

In Question 4 you could represent the velocities of the aeroplane and the wind using a vector diagram, as shown below:

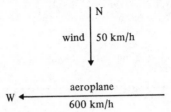

To find the actual velocity of the aeroplane, add the two vectors as shown below:

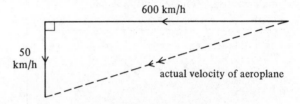

5. Make an accurate scale drawing of the diagram above. Use it to find the actual velocity of the aeroplane. Find its size and its direction.

6. Repeat Question 5 for a wind of:
    (a) 100 km/h coming from the north
    (b) 50 km/h coming from the south
    (c) 100 km/h coming from the south
    (d) 50 km/h coming from the north east

7. A helicopter flies due north at 120 km/h. Suddenly it is struck by a squall of wind, blowing from the west at 50 km/h.
    Find the actual speed of the helicopter, and the direction it will fly in if the pilot does not compensate for the squall.
    What difference would it make if the squall had been of strength 90 km/h?

The speed of an aeroplane in still air is called its *airspeed*. Its actual speed relative to the ground is called its *groundspeed*.
To find the vector representing the groundspeed you must add the vector representing the airspeed to the vector representing the velocity of the wind.

8. An aeroplane has an airspeed of 600 km/h and is travelling on a bearing (or track) of 045°. The velocity of the wind is 100 km/h, coming *from* a bearing of 315°. Draw a vector diagram to find the size and direction of the plane's groundspeed.
    (Remember, bearings are angles measured in a clockwise direction from north.)

9. How long will the aeroplane in Question 8 take to fly 1000 km?

10. A boat can cross from one bank of a river to the other bank at a speed of 8 km/h in still water, i.e. when no current is flowing.
    With a current of 6 km/h the boat will be pushed downstream before it reaches the other bank.
    (a) Draw a diagram to show the addition of the vectors representing the velocity of the boat in still water and the velocity of the current.
    (b) Using the diagram, find the actual velocity of the boat across the water.

Example 1

In which direction must the boat in Question 10 start off if it wants to reach a point on the other bank directly opposite the starting point?

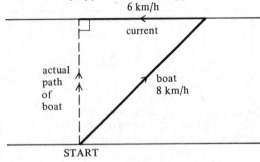

If the boat points upstream, as shown in the diagram, the current will continually push it back onto the dotted line. So it will finish directly opposite the starting point.

---

11. Make an accurate copy of the vector diagram in Example 1 and hence find the vector representing the actual velocity of the boat.

12. What difference would it make in Example 1, if the boat had set off on a path making an angle of 45° with the bank?

13. If the river is 40 metres wide, find how long it will take the boat to reach the other bank, in:
    (a) Question 11   (b) Question 12.

Bearing vectors

We can use a vector to represent a distance travelled along a particular bearing. For example, 5 km NE could be represented by using either an ordered pair or a vector arrow, as shown below:

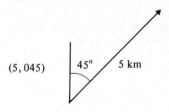

Example 2

Find the distance and direction from his starting position of a man who walks along the bearing vectors (3,090) and (5,045).

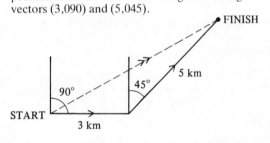

---

14. Make an accurate copy of the drawing in Example 2 to find the distance and direction of the dotted line.

15. A man walks along roads ABCDEF. The bearings of AB, BC, CD, DE, and EF are given by (3,000), (4,045), (2,090), (5,060) and (5,180).
    (a) Make an accurate drawing on squared paper to show this information.
    (b) Find the bearing of F from A by measuring the length and direction of AF.

3.3 Earth distances

Latitude and longitude

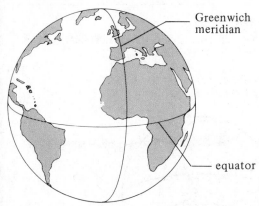

Positions on the Earth are given by the two angles of
latitude and **longitude**.
Latitude gives the position north or south of the
equator. (The equator is at latitude 0°.)
Longitude gives the position east or west of a line called
the Greenwich meridian, which passes through
Greenwich in England. (The Greenwich meridian is at
longitude 0°.)

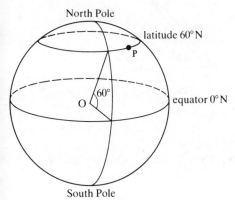

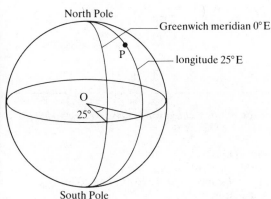

The point P on the diagrams above represents a city. It
lies on a line whose latitude is 60° north of the equator.
It lies on a line whose longitude is 25° east of the
Greenwich meridian. The co-ordinates of P are 60°N,
25°E.

1. (a) Look in your atlas for a map that shows the
         equator. Its latitude is 0°. Find four countries
         that the equator passes through.
    (b) Look for other lines parallel to the equator.
         These are lines of latitude. Find two countries
         that the line 30°N passes through.

2. Say whether each of these is a line of latitude or a
    line of longitude:
    (a) 40°N   (b) 30°W   (c) 50°E   (d) 15°S
    (e) 25°E   (f) 52°S   (g) 23°N   (h) 12°W

3. Find a country that each line of latitude or
    longitude in Question 2 runs through.
    Could you find each line on your map?

4. Use an atlas to find the cities with positions:
    (a) 30°N, 90.1°W
    (b) 43.7°N, 79.4°W
    (c) 43°N, 80°W

5. Which country is found between:
    (a) 10°S and 40°S, 110°E and 155°E
    (b) 49°N and 60°N, 2°E and 8°W
    (c) 36°N and 44°N, 4°E and 10°W
    (d) 19°N and 23°N, 74°W and 85°W?

6. Draw two diagrams to illustrate the position of Q,
    at latitude 25°S, longitude 40°W.

7. (a) What is another way of writing longitude
         180°E?
    (b) What is the latitude of the North Pole?

8. A sphere of clay of radius 10cm has a slice cut off it:

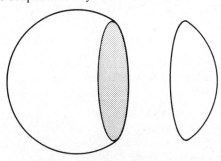

    (a) Will the exposed surface be a circle?
    (b) If the cut is made in a different place, will the
         radius of the circle be different?
    (c) How would you cut the sphere if you wanted
         the largest possible circle?
    (d) What will be the radius of this largest circle,
         and where is its centre?

9. When a circle is drawn on a sphere, it is called a **great circle** if its centre is at the centre of the sphere.
   (a) All lines of longitude are great circles. Are any lines of latitude great circles?
   (b) Draw a diagram to show a great circle which is *not* a line of latitude or longitude.

10. Two pins are stuck in a clay sphere, and joined by a piece of thread.

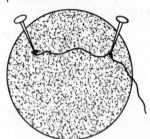

   (a) If the thread is pulled tight, explain why it does not form a straight line but part of a circle.
   (b) Where is the centre of the circle?
   (c) Is the shortest distance between two points on a sphere always along a great circle?

11. A ball is floating in water. When it is lifted out, the edge of the wet area is a circle. How was the ball floating, if the circle is a great circle?

12. An explorer sets out from his camp and walks first 5 km south, then 5 km west and finally 5 km north. Strangely, he finds himself back at his camp site, where a large bear is eating his breakfast.
   (a) Draw a diagram to show where on Earth this could happen.
   (b) What colour was the bear?

Distance along longitudes

All lines of longitude are great circles. The distance between any two points on a line of longitude can easily be found, given the Earth's radius.

Example 1

Find the distance, in km, between X(50°N, 32°E) and Y(20°S, 32°E).

Take the radius of Earth to be 6370 km.
X and Y lie on the line of longitude 32°E.

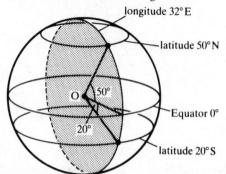

Cutting the Earth along longitude 32° gives the sectional view:

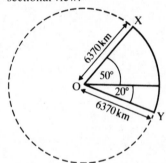

The distance XY is simply the minor arc length XY.

$$\text{Length of arc XY} = \frac{70}{360} \times 2\pi r$$

$$= \frac{70}{360} \times 2 \times \frac{22}{7} \times 6370$$

$$= 7786 \, \text{km}$$

For the rest of this section, where necessary, use 6400 km for the radius of the earth.

13. Find, in km:
   (a) the length of the equator
   (b) the distance from the North Pole to the equator.

14. Find, in km, the distance between:
  (a) (40°S, 37°E) and (10°N, 37°E) along longitude 37°E
  (b) (2°N, 0°) and (3°S, 0°) along the Greenwich meridian
  (c) (0° 140°E) and (0°, 172°W) along the equator.

15. Taking the circumference of the Earth to be 40 000 km, calculate the shortest distance between:
  (a) P (56°S, 35°E) and Q(30°N, 35°E)
  (b) (30°N, 6°W) and the equator
  (c) X (10°N, 15°E) and Y(10°S, 15°E).
  (d) (45°N, 4°E) and the equator.

Example 2

A ship sails 4000 km due north to B from a point A(10°N, 27°W). What is the position of B?
Take the circumference of the Earth to be 40 000 km. A and B lie on the great circle 27°W.

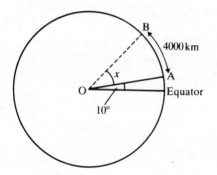

Write AÔB = x
Arc length AB = 4000 km, so

$$4000 = \frac{x}{360} \times \text{circumference}$$

$$4000 = \frac{x}{360} \times 40\,000$$

$$x = \frac{4000 \times 360}{40\,000} = 36°$$

B is at (46°N, 27°W)

---

16. An aeroplane flies due north of X (25°N, 120°E) for 2000 km to a position Y. What is the latitude of Y?

17. A ship sails 15 000 km due west from (0°N, 85°W). What is its new position?
Take the circumference of the Earth to be 40 000 km.

18. From A (15°N, 90°W) a boat sails 8000 km due south to a position B. What is the latitude of B?

Distance along latitudes

Lines of latitude are not great circles. The greater the distance from the equator the smaller is the circle of latitude.

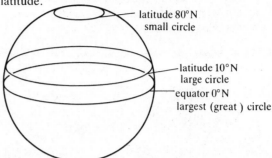

To find the distance between two points along a line of latitude you must first find the radius of the circle of latitude.

Example 3

Find the distance, in kilometres, between A(62°N, 23°E) and B(62°N, 10°W) along latitude 62°N.

Take the Earth's radius to be 6400 km.

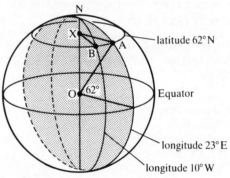

Latitude 62°N is not a great circle.
You must first find its radius. Split the Earth along longitude 23°E through A: the shaded section.

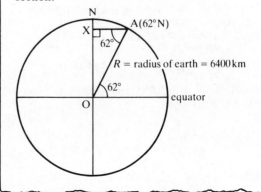

The radius of the latitude is AX.
From the right-angled triangle OAX:
AX = OA cos 62°
   = R cos 62°
   = 6400 × 0.4659
   = 2982 km

To find the distance along 62°N:

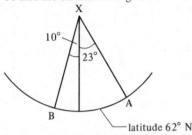

latitude 62° N
Angle at the centre = 10° + 23° = 33°

Arc length AB = $\dfrac{33}{360}$ × 2πr

$= \dfrac{33}{360}$ × 2 π × 2982

≈ 1720 km (3 s.f.)

19. Find the distance, in km, from:
   (a) Moscow (56°N, 38°E) to Edinburgh (56°N, 0°W) along the latitude 56°N.
   (b) Monrovia (6°N, 11°W) to Georgetown (6°N, 58°W) along latitude 6°N.

20. Find the distance between the places (60°S, 27°W) and (60°S, 153°E):
   (a) along latitude 60°S
   (b) across the South Pole.

21. (a) Calculate the radius of latitude 36°N.
   (b) Find the distance along latitude 36°N between Malta (36°N, 14°E) and Gibraltar (36°N, 5°W).

22. Calculate the distance along a line of latitude between:
   (a) Cairo (30°N, 31°E) and New Orleans (30°N, 90°W)
   (b) Vancouver (49°N, 123°W) and Volgograd (49°N, 44°E)
   (c) Krakow (50°N, 20°E) and Krasnokamensk (50°N, 118°E).

23. (a) Calculate the lengths, in kilometres, of a degree of longitude at the equator and a degree of longitude at 60°N.
   (b) What is the distance, in nautical miles, of a degree of longitude at 60°N?

24. Taking the circumference of the equator to be 40 000 km, calculate:
   (a) the length of the Tropic of Cancer (23½°N)
   (b) the distance along latitude 60°S between P (60°S, 10°W) and Q(60°S, 22°E)
   (c) the shortest distance between A(60°N, 45°W) and B(60°N, 135°E).

25. An aeroplane travelling from (80°N, 10°W) to (80°N, 170°E) can either fly over the North Pole, or along latitude 80°N.
   (a) Calculate both distances, in kilometres.
   (b) Is one of these routes along a great circle?

26. Find the distance in kilometres, along a line of latitude, between a point on longitude 10°W and a point on longitude 10°E, if their latitude is:
   (a) 60°N   (b) 30°N   (c) the equator

27. The radius of the moon is approximately 1700 km. Calculate the distance, along latitude 45°N, between two places on the moon whose positions are (45°N, 60°E) and (45°N, 110°W).

28. The radius of Jupiter is 11 times that of Earth. Calculate the length of latitude 60°N on Jupiter.

29. A ship sails 500 km due west from Vancouver (49°N, 123°W). What is its new position?

30. An aeroplane flies 6000 km due east from (36°N, 15°W) to a position Z. What is the longitude of Z?

31. From A (20°N, 25°E) a man drives 1000 km due north to B and then 1000 km due east to C.
   (a) Calculate the positions of B and C.
   (b) What is the shortest distance from C to the North Pole?

3.4 Sines, cosines and tangents in surd form

Angles of 45°

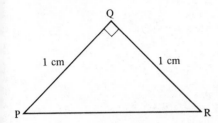

1. (a) Do you agree that PR in the triangle above is √2 cm long?
   (b) What is the size of angle QPR?

2. Using ΔPQR above, write a value for:
   (a) tan 45°   (b) sin 45°   (c) cos 45°

3. Look at the square ABCD on the right.
   (a) Write down the length of AC in square-root form.
   (b) What are the sizes of angles CAB and BCA?

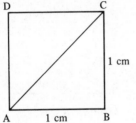

4. For triangle ABC above write down, in square-root form:
   (a) tan 45°   (b) sin 45°   (c) cos 45°

In Questions 2 and 4, you should have found:

$$\tan 45° = 1, \quad \sin 45° = \frac{1}{\sqrt{2}}, \quad \cos 45° = \frac{1}{\sqrt{2}}$$

Sin 45° and cos 45° are written here in square-root form. It is often convenient to leave them in this form, to save time.

5. Using the values given above, write an expression for $(\sin 45°)^2 + (\cos 45°)^2$.
   Show that this is equal to 1.

6. Write down an expression for $\dfrac{\sin 45°}{\cos 45°}$.

   Do you agree that this is equal to tan 45°?

Angles of 30° and 60°

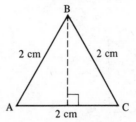   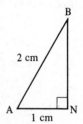

7. Look at triangles ABC and ABN above.
   (a) Explain why angle A is 60° and angle B in triangle ABN is 30°.
   (b) Use Pythagoras' Theorem to show that BN = √3 cm.

8. Using triangle ABN, write down the value of:
   (a) cos 60°   (b) sin 60°   (c) tan 60°
   (d) sin 30°   (e) cos 30°   (f) tan 30°
   (Leave your answers in square-root form.)

You should have found in Question 8 that:

$$\tan 60° = \sqrt{3}, \quad \sin 60° = \frac{\sqrt{3}}{2}, \quad \cos 60° = \frac{1}{2}$$

$$\tan 30° = \frac{1}{\sqrt{3}}, \quad \sin 30° = \frac{1}{2}, \quad \cos 30° = \frac{\sqrt{3}}{2}$$

Note: √2 and √3 are irrational numbers or **surds**. So some of the sines, cosines and tangents above are in **surd form**.

9. Show that $\dfrac{1}{\sqrt{3}}$ can also be written as $\dfrac{\sqrt{3}}{3}$.
   (*Hint:* a multiplication is involved.)

10. Write down an expression for:
    (a) $(\sin 60°)^2 + (\cos 60°)^2$
    (b) $(\sin 30°)^2 + (\cos 30°)^2$
    Show that each of these is equal to 1.

11. Show that:

(a) $\dfrac{\sin 60°}{\cos 60°} = \tan 60°$ (b) $\dfrac{\sin 30°}{\cos 30°} = \tan 30°$

12. Use two or three other values of θ to show that the statement is always true:

(a) $(\sin \theta)^2 + (\cos \theta)^2 = 1$ (b) $\dfrac{\sin \theta}{\cos \theta} = \tan \theta$

13.

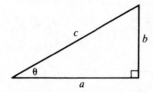

(a) In the triangle above, write down $\sin \theta$, $\cos \theta$ and $\tan \theta$ in terms of a, b and c.

(b) Hence show that: $\dfrac{\sin \theta}{\cos \theta} = \tan \theta$

(c) Use Pythagoras' Theorem to show that:
$$\sin^2 \theta + \cos^2 \theta = 1$$

(Note $(\sin \theta)^2$ is usually written $\sin^2 \theta$)

In Question 13 you proved two important relations namely

[1] $\dfrac{\sin \theta}{\cos \theta} = \tan \theta$ [2] $\sin^2 \theta + \cos^2 \theta = 1$

You can use these two relationships to show the equality of other identities.

Example 1

Prove that $\tan^2 x - \sin^2 x = \tan^2 x \sin^2 x$

L.H.S. $= \tan^2 x - \sin^2 x$

$= \dfrac{\sin^2 x}{\cos^2 x} - \sin^2 x$ $\left(\tan x = \dfrac{\sin x}{\cos x} \right)$

$= \dfrac{\sin^2 x - \sin^2 x \cos^2 x}{\cos^2 x}$

$= \dfrac{\sin^2 x (1 - \cos^2 x)}{\cos^2 x}$

$= \dfrac{\sin^2 x \sin^2 x}{\cos^2 x}$ $(\sin^2 x = 1 - \cos^2 x)$

$= \sin^2 x \tan^2 x$ $\left(\dfrac{\sin x}{\cos x} = \tan x \right)$

$=$ R.H.S

---

14. Prove that:

(a) $\cos^2 x - \sin^2 x = 2 \cos^2 x - 1$

(b) $\tan x + \dfrac{1}{\tan x} = \dfrac{1}{\sin x \cos x}$

(c) $\dfrac{2 \sin x \cos x}{1 + \cos^2 x - \sin^2 x} = \tan x$

(d) $\cos^2 x - \sin^2 x = 1 - 2 \sin^2 x$

(e) $1 + \tan^2 x = \dfrac{1}{1 - \sin^2 x}$

(f) $\dfrac{1 - \tan^2 x}{1 + \tan^2 x} = 2 \cos^2 x - 1$

(g) $\dfrac{\cos^2 x}{\sin x} = \dfrac{1}{\sin x} - \sin x$

(h) $\cos^4 x + \sin^4 x = 1 - 2 \cos^2 x \sin^2 x$

(i) $\cos x + \sin x \tan x = \dfrac{1}{\cos x}$

(j) $\dfrac{2 \sin x \cos x}{\cos^2 x - \sin^2 x} = \dfrac{2 \tan x}{1 - \tan^2 x}$

(k) $\dfrac{1 + \cos x}{1 - \cos x} - \dfrac{1 - \cos x}{1 + \cos x} = \dfrac{4}{\sin x \tan x}$

Example 2

Given $\sin x = \frac{4}{5}$ and x is acute, find without using tables:
(a) $\cos x$ (b) $\tan x$

(a) $\sin^2 x + \cos^2 x = 1$,   so

$\quad (\frac{4}{5})^2 + \cos^2 x = 1$

$\quad\quad\quad \cos^2 x = 1 - \frac{16}{25} = \frac{9}{25}$

$\quad\quad\quad\quad \cos x = \sqrt{\frac{9}{25}} = \frac{3}{5}$

(b) $\tan x = \dfrac{\sin x}{\cos x} = \dfrac{\frac{4}{5}}{\frac{3}{5}} = \frac{4}{3}$

---

15. If x is an acute angle and $\sin x = \frac{3}{5}$, find:
(a) $\cos x$ (b) $\tan x$

16. Given $\sin 60° = \dfrac{\sqrt{3}}{2}$, find:
(a) $\sin 120°$ (b) $\cos 120°$ (c) $\tan 120°$

17. If x is acute and $\tan x = 2$, find:
(a) $\sin x$ $\cos x$

Summary

By the end of this section, these are the things you should know about:

3.1 Lengths and angles in 3-D shapes
(pages 328–330)

How to find lengths in 3-D shapes by using Pythagoras' Theorem.
How to identify and to find the angle between a line and a plane.
e.g.

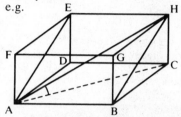

Angle between line AH and plane ABCD is CÂH
How to identify and to find the angle between two planes.

Angle between plane ABCD and plane ABHE is DÂE (or CB̂H)

3.2 Vectors in the real world (pages 331–332)

How to apply vector ideas to simple problems involving velocities and bearings.

3.3 Earth distances (pages 333–336)

What the **latitude** and **longitude** of a place are.
What a **great circle** is.

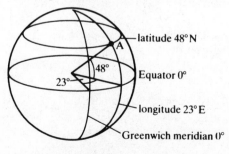

- latitude 48°N
- Equator 0°
- longitude 23°E
- Greenwich meridian 0°

The position of A is (48°N, 23°E).

How to find a distance along a line of longitude.
How to find a distance along a line of latitude.
e.g. The distance between A(48°N, 23°E) and B(48°N, 43°E).

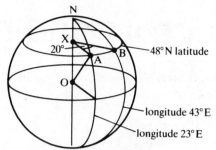

- 48°N latitude
- longitude 43°E
- longitude 23°E

Radius of circle of latitude is AX.
$$AX = OA \cos 48°$$
$$= 6400 \cos 48°$$
$$= 4282 \text{ km}$$

Vertical section

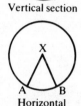

$$\text{Arc AB} = \frac{(43 - 23)}{360} \times 2 \pi \times 4282$$
$$= 1495 \text{ km}$$

Horizontal section

3.4 Sines, cosine and tangents in surd form
(pages 337–338)

You should remember:

$$\sin 30° = \tfrac{1}{2} \qquad \cos 30° = \frac{\sqrt{3}}{2} \qquad \tan 30° = \frac{1}{\sqrt{3}}$$

$$\sin 45° = \frac{1}{\sqrt{2}} \qquad \cos 45° = \frac{1}{\sqrt{2}} \qquad \tan 45° = 1$$

$$\sin 60° = \frac{\sqrt{3}}{2} \qquad \cos 60° = \tfrac{1}{2} \qquad \tan 60° = \sqrt{3}$$

and also that:

$$\tan \theta = \frac{\sin \theta}{\cos \theta} \qquad \sin^2 \theta + \cos^2 \theta = 1$$

You should be able to verify the above results.
How to prove simple identities.
e.g. show that:

$$\frac{\cos x}{\tan x} = \frac{1}{\sin x} - \sin x$$

$$\text{L.H.S.} = \frac{\cos^2 x}{\sin x} \qquad \left(\tan x = \frac{\sin x}{\cos x} \right)$$

$$= \frac{1 - \sin^2 x}{\sin x} \qquad (\cos^2 x = 1 - \sin^2 x)$$

$$= \frac{1}{\sin x} - \sin x = \text{R.H.S.}$$

4 Vectors and matrices 2

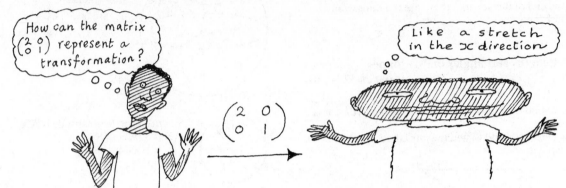

How can the matrix $\begin{pmatrix} 2 & 0 \\ 0 & 1 \end{pmatrix}$ represent a transformation?

Like a stretch in the x direction

$$\begin{pmatrix} 2 & 0 \\ 0 & 1 \end{pmatrix}$$

4.1 The inverse of a matrix

In part 2 you saw how to add, subtract and multiply matrices.
There is no operation of division for matrices. However you can find the **multiplicative inverse** for a matrix.

Recall that for real numbers, 1 is the **identity** under multiplication and that, for example,

$$3 \times \tfrac{1}{3} = 1$$

$\tfrac{1}{3}$ is the multiplicative inverse of 3.
For matrices under multiplication the identity matrix, **I** is given by

$$\mathbf{I} = \begin{pmatrix} 1 & 0 \\ 0 & 1 \end{pmatrix}$$

For any 2×2 matrix, **A**, we are going to look for the inverse matrix **B** such that

$$\mathbf{A} \times \mathbf{B} = \mathbf{I}$$

The inverse of **A** is written $\mathbf{A}^{-1}$

So $$\mathbf{B} = \mathbf{A}^{-1}$$

1. Work out the product $\begin{pmatrix} 7 & 4 \\ 5 & 3 \end{pmatrix}\begin{pmatrix} 3 & -4 \\ -5 & 7 \end{pmatrix}$.

   What matrix is the inverse of $\begin{pmatrix} 7 & 4 \\ 5 & 3 \end{pmatrix}$?

2. Let $\mathbf{A} = \begin{pmatrix} 5 & 7 \\ 2 & 3 \end{pmatrix}$ and $\mathbf{B} = \begin{pmatrix} 3 & -7 \\ -2 & 5 \end{pmatrix}$.
   (a) Work out $\mathbf{A} \times \mathbf{B}$.
   (b) What is the inverse of **B**?
   (c) Write down the matrix $\mathbf{A}^{-1}$.

3. Let $\mathbf{A} = \begin{pmatrix} 7 & 3 \\ 2 & 1 \end{pmatrix}$ and $\mathbf{B} = \begin{pmatrix} 1 & -3 \\ -2 & 7 \end{pmatrix}$.
   (a) Work out $\mathbf{A} \times \mathbf{B}$.

(b) What is the inverse of **A**?
(c) Write down the matrix $\mathbf{B}^{-1}$.

4. Work out the product.
   (a) $\begin{pmatrix} 1 & 2 \\ 5 & 11 \end{pmatrix}\begin{pmatrix} 11 & -2 \\ -5 & 1 \end{pmatrix}$

   (b) $\begin{pmatrix} 3 & 5 \\ 1 & 2 \end{pmatrix}\begin{pmatrix} 2 & -5 \\ -1 & 3 \end{pmatrix}$

   (c) $\begin{pmatrix} 4 & 7 \\ 5 & 9 \end{pmatrix}\begin{pmatrix} 9 & -7 \\ -5 & 4 \end{pmatrix}$

   (d) $\begin{pmatrix} -3 & 8 \\ -2 & 5 \end{pmatrix}\begin{pmatrix} 5 & -8 \\ 2 & -3 \end{pmatrix}$

5. In Question 4 did you obtain the identity matrix in each case? Can you see a pattern for finding the inverse? Write down what you think would be the inverse of $\begin{pmatrix} 4 & 11 \\ 1 & 3 \end{pmatrix}$, and check by multiplication.

Example 1

Find the inverse of $\begin{pmatrix} 3 & 4 \\ 7 & 9 \end{pmatrix}$.

Here is how you do it.
First change over the 3 and the 9:

$$\begin{pmatrix} 3 & \\ & 9 \end{pmatrix} \rightarrow \begin{pmatrix} 9 & \\ & 3 \end{pmatrix}$$

Then change the sign of the 4 and the 7:

$$\begin{pmatrix} & 4 \\ 7 & \end{pmatrix} \rightarrow \begin{pmatrix} & -4 \\ -7 & \end{pmatrix}$$

The inverse is $\begin{pmatrix} 9 & -4 \\ -7 & 3 \end{pmatrix}$.

Check the result!
Unfortunately the steps are not quite so simple for all 2×2 matrices, as you will see later.

6. Let $\mathbf{A} = \begin{pmatrix} 3 & 2 \\ 5 & 4 \end{pmatrix}$ and $\mathbf{B} = \begin{pmatrix} 4 & -2 \\ -5 & 3 \end{pmatrix}$.

(a) Work out the product $\mathbf{A} \times \mathbf{B}$.

(b) Work out the product $\mathbf{B} \times \mathbf{A}$.

(c) Is $\mathbf{B}$ the inverse of $\mathbf{A}$?

(d) Let $\mathbf{C} = \begin{pmatrix} 2 & -1 \\ -2\frac{1}{2} & 1\frac{1}{2} \end{pmatrix}$. Work out $\mathbf{A} \times \mathbf{C}$.

Is $\mathbf{C}$ the inverse of $\mathbf{A}$?

(e) What is the relationship between $\mathbf{C}$ and $\mathbf{B}$?

(f) Write down what you think would be the inverse of $\mathbf{B}$ and check it.

7. To find the inverse of $\begin{pmatrix} 7 & 5 \\ 5 & 4 \end{pmatrix}$, try the matrix

$\begin{pmatrix} 4 & -5 \\ -5 & 7 \end{pmatrix}$. Is it the inverse?

Is the matrix $\frac{1}{3}\begin{pmatrix} 4 & -5 \\ -5 & 7 \end{pmatrix}$ the inverse?

The determinant

Look at these examples:

$\begin{pmatrix} 3 & 4 \\ 2 & 7 \end{pmatrix}\begin{pmatrix} 7 & -4 \\ -2 & 3 \end{pmatrix} = \begin{pmatrix} 13 & 0 \\ 0 & 13 \end{pmatrix} = 13\begin{pmatrix} 1 & 0 \\ 0 & 1 \end{pmatrix}$

$\begin{pmatrix} 4 & 5 \\ 1 & 2 \end{pmatrix}\begin{pmatrix} 2 & -5 \\ -1 & 4 \end{pmatrix} = \begin{pmatrix} 3 & 0 \\ 0 & 3 \end{pmatrix} = 3\begin{pmatrix} 1 & 0 \\ 0 & 1 \end{pmatrix}$

$\begin{pmatrix} 1 & -2 \\ 3 & 8 \end{pmatrix}\begin{pmatrix} 8 & 2 \\ -3 & 1 \end{pmatrix} = \begin{pmatrix} 14 & 0 \\ 0 & 14 \end{pmatrix} = 14\begin{pmatrix} 1 & 0 \\ 0 & 1 \end{pmatrix}$

$\begin{pmatrix} -3 & -2 \\ 1 & 1 \end{pmatrix}\begin{pmatrix} 1 & 2 \\ -1 & -3 \end{pmatrix} = \begin{pmatrix} -1 & 0 \\ 0 & -1 \end{pmatrix} = -1\begin{pmatrix} 1 & 0 \\ 0 & 1 \end{pmatrix}$

In each case, the attempt to find the inverse gives the identity matrix multiplied by a number. This number is the **determinant** of the matrix.

The determinant of $\begin{pmatrix} 3 & 4 \\ 2 & 7 \end{pmatrix}$ is 13.

The determinant can be found quickly from:
$3 \times 7 - 2 \times 4 = 13$

8. Write down statements to show how you would find the determinant for the matrices:

$\begin{pmatrix} 4 & 5 \\ 1 & 2 \end{pmatrix}, \begin{pmatrix} 1 & -2 \\ 3 & 8 \end{pmatrix}$ and $\begin{pmatrix} -3 & -2 \\ 1 & 1 \end{pmatrix}$.

Check your answers with the determinants shown above.

9. Work out the determinant of:

(a) $\begin{pmatrix} 2 & 3 \\ 5 & 9 \end{pmatrix}$ (b) $\begin{pmatrix} 8 & 1 \\ 0 & 2 \end{pmatrix}$ (c) $\begin{pmatrix} -1 & 2 \\ 2 & -3 \end{pmatrix}$

(d) $\begin{pmatrix} 8 & 4 \\ 4 & 2 \end{pmatrix}$ (e) $\begin{pmatrix} 6 & 5 \\ 5 & 4 \end{pmatrix}$ (f) $\begin{pmatrix} 5 & 6 \\ 4 & 5 \end{pmatrix}$

10. Find the value of a if the determinant of $\begin{pmatrix} 6 & 3 \\ 4 & a \end{pmatrix}$

is:

(a) 6   (b) 3   (c) 0   (d) -12

11. Find the value of a if the determinant

of $\begin{pmatrix} a & 8 \\ 2 & a \end{pmatrix}$ is: (a) 0   (b) 9   (c) 84

12. Find the value of a if the determinant of

$\begin{pmatrix} a & 3 \\ 5 & a \end{pmatrix}$ is: (a) 10   (b) 21   (c) 49

Steps for finding the inverse

Let $\mathbf{A} = \begin{pmatrix} a & b \\ c & d \end{pmatrix}$ be any 2×2 matrix.

To find the inverse:

[1] Find the determinant $ad - bc$.

[2] Change $\mathbf{A}$ to $\begin{pmatrix} d & -b \\ -c & a \end{pmatrix}$.

[3] Divide by the determinant.

Example 2

Find $\mathbf{A}^{-1}$ if $\mathbf{A} = \begin{pmatrix} 6 & 2 \\ 10 & 5 \end{pmatrix}$.

Determinant $= 6 \times 5 - 10 \times 2 = 10$

$\mathbf{A}^{-1} = \frac{1}{10}\begin{pmatrix} 5 & -2 \\ -10 & 6 \end{pmatrix} = \begin{pmatrix} 0.5 & -0.2 \\ -1 & 0.6 \end{pmatrix}$

---

13. Find the inverse of:

(a) $\begin{pmatrix} 1 & 2 \\ 1 & 3 \end{pmatrix}$ (b) $\begin{pmatrix} 2 & 1 \\ 5 & 3 \end{pmatrix}$ (c) $\begin{pmatrix} 4 & 1 \\ 10 & 5 \end{pmatrix}$

(d) $\begin{pmatrix} 7 & 3 \\ 4 & 2 \end{pmatrix}$ (e) $\begin{pmatrix} 9 & 3 \\ 5 & 2 \end{pmatrix}$ (f) $\begin{pmatrix} 6 & 2 \\ 4 & 3 \end{pmatrix}$

14. Find the inverse of:

(a) $\begin{pmatrix} 2 & 3 \\ 3 & 4 \end{pmatrix}$ (b) $\begin{pmatrix} 3 & 8 \\ 1 & 2 \end{pmatrix}$ (c) $\begin{pmatrix} 1 & 5 \\ 2 & 5 \end{pmatrix}$

(d) $\begin{pmatrix} 4 & 2 \\ 4 & -3 \end{pmatrix}$ (e) $\begin{pmatrix} -1 & 1 \\ 4 & 0 \end{pmatrix}$ (f) $\begin{pmatrix} 2 & 0 \\ 1 & -1 \end{pmatrix}$

15. Check your answers to Questions 13 and 14 by multiplying each original matrix by its inverse. Is your answer always the identity matrix?

16. (a) What is the determinant of $\begin{pmatrix} 4 & 2 \\ 6 & 3 \end{pmatrix}$?

(b) Find the product $\begin{pmatrix} 4 & 2 \\ 6 & 3 \end{pmatrix}\begin{pmatrix} 3 & -2 \\ -6 & 4 \end{pmatrix}$.

If the determinant of a matrix is zero, the matrix has no inverse. Such a matrix is called a **singular matrix**.

The matrix $\begin{pmatrix} 4 & 2 \\ 6 & 3 \end{pmatrix}$ of Question 16 is a singular matrix.

17. Find whether the matrix is singular. If it is non-singular, find its inverse.

(a) $\begin{pmatrix} 6 & 24 \\ 2 & 8 \end{pmatrix}$ (b) $\begin{pmatrix} 1 & -1 \\ -1 & 1 \end{pmatrix}$ (c) $\begin{pmatrix} 1 & 1 \\ -1 & 1 \end{pmatrix}$

Further exercises

18. Find, if possible, the inverse of:

(a) $\begin{pmatrix} 5 & 7 \\ 2 & 3 \end{pmatrix}$ (b) $\begin{pmatrix} 4 & 2 \\ 5 & 3 \end{pmatrix}$ (c) $\begin{pmatrix} -2 & 3 \\ -3 & 4 \end{pmatrix}$

(d) $\begin{pmatrix} 4 & 2 \\ 10 & 5 \end{pmatrix}$ (e) $\begin{pmatrix} 2 & -1 \\ -2 & 0 \end{pmatrix}$ (f) $\begin{pmatrix} 3 & 9 \\ 2 & -6 \end{pmatrix}$

19. $\mathbf{P} = \begin{pmatrix} 5 & -9 \\ 4 & -8 \end{pmatrix}$, $\mathbf{Q} = \begin{pmatrix} 8 & -9 \\ 4 & -5 \end{pmatrix}$.

Calculate $\mathbf{PQ}$ and use your answer to find $\mathbf{P}^{-1}$ and $\mathbf{Q}^{-1}$.

20. $\mathbf{X} = \begin{pmatrix} 5 & 2 \\ 3 & 1 \end{pmatrix}$, $\mathbf{Y} = \begin{pmatrix} 1 & -2 \\ -3 & 5 \end{pmatrix}$.

Calculate $\mathbf{XY}$ and hence write down the matrix $\mathbf{X}^{-1}$.

21. $\mathbf{A} = \begin{pmatrix} 0 & -1 \\ 2 & 8 \end{pmatrix}$, $\mathbf{B} = \begin{pmatrix} 5 & -3 \\ 2 & -1 \end{pmatrix}$.

(a) Find $\mathbf{A}^{-1}$ and $\mathbf{B}^{-1}$.
(b) Calculate the matrices:
  (i) $\mathbf{AB}$ (ii) $(\mathbf{AB})^{-1}$ (iii) $\mathbf{B}^{-1}\mathbf{A}^{-1}$
(c) What is significant about your answers to (b)?

22. $\mathbf{U} = \begin{pmatrix} 2 & 4 \\ 3 & 5 \end{pmatrix}$, $\mathbf{V} = \begin{pmatrix} 1 & 0 \\ 7 & 3 \end{pmatrix}$.

(a) Write down $\mathbf{U}^{-1}$ and $\mathbf{V}^{-1}$.
(b) Work out the products:
  (i) $\mathbf{UV}$ (ii) $\mathbf{U}^{-1}\mathbf{V}^{-1}$ (iii) $\mathbf{V}^{-1}\mathbf{U}^{-1}$
(c) Calculate the inverse of $\mathbf{UV}$.
(d) Which of these is the true statement?
  (i) $(\mathbf{UV})^{-1} = \mathbf{U}^{-1}\mathbf{V}^{-1}$
  (ii) $(\mathbf{UV})^{-1} = \mathbf{V}^{-1}\mathbf{U}^{-1}$

23. $\mathbf{P} = \begin{pmatrix} 4 & -5 \\ 3 & -4 \end{pmatrix}$.

Find $\mathbf{P}^2$ and hence write down $\mathbf{P}^{-1}$.
Use your answer to write down the matrix:
(a) $\mathbf{P}^4$ (b) $\mathbf{P}^5$

24. $\mathbf{Q} = \begin{pmatrix} -2 & 0 \\ 4 & 2 \end{pmatrix}$. Find $\mathbf{Q}^2$ and hence $\mathbf{Q}^{-1}$.

Use your answers to calculate $\mathbf{Q}^4$ and $\mathbf{Q}^5$.

25. $\mathbf{R} = \begin{pmatrix} 5 & -8 \\ 3 & -5 \end{pmatrix}$. Find $\mathbf{R}^{-1}$.

Use your result to write down:
(a) $\mathbf{R}^2$ (b) $\mathbf{R}^3$ (c) $\mathbf{R}^5$

26. $\mathbf{S} = \begin{pmatrix} -6 & 8 \\ -4 & 6 \end{pmatrix}$. Find $\mathbf{S}^{-1}$.

Use your result to write down:
(a) $\mathbf{S}^2$ (b) $\mathbf{S}^3$ (c) $\mathbf{S}^6$

27. $\mathbf{T} = \begin{pmatrix} k & 1-k \\ 1+k & -k \end{pmatrix}$

(a) Work out $\mathbf{T}^2$.
(b) Write down $\mathbf{T}^{-1}$.
(c) What is $\mathbf{T}^n$ if n is odd?

28. $\mathbf{A} = \begin{pmatrix} 0 & -1 \\ 1 & 0 \end{pmatrix}$. Find $\mathbf{A}^2$, $\mathbf{A}^3$ and $\mathbf{A}^4$.

Hence write down the inverses of $\mathbf{A}$, $\mathbf{A}^2$ and $\mathbf{A}^3$.

29. $\mathbf{R} = \begin{pmatrix} \frac{1}{2} & -\frac{\sqrt{3}}{2} \\ \frac{\sqrt{3}}{2} & \frac{1}{2} \end{pmatrix}$. Find:

(a) the determinant of $\mathbf{R}$
(b) $\mathbf{R}^{-1}$ (c) $\mathbf{R}^2$ (d) $\mathbf{R}^3$ (e) $\mathbf{R}^6$
How many different matrices can be found from powers of $\mathbf{R}$?

30. $\mathbf{A} = \begin{pmatrix} 1 & 1 \\ k & k^3 \end{pmatrix}$. If $\mathbf{A}$ is singular, show that k can have one of three values.

31. If $\mathbf{X} = \begin{pmatrix} 4 & 3 \\ 5 & 2 \end{pmatrix}$ and $\mathbf{I} = \begin{pmatrix} 1 & 0 \\ 0 & 1 \end{pmatrix}$:

(a) find $\mathbf{X}^2$
(b) find $\mathbf{X}^2 - 6\mathbf{X} - 7\mathbf{I}$.

32. $\mathbf{X} = \begin{pmatrix} 1 & 2 \\ -1 & 3 \end{pmatrix}$ and $\mathbf{I} = \begin{pmatrix} 1 & 0 \\ 0 & 1 \end{pmatrix}$.

(a) Find $\mathbf{X}^2$.
(b) Show that $\mathbf{X}^2 - 4\mathbf{X} + 5\mathbf{I} = \mathbf{O}$.
(c) Use $\mathbf{X}^3 - 4\mathbf{X}^2 + 5\mathbf{X} = \mathbf{O}$ to calculate $\mathbf{X}^3$.
(d) Check your answers for $\mathbf{X}^3$ by direct multiplication.

33. $\mathbf{P} = \begin{pmatrix} 0 & 2 \\ 2 & 0 \end{pmatrix}$. Find $\mathbf{P}^2$, $\mathbf{P}^3$ and $\mathbf{P}^4$.

Use your answer to write down:
(a) $\mathbf{P}^5$ (b) $\mathbf{P}^6$

34. Let $\mathbf{X} = \begin{pmatrix} 0 & 1 \\ 1 & 0 \end{pmatrix}$, $\mathbf{Y} = \begin{pmatrix} 0 & -1 \\ -1 & 0 \end{pmatrix}$ and $\mathbf{R} = \mathbf{XY}$.

(a) Find the matrix $\mathbf{R}$ and work out $\mathbf{YX}$.
(b) Find $\mathbf{X}^2$, $\mathbf{Y}^2$ and $\mathbf{R}^2$.
(c) Find $\mathbf{XR}$, $\mathbf{YR}$, $\mathbf{RX}$ and $\mathbf{RY}$ and make up a table of results like this:

$\times$	X	Y	R
X			
Y			
R			

4.2 Simultaneous equations

1. Write as a column matrix:

   (a) $\begin{pmatrix} 2 & 1 \\ 5 & 3 \end{pmatrix}\begin{pmatrix} x \\ y \end{pmatrix}$ (b) $\begin{pmatrix} 4 & 1 \\ 7 & -2 \end{pmatrix}\begin{pmatrix} x \\ y \end{pmatrix}$

2. Complete the statements:

   (a) $\begin{pmatrix} 5x & -y \\ 2x & +y \end{pmatrix} = \begin{pmatrix} 5 & -1 \\ & \end{pmatrix}\begin{pmatrix} x \\ y \end{pmatrix}$

   (b) $\begin{pmatrix} 2x & \\ 3x & -y \end{pmatrix} = \begin{pmatrix} 2 & 0 \\ & \end{pmatrix}\begin{pmatrix} x \\ y \end{pmatrix}$

3. These two column matrices are equal:
   $$\begin{pmatrix} 2x & +3y \\ 5x & -2y \end{pmatrix} = \begin{pmatrix} 5 \\ 3 \end{pmatrix}$$

   What is the value of:
   (a) $2x + 3y$ (b) $5x - 2y$?

4. $\begin{pmatrix} 5 & -1 \\ 7 & 3 \end{pmatrix}\begin{pmatrix} x \\ y \end{pmatrix} = \begin{pmatrix} 4 \\ 10 \end{pmatrix}$

   Multiply out the left side of the equation.
   Write down the value of:
   (a) $7x + 3y$ (b) $5x - y$

5. $4x + 3y = 7$
   $-7x - 2y = -9$
   Rewrite these equations in matrix form by completing:
   $$\begin{pmatrix} & \\ -7 & -2 \end{pmatrix}\begin{pmatrix} x \\ y \end{pmatrix} = \begin{pmatrix} \\ \end{pmatrix}$$

6. Write down two equations from:
   $$\begin{pmatrix} 2 & 1 \\ 3 & -1 \end{pmatrix}\begin{pmatrix} x \\ y \end{pmatrix} = \begin{pmatrix} 4 \\ 7 \end{pmatrix}$$

7. Write down two equations from:
   $$\begin{pmatrix} 3 & 0 \\ 0 & 4 \end{pmatrix}\begin{pmatrix} x \\ y \end{pmatrix} = \begin{pmatrix} 3 \\ 8 \end{pmatrix}$$
   What are the values of x and y?

8. Write down two equations from:
   $$\begin{pmatrix} 0 & 4 \\ 2 & 0 \end{pmatrix}\begin{pmatrix} x \\ y \end{pmatrix} = \begin{pmatrix} 4 \\ 4 \end{pmatrix}$$
   What are the values of x and y?

9. Find x and y if:
   $$\begin{pmatrix} 6 & 0 \\ 1 & 1 \end{pmatrix}\begin{pmatrix} x \\ y \end{pmatrix} = \begin{pmatrix} 12 \\ 3 \end{pmatrix}$$

10. Find x and y if:
    $$\begin{pmatrix} 1 & 1 \\ 0 & 3 \end{pmatrix}\begin{pmatrix} x \\ y \end{pmatrix} = \begin{pmatrix} 4 \\ 9 \end{pmatrix}$$

Example 1

Solve the equations for x and y:
$$2x + y = 1$$
$$5x + 3y = -1$$

First write the equations in matrix form as:

$$\begin{pmatrix} 2 & 1 \\ 5 & 3 \end{pmatrix}\begin{pmatrix} x \\ y \end{pmatrix} = \begin{pmatrix} 1 \\ -1 \end{pmatrix}$$

This is how you find the values of x and y that fit both equations:

The inverse of $\begin{pmatrix} 2 & 1 \\ 5 & 3 \end{pmatrix}$ is $\begin{pmatrix} 3 & -1 \\ -5 & 2 \end{pmatrix} \div 1$

$$= \begin{pmatrix} 3 & -1 \\ -5 & 2 \end{pmatrix}$$

Pre-multiply both sides by the inverse:
$$\begin{pmatrix} 3 & -1 \\ -5 & 2 \end{pmatrix}\begin{pmatrix} 2 & 1 \\ 5 & 3 \end{pmatrix}\begin{pmatrix} x \\ y \end{pmatrix} = \begin{pmatrix} 3 & -1 \\ -5 & 2 \end{pmatrix}\begin{pmatrix} 1 \\ -1 \end{pmatrix}$$

$$\begin{pmatrix} 1 & 0 \\ 0 & 1 \end{pmatrix}\begin{pmatrix} x \\ y \end{pmatrix} = \begin{pmatrix} 4 \\ -7 \end{pmatrix}$$

Multiplying the first two matrices gives:
$$\begin{pmatrix} x \\ y \end{pmatrix} = \begin{pmatrix} 4 \\ -7 \end{pmatrix}$$

So $x = 4$, $y = -7$

---

11. Write down the pair of equations given by the matrix equation: $\begin{pmatrix} 2 & 1 \\ 1 & 1 \end{pmatrix}\begin{pmatrix} x \\ y \end{pmatrix} = \begin{pmatrix} 7 \\ 3 \end{pmatrix}$.

    Multiply both sides of the matrix equation by $\begin{pmatrix} 1 & -1 \\ -1 & 2 \end{pmatrix}$ and find x and y.

12. Write in matrix form the pair of equations:
    $$2x + y = 1$$
    $$5x + 3y = 3$$
    Multiply both sides by $\begin{pmatrix} 3 & -1 \\ -5 & 2 \end{pmatrix}$ and find x and y.

13. Use matrix methods to find x and y:

    (a) $\begin{cases} 3x - 2y = 2 \\ 2x - y = 1 \end{cases}$ (b) $\begin{cases} x + 3y = 4 \\ 2x + 7y = 13 \end{cases}$

    (c) $\begin{cases} 5x + 6y = -1 \\ 4x + 5y = -1 \end{cases}$ (d) $\begin{cases} 7x + 4y = 29 \\ 5x + 3y = 21 \end{cases}$

14. Use matrix methods to find x and y:

    (a) $\begin{cases} 11x - 3y = 1 \\ 4x - y = 1 \end{cases}$ (b) $\begin{cases} 11x - 3y = 3 \\ 4x - y = 2 \end{cases}$

    (c) $\begin{cases} 11x - 3y = 5 \\ 4x - y = 0 \end{cases}$ (d) $\begin{cases} 11x - 3y = 8 \\ 4x - y = 3 \end{cases}$

Example 2

Solve for x and y:
$$2x - y = -2$$
$$x + 2y = 3$$

Write the simultaneous equations in matrix form:

$$\begin{pmatrix} 2 & -1 \\ 1 & 2 \end{pmatrix} \begin{pmatrix} x \\ y \end{pmatrix} = \begin{pmatrix} -2 \\ 3 \end{pmatrix}$$

Pre-multiply both sides of the equation by the inverse:

$$\tfrac{1}{5}\begin{pmatrix} 2 & 1 \\ -1 & 2 \end{pmatrix} \begin{pmatrix} 2 & -1 \\ 1 & 2 \end{pmatrix} \begin{pmatrix} x \\ y \end{pmatrix} = \tfrac{1}{5}\begin{pmatrix} 2 & 1 \\ -1 & 2 \end{pmatrix} \begin{pmatrix} -2 \\ 3 \end{pmatrix}$$

$$\tfrac{1}{5}\begin{pmatrix} 5 & 0 \\ 0 & 5 \end{pmatrix} \begin{pmatrix} x \\ y \end{pmatrix} = \tfrac{1}{5}\begin{pmatrix} -1 \\ 8 \end{pmatrix}$$

$$\begin{pmatrix} x \\ y \end{pmatrix} = \tfrac{1}{5}\begin{pmatrix} -1 \\ 8 \end{pmatrix}$$

So $x = -\tfrac{1}{5}$, $y = \tfrac{8}{5}$

15. Use matrix methods to solve for x and y:

(a) $\begin{cases} 7x + 3y = -3 \\ 2x + y = 2 \end{cases}$ (b) $\begin{cases} 2x - y = -2 \\ x + 2y = 3 \end{cases}$

(c) $\begin{cases} 2x + y = 2 \\ 7x + 4y = 3 \end{cases}$ (d) $\begin{cases} 4x - 2y = 3 \\ 3x + y = -2 \end{cases}$

16. Use matrix methods to solve for x and y:

(a) $\begin{cases} 2x + y = 1 \\ 5x + y = 2 \end{cases}$ (b) $\begin{cases} 5x - 2y = 1 \\ 2x + y = 3 \end{cases}$

(c) $\begin{cases} x + 3y = 2 \\ 2x - 4y = 0 \end{cases}$ (d) $\begin{cases} 4x + 3y = 3 \\ 3x + 2y = 1 \end{cases}$

17. Solve, using any method:

(a) $\begin{cases} x - 3y = -1 \\ x + y = 3 \end{cases}$ (b) $\begin{cases} 4x + 3y = 3 \\ 5x - 5y = 1 \end{cases}$

(c) $\begin{cases} 8x - 5y = 2 \\ 7x - 3y = -1 \end{cases}$ (d) $\begin{cases} 11x + 9y = 1 \\ -5x + 6y = -61 \end{cases}$

18. Solve, using any method:

(a) $\begin{cases} x - 2y = 6 \\ 3x + 2y = 10 \end{cases}$ (b) $\begin{cases} 5x + y = 8 \\ 4x - 2y = 5 \end{cases}$

(c) $\begin{cases} 5x + 8y = 1 \\ 3x + 7y = 5 \end{cases}$ (d) $\begin{cases} 4x - 9y = -2 \\ 8x + 15y = 7 \end{cases}$

19. Use matrix methods to show that the solution set of:
$$\begin{cases} x + 2y = 6 \\ 2x + 3y = k \end{cases}$$
is $\{(x, y) : x = 2k - 18, y = 12 - k\}$.
Find the particular solution when $k = 7$ and check in the original equations.

20. Use matrix methods to find the solution set of:
$$\begin{cases} 3x - 2y = 5 \\ x + y = k \end{cases}$$
where k is any number.
Find the particular solutions for:
(a) $k = 0$ (b) $k = 5$ (c) $k = 15$

Example 3

Solve for x and y:
$$\begin{cases} 4x - 2y = 4 \\ x + 7y = -2 \end{cases}$$

Without finding the determinant, you can proceed like this:

$$\begin{pmatrix} 4 & -2 \\ 1 & 7 \end{pmatrix} \begin{pmatrix} x \\ y \end{pmatrix} = \begin{pmatrix} 4 \\ -2 \end{pmatrix}$$

$$\begin{pmatrix} 7 & 2 \\ -1 & 4 \end{pmatrix} \begin{pmatrix} 4 & -2 \\ 1 & 7 \end{pmatrix} \begin{pmatrix} x \\ y \end{pmatrix} = \begin{pmatrix} 7 & 2 \\ -1 & 4 \end{pmatrix} \begin{pmatrix} 4 \\ -2 \end{pmatrix}$$

$$\begin{pmatrix} 30 & 0 \\ 0 & 30 \end{pmatrix} \begin{pmatrix} x \\ y \end{pmatrix} = \begin{pmatrix} 24 \\ -12 \end{pmatrix}$$

$$30x = 24 \qquad 30y = -12$$
$$x = \tfrac{4}{5} \qquad y = -\tfrac{2}{5}$$

Note that the determinant, which is 30, appears in the working.

21. Use the method of Example 3 to solve for x and y:

(a) $\begin{cases} 3x + 11y = 14 \\ x - 2y = -1 \end{cases}$ (b) $\begin{cases} x + 3y = 14 \\ 4x + y = 23 \end{cases}$

(c) $\begin{cases} 2x + 5y = 9 \\ x - 2y = -3 \end{cases}$ (d) $\begin{cases} 2x + 3y = 8 \\ 6x - 7y = 0 \end{cases}$

22. Solve for x and y:

(a) $\begin{cases} 2x - 3y = 7 \\ x + y = 1 \end{cases}$ (b) $\begin{cases} x + 3y = 30 \\ 3x + 2y = 13 \end{cases}$

(c) $\begin{cases} 4x + 5y = 1.8 \\ x - y = 0 \end{cases}$ (d) $\begin{cases} 7x + 3y = 15 \\ 3x + 4y = 1 \end{cases}$

23. Solve for x and y:

(a) $\begin{cases} 8x - 7y = -12 \\ 8x + 3y = 8 \end{cases}$ (b) $\begin{cases} 5x + 3y = 2 \\ 25x - 12y = 1 \end{cases}$

(c) $\begin{cases} x - 3y = 1 \\ 2x - 5y = 1.7 \end{cases}$ (d) $\begin{cases} 4x - y = -22 \\ 7x + 11y = 38 \end{cases}$

24. Show that the above method does not work if you attempt to solve:
$$\begin{cases} x + 2y = 3 \\ 2x + 4y = 1 \end{cases}$$

Singular matrices

25. (a) What is special about the matrix $\begin{pmatrix} 4 & 6 \\ 6 & 9 \end{pmatrix}$?

(b) Say why matrix methods cannot be used to solve:
$$\begin{cases} 4x + 6y = 24 \\ 6x + 9y = 18 \end{cases}$$

(c) On the same axes, draw graphs of the lines represented by the equations.

(d) How can you tell from the graphs that there are no solutions?

26. This diagram shows the lines with equations:
$$\begin{cases} x - 2y = 1 \\ 2x - 4y = -1 \end{cases}$$

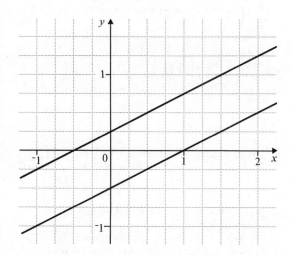

(a) Copy the diagram, and label each line with its corresponding equation.

(b) Write the pair of simultaneous equations in matrix form.

(c) What is the determinant of the matrix $\begin{pmatrix} 1 & -2 \\ 2 & -4 \end{pmatrix}$?

(d) Do you think that the answer to (c) means that the lines are parallel?

27. For each pair of equations:
(a) write them in matrix form
(b) find the determinant of the matrix
(c) find x and y if the matrix is not singular.

   (i) $\begin{cases} 2x - y = 5 \\ 6x - 3y = 10 \end{cases}$ (ii) $\begin{cases} x + y = 1 \\ x - y = 11 \end{cases}$

   (iii) $\begin{cases} 7x - 7y = 32 \\ x + 2y = 8 \end{cases}$ (iv) $\begin{cases} -2x - 6y = 5 \\ 3x + 9y = 1 \end{cases}$

28. For the equation $3x - 2y = 6$:
(a) show that $x = \frac{4}{3}$, $y = -1$ belongs to the solution set

(b) write down two other members of the solution set

(c) show that these values also satisfy the equation $6x - 4y = 12$.

(d) write down three solutions for the pair of simultaneous equations:
$$\begin{cases} 3x - 2y = 6 \\ 6x - 4y = 12 \end{cases}$$

29. The equation in Question 28 can be written as:
$$\begin{pmatrix} 3 & -2 \\ 6 & -4 \end{pmatrix} \begin{pmatrix} x \\ y \end{pmatrix} = \begin{pmatrix} 6 \\ 12 \end{pmatrix}$$

(a) Why can you not use matrix methods to solve the equations?

(b) What can you say about the graphs of the two equations?

30. Find values of x and y to show that there are solutions to the equation:
$$\begin{pmatrix} -1 & -3 \\ 2 & 6 \end{pmatrix} \begin{pmatrix} x \\ y \end{pmatrix} = \begin{pmatrix} -1 \\ 2 \end{pmatrix}.$$

What can you say about the graphs of the lines represented by the equations $-x - 3y = -1$ and $2x + 6y = 2$?

Summary

When solving a pair of simultaneous equations, first check the determinant. If the determinant is zero, the matrix is singular. Then check the lines to see if there are solutions. The results are:

Matrix	Lines	Solution
Non-singular	Intersect	One
Singular	Parallel	None
	Same line	Many

31. Find the value of a for which there is no solution to:
$$\begin{cases} 4x + 2y = 3 \\ 3x + ay = 1 \end{cases}$$

32. Find the value of k which gives solutions for:
$$\begin{cases} 8x - 4y = 12 \\ 6x - 3y = k \end{cases}$$

4.3 Transformation matrices

A matrix can be used to represent a transformation. The unit square in the diagram has vertices at $(0, 0)$, $(1, 0)$, $(1, 1)$, $(0,1)$.

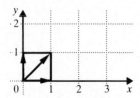

The position vectors of the unit square are:
$$\begin{pmatrix} 0 \\ 0 \end{pmatrix}, \begin{pmatrix} 1 \\ 0 \end{pmatrix}, \begin{pmatrix} 1 \\ 1 \end{pmatrix} \text{ and } \begin{pmatrix} 0 \\ 1 \end{pmatrix}$$
What happens if you multiply each position vector by

the matrix $\begin{pmatrix} 2 & 0 \\ 0 & 1 \end{pmatrix}$?

$$\begin{pmatrix} 2 & 0 \\ 0 & 1 \end{pmatrix}\begin{pmatrix} 0 \\ 0 \end{pmatrix} = \begin{pmatrix} 0 \\ 0 \end{pmatrix} \qquad \begin{pmatrix} 2 & 0 \\ 0 & 1 \end{pmatrix}\begin{pmatrix} 1 \\ 0 \end{pmatrix} = \begin{pmatrix} 2 \\ 0 \end{pmatrix}$$

$$\begin{pmatrix} 2 & 0 \\ 0 & 1 \end{pmatrix}\begin{pmatrix} 1 \\ 1 \end{pmatrix} = \begin{pmatrix} 2 \\ 1 \end{pmatrix} \qquad \begin{pmatrix} 2 & 0 \\ 0 & 1 \end{pmatrix}\begin{pmatrix} 0 \\ 1 \end{pmatrix} = \begin{pmatrix} 0 \\ 1 \end{pmatrix}$$

So the effect of the matrix is to map:

$(0, 0) \rightarrow (0, 0)$	$(1, 0) \rightarrow (2, 0)$
$(1, 1) \rightarrow (2, 1)$	$(0, 1) \rightarrow (0, 1)$

The image of the square is:

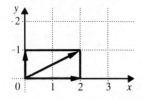

The matrix $\begin{pmatrix} 2 & 0 \\ 0 & 1 \end{pmatrix}$ has transformed the unit square into a rectangle.

The transformation represented by the matrix $\begin{pmatrix} 2 & 0 \\ 0 & 1 \end{pmatrix}$ is a **stretch** in the x direction.
The y co-ordinates have not changed. If (x, y) is any point of the plane, the matrix maps it to $(2x, y)$.

1. Copy the square at the top of the column on the left and draw its image using the transformation matrix:
   (a) $\begin{pmatrix} 1 & 0 \\ 0 & 2 \end{pmatrix}$ (b) $\begin{pmatrix} 0 & 1 \\ 1 & 0 \end{pmatrix}$ (c) $\begin{pmatrix} 2 & 0 \\ 0 & 2 \end{pmatrix}$
   In each case describe the transformation.

2. Draw the quadrilateral with vertices $(0, -1)$, $(2, 0)$, $(2, 2)$, $(0, 3)$.
   Now draw its image using the matrix $\begin{pmatrix} 0 & 1 \\ -1 & 0 \end{pmatrix}$
   How could you describe the transformation?

3. Use the quadrilateral of Question 2 and transform it using the matrix $\begin{pmatrix} 1 & 1 \\ 0 & 1 \end{pmatrix}$.
   Describe the transformation.

4. The matrix $\begin{pmatrix} 3 & 0 \\ 0 & 1 \end{pmatrix}$ represents a stretch in the x direction by a factor 3. Do you agree?
   Write down the matrix that represents a stretch in the y direction by a factor 3.
   Test your answer by transforming the quadrilateral of Question 2.

5. A transformation maps every point (x, y) to $(2x, 3y)$. Find the elements of the matrix of the transformation:
   $$\begin{pmatrix} & \\ & \end{pmatrix}\begin{pmatrix} x \\ y \end{pmatrix} = \begin{pmatrix} 2x \\ 3y \end{pmatrix}$$

6. Use the square with vertices $(0, 0)$, $(1, 0)$, $(1, 1)$, $(0, 1)$ to illustrate a transformation using the matrix $\begin{pmatrix} 3 & 1 \\ 2 & 4 \end{pmatrix}$.
   (a) What is the area of: (i) the square (ii) its image?
   (b) What is the determinant of the matrix?
   (c) Can you see a connection between your answers for (a) and (b)?

7. The matrix $\begin{pmatrix} -2 & 0 \\ 0 & 1 \end{pmatrix}$ is used to transform the triangle $(2, 0)$, $(4, 2)$, $(3, 3)$.
   (a) By what factor does the area of the triangle increase?
   (b) What is the value of the determinant of the matrix?
   (c) What does the negative value of the determinant show?

8. Repeat Question 7 using $\begin{pmatrix} 1 & 0 \\ 0 & -2 \end{pmatrix}$.

9. A right-angled isosceles triangle has vertices $(1, 0)$, $(2, 0)$, $(1, 1)$. Find whether its image is right-angled or isosceles, after a transformation using:
   (a) $\begin{pmatrix} 2 & 0 \\ 0 & 1 \end{pmatrix}$ (b) $\begin{pmatrix} 1 & 0 \\ 0 & 2 \end{pmatrix}$ (c) $\begin{pmatrix} 2 & 0 \\ 0 & 2 \end{pmatrix}$

Enlargement

The unit square has vertices $(0, 0), (1, 0), (1, 1), (0, 1)$.

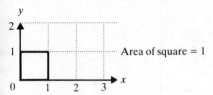

Area of square = 1

The matrix $\begin{pmatrix} 3 & 0 \\ 0 & 1 \end{pmatrix}$ represents a stretch in the x-direction.

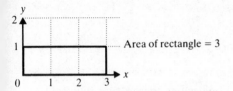

Area of rectangle = 3

The determinant of $\begin{pmatrix} 3 & 0 \\ 0 & 1 \end{pmatrix} = 3$

Notice that:

area of image = determinant × area of object

The matrix $\begin{pmatrix} 1 & 0 \\ 0 & 2 \end{pmatrix}$ represents a stretch in the y-direction.

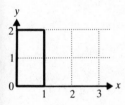

The determinant of $\begin{pmatrix} 1 & 0 \\ 0 & 2 \end{pmatrix} = 2$, so the area of the image is twice the area of the original square.

The matrix $\begin{pmatrix} 3 & 0 \\ 0 & 2 \end{pmatrix}$ represents a **two-way stretch.**

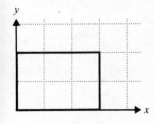

The determinant of $\begin{pmatrix} 3 & 0 \\ 0 & 2 \end{pmatrix} = 6$, so the area of the image is six times the area of the original square.

A two-way stretch with the same stretch in each direction is an **enlargement**.

For example, the matrix $\begin{pmatrix} 2 & 0 \\ 0 & 2 \end{pmatrix}$ represents an enlargement with scale factor 2.

10. Use the matrix $\begin{pmatrix} 2 & 0 \\ 0 & 2 \end{pmatrix}$ to transform a triangle with vertices at $(0, 0), (2, 1), (1, 3)$.
Draw the triangle and its enlargement.

11. Draw a diagram of the quadrilateral with vertices at $(0, 3), (6, 3), (3, 9), (0, 6)$.
Now draw its image using the matrix $\begin{pmatrix} \frac{1}{3} & 0 \\ 0 & \frac{1}{3} \end{pmatrix}$.
Is the second quadrilateral an enlargement of the first?
What is the scale factor of the enlargement?

12. Use the enlargement matrix $\begin{pmatrix} 4 & 0 \\ 0 & 4 \end{pmatrix}$ to find the image of the triangle $(0, -2), (-3, 1), (1, 1)$.
Use the matrix $\begin{pmatrix} \frac{1}{4} & 0 \\ 0 & \frac{1}{4} \end{pmatrix}$ to transform the image.
What do you notice?
What is the inverse of $\begin{pmatrix} 4 & 0 \\ 0 & 4 \end{pmatrix}$?

13. The diagram shows a transformation of the triangle PQR to KLM:

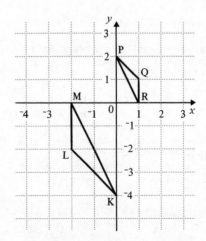

(a) What is the scale factor of the enlargement of PQR to KLM?
(b) What is the scale factor of the enlargement of KLM to PQR?
(c) Write down the matrix for each part (a) and (b).

Reflection

In the diagram, triangle ABC is reflected in the y-axis to A′B′C′.

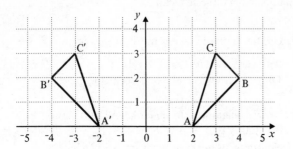

The position vectors of the vertices are mapped as:

$$\binom{2}{0} \to \binom{-2}{0} \qquad \binom{4}{2} \to \binom{-4}{2} \qquad \binom{3}{3} \to \binom{-3}{3}$$

The matrix for this reflection is $\begin{pmatrix} -1 & 0 \\ 0 & 1 \end{pmatrix}$.

For any point (x, y), the image for a reflection in the y-axis is found by:

$$\begin{pmatrix} -1 & 0 \\ 0 & 1 \end{pmatrix} \begin{pmatrix} x \\ y \end{pmatrix} = \begin{pmatrix} -x \\ y \end{pmatrix}.$$

14. (a) Find the image of triangle ABC above, using
the matrix $\begin{pmatrix} 1 & 0 \\ 0 & -1 \end{pmatrix}$.
Plot the image on graph paper.
(b) Is the transformation a reflection? In which axis?
(c) Show how you would find the image, for a reflection in the x-axis, of any point (x, y).

15. The pentagon with vertices at $(0, 1)$, $(1, 2)$, $(0, 3)$, $(-1, 2)$ and $(-1, 1)$ is transformed by a reflection in the y-axis.
(a) What is the transforming matrix?
(b) Draw the pentagon and its image.
(c) Use the same matrix on the image pentagon. What do you notice?

16. A certain transformation produces the mapping
$\binom{x}{y} \to \binom{y}{x}$.
(a) Plot the points $(1, 0)$, $(-2, 3)$, $(4, -1)$, and their images using the transformation.
(b) By drawing the mirror line, show that the transformation is a reflection.
(c) What is the equation of the mirror line?
(d) Find the matrix of the transformation.

17. A reflection in the line $y = -x$ maps:
$(2, 1) \to (-1, -2)$ and $(-2, 1) \to (-1, 2)$.

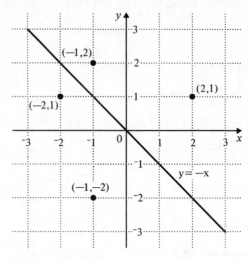

(a) For this reflection, complete the statement
$(x, y) \to (\qquad)$.
(b) Find the matrix for the reflection.

18. A transformation of the plane is represented by
the matrix $\begin{pmatrix} -0.6 & 0.8 \\ 0.8 & 0.6 \end{pmatrix}$.
(a) Find the image of each of the points $(0, 0)$, $(2, -1)$, $(1, 2)$, $(2, 4)$.
(b) What is the image of the point $(k, 2k)$?
(c) Draw a diagram to show that the matrix represents a reflection.
What is the equation of the mirror line?

19. A reflection is represented by the matrix
$\begin{pmatrix} -0.8 & -0.6 \\ -0.6 & 0.8 \end{pmatrix}$.
(a) Find the image of each of the points $(0, 0)$, $(-4, 2)$, $(2, 4)$, $(-1, 3)$.
(b) Plot these points and their images on a graph.
(c) What is the equation of the mirror line?

20. A transformation maps:
$(0, 0) \to (0, 0)$ $(1, 3) \to (1, 3)$
$(4, 2) \to (-2, 4)$ $(-2, 4) \to (4, 2)$
(a) Plot these points and show that the transformation is a reflection.
(b) Find the equation of the mirror line.
(c) Find the matrix that represents the transformation.

Rotation

Example

In the diagram, the image of the triangle ABC under a rotation of 90° about O is the triangle A'B'C'.
Find the matrix which represents this rotation.

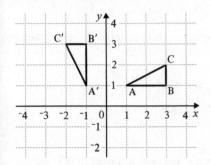

$(1, 1) \rightarrow (-1, 1)$ and $(3, 1) \rightarrow (-1, 3)$.
The matrix for this transformation can be found from:

$$\begin{pmatrix} a & b \\ c & d \end{pmatrix} \begin{pmatrix} 1 & 3 \\ 1 & 1 \end{pmatrix} = \begin{pmatrix} -1 & -1 \\ 1 & 3 \end{pmatrix}$$

This gives the equations:

$\begin{array}{ll} a + b = -1 & c + d = 1 \\ 3a + b = -1 & \text{and} \quad 3c + d = 3 \end{array}$

Solving the simultaneous equations gives:
$a = 0, b = -1, c = 1, d = 0$

So the matrix is $\begin{pmatrix} 0 & -1 \\ 1 & 0 \end{pmatrix}$.

The matrix above represents the rotation of any point (x, y) through 90° about O, in an anticlockwise direction.
You can check by using the point C (3, 2):

$$\begin{pmatrix} 0 & -1 \\ 1 & 0 \end{pmatrix} \begin{pmatrix} 3 \\ 2 \end{pmatrix} = \begin{pmatrix} -2 \\ 3 \end{pmatrix}.$$

C' is at $(-2, 3)$, so the matrix is correct.

21. Copy the triangle ABC above and plot its image after a half-turn rotation about O.
Find the matrix for the rotation.

22. Use the matrix $\begin{pmatrix} 0 & 1 \\ -1 & 0 \end{pmatrix}$ to map the triangle ABC above. Plot its image and describe the transformation.

23. Find the image of the triangle with vertices $(0, 0)$, $(0, 4)$, $(4, 3)$ using the rotation matrix:
$\begin{pmatrix} 0.6 & -0.8 \\ 0.8 & 0.6 \end{pmatrix}$.
Plot the triangle and its image on graph paper and use a protractor to find the angle of rotation.

General rotation matrix

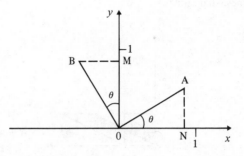

A rotation of the axes through an angle θ takes $(1, 0)$ to A and $(0, 1)$ to B.
The length of OA = 1, so the co-ordinates of A are $(\cos θ, \sin θ)$ from the right-angled triangle OAN.
Similarly, the co-ordinates of B are found from the right-angled triangle OBM to be $(-\sin θ, \cos θ)$.
Thus the rotation maps:
$(1, 0) \rightarrow (\cos θ, \sin θ)$
$(0, 1) \rightarrow (-\sin θ, \cos θ)$

The matrix for this rotation is $\begin{pmatrix} \cos θ & -\sin θ \\ \sin θ & \cos θ \end{pmatrix}$

24. Use the rotation matrix to write down the image of $(-1, 0)$. Draw a diagram like the one above to show that this represents a rotation of angle θ.

25. By using θ = 90°, θ = 180° and θ = 270°, check that this matrix agrees with the results you have already found.

26. What is the matrix for a rotation of 30°?
Use the matrix to find the image of the point $(2, 1)$ under this rotation.

27. (a) Draw a right-angled triangle to show that if θ is an acute angle and sin θ = 0.6, then cos θ = 0.8.
(b) Find the rotation matrix for an acute angle θ where sin θ = 0.6.
(c) Use the matrix to find the image of the triangle with vertices $(0, 0)$, $(1, 2)$, $(2, 2)$, under this rotation. Show your results on a diagram.

28. (a) Find the rotation matrix for an angle θ where sin θ = 0.28 and cos θ = −0.96.
(b) Find the image of the points $(10, 10)$ and $(0, 10)$ under this rotation.
(c) Plot the points $(10, 10)$ and $(0, 10)$ and their images, on graph paper.
(d) Is the angle of rotation an acute angle?
(e) Measure the size of the angle of rotation, to the nearest degree.

shear matrices

The effects of two shear matrices on the unit square are shown in these diagrams:

$\begin{pmatrix} 1 & 2 \\ 0 & 1 \end{pmatrix}$

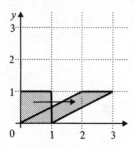

$\begin{pmatrix} 1 & 0 \\ \frac{3}{2} & 1 \end{pmatrix}$

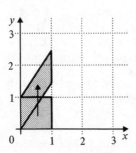

29. Write down the equation of the invariant line of the shear, for each case illustrated above.

30. Use the square $(0, 0)$, $(0, 1)$, $(1, 1)$, $(1, 0)$ and find its image using the shear matrix:

    (a) $\begin{pmatrix} 1 & 3 \\ 0 & 1 \end{pmatrix}$ (b) $\begin{pmatrix} 1 & -1 \\ 0 & 1 \end{pmatrix}$ (c) $\begin{pmatrix} 1 & 0 \\ -2 & 1 \end{pmatrix}$

31. Draw a diagram for each part of Question 30 and write down the equation of the invariant line.

32. Find the matrix of the shear that maps parallelogram P to parallelogram Q.

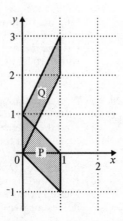

Remember

$\begin{pmatrix} 1 & a \\ 0 & 1 \end{pmatrix}$ is a shear with the x-axis invariant.

$\begin{pmatrix} 1 & 0 \\ a & 1 \end{pmatrix}$ is a shear with the y-axis invariant.

33. What matrix is the inverse of $\mathbf{A} = \begin{pmatrix} 1 & 2 \\ 0 & 1 \end{pmatrix}$?

    Draw a diagram to show the effect of $\mathbf{A}$ and then $\mathbf{A}^{-1}$ on the triangle with vertices $(0, 0)$, $(2, 1)$, $(2, 2)$.

34. $\mathbf{A} = \begin{pmatrix} 1 & 0 \\ 3 & 1 \end{pmatrix}$ and $\mathbf{B} = \begin{pmatrix} 1 & 0 \\ 2 & 1 \end{pmatrix}$ are shear matrices.

    Find the product $\mathbf{AB}$.
    Does this matrix also represent a shear?

35. Draw a diagram to show the image of the parallelogram with vertices $(0, 0)$, $(0, 3)$, $(2, 5)$, $(2, 2)$, using the matrix $\begin{pmatrix} 0 & 1 \\ -1 & 2 \end{pmatrix}$.

    Is the result a shear? What is its invariant line?

36. Transform the square with vertices $(0, 0)$, $(1, 1)$, $(0, 2)$, $(-1, 1)$, using the matrix $\begin{pmatrix} \frac{1}{2} & -\frac{1}{2} \\ \frac{1}{2} & 1\frac{1}{2} \end{pmatrix}$.

    Is the result a shear? What is its invariant line?

37. The parallelogram with vertices $(0, 0)$, $(0, -2)$, $(2, 2)$, $(2, 4)$ is transformed using the matrix

    $\begin{pmatrix} 2 & -1 \\ 1 & 0 \end{pmatrix}$.

    Draw a diagram to show that the transformation is a shear and write down the equation of the invariant line.

38. The vertices of a rectangle are $(0, 0)$, $(5, 0)$, $(5, 10)$, $(0, 10)$. Find the image of these vertices using the matrix $\begin{pmatrix} 0.4 & 0.3 \\ -1.2 & 1.6 \end{pmatrix}$.

    Which of the two vertices are invariant points? What is the invariant line of the shear?

39. Use the rectangle with vertices $(0, 1)$, $(1, 1)$, $(1, -1)$, $(0, -1)$ to illustrate the effect of the transformations represented by the matrix:

    (a) $\begin{pmatrix} 2 & 0 \\ 0 & 1 \end{pmatrix}$ (b) $\begin{pmatrix} 1 & 2 \\ 0 & 1 \end{pmatrix}$ (c) $\begin{pmatrix} 1 & 0 \\ 2 & 1 \end{pmatrix}$

    Which of these matrices represent shears?

4.4 Combining transformations

Enlargements

An enlargement with the origin as centre and scale factor 2 is produced by the mapping:

$$\begin{pmatrix} 2 & 0 \\ 0 & 2 \end{pmatrix}\begin{pmatrix} x \\ y \end{pmatrix} \rightarrow \begin{pmatrix} 2x \\ 2y \end{pmatrix}$$

If this is then followed by an enlargement from the origin with scale factor 3, the mapping is given by:

$$\begin{pmatrix} 3 & 0 \\ 0 & 3 \end{pmatrix}\begin{pmatrix} 2x \\ 2y \end{pmatrix} \rightarrow \begin{pmatrix} 6x \\ 6y \end{pmatrix}$$

Both enlargements can be written as:

$$\begin{pmatrix} 3 & 0 \\ 0 & 3 \end{pmatrix}\begin{pmatrix} 2 & 0 \\ 0 & 2 \end{pmatrix}\begin{pmatrix} x \\ y \end{pmatrix} \rightarrow \begin{pmatrix} 6 & 0 \\ 0 & 6 \end{pmatrix}\begin{pmatrix} x \\ y \end{pmatrix}$$

Note

(a) The matrix $\begin{pmatrix} 2 & 0 \\ 0 & 2 \end{pmatrix}$ appears next to $\begin{pmatrix} x \\ y \end{pmatrix}$

because that enlargement is done first.
(b) Multiplying the two enlargement matrices gives the single enlargement matrix that has the same effect.

1. In the diagram, triangle ABC is enlarged to triangle A'B'C'.

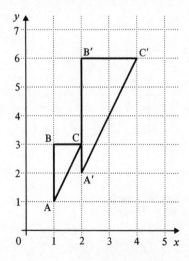

P transforms ABC onto A'B'C'.
   (a) Write down the enlargement matrix **P**.
   (b) Find the matrix **Q** that maps A'B'C' to (6, 6), (6, 18), (12, 18).
   (c) Find the matrix **R** = **QP**.
   (d) Find the image of triangle ABC using the matrix **R**.

2. Two enlargements are given by the matrices:
   $\begin{pmatrix} 4 & 0 \\ 0 & 4 \end{pmatrix}$ and $\begin{pmatrix} 5 & 0 \\ 0 & 5 \end{pmatrix}$.
   (a) Find the matrix that represents the single enlargement obtained by carrying out one enlargement followed by the other.
   (b) If the enlargements are carried out in the reverse order, is the resulting matrix the same?

3. Draw a diagram to illustrate the effect on the square (0, 0), (0, 1), (1, 1), (1, 0) of:
   $\begin{pmatrix} -2 & 0 \\ 0 & -2 \end{pmatrix}$ followed by $\begin{pmatrix} 4 & 0 \\ 0 & 4 \end{pmatrix}$.
   What matrix represents the equivalent transformation?

4. Draw a diagram to illustrate the effect on the square (0, 0), (0, 1), (1, 1), (1, 0) of $\begin{pmatrix} 4 & 0 \\ 0 & 4 \end{pmatrix}$
   followed by $\begin{pmatrix} \frac{1}{2} & 0 \\ 0 & \frac{1}{2} \end{pmatrix}$.
   What matrix represents the equivalent transformation?

5. An enlargement maps $(3, 2) \rightarrow (-6, -4)$.
   A second enlargement maps $(-6, -4) \rightarrow (9, 6)$.
   Write down the matrix for each enlargement, and find their product. Does it represent the enlargement that maps $(3, 2) \rightarrow (9, 6)$?

6. $\mathbf{A} = \begin{pmatrix} -2 & 0 \\ 0 & -2 \end{pmatrix}$ and $\mathbf{B} = \begin{pmatrix} \frac{1}{2} & 0 \\ 0 & \frac{1}{2} \end{pmatrix}$ are enlargement
   matrices.
   (a) What are the scale factors of the enlargement for **A** and **B**?
   (b) What is the geometrical meaning of the negative sign in **A**?
   (c) What is the geometrical meaning of the fraction $\frac{1}{2}$ in **B**?
   (d) Find the images of (2, 1) and (3, 2) using **B**.
   (e) Find the images of the results in (d) using **A**.
   (f) Does the use of **B** followed by **A** produce an enlargement?
   (g) Let **X** = **AB**. Is **X** an enlargement matrix?

7. The product of two enlargement matrices is an enlargement matrix. Show, with examples, that there are special cases where the result may be:
   (a) the identity   (b) a half-turn rotation

...ons and reflections

.ou have met the four rotation matrices:

$$R = \begin{pmatrix} 0 & -1 \\ 1 & 0 \end{pmatrix}$$ 90° about the origin

$$S = \begin{pmatrix} -1 & 0 \\ 0 & -1 \end{pmatrix}$$ 180° about the origin

$$T = \begin{pmatrix} 0 & 1 \\ -1 & 0 \end{pmatrix}$$ 270° about the origin

$$I = \begin{pmatrix} 1 & 0 \\ 0 & 1 \end{pmatrix}$$ 360° or 0° about the origin (the identity matrix)

You have also met the four reflection matrices:

$$X = \begin{pmatrix} 1 & 0 \\ 0 & -1 \end{pmatrix}$$ reflection in x-axis

$$Y = \begin{pmatrix} -1 & 0 \\ 0 & 1 \end{pmatrix}$$ reflection in y-axis

$$Z = \begin{pmatrix} 0 & 1 \\ 1 & 0 \end{pmatrix}$$ reflection in $y = x$

$$W = \begin{pmatrix} 0 & -1 \\ -1 & 0 \end{pmatrix}$$ reflection in $y = -x$

8. In the diagram, the point P(3, 1) is first reflected in the line $y = x$ to P′.
P′ is then reflected in the y-axis to P″.

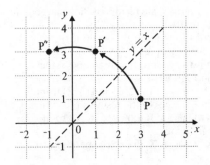

(a) What single transformation maps P to P″?
(b) Work out $\begin{pmatrix} 0 & 1 \\ 1 & 0 \end{pmatrix}\begin{pmatrix} 3 \\ 1 \end{pmatrix}$.
    Does this give the point P′?
(c) What matrix maps P′ to P″?
(d) Work out the product **YZ**, from the list of matrices above. Does the answer map P to P″?
(e) Work out the product **ZY**. Does the answer map P to P″?

9. Work out the product **XY**, using **X** and **Y** from the list opposite. What transformation is it equivalent to? Draw a diagram to illustrate your answer.

10. The product of matrices **XY** represents a reflection in the y-axis followed by a reflection in the x-axis. Note the order.
(a) What does the product **YX** represent?
(b) Is **XY** the same as **YX**?
(c) What does **RX** represent?
(d) Is **RX** the same as **XR**?
(e) Draw a diagram to illustrate the effect of **RX** on the point P(3, 1).
    Show also the effect of **XR** on point P.

11. Show that **ZW** and **WZ** are the same but that **XW** and **WX** are different.
To do this, draw a diagram to show the effect of these mappings on point P (3, 1).

12. The triangle with vertices (1, 0), (2, 1), (1, 3) is rotated through 90° about O. The image is then reflected in the x-axis.
(a) Draw a diagram to show this.
(b) What single transformation could replace the rotation and reflection?
    Write down the corresponding matrix.
(c) Is the matrix equivalent to **XR** or **RX**?
(d) What matrix would map the final image back to the original triangle?

13. In the diagram, triangle A is mapped to triangle B.

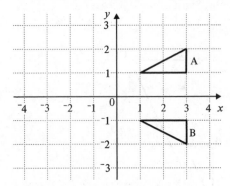

Show that this can be done by using:
(a) matrix **Y** and another matrix
(b) matrix **Z** and another matrix
(c) matrix **W** and another matrix.

14. Show that **X** combined with any of the other reflection matrices will produce a rotation matrix.

Harder problems

15. Draw the rectangle $(0, 0), (0, 1), (3, 1), (3, 0)$ under the following transformations:

(a) $\begin{pmatrix} 0 & 1 \\ 1 & 0 \end{pmatrix}\begin{pmatrix} x \\ y \end{pmatrix} + \begin{pmatrix} 1 \\ -1 \end{pmatrix}$

(b) $\begin{pmatrix} 0 & 1 \\ -1 & 0 \end{pmatrix}\begin{pmatrix} x \\ y \end{pmatrix} + \begin{pmatrix} 2 \\ 0 \end{pmatrix}$

(c) $\begin{pmatrix} 2 & 0 \\ 0 & 2 \end{pmatrix}\begin{pmatrix} x \\ y \end{pmatrix} + \begin{pmatrix} -3 \\ 2 \end{pmatrix}$

Describe the transformation each represents.

16. (a) Show that a matrix $A = \begin{pmatrix} 0 & 1 \\ 1 & 0 \end{pmatrix}$ represents a reflection in the line $y = x$.

(b) What transformation does the matrix $B = \begin{pmatrix} 0 & -1 \\ 1 & 0 \end{pmatrix}$ represent?

(c) Describe fully the transformation represented by: (i) **AB**   (ii) **BA**.

17. (a) Draw $A(1, 2), B(3, 2), C(3, 3)$ and its image $A'B'C'$ under the matrix:

$$U = \begin{pmatrix} 1 & 0 \\ 0 & -1 \end{pmatrix}.$$

(b) The matrix $V = \begin{pmatrix} -1 & 0 \\ 0 & 1 \end{pmatrix}$ maps $A'B'C'$ onto $A''B''C''$. Find and draw the image $A''B''C''$.

(c) What single transformation maps ABC onto $A''B''C''$?

(d) What single transformation maps $A''B''C''$ onto ABC?

18. (a) A transformation **A** maps $(1, 0)$ onto $(3, 4)$ and $(0, 1)$ onto $(2, 3)$. Find the matrix **A**.

(b) What is the image of the triangle $X(2, 1)$, $Y(4, 1), Z(4, 2)$ under **A**?

(c) How is the area of triangle XYZ related to the area of its image under **A**?

19. The parallelogram $A(2, 0), B(-2, 8), C(2, 4)$, $D(6, -4)$ is transformed by the matrix $T = \begin{pmatrix} 1 & \frac{1}{2} \\ 1 & 1 \end{pmatrix}$.

(a) Find and draw the image $A'B'C'D'$ of the parallelogram under **T**.

(b) What is the area of $A'B'C'D'$?

(c) What is the area of ABCD?

20. A transformation **P** is given by:

$$P: \begin{pmatrix} x \\ y \end{pmatrix} \rightarrow \begin{pmatrix} 1.8 & -1.2 \\ 1.2 & 1.8 \end{pmatrix}\begin{pmatrix} x \\ y \end{pmatrix}.$$

(a) Find the image $O'A'B'C'$ of the square $O(0, 0), A(2, 0), B(2, 2), C(0, 2)$ under **P**.

(b) Work out the length of OA' and the angle AOA'.

(c) Calculate the area of $O'A'B'C'$ and the length of $A'C'$.

21. **A** is a reflection in the line $y = -x$; **B** is an anti-clockwise rotation of $90°$ about the origin. Find the image of $(3, 2)$ under:

(a) **A**   (b) **B**   (c) **AB**

(d) **BA**   (e) B^{-1} (f) $A^{-1}B^{-1}$

(g) $(BA)^{-1}$

22. **X** is a reflection in $y = x$; **Y** is a reflection in the y-axis. Find the matrix which represents:

(a) **X**   (b) **Y**

(c) **XY**   (d) **YX**

Describe the single transformations **XY** and **YX**.

23. The square $O(0, 0), A(1, 0), B(1, 1), C(0, 1)$ is transformed by the matrix $Q = \begin{pmatrix} 1 & \frac{1}{2} \\ \frac{1}{2} & 1 \end{pmatrix}$ onto $O'A'B'C'$.

(a) Find the area of $O'A'B'C'$.

(b) Show that OB' and $A'C'$ are perpendicular.

(c) Calculate the size of angle $C'OB'$.

Summary

By the end of this chapter these are the things you
should know about:

4.1 The inverse of a matrix (pages 340–342)

What the **inverse** of a 2×2 matrix is.
If $\mathbf{AB} = \mathbf{I}$, then $\mathbf{B} = \mathbf{A}^{-1}$.
$\mathbf{B}$ is the inverse of $\mathbf{A}$; $\mathbf{I} = \begin{pmatrix} 1 & 0 \\ 0 & 1 \end{pmatrix}$.

The **determinant** of the matrix $\begin{pmatrix} a & b \\ c & d \end{pmatrix}$ is $ad - bc$.

The **inverse** of $\begin{pmatrix} a & b \\ c & d \end{pmatrix}$ is $\dfrac{1}{ad - bc} \begin{pmatrix} d & - & b \\ -c & & a \end{pmatrix}$.

A matrix whose determinant is zero is called a singular
matrix.
e.g. $\begin{pmatrix} 3 & 6 \\ 1 & 2 \end{pmatrix}$ has determinant $3 \times 2 - 1 \times 6 = 0$

A singular matrix has no inverse.

4.2 Simultaneous equations (pages 343–345)

How to write a pair of simultaneous equations in matrix
form.
e.g. $\begin{array}{l} 2x + \ y = 8 \\ x + 4y = 6 \end{array}$ can be written:

$$\begin{pmatrix} 2 & 1 \\ 1 & 4 \end{pmatrix} \begin{pmatrix} x \\ y \end{pmatrix} = \begin{pmatrix} 8 \\ 6 \end{pmatrix} \dots [1]$$

How to use matrices to solve the equations.
e.g. Find the inverse: $\begin{pmatrix} 2 & 1 \\ 1 & 4 \end{pmatrix} = \tfrac{1}{7} \begin{pmatrix} 4 & -1 \\ -1 & 2 \end{pmatrix}$
    Pre-multiply [1] by the inverse:

$$\tfrac{1}{7} \begin{pmatrix} 4 & -1 \\ -1 & 2 \end{pmatrix} \begin{pmatrix} 2 & 1 \\ 1 & 4 \end{pmatrix} \begin{pmatrix} x \\ y \end{pmatrix} = \tfrac{1}{7} \begin{pmatrix} 4 & -1 \\ -1 & 2 \end{pmatrix} \begin{pmatrix} 8 \\ 6 \end{pmatrix}$$

$$\begin{pmatrix} 1 & 0 \\ 0 & 1 \end{pmatrix} \begin{pmatrix} x \\ y \end{pmatrix} = \tfrac{1}{7} \begin{pmatrix} 26 \\ 4 \end{pmatrix}$$

$$\begin{pmatrix} x \\ y \end{pmatrix} = \begin{pmatrix} \frac{26}{7} \\ \frac{4}{7} \end{pmatrix}$$

If a matrix is singular, the equations represent parallel
lines. A singular matrix can mean either:
    (a) no solutions
or (b) an infinite number of solutions

4.3 Transformation matrices (pages 346–350)

Using 2×2 matrix to represent a transformation of the
plane.
The matrix $\begin{pmatrix} a & 0 \\ 0 & 1 \end{pmatrix}$ represents a **one-way stretch** in
the x-direction.
The matrix $\begin{pmatrix} 1 & 0 \\ 0 & b \end{pmatrix}$ represents a **one-way stretch** in
the y-direction.
The matrix $\begin{pmatrix} k & 0 \\ 0 & k \end{pmatrix}$ represents a **two-way stretch**
which is the same in both directions – it is an
enlargement. The scale factor of the enlargement is k.

How to use matrices for reflection and rotation (the
important ones are listed on page 352).
The **general rotation matrix** is $\begin{pmatrix} \cos\theta & -\sin\theta \\ \sin\theta & \cos\theta \end{pmatrix}$ for
an anti-clockwise rotation of angle θ about the origin.

A shear with the x-axis as the invariant line is given
by $\begin{pmatrix} 1 & a \\ 0 & 1 \end{pmatrix}$.
A shear with the y-axis as the invariant line is given
by $\begin{pmatrix} 1 & 0 \\ a & 1 \end{pmatrix}$.

4.4 Combining transformations
(pages 351–353)

The single transformation equivalent to one
transformation followed by another transformation can
be found by **multiplying** the respective matrices.
The **order** of multiplying the matrices is important.
The effect of matrix $\mathbf{A}$ followed by matrix $\mathbf{B}$ is given by
the product $\mathbf{BA}$.
The eight important rotation and reflection matrices
(page 352).

Practice Papers for General CXC examination

Practice Paper A

Multiple choice
Time allowed 90 minutes

1. The value of $60.3 \div 0.03$ is:
  (a) 2.010 (b) 2010 (c) 201.0 (d) 20.10

2. $9x^2 - 4y^2$ is:
  (a) $(3x - 2y)^2$ (b) $(3x + 2y)^2$
  (c) $(3x - 2y)(3x + 2y)$ (d) $(x - y)(9x + 4y)$

3. An example of a many-to-one mapping over the domain $\{^-2, ^-1, 0, 1, 2\}$ is the map:
  (a) $x \rightarrow x + 2$ (b) $x \rightarrow x^2$
  (c) $x \rightarrow 2 - x$ (d) $x \rightarrow 2x + 1$

4. The perimeter of the room shown below is:

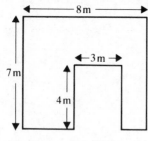

  (a) 30 m (b) 38 m (c) 44 m (d) 46 m

5. The mean of six numbers is 18.
  What is the new mean if 46 is added to the set?
  (a) 22 (b) 25 (c) 28 (d) 32

6. Which transformation does not preserve area?
  (a) reflection (b) shear
  (c) stretch (d) translation

7. The point $\begin{pmatrix} 3 \\ -6 \end{pmatrix}$ is the image of the point $\begin{pmatrix} 3 \\ 6 \end{pmatrix}$
  under:
  (a) a reflection in the x-axis
  (b) a reflection in the y-axis
  (c) a 90° rotation about the origin
  (d) a translation through $\begin{pmatrix} 0 \\ 6 \end{pmatrix}$

8. If nine tables cost $\$x$, the cost of 6 tables is:
  (a) $\$\frac{2}{3}x$ (b) $\$(9x - 6)$
  (c) $\$(\frac{1}{6}x + 6)$ (d) $\$\frac{3}{2}x$

9. The solutions to the equation $x^2 + 5x + 6 = 0$ are:
  (a) $x = 2, x = 3$ (b) $x = 1, x = 6$
  (c) $x = ^-2, x = ^-3$ (d) $x = ^-1, x\,^-6$

10. The force on an object is inversely proportional to its distance away from a point O, and the force is 8 units when the distance from O is 2 m.
  The force on the object when the distance is 4 m is:
  (a) 2 units (b) 4 units
  (c) 8 units (d) 16 units

11. $\sin 120°$ is:
  (a) $\sin 60°$ (b) $-\sin 60°$
  (c) $\cos 60°$ (d) $-\cos 60°$

12. In the right-angled triangle AB = 8 cm and angle ABC = 25°.
  The length of BC is:
  (a) $8 \sin 25°$
  (b) $8 \tan 25°$
  (c) $8 \cos 25°$
  (d) $8 \times 25°$

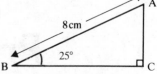

13. A man spends 60% of his salary on food, 30% on rent, and 10% he saves. If this information is to be shown on a pie-chart what angle should represent his expenditure on rent?
  (a) $8\frac{1}{2}°$ (b) 12° (c) 108° (d) 120°

14. The number 48 564 written correct to two significant figures is:
  (a) 48 (b) 49 (c) 49 000 (d) 50 000

15. Which of the following is *not* the net of a cube?
  (a)   (b)

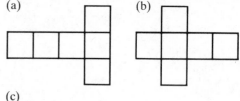

  (c)

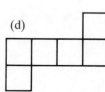

  (d)

16. The histogram shows the weights of a class of school children.
  The total number of children in the class is:

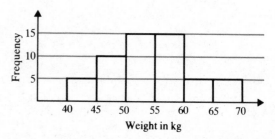

  (a) 15 (b) 30 (c) 55 (d) 60

17. Use the histogram in Question 16.
The modal class is:
(a) 50–55 kg   (b) 50–60 kg
(c) 60–65 kg   (d) 60–70 kg

18. Use the histogram in Question 16.
The probability that a child picked at random has a weight of 60 kg or more is:
(a) $\frac{1}{12}$ (b) $\frac{1}{11}$ (c) $\frac{1}{6}$ (d) $\frac{2}{11}$

19. ABCDEFGH is a cube of side 2 cm.
The length AH is:
(a) $\sqrt{6}$ cm
(b) $\sqrt{12}$ cm
(c) 6 cm
(d) 8 cm

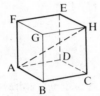

20. The gradient of the line $2x + 3y = 6$ is:
(a) $-\frac{3}{2}$ (b) $-\frac{2}{3}$ (c) $\frac{2}{3}$ (d) $\frac{3}{2}$

21. In the expression $w = x + yz$, y can be written as:
(a) $\dfrac{x - w}{z}$ (b) $\dfrac{w - x}{z}$
(c) $\dfrac{w}{z} - x$ (d) $w - x - z$

22. Consumption tax at 80% is charged on luxury goods and at 30% on clothing.
How much tax is payable on $60 worth of luxury soap and a shirt costing $40?
(a) $50.00   (b) $56.08
(c) $60.00   (d) $110

23. The Venn diagram shows $P, Q \subset U$.

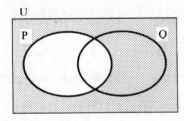

The shaded area represents:
(a) P' (b) Q' (c) $(P \cup Q)'$ (d) P

24. $500 is invested in a deposit account at 4% compound interest.
How much interest is earned after two years?
(a) $40.00   (b) $40.08   (c) $40.80   (d) $48.00

25. The interior angle of a regular pentagon is:
(a) 72°   (b) 108°   (c) 126°   (d) 162°

26. If A = {quadrilaterals} and
B = {four-sided figures with all sides equal in length} then A ∩ B is:
(a) squares   (b) rhombuses
(c) rectangles   (d) parallelograms

27. The graph shows a distance-time graph of a man walking.
His greatest speed during the 40 m walk is:

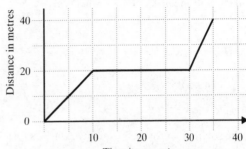

(a) $1\,\text{ms}^{-1}$ (b) $2\,\text{ms}^{-1}$ (c) $3\,\text{ms}^{-1}$ (d) $4\,\text{ms}^{-1}$

28. The value of $\dfrac{38 \times 10^3}{2 \times 10^{-2}}$ written in standard form is:

(a) 19×10^{-5} (b) 1.9×10^{-5}
(c) 1.9×10^1 (d) 1.9×10^6

29. The values of $\dfrac{6m - n}{n - 3}$ where $m = 2$ and $n = {}^{-}3$ is:

(a) $^{-}2\frac{1}{2}$ (b) $^{-}1\frac{1}{2}$ (c) $1\frac{1}{2}$ (d) $2\frac{1}{2}$

30. An electric iron was bought for $120 after a discount of 20%.
The original price was:
(a) $96   (b) $100   (c) $144   (d) $150

31. Given $f : x \to x + 2$, $g : x \to 3x$,
then $fg(4)$ equals:
(a) 4   (b) 9   (c) 14   (d) 18

32. The translation which takes the point $(2, 4)$ to $(1, 6)$ is:
(a) $\begin{pmatrix} -3 \\ 2 \end{pmatrix}$ (b) $\begin{pmatrix} 1 \\ -2 \end{pmatrix}$ (c) $\begin{pmatrix} -1 \\ 2 \end{pmatrix}$ (d) $\begin{pmatrix} 3 \\ 10 \end{pmatrix}$

33. As x becomes very small the value of $\dfrac{1}{x}$ becomes:

(a) very small   (b) close to zero
(c) close to one   (d) very large

34. A large packet of soap powder weighing 1300 g costs $15.31. A smaller packet weighing 400 g costs $4.64.
Which is the best value for money?
(a) the 1300 g packet
(b) the 400 g packet
(c) both are the same
(d) no comparison possible.

35. The scale of 2 cm to $\frac{1}{2}$ km is the same as:
(a) $1:250$ (b) $1:4000$
(c) $1:25\,000$ (d) $1:40\,000$

36. The value of $\frac{3}{8} + \frac{2}{3} \times \frac{1}{4}$ is:
(a) $\frac{13}{24}$ (b) $\frac{25}{96}$ (c) $\frac{2}{7}$ (d) $\frac{1}{4}$

37. Given that A and B are sets, and that $n(A) = 20$, $n(B) = 30$ and $n(A \cap B) = 4$ what is $n(A \cup B)$?
(a) 42   (b) 46   (c) 54   (d) 58

38. If $5! = 5 \times 4 \times 3 \times 2 \times 1$
then $\dfrac{n!}{(n-r)!}$ where $n = 5$ and $r = 3$ is:

(a) 15   (b) 20   (c) 30   (d) 60

39. The solution set for the inequality $2x + 3 > x$ is:
(a) $\{x : x > {}^-3\}$ (b) $\{x : x > {}^-1\}$
(c) $\{x : x > 1\}$ (d) $\{x : x > 3\}$

40. The square OABC is transformed onto the square OA$'$B$'$C$'$ by the transformations:
(a) an enlargement and a 90° rotation
(b) an enlargement and a translation
(c) an enlargement and a reflection in $y = -x$
(d) an enlargement and a reflection in $y = x$

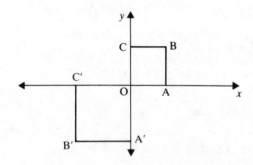

41. A crate of 24 soft drinks can be bought for $12.80 which includes the $2.00 for the crate. How much should a shopkeeper sell a single bottle for if he wishes to make a profit of 20¢ on each bottle sold?
(a) 55¢   (b) 60¢   (c) 65¢   (d) 70¢

42. Which of the following represents a one-to-one mapping over the domain $\{^-1, 0, 1\}$?

(a) $x \to x^2$ (b) $x \to 2x + 1$ (c) $x \to \dfrac{1}{x^2}$

(d) $x \to x^2 + 1$

43. The product of two prime numbers is necessarily:
(a) a prime number   (b) a composite number
(c) a square number   (d) an odd number.

44. The numbers from 1 to 20 inclusive are written on pieces of paper and put into a bag. What is the probability that a number drawn at random from the bag has the number 2 on it?
(a) $\frac{1}{20}$ (b) $\frac{1}{10}$ (c) $\frac{3}{20}$ (d) $\frac{1}{2}$

45. O is the centre of the circle and the larger angle AOC is 220°.
Angle ABC is:
(a) 35°
(b) 70°
(c) 90°
(d) 145°

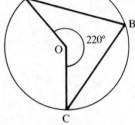

46. A rectangle is drawn to a scale of $1:20$ and has a length of 3 cm and width of 5 cm.
Its actual area is:
(a) 30 cm^2 (b) 300 cm^2 (c) 1500 cm^2
(d) 6000 cm^2

47. $\begin{pmatrix} 1 & 2 \\ 3 & 1 \end{pmatrix}\begin{pmatrix} 3 & 1 \\ 1 & 2 \end{pmatrix}$ is:

(a) $\begin{pmatrix} 3 & 2 \\ 3 & 2 \end{pmatrix}$ (b) $\begin{pmatrix} 5 & 5 \\ 10 & 5 \end{pmatrix}$

(c) $\begin{pmatrix} 10 & 5 \\ 5 & 5 \end{pmatrix}$ (d) $\begin{pmatrix} 3 & 3 \\ 2 & 2 \end{pmatrix}$

48. The number of goals scored in a session of 12 football matches is shown in the table.

Number of goals	0	1	2	3	4
Number of matches	4	2	5	0	1

The mean number of goals per match was:
(a) $\frac{5}{6}$ (b) $\frac{11}{12}$ (c) $1\frac{1}{3}$ (d) $2\frac{1}{2}$

49. The surface area of a sphere is given by the formula $4\pi r^2$.
What is the surface area of a football of radius 7 cm? (Take π as $\frac{22}{7}$.)
(a) 88 cm^2 (b) 176 cm^2 (c) 308 cm^2 (d) 616 cm^2

50. A man makes a 30% profit when he sells a chair for $65. What was the cost price of the chair?
(a) $46.50   (b) $50   (c) $63.05   (d) $80

51. The standard deviation of the numbers $0, 0, 0, 6, 6, 6$ is:
(a) 0   (b) 3   (c) 4   (d) 6

52. $ax + by + ay + bx$ equals:
(a) $(a + b)(x + y)$ (b) $(a - b)(x - y)$
(c) $(1 + ab)(1 + xy)$ (d) $(1 - ab)(1 - xy)$

53. The mapping $f : x \to x^2$ on the domain $\{^-1, 0, 1\}$ is a function since the mapping is:
(a) one-to-one
(b) many-to-one
(c) one-to-many
(d) many-to-many.

54. The area of a rectangle which has one side of length 3 m and a perimeter of 20 m is:
(a) 10m^2
(b) 21m^2
(c) 30m^2
(d) 60m^2

55. Which of the following is an infinite set?
(a) {factors of 36}
(b) {prime numbers}
(c) {even numbers less than 100}
(d) {square numbers between 3 and 36}

56. Which of the following statements is false?
(a) {integers} $\subset$ {fractions}
(b) {fractions} $\subset$ {real numbers}
(c) {integers} $\subset$ {natural numbers}
(d) {positive whole numbers} $\subset$ {natural numbers}

57. The gradient of a line passing through $(2, 3)$ and $(1, 6)$ is:
(a) $^-3$
(b) $^-\frac{1}{3}$
(c) $\frac{1}{3}$
(d) 3

58. $60°$ in radians is:
(a) $\frac{\pi}{6}$
(b) $\frac{\pi}{3}$
(c) $\frac{2\pi}{3}$
(d) $\frac{4\pi}{3}$

59. If $T = \sqrt{\dfrac{a}{b}}$, then b equals:
(a) aT^2
(b) $a^2 T$
(c) $\dfrac{a}{T}$
(d) $\dfrac{a}{T^2}$

60. Given that $y \propto x^2$ and that $y = 8$ when $x = 2$, what is the value of y when $x = 1$?
(a) 1
(b) 2
(c) 4
(d) 6

Practice Paper B

Multiple choice
Time allowed 90 minutes

1. If $A \subset B$ and $B \subset C$ then $A \cup (B \cap C)$ is the same as:
(a) ϕ
(b) A
(c) B
(c) C

2. The graph of the relation $y = 2 + x - x^2$ has the shape of:
(a) a straight line
(b) an exponential curve
(c) a quadratic curve
(d) a circle.

3. The equation of the line with gradient 2 passing through $(0, 6)$ is:
(a) $y = 6x + 2$
(b) $y = 2x + 6$
(c) $y = \dfrac{x}{6} + 2$
(d) $y = \dfrac{x}{2} + 6$

4. $x^2 + 5x - 6$ equals:
(a) $(x - 3)(x + 2)$
(b) $(x - 6)(x + 1)$
(c) $(x + 6)(x - 1)$
(d) $(x + 3)(x - 2)$

5. $f : x \to 3x - 2$, so $f^{-1}(x)$ equals:
(a) $\dfrac{x + 2}{3}$
(b) $\dfrac{x - 2}{3}$
(c) $\dfrac{x}{3} + 2$
(d) $\dfrac{x}{3} - 2$

6. A die is thrown 600 times. How many times would the score on the die be expected to be greater than 4?
(a) 100
(b) 300
(c) 200
(d) 2400

7. An enlargement of scale factor -1, centre the origin, is the same as:
(a) a reflection in the line $y = x$
(b) a rotation about the origin of $180°$
(c) a reflection in the line $y = -x$
(d) a reflection in the x-axis.

8. The expression $\dfrac{x}{6} + \dfrac{6}{x}$ can be written as:
(a) 1
(b) $\dfrac{6x}{6 + x}$
(c) $\dfrac{6 + x}{6x}$
(d) $\dfrac{x^2 + 36}{6x}$

9. A man takes EC \$270 from Dominica to Barbados and spends BDS \$50.
If EC \$1.35 = BDS \$1, how much money does he have left on his return to Dominica?
(a) EC \$67.50
(b) EC \$200
(c) EC \$202.50
(d) EC \$220

10. A man gets a bank loan of EC $15 000 to buy a car. If the bank charges simple interest of 8% per annum, how much is he required to pay (to the nearest dollar) each month, if the bank gives him 3 years to pay?
(a) $417   (b) $450   (c) $517   (d) $620

11. If $n(A) = 8$, $n(B) = 12$ and $n(A \cup B) = 17$ then $n(A \cap B)$ is:
(a) 3   (b) 4   (c) 5   (d) 9

12. A mechanic earns $270 a week of which he spends $110 on food, $60 on entertainment, $40 on rent and he saves the rest.
If this information was shown on a pie chart what angle would represent his savings
(a) $55\frac{1}{3}°$ (b) 80°   (c) 100°   (d) $126\frac{2}{3}°$

13. If x and y are positive whole numbers which of the following are necessarily positive whole numbers?
(a) $x - y$ (b) xy (c) $x \div y$ (d) $x^2 - y^2$

14. In the expression $P = mf - mg$, m written in terms of P, f and g is:
(a) $\dfrac{P}{f} + g$ (b) $P - f + g$

(c) $\dfrac{P}{g} - f$ (d) $\dfrac{P}{f - g}$

15. The perimeter of the running track shown with semi-circular ends is:
(a) 230 m
(b) 340 m
(c) 480 m
(d) 1660 m

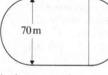

16. If $3x - 2 = 7 - 2(4 - x)$, then x equals:
(a) $^-1$ (b) $\frac{1}{5}$ (c) 1   (d) $2\frac{3}{4}$

17. If $a * b = 3a + b + 2$ then $-3 * 1$ is:
(a) $^-6$ (b) $^-4$ (c) 2   (d) 6

18. If $f : x \to \dfrac{4}{3 - x}$ then $f(1)$ is:

(a) $^-2$ (b) $^-1$ (c) 1   (d) 2

19. If $2x + 3 < 4x - 3$, then the solution set is:
(a) $\{x : x > 0\}$ (b) $\{x : x < 3\}$
(c) $\{x : x > 1\}$ (d) $\{x : x > 3\}$

20. The number of square millimetres in $3\,\text{m}^2$ is:
(a) 9   (b) 3000
(c) 3 000 000   (d) 9 000 000

21. ABCD can be mapped onto A'B'C'D' by:

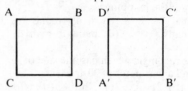

(a) a translation   (b) a reflection
(c) an enlargement
(d) a reflection and a translation

22. The number 0.003 84 written in standard form is:
(a) 0.384×10^{-3} (b) 3.84×10^2
(c) 3.84×10^{-3} (d) 38.4×10^{-2}

23. The minimum length of a piece of paper 15 cm long measured to the nearest mm is:
(a) 14 cm   (b) 14.9 cm
(c) 14.95 cm   (d) 14.99 cm

24. The smallest of the numbers
$\frac{1}{7}, 1.3 \times 10^{-1}, 0.125, 1.4\%$ is:

(a) $\frac{1}{7}$ (b) 1.3×10^{-1}
(c) 0.125   (d) 1.4%

25. In the simultaneous equations $x + y = 4$ and $x - y = 1$, the value of y, when x is $2\frac{1}{2}$, is:
(a) $^-3\frac{1}{2}$ (b) $^-1\frac{1}{2}$ (c) $\frac{2}{3}$ (d) $1\frac{1}{2}$

26. $x^{-\frac{3}{2}} \times x^{\frac{1}{2}}$ is:

(a) $\dfrac{1}{x^2}$ (b) $\dfrac{1}{x}$ (c) x (d) x^2

27. In the triangle ABC, angle ABC = 90°, AB = 2 cm and AC = 5 cm.
The length of BC is:

(a) 3 cm
(b) $\sqrt{21}$ cm
(c) $\sqrt{29}$ cm
(d) 7 cm

28. A glide reflection consists of
a reflection in the line $y = x$ followed by
a translation through $\begin{pmatrix} 2 \\ -1 \end{pmatrix}$.

The image of $(3, 2)$ under the glide reflection is:
(a) $(0, 4)$ (b) $(^-1, ^-2)$ (c) $(0, ^-4)$ (d) $(4, 2)$

29. Given $a^2 + b^2 = 5$ and $(a - b)^2 = 1$, what is the value of ab?
(a) -2 (b) 2   (c) 4   (d) 6

30. 56 expressed as a product of prime factors is:
(a) 7×8 (b) 7×2^3
(c) $2 \times 4 \times 7$ (d) 1×56

31. The simple interest on $400 invested for 5 years is $120. The rate of interest per annum is:
(a) 3%   (b) 5%   (c) 6%   (d) 7%

32. A machine depreciates at a rate of 10% per annum. If it was bought for $10 000, what is its value after two years?
(a) $8000 (b) $8100 (c) $11 900   (d) $12 000

33. If $\begin{pmatrix} 2 & 1 \\ 6 & -1 \end{pmatrix}\begin{pmatrix} x \\ 2 \end{pmatrix} = \begin{pmatrix} 8 \\ y \end{pmatrix}$ then:

(a) $x = 3, y = 7$ (b) $x = 3, y = 16$
(c) $x = 4, y = {}^-12$ (d) $x = 4, y = 4$

34. The number of bacteria in a jar doubles every ten minutes. Its population can be said to grow:
(a) exponentially   (b) linearly
(c) proportionally to the square of the time
(d) inversely with time.

35. The diagam shows a region between two circles of radius 3 cm and 5 cm, respectively, with the same centre O.
If P is any point in the region, then P can be represented by:

(a) $\{P : 3\,cm < OP\}$

(b) $\{P : 5\,cm > OP\}$

(c) $\{P : 3\,cm < OP < 5\,cm\}$

(d) $\{P : OP = 3\,cm, OP = 5\,cm\}$

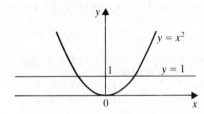

36. The graphs show the relations $y = x^2$ and $y = 1$.

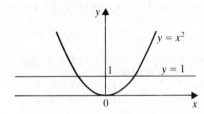

The complete solution of these two equations is:
(a) $x = 1, y = 0$ (b) $x = 1, y = 1$
(c) $x = 1, y = {}^-1$ and $x = 1, y = 1$
(d) $x = -1, y = 1$ and $x = 1, y = 1$

37. $x^2 - 8x + 2$ equals:
(a) $(x - 4)^2 + 18$ (b) $(x - 4)^2 - 18$
(c) $(x - 4)^2 + 14$ (d) $(x - 4)^2 - 14$

38. The probability of throwing a double six or a double five with two dice is:
(a) $\frac{1}{18}$ (b) $\frac{1}{12}$ (c) $\frac{1}{6}$ (d) $\frac{1}{3}$

39. In the triangle ABC, AB = 3 cm, AC = 4 cm and BC = 5 cm. The angle ABC is:
(a) 36.9°   (b) 53.1°   (c) 90°   (d) 120°

40. A truck travels at 20 km/h for 3 hours and then at 30 km/h for 2 hours. The average speed is:
(a) 10 km/h   (b) $21\frac{3}{5}$ km/h
(c) 24 km/h   (d) 25 km/h

41. Three boys share $24 in the ratio 2 : 3 : 4. How much does the boy with the greatest share receive?
(a) $4.00   (b) $5.33   (c) $8.00   (d) $10.67

42. When the income tax was levied at 20% a man paid $400 in tax. His taxable income was:
(a) $2000   (b) $3200   (c) $8000   (d) $20 000

43. In the triangles ABE and ACD, BE and CD are parallel; AD = 9 cm, BE = 4 cm and ED = 3 cm. The length of CD is:
(a) 5 cm
(b) 6 cm
(c) 8 cm
(d) 9 cm

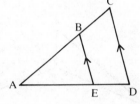

44. $x = 1$ and $x = {}^-1$ are the solutions of the equation:
(a) $(x - 1)^2 = 0$ (b) $(x + 1)^2 = 0$
(c) $(x - 1)(x + 1) = 0$ (d) $x(x - 1) = 0$

45. In the Venn diagram $n(A \cap B) = 3$, $n(A) = 12$, $n(B) = 8$ and $n(U) = 30$.
$n(A \cup B)$ is:
(a) 10
(b) 17
(c) 20
(d) 23

46. Use the data in Question 45.
$n(A' \cap B')$ is:
(a) 7   (b) 10   (c) 13   (d) 20

47. Use the diagram in Question 45.
The shaded region represents:
(a) A'   (b) $A \cap B'$ (c) $B \cap A'$ (d) B'

48. If n is an integer, then $n(n + 1)$ is always:
(a) an odd number   (b) a prime number
(c) an even number   (d) a square number

49. A cylinder has a radius of 7 cm and a volume of 308 cm³. (Use π as $\frac{22}{7}$).
The height of the cylinder is:
(a) 2 cm   (b) 4 cm   (c) 7 cm   (d) 14 cm

50. In the diagram O is the centre of the circle and AB = CD.
ABCD is most accurately described as:
(a) a parallelogram
(b) a square
(c) a quadrilateral
(d) a rectangle.

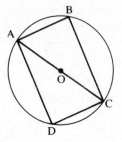

51. In the figure BC = BD and angle ABC = angle ABD.
Which of the following statements is true?

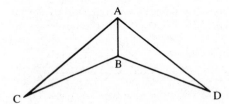

(a) triangle ABC and ABD are congruent
(b) triangles ABC and ABD are isosceles
(c) angle ABC = 90°
(d) triangle ACD is equilateral.

52. The point (3, 1) is first reflected in the line $x = 2$ and then reflected in the line $y = 2$.
Its final image is:
(a) $(^-3, ^-1)$ (b) $(^-3, 1)$ (c) $(1, 3)$
(d) $(1, ^-3)$

53. In the figure OA = 8 cm,
angle AOB = $\dfrac{\pi}{8}$ radians.
The area of the sector AOB is:

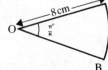

(a) $\dfrac{\pi^2}{16}$ cm² (b) $\dfrac{\pi^2}{8}$ cm² (c) π cm² (d) 4π cm²

54. Which of the following is the largest number?
(a) 110 (base two)   (b) 101 (base four)
(c) 111 (base three)   (d) 60 (base ten)

55. The position vectors of the points P and Q are
$\mathbf{OP} = \begin{pmatrix} 2 \\ 3 \end{pmatrix}$ and $\mathbf{OQ} = \begin{pmatrix} 1 \\ -2 \end{pmatrix}$ respectively.

The vector **PQ** is:

(a) $\begin{pmatrix} 3 \\ 1 \end{pmatrix}$ (b) $\begin{pmatrix} 1 \\ 5 \end{pmatrix}$ (c) $\begin{pmatrix} -1 \\ -5 \end{pmatrix}$ (d) $\begin{pmatrix} -3 \\ -1 \end{pmatrix}$

56. A measure of the deviation from the median of a set of data is:
(a) the mode   (b) the interquartile range
(c) the frequency (d) the range.

57. In triangle ABC, AB = 8 cm, AC = 6 cm and angle BAC = 30°.

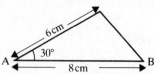

The area of the triangle is:
(a) 10.4 cm² (b) 12 cm² (c) 20.8 cm²   (d) 24 cm²

58. ABCD is a parallelogram.

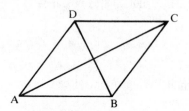

The transformation which maps triangle ABD onto triangle ABC is:
(a) a rotation about B
(b) a reflection in the line AC
(c) a shear with invariant line AB
(d) a stretch with invariant line AD.

59. The probability that a man dies of cancer is $\frac{1}{30}$.
In a group of 60 men how many will be expected to die of cancer?
(a) 2   (b) 4   (c) 10   (d) 20

60. Two numbers x and y are inversely proportional to each other. If y is trebled then x:
(a) is trebled   (b) is divided by 3
(c) has 3 added   (d) has 3 subtracted

Practice Paper 1

Longer questions
Time allowed $2\frac{1}{2}$ hours

Section 1 Attempt all questions

1. (a) In a certain class 20 students study Physics, 16 study Chemistry and 4 study neither. If the class has 32 students, how many students do both subjects?
    Draw a Venn diagram to illustrate this.
   (b) Write down all the subsets of set A when A = {a, b, c}

2. (a) A rectangular piece of land has a width 30 m shorter than its length. If the area of the land is 1800 m², what are its dimensions?
   (b) Write the equation $T = 2\pi\sqrt{\dfrac{l}{g}}$ in terms of g.
    Find the value of g if $T = 13.5$, $l = 50$ and $\pi = 3.14$.

3. (a) Calculate: (i) $10.8 \div 0.03 + 6$
                        (ii) $3\frac{1}{4} - 2\frac{5}{8}$
   (b) A permanent secretary receives an annual salary of $27 192 after a 10% wage rise. Calculate his salary before the increase. What will his salary be in two years time if he receives annual increases of 10%?

4. The function $f(x) = \dfrac{1-x}{1+x}$.
   (a) Calculate $f(\frac{1}{4})$
   (b) Given that $f(f(x)) = f^2(x)$, show that $f^2(x) = x$.
   (c) Write down $f^{-1}(x)$.

5. ABCD is a parallelogram with AB = 8 cm, AD = 7 cm and angle DAC = 43°

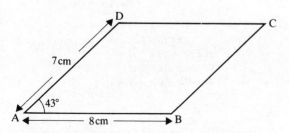

Calculate the lengths of the diagonals AC and BD.

6. The weights of 300 boys were as follows:

Weight (kg)	40–44	45–49	50–54
Number of boys	6	28	56

55–59	60–64	65–69	70–74	75–79
80	73	37	18	2

   (a) Draw a cumulative frequency curve for this data.
   (b) From the graph estimate the median weight and find the semi-interquartile range.
   (c) What is the probability that a boy picked at random weighs 65 kg or more?

7. (a) Find the equation of the line passing through the points $(2, 1)$ and $(-3, 4)$.
   (b) Find where the line perpendicular to the one in (a) and passing through the point $(2, 1)$ cuts the x-axis.

8. Using a ruler and compasses only, construct the triangle ABC with angle ABC = 30°, angle BCA = 90° and BC = 8 cm. Measure the length of AC.

Section II Attempt two questions

9. A farmer makes a composite feed from two different feeds so that the vitamin content of the final feed is at least:
    Vitamin A 6 units,   Vitamin B 8 units
    Vitamin C 3 units,   Vitamin D 8 units
    The vitamin content of each feed per kilogram is:

	Vitamin A	Vitamin B	Vitamin C	Vitamin D
Feed 1	3	2	1	1
Feed 2	1	2	1	4

If the costs of each feed per kilogram are 40 cents and 30 cents respectively, find how the farmer should make his feed up to keep his costs to a minimum.

Practice Paper 2

Longer questions
Time allowed $2\frac{1}{2}$ hours

Section I Attempt all questions

10. Find the latitude and longitude of a point which is:
    (a) 1400 km due north of Moscow (56°N, 38°E)
    (b) 1400 km due west of Moscow.
    Assume the radius of the Earth is 6400 km
    and $\pi = \frac{22}{7}$.

11. (a) If the matrix **T** represents a rotation of 60°, find
        the image of the unit square $(0, 0)$, $(0, 1)$, $(1, 0)$,
        and $(1, 1)$ under **T**.
    (b) Where is the image of the square under $\mathbf{T}^3$?
    (c) Find the value of n such that $\mathbf{T}^n = \mathbf{I}$.

12. The base UVWXYZ of the right pyramid
    OUVWXYZ is a regular hexagon of side 5 cm.
    OU, OV, OW, OX, OY and OZ are each of length
    6 cm.
    Giving your answers to two significant figures,
    calculate:
    (a) the height of the pyramid
    (b) the volume of the pyramid
        (The volume of a pyramid is $\frac{1}{3}$ area of the
        base × height)

13. (a) Find the values of a, b and c such that:
        $$3x^2 - 6x + 2 = a(x + b)^2 + c$$
    (b) Determine the minimum value of $3x^2 - 6x + 2$
    (c) Solve correct to 2 decimal places:
        $$3x^2 - 6x + 2 = 0$$

14. (a) Find the values of a and b such that:
        $$\begin{pmatrix} 2 & a \\ b & 3 \end{pmatrix}\begin{pmatrix} 1 & -2 \\ 4 & 1 \end{pmatrix} = 3\begin{pmatrix} 6 & 0 \\ 6 & -3 \end{pmatrix}$$
    (b) Find the inverse of $\begin{pmatrix} 3 & -1 \\ 4 & -2 \end{pmatrix}$
        and hence find the point of intersection of the
        lines $3x - y = 2$ and $4x - 2y = 6$.

1. (a) Without using tables or calculator, evaluate
       correct to three significant figures:
       $$\frac{2.91^2 - 0.09^2}{33}$$
   (b) A man sells a table for $250 at a profit of 25%.
       What was the cost price of the table?

2. The scores of 82 children in an exam are shown in
   the table below.

Score	0–9	10–19	20–29	30–39	40–49
Frequency	2	5	13	13	15

Score	50–59	60–69	70–79	80–89	90–99
Frequency	15	8	6	4	1

   (a) Estimate the mean score.
   (b) Determine an estimate for the standard
       deviation.

3. (a) 200 cm³ of water is poured into a hollow
       cylindrical container. If the container has a
       radius of 6 cm, how high will the water level
       rise up the cylinder? ($\pi = 3.14$)
   (b) If the cylinder in (a) has an actual height of
       8 cm, how much more water is needed to fill the
       container?

4. (a) Solve the equation giving your answers correct
       to two decimal places.
       $$7x^2 = 7 - 6x$$
   (b) Re-arrange the formula so as to make V the
       subject:
       $$R = \frac{C - V}{D - V}$$

5. (a) From a pack of cards two cards are drawn.
       What is the probability that:
       (i) both cards are aces,
       (ii) both cards are spades,
       (iii) one card is the king of hearts and the other
             the two of clubs?
   (b) A man invests $5000 at 6% compound interest
       for 3 years. How much interest does he receive
       at the end of this period?

6. In the triangle ABC, AB = 6 cm, AC = 8 cm and angle BAC = 40°.

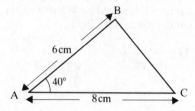

Find:
(a) the length of BC
(b) the angle BCA

7. f is the function defined by $f(x) = \dfrac{2x + 3}{x + 1}$

Find:
(a) $f(4)$
(b) the inverse of f, f^{-1}
(c) $f^{-1}(2)$

Section II Attempt two questions

8. The speed v of a particle with respect to time t is given by the relation:

$$v = 6t - t^2$$

(a) Draw a graph of this relation for $0 \leqslant t \leqslant 6$
(b) What is the maximum speed attained by the particle?
(c) Calculate the distance travelled during the six seconds of motion, if v is measured in m s^{-1}.

9. (a) Write $6 + 5x - 2x^2$ in the form $a(x + b)^2 + c$
(b) Sketch the graph of $y = 6 + 5x - 2x^2$ for $^-3 \leqslant x \leqslant 3$
(c) Find the maximum value of y.

10. Taking the radius of the Earth to be 6400 km, calculate:
(a) the distance from the North Pole to the South Pole
(b) the distance along a line of latitude between Cairo (30°N, 31°E) and New Orleans (30°N, 90°W).

11. The current in a river flows downstream at 2 km/hr. A man wishes to cross to a point directly opposite him on the other bank.
If the man can swim at 4 km/hr in what direction should he swim?
The distance across the river where the man swims is $\frac{1}{2}$ km. How long should his swim take him?

12. (a) Given $\mathbf{A} = \begin{pmatrix} 2 & 6 \\ -1 & 4 \end{pmatrix}$ and $\mathbf{B} = \begin{pmatrix} 1 & 4 \\ 2 & 2 \end{pmatrix}$
show that $\mathbf{AB} \neq \mathbf{BA}$.
(b) Determine $(\mathbf{AB})^{-1}$ and show that
$$(\mathbf{AB})^{-1} = \mathbf{B}^{-1}\mathbf{A}^{-1}.$$
(c) Find x and y if $[\mathbf{B}(\mathbf{AB})^{-1}]\begin{pmatrix} x \\ y \end{pmatrix} = \begin{pmatrix} 1 \\ 0 \end{pmatrix}$.

13. (a) In the parallelogram ABCD,
$\overrightarrow{AB} = \mathbf{a}$ and $\overrightarrow{AD} = \mathbf{b}$.

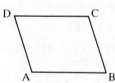

Write in terms of $\mathbf{a}$ and $\mathbf{b}$
(i) $\overrightarrow{BD}$ (ii) $\overrightarrow{AC}$
(b) The position vectors of the points X, Y and Z are:

$$\overrightarrow{OX} = \begin{pmatrix} 3 \\ 0 \end{pmatrix}, \overrightarrow{OY} = \begin{pmatrix} 3 \\ 3 \end{pmatrix} \text{ and } \overrightarrow{OZ} = \begin{pmatrix} 0 \\ 3 \end{pmatrix},$$

where O is the origin.
(i) Write down the images of these position vectors under the transformation represented by $\begin{pmatrix} 1 & -2 \\ 0 & 1 \end{pmatrix}$.
(ii) On graph paper draw the position vectors and their images.
(iii) Describe fully the transformation represented by $\begin{pmatrix} 1 & -2 \\ 0 & 1 \end{pmatrix}$

Practice Paper 3

Longer questions
Time allowed $2\frac{1}{2}$ hours

Section I Attempt all questions

1. (a) Without using tables or calculator, evaluate:
$$\frac{3^2 - 1.8^2}{0.024}$$

   (b) During the Christmas period from a class of 35, 18 children stayed in town and 15 stayed in the country for some of the holidays. Nine spent some time in both the town and the country, the remainder went overseas.
   - (i) Draw a Venn diagram to illustrate this information.
   - (ii) Find the number of children who went overseas.

2. (a) Solve the equations:
$$2x - 3y = 1, \quad -3x + 5y = 2$$
   (b) Solve the equation:
$$2y^2 = y + 5$$
   (c) Find the solution set for the inequality:
$$2x - 3 < 3 + 4x$$

3. Using a ruler and compasses only, construct the rhombus ABCD with AB = 8 cm and angle DAB = 45°.
   (a) Measure the length DB.
   (b) Construct the image of the triangle DBC when it is reflected in the line BC.

4. The table shows the heights of a group of 40 boys.

Heights (cm)	141–145	146–150	151–155
Number of boys	3	9	15
Heights (cm)	156–160	161–165	
Number of boys	12	1	

   (a) Estimate the mean height of the group.
   (b) What percentage of the boys have a height less than the mean?
   (c) What is the probability that a boy picked at random is 156 cm or taller?

5. (a) A regular pentagon has a side of 5 cm. Find its area.
   (b) The volume of a cone is given by the formula
$$V = \tfrac{1}{3}\pi r^2 h$$
   where r is the radius of the base and h is the height of the cone.
   If a golden cone is melted down to form a cylinder which has the same base radius as the cone, find the height of the cylinder.

6. A car bought for $20 000 depreciates in value by 10% each year.
   (a) How much will the car be worth after 2 years?
   (b) If after that time it is resold for $15 000 what is the percentage loss to the seller?

7. Given that $f(x) = 2x + 3$ and $g(x) = 3 - 2x$, find:
   (a) $f(2)$ (b) $gf(2)$ (c) $fg(2)$
   (d) $f^{-1}(x)$ (e) $g^{-1}(x)$ (f) $f^{-1}g^{-1}(2)$

Section II Attempt two questions

8. A factory manager is planning to buy two types of machine.
   Type X needs $3\,m^2$ of floor space, type Y needs $2\,m^2$ of floor space, and he has $40\,m^2$ available. The cost of type X is $20 and type Y $100, and he can spend up to $900.
   Find the number of each type he should buy if he wants the greatest possible number of machines.

9. (a) Sketch the graph of $y = x^2 - 3x - 1$.
   (b) Hence state whether the curve possesses a maximum or minimum value of y.
   (c) Find this value and the value of x which gives this value of y.

10. Find the latitude and longitude of a point 3000 km due west of Caracas (10°N, 66°W). Assume that the Earth is spherical and has a radius of 6000 km and that $\pi = 3.14$.

11. A surveyor measures the angle of elevation of a tower to be 60°, when the tower is on a bearing of 310° from himself. The surveyor then moves to a position 150 m away from the tower on a bearing of 030° from the tower.
   If the new angle of elevation is 30°, find the height of the tower and the distance between the two positions of the surveyor.

Practice Paper 4

Longer questions
Time allowed $2\frac{1}{2}$ hours

Section I Attempt all questions

12. A triangle has co-ordinates, P(1, 0), Q(2, 1) and R(3, 1).

    The matrix $\mathbf{A} = \begin{pmatrix} 0 & 1 \\ -1 & 0 \end{pmatrix}$ transforms PQR into

    P'Q'R' and the matrix $\mathbf{B} = \begin{pmatrix} 1 & 3 \\ 0 & 1 \end{pmatrix}$

    transforms P'Q'R' into P"Q"R".
    (a) Find the co-ordinates of P'Q'R' and P"Q"R".
    (b) Find the matrix which transforms PQR into P"Q"R" and the matrix which transforms P"Q"R" into PQR.

13. (a) Given that: $\mathbf{L} = \begin{pmatrix} 1 & 0 \\ 0 & -1 \end{pmatrix}$ and $\mathbf{M} = \begin{pmatrix} 0 & -1 \\ 1 & 0 \end{pmatrix}$
    describe fully the geometrical transformation each represents.
    (b) Calculate (i) **LM** (ii) **ML**
    (c) Describe each transformation in (b).
    (d) Show that: $(\mathbf{LM})^2 = \mathbf{I}$

1. A radio can be bought for $80.00 cash or by a deposit of $25 and 12 monthly payments of $5.85. By what percentage does this hire purchase cost exceed the cash cost?

2. U = {animals}, D = {dogs} and T = {animals with long teeth}
   (a) Draw a diagram to illustrate this information.
   (b) Give a meaning to $D \cap T' \neq \phi$

3. (a) Using a scale of 2 cm to 1 unit on each axis, draw a graph to represent the region described by the four inequalities:
   $x \geqslant 0, \quad y \geqslant 0, \quad x + y \leqslant 6, \quad x + 2y \leqslant 8$
   (b) Shade the region described and write down the largest value of x which satisfies the inequalities.

4. The table shows the number of children in each of 100 families.

Number of children per family	0	1	2	3	4
Number of families	7	15	21	18	16

Number of children per family	5	6	7	8
Number of families	3	8	12	0

   (a) Find the mean number of children in each family.
   (b) Find the standard deviation.

5. (a) Solve the equation: $\dfrac{p+2}{6} - \dfrac{p-3}{3} = p$

   (b) A piece of wire of length 24 cm is cut into two pieces, each of which is bent into the form of a square.
   If the length of the side of one square is x cm, find an expression for the length of the side of the other square.
   Given that the total area of the two squares is $18\frac{1}{2}$ cm², find the lengths of each of the two pieces of wire.

6. The ratio of the lengths of a scale model of a ship is 1 : 200. The height of the mast of the model is 100 mm and the area of its deck is 90 000 mm²
   (a) Calculate the height of the mast and the deck area of the actual ship.
   (b) If the capacity of the hold of the ship is 1600 m³, calculate the capacity of the hold of the model.

7. (a) Find the value of x for which: $3^{2x} = 27$
   (b) Simplify: (i) $27^{-\frac{2}{3}}$ (ii) $\sqrt{x} \times x^{\frac{3}{2}}$
   (c) $f : x \rightarrow 3x - 4$. Find $f^{-1}(2)$

8. AB is the diameter of a circle, and C is a point on the circumference such that the angle ABC = 60°. If the radius of the circle is 3 cm, calculate the lengths of the chords AC and BC.

Section II Attempt two questions

9. The distance s travelled by a stone rolling down a hill at any time t is given by the formula:

$$s = ut + \tfrac{1}{2} at^2$$

   where u is the initial speed of the stone and a is its acceleration.
   (a) If initially $u = 5\,\text{ms}^{-1}$ and $a = 6\,\text{ms}^{-2}$ plot a distance-time graph for the stone's motion during the first 5 seconds.
   (b) By drawing a tangent to the graph, find the speed of the stone after 3 seconds.

10. Find the value of p which makes $6p^2 - p + 2$ a minimum.
    What is this minimum value?

11. Use the definitions of sine, cosine, and tangent to prove that:
    (a) $\dfrac{\sin x}{\cos x} = \tan x$

    (b) $\sin^2 x + \cos^2 x = 1$
    (c) Hence or otherwise find the value of $\tan x$ if $\sin x = \tfrac{1}{2}$

    (d) Prove that $\tan^2 x = \dfrac{1}{1 - \sin^2 x} - 1$

12. Two towns are 1500 km apart on the parallel of latitude 24°S.
    If the first town has a longitude of 165°W what is the longitude of the second town, assuming that it is due west of the first?
    Assume the circumference of the Earth is 40000 km.

13. The triangle PQR, given by the points $(0,0)$, $(0,1)$, $(2,0)$ respectively, is reflected first in the x-axis and then rotated 90° clockwise about $(0,0)$.
    (a) Calculate the final image points P′Q′R′.
    (b) Find the single matrix which transforms PQR onto P′Q′R′.

14. (a) If $A = \begin{pmatrix} 1 & 3 \\ 0 & -1 \end{pmatrix}$ find the value of x and y such that $A\begin{pmatrix} x \\ y \end{pmatrix} = \begin{pmatrix} 2 \\ 0 \end{pmatrix}$

    (b) Find the value of A^2, and hence write down the matrix A^n when:
       (i) n is even   (ii) n is odd

Practice Paper 5

Longer questions
Time allowed $2\frac{1}{2}$ hours

Section I Attempt all questions

1. (a) A man runs 400m in 46.6 sec (to the nearest tenth of a second).
Find his greatest possible speed in metres per second.
   (b) Work out:
$$\frac{0.00362 \times 792 \times 1.83^2}{0.0495}$$
Give your answer correct to one significant figure.

2. (a) If $V = d^2h$ find V when $d = 0.2$ and $h = 1.44$
   (b) Use the expression in (a) to express h in terms of d and V.
   (c) Find the positive number x which satisfies the equation $2x^2 = x + 3$
   (d) Find the solution set for the inequality $3 < 2x + 1 < x + 4$.

3. Out of 40 boys in a class 30 play cricket, 25 play football and 10 play neither game.
Draw a Venn diagram to illustrate these facts.
Find the probability that a boy chosen at random plays:
   (a) cricket only
   (b) either cricket or football but not both.

4. (a) Using a scale of 2 cm for 1 unit on each axis, draw the graph of the function:
$$f(x) = x + \frac{6}{x} - 2 \text{ for } 1 \leqslant x \leqslant 6$$
   (b) On the same graph represent the function $g(x) = x$.
   (c) Hence or otherwise show that $f(x) = g(x)$ when $x = 3$.

5. (a) The position vectors of the points P, Q and R are given by the vectors:
$$\overrightarrow{OP} = \begin{pmatrix} 1 \\ 2 \end{pmatrix}, \overrightarrow{OQ} = \begin{pmatrix} 4 \\ 1 \end{pmatrix} \text{ and } \overrightarrow{OR} = \begin{pmatrix} 5 \\ 6 \end{pmatrix}$$
respectively.
Find the vector $\overrightarrow{PQ}$ and hence the position vector of the point S, where PQRS is a parallelogram.
   (b) OABCDE is a regular hexagon.
If $\overrightarrow{OA} = \mathbf{a}$, $\overrightarrow{OB} = \mathbf{b}$, find $\overrightarrow{OC}$ and $\overrightarrow{OE}$ in terms of $\mathbf{a}$ and $\mathbf{b}$.

6. (a) Find the equation of the straight line joining the points ($^-2$, 1) and (3, 4).
   (b) Work out the equation of the line passing through (3, 4) which is perpendicular to the line in (a).
   (c) Calculate the distance between the point ($^-2$, 1) and the point where the line in (b) meets the y-axis.

7. A shoe store sells 50 pairs of shoes of the following sizes in one day.

Size	4	5	6	7	8	9	10
Frequency	1	3	4	13	21	6	2

   (a) Draw a histogram to show the data.
   (b) Calculate the mean shoe size.
   (c) Find the median size.

Section II Attempt two questions

8. A group of school children have $15 with which to buy soft drinks and cakes. At least twice as many cakes as soft drinks are bought.
If the cost of a cake is $1.00, and a soft drink is 50c, what is the maximum total number of items that can be bought?

9. Solve the inequality $2x^2 - 3 > x$ where:
   (a) x is real
   (b) x is an integer.

10. O is the centre of a circle of radius 6 cm. AB is a minor arc of the circle whose length is 12 cm.

   (a) Find the angle BOA in radians.
   (b) Calculate the area of the minor sector AOB.
   (c) Determine the ratio of the area of the major sector AOB to the area of the minor sector AOB.

Practice Paper 6

Longer questions
Time allowed 2½ hours

Section I Attempt all questions

11. The diagram shows a pyramid PQRSV with a horizontal rectangular base PQRS and with vertex V; PQ = 5 cm, QR = 12 cm and VP = 10 cm.

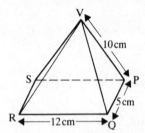

Calculate:
(a) the length PR   (b) the angle VPR
(c) the vertical height of V above the base PQRS.

12. (a) Draw the rectangle ABCD given by A(0, 0), B(0, 1), C(2, 1) and D(2, 0) and its image A'B'C'D' under the transformation:
$$\begin{pmatrix} 0 & 1 \\ -1 & 0 \end{pmatrix}\begin{pmatrix} x \\ y \end{pmatrix} + \begin{pmatrix} 0 \\ 2 \end{pmatrix}$$
(b) Describe fully the single transformation represented.
(c) What transformation will transform A'B'C'D' back to ABCD?

13. (a) Find the value of a to make the matrix $\begin{pmatrix} 4 & 6 \\ 2 & a \end{pmatrix}$ singular.
(b) Calculate the inverse of $\begin{pmatrix} 4 & 6 \\ 2 & 4 \end{pmatrix}$ and use it to solve the equations: $4x = 2 - 6y$
$2x = 3 - 4y$

1. U = {people}, M = {mathematicians} and I = {intelligent people}
Draw a Venn diagram to represent these sets.
(a) On the diagram mark, with an i, Ivan who is an intelligent mathematician.
(b) Describe the set I ∩ M', and shade the region it represents on the diagram.

2. Given that f is a function defined by $f : x \rightarrow x^2 - 1$ and that g is a function defined by $g : x \rightarrow 1 - 2x$
(a) find the value of x such that $f(x) = 8$
(b) find the value of $gf(2)$
(c) find the value of $fg(2)$
(d) write down the inverse of g and hence find the value of $fg^{-1}(2)$.

3. (a) A cone P is similar to a cone Q. The height of P is three times the height of the cone Q.
Find the ratios of:
   (i) their volumes
   (ii) their diameters.
(b) The radius of a circle is 1 m measured correct to the nearest centimetre.
Calculate the largest possible values for:
   (i) the circumference
   (ii) the area.
Give your answers as multiples of π.

4. In the figure, OAB is a sector of a circle centre O, radius 8 cm, angle BOA = 40°.

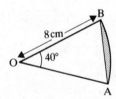

(a) Calculate the area of triangle OAB
(b) Determine the area of the shaded region bounded by the line AB and the minor arc AB.

5. (a) Solve for x, giving your answers correct to two decimal places:
$$5x + 7 = \frac{2}{x}$$
(b) A mother is three times as old as her daughter. Six years ago she was five times as old. How old is the daughter now?

6. A number of students were given a task to complete. The table below shows the percentage p of the students who had completed the task after t minutes.

t	0	5	10	15	20	25	30
p	0	3	15	40	80	90	100

(a) Represent the above information on a graph using a cumulative frequency polygon.
(b) Estimate the median of the times taken by the students to complete the task.

7. (a) Prove the sine rule for triangles. Hence find the angle ABC in triangle ABC where AB = 9 cm, BC = 8 cm and angle ACB = 53°.
(b) A car initially worth $20 000 depreciates by 5% each year. Find its value after three years.

Section II Attempt two questions

8. The number of bacteria N in a pond at any time t is given by the table below.

N	5	10	20	40	80	160	320
t sec	0	10	20	30	40	50	60

(a) Draw a graph of the data using suitable axes.
(b) Find an expression relating N in terms of t.
(c) From the graph estimate the rate at which the bacteria are producing during the 25th second.

9. Find the greatest value of the function defined by
$$f : x \rightarrow 6 - 3x - 5x^2$$

10. Two towns on the same line of latitude are 1200 km apart. If their longitudinal parallels are 60°E and 105°E respectively, find their parallel of latitude. Assume the circumference of the Earth is 40 000 km.

11. A wedge is made by cutting a cuboid in two and has angle CED = 60°, angle AEC = 25° and AB = 15 cm as shown below.

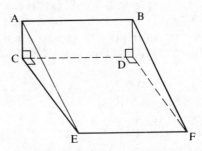

Find
(a) the length BD
(b) the angle AEB

12. A geometrical transformation **T** is defined by:
$$\mathbf{T} : \begin{pmatrix} x \\ y \end{pmatrix} \rightarrow \begin{pmatrix} 1 & 2 \\ 0 & 1 \end{pmatrix} \begin{pmatrix} x \\ y \end{pmatrix}$$
The rectangle OABC has vertices $O(0, 0)$, $A(2, 0)$, $B(2, 1)$ and $C(0, 1)$.
(a) Draw a diagram showing OABC and its image $O'A'B'C'$ under **T**.
(b) Describe fully the geometrical transformation **T**.
(c) Find the matrix which sends $O'A'B'C'$ back to OABC.

13. (a) If $\mathbf{A} = \begin{pmatrix} 3 & 2 \\ 4 & 3 \end{pmatrix}$ and $\mathbf{B} = \begin{pmatrix} 8 & 5 \\ 3 & 2 \end{pmatrix}$, find the matrix **X** where $\mathbf{AX} = \mathbf{B}$
(b) **P**, **Q** and **R** are 2×2 non-singular matrices. Prove that, if $\mathbf{P}^{-1}\mathbf{QP} = \mathbf{R}$, then $\mathbf{Q} = \mathbf{PRP}^{-1}$.

Answers to Part I

I Sets I

page 2 **Revision** (1.1)

1. (a) {Odd numbers less than 10}   (b) {Square numbers up to and including 25}
   (c) {First five letters of the alphabet}   (d) {Vowels}
2. (a) {7,14,21,28}   (b) {1, 2, 3, 4, 6, 12}   (c) {Diamonds, Hearts, Clubs, Spades}
   (d) {January, March, May, July, August, October, December}
3. (a) $\in$ (b) $\notin$ (c) $\in$ (d) $\notin$ 4. (a) True   (b) True
5. (a) {1,2,3,4,6,12}, {3,6,9,12}   (b) 6   6. (a) 4   (b) 7   7. (a) 6   (b) 4   (c) 12   (d) 6
8. None   9. (a) An empty set   (b) An empty set
10. (a) $\subset$ (b) $\not\subset$ 11. (a) True   (b) False   (c) True   (d) True

page 3

12. (a) {3,6,9}   (b) {1,2,5,10}   (c) {1,2,3,4}   (d) {2,3,5,7}   (e) {1,4,9}
    (f) {1,2,3,4,5,6,7,8,9,10}
13. (a) 3   (b) 4   (c) 4   (d) 4   (e) 3   (f) 10   14. Multiples of two.
16. (a) 9   (b) 4   (c) 10   (d) 3   17. (a) {Prime numbers}, {Square numbers}
18. (a) Yes   (b) No   (c) Yes   (d) No
19. (a) (i) {4,8,12,16,20}   (ii) {1,2,3,5,6,7,9,10,11,13,14,15,17,18,19}   (b) (i) 20   (ii) 5   (iii) 15
    (c) They are disjoint
20. (a) Finite   (b) Finite   (c) Infinite

page 4

21. (a) (i) {First 12 letters of the alphabet}   (ii) {Vowels}   (iii) {Consonants}
22. (a) (i) {Numbers from 1 to 12}   (ii) {Prime numbers}
    (iii) {Numbers which have other than two different factors}
23. (a) {1,2,4,5,7,8,10}   (b) {b,y,c,x,w}   (c) {g,i,j,l,m}   (d) {4,6,8,10,12}
    (c) {Monday, Wednesday, Friday, Saturday, Sunday}
24. {girls in form 4}
25. {Bob, Ronald, Marvin}   26. (a) {1,3,5,7,9}   (b) {Odd numbers less than 10}
27. (a) True   (b) True   (c) True   (d) True   (e) True   (f) False
28. (a) (i) 12   (ii) 3   (iii) 9   (b) $n(V) + n(V') = n(U)$ 29. (a) (i) 10   (ii) 3   (iii) 7   (b) Yes
30. (a) 3   (b) 8   (c) 10   (d) 1   31. $T' = \{\ \ \}$
33. (a) (i) {2,4}   (ii) {a,e}   (iii) {Sunday}   (b) (i) {3, 9}   (ii) {l,p}   (iii) {1,2,4}
34. (a) {1,3,5}   (b) {a,e,i}   (c) {3,6}

page 5

35. (a) {Multiples of 2 only}   (b) {Multiples of 3 only}
    (c) {Numbers which are neither multiples of 2 nor multiples of 3}
36. (b) {Multiples of 2 only}, {Multiples of 5 only}, {Numbers which are neither multiples of 2 nor
    multiples of 5}, {Numbers which are multiples of both 2 and 5}
37. (a) (i) {1,2,3,4,5,6,7,8,9,10}   (ii) {a,b,c,d,e,i,o,u}   (ii) {Monday, Friday, Saturday, Sunday}
    (b) (i) {1,2,4,6,8,9,10,16}   (ii) {p,q,r,s,t,v,x}   (iii) {1,2}
38. (a) {1,3,5,6,7,9,12,15}   (b) {a,c,e,g,i,o,u}   (c) {1,3}   39. (b) {1,2,4,5,10,15,20}
40. (a) Yes   (b) Yes   (c) Yes   (d) Yes   (e) Yes

page 6   **More about union and intersection** (1.2)

2. (a) P ∩ Q   (b) S′   (c) X ∪ Y   (d) (L ∪ M)′ or L′ ∩ M′

4. (a) {2,3,5,6,7,8,10}   (b) {2,4,5,7,8,9}   (c) {2,5,7,8}   (d) {1}   (e) {1,3,4,6,9,10}
   (f) {2,5,7,8}

5. Yes   **6.** Yes,   (c) Yes

page 7

7. (a) {1,3,5,7,9}   (b) {1,2,3,4,6,7,8,9}   (c) {1,2,3,4,5,6,7,8,9}   (d) {1,3,5,7,9,10}   (e) {10}
   (f) {1,2,3,4,5,6,7,8,9}

8. Yes

10. (a) {Clive}   (b) {Sonia}   (c) {Clive, Sonia, David, Gregg, Sandra}   (d) {Andy, Tina}
   (e) { }   (f) {Paula}

11. (a) {Clive}   (b) {Andy, Tina, Sonia, Clive, David, Gregg, Sandra, Fatima}
   (c) {Sonia, Clive}   (d) {Sandra, Clive}   (e) {Paula}

12. (b) (i) { }   (ii) {1,2,3,4,6,9,12,15,16,18}   (iii) {3,6,12}   (iv) {1,4}
   (v) {5,7,8,10,11,13,14,17,19,20}
   (c) {Numbers which are neither square, multiples of 3 nor factors of 12}

13. (b) (i) {4,16}   (ii) {1,2,4,8,9,12,16,20}   (iii) {3,5,6,7,10,11,13,14,15,17,18,19}
   (iv) {1,2,3,5,6,7,8,9,10,11,12,13,14,15,17,18,19,20}
   (c) (i) {Square numbers which are multiples of 4 and factors of 16}
   (ii) {Numbers which are either square, multiples of 4 or factors of 16}
   (iii) {Numbers which are neither square, multiples of 4 nor factors of 16}
   (iv) {Numbers which are not square, multiples of 4 and factors of 16}

14. (a) (i) {B,C,D,E,H,I,K,O,X}   (ii) {A,H,I,M,O,T,U,V,W,X,Y}   (iii) {H,I,N,O,S,X,Z}

page 8

15. (a) (i) {H,I,O,X}   (ii) {A,B,C,D,E,H,I,K,M,N,O,S,T,U,V,W,X,Y,Z}

17. (a) (i) (A ∩ B) ∩ C′   (ii) C ∩ A′ ∩ B′ or C ∩ (A ∪ B)′

18. (a) {2,3,4,6,8,12,24}   (b) {2,3,4,6,9,12,18,36}   (c) {2,3,4,5,6,10,12,15,20,30,60}
   (d) {2,3,4,6,12}   (e) {2,3,4,6,8,9,12,18,24,36}
   (f) {the whole numbers from 2 to 60 except 2,3,4,6,12}
   (g) {the whole numbers from 2 to 60 except 2,3,4,6,8,9,12,18,24,36}
   (h) {the whole numbers from 2 to 60 except 2,3,4,5,6,10,12,15,20,30,60}   (i) {8,24}   (j) { }
   (k) {2,3,4,6,12}   (l) {5,10,15,20,30,60}   (m) {9,18,36}

19. (a) P ∩ Q ∩ R   (b) Q ∩ P′ ∩ R′ or (P ∪ R)′ ∪ Q   (c) P ∩ Q′ ∩ R′ or (Q ∪ R)′ ∩ P
   (d) R ∩ P′ ∩ Q′ or (P ∪ Q)′ ∩ R

20. (a) True   (b) True   (c) True   (d) False   (e) True   (f) False   (g) True   (h) True

21. (a) Students in Form Four who belong to the debating society *and* either the chess club or the cricket
   team
   (b) {C ∩ S) ∪ (T ∩ S)} or {C ∪ T) ∩ S}

page 9

22. (a) 4   (b) 4   (c) 2   (d) 6   (e) 2   (f) 2   (g) 10; Square numbers, Multiples of 4

23. (a) 4   (b) 4   (c) 2   (d) 6   (e) 2   (f) 2   (g) 10

24. (a) 6   (b) 4   (c) 1   (d) 9   (e) 5   (f) 3   (g) 20   (h) 14   (i) 17   (j) 5   (k) 17

25. (a) 15   (b) 7   (c) 27

26. (a) 2   (b) 7   (c) 5   (d) 6   (e) 9   (f) 7   (g) 14   (h) 20   (i) 11   (j) 13

27. (a) (i) 9   (ii) 12   (iii) 18   (iv) 3   (b) Yes

page 10   **Problems using two sets** (1.3)

1. (b) (i) 8   (ii) 12   (iii) 80   (iv) 13   (v) 20   **2.** (b) (i) 400   (ii) 250   (iii) 350

3. (b) (i) 62   (ii) 73   (iii) 28   (iv) 135   **4.** 13   **5.** 39

page 11

6. 13, Yes **7.** 8 **8.** 21 **9.** (a) 24 (b) 3 **10.** 5 **11.** 5

12. (a) 3 (b) 15 (c) 12 (d) The number who neither cycle to school nor wear glasses

page 12 **Number of subsets** (1.4)

1. (a) {Joyce, Taraben, Joe} (b) {Joyce, Joe} (c) {Joyce, Taraben} (d) {Joyce, Joe}
  (e) {Joe} (f) {Taraben} (g) {Taraben} (g) {   }

2. Yes. Yes. There are two. There is one. **3.** Yes, {Taraben, Joe} and {Joyce}

4. (a) {p,q,r}, {p,q}, {p,r}, {q,r}, {p}, {q}, {r}, {   } (b) {1,2,3}, {1,2}, {1,3}, {2,3}, {1}, {2},
  {3}, {   }

5. (a) {p,q}, {p}, {q}, {   } (b) {1,2}, {1}, {2}, {   } **6.** Yes

7. {q,r,s}, {p,r,s}; {p,s}, {q,r}, {q,s}, {r,s}; {q}, {r}, {s}

8. {1,2,3,4}; {1,2,3}, {1,2,4}, {1,3,4}, {2,3,4}; {1,2}, {1,3}, {1,4}, {2,3}, {2,4}, {3,4}; {1}, {2}, {3},
  {4}; {   }

9. (a) Yes (b) Yes

10.	No. of elements	1	2	3	4	5	6
	No. of subsets	2	4	8	16	32	64

11. (a) 8 (b) 32 (c) 256 **12.** (a) {1} and {   }; {1,a}, {1,b}, {1}, {a}, {b} and {   }

page 13

13. (a) (i) 4 (ii) 4 (iii) 2

14. (a) {1,2,p}, {1,2}, {1,p}, {2,p}, {1}, {2}, {p} and {   }; 8
  (b) {1,2,q}, {1,2}, {1,q}, {2,q}, {1}, {2}, {q} and {   }; 8 (c) {1,2}, {1}, {2} and {   }; 4
  (d) {1,2,p}, {1,2,q}, {1,p}, {1,q}, {2,p}, {2,q}, {p}, {q}, {1,2}, {1}, {2} and {   }; 12

15. The $\cap$ of {   } with any set is always {   }
  The $\cap$ of any set with itself is always the same set
  The $\cup$ of {a,b} with any set is always {a,b}
  The $\cup$ of any set with itself is always the same set

2 Mapping and functions

page 14 **Mapping diagrams** (2.1)

2. (a) (28, February); (30, April); (30, June); (31, March); (31, July); (31, August)
  (b) (4,12); (4,24); (3,12); (3,18); (3,24); (3,30), (6,12), (6,18); (6,24); (6,30); (5,30); (5,25); (5,35)

page 15

4. (a) (1-M) (b) (1-M) (c) (1-1) (d) (M-1)

5. 1. (a) to 1. (e) (1-1), 1. (f) and 1. (g) (1-M), 1. (h) (1-1), 1. (i) and 1. (g) (1-M),
  2. (a) and 2 (b) (1-M), 3. (a) (M-M), 3. (b) (M-M)

6. (a) (1-1) (b) (M-M) (c) (1-M) (d) (M-1)

7. (a) 8, No (b) 4 or ⁻4, Yes (c) Any multiple of 16, Yes (d) 13, No
  (e) Any number greater than 16, Yes

8. Yes, Yes **10.** (a) Yes (b) They are (1-M) mappings.

page 16

11. (a) and (b) **12.** (b) Yes, Yes **13.** $x+4$, $3x$

page 16 **Function notation** (2.2)

2. (a) (i) $f:x \rightarrow 6x$ where $x \in$ {1,2,3,4,5} (ii) $g:x \rightarrow x-1$ where $x \in$ {1,3,6,10,15} (b) (i) 18 (ii) 2

4. (a) 8 (b) 14 (c) 1 (d) 3

page 17

5. (a) (1,2); (3,4); (4,5); (6,7)   (b) (i) {1,3,4,6}   (ii) {2,4,5,7}   (c) Yes, add 1   (d) $f{:}x \to x+1$

6. (a) 4   (b) 7   (c) 1   (d) 4   **7.** (a) 2,0   (b) 1,1   (c) 0,2   (d) 0,0   (e) 12,2

8. (a) Yes, it is a (1-1) mapping   (b) "Is the capital city of"   (c) Port of Spain   (d) Jamaica
   (e) Cuba   (f) Georgetown   (g) Yes   (h) (i) Trinidad   (ii) Barbados

9. Yes,   (a) 4   (b) 7   (c) 12, 2 or ⁻2   **10.** Yes, (a) 15   (b) 21   (c) 27, 5

11. (a) 31   (b) 30, February

12. (a) No; it does not give the domain.   (b) (i) 11   (ii) 26   (iii) 501   (iv) $3\frac{1}{2}$ (v) $5a+1$
   (vi) $5k+6$ (c) 8

page 18

13. (a) 0   (b) ⁻3   (c) ⁻3   (d) 0   (e) 5

14. (i) (a) 10   (b) 45   (c) ⁻4   (d) ⁻25   (ii) (a) 27   (b) 47   (c) 19   (d) 7   (iii) (a) ⁻9
   (b) ⁻34   (c) 1   (d) 16   (iv) (a) ⁻2   (b) ⁻17   (c) 4   (d) 13

15. (i) (a) 6   (b) 9   (c) 21   (d) $5\frac{1}{4}$ (ii) (a) 0   (b) 2   (c) 12   (d) $-\frac{1}{4}$ (iii) (a) 0   (b) ⁻7
   (c) ⁻63   (d) $\frac{7}{8}$ (iv) (a) 2   (b) $2\frac{1}{2}$ (c) $4\frac{1}{4}$ (d) $2\frac{1}{2}$

17. (a) 7   (b) 14   (c) ⁻4   **19.** (a) 39   (b) ⁻23   (c) ⁻4   (d) 20

20. (i) (a) 29   (b) 125   (c) ⁻31   (d) 5   (ii) (a) 2   (b) ⁻38   (c) 27   (d) 12
   (iii) (a) 2   (b) 90   (c) 12   (d) 0

21. (a) ⁻2   (b) ⁻$2\frac{1}{2}$ (c) ⁻1   (d) 0

22. (a) 5   (b) 13   (c) 6   **23.** 7

24. (a) 5, 25   (b) 20, 23   **25.** 7   **26.** (a) 17, 67   (b) 43, 89

page 19   **Relations, equations and graphs** (2.3)

3. (1,9); (2,8); (3,7); (4,6); (5,5); (6,4); (7,3); (8,2); (9,1)

4. Their sum is 10.   **5.** □ + △ = 10

6. Yes, {1,2,3,4,5,6,7,8,9}, {9,8,7,6,5,4,3,2,1}

7. (a) (1,7); (2,6); (3,5); (4,4); (5,3)   (b) (1,4); (2,3); (3,2); (4,1); (5,0)
   (c) (1,60); (2,30); (3,20); (4,15); (5,12)

8. (a) {7,6,5,4,3}   (b) {4,3,2,1,0}   (c) {60,30,20,15,12}

page 20

10. (a) $1\,\text{cm}^2$ (b) $36\,\text{cm}^2$

11.	Length of first side (cm)	12	9	6	4	3
	Length of second side (cm)	3	4	6	9	12
	Area of rectangle (cm²)	36	36	36	36	36

12. The third is the product of the other two.   The area is the product of the two side lengths

13. (12,3); (9,4); (6,6); (4,9); (3,12)   **14.** Yes, {12,9,6,4,3}, {3,4,6,9,12}

16. Question 9 gives a straight line graph, question 15 gives a curved line graph.

17. (b) $f{:}x \to 2x$, where $x \in \{1,2,3,4\}$; $f(x) = 2x$ **18.** (b) Yes   (c) Yes

page 21

19. (a) (i) {1,2,3,4}, {All values between 1 and 4}   (ii) {2,4,6,8}, {All values between 2 and 8}

22. The graph lines would be continuous

23. 4   **24.** (a) (6,9); (7,8); (8,7); (9,6)   (b) $F+S=15$ **25.** (a) {6,7,8,9}   (b) {9,8,7,6}

26. (a) (3,9); (4,8); (5,7); (6,6); (7,5); (8,4); (9,3)   (b) (8,9); (9,8)   (c) (3,8); (4,6); (6,4); (8,3)

27. (i) (a) {3,4,5,6,7,8,9}   (b) {8,9}   (c) {3,4,6,8}   (ii) (a) {9,8,7,6,5,4,3}   (b) {9,8}
   (c) {8,6,4,3}

29. (a)

F	1	2	3	4	5	6	7
S	3	4	5	6	7	8	9

(b) $S=F+2$

30. (a)

F	4	5	6	7	8	9
S	1	2	3	4	5	6

31. (a) {1,2,3,4,5,6,7}, {4,5,6,7,8,9}   (b) {3,4,5,6,7,8,9}, {1,2,3,4,5,6}
page 22
32. (a) The set of ordered pairs (F,S) such that $F + S = 12$, where F and S both belong to the set N, and so on.
33. (a) (3,9); (4,8); (5,7); (6,6); (7,5); (8,4); (9,3)   (b) (1,3); (2,4); (3,5); (4,6); (5,7); (6,8); (7,9)
   (c) (1,2); (2,4); (3,6); (4,8); (5,10); (6,12); (7,14)
   (d) (1,1); (2,3); (3,5); (4,7); (5,9)
   (e) (1,⁻1); (2,1); (3,3); (4,5); (5,7); (6,9); (7,11); (8,13); (9,15)
   (f) $(1,1\frac{1}{2})$; (2,2); $(3,2\frac{1}{2})$; (4,3); $(5,3\frac{1}{2})$; (6,4); $(7,4\frac{1}{2})$; (8,5); $(9,5\frac{1}{2})$
34. (a) The set of ordered pairs (x,y) such that $x + y = 7$, where x belongs to set W
   (b) The set of ordered pairs (x,y) such that $y = 3x$, where x belongs to the set U
   (c) The set of ordered pairs (x,y) such that $y = x - 1$, where x belongs to set T
35. (a) (1,6); (2,5); (3,4); (4,3); (5,2); (6,1)   (b) (0,0); (1,3); (2,6); (3,9); (4,12)
   (c) (1,0); (2,1); (3,2); (4,3); (5,4); (6,5); (7,6); (8,7); (9,8); (10,9)
36. (a) $y=x^2$ (b) $y=x^2+1$ (c) $y= 5 - x$ (d) $y=4x$
37. (a) $\{(x,y): y=x^2, x \in U\}$ where $U = \{0,1,2,3,4\}$
   (b) $\{(x,y) :y=x^2+1, x \in U\}$ where $U = \{0,1,2,3,4\}$
   (c) $\{(x,y) : y=5-x, x \in U\}$ where $U = \{0,1,2,3,4\}$ (d) $\{(x,y) : y=4x, x \in U\}$ where $U = \{0,1,2,3,4\}$
38. (a) (1,2); (2,3); (3,4); (4,5); (5,6); (6,7)   (b) $y=x+1$
39. (a) {1,2,3,4,5,6}   (b) {2,3,4,5,6,7}
40. $\{(x,y) : y=x+1, x \in P\}$ where $P = \{1,2,3,4,5,6\}$

page 23   **Converting measurements** (2.4)
   2. (a) Yes. For each element in the domain there is only one image.
   (b) $\{(x,y) : y = \frac{5.1x}{2}, x \in Q\}$ where $Q = \{2,4,6,8\}$
   3. (a) Yes, any length can be converted from inches to centimetres   (b) {All lengths from 2″ to 8″}
   (c) {All lengths from 5.1 cm to 20.4 cm}
   4. (a) 5.1 cm   (b) 15.3 cm   (c) 20.4 cm   (d) 2.55 cm   (e) 7.65 cm   (f) 17.85 cm
   5. (a) 1.6″   (b) 2.7″   (c) 4.7″   (d) 6.7″
   7. (a) 1.6″   (b) 4.7″   (c) 6.7″   (d) 3.5″   (e) 5.5″   (f) 8.6″
   10. (a) Yes. For each element in the domain there is only one image
   (b) ($10,£2.10); ($20,£4.20); ($30,£6.30); ($40,£8.40); ($50,£10.50)
   (d) Yes; even fractional values of $Bd can be converted to £. e.g. $2.81 = £0.59
   (e) (i) £3.15   (ii) £5.25   (iii) £8.82   (f) (i) $23.81   (ii) $11.90   (iii) $41.67
   12. (a) $\{(x,y) : y=0.16x, x \in A\}$ where $A = \{$10,$20,$30,$40,$50\}$
   (b) $\{(x,y) : y=0.17x, x \in B\}$ where $B = \{$10,$20,$30,$40,$50\}$
   14. (a) J$4.35   (b) U.S. $2.38   (c) J$1 = U.S. $0.55
   15. (a) $\{x,y : y = \frac{23x}{42}, x \in C\}$ where $C = \{$10,$20,$30,$40,$50\}$
   (b) (J$10,U.S.$5.48); (J$20,U.S.$10.95); (J$30,U.S.$16.43); (J$40,U.S.$21.90);
      (J$50,U.S.$27.38)   (d) (i) U.S.$8.21   (ii) U.S.$20.81   (iii) U.S.$25.74

3 Graphs I

page 25 **Revision** (3.1)
1. (a) 6 a.m. (b) 28°C (c) 2 p.m. (d) 11 a.m. and 4 p.m.
2. (a) 1.7 h (b) 2.4 kg (c) 3.4 h
page 26
3. (a) 3.75 km (b) Walking at 3.75 km/h (c) $4\frac{3}{4}$ h (d) Between 4.30 and 5.00 p.m.
4. (a) 30 000 (b) 140 000 (c) After 3.7 minutes (d) 90 000
5. (a) 1 minute (b) 58° (c) During the first minute (d) The liquid is solidifying
page 27
6. (a) 1.7 A (b) 4.2 V (c) 1.3 V 7. (b) 6.05 s 8. (b) $101.25 (c) 2.6
9. (b) 3.6 cm (c) $41\frac{1}{2}$ days 10. (b) 85.5 g (c) 0.855 g 11. (b) 19.6 cm^3 (c) 82.7 cm of mercury

page 28 **Linear Relations** (3.2)
1. All represent a linear relation except (e)
2. (a) $y=2x$ (b) $y=x+1$ (c) $y=x-1$ (d) $y=2x+2$ (e) $y=2x-3$ (f) $y=3$

3.

x	$^-2$	$^-1$	0	1	2	3	4
$3x$ +2	$^-6$ $^+2$	$^-3$ $^+2$	0 $^+2$	3 $^+2$	6 $^+2$	9 $^+2$	12 $^+2$
y	$^-4$	$^-1$	2	5	8	11	14

4. (a)

x	$^-2$	$^-1$	0	1	2	3	4
$2x$	$^-4$	$^-2$	0	2	4	6	8
y	$^-4$	$^-2$	0	2	4	6	8

(b)

x	$^-2$	$^-1$	0	1	2	3	4
x +4	$^-2$ $^+4$	$^-1$ $^+4$	0 $^+4$	1 $^+4$	2 $^+4$	3 $^+4$	4 $^+4$
y	2	3	4	5	6	7	8

(c)

x	$^-2$	$^-1$	0	1	2	3	4
$2x$ +4	$^-4$ $^+4$	$^-2$ $^+4$	0 $^+4$	2 $^+4$	4 $^+4$	6 $^+4$	8 $^+4$
y	0	2	4	6	8	10	12

(d)

x	$^-2$	$^-1$	0	1	2	3	4
$3x$ -4	$^-6$ $^-4$	$^-3$ $^-4$	0 $^-4$	3 $^-4$	6 $^-4$	9 $^-4$	12 $^-4$
y	$^-10$	$^-7$	$^-4$	$^-1$	2	5	8

page 29

8. (b)

x	$^-2$	$^-1$	0	1	2	3	4
4	4	4	4	4	4	4	4
$-\frac{1}{2}x$	1	$\frac{1}{2}$	0	$\frac{1}{2}$	$^-1$	$^-1\frac{1}{2}$	$^-2$
y	5	$4\frac{1}{2}$	4	$3\frac{1}{2}$	3	$2\frac{1}{2}$	2

10. (a)

Number of gallons (g)	0	1	2	3	4	5	6
Cost (c) $	0	6.50	13.00	19.50	26.00	32.50	39.00

(c) (i) $29.25 (ii) 3.08 gallons (d) $c = \frac{13}{2}g$
11. (a) Yes (b) Yes (c) No (d) No 12. (a) $y=22x$ (c) $y=12x+50$

page 30
13. (a) 249, 415, 581 (b) 40.00, 75.00, 92.50, 127.50 (c) 200, 144, 88, 4
14. (a) $y=83x$ (b) $y=\frac{35}{2}x+5$ (c) $y=200-28x$
15. (a) is a linear relation, (b) is not a linear relation.

page 30 **Solving simultaneous equations graphically** (3.3)
 1. (2,3)
 2. (a) (1,5) (b) (0,3) (c) (1,2) (d) ($^-6,^-11$) (e) (2,4) (f) (2,5)
 3. (a) ($2\frac{2}{3},5\frac{1}{3}$) (b) (5,6) (c) (3,7) (d) ($2\frac{1}{2},7$) **4.** (a) (2,3) (b) (2,7) (c) $1\frac{1}{2},3\frac{1}{2}$ (d) ($2\frac{1}{2},4\frac{1}{2}$)
 5. The two graph lines are parallel.
 6. (a) $y=2x, y=6-x$ (b) $y=2x+3, y=3x-2$ **7.** (a) $y=7-x, y=3x+1$ (b) $y=2x + 1, y=4x-4$
 8. (a) ($^-4,^-11$) (b) ($\frac{1}{2},1\frac{1}{2}$) (c) (1,1) (d) ($1\frac{1}{4},3\frac{1}{2}$) **9.** (a) $2\frac{3}{4}$ (b) $1\frac{3}{4}$
 10. (a) (0,−1) (b) (1,0) (c) (0,10) (d) ($3\frac{1}{3},0$) **11.** (a) (4,1) (b) (1,2)

page 32 **Gradients** (3.4)
 1. $y=4x$ **2.** They are all the same
 3. (a) 1, 2, 3 and 4 (c) The gradient is the coefficient of x.
 4. All are equal to 2 **5.** (c) 1 **6.** (a) 2 (b) 2 (c) 1 (d) $1\frac{2}{3}$ (e) 0 (f) Infinity
page 33
 7. (a) Yes (b) (0,10) (c) 3 (d) $y=3x+10$ **8.** (b) 20 cm (c) $\frac{2}{5}$ (d) $\frac{2}{5}$cm
 9. $E = 20, R = 7.5$ **10.** (a) $s = 13.6t$ (b) $s = 3.5t$ **11.** (a) $I = 10, P = 5.3$
 12. (19,11.1), correct value of E is 12.7
 13. $a = \frac{-95}{27}, b = 9.5$. Corrected ordered pairs are (1.1,5.6) and (2.7,0)

4 Computation and number

page 35 **Calculating with fractions – revision** (4.1)
 1. (a) 1 (b) $\frac{7}{8}$ (c) $\frac{11}{12}$ (d) $\frac{13}{15}$ (e) $\frac{2}{5}$ (f) $\frac{5}{8}$ (g) $\frac{13}{24}$ (h) $\frac{5}{9}$
 2. (a) $3\frac{9}{20}$ (b) $4\frac{3}{8}$ (c) $6\frac{1}{6}$ (d) $22\frac{1}{8}$ (e) $\frac{1}{2}$ (f) $1\frac{5}{8}$ (g) $\frac{3}{8}$ (h) $\frac{9}{20}$
 3. (a) $\frac{2}{9}$ (b) $\frac{1}{3}$ (c) $\frac{1}{2}$ (d) 1 (e) 2 (f) $1\frac{1}{2}$
 4. (a) $\frac{2}{3}$ (b) $1\frac{7}{8}$ (c) 2 (d) $\frac{3}{8}$ (e) $\frac{1}{2}$ (f) $\frac{1}{3}$
 5. (a) $2\frac{1}{4}$ (b) $1\frac{1}{8}$ (c) 19 (d) $1\frac{25}{48}$ (e) $2\frac{3}{8}$ (f) $\frac{13}{72}$
 6. (a) $1\frac{37}{44}$ (b) $\frac{9}{16}$ (c) $1\frac{2}{3}$ (d) $1\frac{2}{3}$ (e) $\frac{14}{15}$ (f) $\frac{5}{12}$ (g) $1\frac{23}{26}$ (h) $\frac{10}{27}$
 7. (a) 12 (b) 13, Yes $\frac{1}{2}$ metre **8.** (a) 64 (b) 9 (c) 1 (d) $\frac{9}{10}$
 9. (a) $600 (b) $60

page 36 **Calculating with decimals – revision** (4.2)
 1. (a) 3.8 (b) 6.2 (c) 1.2 (d) 3 (e) 45.1 (f) 13.6
 2. (a) 5.59 (b) 7 (c) 16.21 (d) 5.12 (e) 1.62 (f) 32.3
 3. (a) 5.38 (b) 14.31 (c) 10.48 (d) 1.763 (e) 8.872 (f) 0.141
 4. (a) 2.1 (b) 4.8 (c) 50.4 (d) 0.63 (e) 22.08 (f) 155.34 (g) 12.6 (h) 190 (i) 115
 5. (a) 0.12 (b) 0.72 (c) 0.31 (d) 3.751 (e) 17.225 (f) 13.44 (g) 0.3216 (h) 0.438
 (i) 3.8734
 6. (a) 0.2 (b) 0.8 (c) 0.4 (d) 0.16 (e) 0.02 (f) 0.312
 7. (a) 70 (b) 800 (c) 23 000 (d) 40 (e) 200 (f) 600
 8. (a) 4 (b) 8 (c) 12 (d) 40 (e) 80 (f) 270
 9. (a) 4 (b) 9 (c) 0.4 (d) 1.52 (e) 0.8 (f) 32.5
 10. (a) 6 (b) 10 (c) 400

page 37 **Fractions and decimals** (4.3)
 1. (a) 0.25 (b) 0.625 (c) 0.75 (d) 0.4

2. (a) 0.075 (b) 0.16 (c) 0.12 (d) 0.1875 **3.** (a) $\frac{7}{20}$ (b) $\frac{4}{5}$ (c) $\frac{19}{20}$ (d) $\frac{6}{25}$
4. (a) $\frac{5}{8}$ (b) $\frac{3}{40}$ (c) $\frac{23}{125}$ (d) $\frac{1}{125}$
5. 0.125, (a) 0.25 (b) 0.375 (c) 0.5 (d) 0.625 (e) 0.75 (f) 0.875
6. 0.0625, (a) 0.3125 (b) 0.5625 (c) 0.4375 (d) 0.6875 (e) 0.9375
7. $\frac{1}{16} = 0.0625$, $\frac{1}{32} = 0.03125$, (a) 0.09375 (b) 0.96875 (c) 0.046875 (d) 0.0234375
8. (a) 0.66666 (b) 0.16666 (c) 0.83333 (d) 0.44444 (e) 0.08333
9. (a) $\frac{2}{11}$ (b) $\frac{3}{11}$ (c) $\frac{9}{11}$ (d) $\frac{10}{11}$
11. (a) 2.89, 3.24 (b) 2.9929 and 3.0276 (c) 2.999824 and 3.003289, 1.732
12. 4, 8 m **13.** $4\frac{5}{12}$ km
page 38
14. 1 g **15.** 1 litre **16.** 0.5958 kg **17.** 16.3 g **18.** 16 cm **19.** \$1.72
20. 6 **21.** $\frac{23}{42}$ litre **22.** 22.4 cm, $\frac{17}{25}$ **23.** (a) 27.27 (b) 27 (c) $\frac{3}{11}$
24. (a) $\frac{34}{99}$ (b) $\frac{86}{99}$ (c) $\frac{1}{3}$ (d) $\frac{1}{9}$ **25.** (a) $\frac{41}{99}$ (b) $\frac{217}{999}$ **26.** 12, 8 and 4

page 38 **Significant figures** (4.4)
1. (a) 60 (b) 50 (c) 70 (d) 70 (e) 70 (f) 140 (g) 290 (h) 1410 (i) 1050 (j) 2540
  (k) 13 790 (l) 14 300
2. (a) 200 (b) 800 (c) 1500 (d) 2500 (e) 4600 (f) 4500 (g) 11 700 (h) 12 100
  (i) 13 000 (j) 20 100 (k) 130 500 (l) 220 100
4. (a) 1.3 (b) 1.4 (c) 1.4 (d) 3.7 (e) 5.5 (f) 2.2 (g) 12.4 (h) 13.0 (i) 0.1
5. (a) 1.44 (b) 2.50 (c) 10.40 (d) 0.30 (e) 10.09 (f) 0.01 (g) 0.11 (h) 13.33 (i) 15.40
7. (a) 900 (b) 9000 (c) 40 000 (d) 40 000 (e) 0.8 (f) 0.07 (g) 0.007 (h) 9 (i) 0.0004
8. (a) 540 000 (b) 42 000 (c) 0.037 (d) 0.000 22 (e) 12 (f) 1.1 (g) 0.0048 (h) 1400
  (i) 0.31
9. (b) 0.00571 (d) 509 000 (f) 0.0101
10. (a) 18.4 (b) 158 000 (c) 10 500 (d) 0.0301 (e) 15.1 (f) 113 (g) 21 500 (h) 13.4
  (i) 21.0
11. (a) Exact (b) Approximate, 15 300 (c) Approximate, 3 000 000 (d) Exact (e) Exact
  (f) Exact (g) Approximate, 384 400 km (h) Exact

page 40 **Indices** (4.5)
1. (a) 5^1 (b) 7^1 (c) 9^1 (d) 10^1 (e) 3^4 (f) 7^3 (g) 5^5 (h) p^4 (i) q^3 (j) y^5
2. (a) $3 \times 3 \times 3 \times 3 \times 3$ (b) $7 \times 7 \times 7 \times 7$ (c) $6 \times 6 \times 6$ (d) 9×9 (e) $p \times p \times p \times p \times p$
  (f) $q \times q \times q \times q$ (g) $r \times r \times r$ (h) $y \times y$
3. (a) $3^4 = 3 \times 3 \times 3 \times 3 = 81$ (b) $5^4 = 5 \times 5 \times 5 \times 5 = 625$
  (c) $2^7 = 2 \times 2 \times 2 \times 2 \times 2 \times 2 \times 2 = 128$
  (d) $25 = 5^2 = 5 \times 5$ (e) $49 = 7^2 = 7 \times 7$ (f) $8 = 2^3 = 2 \times 2 \times 2$ (g) $81 = 3^4 = 3 \times 3 \times 3 \times 3$
  (h) $10\,000 = 10 \times 10 \times 10 \times 10 = 10^4$ (i) $1\,000\,000 = 10 \times 10 \times 10 \times 10 \times 10 \times 10 = 10^6$
4. (a) 5^1 (b) 9^1 (c) 5^3 (d) 8^2 (e) 3^3 (f) 2^5 (g) 4^4 (h) 11^3
5. (a) 3^6 (b) 2^8 (c) 7^6 (d) 5^{10} **6.** (a) 2^7 (b) 3^7 (c) 4^7 (d) 5^{10} (e) 6^6 (f) 7^{15}
7. (a) 6^{10} (b) 7^{23} (c) 3^{17} (d) 10^5
8. (a) a^5 (b) q^8 (c) r^{10} (d) s^{15} (e) p^8 (f) j^{19} (g) a^{m+n} (h) p^{a+b} (i) m^{a+b+c} (j) x^{a+m+c}
9. (a) 2^{13} (b) 2^5 (c) Not possible, 4 and 5 are not powers of 2. (d) a^5
  (e) Not possible, b is not a power of a (f) $p^5 \times q^2$ (g) $2p^5$ (h) $2p^6 \times q^3$
10. (a) 3^2 (b) 5^4 (c) 7^6 **11.** (a) 2^3 (b) 3^3 (c) 4^5 (d) 7^5 (e) 9^6 (f) 5^4
12. p^3 (b) q^5 (c) r^{14}

page 41

13. (a) 6^1 (b) 5^3 (c) 12^3 (d) 7^4 (e) 20^5 (f) q^1 (g) b^1 (h) p^5 (i) y^{4-m}

14. (a) Yes (b) $4^0 = 1$

15. (a) $2^3 \div 2^3 = 2^0 = 1$ (b) $3^5 \div 3^5 = 3^0 = 1$ (c) $7^2 \div 7^2 = 7^0 = 1$ (d) $9^{10} \div 9^{10} = 1$

16. Yes

17. (a) 1 (b) 1 (c) 1 (d) 1

18. (a) $\frac{1}{4}$ (b) $4^5 \div 4^6 = 4^{(5-6)} = 4^{-1}$ (c) $\frac{1}{4} = 4^{-1}$

19. (a) $\frac{1}{5}$ (b) $5^6 \div 5^7 = 5^{(6-7)} = 5^{-1}$
(c) $\frac{1}{5} = 5^{-1}$

20. (a) $\frac{1}{7}$ (b) $\frac{1}{3}$ (c) $\frac{1}{4}$ (d) $\frac{1}{8}$

21. (a) 6^{-1} (b) 2^{-1} (c) 20^{-1} (d) 100^{-1}

22. (a) 5^{-2} (b) p^{-3} $1/5^2$ and $1/p^3$

26. (a) 1 (b) $\frac{1}{4}$ (c) $1\frac{1}{2}$ (d) 4 (e) 1 (f) $\frac{1}{3}$ (g) $\frac{3}{4}$ (h) $\frac{1}{36}$ (i) $2\frac{1}{4}$ (j) 8

27. (a) $3(1-a)(1+a)$ (b) $a(a-1)(a+1)$ (c) $(1-a)(1+a)(1+a^2)$ (d) $a^4(a+1)$ (e) $2\frac{8}{9}a$ (f) $4 + \dfrac{1}{a}$

28. $0.001 = \frac{1}{1000} = 10^{-3}, 0.0001 = \frac{1}{10\,000} = 10^{-4}, 0.00001 = \frac{1}{100\,000} = 10^{-5}$

29. (a) 10^{-3} (b) 10^{-4} (c) 10^{-6} (d) 10^{-7} (e) 10^{-3} (f) 10^{-3}

30. The size of the index equals the number of digits after the decimal point.

31. (a) 0.01 (b) 0.000 001 (c) 0.000 0001 (d) 0.000 000 01 (e) 0.0001 (f) 0.000 000 0001
(g) 0.000 000 000 01 (h) 0.000 000 000 001

page 42 **Standard form** (4.6)

1. (a) 4×10^3 (b) 2×10^4 (c) 7×10^7 (d) 3×10^5 (e) 9×10^3 (f) 1×10^4 (g) 8×10^4
(h) 1×10^5 (i) 1×10^6

2. (a) 30 000 000 (b) 4 000 000 (c) 7 000 000 000 (d) 50 000 (e) 3 000 000 000 (f) 6 000 000

3. (a) 4.01×10^2 (b) 2.17×10^3 (c) 3.401×10^3 (d) 9.082×10^3 (e) 1.12×10^4 (f) 2.5×10^4
(g) 6.741×10^3 (h) 5.82×10^4 (i) 3.4761×10^4

4. (a) 3.27×10^3 (b) 4.3×10^3 (c) 1.04×10^5 (d) 3.57×10^5 (e) 8.314×10^5 (f) 1.74×10^6
(g) 2.801×10^6 (h) 1.35×10^7

5. (a) 1500 (b) 632 (c) 16 280 (d) 3 940 000 (e) 54 100 000 000 (f) 9 999 000 000 000

6. (a) 5×10^{-1} (b) 8×10^{-1} (c) 4×10^{-2} (d) 7×10^{-2} (e) 6×10^{-3} (f) 3×10^{-3}
(g) 1×10^{-3} (h) 5×10^{-4} (i) 9×10^{-3}

page 43

7. (a) 0.7 (b) 0.03 (c) 0.0004 (d) 0.0009 (e) 0.000 06 (f) 0.000 005

8. (a) 1.6×10^{-1} (b) 3.7×10^{-1} (c) 2.2×10^{-2} (d) 9.4×10^{-2} (e) 8.7×10^{-2} (f) 6.4×10^{-3}
(g) 9.6×10^{-3} (h) 3.7×10^{-3} (i) 9.1×10^{-4}

9. (a) 3.2×10^{-3} (b) 9.46×10^{-3} (c) 8.74×10^{-4} (d) 3.77×10^{-6} (e) 9.99×10^{-7}
(f) 6.21×10^{-10} (g) 8.046×10^{-7} (h) 9×10^{-13}

10. (a) 0.036 (b) 0.007 409 (c) 0.000 611 (d) 0.019 99 (e) 0.002 6741 (f) 0.000 005 47
(g) 0.000 000 016 77 (h) 0.000 000 000 3084

11. $1.5 \times 10^7, 6 \times 10^{13}, 1 \times 10^{20}, 6.023 \times 10^{23}, 1 \times 10^{-5}, 2.88 \times 10^{-7}, 3.3 \times 10^{-22}$

12. (a) 10^4 (b) 6.87×10^8 (c) 10^{10} (d) 10^{-6}

13. (a) 10^{-3} (b) 1.009×10^{-6} (c) 6.3×10^{-8} (d) 590 000

page 43 **Error in measurements** (4.7)

1. (a) 12.37 (b) 12.37 (c) 12.36 and 42 seconds (d) 12.36.71

2. (a) d (b) Yes

3. (a) Watch (d) would be best because it shows hundredths of a minute. But a stop-watch would be better than any of these

(b) Any of them   (c) Watch (c) or (d)   (d) Watch (c) or (d)   (e) Watch (e) or (d)

page 44

4. (a) and (f) are too small to be measured with a ruler   (c) is too large to be measured with a ruler.

5. (a) 3 cm, 3 cm, 6 cm, 5 cm, 3 cm   (b) 33 mm, 32 mm, 59 mm, 48 mm, 25 mm

6. (a) No   (b) Yes; AB, EF and IJ

7. (a) No   (b) 3 cm, 3 cm, 3 cm   (c) Yes; Yes

8. (a) 4 cm, 4 cm, 4 cm, 4 cm, 3 cm   (b) 36 mm, 44 mm, 37 mm, 39 mm, 28 mm

9. 4 mm, 4 mm, 3 mm, 1 mm, 2 mm   **10.** (a) Yes   (b) Yes   (c) Yes

11. (a) 4.5 cm   (b) 6.5 cm   (c) 11.5 cm; 0.5 cm   **12.** (a) 5.55 cm   (b) 4.05 km   (c) 0.95 m

page 45

13. (a) 31.5 min   (b) 115 miles   (c) 0.245 s   (d) 1.25 cm

14. (a) 36 mm, 28 mm, 63 mm   (b) 4 cm, 3 cm, 6 cm   **15.** Yes   (a) Yes

16. (a) The time is only correct to the nearest hundredth of a second

(b) To the nearest one hundredth of a second   (c) 39.125 s   (d) 39.135 s

page 45   **Calculations and degrees of accuracy** (4.8)

1. (d) because it is expressed to two decimal places rather than one.

2. 150.2 cm and 145.5 cm, because they are expressed to the nearest millimetre rather than to the nearest centimetre

3. (a) 52.14 s and 50.32 s   (b) To ensure that the error is the same for all.

(c) 48.3 s, 52.1 s, 50.3 s, 49.8 s, 50.6 s

(d) 50.22 s or 50.2 s to three significant figures. The average must be given to the same degree of accuracy as the individual values.

4. (a) No   (b) Yes, 5.4 cm − 1.2 cm = 4.2 cm

(c) Yes, 11.5 cm + 17.3 cm + 18.2 cm. Average = 47.0 cm ÷ 3 = 15.7 cm   (d) No; Average

5. (a) 9.35 cm and 9.25 cm, 10.45 cm and 10.35 cm, 11.15 cm and 11.05 cm   (b) 30.95 cm and 30.65 cm

6. (a) 95.5 cm and 94.5 cm   (b) 58 cm and 56 cm   **7.** (a) 12.5 m and 11.5 m   (b) 4.5 m and 3.5 m

page 46

8. (a) $48 \text{m}^2, 56 \text{m}^2, 40 \text{m}^2$ (b) 8m^2 **9.** (a) 17.92cm^2 (b) 18.36cm^3 (c) 17.48cm^2 (d) 0.44cm^2

10. (a) To one decimal place

(b) Yes, because if the sides of a square are each divided up into ten equal parts the square is divided up into one hundred equal parts.

11. (a) 4.5 cm and 3.5 cm   (b) (i) 91cm^3 (ii) 43cm^3 (c) 2.430cm^3

page 46   **Number bases** (4.9)

1. (a) 40   (b) 42   (c) 43   (d) 101   (e) 120   (f) 1011

2. (a) 11   (b) 13   (c) 4   (d) 34   (e) 123   (f) 34

3. (a) 3   (b) 43   (c) 100   (d) 100   (e) 400

4. $3 \times 1 = 3$ $3 \times 2 = 11$ $3 \times 3 = 14$ $3 \times 4 = 22$ $4 \times 1 = 4$ $4 \times 2 = 13$ $4 \times 3 = 22$ $4 \times 4 = 31$

page 47

5. (a) 31   (b) 124   (c) 1104   (d) 3243   (e) 20141   (f) 1034

6. (a) 0   (b) 1   (c) 4   (d) 14   (e) 31; No   **7.** Yes, 41 − 14 = 22 and 30 − 03 = 22

8. Yes 143

9. (a) 9   (b) 17   (c) 28   (d) 36   (e) 79   (f) 65   (g) 175   (h) 194

10. (a) 7   (b) 10   (c) 19   (d) 41   **11.** (a) 4   (b) 7   (c) 10   (d) 23

12. (a) 21   (b) 26   (c) 37   (d) 61   (e) 70   (f) 121   (g) 130   (h) 140   (i) 250   (j) 370

(k) 624   (l) 625

13. (a) 21   (b) 32   (c) 100   (d) 120   (e) 331   (f) 1103   (g) 3333   (h) 10000

14. (a) 101 (b) 1000 (c) 10110 **15.** (a) 11 (b) 111 (c) 1011
16. (a) 7 (b) 21 (c) 17 (d) 31
17. (a) 100 (b) 10000 (c) 10111 (d) 100000 (e) 111100 (f) 111111 (g) 1111111
(h) 10000000 (i) 111110100 (j) 10000000000
18. 255

5 Measurement

page 49 **Area – revision** (5.1)
1. (a) 7 squares (b) 8 squares (c) 8 squares (d) 18 squares
3. (a) (i) 8 cm (ii) $7\frac{1}{2}$ cm^2 (b) Area = Length × Width
4. (a) 5.25 cm^2 (b) 15.08 cm^2 **5.** (a), (b), (c) and (e)
6. (a) 1 cm^2 (b) (i) 0.04 cm^2 (ii) 4 mm^2 **7.** (a) 24 cm^2 (b) 2400 mm^2 (c) 0.0024 m^2
8. (a) 26 m^2 (b) 63 m^2 (c) 33 m^2 (d) 40 m^2
9. 10^2 or 100 **10.** 3.1 hectares **11.** 24 mm^2
12. 2360.76 cm^2

page 51 **Circles** (5.2)
1. (a) 12.56 cm (b) 31.4 cm (c) 62.8 cm **2.** (a) 12.56 cm^2 (b) 78.5 cm^2 (c) 314 cm^2
3. (a) 77 cm^2 (b) 4928 mm^2 (c) 1925 mm^2 **4.** (a) 12.568 cm (b) 31.42 cm (c) 0.3142 m^2
5. (a) 20.56 cm (b) 25.12 cm^2
6. (a) 14.13 cm^2 (b) 39.25 cm^2 (c) 30.96 cm^2 (d) 64.26 cm^2 (e) 49.0625 cm^2
7. (a) 25.7 m **8.** (a) 87.92 cm (b) 94.2 cm **9.** (a) 37 680 km (c) 6.28 m

page 52 **Arcs and sectors** (5.3)
1. (a) 15.7 cm (b) 314 cm^2 (c) 78.5 cm^2 **2.** (a) 45° (b) 56.52 cm^2
3. (a) $\frac{1}{8}$ (b) $\frac{1}{10}$ (c) $\frac{1}{6}$ (d) $\frac{1}{3}$ **4.** 12.56 cm, 1.57 cm, 1.256 cm, 2.093 cm, 4.187 cm, 9.42 cm
5. 1.57 cm^2, 1.256 cm^2, 2.093 cm^2, 4.187 cm^2, 9.42 cm^2 **6.** 3.14×10^{12} km

page 53 **Triangles and quadrilaterals** (5.4)
1. (a) 16 cm^2 (b) 6.3 m^2 (c) 2.16 cm^2 (d) 24 cm^2
2. (a) 10 squares (b) $10\frac{1}{2}$ squares (c) 4 squares (d) 3 squares
3. (a) 12 squares (b) 8 squares (c) 12 squares (d) 9 squares (e) $17\frac{1}{2}$ squares (f) 15 squares
(g) $7\frac{1}{2}$ squares
4. (a) 25 squares (b) 14 squares (c) 24 squares (d) $10\frac{1}{2}$ squares (e) 4 squares
page 54
5. 18.505 cm^2 **6.** (a) 10 cm (b) 24 cm^2, 20 cm^2 (c) 44 cm^2 **7.** 57.25 cm^2
8. (a) 13 cm (b) 56 cm^2 **9.** 60 cm^2 **10.** 20 cm^2 **11.** (a) 1.732 cm (b) 1.732 cm^2
12. (b) 10.39 cm^2 (c) 2 cm (d) 12.56 cm^2 (e) 2.17 cm^2 **13.** 65.5 cm^2 **14.** 42.14 cm^2

page 55 **Solids – surface area** (5.5)
1. (a) 6 cm^2 (b) 24 cm^2 **2.** 54 cm^2, 216 cm^2; It is quadrupled.
3. (a) 22 cm^2 (b) 125 m^2 (c) 5800 mm^2 **4.** (a) 5 (b) 132 cm^2 **5.** (b) 660 cm^2
6. (a) 21.98 cm (b) 219.8 cm^2 **7.** (a) 188.4 cm^2 (b) 452.16 mm^2 (c) 6280 cm^2 (d) 0.942 m^2
8. (a) 244.92 cm (b) 678.24 mm^2 (c) 6437 cm^2 (d) 1.0833 m^2 **9.** (a) 153.86 cm^2 (c) 230.79 cm^2
10. (a) 62.8 cm^2 (b) 251.2 cm^2
page 56
11. (a) 615.44 cm^2 (b) 50.24 cm^2 (c) 1256 cm^2 (d) 314 mm^2
12. (a) 498 506 400 km^2 (b) 144 566 856 km^2 **13.** 38 465 000 km^2
14. (a) 6.28 cm^2 (b) 25.12 cm^2 (c) 109.9 cm^2 (d) 4.71 m^2 **15.** (a) 2 cm (b) 94.2 cm^2
16. (a) 78.5 cm^2 (b) 188.4 cm^2 (c) 266.9 cm^2 **17.** $\pi r(l+r)$, 65.94 cm^2 **18.** 1356.48 cm^2

page 56 **Volume** (5.6)
1. 18 cm   2. (b) 55 cm by 14 cm by 3.4 cm, 2618 cm^3 3. 192 cm^2

page 57
4. (b) 60 cm^3 5. 252 cm^3
6. (a) 6.28 cm^3 (b) 1538.6 cm^3 (c) 9.42 cm^3 (9420 mm^3)   (d) 0.07065 m^3
7. (a) 1 cm, 0.2 cm   (b) 62.8 cm^3
8. (a) 4.187 cm^3 (b) 113.04 mm^3 (c) 2.144 m^3 9. 4187 mm^3
10. (a) 1437$\frac{1}{3}$ cm^3 (b) 6707$\frac{5}{9}$ cm^3 11. (a) 1848 cm^3 (b) 1348 cm^3 (c) 938
12. (a) 33 493 cm^3 (b) 33.493 litres   (c) 187.5   13. (a) 757 m^3 (b) 757 000 litres

page 58
14. 20.93 cm^3 15. (a) 75 cm^3 (b) 116.7 cm^3
16. 2 555 000 m^3 17. (a) 4.8 cm   (b) 65.11104 cm^3 18. (a) 2 cm   (b) 9.220 cm
19. (i) 5.657 cm   (ii) 2.828 cm   (iii) 2.828 cm   20. 15.08 cm^3 21. 235.7 cm^3
22. (a) 166.3 cm^3 (b) 12.65 cm   23. (a) 1047 cm^3 (b) 154.5 cm^3 (c) 118.1 cm^3

page 59 **Measurement and scales** (5.7)
1. 15 km   2. 7.2 cm (108 km)   (b) 2.5 cm (37.5 km)   3. 195 km   4. 8$\frac{1}{3}$ cm
5. (a) 0.5 km   (b) 2.5 km   (c) 0.25 km   (d) 10 cm   (e) 20 cm   (f) 2 cm
6. (a) 200 m   (b) 20000 cm   (c) 1 : 20 000
7. 1 : 50 000 = 2 cm : 1 km; 1 : 100 000 = 1 cm : 1 km, 1 : 1 250 000 = 2 cm : 25 km;
   1 : 10 000 = 10 cm : 1 km, 1 : 4 000 000 = 1 cm : 40 km; 1 : 400 000 = 1 cm : 4 km.
8. (a) 500 m   (b) 2 km   (c) 50 m   (d) 12.5 km   (e) 50 km
9. (a) 750 m   (b) 750 000 m^2 (c) 75 hectares

page 60
10. (a) 7 cm^2 (b) 1.75 km^2
11. (a) 120 000 cm^2 (b) 48 : 120 000 = 1 : 2500   (c) The former is the square of the latter
12. 20 m^2 13. (a) 80 000 000 cm^2 (b) 100 000 000 : 1   (c) 1 : 10 000
14. (a) 4 cm   (b) 12.56 cm^2 (c) 1 : 10 000   (d) 37.68 cm^3 (e) 1 : 1 000 000
15. (a) 1 cm^2 = 100 mm^2 (b) 1 m^2 = 10 000 cm^2 (c) 1 km^2 = 1 000 000 m^2
    (d) 1 km^2 = 10 000 000 000 cm^2 (e) 1 cm^3 = 1000 mm^3 (f) 1 m^3 = 1 000 000 cm^3
    (g) 1 km^3 = 1 000 000 000 m^3 (h) 1 km^3 = 1 000 000 000 000 000 cm^3
16. (a) 40 m   (b) 1600 m^2 (c) 64 000 m^3

6 Geometry

page 62 **Constructions** (6.1)
1. (a) Scalene   (b) Isosceles   (c) Right-angled   2. (a) 3.1 cm   (b) 5 cm   (c) 8.3 cm
3. (a) 3.4 cm, 5 cm   (b) 3.5 cm, 3.5 cm   (c) 3 cm, 5.2 cm
4. (f) All are equal to 45°. The lines are parallel.   5. 90°
6. Yes, using the sides AC and BC
7. 45°, 45°, 90°   10. PQ̂R = 90°   11. 60°
13. (c) (i) It is a parallelogram.   (ii) They are parallel

page 64 **Bisecting** (6.2)
3. (c) The three bisectors all meet at one point.   6. 10 cm   7. 3.6 cm, 6.4 cm, 4.8 cm
8. They all meet at one point   12. (c) They are perpendicular.

page 66 **Constructing angles** (6.3)
2. (a) 4   10. (b) 10.4 cm, 31.2 cm^2, 12 cm
14. (b) Yes, 50 cm^2 (c) QS is parallel to PR and equal to 14.1 cm.

page 67   **Ratios and similar triangles** (6.4)
 1. (a) (i) $\hat{R}$ (ii) $\hat{B}$ (iii) $\hat{C}$ (b) Yes   (c) (i) BC   (ii) AC   (iii) RQ   (d) Yes
 2. (a) Yes   (b) Yes
page 68
 3. (a) (i) $\hat{Q}$ (ii) $\hat{O}$ (iii) AB   (iv) OB
    (b) Both are 78°; Yes, because two pairs of corresponding angles are equal
 4. (a) 2.1 cm, 6.3 cm   (b) 2.1 cm, 6.3 cm   (c) 1 cm, 3 cm; The corresponding side ratio is always 1 : 3
 5. All ratios are 1 : 3   6. All ratios are 1 : 4
 7. (b) In Question 2(a) all ratios are 4 : 3. In Question 2(b) all ratios are 5 : 4.
 9. (a) 16 cm   (b) 8 cm
10. (a) 9 cm, 12 cm   (b) 90 cm, 54 cm   (c) 6 cm, 48 cm
11. Two pairs of corresponding angles are equal. OL and OA, OM and OB, LM and AB.
    (a) 49 cm   (b) 18 cm   (c) 6 cm   (d) $2x$

page 69   **Congruency** (6.5)
 1. Yes   2. (a) No   (b) Yes   (c) Yes   3. (a) Yes   (b) Yes
page 70
 4. (a) ΔABC and ΔPQR, ΔDEF and ΔNVW, ΔKLM and ΔGHJ, ΔXYZ and ΔSTU.
    (c) All pairs except ΔABC and ΔPQR
 5. (a) Yes   (b) $\hat{B} \to \hat{R}, \hat{C} \to \hat{P}$
 6. $\hat{D} \to \hat{N}, \hat{E} \to \hat{V}, \hat{F} \to W; \hat{K} \to \hat{G}, \hat{L} \to \hat{J}, \hat{M} \to \hat{H}; \hat{X} \to \hat{T}, \hat{Y} \to \hat{S}, \hat{Z} \to \hat{U}$
 7. (a) Yes   (b) BC $\to$ RP, AC $\to$ QP
 8. DE $\to$ VN, DF $\to$ NW, EF $\to$ VW; KL $\to$ GJ, KM $\to$ GH, LM $\to$ HJ; XY $\to$ ST, XZ $\to$ UT, YZ $\to$ SU
 9. (a) Yes, Yes   (b) Yes, because three pairs of corresponding sides and angles are equal
    (c) $\hat{A} \to \hat{F}, \hat{B} \to \hat{E}, \hat{C} \to \hat{D}$ (d) AB $\to$ EF, BC $\to$ DE, CA $\to$ DF
    (e) Because the two triangles are equal in every respect
page 71
10. (a) Yes   (b) $\hat{H} \to \hat{N}, J \to \hat{M}, \hat{K} \to \hat{L}$; HJ $\to$ MN, JK $\to$ LM, KH $\to$ LN   (c) ΔHJK $\equiv$ ΔLMN
11. (a) 6.3 cm, 5 cm   (b) 65°, 70°   (c) U$\hat{W}$V, 45°   (d) ST
12. (a) 22°   (b) 106°, 52°, 22°   (c) KL = 6 cm, KM = 12 cm
13. ΔABC has sides of length 5 cm and 7 cm with an included angle of 100°.
14. (a) ΔDEF and ΔKLM, (S.A.S); ΔABC and ΔPQR, (R.H.S.); ΔLMN and ΔXYZ (A.A.S.)
    (b) $\hat{D} = \hat{M}, \hat{E} = \hat{K}, \hat{F} = \hat{L}$, DE = KM, DF = LM, EF = KL; $\hat{A} = \hat{Q}, \hat{B} = \hat{R}, \hat{C} = \hat{P}$,
    AB = QR, AC = PQ, BC = PR; $\hat{L} = \hat{Z}, \hat{M} = \hat{Y}, \hat{N} = \hat{X}$, LM = YZ, LN = XZ, MN = XY
15. ΔLMN $\equiv$ ΔXYZ, ΔDEF $\equiv$ ΔKLM
page 72
17. (a) No, Yes   (b) Same answer as part (a) for all three cases.
18. 30° is not the included angle between the two given sides
19. $\hat{B} = 38.2°, \hat{C} = 60°$, AC = 5 cm; $\hat{X} = 81.8°$, XY = 5 cm; $\hat{L} = 81.8°, \hat{N} = 60°$, LM = 7 cm
20. They are both right-angled, have the same hypotenuse and the corresponding sides are equal.

page 72   **Angles in circles** (6.6)
 1. (d) All are the same.   2. (c) All are the same.   3. 180°   4. (c) The sum is 180°
 5. (b) Yes   (c) The sum is 180°
page 73
 6. (a) 180°   (b) 180°   (c) The sum is always 180°   7. (a) Yes   (b) Yes   (c) Yes   (d) 180°
 8. (c) A$\hat{O}$B = 2A$\hat{X}$B   10. (a) 60°   (b) 50°   (c) 110°   (d) 90°   (e) 45°, 68°   (f) 80°
11. (a) 125°   (b) 260°   (c) 130°   (d) 65°, 65°
12. (a) Semicircular   (b) 180°   (c) 90°   (d) 90°, Yes

page 74
13. (b) Yes   (c) Yes   (d) An angle in a semicircle is a right angle.
14. (a) $90°, 90°, 64°$ (b) (i) $X\hat{O}Y, 128°$ (ii) $X\hat{O}Y$ (reflex), $232°$
15. (a) $L\hat{M}X$ (b) $Y\hat{M}L$
16. (a) $132°$ (b) $120°$ (c) $90°, 40°$ (d) $60°, 120°$ (e) $100°, 100°$ (f) $50°, 50°$
17. (a) p and y (b) Yes, the interior opposite angle.   **18.** $y, x, 50°$ **19.** $65°, 130°, 110°$
20. (a) $30°$ (b) $20°$ (c) $90°$ (d) $40°$ (e) $90°$ (f) $130°$

page 75   **Quadrilaterals** (6.7)
 3. It is isosceles, because AD = AY.   **4.** (a) and (d)
 6. (a) $\triangle ACX$ is isosceles and right-angled with $\hat{X} = 90°$.
     (b) $\triangle ACX$ is isosceles but not right-angled and AX = XC.
     (c) $\triangle ACX$ is isosceles but not right-angled and CA = CX.
page 76
 7. (a) Kite   (b) Parallelogram   (c) Rectangle   **8.** (a) Rectangle   (b) Rhombus   (c) Square
 9. (a) B   (b) A   (c) C   (d) B   (e) C   **10.** (a) A   (b) B   (c) C   (d) A   (e) B
11. $35°, 145°, 145°$ **12.** $70°, 110°, 110°$ **13.** $130°, 43°$

page 76   **Plans and elevations** (6.8)
 1. (c) 3 doors, 8 windows   **2.** Yes   **3.** $12\,m, 7\,m, 84\,m^2$ **4.** From directly above.   **5.** $12\,m$
 6. $42\,m^2$ **7.** $15\,cm$
 9. (e) L is 3.1 miles from A, B or C. L is the centre of the circle which passes through A, B and C.
10. 1.4 miles from the town nearer to the school.
11. (i) C   (ii) A   (iii) B   **12.** C   **13.** B   **14.** A
page 78
16. (a) The holes   (b) The holes are in line when the brick is viewed from the end.
page 79
21. (a) Yes   (b) The line can be seen from above.   **23.** (b) A square-based pyramid.

7   Consumer arithmetic

page 82   **Money management** (7.1)
 1. Yes, (a) \$4.93   (b) \$10.73   (c) \$8.41   (d) \$1.74   (e) \$4.64   (f) \$6.38
 2. Yes, (a) \$26.10   (b) \$261; Multiply by 10 and 100 respectively
 3. (a) \$20.30   (b) \$52.20   (c) \$522   (d) \$1073
 5. (a) \$12.47   (b) \$13.34   (c) \$13.92   (d) \$124.70   (e) \$127.31   (f) \$118.61
 6. (a) \$16.24   (b) \$18.56   (c) \$28.71   (d) \$96.86   (e) \$80.04   (f) \$44.66   (g) \$290
     (h) \$871.16   (i) \$507.50
page 83
 7. (a) \$9   (b) \$15   (c) \$15.20   (d) \$22   **8.** (a) \$0.35   (b) \$0.30   (c) \$0.25
 9. (a) \$24   (b) \$61   (c) \$75   (d) \$75.30   (e) \$127.50   (f) \$142.50   (g) \$285   (h) \$535
10. \$53.58   **11.** 116   **12.** (a) 100   (b) 127.25   (c) 287   (d) 402   (e) 474   (f) 508
13. (a) 0   (b) 10   (c) 36   (d) 119   **14.** Calls which are dialled directly
15. \$189, \$308, \$46.20, \$354.20   **16.** \$825.26   **17.** \$1182.59   **18.** \$540.30
    page 84
19. 5 days   **20.** (a) \$18   (b) \$28.50   (c) \$78   (d) \$126   (e) \$242

21.

Week	Food $	Clothing $	Rent $	Sundries $	Totals $
1	26.10	14.25	35.00	10.40	85.75
2	21.32	29.95	35.00	18.00	104.27
3	19.90	3.95	35.00	14.60	73.45
4	21.75	9.75	35.00	8.70	75.20
Totals $	89.07	57.90	140.00	51.70	338.67

22. (a) $84.67, $4402.71   (b) $5042.71
23. (a) EC$81   (b) EC$34   (c) EC$22   (d) EC$651
24. (a) Bds$100   (b) Bds$500   (c) Bds$666.67   (d) Bds$62.22
25. (a) TT$1.82   (b) J$2.94   (c) US$0.50   (d) G$3.70
26. (a) Bds$110   (b) Bds$100   (c) Bds$73.75   (d) Bds$810   (e) Bds$232.56   (f) Bds$156.50
27. (a) J$88.24   (b) US$50   (c) G$981.48   (d) UK£1355.93   (e) TT$119.09
28. Barbados by Bd$3.00
page 85
29. (a) Bds$330   (b) Bds$451   **30.** (a) Bds$272.25   (b) Bds$560.84
31. (a) TT$36 363.63   (b) EC$4.05   (c) US$540   (d)US$368.75   (e) EC$5.27
32. TT$567.27   **33.** £126.84
34. (a) US$20   (b) US$33.33   (c) EC$94.50   (d) EC$22.95
35. (a) £3.53   (b) £8.82   (c) J$102   (d) J$53.55
36. (a) £13.42   (b) £30.87   (c) US$35.76   (d) US$74.50

page 86   **Profit and loss** (7.2)
  1. (a) $20   (b) 25%   **2.** (a) $5   (b) $33\frac{1}{3}$%   **3.** (a) $150   (b) $33\frac{1}{3}$%   **4.** (a) $0.10   (b) 50%
  5. 4% loss   **6.** 25% profit

7.

Item	Cost price $	Selling price $	Percentage profit
Calculator	120	140	$16\frac{2}{3}$
Pencil	0.35	0.40	$14\frac{2}{7}$
T.V.	850	1020	20
Bed	600	480	−20
Book	6.75	10.25	$51\frac{23}{27}$

  8. (a) $36   (b) $336   **9.** (a) $5350   (b) $21 400   **10.** (a) $50.40   (b) $669.60   **11.** $43.75
12. $160   **13.** $8.12   **14.** $19.57
page 87

15.

Item	Cost price $	Selling price $	Percentage profit
Table	260	357.50	$37\frac{1}{2}$
Dress	95	100.70	6
Carpet	1060	1197.80	13
Umbrella	26	27.17	$4\frac{1}{2}$
Ruler	0.80	1.26	$57\frac{1}{2}$

16. (c), the incomes are: (a) $7000   (b) $7200   (c) $7500   **17.** $10   **18.** $70   **19.** $200
     20. $20 000   **21.** $60   **22.** $42.86   **23.** $20   **24.** $11 000   **25.** $69   **26.** $36   **27.** $92

28.

Item	Cost price	Selling price	Percentage profit	Percentage loss
Curtains	$120	$130	$8\frac{1}{3}\%$	
Mat	$20	$25	25%	
Tiles	$180	$172.80		4%
Sofa	$1000	$980		2%
Bookcase	$620	$530		$14\frac{16}{31}\%$
Cabinet	$900	$960.75	$6\frac{3}{4}\%$	
Centre table	$204	$168.30		$17\frac{1}{2}\%$

29. $1125 **30.** $162.50 **31.** $18 666.67 **32.** (a) $22.50 (b) £4.50

page 88 **Interest and investment**(7.3)
1. (a) $84 (b) $1600 (c) $1806 (d) $40 (e) $756 **2.** $972 **3.** (a) $1040 (b) 3040
4. (a) $300 (b) $384 (c) $432 (d) $2625 **5.** (a) $3000 (b) $2250 (c) $2187.50 (d) $1925
6. (a) $250 (b) $500 (c) $480 **7.** (a) 3 years (b) $2\frac{1}{2}$ years (c) $3\frac{1}{2}$ years **8.** 6 years 8 months
page 89
9. (a) 9% (b) $9\frac{1}{2}\%$ (c) $13\frac{1}{2}\%$
11. (a) $105 (b) $264 (c) $102.50 (d) $297.90 (e) $2083.50
12. (a) $605 (b) $864 (c) $1102.50 (d) $1197.90 (e) $6083.50
13. $2249.73 **14.** $30 417.50
15. (a) $726 (b) $714.61, therefore (a) is the better investment.
16. $59 550.80 **17.** $28 350 **18.** $30 720 **19.** 3842 **20.** 25 g
page 90
21. (a) $1.44 (b) $2.50 (c) $2.56 (d) $1.77
22. (a) $31.10 (b) $269 (c) $2510 (d) $440 (e) $2177
23. (a) $222 433.28 (b) $1853.61

page 90 **Hire Purchase and mortgages** (7.4)
1. $2530 **2.** (a) $893, $1041 (b) $101 **3.** (a) $3244 (b) $224 (c) 7.417%
4. (a) $9300 (b) $900 (c) 10.71% **5.** (a) $1650 (b) $137.50
6. (a) $288 (b) $228 (c) $19
7. (a) $63 000 (b) $59 500 (c) $64 750 (d) $43 750 **8.** (a) $3000 (b) $75 600 (c) $78 600
9. (a) $50 000 (b) $396 000 (c) $446 000
page 92
10. (a) $495 (b) $472.50 (c) $450
11. (a) $577.50 (b) $556.50 (c) $441 (d) $446.25 (e) $1260 (f) $1370.25
12. (a) $15 000 (b) $85 000 (c) $850 (d) $270 000
13. (a) $12 500 (b) $112 500 (c) $1125 (d) $350 000

page 92 **Rates and taxes** (7.5)
3. (a) $5000 (b) $8500 **4.** (a) $6500 (b) $0
5. The difference between his taxable income and $5000.
6. (a) $525 (b) $1350 (c) $2475 **7.** (a) $5000 (b) $4350
8. (a) $5900 (b) $2625 (c) $17 375 **9.** (a) $180 (b) $6020
10. (a) $2700 (b) $4000 (c) $400 (d) $6300
11. (a) $5200 (b) $3000 (c) $300 (d) $7900 **12.** (a) $4700 (b) $4200

page 94
13. (a) $29 000   (b) $23 500   **14.** $8200
15. A $1690   B $1690   C $1840; therefore C pays most tax.
16. (a) Rateable value   (b) $429   (c) Yes   (d) $107.25
17. (a) $550   (b) $319   (c) $792   **18.** (a) $2000   (b) $2500   (c) $3250
19. (a) 0.7%   (b) 18%   **20.** (a) $500 000   (b) 20%   (c) 4%
21. (a) $32 000 000   (b) 29%   **22.** $820 000

8   Statistics I

page 97   **Bar and pie charts – revision** (8.1)
1. (b) 27.4   **2.** (b) 79   (c) 2.633   **3.** (a) 110   (b) 7.909   (c) 8
4. (a) 35   (b) 108   (c) 3.086   (d) 2

5. (a)

Score	4	5	6	7	8	9	10
Frequency	2	1	4	6	4	2	1

(c) 6.95   (d) 7   (e) 7   (f) $\frac{7}{20}$

6. (a)

Cars sold	0	1	2	3	4	5	6
Frequency	2	7	8	6	4	2	1

(c) 2.433   (d) 2,2

7. (a) $55 250   (b) $79 000   **8.** Sector angles are : 225°, 15°, 90°, 30°
9. Sector angles are : 132°, 192°, 24°, 12°
10. (a) Sector angles are : 45°, $22\frac{1}{2}°$, 135°, $67\frac{1}{2}°$, 90°   (b) $12\frac{1}{2}$%
11. (a) Sector angles are : 162°, 90°, 36°, 36°, 18°, 18°   (b) $60 000   **12.** (a) $\frac{1}{6}$ (b) 344
13. (a) Sector angles are : 108°, 79.2°, 86.4°, 32.4°, 54°   (b) $40 million
   (c) $12 million, $8.8 million, $9.6 million, $3.6 million, $6 million
14. (a) $15\frac{5}{18}$%   (b) 54°, 131°   **15.** (a) Sector angles are : 198°, 115.2°, 36°, 10.8°   (b) 0.61

page 99   **Histograms** (8.2)
1. (b) 4   **2.** (b) 2.9

3. (a)

Shoe size	2	3	4	5	6	7
Frequency	2	2	6	6	6	3

(c) 5

4. (a) 140–144 cm   (b) 145–149 cm   (c) 150–154 cm   (d) 160–164 cm   (e) 165–169 cm
   (f) 140–144 cm
5. (a) 160–164 cm   (b) 140–144 cm   (c) 145–149 cm   **6.** 159.5 cm, 154.5 cm
8. (a) 134.5–139.5 cm   (b) 139.5–144.5 cm   (c) 144.5–149.5 cm   (d) 149.5–154.5 cm
10. (a) 15   (b) They are the least and greatest values for the interval.

11.

Mass (g)	90–99	100–109	110–119	120–129	130–139	140–149	150–159
Frequency	0	2	15	45	27	7	4

page 101
12. (a) 19.5–24.5 mm, 24.5–29.5 mm, 29.5–34.5 mm, 34.5–39.5 mm, 39.5–44.5 mm, 44.5–49.5 mm,
   49.5–54.5 mm, 54.5–59.5 mm, 59.5–64.5 mm

13. (a)

Height (cm)	160–161	162–163	164–165	166–167	168–169	170–171	172–173
Frequency	9	15	38	52	29	9	2

(b) 163.5 cm and 165.5 cm (c) 167.5 cm

14. (a)

Marks %	0–19	20–39	40–59	60–79	80–99
Frequency	5	19	46	24	6

(b) ⁻0.5–19.5, 19.5–39.5, 39.5–59.5, 59.5–79.5, 79.5–99.5
16. (a) 524.5 kg   **17.** (a) 160   (b) 22 is the mean of 19.5 and 24.5

page 102   **Medians and quartiles** (8.3)
1. (a) 5   (b) 4   (c) 4   **2.** (a) 9,11,5   (b) 4,6,2   (c) 7,9,2   **3.** (a) 6   (b) 4   (c) 7
4. (a) 70 kg   (b) 61,79   (c) 18   **5.** (a) 7   (b) 6,8   **6.** (a) 15   (b) 14,15   (c) 1
7. (a) 6   (b) 3   **8.** (a) 4   (b) 5,2

page 103   **Cumulative frequency** (8.4)
2. (a) 67   (b) Wednesday   **3.** (a) Tuesday

5.

Length (mm)	20–24	25–29	30–34	35–39	40–44	45–49	50–54	55–59	60–64
Running total	1	5	13	31	56	80	97	99	100

(a) 56   (b) 49.5 mm
page 104

6.

Upper height limit (cm)	139.5	144.5	149.5	154.5	159.5	164.5	169.5
Cumulative frequency	1	4	8	15	20	24	25

7. (a) 20   (b) Below 149.5 cm   (c) Above 159.5 cm
8. (a) 134.5 cm is the lower limit of the lowest interval   (c) 153 cm   (d) Median

9. (a)

Upper length limit (mm)	29.5	34.5	39.5	44.5	49.5	54.5	59.5	64.5
Cumulative frequency	3	15	35	69	94	98	99	100

(b) 34.5 mm   (d) 41.5 mm

10.

Upper mass limit (kg)	74.5	79.5	84.5	89.5	94.5	99.5
Cumulative frequency	6	19	43	73	89	100

(a) 31   (b) 36   (c) 85.5 kg

page 105   **Using cumulative frequency graphs** (8.5)
1. (a) 129 g   (b) 124.5 g   (c) 137 g

2. (a)

Upper length limit (cm)	30.5	31.5	32.5	33.5	34.5	35.5	36.5
Cumulative frequency	2	10	26	51	68	77	80

(c) 33.1 cm   (d) 32.1 cm   (e) 34 cm

3. (a)

Score interval	0.5–10.5	10.5–20.5	20.5–30.5	30.5–40.5	40.5–50.5
Frequency	2	10	19	13	6

(c) 27.5, 20.5, 35.5

4. (a)

Upper mark limit	9.5	19.5	29.5	39.5	49.5	59.5	69.5	79.5	89.5	99.5
Cumulative frequency	2	5	11	24	46	70	86	94	97	100

(c) 40%, 62.5%, 51% (d) 47% (e) 72%

5. Machine B the mean is nearer to 1000 ml and the range is smaller.

page 107

6. (a) 46 kg and 54 kg (b) 9 kg, 6 kg (c) Group 1 (d) Group 2 (e) No

7. (a) The 13th (b) Yes (c) 25–19½ is equal to 6½–1 (d) (i) 49.6 kg (ii) 51.2 kg

(e) Yes, because $51.2 - 49.6 = 1.6$

8. For the blocks in the middle, yes **9.** (a) 49.4 kg, 51.6 kg (b) 2.2 kg **11.** 60 g, 12 g

page 108

12. (a)

Reading A (g)	99.97	99.98	99.995	100.00	100.01	100.02	100.03	100.04
Cumulative frequency	12	60	89	100	100	100	100	100

Reading B (g)	99.97	99.98	99.99	100.00	100.01	100.02	100.03	100.04
Cumulative frequency	3	11	30	58	81	91	98	100

(c) (i) 99.983 g, 100.002 g (ii) 0.04 g, 0.08 g (iii) 0.012 g, 0.02 g

(d) A, the range and interquartile range are both smaller.

13. 39.8 g **14.** (b) 51% (c) 65% (d) 62%, 31%; 73%, 18%

15. The semi-interquartile range is half of the interquartile range

16. 6 g **17.** 0.006 g, 0.01 g **18.** 69 kg, 19.5 kg, 9.75 kg

9 Probability I

page 110 **The idea of probability** (9.1)

1. Neither **5.** (a) Impossible (b) Certain

page 111 **Experimental probability** (9.2)

3. (c)

4. (a) $\frac{1}{2}$, because the chances of the event happening and not happening are the same

5. $\frac{7}{10}$ (b) $\frac{3}{10}$ (c) 1

page 112

6. (a) $\frac{6}{25}$ (b) $\frac{19}{25}$ **7.** (a) $\frac{1}{20}$ (b) $\frac{4}{25}$ (c) $\frac{1}{25}$ **8.** (a) 200 (b) $\frac{1}{40}$ (c) $\frac{39}{40}$ **9.** (a) 75 (b) $\frac{2}{15}$ (c) $\frac{4}{15}$

10. (a) $\frac{9}{32}$ (b) $\frac{3}{32}$ **11.** (a) $\frac{4}{25}$ (b) $\frac{1}{25}$ (c) $\frac{3}{10}$ (d) $\frac{3}{50}$ **12.** (b) (i) $\frac{1}{6}$ (ii) $\frac{1}{2}$

page 113 **Theeoretical probability** (9.3)

1. (a) 6 (b) $\frac{1}{6}$ **2.** $\frac{1}{13}$ **3.** (a) $\frac{2}{5}$ (b) $\frac{3}{5}$ **4.** (a) $\frac{2}{11}$ (b) $\frac{2}{11}$ **5.** (a) 4 (b) $\frac{1}{13}$ (c) 13 (d) $\frac{1}{4}$

6. (a) 4 (b) $\frac{1}{10}$ (c) 20 (d) $\frac{1}{2}$ **7.** (a) Green (b) Red

8. (a) 30 (b) (i) $\frac{4}{15}$ (ii) $\frac{1}{6}$ (iii) $\frac{1}{5}$ (iv) $\frac{2}{15}$ **9.** (a) 100

(b) (i) $\frac{1}{10}$ (ii) $\frac{1}{5}$ (iii) $\frac{2}{5}$ (iv) $\frac{3}{10}$

10. (a) $\frac{3}{20}$ (b) $\frac{17}{20}$ **11.** (a) $\frac{1}{6}$ (b) $\frac{1}{6}$ (c) $\frac{1}{2}$ (d) $\frac{1}{2}$ (e) $\frac{2}{3}$ (f) $\frac{2}{3}$ (g) $\frac{1}{3}$ (h) $\frac{2}{3}$

12. (a) $\frac{1}{3}$ (b) $\frac{2}{3}$ **13.** (a) A girl (b) The sum equals 1 (c) A certainty

page 114 **Using your knowledge** (9.4)

1. $\frac{15}{1000}$ **2.** (a) $\frac{9}{1000}, \frac{8}{1000}$ (b) 16   (c) 21   **3.** (a) 3   (b) 18   (c) \$75 000, \$450 000

4. (a) \$450 000   (b) \$540 000   (c) \$90   (d) \$7.50   **5.** \$42.92, \$32.50, \$27.29, \$20, \$17.92

6. (a) (i) 16   (ii) 21

(b) The probability of an imminent death is not the same for any two age groups

7. (a) $\frac{1}{6}$ (b) $\frac{1}{6}$ (c) Yes   **8.** (a) 10¢   (b) $1\frac{2}{3}$¢   (c) \$1.67   (d) \$2.00   (e) Loss of 33¢

9. (a) (i) $\frac{2}{25}$ (ii) $\frac{2}{25}$ (iii) $\frac{1}{25}$ (b) The probability of this event is smaller   (c) \$2.50   (d) \$1.30

(e) A loss of \$1.20

10. (a) $\frac{4}{52} \times \frac{48}{51}$ (b) $\frac{4}{52} \times \frac{3}{51}$ (c) $\frac{2 \times 4 \times 48}{52 \times 51}$ (d) $\frac{48}{52} \times \frac{47}{51}$ (e) $\frac{2 \times 4 \times 48}{52 \times 51}$ (f) $\frac{4}{52} \times \frac{3}{51}$

page 116

11. (a) $\frac{1}{10}$ (b) $\frac{1}{10}$

12. (a) 50   (b) (i) $\frac{2}{25}$ (ii) $\frac{17}{50}$ (iii) $\frac{11}{25}$ (c) (i) $\frac{1}{100\,000}$ (ii) $\frac{1}{100\,000}$ (iii) $\frac{1}{100\,000}$ (d) Yes, Yes

(c) Yes, it was only conducted over a limited sample of numbers

10 Algebra I

page 117 **Revision** (10.1)

1. (a) $4a$ cm   (b) $3a$ cm   (c) $6a$ cm   **2.** (a) 20 cm   (b) 21 cm   (c) 72 cm

3. (a) $2(b+l)$ cm   (b) $2(3x+2y)$ cm   **4.** (a) Yes   (b) Yes   (c) Yes   **5.** (a) 18 cm   (b) 34 cm

6. (a) 38 cm   (b) 88 cm   **7.** (a) $5x$ (b) $16y$ (c) $20z$ (d) $6x$ (e) $5y$ (f) z

8. (a) 15   (b) 128   (c) 240   (d) 18   (e) 40   (f) 12

9. (a) $10mn$ (b) pxy^2 (c) $2abc^2$ (d) $-6abc$

page 118

10. (a) $6a$ (b) $20b$ (c) $12ab$ (d) $14a^2$ (e) $24bc$ (f) $30abc$ (g) $-21y$ (h) $30p$ (i) $-12pq$

(j) $15y^2$ (k) $6a^3$ (l) $40x^3$

11. (a) $3a$ (b) 2   (c) $2\frac{1}{2}$ (d) $4p$ (e) 3   (f) $4p$ (g) $\dfrac{5}{x}$ (h) $\dfrac{1}{2y}$ (i) a (j) a (k) $\dfrac{7b^3}{3a^2}$ (l) $\dfrac{4x}{y}$

12. (a) 39   (b) 144   (c) 120   (d) 12   (e) 32   (f) 25   (g) 14   (h) 32

13. (a) $8x$ (b) $10a$ (c) $12b$ (d) $-3y$ (e) $9a$ (f) $3b$ (g) $-8p$ (h) $17ab$ (i) $9a^2$ (j) $7b^2$

(k) $11x^2$ (l) $2y^3$

14. (a) $7a + 12b$ (b) $11a + 5b$ (c) $2a + 6b$ (d) $4x + 4y$ (e) $-7x - 10y$ (f) $2xy - 3z$

(g) $2ab + 6pq$ (h) $7a^2 - 2b^2$ (i) $3a^3 + 4a$

15. (a) $7a + 12b$ (b) $2p + 6q$ (c) $3z - z^3$ (d) $7a^2 - 2b^2$ (e) $8pq - 3p^2$

16. (a) $22xy$ (b) $17p^2q + 7lm$ (c) $pqr + mny + 6abx$ (d) $4pq - 13ab$ (e) $4x^2y^2 + 9xy$

17. (a) $11x^2$ (b) $4mn$ (c) $-3l^2m^2$ (d) $-16pqr$ (e) $-15m$ (f) $66ab$ (g) $21a^5$ (h) $8p^3q^4$

(i) $5m^2$ (j) $\dfrac{7ab^2}{2}$ (k) $\dfrac{4}{7x^3}$ (l) $\dfrac{2n^2}{3l^2}$

18. (a) $5a + 5b$ (b) $4p + 8q$ (c) $3m^2 + 6n$ (d) $10p + 10q^2 + 20r$ (e) $4b - 2a$ (f) $9a - 12b^2$

(g) $-mn - m^2$ (h) $8y - 12xy$

19. (a) $3(x + y)$ (b) $-1(x - y)$ (c) $5(l + 2m)$ (d) $p^2(q - p)$ (e) $r^2(p + q)$ (f) $m(m^2 - m)$

page 119

20. (a) $2a + 2b$ (b) $3x + 6y$ (c) $12p - 20q$ (d) $5ab + 5ac$ (e) $3pq - 6pr$ (f) $5a - 10b + 15c$

(g) $2xy - 4x + 6wx$ (h) $-6l - 3m$ (i) $10ln - 2lm$ (j) $p^2 + 3pq - 5pr$ (k) $8y - 12xy$

(l) $4x^3 - 4x^2 + 4x$

21. (a) $5x + y$ (b) $7l + 9m$ (c) $2p - 10q + 4r$ (d) $4ab + 10ac + 2bc - 4a^2$ (e) $4m^2 + 7m + 5$

(f) $8n - 3m - 7mn$

22. (a) $3m - 3n + mn$ (b) $31 - 5x^2 - 4x^3$ (c) $p^3q + 2pq + \dfrac{q}{p}$ (d) $\dfrac{y}{x^2} + x^2y + 15xy + \dfrac{5x}{y^2}$

(e) $p - p^2 + q + pq$ (f) $2p^3 - \dfrac{p}{3} + \dfrac{5}{3p}$

23. (a) $5x + y$ (b) $10x + 19y$ (c) $2a - 5b$ (d) $11x - 8$ (e) $3x^3 + 11x$ (f) $-5a - 4ab$

24. (a) $-18x - 3y - 2z$ (b) $6m + 5n$ (c) $3x^3 + 2x^2 - 6x$

25. (a) $3(x + y)$ (b) $5(a - b)$ (c) $4(x + y + z)$ (d) $6(a - b + c)$ (e) $2(x + 3y)$ (f) $4(2a - b)$
(g) $3(x + 2y + 3z)$ (h) $5(5a - 2b - c)$

26. (a) $a(x + y)$ (b) $p(a - b)$ (c) $p(x + y + z)$ (d) $r(a - b + c)$ (e) $q(x + 3y)$ (f) $s(5a - b)$
(g) $t(2x + 5y + z)$ (h) $l(7a - 4b - c)$

27. (a) $(p + q)x$ (b) $(a - b)s$ (c) $(p + q + r)x$ (d) $(r - s + t)a$ (e) $(3l + 2m)y$ (f) $(6f - 5g)h$
(g) $(4x + 9y + z)t$ (h) $(2l - 7m - 3n)g$

28. (a) $2(a + b)$ (b) $3(a - b)$ (c) $4(x + 3y)$ (d) $3(3p - 2q)$ (e) $p(x + y)$ (f) $r(a - b)$
(g) $s(7x + 4y)$ (h) $t(2a - 7b)$ (i) $x(a + b + c)$ (j) $l(a - b - c)$ (k) $r(4x + 5y + z)$
(l) $p(a - 6b + 8c)$

29. (a) $x(l + m)$ (b) $n(a - b)$ (c) $y(7p + 2q)$ (d) $t(r - 5s)$ (e) $t(p + q + r)$ (f) $n(a + b + c)$
(g) $x(5l + m + 2n)$ (h) $g(4k - 2l - m)$

30. (a) $m(3 + 5n + m)$ (b) $p(2 + 3r + p)$ (c) $2l(3 + m + l)$ (d) $5rs(1 + 10s + 3r)$

31. (a) $2p(2 + r + 3z)$ (b) $5m(1 + 3p + 5g)$ (c) $3s(3r + 1 + 2s)$ (d) $2m(2l + n + 4pn)$
(e) $ab^2(1 + 6b + 2a)$ (f) $3xy^2(x + 1)$

32. (a) $x(x + 3)$ (b) $y(y - 5)$ (c) $z(2z + 3)$ (d) $m(4m - 1)$ (e) $x(x^2 + 2y)$ (f) $y^2(4z - y)$
(g) $ab(b + a)$ (h) $xyz^2(x - z)$ (i) $\pi r(r + 2h)$ (j) $2lm(m + 4l)$ (k) $x^2(x^2 + x + 1)$
(l) $8y(4 + 2y^2 + y^4)$

page 120

33. (a) $ab(c^2 + b + a)$ (b) $pq^2r(p^2 + pr + r^2)$ (c) $7xy(a + 2b + 3c)$ (d) $8x^3(x^3 + 2x + 6)$
(e) $lm(2p - 1 + 5m)$ (f) $fg^2(f^3 - 6fg + 2g^2)$ (g) $5cd(ab + 7be)$ (h) $8klm^2n(3k - 4ln^2)$
(i) $4cx(4ab - 7bd - 5de)$

34. (a) $\frac{1}{4}(p - \dfrac{q}{2} + \dfrac{r}{3})$ (b) $\dfrac{6}{x}(2a - b - 4c)$ (c) $\dfrac{lm}{n}(l + \dfrac{m}{n} + \dfrac{lm}{n^2})$

35. (a) $7(x - 4)$ (b) $11x(1 - y)$ (c) $c(a + b + 3)$ (d) $7lm(l + m)$

36. (a) $xy(x + 3 + 4y)$ (b) $2rs(1 + 9t + 4rs + 5t^2)$ (c) $2mn(7n + 1 + 4m + 4mn)$
(d) $\frac{1}{3}g^2h(1 + 5g + 6gh^2)$ (e) $\frac{1}{2}xy(x + 4y + 2xy^2 + 3x^3y^3)$

37. (a) $(x + y)(p + q)$ (b) $(x + y)(a - b)$ (c) $(u + v)(t^2 + s)$ (d) $(x - y)(2l + m)$

38. (a) $(r + s)(x + y)$ (b) $(s + 2r)(x + y)$ (c) $(x + y)(3a + b)$ (d) $2(a + b)(p + q)$
(e) $2(4a + b)(p + q)$

39. (a) $(3t^2 + z)(x + 2y)$ (b) $(2a + 3b)(x - y)$ (c) $(p^2 - 2q)(m + n)$ (d) $(g - 2h)(x + 2y)$
(e) $(l - m)(a^2 + b^2)$

40. (a) $(x + y)(p + q - r)$ (b) $(a + b)(x^2 - y - z^3)$ (c) $f + g)(2x + y - 3z)$
(d) $2(4m - 5n)(x - y)$ (e) $(3m^2 + 4n^3)(x - y^2)$

41. (a) $\frac{7}{8}$ (b) $\frac{11}{12}$ (c) $\frac{1}{2}$ (d) $\frac{25}{84}$

42. (a) $\dfrac{8a}{15}$ (b) $\dfrac{19a}{45}$ (c) $\dfrac{11a}{3}$ (d) $\dfrac{11a}{12}$ (e) $\dfrac{-11a}{21}$ (f) $\dfrac{215a}{231}$

43. (a) $\dfrac{4x + y}{6}$ (b) $\dfrac{11x + 9y}{33}$ (c) $\dfrac{4x + 5y + 5z}{10}$ (d) $\dfrac{x + 2y^2}{4}$ (e) $\dfrac{6x + 10y^2 + y}{4}$ (f) $\dfrac{7x^2 + 18y}{63}$

page 121

44. (a) $1\frac{5}{6}$ (b) $1\frac{16}{33}$ (c) $4\frac{3}{10}$ (d) 5 (e) $26\frac{1}{4}$ (f) $1\frac{19}{63}$

45. (a) $\dfrac{p^2 + 6q^2}{3pq}$ (b) $\dfrac{15 + 4l}{3m}$ (c) $\dfrac{5x + 12z}{4x}$ (d) $\dfrac{r + 3pq}{pqr}$ (e) $\dfrac{xy^2 + az^2}{yz}$ (f) $\dfrac{4a^2b + 5bc^2}{20ac}$

47. (a) $\dfrac{4(2x + 1)}{(x + 3)(x - 1)}$ (b) $\dfrac{2(x - 11)}{(x + 1)(x - 3)}$ (c) $\dfrac{2x}{(x - 1)(x + 1)}$ (d) $\dfrac{9x + 11}{20}$ (e) $\dfrac{-3(x + 3)}{35}$

(f) $\dfrac{7x + 11}{(x + 1)(x + 2)}$

48. (a) $x + y$ (b) $2n - 3m$ (c) $2z - 4x$ (d) $p + 2$ (e) $ab^2 + a^5$ (f) $h + 1$

49. $\dfrac{48p + 51q}{p + q}$

50. $\dfrac{2(7x + 5y)}{xy}$ hours

51. (a) $\dfrac{145}{b}$ (b) $\dfrac{235}{a}$ (c) $\dfrac{145a + 235b}{ab}$ ¢

page 121 **Binary operations** (10.2)

1. (a) 18 (b) 22 (c) 20 (d) 56 (e) 32, No, No

2. (a) 72 (b) 72 (c) 36 (d) 432 (e) 432, $a \square b = b \square a$, $9abc$, $9abc$

3. (a) 13 (b) 13 (c) 25 (d) 185 (e) 629, Yes, $p * q = q * p$; No, $(p * q) * r \neq p * (q * r)$

4. (a) 36 (b) 36 (c) 144 (d) 20 736

   (e) 82 944, Yes, $p \square q = q \square p$; No, $(p \square q) \square r \neq p \square (q \square r)$

5. (a) 3, 4 (b) x, x

6. (a) 13, 3, $a \circ b = b \circ a$ (b) 13, 13, Yes

7. (a) $\frac{1}{17}, \frac{1}{17}, a \circ b = b \circ a$ (b) $\frac{7}{85}, \frac{16}{49}$, No, $\dfrac{a + b}{ac + bc + 1}$, $\dfrac{b + c}{ab + ac + 1}$

8. (a) 11, 11, $p * q = q * p$ (b) 59, 59, Yes

9. (a) 21, 21, Yes (b) 129, 387, No

page 122 **Linear equations** (10.3)

2. (a) 8 (b) 12 (c) 9 **3.** (a) 16 (b) 16 (c) 7

4. (a) 7 (b) 9 (c) 11 (d) 1 (e) ⁻2 (f) ⁻1 (g) $2\frac{1}{2}$ (h) $1\frac{1}{5}$

5. (a) 7 (b) 20 (c) 5 (d) 12 (e) 67 (f) 20 **6.** (a) 9 (b) 8 (c) 6 (d) 6

7. (a) 15 (b) 13

page 123

8. $2(5x + 9) = 188, 17$ **9.** (a) 14 (b) 8 (c) 22 (d) ⁻4 (e) ⁻27

10. (a) 24 (b) 16 (c) 149 (d) ⁻5 (e) 1 **11.** (a) 4 (b) 12 (c) 9 (d) $\frac{1}{2}$ (e) $\frac{1}{5}$

12. (a) 10 (b) 42 (c) 38 (d) ⁻12 (e) ⁻66 **13.** (a) 3 (b) 7 (c) 11 (d) 8 (e) 4

14. (a) 12 (b) 63 (c) 108 (d) 160 (e) 121 **15.** (a) 8 (b) 7

16. (a) 13 (b) 4 (c) ⁻8 (d) $1\frac{2}{3}$

17. (a) 6 (b) 2 (c) 9 (d) 5 (e) ⁻6 (f) ⁻7 (g) $\frac{3}{5}$ (h) ⁻3

18. (a) 1 (b) 5 (c) 4 (d) ⁻3 (e) 7 (f) $4\frac{4}{5}$ (g) 22 (h) ⁻$5\frac{1}{7}$ **19.** (a) 3 (b) 4 (c) 7 (d) 1

20. (a) 7 (b) 10 (c) 13 (d) 8 **21.** (a) 1 (b) 4 (c) 6 (d) 6

page 124

22. (a) 20 (b) 54 (c) 70 (d) $7\frac{7}{11}$ **23.** (a) 21 (b) 165 (c) 4 (d) 148

24. (a) 35 (b) 45 (c) 23 (d) $5\frac{1}{2}$ **25.** (a) 8 (b) 10 **26.** 7

27. 55 **28.** (a) ⁻$1\frac{1}{4}$ (b) 29

page 124   **Linear inequalities** (10.4)

1. (a) $x < 4$ (b) $x \geqslant 17$ (c) $x < ^-5$ (d) $x > 13$ (e) $x < 6$ (f) $x > 5$ (g) $x \leqslant 4$ (h) $x > 7$

2. (a) $\{1,2,3\}$ (b) $\{\quad\}$ (c) $\{\quad\}$ (d) $\{\quad\}$ (e) $\{1,2,3,4,5\}$ (f) $\{6,7,8,9\}$
   (g) $\{1,2,3,4\}$ (h) $\{8,9\}$

3. (a) $x > 4$ (b) $x \leqslant 6$ (c) $x < 3$ (d) $x > 4$ (e) $x \geqslant 4\frac{1}{2}$ (f) $x < ^-2$ (g) $x \leqslant 4$ (h) $x > ^-2$

4. (a) $\{5\}$ (b) $\{^-5,^-4,^-3,^-2,^-1,0,1,2,3,4,5\}$ (c) $\{^-5,^-4,^-3,^-2,^-1,0,1,2\}$ (d) $\{5\}$ (e) $\{5\}$
   (f) $\{^-5,^-4,^-3\}$ (g) $\{^-5,^-4,^-3,^-2,^-1,0,1,2,3,4\}$ (h) $\{^-1,0,1,2,3,4,5\}$

5. (a) $x \geqslant 6$ (b) $x < 2$ (c) $x > 12$ (d) $x < 4$ (e) $x \leqslant ^-3$ (f) $x > ^-5$

7. (a) $x \geqslant 3$ (b) $x \leqslant 1$ (c) $x > ^-4$ (d) $x < 5$ (e) $x > 3$ (f) $x \leqslant ^-2$

9. (a) $x \geqslant 6$ (b) $x \leqslant 1\frac{1}{3}$ (c) $x > 4$ (d) $x \leqslant 6$ (e) $x > 2$ (f) $x \leqslant ^-2$ (g) $x > 2$ (h) $x \leqslant ^-\frac{1}{3}$
   (i) $x < 5$

10. (a) $x > 4$ (b) $x \geqslant ^-4$ (c) $x < 5$ (d) $x \leqslant ^-5$

11. (a) $x > 4$ (b) $x \geqslant ^-4$ (c) $x < 5$ (d) $x < ^-5$

12. (a) $x < 1$ (b) $x \geqslant ^-6$ (c) $x \leqslant 3$ (d) $x > 5$

13. (a) $\{^-4,^-3,^-2,^-1,0\}$ (b) $\{^-4,^-3,^-2,^-1,0,1,2,3,4\}$ (c) $\{^-4,^-3^-2,^-1,0,1,2,3\}$ (d) $\{\quad\}$

14. (a) $x < 1$ (b) $x > 1$ (c) $x \leqslant 6$ (d) $x \geqslant ^-4$ (e) $x > 3$ (f) $x \geqslant ^-5$

15. (a) $x > 8$ (b) $x \geqslant 1\frac{1}{2}$ (c) $x \geqslant ^-2$ (d) $x > 7$ (e) $x \geqslant 4\frac{3}{5}$ (f) $x > 2$

16. (a) $x < 5$ (b) $x > \frac{1}{2}$ (c) $x \leqslant \frac{1}{4}$ (d) $x > 6$ **17.** It is greater than $7\,\text{cm}$

18. It is less than $4\,\text{cm}$.   **19.** (a) $\{1\}$ (b) $\{3,4\}$ (c) $\{^-1,^-2,^-3,^-4\}$

20. (a) $\{0\}$ (b) $\{^-4,^-3,^-2,^-1\}$ (c) $\{1,2,3,4\}$ **21.** (a) $\{1,2,3,4\}$ (b) $\{2,3,4\}$

page 126

23. (a) $\{\quad\}$ (b) $\{x \text{ must be less than } 1\frac{1}{3}\}$ (c) $\{x \text{ lies between } \frac{1}{2} \text{ and } 4\}$

24. (a) $\{0,1,2,3,4\}$ (b) $\{4,5,6,7,8,9,10\}$ (c) $\{0,1,2,3\}$ (d) $\{7,8,9,10\}$

25. (a) $\{0,1,2,3,4,5,6,7,8,9,10\}$ (b) $\{15,16,17,18,19,20\}$ (c) $\{0,1,2,3,4,5,6\}$
   (d) $\{8,9,10,11,12,13,14,15,16,17,18,19,20\}$

26. (a) $\{x : x > 6\}$ (b) $\{x : x < 22\}$ (c) $\{x : x > 7\}$ (d) $\{x : x < 8\}$ (e) $\{x : x < 5\}$

27. (a) $\{x : x < 5\}$ (b) $\{x : x > 4\}$ (c) $\{x : x > 4\}$ (d) $\{x : x > 7\}$ (e) $\{x : x < 9\}$

28. (a) $\{x : 5 \leqslant x < 9\}$ (b) $\{x : 2 < x < 12\}$ (c) $\{x : 6 \leqslant x \leqslant 14\}$ (d) $\{x : 2 \leqslant x \leqslant 19\}$

29. (a) $\{x : 3 \leqslant x \leqslant 6\}, \{x : 1 < x \leqslant 4\}, \{x : 4 < x < 9\}, \{x : 2 \leqslant x < 6\}$
   (b) $\{x : ^-1 < x < 3\}, \{x : ^-2 \leqslant x \leqslant 5\}, \{x : ^-3 < x \leqslant 2\}, \{x : 1 \leqslant x < 7\}$

30. (a) $\{x : 3 \leqslant x \leqslant 4\}, \{x : ^-1 < x < 3\}$ (b) $\{x \text{ assumes no values}\}, \{x : ^-2 \leqslant x \leqslant 2\}$
   (c) $\{x : 4 < x < 6\}, \{x : 1 \leqslant x \leqslant 2\}$ (d) $\{x : 1 < x \leqslant 6\}, \{x : ^-2 \leqslant x \leqslant 5\}$
   (e) $\{x : 1 < x < 9\}, \{x : ^-3 < x \leqslant 5\}$
   (f) $\{x : 2 \leqslant x < 9\}, \{x : ^-3 < x < 7\}$ (g) $\{x : 6 \leqslant x < 9\}, \{x : ^-3 < x < 1\}$

31. (a) $\{x : 6 < x < 12\}$ (b) $\{x : x < 10\}$ (c) $\{x : 6 < x < 13\}$ (d) $\{x : x \leqslant 9\}$
   (e) $\{x : 5 < x < 9\}$ (f) $\{x \text{ assumes all values}\}$ (g) $\{x : x \geqslant 3\}$

page 127   **Simultaneous equations** (10.5)

1. (a) $(8,0), (6,1), (4,2), (2,3), (0,4)$ (b) $(5,0), (4,2), (3,4), (2,6), (1,8), (0,10), (4,2)$

2. (a) $(5,0), (4,2), (3,4), (2,6), (1,8), (0,10)$ (b) $(8,0), (6,1), (4,2), (2,3), (0,4)$

3. $(4,2)$ **4.** (c) (i) $(2,3)$ (ii) $(3,4)$

6. (a)

x	0	1	2	3	4
y	1	3	5	7	9

(b)

x	0	1	2	3	4
y	$^-2$	1	4	7	10

(c) $(3,7)$

8. (a)

x	0	1	2	3	4
y	1	4	7	10	13

x	0	1	2	3	4
y	3	5	7	9	11

(2,7)

(b)

x	0	1	2	3	4
y	8	7	6	5	4

x	0	1	2	3	4
y	$^-1$	1	3	5	7

(3,5)

(c)

x	0	1	2	3	4
y	$^-5$	$^-1$	3	7	11

x	0	1	2	3	4
y	4	$3\frac{1}{2}$	3	$2\frac{1}{2}$	2

(2,3)

9. Yes, because the point of intersection lies on both graph lines. $x = 3$ and $y = 7$.
10. Yes, because at the point of intersection y equals both $2x - 1$ and $8 - x$. $x = 3$ and $y = 5$
11. $x = 2$ and $y = 7$ **12.** $x = 2$ and $y = 3$
13. (a) $x = 1, y = 5$ (b) $x = 7, y = 23$ (c) $x = 3, y = 11$ (d) $x = 1, y = 5$
page 128
14. (a) $x = 5, y = 1$ (b) $x = 2, y = 7$
15. (a) $x = {}^-2, y = 16$ (b) $x = 4, y = {}^-1$ (c) $x = {}^-1, y = 5\frac{2}{3}$
16. (a) $x = 5, y = 2$ (b) $x = {}^-1, y = 2$
17. (a) $x = 6, y = 4$ (b) $x = {}^-2, y = 4$ (c) $x = 5, y = {}^-3$
18. (a) $x = 3, y = 4$ (b) $x = 2, y = {}^-3$ (c) $x = 5, y = 1$
19. (a) $x = 6, y = 1$ (b) $x = 5, y = 3$
20. (a) $x = 2, y = 5$ (b) $x = 5, y = 6$ (c) $x = 3, y = {}^-4$ (d) $x = 2, y = 3$ (e) $a = 7, b = {}^-2$
   (f) $p = 3\frac{2}{3}, q = 1\frac{1}{3}$
page 129
21. (a) $x = {}^-7, y = {}^-11$ (b) $x = 3, y = 7$ (c) $x = 1, y = 2$
22. (a) $x = 2, y = 3$ (b) $x = 7, y = 1$ (c) $x = {}^-2, y = 3$
24. (a) $x = 4, y = 3$ (b) $x = 3, y = {}^-2$ (c) $x = 3, y = {}^-4$ (d) $x = 4, y = 3$ (e) $x = 1\frac{1}{2}, y = 2$
   (f) $x = {}^-5.8, y = {}^-6.2$ (g) $x = 2, y = 1$ (h) $x = 2, y = {}^-1$
25. (a) $x = 7, y = {}^-2$ (b) $x = 8\frac{9}{13}, y = \frac{11}{13}$ (c) $x = 7, y = 2$ (d) $x = 5, y = 12$
26. (a) $x = 11, y = 3$ (b) $x = \frac{1}{2}, y = 5$

page 129 **Word problems** (10.6)
 1. 21 cm, 28 cm, 21 cm, 28 cm
 2. 9 cm, 27 cm, 9 cm, 27 cm   **3.** 25, 26, 27
page 130
 4. 34, 36, 38   **5.** 3.1 m, 5.4 m, 3.1 m, 5.4 m   **6.** 5.1 m, 8.2 m, 5.1 m, 8.2 m, No
 7. $28 and $5   **8.** $24 and $48   **9.** 65   **10.** 11   **11.** 26¢ per litre
12. 115, method (i)   **13.** $7500   **14.** $8.50, $13, $6.50   **15.** (a) 9 g   (b) 15 g
16. (a) $9000   (b) $7500
page 131
17. (a) 17 cm   (b) 12 cm   **18.** (a) $15   (b) $6.50   **19.** 87 and 14   **20.** 20 and 5
21. 51 and 26   **22.** 8¢ and 12¢ respectively   **23.** $2.25 and $1.20   **24.** 90 km and 200 km
25. 360 cars and 8 coaches   **26.** 121 stamps by 7¢, 59 by 9¢; 112 stamps by 7¢, 66 by 9¢.
27. 8 cm, 4 cm   **28.** $18   **29.** $28.80, $20.16; $486, $380.30   **30.** 7 and 8

11   Graphs 2

page 133   **Quadratic graphs** (11.1)
1. (a) Quadratic   (b) Non-linear

(c)

x	$^-3$	$^-2$	$^-1$	0	1	2	3
x^2	9	4	1	0	1	4	9
1	1	1	1	1	1	1	1
y	7	3	1	1	3	7	13

2. No. Yes, a smooth curve can be drawn through the points.
5. Missing values of y are 5 and 2. The curve rises to a maximum.
page 134
7. (a) $y : 4, 0, ^-2, ^-2, 0, 4, 10$ 8. (a) $y : ^-12, ^-10, ^-6, 0, 8, 18, 30$
9. (a) $y : 30, 20, 12, 6, 2, 0, 0$ (b) $y : ^-6, 0, 4, 6, 6, 4, 0$ (c) $y : 18, 7, 0, ^-3, ^-2, 3, 12$
    (d) $y : ^-16, ^-3, 4, 5, 0, ^-11, ^-28$
11. (a) $(1,0), (3,0)$ (b) Yes   12. (a) $^-4$ and 2, $^-3$ and 2, $^-5$ and 2, $^-1$ and 3

page 134   **Solving quadratic equations graphically** (11.2)
1. (b) $(^-2.45,6), (2.45,6)$ (c) $x = ^-2.45$ or 2.45
2. (a) Yes   (b) $(^-1,1), (2,4); x = ^-1$ and $y = 1$ or $x = 2$ and $y = 4$
3. (b) $(2,4), (1,1)$ (c) Yes   (d) $x = 2$ or 1
4. (a) $(1,0)$ and $(4,0)$ (b) $x = 1$ or 4   (c) $(0,4)$ and $(5,4), x = 0$ or 5
5. (c) (i) $x = 2$ or 1   (ii) $x = 3$ or 0   (iii) $x = 3.6$ or $^-0.6$
6. (b) (i) $x = 3$ or $^-1$ (ii) $x = 4$ or $^-2$ (iii) $x = 1$
7. (b) $x = 2$ or 3   (d) $x = 1$ or 6, The x-coordinates of the intersection points.
8. (a) y has a minimum value   (b) y has a maximum value

page 136   **Non-linear relations** (11.3)
1. Yes   2. (b) 512   (c) 3 weeks and 2 days   (d) Yes
3. (c) 5.32   (d) 5.66   4. (b) After 2 years and 10 months   (c) 26 800
5. (b) After 4 years and 3 months   (c) $177
7. (a) Missing values are 16, 32 and 64 sheets   (c) 5.12 cm   (d) 10 737 418 cm
8. (c) Yes   (d) It never crosses either axis, y gets very small.

page 137   **Variation** (11.4)
1. (a) $\frac{5}{9}$ (b) $\frac{4}{9}$ 2. $4 : 5$
                          3. (a) $1 : 9$ (b) $1 : 3$ (c) $2 : 3$ (d) $7 : 15$ (e) $3 : 11$ (f) $5 : 3$
4. (a) 1.6 km   (b) 16 km   (c) 32 km   (d) 76.8 km
5. (a) 0.625 miles   (b) 6.25 miles   (c) 35 miles   (d) 45 miles   (e) 57.5 miles   (f) 120.625 miles
6. 195 brown and 91 white

7. (a) 12   (b) 10   8. (a) $\dfrac{p}{q} = \dfrac{x}{y}$ (b) $\dfrac{p}{x} = \dfrac{q}{y}$ (c) $py = qx$

9. Yes   10. $5 : 6$
11. (a) 12.56 cm   (b) 31.4 cm   (c) 62.8 cm   (d) 125.6 cm, All the ratios are $1 : 6.28$
12. (i) Yes   (ii) Yes   (iii) No   (iv) Yes
page 138
13. (a) (i), (ii) and (iv); $k = 4, 1.5$ and 3.2 respectively.
    (b) (i) 40, 84; 12, 25.   (ii) 18, 117; 20, 94   (iv) 19.2, 64; 12, 30

15. (a) Yes (b) Yes (c) Yes

16. $24\,\text{cm}^2, 6\,\text{cm}^2, 54\,\text{cm}^2$; No **17.** (b) $s = 6l^2$ (c) Yes, Yes

18. (a) 5 (b) 3 (c) 0.5 (d) $\frac{1}{3}$ **19.** (a) 1 (b) 1 (c) 3 (d) $\frac{1}{256}$

20. π **21.** $A = \pi r^2, \pi \approx 3.14$ **22.** 48

page 139

23. $1\frac{3}{7}$ **24.** 125 km **25.** 150 **26.** 4 or $^-4$ **27.** $S = kl^2, k = 6, 96\,\text{cm}^2$ **28.** 2.7

29. 12 **30.** 2 seconds **31.** (a) 6 (b) 2.4 **32.** (a) 0.6 (b) 20 or $^-20$ **33.** 5 amps

35. 105 **36.** (a) $F = \frac{c}{d^2}$ (b) 7.2 (c) 5

page 139 **Variation and graphs** (11.5)

1. No, Yes, 31.4 **2.** The graph in part (b)

3. (a) $12.56\,\text{cm}^3, 25.12\,\text{cm}^3, 37.68\,\text{cm}^3, 50.24\,\text{cm}^3, 62.8\,\text{cm}^3, 75.36\,\text{cm}^3$ (b) Yes (c) Yes, 12.56

4. (a) 2 (b) 54

page 140

6. The graph in part (c). $V = x^3$ **7.** (a) 8 (b) 2 (c) $\frac{1}{2}$ (d) 16

8. (a) 72, 162, 364.5, 48 (b) $\frac{1}{16}, \frac{1}{2}, 1, \frac{1}{1024}$ **9.** 2, 3 **10.** 0.2, 3.4

11. (a) Yes, but inversely (b) 360 km **12.** (a) 12,9,6,5.1,4.5,4

13. Yes (a) Yes, Yes (b) 360

page 141

14. (b)

1/R	0.05	0.025	0.02	0.0125	0.01	0.005
Current, I amps	10	5	4	2.5	2	1

(c) Yes (d) 200

17. 30

18. (a) 60, 120, 40 (b) Part 1, 60 km/h; Part 2, 120 km/h; Part 3, 40 km/h (c) 30 minutes, 45 minutes, 60 minutes, 2 hours and 15 minutes (d) 160 km

page 142

19. (a) The y intercept, 2 (b) 3 **20.** 3.2

21. $k = 5.4\, c = 3$ **22.** $n = 1.5, k = 4, v = 11.3$ if $p = 2$

12 Transformations I

page 144 **Translations** (12.1)

1. (a) $\binom{12}{-1}$ (b) $\binom{20}{1}$ (c) $\binom{-20}{-1}$ **2.** (c) $\binom{9}{5}$

3. (a) $\binom{3}{-2}$ (b) Not a translation (c) Not a translation (d) $\binom{-1}{0}$ (e) $\binom{1}{-1}$

4. (a) No (b) Yes (c) No **5.** (a) (1,1) (b) (5,4) (c) $\binom{1}{1} + \binom{4}{3} = \binom{5}{4}$

6. (5,4) (b) (8,8); (6,7) (d) Yes (e) Yes **7.** (b) S(6,3); T(9,7); U(7,6)

8. $\binom{5}{2}, \binom{4}{3} + \binom{1}{-1} = \binom{5}{2}$ **9.** (a) $\binom{3}{1}$ (b) $\binom{-3}{-1}$

page 145 **Relations** (12.2)

1. (a) 90°, A (b) 90°, B (c) 90°, C (d) 270°, C (e) 180°, B (f) 270°, A

2. (a) A(7,9); B(4,5); C(6,6) (b) A(5,3); B(1,6); C(2,4) (c) A(1,1); B($^-$3,4); C(2,2)

3. (a) A(8,0); B(4,3); C(5,1) (b) A(11,9); B(8,5); C(10,6)

4. It has rotational symmetry order 4.

page 147

6. (a) (2,0); 90° (b) (3,0); 180° (c) (2,0); 270° (d) (3,1); 270°

7. (0,2) and (0,0) **8.** (a) 120° (b) 3 (c) 3

9. (a) (i) 72° (ii) 45° (b) (i) 5 (ii) 8 **10.** (a) 4 (b) 2 (c) 1 (d) 2

page 147   **Reflections** (12.3)
1. Yes   2. On the mirror line   3. $y = 2$
5. (a) $(^-1,1)$ (b) $A(1,1) \rightarrow P(^-1,1)$ (c) $B(4,6) \rightarrow Q(^-4,6)$; $C(2,5) \rightarrow R(^-2,5)$ (d) $(x,y) \rightarrow (^-x,y)$
6. (a) $(5,1)$; $(2,6)$; $(4,5)$ (b) $(1,5)$; $(2,1)$; $(4,0)$ (c) $(4,4)$; $(^-1,1)$; $(0,3)$
7. Yes   8. $y = x + 5$ 9. $y = 2$
10. (a) A translation   (b) $\binom{4}{0}$ (c) Two lateral inversions
11. (a) Yes   (b) $\binom{2}{0}$ (c) The x displacement is twice as much
12. (a) $\binom{8}{0}$ 13. (a) The same square   (b) 4   (c) 4
page 149
14. (a) The same isosceles triangle   (b) 1   (c) 1
15. 6   16. (a) 3   (b) 1   (c) 5   (d) 2

page 149   **Enlargements** (12.4)
1. (a) $OQ = 2OP$ (b) 3 units and 2 units; 6 units and 4 units   (c) It doubles them
2. Scale factor $\frac{1}{2}$ 3. (a) 3   (b) $SF = 3SC$ (c) 9 units   (d) 4 units
4. (a) Yes   (b) $(0,2)$ (c) 2   5. (a) $(8,2)$ (b) The translation $\binom{-4}{0}$ (c) The translation $\binom{4}{0}$
6. (a) 2.5   (b) 7.5 cm   (c) 7.5 cm   (d) 12.5 cm   7. (b) $(3,5)$ 8. $^-2$
page 151
9. (a) 4.5 cm, 7.5 cm   (b) 3 cm, 5 cm   (c) 4.2 cm   10. The translation $\binom{0}{6}$
11. A rotation of $180°$ 12. (a) 1.5   (b) 4cm^2 and 9cm^2 (c) 2.25   13. (a) and (d)
page 152
14. (b) and (d)   15. (a), (c), (d) and (f)   16. (b) X (c) 16 cm   (d) 4cm^2

13   Trigonometry I

page 153   **Sine and cosine** (13.1)
1. (a) $18°$ (b) $31.4°$ (c) $36°$ (d) $71.4°$ (e) $90°$ (f) $0°$
2. (a) 0.6   (b) 0.6   (c) 0.8   (d) 0.8   3. (a) $30°$ (b) $25.8°$ (c) $23.6°$ (d) $39.8°$
4. (a) $48.6°$ (b) $66.4°$ (c) $53.1°$ (d) $68°$
5. (a) 9.4 cm   (b) 2.29 cm   (c) 2.1 cm   (d) 1.06 cm
6. (a) 1.618 cm   (b) 2.113 cm   (c) 3.564 cm   (d) 5 cm   (e) 3.396 cm   (f) 5.46 cm

page 154   **Tangent** (13.2)
1. (a) $31°, 59°$ (b) $54.8°, 35.2°$ (c) $37.8°, 52.2°$ (d) $74.1, 15.9°$ 2. $26.6°$
3. (a) $70°$ (b) $75.1°$ 4. $0.176, 0.364, 0.577, 0.839, 1.192, 1.732, 2.145$
5. (a) 2.747   (b) 5.671   (c) 11.43   (d) 19.08   (e) 28.63   (f) 38.19   (g) 57.29   (h) 114.6
6. 573 units
7. (a) 1.82 cm   (b) 2.42 cm   (c) 5.2 cm   (d) 7.29 cm
8. (a) 13.1 cm   (b) 6.87 cm   (c) 100 cm   (d) 15.14 cm   (e) 6.97 cm
page 156
9. 23.8 m   10. 41.2 m   11. 9.33 m   12. (a) 30 m   (b) 52 m   (c) 170 m   13. 700 m
14. (a) $88.3°$ (b) 60 m   (c) 2022 m   15. 2291 m   16. 346.5 m, 179.7 m, 166.8 m

page 157   **Bearings** (13.3)
1. (a) 74.3 km East, 66.9 km South   (b) 24.2 km East, 43.7 km South
   (c) 5.18 km East, 19.3 km South
2. (a) 50.0 km West, 86.6 km South   (b) 41.5 km West, 28.0 km South
   (c) 19.8 km West, 3.13 km South
3. (a) 92.1 km West, 39.1 km North   (b) 37.7 km West, 32.8 km North
   (c) 4.95 km West, 21.4 km North

4. (a) (i) East 7.66 km (ii) West 11.5 km (iii) West 20 km (b) (i) South 6.43 km
(ii) South 16.4 km (iii) North 34.6 km; North 11.8 km, West 23.8 km
5. 153.4° **6.** 22.4 km
7. (a) 116.6° (b) 213.7° (c) 346° (d) 303.7° (e) 116.6°
8. (a) 9.14 km East, 4.07 km North (b) 16.2 km East, 11.8 km South
(c) 38.8 km West, 9.68 km South (d) 44.9 km West, 21.9 km North
(e) 16.1 km West, 19.2 km North (f) 7.18 km West, 15.4 km North
9. (a) (i) 30.6 km East, 25.7 km South (ii) 34.6 km West, 20.0 km South
(iii) 21.3 km East, 36.9 km North; 17.3 km East, 8.8 km South

page 158 **Pythagoras' Theorem** (13.4)
1. (a) 10 cm (b) 26 cm (c) 25 cm **2.** (a) 11 cm (b) 0.9 cm (c) 2 cm
3. (a) 1.41 cm (b) 14.1 cm (c) 141 cm **4.** 10.6 cm **5.** 10.9 cm, 54.5 cm^2 **6.** 8.66 cm
7. (a) 9 cm (b) 111.8 cm **8.** No, the longest that will fit is 17.32 cm
9. (a) 8.66 cm (b) 34.64 cm (c) 13.86 cm **10.** 4 cm **11.** (a) 13 cm, 5 cm (b) Yes
12. 2.65 cm

page 159 **Angles in solids** (13.5)
1. (a) 16.97 cm (c) 59°, 49.7° **2.** (a) 14.14 cm (c) 54.7°, 35.3°
3. (b) 26.6°, 33.7° (c) 2.5 cm (e) 21.8° **4.** (a) 56.7 m (b) 27.5 m (c) 63.0 m

page 162 **Practice Paper A**
1. (b) **2.** (b) **3.** (c) **4.** (c) **5.** (a) **6.** (c) **7.** (b) **8.** (c) **9.** (c) **10.** (b) **11.** (d)
12. (b) **13.** (b) **14.** (c) **15.** (b) **16.** (b) **17.** (d) **18.** (c) **19.** (c) **20.** (d) **21.** (b)
22. (c) **23.** (b) **24.** (c) **25.** (c) **26.** (b) **27.** (a) **28.** (b) **29.** (c) **30.** (d) **31.** (b)
32. (c) **33.** (c) **34.** (c) **35.** (a) **36.** (d) **37.** (d) **38.** (c) **39.** (a) **40.** (b) **41.** (c) **42.** (a)
43. (b) **44.** (c) **45.** (a) **46.** (c) **47.** (c) **48.** (b) **49.** (c) **50.** (a) **51.** (a) **52.** (d)
53. (c) **54.** (b) **55.** (d) **56.** (c) **57.** (b) **58.** (c) **59.** (d) **60.** (d)

page 164 **Practice Paper B**
1. (a) **2.** (c) **3.** (b) **4.** (c) **5.** (b) **6.** (c) **7.** (b) **8.** (a) **9.** (c) **10.** (a) **11.** (d) **12.** (d)
13. (b) **14.** (b) **15.** (a) **16.** (c) **17.** (d) **18.** (b) **19.** (c) **20.** (a) **21.** (c) **22.** (c)
23. (d) **24.** (b) **25.** (d) **26.** (d) **27.** (d) **28.** (a) **29.** (c) **30.** (d) **31.** (b) **32.** (a)
33. (d) **34.** (a) **35.** (b) **36.** (d) **37.** (d) **38.** (a) **39.** (a) **40.** (b) **41.** (a) **42.** (d)
43. (d) **44.** (b) **45.** (a) **46.** (b) **47.** (a) **48.** (c) **49.** (b) **50.** (b) **51.** (c) **52.** (c)
53. (b) **54.** (b) **55.** (c) **56.** (c) **57.** (b) **58.** (b) **59.** (a) **60.** (d)

page 168 **Practice Paper 1**
1. (a) 48.6 (b) $31\frac{1}{9}$ **2.** (a) $4w+10$ (b) 35 m **3.** (a) 10 cm (b) 5 cm
4. (a) ($^-$2,3) (b) $x = 0, y = {}^-2$ (c) (i) ($^-$2,1) (ii) ($^-$1,$^-$2)
5. (a) \$266.67 (b) \$1304.35 **6.** (a) $\frac{1}{6}$ (b) $\frac{1}{36}$
7. (a) (i) 3 km (ii) 0.1536 cm^2 (b) (i) 15.5 kg (ii) 421.875 cm^3
8. (a) EC\$80 000 000 (b) Sector angles are : 67.5°, 112.5°, 103.5°, 54°, 22.5° (c) $31\frac{1}{4}$%
9. (0,0); (3,0); (3,5); (0,8), 8 **10.** (a) 4 (b) 2

page 169 **Practice Paper 2**
1. (a) $4\frac{5}{28}$ (b) 104.17 **2.** (a) $1437\frac{1}{3}$cm^3 (b) (i) 23 (ii) 20 (iii) 68
3. (a) \$300 (b) \$32 (c) (i) £0.27 (ii) EC\$1687.50 **4.** (a) 411.2 (b) 24.67 km/h **5.** 9.434 cm
6. (a) 33 (b) 72 (c) $\frac{5}{33}$ (d) $\frac{14}{33}$ **7.** (a) $2\frac{1}{4}$ (b) $x = \frac{1}{3}, y = 2$

8.

x	$^-2$	$^-1$	$^-\frac{1}{2}$	$^-\frac{1}{4}$	$\frac{1}{4}$	$\frac{1}{2}$	1	2
y	$^-2$	$^-4$	$^-8$	$^-16$	16	8	4	2

1.69 and $^-$1.19

9. 0.0237   **10.** 60°, 120°, 180°, 100°, 80°

page 170   **Practice Paper 3**
1. (a) $1 \times 10°$ (b) 2.36 miles   **2.** (a) EC$54.88   (b) (i) $6200   (ii) $2080
3. (a) $4   (b) {3,4}   **4.** (a) $1.32 \, m^2$ (b) $10.56 \, m^3$ **5.** (a) 4.65, 6, 5   (b) 9.5, 3   (c) $\frac{3}{20}$
6. (a) 5 doors and 7 windows   (b) $7.5 \, m \times 5 \, m$ (c) $200 \, m^2$ **7.** (b) 28   (c) $N = 5(2^t)$
8. (a) 25%   (b) 240 km/h   **9.** 6.93 cm   **10.** (a) 6 cm   (b) 50.2°

page 171   **Practice paper 4**
1. (a) $8.33, $5, $1.67   (b) 16%   **2.** (a) $2\frac{1}{3}$ (b) 3.742 cm
3. (a) $25   (b) 111   (c) $26.70   **4.** (b) $2.4675 \, m^3$ **5.** (b) $\frac{3}{10}$
6. (a) (i) $2315.25   (ii) $2360   (b) $79.71   **7.** (a) 10.47 cm   (b) 1.67 cm
8. (a) $6x + 3y = 8.40, 4x + 5y = 6.80$ (b) $1.20 and $0.40
9. (b) $4.90   **10.** (a) $1 \, km^2$ (b) 34.62 km/h, 34.96 km/h

page 172   **Practice Paper 5**
1. (a) $1\frac{19}{87}$ (b) 477   **2.** (a) $37.05   (b) $57.60   **3.** 6 cm, 5.67 cm
4. (a) $8900   (b) $4155   (c) $6845   **5.** (a) (i) 19.2 m   (ii) $20.3175 \, m^2$ (b) $8000 \, m^2$
6. (a) Frequency figures are 3, 5, 6, 6, 7, 1, 1, and 1   (b) 70–74 kg   (c) 65.5 kg
7. (a) $(4,^-2); (6,^-2); (6,^-4); (4,^-4)$ (b) $(^-4,^-2); (^-6,^-2); (^-6,^-4); (^-4,^-4)$
8. y values are 1, 4, 10, 28, 82 and 244; 0.1 and 3.95
9. (a) 76 m   (b) 16 m   **10.** (a) 26   (b) $^-23$ (c) $x = 3, y = 4$

page 173   **Practice Paper 6**
2. (c) 4   **3.** (a) $8\frac{1}{3}$ cm   (b) 3 : 2   (c) 9 : 25   **4.** (a) $1615   (b) $107.50   **5.** 8.62 cm
6. (a) 67.5 km/h   (b) $26\frac{2}{3}$ kg   (c) 9.741
7. (a) 198°, 18°, 36°, 54°, 27°, 27°   (b) (i) $\frac{1}{3}$ (ii) $\frac{2}{3}$ (iii) $\frac{7}{9}$
8. (a) $0.25   (b) $x < {}^-3\frac{1}{2}$ **9.** 1.54, $^-0.87$ **10.** (a) $44 \, cm^2$ (b) $56 \, cm^2$

Answers to Part 2

I Sets 2

page 176 **More about sets** (1.1)

1. (a) (i) Yes (ii) Yes (iii) Yes (iv) Yes (v) Yes (b) Yes

3. (a) (i) 60 (ii) 35 (iii) 10 (iv) 85 (b) Yes **4.** (a) 16 (b) 5 **6.** 6

7. (c) (i) Yes (ii) Yes

8. (a) (i) {3,6,9} (ii) {1,4,9} (iii) {9} (iv) {1,2,4,5,7,8,10} (v) {2,3,5,6,7,8,10}
(vi) {1,3,4,6,9} (b) (i) {2,5,7,8,10}, {2,5,7,8,10}
(ii) {1,2,3,4,5,6,7,8,10}, {1,2,3,4,5,6,7,8,10} (c) Yes

11. (b) Yes **12.** (a) {3,6} (b) {6} (c) {3,6} (d) {1,2,3,4,6,8,10} (e) {3,6}

13. Yes **14.** (c) Yes (d) Both are equal to {3,6,9,10}

page 178 **Problems using three sets** (1.2)

1. 3 **2.** (a) 8 (b) 5 **3.** 2 **5.** 7 **6.** 5,119 **7.** 10

page 179

8. (a) 13 (b) 17 (c) 23 (d) 17 (e) 7

9. (a) 11 (b) 17 (c) 13 (d) 7 (e) 21 (f) 10 (g) 2 (h) 11 (i) 4 (j) 28

10. 36 **12.** (a) 2 (b) 5 (c) 3 (d) 6 **13.** (a) 16 (b) 15 (c) 7 (d) 28

14. (a) 11 (b) 13 (c) 13 **15.** 21

16. (a) 36 (b) 31 (c) 26 (d) 11 (e) 31 (f) 5 **17.** 3 **18.** 8

page 180

19. 3, 8 **20.** 8 **21.** 7 **22.** 102 **23.** 36

24. (a) Yes (b) (i) $7 - x$ (ii) $6 - x$ (c) 4 **25.** (b) $13 - x, 7 - x, 6 - x$ (c) 4

26. (a) 6 (b) 2 **27.** 3 **28.** (b) 2 **29.** (a) 6 (b) 5 (c) 10 (d) 24 **30.** (b) 3 (c) 33

page 181 **Sets and logic** (1.3)

2. (b), (c) and (e) **3.** (a), (b) and (e)

5. It is red but not even numbered. It is even numbered but not red. It is neither even numbered nor red.

6. (a) Sam is in the football team. (untrue) (b) Sam is not a tall boy (untrue)
(c) Sam is a tall boy and he is in the football team (untrue)
(d) Sam is not both a tall boy and a member of the football team (true)

7. (a) $n \in E$ (untrue) (b) $n \notin E$ (true) (c) $n \notin T$ (untrue) (d) $n \in (E \cap T)$ (untrue)

8. (a) Certainly false (b) Certainly false (c) May be true (d) Certainly true (e) May be true
(f) Certainly true

9. (a) (iii) (b) (i) (c) (v) (d) (ii) (e) (iv)

page 183

11. (a) True (b) May be true (c) May be true (d) May be true (e) True (f) True

12. Yes **13.** No **14.** Yes

15. (a) Must be true (b) Must be wrong (c) Must be wrong (d) Must be true

16. The argument is valid. **17.** The argument is not valid.

18. (a) Some men are not wise (b) Some cats do not love milk (c) Some cats sleep at night
(d) No parrots are blue

19. No mice are tall.

20. Some snakes should be avoided. **21.** (a) is valid (b) is not valid

2 Relations and functions I

page 185 **Facts about functions** (2.1)
1. $\{^-2, ^-1, 0, 1, 2\}$ **2.** Yes
3. (a) $\{4, 5, 6, 7, 8\}$ (b) It is the same as the co-domain.   **4.** (a) $g : x \rightarrow x^2$ (b) $g(x) = x^2$
5. (a) 5   (b) 4   (c) 8   (d) 4
page 186
6. $g : x \rightarrow x^2$ or $g(x) = x^2$, where $x \in \{^-2, ^-1, 0, 1, 2\}$; $(^-2,4), (^-1,1), (0,0), (1,1), (2,4)$

7.

x	$^-2$	$^-1\frac{1}{2}$	$^-1$	$^-\frac{1}{2}$	0	$\frac{1}{2}$	1	$1\frac{1}{2}$	2
$g(x)$	4	$2\frac{1}{4}$	1	$\frac{1}{4}$	0	$\frac{1}{4}$	1	$2\frac{1}{4}$	4

8. It would be a smooth curve.
9. (a) $g : \frac{1}{2} \rightarrow \frac{1}{4}$ (b) $g : ^-1\frac{1}{2} \rightarrow 2\frac{1}{4}$ (c) $g(^-\frac{1}{2}) = \frac{1}{4}$ (d) $g(1\frac{1}{2}) = 2\frac{1}{4}$ **10.** Yes, 2
11. (a) 3   (b) 9   (c) 11   (d) 2   (e) 3   **12.** $(1,1), (2,4), (3,7), (4,10), (5,13)$
13. (b) They lie on a straight line   (c) The straight line would be continuous.
14. (a) $\{0, 1, 2, 3, 4, 5\}$ (b) $\{0, 3, 6, 9, 12, 15\}$ (c) 6   (d) 4   (e) (i) $l : x \rightarrow 3x$ (ii) $l(x) = 3x$
16. (a) $(1,^-4), (2,^-2), (3,0), (4,2), (5,4), (6,6)$ (b) $m(x) = 2x - 6$ (c) $\{1, 2, 3, 4, 5, 6\}$
    (d) (i) 4   (ii) 0   (e) 2

page 187 **Some special functions** (2.2)
1. (a) is a function; it is 1-1,   (b) is a function; it is M-1,
   (c) is not a function; because one element has no image,   (d) is not a function; it is 1-M
2. (a) $f : x \rightarrow 5 - x, f : x \rightarrow 0, f : x \rightarrow \sqrt{x}, f : x \rightarrow$ multiples of x (b) Each has zero for its image
   (c) $f(x) = \sqrt{x}$ is not defined if $x < 0$
   (d) the image set does not include any multiple of 4 or 6 other than 4 and 6 themselves.
4. 2
5. Yes
6. There are nine such functions in all
7. 8
8. 2
10. (a) $f : x \rightarrow 1$ (b) $f : x \rightarrow 2$ (c) $f : x \rightarrow 3$
11. (a) $(0,2), (1,2), (2,2), (3,2), (4,2)$ (b) M-1   (c) $\{0, 1, 2, 3, 4\}$ (d) 2   (e) $f : x \rightarrow 2$
Page 188
12. It would be a continuous straight line
14. (a) A set of dots on the x-axis   (b) A continuous line on the x-axis
15. (a) All scored full marks   (b) All scored zero marks
16. If all chose the same sport
17. $(p,p), (q,q), (r,r)$; Each ordered pair contains two identical numbers.
18. The image set is the same as the domain
19. (a) 3   (b) 5   (c) Missing numbers for $g(x)$ are 2, 3, 4 and 5   (d) Yes
    (e) The dots lie on a line which is inclined at 45° to either axis
20. (a) $(0,0), (1,1), (2,2), (3,3), (4,4)$ (b) 4   (c) 1   (d) Yes   (e) $h(x) = x$

page 189 **The inverse of a function** (2.3)
1. (a) Yes   (b) Interchange the domain and co-domain   (c) (i) add 5   (ii) subtract 5
   (e) $f(x) = x + 5, g(x) = x - 5$
2. (a) The inverse is a function   (b) The inverse is not a function   (c) The inverse is not a function
   (d) The inverse is not a function
3. (a) subtract 3   (b) divide by 4   (c) not possible   (d) square root

4. (a) Yes (b) Yes (c) Yes (d) Yes
5. (a) (i) $\{4, 5, 6, 7\}$ (ii) $f^{-1}(x) = x - 4$ (b) (i) $\{3, 6, 9, 12\}$ (ii) $g^{-1}(x) = \frac{1}{3}x$ (c) (i) $\{3, 4, 5, 6\}$
  (ii) $h^{-1}(x) = x + 3$ (d) (i) $\{1, 2, 3, 4\}$ (ii) $k^{-1}(x) = 5x$
6. (a) $f(x) = 3x + 1$ (b) $f^{-1}(x) = \frac{1}{3}(x - 1)$, $\{4, 7, 10, 13, 16\}$

page 190
7. (a) $(1,2), (2,3), (3,4), (4,5)$ (b) $f(x) = x + 1$ (c) Yes (d) $f^{-1}(x) = x - 1$, $\{2, 3, 4, 5\}$
8. (a) $g(x) = 2$ (b) M-1 (c) $(2,1), (2,2), (2,3), (2,4), (2,5), (2,6)$ (d) No
9. It is the same as the function itself.
10. (a) $\{7, 8, 9, 10, 11, 12\}$ (b) $\{0, 4, 8, 12, 16, 20\}$ (c) $\{7, 11, 15, 19, 23, 27\}$
11. (a) $f(x) = x + 7, g(x) = 4x, h(x) = 4x + 7$
  (b) $\{7, 8, 9, 10, 11, 12\}, f^{-1}(x) = x - 7, \{0, 4, 8, 12, 16, 20\}$;
  $g^{-1}(x) = \frac{1}{4}x; \{7, 11, 15, 19, 23, 27\}, h^{-1}(x) = \frac{1}{4}(x - 7)$
12. (a) $f^{-1}(x) = x + 4$ (b) $g^{-1}(x) = \frac{1}{5}x$ (c) $h^{-1}(x) = \frac{1}{5}(x + 4)$
13. (a) True (b) True (c) False (d) True (e) True (f) False
14. (a) $f^{-1}(x) = \frac{1}{7}x$ (b) 3 (c) $g^{-1}(x) = x + 8$ (d) 25
15. (a) 13 (b) 41 (c) 48 (d) $h^{-1}(x) = \frac{1}{7}(x + 8)$ (e) 3 (f) 7 (g) 8

page 191 **The composition of functions** (2.4)
1. (a) $x \to 3x + 6$ (b) $x \to 5x - 3$ (c) $x \to 7x - 28$
2. (a) $x \to x^2 + 4$ (b) $x \to (x + 4)^2$ (c) $x \to \frac{1}{x+1}$
3. (a) $x \to 5x - 15$ (b) $x \to 2x + 5$ (c) $x \to (x - 2)^2$ (d) $x \to \frac{1}{x+3}$
4. (a) $\{^-25, ^-20, ^-15, ^-10, ^-5\}$ (b) $\{1, 3, 5, 7, 9\}$ (c) $\{16, 9, 4, 1, 0\}$ (d) $\{1, \frac{1}{2}, \frac{1}{3}, \frac{1}{4}, \frac{1}{5}\}$
5. (a) $x \to 6x + 9$ (b) $x \to 6x - 16$ (c) $x \to 20x + 1$ (d) $x \to 16x^2 - 8x + 3$
6. (a) $\{9, 15, 21, 27, 33, 39\}$ (b) $\{^-16, ^-10, ^-4, 2, 8, 14\}$ (c) $\{1, 21, 41, 61, 81, 101\}$
  (d) $\{3, 11, 51, 123, 227, 363\}$
7. (d) **8.** Yes, it is (c) **9.** (c) **10.** Yes, it is (c) **11.** Yes, $\{23, 35, 47, 59, 71\}$
12. (a) 8, 15 (b) 20,27 (c) 0,7 **13.** (a) 15 (b) 27 (c) 7 **14.** (a) 15 (b) 27 (c) 7
15. Yes, $x \to 4x + 7$ **16.** $g(f(x))$ or gf
page 192
17. (a) $x \to 2x$ (b) $x \to x + 1$ (c) $x \to 2x + 1$ **18.** (a) $x \to x + 1$ (b) $x \to 2x$ (c) $x \to 2x + 2$
19. Yes **20.** (a) 6 (b) 3 (c) 3 (d) 5 (e) 10 (f) 10, $x \to 2x - 3, x \to 2x - 6$
21. (a) 25 (b) 24 (c) 24 (d) 3 (e) 9 (f) 9, $x \to x^2 - 1, x \to (x - 1)^2$
22. $x \to 3x + 2, x \to 3x + 6$, (a) 8 (b) 23 (c) 35 (d) 12 (e) 27 (f) 39
23. $x \to 4x^2, x \to 16x^2$, (a) 36 (b) 400 (c) 64
page 193
24. (b) $\{1, 2, 3, 4, 5\}$ (c) $\{5, 6, 7, 8, 9\}$ (d) $\{15, 18, 21, 24, 27\}$ (e) (i) $x \to x + 4$, (ii) $x \to 3x$
  (iii) $x \to 3x + 12$ (f) (i) 7 (ii) 18 (iii) 27
25. (b) $\{5, 6, 7, 8, 9\}$ (c) $\{11, 14, 17, 20, 23\}$ (d) $x \to x - 4, x \to 3x - 4$ (e) (i) 17 (ii)14
26. (a) 11 (b) 14 (c) 17 (d) 20 (e) 23, Yes, (i) 14 (ii) 23
27. (e) 23 (f) 20 (g) 25 (h) 4 (i) $x \to 4x + 3$ (j) $x \to 4x + 12$ (k) $x \to 4x - 3$
  (l) $x \to 4x - 12$
28. (a) $x \to 4x + 9$ (b) $x \to 4x - 9$ (c) $x \to x$
  (d) $x \to x$ Each element of the domain will be its own image. The functions are identity functions
29. (a) 7 (b) 49 (c) 49 (d) 99 (e) 225 (f) 19, $x \to (2x + 1)^2, x \to 2x^2 + 1$
30. (a) 8 (b) 64 (c) 64 (d) 318 (e) 1444 (f) 18, $x \to (5x - 2)^2, x \to 5x^2 - 2$
31. $x \to 6x - 9, x \to 6x + 8$, (a) 3 (b) 20 $^-27$ (d) $^-10$
32. $x \to 6x - 16, x \to 6x + 3$, (a) 8 (b) 9 (c) $^-16$ (d) $^-9$
33. (a) $gf(x) = (3x - 1)^2$ (b) $fg(x) = 3x^2 - 1$ (c) $gg(x) = x^4$ (d) $ff(x) = 9x - 4$
34. (a) $fg(x) = (4x + 1)^2$ (b) $gf(x) = 4x^2 + 1$ (c) $ff(x) = x^4$ (d) $gg(x) = 16x + 5$
35. (a) $kh(x) = 2x - 1)^3$ (b) $hk(x) = 2x^3 - 1$ (c) $kk(x) = x^9$ (f) $hh(x) = 4x - 3$

36. (a) $hk(x) = (1 - x)^3$ (b) $kh(x) = 1 - x^3$ (c) $kh(x) = x^9$ (d) $kk(x) = x$

37. (a) gf (b) fg (c) gg (d) ff

38. (a) hk (b) kh (c) kkk (d) hkh

39. (a), (b) and (d)

42. (a) $4x + 3$ (b) $8x + 7$ (c) $16x + 15$

page 194   **Composition and inverses** (2.5)

1. (a) $x \to 3x + 2$ (b) $x \to 4x - 3; x \to \frac{1}{3}(x - 2), x \to \frac{1}{4}(x + 3)$

2. (a) $x \to 4(x - 5)$ (b) $x \to \frac{1}{3}(x + 2); x \to \frac{1}{4}x + 5, x \to 3x - 2$

3. (a) $x \to \frac{1}{4}(x - 7)$ (b) $x \to \frac{1}{3}(x + 5)$ (c) $x \to \frac{1}{2}x - 2$ (d) $x \to \frac{1}{2}x + 5$

4. (a) $x \to \frac{1}{6}(x + 1)$ (b) $x \to 2x - 3$ (c) $x \to \sqrt{x - 3}$ (d) $x \to \sqrt{x} - 1$

5. (a) $x \to \frac{1}{3}(x + 7)$ (b) $x \to \frac{1}{2}x - 5$ (c) $x \to 3x - 2$ (d) $x \to 3x + 4$

6. (a) $x \to \frac{1}{2}(x - 3)$ (b) $x \to \frac{1}{4}x + 5$ (c) $x \to \frac{1}{4}(x - 10)$ (d) $x \to \frac{1}{2}(\frac{x}{3} - 1)$ (e) $x \to 3x + 5$

page 195

7. (a) 20   (b) 5

8. (a) 13   (b) 8   (c) 22   (d) 27   (e) 5   (f) 7   (g) 3   (h) 4

9. (a) $f^{-1}(x) = \frac{1}{4}(x - 1)$ (b) 9   (c) 2   (d) $\frac{1}{4}$

10. (a) $g^{-1}(x) = \frac{1}{2}x - 5$ (b) 12   (c) 1   (d) $^-4\frac{1}{2}$

11. (a) $h^{-1}(x) = 2x + 3$ (b) 0   (c) 3   (d) 9

12. (a) $k^{-1}(x) = \sqrt{x + 4}$ (b) 21   (c) 5   (d) 3

13. (a) $f^{-1}(x) = \frac{1}{6}(x - 7)$ (b) 25   (c) 3   (d) $\frac{-1}{2}$

14. (a) $x \to 3x + 2$ (b) $x \to \frac{1}{3}x$ (c) $x \to x - 2$ (d) $x \to \frac{1}{3}(x - 2), x \to 3x + 6$

15. (a) $x \to 4x - 12$ (b) $x \to \frac{1}{4}x$ (c) $x \to x + 3$ (d) $x \to \frac{1}{4}(x + 12), x \to 4x - 3$

16. (a) $x \to 12x + 8$ (b) $x \to \frac{1}{12}(x - 8)$ (c) $x \to 12x + 2$ (d) $x \to \frac{1}{12}(x - 2)$

17. (a) $x \to 2x + 4$ (b) $x \to \frac{1}{2}(x - 4)$ (c) $x \to 2x + 9$ (d) $x \to \frac{1}{2}(x - 9)$

18. (a) 19   (b) 6   (c) 4   **19.** (a) 3   (b) 4   **20.** 5   **21.** 3   **22.** (a) 7   (b) 7   (c) $^-1$ (d) $3\frac{1}{2}$

23. (a) 7   (b) 11   (c) $^-1$ (d) $^-3$ **24.** (a) 4   (b) 7   (c) $^-2$

25. (a) 3   (b) 11   (c) $^-4$ **26.** (a) $\frac{1}{2}$ (b) $^-2$ (c) 62

page 196

27. $x \to \frac{1}{7}(x + 8), 4, 2$ **28.** $x \to \frac{1}{24}(x + 5), 7$

29. (a) $x \to 3x, x \to \frac{1}{3}x$ (b) (i) $\{1, 2, 3, 4\}, \{1, 2, 3, 4\}$ (c) $x \to x$ (d) An identity function

30. (c) It is an identity function   **31.** $f^{-1}f : x \to x$ **32.** $ff^{-1} : x \to x$

33. (b) h is the inverse of g and vice-versa.   (d) (i) $h = g^{-1}$ (ii) $hg : x \to x$

34. $gh : x \to x$ **35.** (a) 4   (b) 6   (c) 3   (d) 1   **36.** (a) 8   (b) 9   (c) 2   (d) 8

37. (a) 17   (b) 2   (c) 1   (d) 9   (e) 4   (f) 25   (g) 17   (h) 4   (i) $x \to \frac{1}{4}(x - 5)$ (j) $x \to 4x + 5$ (k) $x \to x$ (l) $x \to x$

38. (a) $x \to 2x + 2$ (b) $x \to 2x + 1$ (c) $x \to (x + 1)^2$ (d) $x \to x^2 + 1$ (e) $x \to 2x^2$ (f) $x \to 4x^2$ (g) $x \to 4x$ (h) $x \to x + 2$

39. (a) $10, x \to x + 3$

40. (a) $x \to 3x$ (b) $x \to x + 2$ (c) $x \to \frac{1}{3}x$ (d) $x \to x - 2$ (e) $x \to 3x + 2$ (f) $x \to \frac{1}{3}(x - 2)$, Yes

page 197

41. (a) $x \to 5x - 2, x \to \frac{1}{5}(x + 2)$ (b) $x \to x + 2, x \to \frac{1}{5}x, x \to \frac{1}{5}(x + 2)$

42. (a) $x \to 4 - x$ (b) $x \to 4 - x, x \to 4 - x$ (c) Yes, Yes

43. (a) 1,5   (b) 4,2   (c) $\frac{1}{3}, 3$ (d) $\frac{1}{4}, 4; gg : x \to x, hh : x \to x$, they are self-inverse functions.

3 Graphs 3

page 199 **Revision** (3.1)

2. (a) $y = x + 2$ (b) $y = 2x$ (c) $y = 3x - 1$ (d) $y = 6 - x$

3. (a)

x	$^-2$	$^-1$	0	1	2	3	4	5	6
y	1	2	3	4	5	6	7	8	9

(b)

x	$^-2$	$^-1$	0	1	2	3	4	5	6
y	$^-6$	$^-3$	0	3	6	9	12	15	18

(c)

x	$^-2$	$^-1$	0	1	2	3	4	5	6
y	$^-1$	1	3	5	7	9	11	13	15

(d)

x	$^-2$	$^-1$	0	1	2	3	4	5	6
y	9	8	7	6	5	4	3	2	1

4. (a) Gradient is equal to one and the intercept on the y-axis is positive
(b) Both pass through the origin   (d) Both have a gradient of $^-1$.
5. (a) $y = x + 5$ (b) $y = 4x$ (c) $y = 5 - x$ (d) $y = 3x - 2$ (e) $y = 10 - 2x$ (f) $y = \frac{1}{2}x + 3$
page 200

6. (a)

x	$^-2$	$^-1$	0	1	2	3	4	5	6
y	$^-13$	$^-8$	$^-3$	2	7	12	17	22	27

(b)

x	$^-2$	$^-1$	0	1	2	3	4	5	6
y	10	7	4	1	$^-2$	$^-5$	$^-8$	$^-11$	$^-14$

(c)

x	$^-2$	$^-1$	0	1	2	3	4	5	6
y	$^-\frac{1}{2}$	0	$\frac{1}{2}$	1	$1\frac{1}{2}$	2	$2\frac{1}{2}$	3	$3\frac{1}{2}$

(d)

x	$^-2$	$^-1$	0	1	2	3	4	5	6
y	$^-12$	$^-9$	$^-6$	$^-3$	0	3	6	9	12

7. 5 (f) and 6 (c), 5 (d) and 6 (d)   **8.** (1,1)

9. (a)

x	$^-2$	$^-1$	0	1	2	3
x^2	4	1	0	1	4	9
$x^2 - 2$	2	$^-1$	$^-2$	$^-1$	2	7

(c) $^-1.4$ and 1.4

10. (c) $y = x^2 + 4$

11. (a)

x	$^-5$	$^-4$	$^-3$	$^-2$	$^-1$	0	1	2	3	4	5
y	24	15	8	3	0	$^-1$	0	3	8	15	24

(b)

x	$^-5$	$^-4$	$^-3$	$^-2$	$^-1$	0	1	2	3	4	5
y	21	12	5	0	$^-3$	$^-4$	$^-3$	0	5	12	21

(c)

x	$^-5$	$^-4$	$^-3$	$^-2$	$^-1$	0	1	2	3	4	5
y	18	9	2	$^-3$	$^-6$	$^-7$	$^-3$	2	9	18

12. (b) $x = {}^-1$ and 1, $x = {}^-2$ and 2, $x = {}^-2.6$ and 2.6 (c) 2.6
13. (a) All three were of exactly the same shape   (b) Move the first curve down the y-axis   (c) $\binom{0}{-6}$
(d) $\binom{0}{3}$

14. (a)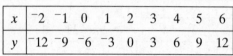

x	$^-5$	$^-4$	$^-3$	$^-2$	$^-1$	0	1	2	3	4	5
y	$^-21$	$^-12$	$^-5$	0	3	4	3	0	$^-5$	$^-12$	$^-21$

(b) $^-2$ and 2   (c) One is a reflection of the other in the x-axis

15. (a) $(0,4), (1,0), (2,{}^-2\frac{1}{4}), (4,0), (5,4)$ (b) 0   (c) 1 and 4

16.

x	$^-5$	$^-4$	$^-3$	$^-2$	$^-1$	0	1	2	3	4	5
y	$^-24$	$^-14$	$^-6$	0	4	6	6	4	0	$^-6$	$^-14$

(b) $^-2$ and 3

17. (a)

x	‾3	‾2	‾1	0	1	2	3	4	5	6
y	‾5	‾8	‾9	‾8	‾5	0	7	16	27	40

(b)

x	‾3	‾2	‾1	0	1	2	3	4	5	6
y	0	‾4	‾6	‾6	‾4	0	6	14	24	36

(c)

x	‾3	‾2	‾1	0	1	2	3	4	5	6
y	‾10	‾12	‾12	‾10	‾6	0	8	18	30	44

(d)

x	‾3	‾2	‾1	0	1	2	3	4	5	6
y	12	5	0	‾3	‾4	‾3	0	5	12	21

(e)

x	‾3	‾2	‾1	0	1	2	3	4	5	6
y	7	0	‾3	‾2	3	12	25	42	63	88

(f)

x	‾3	‾2	‾1	0	1	2	3	4	5	6
y	49	24	5	‾8	‾15	‾16	‾11	0	17	40

(g)

x	‾3	‾2	‾1	0	1	2	3	4	5	6
y	‾9	0	5	6	3	‾4	‾15	‾30	‾49	‾72

(h)

x	‾3	‾2	‾1	0	1	2	3	4	5	6
y	‾48	‾13	10	21	20	7	‾18	‾55	‾104	‾165

18. (b) ‾4 and 2, ‾3 and 2, ‾5 and 2, ‾1 and 3, ‾2 or $\frac{1}{2}$, ‾$\frac{2}{3}$ and 4, ‾2 and $1\frac{1}{2}$, ‾$1\frac{1}{2}$ and $2\frac{1}{3}$

page 201 **Graphs of functions** (3.2)

1.

x	0	1	2	3	4	5
f(x)	3	5	7	9	11	13

2. Yes, Yes　(a) $x \to \frac{1}{2}(x - 3)$　(b) 4

3.

x	‾3	‾2	‾1	0	1	2	3
g(x)	7	2	‾1	‾2	‾1	2	7

4. (a) Yes　(b) {‾3, ‾2, ‾1, 0, 1, 2, 3}　(c) {7, 2, ‾1, ‾2}　(d) They both equal 7　(e) M-1
(f) ‾2 or 2　(g) It is 1-M

5.

x	‾3	‾2	‾1	0	1	2	3
h(x)	‾27	‾8	‾1	0	1	8	27

6. (c), it is neither a straight line function nor a quadratic function
7. (a) {‾27, ‾8, ‾1, 0, 1, 8, 27}　(b) 1-1　(c) Yes　(d) {‾27, ‾8, ‾1, 0, 1, 8, 27}　(e) $x \to {}^3\sqrt{x}$
8. (b) {0, 1, 2, 3, 4, 5}　(c) {1, 2, 4, 8, 16, 32}　(d) (i) 8　(ii) 16　(e) Yes

page 202 **Graphs of inequalities** (3.3)
1. (a) 5, 3, 7　(b) 10, 12, 14　(c) Thos in (a) are smaller, those in (b) are bigger
2. (a) Yes　(b) Yes
3. (a) Yes
　(b) All points representing scores lower than 7 lie below the line of dots and all points representing
　scores higher than 7 lie above the same line
4. (1,6), (2,3), (3,2), (4,7), (3,8), (5,6), (6,4)　(a) For P and T; $y > 2x - 1$, for R, U and V; $y < 2x - 1$,
　for Q and S; $y = 2x - 1$
　(b) (i) $y < 2x - 1$　(ii) $y > 2x - 1$　(c) Yes
5. (a) Q, R and W　(b) P, T, U and V　(c) S only　**6.** (a) Q, R and W　(b) P, T, U and V
8. (c) $x + y < 5$ and $y < 2x - 2$　**9.** Any two of (2,0), (2,1), (3,0), (3,1) and (4,0)
10. Yes　(a) The shaded part to the left of the line $x = 3$
　(b) Any three points to the right of the line $x = 3$ and below the line $y = 4$

page 204
11. (a) $x = 2, y = 1, x + y = 6$ (b) $x > 2, y > 1, x + y < 6$
12. (a) D   (b) A   (c) B   (d) C
14. (a) A right angled triangle   (b) $x + y < 6, y < 3x, y > x + 1$ (c) Yes
16. $(0,0), (0,^-1), (0,^-2)$ **21.** $x + y \leqslant 7, y \leqslant \dfrac{6}{x}$ **22.** $y < 4 - x^2, y \leqslant (x - 1)^2$

page 205   **Finding roots using graphs** (3.4)
1. (a) 1 and 5   (b) 0 and 6   (c) 2 and 4   (d) 3   **2.** (a) 2 and 4   (b) 1 and 5   (c) 3   (d) 0 and 6

3.(a)

x	0	1	2	3	4	5	6
x^2	0	1	4	9	16	25	36
$6x$	0	6	12	18	24	30	36
$x^2 - 6x + 5$	5	0	‾3	‾4	‾3	0	5

(d) 0 and 6, 1 and 5, 2 and 4, 3

4. (a) 1 or 5   (b) 2 or 4   (c) 3   (d) 0 or 6
5. (a) Find the x-coordinate of each of the two points where the curve meets the line $y = 5$
   (b) Find the x-coordinate of each of the two points where the curve meets the line $y = 2$
page 206
6. (b) $x = 2$ or 5   (c) $x = 1$ or 6

7. (a)

x	0	1	2	3	4	5	6
$4x^2$	0	4	16	36	64	100	144
$8x$	0	8	16	24	32	40	48
$4x^2 - 8x + 3$	3	‾1	3	15	35	63	99

(c) $x = \frac{1}{2}$ or $1\frac{1}{2}$

8.(a)

x	‾3	‾2	‾1	0	1	2	3	4	5
y	15	8	3	0	‾1	0	3	8	15

(c) (i) ‾1 and 3   (ii) ‾2 and 4
(iii) ‾3 and 5   (iv) 0 and 2
(v) 1   (vi) No solutions

$x^2 - 2x + 1 = 0$ has just one solution, $x^2 - 2x = -2$ has no solutions.
9. (a) ‾1 or 2   (b) ‾2.45 or 2.45   (c) ‾1.4 or 1.4   (d) 1
10. (a) 0 or 1   (b) ‾3 or 2   (c) ‾2 or 1   (d) 2   **11.** (a) ‾2 or 4   (b) 0 or 3   (c) ‾1 or 4
12. (a) ‾1 or 5   (b) 1 or 4   (c) ‾1 or 4   **13.** (a) ‾2 or 5   (b) ‾1 or 5   (c) ‾2 or 4
14. (a) $\{^-2,2\}$ (b) $\{^-4,3\}$ (c) $\{^-1,2\}$
page 207
15. (a) $8 + 2x - x^2 = x + 6$ (b) $8 + 2x - x^2 = 8 - x$ (c) $8 + 2x - x^2 = 2$ **16.** ‾1 or 4
17. $x = 1, y = 4$ or $x = 3, y = 12$ **18.** (a) $\{3\}$ (b) $\{^-3,3\}$ (c) $\{^-1.7,1.7\}$
19. (a) $\{^-5,2\}$ (b) $\{^-2$ or $5\}$ **21.** $\{^-0.35,1.35\}$
22. (a) $\{^-1,0,1\}$ (b) $\{^-2,0,2\}$ (c) $\{^-3,0,3\}$ **23.** $\{^-3,1,2\}$

4   Gradients

page 209   **Gradients of straight lines** (4.1)
2. (a) Yes   (b) Yes   **3.** $y = 3x - 3$ **4.** $(0,1), (0,4), (0,^-1)$ **5.** $1, 3, \frac{1}{2}$
6. Divide both sides of the equation by 2
7. (a) $3, 2$ (b) ‾2, 3   (c) $\frac{1}{3}, 1\frac{1}{3}$ (d) $4, ^-2$ (e) $\frac{1}{3}, ^-\frac{1}{2}$ (f) $^-2\frac{1}{2}, 2$

page 210

8. (a) 2   (b) 3   (c) 2   (d) $\frac{1}{2}$ **10.** (a) $^-2$ (b) $^-2$ (c) 2   (d) $\frac{-1}{2}$
11. (a) 2   (b) $\frac{1}{2}$ (c) $^-2$ (d) 2   (e) $\frac{1}{2}$ (f) $^-2$ **12.** (a) a and d, b and e, c and f   (b) c and f
13. a, c and e; b, d and f   **14.** a and b, d and e

page 211

15. b, d and f   **16.** c
17. (a) $y = 1x + 3$ (b) $y = 5x - 1$ (c) $y = 5x + 3$ (d) $y = 3x + 5$
18. (a) a and c   (b) b and c
19. (a) (1,2)   (b) (2,6)   (c) (4,4)   (d) $\frac{2}{3}$ (e) 4
   (f) $^-1$; PQ = 4.123 units, QR = 2.828 units, PR = 3.606 units
20. (a) $\frac{3}{4}$ (b) 5 units   **21.** (a) Yes   (b) Yes; $\sqrt{13}$, $\sqrt{13}$ and $\sqrt{26}$ units
22. Their product is $^-1$ **23.** (b) 3, $-\frac{1}{3}$ (c) $\sqrt{10}$, $\sqrt{10}$ and $\sqrt{20}$ units   (d) Yes
24. a and c, b and f, d and e   **25.** $\frac{1}{4}$, $^-4$, $1\frac{2}{3}$; PQ and QR

page 212   **Equations of straight lines** (4.2)

1. $(^-8,^-2)$, $(^-6,0)$, $(^-4,2)$, $(^-2,4)$, $(0,6)$, $(2,8)$, $(4,10)$, $(6,12)$, $(8,14)$, $y = x + 6$; $(0,^-8)$, $(2,^-4)$, $(4,0)$,
   $(8,8)$, $(10,12)$, $y = 2x - 8$; $(^-2,1)$, $(2,3)$, $(4,4)$, $(8,6)$, $(10,7)$, $(12,8)$, $y = \frac{1}{2}x + 2$
2. (a) $6,^-8,2$ (b) $1,2,\frac{1}{2}$ **3.** $y = x + 6$, $y = 2x - 8$, $y = \frac{1}{2}x + 2$
5. (a) $y = 2x$ (b) $y = 2x + 1$ (c) $y = 2x + 5$ (d) $y = 2x - 3$ (e) $y = 2x + \frac{3}{2}$
6. (a) $y = 3x + 2$ (b) $y = 5x + 2$ (c) $y = \frac{1}{2}x + 2$ (d) $y = 2 - 2x$ (e) $y = 2$
7. (a) $y = 3x + 5$ (b) $y = 4x - 2$ (c) $y = 1 - x$
8. (a) $3, y = 3x + 2$ (b) $2, y = 2x + 4$ (c) $4, y = 4x - 1$ (d) $4, y = 4x - 3$
9. $(3\frac{1}{2},5)$, 5 units

page 213

10. $y = 3x - 5$
12. (a) $y = 4x - 5$ (b) $y = 3x - 11$ (c) $y = 2x + 3$ (d) $y = \frac{1}{2}x + 1$ (e) $y = 7 - 2x$
14. (a) $y = 4x - 15$ (b) $y = 2x + 3$ (c) $y = \frac{1}{2}x + 1$ (d) $y = 7 - 2x$
16. (a) $y = 5 - \frac{5}{3}x$ (b) $y = 7 - \frac{7}{4}x$ (c) $y = \frac{5}{2}x - 5$
17. (a) $y = 6 - 2x$ (b) $y = 6 - 2x$ (c) $y = 6 - 2x$, all are the same line.

page 213   **Gradients of curves** (4.3)

1. (a) Point Q   (b) Find the gradient of the tangent at each point
2. (b) PQ has a gradient greater than that of the tangent at P, but less than that of the tangent at Q.
   (c) Join PQ and measure it directly.

page 214

3. (a) 1   (b) 2 and $\frac{1}{2}$ (c) Yes

4. (a)

x	0	1	2	3	4	5	6
y	0	1	4	9	16	25	36

(b) 5   (d) 2, 8

5. (a) 25 km/h   (b) 25 km/h   (c) 50 km/h
   (d) 25 km/h. The third hour, because BC has steeper gradient than OA, AB, CD or DE.
6. (b) 50 km/h, 50 km/h   (c) 96 km/h
7. (a) and (b) 20 km/h, 40 km/h, 40 km/h, 20 km/h, 0 km/h
   (c) The third hour, because BC has a gradient steeper than any other chord.
   (d) EF has zero gradient

page 215   **Rates of change** (4.4)

1. (a) 4   (b) 2   (c) $\frac{1}{2}$ **2.** 21   **3.** (a) 4   (b) 14   (c) 9
4. (a) 60 km/h   (b) 48 km/h   (c) 151.2 km/h   **5.** (a) 44 km/h^2 (b) 540 km/h^2

page 216
6. (a) $12\pi\,\text{cm}^2/\text{cm}$ (b) $2.7\pi\,\text{cm}^2/\text{cm}$ (c) $4\pi\,\text{cm}^2/\text{cm}$
7. (a) $52\,\text{cm}^3/\text{cm}$ (b) $4.33\,\text{cm}^3/\text{cm}$ (c) $2.77\,\text{cm}^3/\text{cm}$ **8.** $84\pi\,\text{cm}^3/\text{cm}, 504\pi\,\text{cm}^3/\text{s}$
9. (a) 5   (b) 9   **10.** 6   **11.** (a) 5   (b) 7   (c) 11   (d) 15
12. (a) 6   (b) 18   (c) 24   (d) 36   **13.** (a) $6\pi\,\text{cm}^2/\text{cm}$ (b) $10\pi\,\text{cm}^2/\text{cm}$ (c) $12\pi\,\text{cm}^2/\text{cm}$
14. $16\pi\,\text{cm}^3/\text{cm}$ (b) $64\pi\,\text{cm}^3/\text{cm}$ (c) $100\pi\,\text{cm}^3/\text{cm}$

5   Transformations 2

page 218   **Revision** (5.1)
 1. (a) $(2,^-3)$ (b) $(^-2,^-3)$ (c) $(2,3)$ (d) $(^-2,3)$ (e) $(0,0)$
 2. (a) $(^-2,3)$ (b) $(2,3)$ (c) $(^-2,^-3)$ (d) $(2,^-3)$ (e) $(0,0)$
 3. (a) $A(2,^-1), B(4,^-1), C(4,^-5)$ (b) $A(^-2,1), B(^-4,1), C(^-4,5)$ (c) $A(8,1), B(6,1), C(6,5)$
     (d) $A(0,1), B(^-2,1), C(^-2,5)$ (e) $A(2,9), B(4,9), C(4,5)$ (f) $A(2,5), B(4,5), C(4,1)$
 4. (c) (i) $(3,2)$ (ii) $(3,3)$ (iii) $(4,^-1)$ (iv) $(^-1,4)$ (v) $(^-2,^-5)$ (vi) $(5,2)$
     (d) Yes, the coordinate figures are interchanged   (e) (b,a)
 5. (c) (i) $(^-4,^-3)$ (ii) $(^-3,^-4)$ (iii) $(3,4)$ (iv) $(1,2)$ (v) $(^-2,^-1)$ (vi) $(^-1,3)$
     (d) Yes, the coordinate figures and signs are interchanged   (e) $(^-b,^-a)$
 7. (c) $y = -x$ **8.** (a) $y = 4$ (b) $x = 2$ (c) $y = 1\frac{1}{2}$ (d) $y = x$ (e) $y = -x$
 9. $y = x$ **10.** $y = x + 2$
11. (a) $(^-1,3)$ (b) $(^-1,^-1)$ (c) $(0.2,4)$ (d) $(2,6.9)$ (e) $^-1.3,0.7)$
12. (a) $A(2,^-1), B(2,2), C(0,2)$ (b) $A(^-1,2), B(^-1,5), C(^-3,5)$ (c) $A(1,4), B(1,7), C(^-1,7)$
     (d) $A(4,^-1), B(4,2), C(2,2)$
page 220
13. (a) Rotation of $90°$ (anticlockwise) about $(2,5)$ (b) Both pairs are equal   (c) Yes, X only
     (d) Rotation of $90°$ (clockwise) about $(2,5)$ (d) They meet at X   (e) Yes
14. (a) A rotation of $180°$ about $(2,5)$ (b) Yes   **15.** (c) $(3,2)$ (d) $90°$ (e) $90°$ (anticlockwise)
16. (a) Yes   (b) (i) $90°$ (ii) $90°$, Yes   **18.** (b) $(0,^-1)$ (c) $90°$ (anticlockwise)
19. (b) $(0,1)$ (c) $90°$ (anticlockwise)   **20.** $(1,^-1), 90°$ anticlockwise

page 221   **Glide reflections** (5.2)
 1. Yes, yes.   **2.** Opposite image, yes   **4.** Yes   **5.** (a) No   (b) No
 9. (a) Yes   (b) $(3,4), (3,2), (3,6)$ (c) $x = 3$
     (d) Translation $\binom{0}{4}$ followed by a reflection in $x = 3$ (or vice versa)
page 222
10. (b) Yes. Triangle PMN has side lengths equal to half of those of triangle PQQ'.   **11.** $y = -x$
12. (a) $90°$ rotation (clockwise) about $(3\frac{1}{2},\frac{1}{2})$ (b) Translation $\binom{3}{3}$ (c) Reflection in the line $x + y = 4$
     (d) Translation $\binom{3}{0}$ followed by a reflection in $y = 2$, or the translation $\binom{0}{3}$ followed by a reflection in
     $x = 2$ (or vice versa for both cases)
13. (b) A rotation of $180°$ about $(0,1\frac{1}{2})$ **14.** (a) $A(^-1,3), B(^-1,5), C(0,5)$ (b) No
15. (a) $A(^-1,^-3), B(^-1,^-5), C(0,^-5)$ (b) No   **16.** (b) $8.5\,\text{cm}$ (c) $18.5°$

page 223   **Shears and stretches** (5.3)
 1. (a) $35\,\text{cm}^2$ (b) $35\,\text{cm}^2$ (c) $17.5\,\text{cm}^2$ (d) $17.5\,\text{cm}^2$ (e) $8.75\,\text{cm}^2$ (f) $8.75\,\text{cm}^2$, No
 2. (a) PQEF   (b) A   (c) Extend object and image lines until they meet
 3. (a) They are all the same   (b) AB   (c) A shear with XYZ as the invariant line
     (d) XZA and XZB or YZA and YZB
 4. (b) Those along the x-axis.   **5.** $(1,2) \rightarrow (4,2), (2,2) \rightarrow (8,2), (2,1) \rightarrow (4,1), (1,1) \rightarrow (2,1)$
 6. (a) They are both equal to $4\,\text{cm}$ (b) A line through A which is parallel to BC

page 224
7. (a) No   (b) No
9. (a) Shear, rotation of 90° (anticlockwise), shear   (b) Yes   (d) 170 cm², $\sqrt{170}$ or 13.04 cm
page 225
10. (a) Scale factor 7, invariant line WX   (b) Scale factor 2, invariant line PQ
  (c) Scale factor 3, invariant line AB   (d) Scale factor 2, invariant line RS.
11. (a) A → (2,0), B → (2,1)   (b) B → (1,3), C → (0,3)   (c) O → (⁻1,0), C → (⁻1,1)
  (d) O → (0,⁻1½), A → (1,⁻1½)
12. (c) A → (2,6), B(5,6), C(5,8)
13. (a) Scale factor 3 parallel to AB, scale factor 2 parallel to AD
  (b) Scale factor 3 parallel to AB, scale factor 2 parallel to AC
14. X'(4,4), Y'(12,4), Z'(12,12)

page 226   **Combining transformations** (5.4)
1. The translation $\binom{4}{0}$ **2.** Reflection in $x = 4$
3. (b) (3,1)   (c) (8,6)   **4.** (b) (8,0)   (c) ⁻8,0), Yes
  5. (b) and (d)   **6.** A(⁻3,2), B(⁻3,5), C(⁻4,6)   **7.** W(1,⁻1), X(1,⁻3), Y(3,⁻4), Z(5,⁻1)
8. (a) P(8,0), Q(4,0), R(4,2)   (b) P(0,0), Q(⁻4,0), R(⁻4,2)   (c) P(⁻4,2), Q(⁻8,2), R(⁻8,0)
  (d) P(6,0), Q(10,0), R(10,⁻2)
9. (a) (15,3)   (b) (⁻3,⁻3)
10. (a) A(⁻1,3), B(⁻1,9), C(⁻2,9), D(⁻2,1)   (b) A(⁻3,1), B(⁻3,3), C(⁻6,3), D(⁻6,1)

6   Trigonometry 2

page 228   **Graphs of trigonometric functions** (6.1)
1. (a) 0.577 units   (b) 1.732 units   **2.** (a) Yes   (b) Yes, yes   **3.** (c) 0.58 units
4. (c) 1.73 units   **5.** (a) 1 unit   (b) None   **6.** It is very large indeed   **7.** Yes
8. ⁻1 unit   **9.** Yes
10. Yes, because the length that 135° cuts off on a tangent to a circle of unit radius is ⁻1 unit.
11. (a) ⁻1.73 units   (b) ⁻0.58 units   **12.** (a) Yes   (b) Yes
13. (a) tan 300° = ⁻tan 60°   (b) tan 315° = ⁻tan 45°   (c) tan 330° = ⁻tan 30°
14. (a) The length cut off by the angle θ is equal to that cut off by the angle (180−θ)°, but is measured in the opposite direction
  (b) the length cut off by the angle θ is equal to that cut off by the angle (θ−180)°
  (c) The length cut off by the angle θ is equal to that cut off by the angle (360−θ)°, but is measured in the opposite direction.

15.

Angle	0°	15°	30°	45°	60°	75°	90°	105°	120°	135°	150°	165°	180°
Tangent	0	0.27	0.58	1.00	1.73	3.73	∞	⁻3.73	⁻1.73	⁻1.00	⁻0.58	⁻0.27	0

Angle	195°	210°	225°	240°	255°	270°	285°	300°	315°	330°	345°	360°
Tangent	0.27	0.58	1.00	1.73	3.73	∞	⁻3.73	⁻1.73	⁻1.00	⁻0.58	⁻0.27	0

16. Answers are the same as those for question 15   **17.** (a) tan 90° = ∞   (b) tan 270° = ∞
18. (a) 210°   (b) 240°   (c) 300°   **19.** (a) 225°   (b) 251°   (c) 307°
20. (a) 1.00   (b) 1.00   (c) ⁻1.00   (d) 0.364   (e) 0.364   (f) ⁻0.364   (g) 2.75   (h) ⁻2.75
  (i) 2.75   (j) 0.700   (k) ⁻0.700   (l) ⁻0.700   (m) 3.73   (n) ⁻3.73   (o) 3.73
page 230
21. Yes   (b) Yes   **22.** (a) 330°   (b) 310°   (c) 270°   (d) 230°

23.

Angle	0°	⁻15°	⁻30°	⁻45°	⁻60°	⁻75°	⁻90°	⁻105°	⁻120°	⁻135°	⁻150°	⁻165°	⁻180°
Tangent	0	⁻0.27	⁻0.58	⁻1.00	⁻1.73	⁻3.73	∞	3.73	1.73	1.00	0.58	0.27	0

Angle	⁻195°	⁻210°	⁻225°	⁻240°	⁻255°	⁻270°	⁻285°	⁻300°	⁻315°	⁻330°	⁻345°	⁻360°
Tangent	⁻0.27	⁻0.58	⁻1.00	⁻1.73	⁻3.73	∞	3.73	1.73	1.00	0.58	0.27	0

24. Answers are the same as those for question 23.
25. (a) 200°, ⁻160°, ⁻340° (b) 30°, ⁻150°, ⁻330° (c) ⁻220°, 320°, 140° (d) ⁻20°, 160°, 340°; 4
26. (a) 0.5 (b) 0.87, Yes, Yes   **27.** (a) 0.87 (b) 0.5
28. Yes, because the sine is defined by that distance
29. It changes from being positive to negative every half revolution
30. (a) 0.5 (b) ⁻0.87   **31.** (a) sin 150° = sin 30° (b) cos 150° = ⁻cos 30°
32. (a) Yes (b) Yes
33. (a) sin 210° = ⁻sin 150° = ⁻sin 30° (b) cos 210° = cos 150° = ⁻cos 30°
34. (a) Yes (b) Yes
page 231
35. (a) 210° (b) 30° and 150° (c) 30° (d) 210° and 150°
36. (a) 240° (b) 60° and 120° (c) 60° (d) 240° and 120°
37. (a) positive (b) negative (c) negative (d) negative, positive
38. (a) positive (b) negative (c) positive (d) negative

39.

Angle	0°	15°	30°	45°	60°	75°	90°	105°	120°	135°	150°	165°	180°
Sine	0	0.26	0.50	0.71	0.87	0.97	1	0.97	0.87	0.71	0.50	0.26	0
Cosine	1	0.97	0.87	0.71	0.50	0.26	0	⁻0.26	⁻0.50	⁻0.71	⁻0.87	⁻0.97	⁻1

Angle	195°	210°	225°	240°	255°	270°	285°	300°	315°	330°	345°	360°
Sine	⁻0.26	⁻0.50	⁻0.71	⁻0.87	⁻0.97	⁻1	⁻0.97	⁻0.87	⁻0.71	⁻0.50	⁻0.26	0
Cosine	⁻0.97	⁻0.87	⁻0.71	⁻0.50	⁻0.26	0	0.26	0.50	0.71	0.87	0.97	1

40. Answers are the same as those for question 39.
41. (a) 90° or ⁻2.70° (b) 0°, 180°, 360°, ⁻180°, ⁻360°
42. (a) 150°, ⁻330°, ⁻210° (b) 120°, ⁻300°, ⁻240° (c) 330°, ⁻150°, ⁻30° (d) 300°, ⁻120°, ⁻60°
43. (a) 135°, ⁻315°, ⁻225° (b) 109°, ⁻289°, ⁻251° (c) 313°, ⁻133°, ⁻47° (d) 260°, ⁻80°, ⁻100°
44. (a) 0.602 (b) 0.602 (c) ⁻0.602

45.

Angle	0°	⁻15°	⁻30°	⁻45°	⁻60°	⁻75°	⁻90°	⁻105°	⁻120°	⁻135°	⁻150°	⁻165°	⁻180°
Sine	0	⁻0.26	⁻0.50	⁻0.71	⁻0.87	⁻0.97	⁻1	⁻0.97	⁻0.87	⁻0.71	⁻0.50	⁻0.26	0
Cosine	1	0.97	0.87	0.71	0.50	0.26	0	⁻0.26	⁻0.50	⁻0.71	⁻0.87	⁻0.97	⁻1

Angle	⁻195°	⁻210°	⁻225°	⁻240°	⁻255°	⁻270°	⁻285°	⁻300°	⁻315°	⁻330°	⁻345°	⁻360°
Sine	0.26	0.50	0.71	0.87	0.97	1	0.97	0.87	0.71	0.50	0.26	0
Cosine	⁻0.97	⁻0.87	⁻0.71	⁻0.50	⁻0.26	0	0.26	0.50	0.71	0.87	0.97	1

46. Answers are the same as those for question 45.
47. (a) 160°, ⁻340°, ⁻200° (b) 330°, ⁻150°, ⁻30° (c) ⁻140°, 320°, 220° (d) ⁻340°, 160°, 20°; 4

page 232

49. The translation $\begin{pmatrix} -90° \\ 0 \end{pmatrix}$ maps the sine curve onto the cosine curve.

50. (a) 45°, ⁻315°   (b) 135°, 225°, 315°, ⁻225°, ⁻135°, ⁻45°

51. (a) 330°, ⁻330°, ⁻30°   (b) 120°, ⁻120°, ⁻240°   (c) ⁻300°, 300°, 60°   (d) ⁻260°, 260°, 100°; 4

52. (a) 0.799   (b) ⁻0.799   (c) ⁻0.799   **53.** (a) 0°, 360°, ⁻360°   (b) 180°, ⁻180°

54. (a) No   (b) No   **55.** (a) 90°, ⁻270°, ⁻360°   (b) 0°, 180°, 360°, ⁻180°, ⁻360°

56. (a) 0°, 360°, ⁻360°   (b) 90°, 270°, ⁻90°, ⁻270°   **57.** (a) 1   (b) ⁻1   (c) 0   (d) 1   (e) ⁻1   (f) 0

58. (a) 30°, 150°, ⁻330°, ⁻210°   (b) 210°, 330°, ⁻150°, ⁻30°

59. (a) 60°, 300°, ⁻300°, ⁻60°   (b) 120°, 240°, ⁻240°, ⁻120°

60. (a) $\frac{1}{2}$ (b) $\frac{1}{2}$ (c) $-\frac{1}{2}$ (d) $\frac{1}{2}$ (e) $-\frac{1}{2}$ (f) $-\frac{1}{2}$ **61.** (a) True   (b) True   (c) True   (d) True, Yes

page 233   **Using tables and calculators** (6.2)

1. (a) 0.530   (b) 0.731   (c) 1.38

2. (a) 0.530, ⁻0.530, ⁻0.530   (b) ⁻0.731, ⁻0.731, 0.731   (c) ⁻1.38, 1.38, ⁻1.38

3. (a) ⁻0.946   (b) 0.946   (c) ⁻0.946   **4.** (a) ⁻0.927   (b) 0.927   (c) ⁻0.927

5. (a) ⁻0.754   (b) ⁻0.754   (c) 0.754

6. (a) 0.940   (b) ⁻0.500   (c) ⁻0.766   (d) ⁻0.515   (e) ⁻0.755   (f) 0.875   (g) ⁻0.424   (h) 2.25
(i) ⁻0.466

7. (a) True   (b) True   (c) True, No

page 234

8. (a) 0.719   (b) 14.3   (c) ⁻0.469   (d) 0.819   (e) 0.105   (f) ⁻0.259   (g) ⁻0.454   (h) ⁻0.156
(i) ⁻0.643   (j) ⁻0.306   (k) 0.699   (l) 0.532

10. (a) 30° or 330°   (b) 30° or 150°   (c) 150° or 210°   (d) 7.1° or 172.9°   (e) 108.3° or 251.7°
(f) 198.3° or 341.7°   (g) 169.1° or 190.9°   (h) 357.6° or 182.4°

page 234   **The sine and cosine rules** (6.3)

1. (a) Missing term is a   (b) Missing term is sin 75°   **2.** (a) 4.23 cm   (b) 4.508 cm

3. (a) 45.5°   (b) 63.1°

4. (a) 6.203 cm, 7.724 cm   (b) 6.305 cm, 5.347 cm   (c) 3.340 cm, 5.602 cm

5. (a) $p = 7.607$ cm, $r = 9$ cm, $\hat{R} = 65°$ (b) $\hat{T} = 53.7°$, $\hat{S} = 56.3°$, $s = 12.40$ cm
(c) $u = 18.90$ cm, $v = 14.61$ cm, $\hat{V} = 44°$ (d) $\hat{Z} = 49.5°$, $\hat{Y} = 74.5°$, $y = 13.95$ cm

6. (a) $c \sin A$ (b) $c \cos A$ (c) $b - c \cos A$

page 236

7. $(c \sin A)^2 + (b - c \cos A)^2$ **8.** 4.583 cm   **9.** 4.001 cm

10. (a) 5.734 cm   (b) 10.41 cm   (c) 10.12 cm   (d) 4.233 cm   **11.** 36.2°   **12.** 43.5°

13. 19.2°   **14.** 101.5°   **15.** (a) 48.5°   (b) 5.040 cm   (c) 23.6°   (d) 19.49 cm

page 237

16. (a) 33.6°   (b) 117.3°   (c) 90°   (d) 22.3°   **17.** (a) 9.511 cm²   (b) 22.94 cm²   **18.** 11.05 cm²

19. 10.28 cm²

20. 93.53 cm²   **21.** (a) 6.928 cm²   (b) 6 cm²

22. (a) BC = 10.06 cm, $\hat{B} = 52.3°$, $\hat{C} = 43.8°$ (b) $\hat{C} = 127°$, AC = 3.66 cm, BC = 7.360 cm
(c) AB = 14.75 cm, $\hat{A} = 20°$, $\hat{B} = 26°$

23. (a) 52°   (b) 6.395 cm   (c) 12.61 cm

page 238

24. (a) 8.771 cm   (b) 16.48 cm   **25.** (a) 11.08 cm   (b) 76.13 cm²   **26.** 30°   **27.** 56.4°

28. (a) 4.243 cm   (b) 4.098 cm   **29.** 9.298 km   **30.** 391.6 km   **31.** (a) 026.3°   (b) 13.54 km

32. 12.12 m   **33.** 61.94 cm²

page 239   **Radians** (6.4)

1. (a) 45°   (b) 30°   (c) 120°   (d) 270°   (e) 135°

2. (a) $\frac{\pi}{3}$ (b) $\frac{5\pi}{4}$ (c) $\frac{7\pi}{6}$ (d) $\frac{5\pi}{3}$ (e) $\frac{7\pi}{4}$

3. (a) 0.35 (b) 1.31 (c) 0.96 (d) 1.43 (e) 0.52
4. (a) 3.50 (b) 2.62 (c) 2.88 (d) 2.86 (e) 5.72
5. (a) 28.65° (b) 57.30° (c) 114.59° (d) 68.75° (e) 137.51°
6. (a) 0.500 (b) 0.866 (c) 1.00 (d) 1.73

7. (a)

x	0	$\frac{\pi}{4}$	$\frac{\pi}{2}$	$\frac{3\pi}{4}$	π	$\frac{5\pi}{4}$	$\frac{3\pi}{2}$	$\frac{7\pi}{4}$	2π
$\sin x$	0	0.707	1	0.707	0	⁻0.707	⁻1	⁻0.707	0

8. (a)

x	1	$\frac{\pi}{4}$	$\frac{\pi}{2}$	$\frac{3\pi}{4}$	π	$\frac{5\pi}{4}$	$\frac{3\pi}{2}$	$\frac{7\pi}{4}$	2π
$\cos x$	1	0.707	0	⁻0.707	⁻1	⁻0.707	0	0.707	1

(b)

x	0	$\frac{\pi}{4}$	$\frac{\pi}{2}$	$\frac{3\pi}{4}$	π	$\frac{5\pi}{4}$	$\frac{3\pi}{2}$	$\frac{7\pi}{4}$	2π
$\tan x$	0	1	∞	⁻1	0	1	∞	⁻1	0

page 240
10. (a) 10 cm (b) 0.4 m (c) 0.05 km **11.** (a) 0.5 (b) 0.1 (c) $\frac{\pi}{2}$ **12.** 14.12 cm
13. (a) 0.0873 (b) 0.873 m (c) 0.872 m (d) Yes **14.** (a) 0.0698 (b) 0.698 km
15. (a) 0.00873 (b) 3316 km **16.** 1 309 000 km

page 241 **Sectors and segments** (6.5)
1. (a) 9 cm^2 (b) 3.75 cm^2 (c) 19.24 cm^2 (d) 37.70 cm^2 **2.** (a) 12.5 cm (b) 156.25 cm^2
3. 2.52 m^2 **4.** 140 m^2
5. (a) 339 mm^2 (b) 11.59 mm^2 (c) 3.840 (d) 69.12 mm^2 (e) 419.7 mm^2 **6.** (c)
page 242
7. (a) 26.18 cm^2 (b) 9.817 cm^2 (c) 9.6 cm^2 (d) 23.53 cm^2
8. (a) 201.1 cm^2 (:b) 0.6428 (c) 2.443 (d) 57.62 cm^2 (e) 143.3 cm^2
9. (b) 12 cm^2 (c) 106.3° (d) 11.18 cm^2
10. (a) 48 cm^2, 73.7°, 16.32 cm^2 (b) 43.3 cm^2, 60°, 9.060 cm^2
11. 36.23 cm^2
12. (b) 57.08 cm^2

7 Algebra 2

page 244 **Revision** (7.1)
1. (a) $9x$ (b) $24y^3$ (c) $2p + q$ (d) $4ab$ **2.** (a) x^9 (b) p^9 (c) y^{-4} (d) q^3
3. (a) x^6 (b) p^{-8} (c) $81y^8$
4. (a) $\dfrac{1}{p^5}$ (b) $\dfrac{1}{x^3}$ (c) $\dfrac{1}{q^7}$ (d) y^0 (e) $\dfrac{1}{k^6}$
5. (a) lm^2 (b) $\dfrac{x^5 z}{y}$
6. (a) $\dfrac{p^2}{q^3}$ (b) $\dfrac{x^3}{yz}$ (c) $k^3 m^2$
7. (a) $7x + 3y$ (b) $2p - 6q$ (c) $2l - 3m$ (d) $6k - 6n$
8. (a) 11 (b) $-3p - 7q$ (c) $-7l + 2m$ (d) $2ab - 2bc$
9. (a) $8pq - 3pr$ (b) $-6mn$ (c) $6kl - 8l$ **10.** (a) xz (b) $6pqr - 10pq + qr - 6pr$
page 245
11. (a) $3(x + 2y)$ (b) $t(2s - 1)$ (c) $k(l + m + n)$ (d) $qr(p - s)$ (e) $xy(2x + yz + z^2)$

12. (a) $(a-b)(x+y)$ (b) $(p+q)(x-y)$ (c) $(u+v)(t+s)$ (d) $(u+v)(t^2-s)$

    (e) $(2l+m)(x-y)$ (f) $(p-q)(r+3s)$

13. (a) $(s+5t)(x+y)$ (b) $(m-2l)(a+b)$ (c) $(u^2+4v)(s+t)$ (d) $(a^2+b^2)(l-m)$

    (e) $(2b+3c)(x+y)$ (f) $(3z-y^2)(w^2+t)$

14. (a) $(x+y)(a+b-c)$ (b) $(p+q)(x^2-y-z^3)$ (c) $s+t)(l+m+n)$ (d) $(f+g)(2x+y-3z)$

15. (a) $(3m^2+4n^3)(x-y^2)$ (b) $(4a-5b)(x-y)$ (c) $(2a+b)(c-2d)$ (d) $(5p-s)(2q-r)$

16. (a) $(x+y)(p+q)$ (b) $(3l-2m)(p+q)$ (c) $(w+2z)(2x-y)$ (d) $(3x-2y)(2p+q)$

    (e) $(l+2m)(x+y-z)$ (f) $(p-2q)(r+s+2t)$ (g) $(2x-n)(x-m)$ (h) $(m-3)(2l-1)$

17. (a) $\dfrac{5x}{6}$ (b) $\dfrac{13}{12p}$ (c) $\dfrac{kl+6}{2l}$ (d) $\dfrac{yz+6xz-8xy}{2xyz}$

18. (a) $\dfrac{-x-10}{12}$ (b) $\dfrac{p^2+q^2r}{pqr}$ (c) $\dfrac{m^2}{n^2}$ (d) $\dfrac{-x}{12}$

19. (a) $\dfrac{2x+1}{(x-2)(x+3)}$ (b) $\dfrac{-a-5b}{(a+b)(a-b)}$ (c) $\dfrac{l^2-m^2-6}{3(l-m)}$ (d) $\dfrac{7p+13q}{2r}$

page 246

20. (a) $^-22$ (b) 87   (c) $^-50$ (d) $^-3$ **21.** (a) $1\frac{1}{2}$ (b) $\frac{3}{7}$ (c) $2\frac{4}{5}$ (d) 3.162   (e) 288   (f) $^-3$

page 246   **Fractional indices** (7.2)

1. (a) 4   (b) 3   (c) 3   (d) 1   (e) 64   (f) 125   (g) $\frac{1}{2}$ (h) $\frac{1}{1000}$ (i) $1\frac{1}{2}$ (j) $\frac{1}{25}$ (k) $2\frac{10}{27}$ (l)$1\frac{91}{125}$

2. (a) 3   (b) 8   (c) $\frac{1}{4}$ (d) 1   (e) $\frac{1}{3}$ (f) $\frac{1}{49}$ (g) 3   (h) 36   (i) $\frac{1}{16}$ (j) 0.3489   (h) $2\frac{10}{27}$ (l)$\frac{1}{64}$

3. (a) $4a^2$ (b) $\dfrac{1}{4a^2}$ (c) xy (d) $\dfrac{y}{3x}$ (e) $8a^{12}$ (f) $16x^6$ (g) $16a^3$ (h) $\dfrac{x^2}{y}$

    (i) $\dfrac{2}{5x^2y}$ (j) $\dfrac{1}{64x^3y^9}$ (k) $\dfrac{x^4y^6}{z}$ (l) $\dfrac{1}{4x^4y^2z^2}$

4. (a) $\dfrac{y}{x}$ (b) x (c) $rq^{\frac{4}{3}}$ (d) $r^2s^{-\frac{1}{2}}$ (e) xy^4 (f) $a^{-5}b^{-4})^{\frac{1}{3}}$ (g) b^{-1} (h) $\frac{1}{8}a^{-\frac{3}{2}}$

5. (a) 16   (b) $\frac{1}{16}$ (c) 25   (d) 64   (e) 729   (f) 16   (g) 256   (h) 64

6. (a) 2   (b) $1\frac{1}{2}$ (c) 5   (d) 3   (e) 3   (f) $\frac{1}{3}$ (g) 1   (h) 3

page 247   **Changing the subject of a formula** (7.3)

1. (a) $C=2\pi r=31.4\,\text{cm}$ (b) $A=\pi r^2=78.5\,\text{cm}^2$ **2.** (a) 10 cm   (b) 5 cm   **3.** 0.897

5. 2   **7.** (b) (i) 5°   (ii) 15°   (iii) 30°   (iv) 100°

8. (b) $F=32+\dfrac{9C}{5}$ (c) (i) 122°   (ii) 212°

page 248

9. (a) 12 000   (b) 140   (c) 251.2   (d) 65   (e) $25\frac{5}{9}$ (f) 0.628

11. (a) $l=\dfrac{v}{bh}$ (b) $r=\dfrac{S}{2\pi h}$ (c) $t=\dfrac{v-u}{a}$ (d) $r=\sqrt{\dfrac{V}{\pi k}}$ (e) $h=\dfrac{S-\pi r^2}{2\pi r}$

    (f) $F=32+\dfrac{9C}{5}$ (g) $C=\frac{5}{9}(F-32)$ (h) $a=\dfrac{2(s-ut)}{t^2}$

12. (a) $314\,\text{cm}^3$ (c) $R=\sqrt{\dfrac{\pi hr^2+V}{\pi h}}$

13. 6.745 cm

14. (b) $T = \dfrac{I \times 100}{p \times R}$

15. (ii) (a) $x = \dfrac{y - q}{p}$ (b) $x = \dfrac{y + kl}{k}$ (c) $x = \dfrac{sr + y - t}{r}$ (d) $x = \dfrac{y - lm}{mn}$

16. (a) $r = \dfrac{A}{h}$ (b) $r = \dfrac{A}{2\pi h}$ (c) $r = \sqrt{\dfrac{V}{\pi h}}$ (d) $r = \dfrac{S - \pi h R}{\pi h}$

(e) $r = \sqrt[3]{\dfrac{3V}{4\pi}}$ (f) $r = \dfrac{100(A - P)}{P}$

17. (a) $R_2 = \dfrac{V - R_1 I}{I}$ (b) $I = \dfrac{V}{R_1 + R_2}$

18. (a) $R = \dfrac{100I}{PT}$ (b) $P = \dfrac{100I}{RT}$

19. (a) $P_0 = \dfrac{P}{1 + \alpha t}$ (b) $\alpha = \dfrac{P - P_0}{P_0 t}$ (c) $t = \dfrac{P - P_0}{P_0 \alpha}$

page 249

20. (a) $k = d(P - mv)$ (b) $V = \dfrac{Pd - k}{md}$

21. (a) $t = \dfrac{m}{P}(v - u)$ (b) $m = \dfrac{Pt}{v - u}$ (c) $v = \dfrac{Pt + mu}{m}$ (d) $u = \dfrac{mv - Pt}{m}$

22. (a) $x = \dfrac{pq - py}{q}$ (b) $y = \dfrac{pq - qx}{p}$ (c) $p = \dfrac{qx}{q - y}$ (d) $q = \dfrac{py}{p - x}$

23. (a) uvf (b) (i) $u = \dfrac{vf}{v - f}$ (ii) $v = \dfrac{uf}{u - f}$ (iii) $f = \dfrac{uv}{u + v}$

25. (a) $l = \dfrac{A}{b}$ (b) $r = \dfrac{C}{2\pi}$ (c) $I = \dfrac{V}{R}$ (d) $L = \dfrac{S}{\pi r}$ (e) $\dfrac{v - u}{t}$ (f) $\dfrac{y - c}{m}$ (g) $T = \dfrac{PV}{R}$

(h) $R = \dfrac{E}{I}$ (i) $m = \dfrac{Pt}{v - u}$ (j) $r = \sqrt{\dfrac{V}{\pi h}}$ (k) $u = \sqrt{v^2 - 2as}$ (l) $x = \sqrt{r^2 - y^2} + a$ (m) $g = \dfrac{4\pi^2 l}{T^2}$

26. (a) $r = \sqrt{\dfrac{S}{4\pi}}$ (b) $r = \dfrac{V}{3\pi h}$ (c) $r = \dfrac{2A - rh}{h}$ (d) $r = \sqrt{\dfrac{\pi h R^2 - V}{\pi h}}$

27. (a) $t = \dfrac{2s}{u + v}$ (b) $t = \dfrac{v - u}{f}$ (c) $t = \dfrac{PV}{mR}$ (d) $t = \dfrac{T - \beta k}{\alpha k}$

28. (a) $x = \dfrac{y + am}{m}$ (b) $x = \dfrac{a(b - y)}{b}$ (c) $x = \dfrac{c + ay}{y}$ (d) $x = \dfrac{1}{1 - y}$

29. (a) $R = \dfrac{100(A - P))}{P}$ (b) $R = \dfrac{t}{t - 2}$ (c) $R = \dfrac{Vr}{V - 1}$ (d) $R = \dfrac{1 - 2K}{K - 1}$

page 250

30. (c) **31.** (b) **32.** (b) or (d) **33.** (c) **34.** (c)

page 250   **The product of two brackets** (7.4)
 1. (a) It is square, x^2 (b) $3x, 2x, 6$ (c) $x^2 + 5x + 6$ (d) $(x + 3)(x + 2)$
 2. (a) $x^2 + 7x + 12$ (b) $x^2 + 8x + 12$ (c) $x^2 + 8x + 15$ (d) $x^2 + 9x + 14$ (e) $x^2 + 4x + 3$
    (f) $x^2 + 3x + 2$
 3. Yes
 4. (a) Add the numbers in the two brackets   (b) Multiply the numbers in the two brackets
 6. (a) Yes   (b) Yes
 7. (a) $x^2 + 5x - 14$ (b) $x^2 + 2x - 15$ (c) $x^2 - 3x - 10$ (d) $x^2 + x - 56$ (e) $x^2 - 4x - 21$
    (f) $x^2 - x - 6$
 8. (a) $x^2 - 7x + 12$ (b) $x^2 - 7x + 10$ (c) $x^2 - 10x + 21$ (d) $x^2 - 16x + 63$ (e) $x^2 - 4x + 4$
    (f) $x^2 - 2x + 1$
 9. (a) $x^2 + 12x + 27$ (b) $x^2 - x - 20$ (c) $x^2 + x - 42$ (d) $x^2 - 11x + 28$ (e) $x^2 - 15x + 44$
    (f) $x^2 - 7x - 30$
11. $ac + ad + bc + bd$ 12. (a) Yes   (b) Yes
13. (a) $2pr + 6ps + qr + 3qs$ (b) $2ac + ad + 6bc + 3bd$ (c) $18x + 15mx + 6y + 5my$
    (d) $2pl + 2pm + 5ql + 5qm$ (e) $20ac + 5ad + 4bc + bd$ (f) $xp + 7xq + 3yp + 2lyq$
14. (a) $\dfrac{c}{3a} + \dfrac{d}{2a} + \dfrac{bc}{18} + \dfrac{bd}{12}$ (b) $\dfrac{3x}{4z} + \dfrac{3x^2z}{20} + \dfrac{y}{z^2} + \dfrac{xy}{5}$ (c) $\dfrac{12}{a} + \dfrac{4b}{a} + \dfrac{15}{ab} + \dfrac{5}{a}$
    (d) $\dfrac{4x}{3a} + \dfrac{bx}{9} + \dfrac{4y}{3a} + \dfrac{by}{9}$ (e) $\dfrac{6a}{5x} + \dfrac{6}{xab} - \dfrac{a}{y} - \dfrac{5}{yab}$
15. Yes   17. Yes. (a) 1681   (b) 2601   (c) 529   (d) 5184
page 252
20. Yes, (a) 1521   (b) 2401   (c) 729   (d) 4624
23. (a) $(8 + 3) \times (8 - 3) = 55$ (b) $(37 + 27) \times (37 - 27) = 640$ 24. (a) 121   (b) 1000
25. (a) $(x + y)(x - y)$ (b) $(p + q)(p - q)$ (c) $(m + 3)(m - 3)$ (d) $(2p + q)(2p - q)$
    (e) $(x + 3y)(x - 3y)$ (f) $(2d + 3m)(2d - 3m)$
26. (a) $\left(\dfrac{1}{x} + \dfrac{3}{a}\right)\left(\dfrac{1}{x} + \dfrac{3}{a}\right)$ (b) $\left(\dfrac{a}{x} + 2y\right)\left(\dfrac{a}{x} - 2y\right)$ (c) $\left(\dfrac{mn}{2} + 1\right)\left(\dfrac{mn}{2} - 1\right)$
    (d) $\left(5 + \dfrac{ab}{4c^2}\right)\left(5 - \dfrac{ab}{4c^2}\right)$

page 252   **Completing the square** (7.5)
 1. (a) $7^2 + (2 \times 7 \times 8) + 8^2$ (b) $5^2 + (2 \times 5 \times 9) + 9^2$ (c) $8^2 - (2 \times 8 \times 3) + 3^2$
    (d) $11^2 - (2 \times 11 \times 7) + 7^2$
 2. (a) $20^2 + (2 \times 20 \times 1) + 1^2 = 441$ (b) $50^2 + (2 \times 50 \times 2) + 2^2 = 2704$
    (c) $30^2 - (2 \times 30 \times 1) + 1^2 = 841$ (d) $80^2 - (2 \times 80 \times 3) + 3^2 = 5929$
 3. (a) $9^2 + (2 \times 9 \times 0.1) + 0.1^2 = 82.81$ (b) $12^2 + (2 \times 12 \times 0.3) + 0.3^2 = 151.29$
    (c) $5^2 - (2 \times 5 \times 0.1) + 0.1^2 = 24.01$ (d) $20^2 - (2 \times 20 \times 0.2) + 0.2^2 = 392.04$
 4. (a) $l^2 + 2m + m^2$ (b) $x^2 - 2xy + y^2$ (c) $4p^2 + 4pq + q^2$ (d) $a^2 - 6ab + 9b^2$
    (e) $16m^2 + 24mn + 9n^2$
 5. (a) $x^2 + 12x + 36$ (b) $x^2 + 22x + 121$ (c) $x^2 - 10x + 25$ (d) $x^2 - 26x + 169$
    (e) $4x^2 + 4x + 1$ (f) $25x^2 + 10x + 1$ (g) $9x^2 - 6x + 1$ (h) $49x^2 - 14x + 1$ (i) $9x^2 + 30x + 25$
    (j) $16x^2 - 56x + 49$
 6. (a) $(7 + 5)^2 = 144$ (b) $(8 + 3)^2 = 121$ (c) $(6 - 4)^2 = 4$ (d) $(9 - 6)^2 = 9$
 7. (a) $(p + q)^2$ (b) $(l - m)^2$ (c) $(x + 6)^2$ (d) $(y - 9)^2$
 8. (a) $(x + 4)^2$ (b) $(x + 10)^2$ (c) $(x - 7)^2$ (d) $(x - \frac{1}{2})^2$ (e) $(3x + 1)^2$ (f) $(5x + 1)^2$
    (g) $(4x - 1)^2$ (h) $(6x - 1)^2$
 9. (a) $(x + 3y)^2$ (b) $(2l + m)^2$ (c) $(a + 5b)^2$ (d) $(p - 4q)^2$ (e) $(8x - y)^2$ (f) $(10l - m)^2$
    (g) $(2a + 3b)^2$ (h) $(4p - 3q)^2$

11. $m^2 - n^2, 2mn, m^2 + n^2; 3, 4, 5$

12. (a) $3x^2 + 12x + 14$ (b) $4x^2 + 20$ (c) $2x^2 + 2y^2 + 2z^2 + 2xy + 2xz + 2yz$ (d) $-4x^2 + 20xy + y^2$

13. (a) $(x + 2)^2 - 4$ (b) $(x + 4)^2 - 16$ (c) $(x + 6)^2 - 36$ (d) $(x + 10)^2 - 100$ (e) $(x - 3)^2 - 9$
(f) $(x - 5)^2 - 25$ (g) $(x - 2)^2 - 4$ (h) $(x - 7)^2 - 49$

14. (a) $(x + 1)^2 + 4$ (b) $(x + 3)^2 + 3$ (c) $(x + 8)^2 + 36$ (d) $(x + 9)^2 + 19$ (e) $(x + 5)^2 - 22$
(f) $(x - 4)^2 + 9$ (g) $(x - 6)^2 + 4$ (h) $(x - 8)^2 - 54$

15. (a) $(x + 7)^2 - 49$ (b) $(x + 11)^2 - 121$ (c) $(x - 9)^2 - 81$ (d) $(x - 10)^2 - 100$ (e) $(x + \frac{3}{2})^2 - \frac{9}{4}$
(f) $(x + \frac{1}{2})^2 - \frac{1}{4}$ (g) $(x - \frac{3}{2})^2 - \frac{9}{4}$ (h) $(x - \frac{5}{2})^2 - \frac{25}{4}$

16. (a) $(x + 3)^2 + 8$ (b) $(x + 5)^2 - 5$ (c) $(x - 4)^2 + 5$ (d) $(x - 12)^2 - 244$ (e) $(x + \frac{3}{2})^2 + \frac{11}{4}$
(f) $(x + \frac{5}{2})^2 - \frac{13}{4}$ (g) $(x - \frac{3}{2})^2 + \frac{17}{4}$ (h) $(x - \frac{1}{2})^2 + \frac{15}{4}$

17. (a) $(2x + 1)^2 + 2$ (b) $(3x + 2)^2 - 7$ (c) $(2x - 3)^2 - 1$ (d) $(4x - 3)^2 - 23$ (e) $(5x - 2)^2 - 10$
(f) $(3x - 2)^2 + 13$

18. (a) $2(x + \frac{3}{2})^2 - \frac{5}{2}$ (b) $4(x - \frac{1}{2})^2 - 18$ (c) $6(x - \frac{1}{3})^2 + \frac{16}{3}$ (d) $5(x - \frac{6}{5})^2 + \frac{4}{5}$ (e) $5(x - \frac{3}{10})^2 + \frac{31}{20}$
(f) $3(x - \frac{7}{3})^2 - \frac{40}{3}$

page 254 **The difference between two squares** (7.6)

1. (a) $(7 - 3)(7 + 3) = 40$ (b) $(14 - 6)(14 + 6) = 160$ (c) $(89 - 11)(89 + 11) = 7800$
(d) $(28 - 18)(28 + 18) = 460$ (e) $(53 - 33)(53 + 33) = 1720$ (f) $(72 - 42)(72 + 42) = 3420$

2. (a) $(8.6 - 1.4)(8.6 + 1.4) = 72$ (b) $(5.9 - 4.1)(5.9 + 4.1) = 18$ (c) $(6.2 - 3.8)(6.2 + 3.8) = 24$
(d) $(4.7 - 2.7)(4.7 + 2.7) = 14.8$ (e) $(5.9 - 3.9)(5.9 + 3.9) = 19.6$
(f) $(7.5 - 3.5)(7.5 + 3.5) = 44$

3. (a) $6 \times 10 = 60$ (b) $4 \times 20 = 80$ (c) $6 \times 100 = 600$ (d) $20 \times 162 = 3240$
(e) $54 \times 200 = 10\,800$ (f) $200 \times 318 = 63\,600$ (g) $262 \times 500 = 131\,000$ (h) $50 \times 502 = 25\,100$

4. (a) $1.4 \times 10 = 14$ (b) $6.2 \times 10 = 62$ (c) $1.2 \times 4 = 4.8$ (d) $2 \times 9.4 = 18.8$
(e) $2.6 \times 11 = 28.6$ (f) $5 \times 10.8 = 54$ (g) $0.32 \times 10 = 3.2$ (h) $6.58 \times 10 = 65.8$

5. (a) $(p - q)(p + q)$ (b) $(l - m)(l + m)$ (c) $(p - 2q)(p + 2q)$ (d) $(3l - m)(3l + m)$
(e) $(3p - 2q)(3p + 2q)$ (f) $(4l - 3m)(4l + 3m)$

6. (a) $(x - y)(x + y)$ (b) $(s - t)(s + t)$ (c) $(2a - b)(2a + b)$ (d) $(l - 3m)(l + 3m)$
(e) $(4a - b)(4a + b)$ (f) $(p - 5q)(p + 5q)$ (g) $(4a - 5b)(4a + 5b)$ (h) $(7p - 4q)(7p + 4q)$

7. (a) $(b - c)(b + c)$ (b) $(9x - y)(9x + y)$ (c) $(p - 10q)(p + 10q)$ (d) $(10a - 9b)(10a + 9b)$
(e) $(xy - z)(xy + z)$ (f) $(a - bc)(a + bc)$ (g) $(2p - qr)(2p + qr)$ (h) $(3lm - n^2)(3lm + n^2)$

8. (a) $(ab - cd)(ab + cd)$ (b) $(xyz - w)(xyz + w)$ (c) $(4pq - 9r)(4pq + 9r)$ (d) $(l^2 - n^2)(l^2 + n^2)$
(e) $(a + b - c)(a + b + c)$ (f) $(p - q - r)(p + q + r)$ (g) $(x - z)(x + 2y + z)$ (h) $(2m)(2l)$

9. (a) 5 cm (b) 24 cm (c) 40 cm

10. (a) 60 cm (b) 84 cm (c) 3.6 cm (d) 2.966 cm

page 255

11. (a) $14 \, \text{cm}^2$ (b) $128 \, \text{cm}^2$ (c) $40.32 \, \text{cm}^2$ **12.** (a) $600\pi \, \text{cm}^2$ (b) $272\pi \, \text{cm}^2$ (c) $21.12\pi \, \text{cm}^2$

13. (a) $95.16 \, \text{cm}^3$ (b) $10.075 \, \text{m}^2$ (c) $283.05 \, \text{cm}^2$

14. (a) $28.94 \, \text{cm}^3$ (b) $1\,213\,300 \, \text{cm}^3$ (c) $3006.9 \, \text{cm}^3$ **15.** (a) $2166.3 \, \text{cm}^3$ (b) $205\,455 \, \text{cm}^3$

16. 7.253 cm

page 255 **Factorising quadratic expressions** (7.7)

1. (a) $(x + 6)(x + 1)$ (b) $(x + 1)(x + 15)$ (c) $(x + 5)(x + 3)$ (d) $(x + 5)(x + 4)$
(e) $(x + 3)(x + 2)$

2. (a) $(x + 5)(x + 1)$ (b) $(x + 11)(x + 1)$ (c) $(x + 3)(x + 7)$ (d) $(x + 2)(x + 5)$
(e) $(x + 8)(x + 2)$ (f) $(x + 6)(x + 3)$

3. positive

4. (a) $(x - 2)(x - 4)$ (b) $(x - 3)(x - 5)$ (c) $(x - 1)(x - 4)$ (d) $(x - 8)(x - 1)$
(e) $(x - 3)(x - 3)$ (f) $(x - 2)(x - 3)$

page 256

5. (a) $(x - 1)(x - 7)$ (b) $(x - 1)(x - 5)$ (c) $(x - 5)(x - 2)$ (d) $(x - 2)(x - 9)$

(e) $(x - 4)(x - 4)$ (f) $(x - 3)(x - 3)$

6. negative

7. (a) $(x + 8)(x - 1)$ (b) $(x + 1)(x - 6)$ (c) $(x + 6)(x - 2)$ (d) $(x - 7)(x + 2)$ (e) $(x - 2)(x + 7)$

8. (a) $(x + 11)(x - 1)$ (b) $(x - 3)(x + 7)$ (c) $(x + 5)(x - 7)$ (d) $(x + 3)(x - 7)$
   (e) $(x + 30)(x + 2)$ (f) $(x + 1)(x - 2)$

9. (a) $(x + 5)(x + 11)$ (b) $(x + 16)(x + 2)$ (c) $(x + 1)(x + 18)$ (d) $(x + 4)(x + 9)$
   (e) $(x + 6)(x + 15)$ (f) $(x + 5)(x + 5)$

10. (a) $(x - 5)(x - 7)$ (b) $(x - 3)(x - 16)$ (c) $(x - 1)(x - 8)$ (d) $(x - 10)(x - 6)$
   (e) $(x - 16)(x - 6)$ (f) $(x - 6)(x - 6)$ (g) $(z - 2)(z - 8)$ (h) $(x + 9)(x - 3)$
   (i) $(y - 18)(y + 3)$ (j) $(z - 2)(z - 10)$

11. (a) $(x + 11)(x - 2)$ (b) $(x + 6)(x - 2)$ (c) $(x + 17)(x - 1)$ (d) $(x - 11)(x + 3)$
   (e) $(x - 8)(x + 3)$ (f) $(x - 7)(x + 7)$

12. (a) $(x + 1)(x + 1)$ (b) $(x - 1)(x + 1)$ (c) $(x - 1)(x - 1)$ (d) $(x - 3)(x - 1)$
   (e) $(x + 4)(x - 2)$ (f) $(x + 7)(x - 3)$ (g) $(x - 10)(x + 10)$ (h) $(x - 8)(x + 8)$
   (i) $(x - 7)(x + 6)$ (j) $(x + 13)(x + 2)$

13. (a) $(3x + 1)(5x + 1)$ (b) $(11x + 1)(x + 1)$ (c) $(2x + 1)(12x - 1)$ (d) $(8x - 1)(2x + 1)$
   (e) $(5x - 1)(6x + 1)$ (f) $(7x - 1)(7x - 1)$

14. (a) $(3x + 1)(6x + 1)$ (b) $(3x + 1)(11x - 1)$ (c) $(4x - 1)(10x + 1)$ (d) $(8x - 1)(9x + 1)$
   (e) $(6x - 1)(6x + 1)$ (f) $(11x + 1)(11x + 1)$

page 257

15. (a) $(5x + 7)(x + 1)$ (b) $(2x + 1)(4x + 5)$ (c) $(11x 3)(x + 2)$ (d) $(7x - 15)(x - 1)$
   (e) $(10x - 1)(x + 3)$ (f) $(4x + 1)(x - 13)$ (g) $(7x + 3)(x + 8)$ (h) $(5x + 18)(x - 1)$
   (i) $(5x + 2)(5x + 2)$ (j) $(3x - 7)(3x - 7)$

16. (a) $(3x + 2)(x + 7)$ (b) $(6x + 1)(x + 5)$ (c) $(8x - 15)(x - 1)$ (d) $(7x - 6)(x - 3)$
   (e) $(4x - 3)(x + 2)$ (f) $(5x - 1)(5x + 9)$ (g) $(5x + 3)(x - 8)$ (h) $(6x + 7)(2x - 3)$
   (i) $(6x + 5)(6x + 5)$ (j) $(7x - 4)(7x - 4)$ (k) $(5x + 7)(3x - 2)$ (l) $(5x - 13)(3x + 1)$

page 257 **Solving quadratic equations** (7.8)

1. Yes   **2.** Yes   **3.** Yes, because either $x - 3 = 0$ or $x + 1 = 0$

4. (a) 3 and 4   (b) 5 and 6   (c) 5 and $^-2$ (d) 2 and $^-5$ (e) $^-4$ and 7   (f) $^-6$ and 3

5. (a) 3 and 4   (b) $^-5$ and 2   (c) $^-2$ and $^-9$ (d) $\frac{1}{2}$ and 3   (e) $\frac{1}{4}$ and $\frac{1}{3}$ (f) 0 and 3   (g) $^-\frac{1}{7}$ and $^-\frac{1}{4}$
   (h) $1\frac{1}{2}$ and $\frac{2}{3}$

6. (a) 5 and 1   (b) 6 and 4   (c) 7 and 8   (d) 2 and 4   (e) 4 and 8   (f) 4 and 5

7. (a) 5 and 1   (b) 3 and 2   (c) 5 and 2   (d) $^-2$ and $^-6$ (e) $^-1$ and $^-3$ (f) $^-2$ and $^-8$
   (g) 1 and $^-7$ (h) 2 and $^-7$ (i) 4 and $^-7$ (j) 6 and $^-1$ (k) 8 and $^-2$ (l) 13 and $^-3$

8. (a) $\{2,5\}$ (b) $\{3,4\}$ (c) $\{3,7\}$ (d) $\{6,7\}$ (e) $\{4,9\}$ (f) $\{2\}$

9. (a) 7 and $^-3$ (b) $\frac{1}{3}$ and $^-4$ (c) 0 and $^-\frac{1}{3}$ (d) $\frac{2}{7}$ and $^-1\frac{1}{3}$ (e) 2 and 5   (f) 3 and $^-4$

page 258

10. (a) $\{8, ^-1\}$ (b) $\{3, ^-5\}$ (c) $\{\frac{1}{3}, \frac{1}{2}\}$ (d) $\{1, \frac{1}{5}\}$ (e) $\{1\frac{2}{3}, 1\}$ (f) $\{1\frac{2}{5}, 1\}$ (g) $\{1\frac{1}{2}, ^-3\}$ (h) $\{2, ^-\frac{4}{7}\}$
   (i) $\{13, ^-\frac{1}{4}\}$ (j) $\{1, ^-3\frac{3}{5}\}$ (k) $\{\frac{1}{3}\}$ (l) $\{^-\frac{2}{5}\}$ (m) $\{1, ^-\frac{1}{9}\}$ (n) $\{2\frac{1}{2}\}$

11. (a) $\frac{1}{2}$ and 1   (b) $\frac{1}{2}$ and $\frac{1}{3}$ (c) $\frac{1}{2}$ and $\frac{1}{4}$ (d) $^-1$ and $^-\frac{1}{7}$ (e) $\frac{1}{2}$ and $\frac{1}{5}$ (f) $\frac{1}{4}$ and $\frac{1}{3}$ (g) $\frac{1}{2}$ and 4
   (h) 5 and $\frac{1}{3}$ (i) 1 and $\frac{3}{4}$ (j) 3 and $^-\frac{1}{2}$ (k) $^-\frac{2}{3}$ and 1   (l) $\frac{3}{4}$ and $^-2$

12. (a) 3 and 4   (b) 3 and $^-4$ (c) 2 and $^-5$ (d) $\frac{1}{3}$ and $^-2$ (e) 3 and $^-\frac{1}{2}$ (f) $1\frac{1}{2}$ and $^-\frac{1}{4}$

13. (a) $^-3$ and $^-4$ (b) 2 and $^-7$ (c) $^-2$ and $^-3$ (d) 9 and $^-1$ (e) $^-6$ and $^-1$ (f) $^-4$ and 6

14. (a) 3 and $^-6$ (b) $^-7$ and 7   (c) 4 and $^-5$ (d) 11 and $^-8$ (e) 4 and $^-15$ (f) $^-10$ and $^-11$

15. (a) Yes   (b) $^-2$ and $^-1$, $^-2$ and $^-1$, the second one, yes

16. (a) 9 and $^-2$ (b) 1 and $^-1$ (c) 3 and $^-3$ (d) 2 and 8   (e) 1 and 6   (f) 7 and $^-2$

17. Yes, (a) 2 and $^-2$ (b) 2 and $^-2$ **18.** (a) Yes   (b) (i) $\{4, ^-4\}$ (ii) $\{5, ^-5\}$ (iii) $\{9, ^-9\}$

19. (a) $\{3, ^-1\}$ (b) $\{8, ^-2\}$ **20.** (c) Impossible   (d) Yes, $1 + \sqrt{3}$ and $1 - \sqrt{3}$

21. (a) 6 and $^-6$ (b) $\sqrt{5}$ and $^-\sqrt{5}$ (c) Impossible

22. (a) 2   (b) 1   (c) 3   (d) 5   (e) $^-4$ (f) $^-6$ (g) $^-2$ (h) $^-3$ (i) $\frac{1}{2}$ (j) $^-\frac{1}{3}$

page 259

23. (a) $(x+3)^2+1$ (b) $(x+2)^2+6$ (c) $(x+4)^2+2$ (d) $(x+5)^2+2$ (e) $(x+1)^2+4$
(f) $(x+6)^2-41$ (g) $(x+9)^2+19$ (h) $(x+8)^2-24$

24. (a) $(x-3)^2+1$ (b) $(x-2)^2+6$ (c) $(x-5)^2+5$ (d) $(x-4)-17$ (e) $(x-1)^2+2$
(f) $(x-6)^2+0$ (g) $(x-\frac{1}{2})^2+0$ (h) $(x-4)^2-26$

25. (a) 7 and $^-3$ (b) 13 and $^-3$ (c) 7 and $^-1$ (d) $^-3$ and $^-5$ (e) 1 and $^-13$ (f) 0 and $^-4$

26. (a) 2 and $^-8$ (b) 1 and $^-11$ (c) 2 and $^-10$ (d) 3 and $^-15$ (e) 1 and 5 (f) 2 and 8

27. (a) 2 and 4 (b) 11 and 1 (c) 12 and 2 (d) $^-6$ and $^-2$ (e) 3 and $^-13$ (f) 7 and $^-9$

28. (a) $1\pm\sqrt5$ (b) $4\pm\sqrt7$ (c) $6\pm\sqrt{11}$ (d) $^-2\pm\sqrt3$ (e) $^-5\pm\sqrt2$ (f) $^-1\pm\sqrt{13}$

29. (a) $3\pm2\sqrt2$)b) $8\pm\sqrt{61}$ (c) $2\pm\sqrt3$ (d) $^-1\pm2\sqrt2$ (e) $^-3\pm\sqrt{21}$ (f) $^-7\pm2\sqrt{13}$

30. (a) $^-5\pm2\sqrt{10}$ (b) $^-5\pm2\sqrt{10}$ (c) $^-4\pm2\sqrt{10}$ (d) $3\pm2\sqrt{10}$ (e) $^-3\pm2\sqrt5$ (f) $6\pm2\sqrt5$

31. (a) 2 and 1 (b) 1 and $\frac{1}{2}$ (c) 3 and $^-1$ (d) 1 and $\frac{1}{4}$ (e) $\frac{1}{2}$ and 3 (f) 3 and $\frac{1}{4}$ (g) 5 and $^-3$
(h) $^-2$ and $^-\frac{1}{5}$ (i) $\frac{1}{3}$ and 3 (j) $^-\frac{1}{2}$ and $^-2$ (k) $1\frac{2}{3}$ and 1 (l) $^-3\frac{1}{2}$ and $^-1$

page 260

32. (a) 2 and $\frac{1}{3}$ (b) 1 and $\frac{3}{5}$ (c) $\dfrac{-2\pm\sqrt{10}}{3}$ (d) $\dfrac{-11\pm\sqrt{65}}{14}$

33. (a) 2 and $^-8$ (b) 1 and 5 (c) 2 and $^-10$ (d) 2 and 8 (e) 1 and $^-11$ (f) 3 and $^-15$

34. (a) $^-1$ and $^-3$ (b) 2 and 7 (c) 3 and $\frac{1}{2}$ (d) $^-2$ and $^-5$ (e) 2 and $^-10$ (f) $\frac{1}{4}$ and $^-3$

35. (a) $\dfrac{5\pm\sqrt{21}}{2}$ (b) $\dfrac{7\pm\sqrt{37}}{2}$ (c) $^-2\pm\sqrt{13}$ (d) $^-3\pm\sqrt7$ (e) $\dfrac{1\pm\sqrt{19}}{3}$ (f) $\dfrac{9\pm\sqrt{61}}{10}$

36. (a) 2 and $^-12$ (b) $\frac{1}{2}$ and $^-7$ (c) $1\frac{1}{2}$ and $2\frac{1}{2}$ (d) $^-\frac{1}{2}$ and $^-2$

37. (a) $\frac{1}{10}$ and 1 (b) $^-4$ (c) $^-1\frac{1}{2}$ and $1\frac{1}{2}$ (d) No solution

38. 81, 0, 144, $^-3$ (a) Yes (b) Yes (c) Yes

39. (a) $^-8$, none (b) 77, two (c) 0, one (d) $^-16$, none

page 261 **Word problems** (7.9)

1. (a) 17,66 (b) $^-7,^-60$ (c) 1,$^-56$ (d) $^-11,8$ **2.** (a) 5,7 (b) 1,5 (c) 5,$^-3$ (d) $^-3,^-7$

3. (a) 3,4 (b) 3,2 (c) 3,1 **4.** (a) 5,$^-2$ (b) 11,$^-7$ (c) 5,$^-6$

5. (a) $^-4,^-5$ (b) $^-2,^-5$ (c) $^-1,^-4$ **6.** 4 cm and 14 cm **7.** 7 cm and 12 cm

8. 16.37 m, 20.37 m **9.** 5 cm, 12 cm, 13 cm **10.** 3 cm, 4 cm, 5 cm **11.** 13 cm, 12 cm, 5 cm

page 262

12. 5 and 7 **13.** 4, 5 and 6 **14.** 5, 6 and 7 **15.** 50 km/h **16.** 90 km/h **17.** 11 cm

page 263 **Simultaneous equations** (7.10)

1. (1,0) and (3,2), yes **2.** (a) 3 and 1 (b) 0 and 2 (c) The figures are the same

3. (a) (0,2) and (4,6) **4.** (a) and (b) (1,0) and (4,6) **5.** (2,0) and (4,6)

6. (b) and (c) (4,3) and (2,$^-1$)

7. (a) (4,3) and ($^-3,^-4$) (b) (5,3) and ($^-3,^-5$) (c) (1,1) and ($^-1,^-1$) (d) ($^-1,^-2$) and ($2\frac{1}{5},^-\frac{2}{5}$)

8. (a) ($\sqrt2,2$) (b) $\sqrt6,3$) **9.** (a) Yes (b) ($^-1,1$) and (2,4) (c) ($^-1,1$) and (2,4)

10. (a) (3,12) and (1,2) (b) ($^-1,8$) and ($^-2,13$) **11.** (a) ($^-1,8$) and (2,$^-1$)

8 Statistics 2

page 265 **Revision** (8.1)

2. (a) 26 (b) 13 (c) 19.5 (d) 16 (e) 23.5

3. (a)

Mark	$\leqslant2$	$\leqslant4$	$\leqslant6$	$\leqslant8$	$\leqslant10$
Cumulative frequency	3	10	18	23	25

(c) 4.5, 3.1, 6.3 (d) 3.2, 1.6

4. (a)

Height (cm)	16	17	18	19	20	21	22	23	24	25	20cm
Cumulative frequency		3	8	18	34	58	79	94	103	108	110

5. (a)

Engine size (c.c)	⩽ 600	601–800	801–1000	1001–1200	1201–1400	1401–1600
Cumulative frequency	6	19	44	70	84	100

  (c) 1050 c.c., 860 c.c., 1280 c.c (d) 210 c.c.
  (e) No change to median, but the interquartile range is reduced from 420 c.c. to 370 c.c.
6. (a) The 16th, the 8th and the 24th (b) 175.5 cm, 9.5 cm
  (c) More of the interquartile range lies to the right of the median.
7. (a) 44 (b) 34, 52

page 267 **The mean** (8.2)
  1. 218.8 **2.** 15.2 **3.** 20.03
page 268
  4. 7.25 **5.** (a) 300 cm (b) 30 cm
  7. (a) 7 (b) Missing values for $f \times d$ are: $^-$21, $^-$16, $^-$12, 0, 16, 32, 36, 28 and 10 (c) 100, 52
  (d) 7.52
  9. (c) 6840 cm **12.** 83.02 h **13.** 1 **14.** 99.896 **15.** (a) 198.26 mm (b) 197.825 mm

page 269 **Grouped frequencies** (8.3)
  1. 154 cm **2.** (a) 997.5 mm, 996.5 mm, 996.5 mm to 997.5 mm or 997 mm (b) 998.45 mm
  3. (a) 2.5 km (b) 1.614 km
  4. (a) 15 years (b) 31.4 years
page 270
  5. 57.5 **6.** (a) 25.5 (b) 62.4, 72.3

page 270 **Standard deviation** (8.4)
  1. 3.32 cm **2.** The standard deviation is smaller for Set 2.
  3. 7, 3.77 **4.** 17, 3.77 **5.** 10, 3.46 **6.** 12, 2.58
  7. (b) 1.44 (c) 8 **8.** (a) 7 (b) 2.34
page 272
  9. (a) 20 (b) 3, the mean (c) 1.45 (d) 70% **10.** 16, 1.77 **11.** 84 cm, 1.87 cm
  12. (a) 8 (b) 2.35 **13.** (a) 24.25 years (b) 17.96 years
page 273
  14. 134 cm, 15.75 cm **15.** (a) 134 cm, 15.75 cm (b) Yes (c) 134.5 cm **16.** 42.93, 19.54
  17. (a) 48.65 kg, 8.45 kg (b) 30 **18.** (a) 6.034 cm, 2.27 cm (b) 42 **19.** 2.36, 1.073
  20. 5.12, 2.39

page 274 **Using standard deviation** (8.5)
  1. 23 **2.** 86 **3.** He did better in Test 2 **4.** She did better in Test 2, so she thought wrong.
  5. Yes
  6. (a) 40 and 60 (b) 65 and 85 (c) Mean minus standard deviation (d) 70 on the practical
  7. (a) 70, 65 (b) Between 40 and 80 (practical), 20 and 80 (written)
  (c) Mean plus half of the standard deviation (d) 57.5
  9. (a) 10, 3 (b) 20, 24, 32, 40, 40, 40, 48, 56, 60 **10.** (a) 45, 18 (b) 80 (c) 36
  11. (a) Vishnu: 45 (History), 65 Geography; Michael: 65 (History), 35 (Geography) (b) No, Michael
      has 100, Vishnu has 110.
  12. (a) 50, 50, 70, 40 (b) Caleb 130, Ben 120, Anab 100, Daniel 70

9 Probability 2

page 278 **Revision** (9.1)

1. (a) 1   (b) 0   (c) 0   (d) 1   (e) 0   **2.** (a) $\frac{1}{2}$ (b) (i) $\frac{1}{2}$ (ii) $\frac{1}{4}$ (iii) $\frac{1}{13}$ (c) $\frac{1}{6}$ (d) $\frac{1}{5}$
3. (b) 3   (c) (i) $\frac{1}{4}$ (ii) $\frac{1}{6}$ (iii) $\frac{1}{12}$ (iv) 0   **4.** (b) (i) $\frac{2}{7}$ (ii) $\frac{2}{7}$ (iii) $\frac{1}{7}$ (iv) 0
6. (a) $\frac{3}{8}$ (b) $\frac{3}{8}$ (c) $\frac{3}{8}$ (d) $\frac{1}{8}$ **7.** (a) $\frac{1}{2}$ (b) $\frac{1}{4}$ (c) $\frac{1}{2}$ (d) $\frac{1}{4}$
8. $\frac{1}{8}$ **9.** (a) $\frac{7}{8}$ (b) Their total is one   **10.** $\frac{3}{4}$ **11.** $Pr(E) + Pr(E') = 1$
12. The probability of getting a multiple of 3 is $\frac{2}{6}$.   **13.** $\frac{2}{3}$ **14.** $\frac{5}{8}$
15. (a) $\frac{1}{2}$ (b) $\frac{1}{6}$ (c) $\frac{1}{6}$ (d) $\frac{5}{6}$ **16.** (a) $\frac{1}{13}$ (b) $\frac{1}{2}$ (c) $\frac{3}{13}$ (d) $\frac{5}{13}$ (e) $\frac{2}{13}$ (f) $\frac{3}{13}$

page 280 **Probability of compound events** (9.2)

1. (a) $\frac{1}{3}$ (b) $\frac{1}{2}$ (c) $\frac{5}{6}$ **2.** Yes   **3.** (a) $\frac{1}{4}$ (b) $\frac{1}{2}$ (c) $\frac{1}{13}$ (d) $\frac{3}{13}$ (e) $\frac{1}{2}$ (f) $\frac{2}{13}$
4. (a) Yes   (b) Yes   **5.** (a) $\frac{3}{4}$ (b) $\frac{1}{2}$ (c) $\frac{4}{13}$ (d) $\frac{3}{13}$
6. (a) $Pr(C) + Pr(R)$ (b) $Pr(R)$ (c) $Pr(A) + Pr(P)$ (d) $Pr(P)$
7. (a) 16   (b) 28   (c) $\frac{4}{13}$ (d) $\frac{7}{13}$ **8.** (a) Yes   (b) Yes
9. (a) 1   (b) 2. It is possible for a card to be both a heart and a queen, similarly a card could be both a red and an ace.
10. (a) $\frac{3}{4}$ (b) $\frac{3}{13}$ (c) $\frac{7}{13}$ (d) $\frac{7}{13}$ (e) $\frac{8}{13}$ **11.** (a) $\frac{1}{2}$ (b) 1   (c) $\frac{2}{3}$
12. (a) $\frac{2}{5}$ (b) $\frac{3}{5}$ (c) $\frac{1}{5}$ (d) $\frac{1}{5}$ (e) $\frac{2}{5}$ (f) $\frac{1}{5}$ **13.** (i) They total one   (ii) They total one
14. (a) $\frac{2}{5}$ (b) $\frac{3}{5}$ (c) $\frac{1}{10}$ (d) $\frac{9}{20}$ (e) $\frac{7}{10}$ (f) $\frac{2}{5}$ (g) $\frac{1}{4}$ (h) $\frac{3}{5}$ **15.** (a) $\frac{1}{36}$ (b) 0   (c) $\frac{1}{6}$ (d) $\frac{1}{6}$
page 282
16. $\frac{1}{12}$ **17.** $3, \frac{1}{4}$ **18.** $\frac{1}{4}$ **19.** (b) 36   (c) 6   (d) $\frac{1}{6}$
20. (a) Yes   (b) Doubles   (c) $\frac{1}{6}$ (d) The sum equals seven   (e) $\frac{1}{6}$
21. (a) (3,6), (4,5), (5,4), (6,3)   (c) 4   (d) $\frac{1}{9}$ **22.** (a) $\frac{1}{4}$ (b) $\frac{1}{12}$ (c) $\frac{5}{18}$ (d) $\frac{7}{12}$ (e) $\frac{5}{6}$

page 283 **Using tree diagrams** (9.3)

1. $\frac{1}{2}$ **2.** $\frac{1}{4}$ **4.** 36   (b) $\frac{1}{36}$ (c) $\frac{11}{36}$ (d) $\frac{25}{36}$ (e) $\frac{1}{6}$ (f) $\frac{1}{18}$ (g) $\frac{25}{36}$ (h) $\frac{1}{6}$
5. (a) $\frac{1}{36}$ (b) $\frac{1}{18}$ (c) $\frac{1}{6}$ (d) $\frac{1}{12}$ **6.** Yes
7. (a) 1,2,3,4,5,6; 2,4,6,8,10,12; 3,6,9,12,15,18; 4,8,12,16,20,24; 5,10,15,20,25,30; 6,12,18,24,30,36
   (b) Yes   (c) (i) $\frac{1}{36}$ (ii) $\frac{1}{9}$ (iii) $\frac{1}{12}$ (iv) $\frac{7}{8}$
9. (a) $\frac{1}{8}$ (b) $\frac{3}{8}$ (c) $\frac{1}{8}$ (d) $\frac{7}{8}$ (e) $\frac{7}{8}$ **10.** (a) $\frac{1}{4}$ (b) $\frac{3}{8}$ (c) $\frac{1}{16}$ (d) $\frac{15}{16}$ (e) $\frac{11}{16}$
page 284
13. (a) $\frac{657}{1000}$ (b) $\frac{27}{125}$ **14.** (a) $\frac{2}{9}$ (b) $\frac{1}{3}$ **17.** $\frac{1}{120}$ **19.** (a) $\frac{343}{8000}$ (b) $\frac{7}{228}$

page 285 **Mutually exclusive events** (9.4)

1. (a) $\frac{1}{7}$ (b) $\frac{2}{7}$ (c) $\frac{3}{7}$ **2.** (a) Yes   (b) Yes   **3.** (b) (i) 2   (ii) 3   (iii) 1
4. (a) $\frac{2}{7}$ (b) $\frac{3}{7}$ (c) $\frac{4}{7}$ **5.** (a) Yes   (b) Yes
6. (a) 2,2,2   (i) $\frac{1}{6}$ (ii) $\frac{1}{6}$ (iii) $\frac{1}{6}$ (b) 4,3   (i) $\frac{1}{3}$ (ii) $\frac{1}{4}$
7. (a) Yes   (b) No   (c) No   (d) Yes   (e) Yes   (f) No
8. (a) (i) $\frac{1}{4}$ (ii) $\frac{1}{4}$ (iii) $\frac{1}{2}$ (b) (i) $\frac{1}{2}$ (ii) $\frac{1}{6}$ (iii) $\frac{1}{2}$ (c) (i) $\frac{5}{36}$ (ii) $\frac{2}{9}$ (iii) $\frac{7}{9}$ (d) (i) $\frac{1}{2}$ (ii) $\frac{1}{2}$
   (iii) 1
9. (a) and (d)
page 286
10. (a) Yes   (b) Yes   (c) Yes   **11.** (a) All are equal to $\frac{1}{12}$ (b) Yes   **12.** (a) Yes   (b) Yes
13. (a) $\frac{1}{12}, \frac{1}{12}, \frac{5}{12}, \frac{5}{12}$ (b) There are only four possible outcomes.   **14.** $\frac{5}{12}$
15. (a) $\frac{1}{5}$ (b) $\frac{5}{6}$ (c) $\frac{11}{30}$ (d) $\frac{3}{5}$ (e) $\frac{13}{30}$ **16.** (a) $\frac{2}{5}$ (b) $\frac{7}{10}$ (c) $\frac{7}{10}$ (d) $\frac{3}{5}$
17. (a) $\frac{1}{10}$ (b) $\frac{27}{50}$ (c) $\frac{2}{5}$ (d) $\frac{19}{20}$ (e) $\frac{243}{425}$ (f) $\frac{182}{425}$ **18.** (a) $\frac{1}{2}$ (b) $\frac{1}{4}$ (c) $\frac{3}{4}$ (d) $\frac{1}{2}$ (e) $\frac{3}{5}$ (f) $\frac{3}{5}$ (g) $\frac{7}{10}$

page 287 **Independent and dependent events** (9.5)

1. (a) $\frac{1}{169}$ (b) $\frac{1}{13}$ (c) $\frac{16}{2704} = \left(\frac{4}{52}\right)^2$ **2.** (a) $\frac{1}{36}$ (b) Yes   (c) $\frac{1}{36} = \left(\frac{1}{6}\right)^2$ **3.** $\frac{1}{4}$
4. (a) Yes   (b) (i) $\frac{1}{8}$ (ii) $\frac{1}{8}$ **5.** (a) $\frac{1}{24}$ (b) $\frac{1}{24}$ (c) $\frac{1}{8}$
6. (a) $\frac{1}{216}$ (b) $\frac{1}{8}$ (c) $\frac{1}{27}$ (d) $\frac{1}{72}$ (e) $\frac{1}{36}$ **7.** (a) Yes   (b) (i) $\frac{1}{6}$ (ii) $\frac{7}{20}$

page 288

8. (a) $\frac{1}{16}$ (b) $\frac{1}{16}$ (c) $\frac{1}{169}$ (d) $\frac{1}{52}$ (e) $\frac{1}{169}$ (f) $\frac{3}{52}$ **9.** (a) $\frac{12}{25}$ (b) $\frac{6}{25}$ (c) $\frac{6}{25}$ (d) $\frac{1}{25}$ (e) $\frac{2}{5}$

10. (a) Yes   (b) (i) $\frac{1}{75}$ (ii) $\frac{7}{150}$ (iii) $\frac{7}{25}$

11. (a) $\frac{7}{120}$ (b) $\frac{1}{15}$ (c) $\frac{7}{15}$ **12.** (a) $\frac{1}{100}$ (b) $\frac{3}{50}$ (c) $\frac{3}{10}$

13. (a) $\frac{2}{15}$ (b) $\frac{4}{15}$ (c) $\frac{4}{15}$ (d) $\frac{2}{15}$ **14.** $\frac{1}{221}$ **15.** (a) $\frac{1}{5525}$ (b) $\frac{8}{16\,575}$ (c) $\frac{4324}{5525}$

16. (a) $\frac{1}{270\,725}$ (b) $\frac{38\,916}{54\,145}$

page 289

17. (a) $\frac{1}{10}$ (b) $\frac{1}{100}$ **18.** (a) 1326   (b) 325   (c) 6   (d) 1   **19.** (a) $\frac{1}{1326}$ (b) $\frac{1}{221}$ (c) $\frac{1}{1326}$

20. $\frac{4}{49}$ **21.** (a) $\frac{3}{5}$ (b) $\frac{18}{25}$ (c) $\frac{2}{25}$ (d) $\frac{17}{25}$

22. (a) 4950   (b) (i) $\frac{142}{275}$ (ii) $\frac{59}{165}$ (iii) $\frac{112}{275}$ (iv) $\frac{106}{165}$ (v) $\frac{17}{33}$

23. (a) $\frac{7}{29}$ (b) $\frac{26}{145}$ (c) $\frac{2}{87}$ (d) $\frac{3}{29}$ (e) $\frac{7}{145}$

10   Vectors and matrices I

page 291   **Vectors** (10.1)

1. (a) $\binom{4}{2}$ (b) $\binom{-3}{-2}$ (c) $\binom{4}{0}$ (d) $\binom{1}{-2}$ (e) $\binom{-3}{2}$ (f) $\binom{-2}{0}$ (g) $\binom{-4}{-2}$ (h) $\binom{-1}{3}$ (i) $\binom{0}{-2}$ (j) $\binom{-2}{1}$

page 292

3. (a) **a** and **e**; **b**, **d** and **g**   (b) $\mathbf{b} = \frac{1}{2}\mathbf{d}$, $\mathbf{g} = 3\mathbf{b} = \frac{3}{2}\mathbf{d}$ **4.** $\mathbf{p} = -\mathbf{a}$, $\mathbf{q} = 2\mathbf{a}$, $\mathbf{r} = -\frac{1}{2}\mathbf{a}$, $\mathbf{s} = -\frac{3}{2}\mathbf{a}$, $\mathbf{t} = \mathbf{a}$

5. (a) $\binom{2}{4}$ (b) $\binom{3}{6}$ (c) $\binom{-1}{-2}$ (d) $\binom{-4}{-8}$ (e) $\binom{4}{1}$ (f) $\binom{-2}{-4}$ **6.** (a) $\binom{4}{3}$ (b) $\binom{2}{-1}$ (c) $\binom{5}{0}$

7. (a) $\binom{3}{1}$ (b) $\binom{-1}{-3}$ (c) $\binom{-4}{-2}$ **8.** (a) D   (b) B   (c) S   (d) A   **9.** They are the same

10.

	Translation	Vector	Translation	Vector
(a)	A → B	$\binom{0}{1}$	B → A	$\binom{-3}{-1}$
(b)	B → D	$\binom{1}{-3}$	D → B	$\binom{-1}{3}$
(c)	C → B	$\binom{2}{4}$	B → C	$\binom{-2}{-4}$

11. One is the negative of the other

page 293

12.

	Translation	Translation	Translation
(a)	S → A $\binom{1}{2}$	A → B $\binom{3}{1}$	S → B $\binom{4}{3}$
(b)	C → B $\binom{2}{4}$	B → D $\binom{1}{-3}$	C → D $\binom{3}{1}$
(c)	S → D $\binom{5}{0}$	D → C $\binom{-3}{-1}$	S → C $\binom{2}{-1}$

13. (a) The corresponding numbers are added   (b) The third vector is the sum of the other two

14. (a) $\binom{2}{3}, \binom{4}{1}$ (b) $\binom{6}{4}$

15. (a) $\binom{-1}{1}$ (b) $\binom{-1}{1}$ (c) $\binom{1}{3}$ (d) $\binom{1}{3}$ (e) $\binom{-5}{-1}$ (f) $\binom{-3}{1}$ (g) $\binom{0}{-4}$ (h) $\binom{-3}{-5}$

page 294

16. (a) $\binom{3}{1}$ (b) $\binom{-1}{2}$

20. (a) (i) $\binom{1}{-5}$ (ii) $\binom{-4}{3}$ (iii) $\binom{-3}{15}$ (c) (i) $\binom{6}{-13}$ (ii) $\binom{13}{-14}$ (iii) $\binom{1}{-5}$ (iv) $\binom{2}{-10}$ (v) $\binom{1}{-39}$

21. Yes   **22.** (a) $\binom{2}{2}$ (b) $\binom{-2}{-2}$ (c) $\binom{7}{8}$ (d) $\binom{9}{10}$

23. (a) $x = y = 2$ (b) $x = -5, y = 3$ (c) $x = 3, y = 1$

page 295   **Using vectors in geometry** (10.2)
1. (a) $2\mathbf{a}$ (b) $\mathbf{a}$ (c) $\mathbf{a}+\mathbf{b}$ (d) $2\mathbf{a}+\mathbf{b}$ (e) $\mathbf{a}-\mathbf{b}$ (f) $-(2\mathbf{a}+\mathbf{b})$
2. (a) $\overrightarrow{AM}=\frac{1}{2}(\overrightarrow{AB})$ (b) $\overrightarrow{AN}=\frac{1}{2}(\overrightarrow{AC})$ (c) $\overrightarrow{AB}+\overrightarrow{BC}=\overrightarrow{AC}$ (d) $\overrightarrow{AM}+\overrightarrow{MN}=\overrightarrow{AN}$
3. (a) $\frac{1}{2}\mathbf{p}$ (b) $\frac{1}{2}\mathbf{q}$ (c) $\mathbf{q}-\mathbf{p}$ (d) $\frac{1}{2}(\mathbf{q}-\mathbf{p})$
4. Its direction is the same as that of $\overrightarrow{BC}$ and its magnitude is half of that of $\overrightarrow{BC}$.
5. (a) $\overrightarrow{AB}+\overrightarrow{BC}=\overrightarrow{AC}$ (b) $\overrightarrow{CD}+\overrightarrow{DE}=\overrightarrow{CE}$ (c) $\overrightarrow{AC}+\overrightarrow{CE}=\overrightarrow{AE}$
6. (a) $\overrightarrow{AB}+\overrightarrow{BC}=\overrightarrow{AC}$ (b) $\overrightarrow{AC}+\overrightarrow{CD}=\overrightarrow{AD}$ (c) $\overrightarrow{AD}+\overrightarrow{DE}=\overrightarrow{AE}$ (d) $\overrightarrow{AE}+\overrightarrow{EF}=\overrightarrow{AF}$
7. The net displacement is zero.

page 296
8. (a) $\mathbf{a}$ (b) $\mathbf{a}$ (c) $\mathbf{b}$ (d) $-2\mathbf{b}$ (e) $\mathbf{a}+3\mathbf{b}$ (f) $2\mathbf{a}+\mathbf{b}$ (g) $2(\mathbf{a}-\mathbf{b})$ (h) $\mathbf{a}-2\mathbf{b}$
9. (a) $-\mathbf{a}$ (b) $\mathbf{b}-\mathbf{a}$ (c) $\mathbf{a}-\mathbf{b}$ **10.** (a) $\mathbf{v}$ (b) $-\mathbf{u}$ (c) $\mathbf{u}+\mathbf{v}$
11. (a) $\mathbf{b}-\mathbf{a}$ (b) $2\mathbf{b}-\mathbf{a}$ (c) $2\mathbf{b}-\mathbf{a}$ **12.** $\mathbf{v}+9\mathbf{u},\mathbf{v}+5\mathbf{u}$
13. (a) $-\mathbf{a}$ (b) $\mathbf{b}-\mathbf{a}$ (c) $\frac{1}{2}(\mathbf{b}-\mathbf{a})$ (d) $\frac{1}{2}(\mathbf{a}+\mathbf{b})$
page 297
14. (a) (i) $2\mathbf{q}+2\mathbf{r}-2\mathbf{p}$ (ii) $\mathbf{q}+\mathbf{r}-\mathbf{p}$ (iii) $\mathbf{p}$ (iv) $\mathbf{q}+\mathbf{r}$ (b) (i) $\mathbf{q}$ (ii) $\mathbf{r}$ (iii) $\mathbf{q}+\mathbf{r}$
   (c) Yes, yes
   (d) $\mathbf{p}-\mathbf{q},\mathbf{p}-\mathbf{q}$ KLMN is a parallelogram because it has two pairs of equal and parallel sides
15. (a) $\overrightarrow{PQ}=\overrightarrow{PO}+\overrightarrow{OQ}=-\overrightarrow{OP}+\overrightarrow{OQ}=\binom{-2}{-3}+\binom{4}{1}=\binom{2}{-2}$ (b) $\binom{-2}{-2}$ (c) $\binom{-1}{-1}$
   (d) $\overrightarrow{OM}=\overrightarrow{OP}+\overrightarrow{PM}$ (e) $\binom{3}{2}$
16. Take the mean of the corresponding figures
17. (a) $\mathbf{s}-\mathbf{r}$ (b) $\overrightarrow{RM}=\frac{1}{2}(\mathbf{s}-\mathbf{r}),\overrightarrow{OM}=\frac{1}{2}(\mathbf{r}+\mathbf{s})$ **18.** (a) $\binom{1}{3}$ (b) $\binom{-1}{4}$ (c) $\binom{-2}{1}$
19. (a) $\binom{3}{-2}$ (b) $\binom{5}{2}$ (c) $(5,2)$
20. (a) $\binom{4}{1}$ (b) $\binom{6}{-2},\binom{8}{-1}$ (c) $\binom{6}{2}$
page 298
21. (a) $\binom{2}{6},\binom{-3}{-1},\binom{4}{2}$ (b) $\binom{1}{11\frac{1}{2}},\binom{1}{3}$ **22.** $(5,9)$ **23.** (a) $(8,8)$ (b) $(3,6)$
24. (a) $(1,2)$ (b) $(3,2)$ (c) $(2,2)$ **25.** (b) (i) $(3,5)$ (ii) $(2,6)$ (iii) $(3,^-2)$ (iv) $(2,1)$
26. (a) 5   (b) 13   (c) 10   (d) 25   **27.** (a) 5   (b) 10   (c) 13   (d) $4\sqrt{2}$ (e) 17   (f) 25
28. (a) 1   (b) 1   (c) 1   (d) 1
29. (a) 1, yes   (b) 1, yes   (c) $\sqrt{2}$, no   (d) $\sqrt{2}$, no   (e) 1, yes   (f) 1, yes
30. (a) $\binom{3}{4}$ (b) (i) $4\mathbf{i}+3\mathbf{j}$ (ii) $3\mathbf{i}-2\mathbf{j}$

page 299   **Matrices** (10.3)
1. 48   **2.** 58   **3.** (a) 25   (b) 23
4.
$$\begin{pmatrix} 25 & 13 & 22 & 16 \\ 13 & 11 & 35 & 30 \\ 14 & 31 & 23 & 27 \\ 18 & 33 & 17 & 18 \\ 21 & 16 & 1 & 38 \end{pmatrix}$$
5. (a) 1×3 (b) 2×2 (c) 2×1 (d) 2×3 (e) 3×2 (f) 3×3
6. (a) $\binom{5\ \ 0}{14\ \ 15}$ (b) $\binom{2\ 4}{3\ 9}$ (c) $\binom{5\ \ 0}{14\ \ 15}$ (d) Impossible   (e) Impossible   (f) $\binom{0\ 0}{0\ 0}$
7. (a) A, B, C and D   (b) The other matrix is unaffected   (c) Their sum is the 2×2 zero matrix
   (d) No, they are not the same type of matrix   (e) Yes
8. (a) $\binom{2\ 4}{3\ 9}$ (b) $\binom{2\ 4}{3\ 9}$, yes, yes
9. (a) The corresponding numbers are separately subtracted
   (b) (i) $\binom{-1\ \ 8}{-8\ \ 3}$
   (ii) $\binom{-2\ -4}{-3\ -9}$ (iii) Impossible   (iv) Impossible   (v) $\binom{2\ 4}{3\ 9}$ (vi) $\binom{-6\ \ 8}{-22\ -12}$

10.

	Size	
	Large	Small
Chocolate	20	44
Rum	30	72

11. $\begin{pmatrix} 20 & 44 \\ 30 & 72 \end{pmatrix}$ **12.** Multiply each figure by three separately. **13.** $\begin{pmatrix} 20 \\ 8 \end{pmatrix}$, yes

14. (a) $\begin{pmatrix} 6 & 0 \\ 0 & 2 \end{pmatrix}$ (b) $\begin{pmatrix} 15 \\ 20 \end{pmatrix}$ (c) $\begin{pmatrix} 7 & 5 \\ -2\frac{1}{4} & 3 \end{pmatrix}$

15. (a) $a = 2, b = 8$ (b) $c = 1\frac{1}{3}, d = 4$ (c) $e = 4, f = {}^-4, g = 4\frac{1}{2}$
 (d) $h = 4$ or $^-4, k = {}^-1, i = 2$ or $^-2, j = 0$ or 24

page 301 **Multiplying matrices** (10.4)
 1. (a) 30 (b) 42 (c) 17 **2.** (a) 47 (b) 51

3.

	Woodwork
First	47
Second	51

4. $\begin{pmatrix} 47 \\ 51 \end{pmatrix}$
6. (a) Total number of pieces of woodwork completed by first year pupils.
 (b) Total number of pieces of woodwork completed by second year pupils.
7. (a) 105 (b) 73 **8.** $\begin{pmatrix} 10 & 17 \\ 14 & 9 \end{pmatrix} \times \begin{pmatrix} 2 \\ 5 \end{pmatrix} = \begin{pmatrix} 105 \\ 73 \end{pmatrix}$
9. (a) $\begin{pmatrix} 23 \\ 53 \end{pmatrix}$ (b) $\begin{pmatrix} 5 \\ 10 \end{pmatrix}$ (c) $\begin{pmatrix} 3 \\ 9 \end{pmatrix}$ (d) $\begin{pmatrix} -7 \\ 6 \end{pmatrix}$ (e) $\begin{pmatrix} 3 \\ 4 \end{pmatrix}$ (f) $\begin{pmatrix} 4 \\ 3 \end{pmatrix}$ **10.** $\begin{pmatrix} 47 & 105 \\ 51 & 73 \end{pmatrix}$
page 302
11. $\begin{pmatrix} 10 & 35 \\ 8 & 17 \end{pmatrix}$
12. (a) $\begin{pmatrix} 24 & 52 \\ 29 & 50 \end{pmatrix}$ (b) $\begin{pmatrix} 46 & -6 \\ -1 & 15 \end{pmatrix}$ (c) $\begin{pmatrix} 2 & 3 \\ 4 & 2 \end{pmatrix}$ (d) $\begin{pmatrix} 6 & 18 \\ 12 & 12 \end{pmatrix}$ (e) $\begin{pmatrix} 3 & 1 \\ -2 & 1 \end{pmatrix}$ (f) $\begin{pmatrix} -4 & -6 \\ 10 & 13 \end{pmatrix}$ (g) $\begin{pmatrix} 2 & 9 \\ 4 & 3 \end{pmatrix}$
 (h) $\begin{pmatrix} -5 & 5 \\ -4 & -8 \end{pmatrix}$
13. (a) $a = 1, b = 4$ (b) $c = 6, d = 2$ (c) $e = 1, f = 0$ (d) $g = 3, h = 1, i = 14, j = 4$
 (e) $k = 0, l = 8\frac{1}{2}, m = n = 0$ (f) $p = 3, q = 5, r = 5$
14. $2\frac{2}{3}$
15. $^-1$ or 1 **16.** (a) $\begin{pmatrix} 5 & 8 \\ 13 & 16 \end{pmatrix}$ (b) $\begin{pmatrix} 3 & 6 \\ 13 & 18 \end{pmatrix}$ (c) $\begin{pmatrix} 2 & 0 \\ 0 & 2 \end{pmatrix}$ (d) $\begin{pmatrix} 2 & 0 \\ 0 & 2 \end{pmatrix}$ (e) $\begin{pmatrix} -12 & 6 \\ 8 & -2 \end{pmatrix}$ (f) $\begin{pmatrix} -10 & 8 \\ 8 & -4 \end{pmatrix}$
17. No **18.** (a) $\begin{pmatrix} 4 & 2 \\ -4 & 10 \end{pmatrix}$ (b) $\begin{pmatrix} 4 & 2 \\ -4 & 10 \end{pmatrix}$ (c) $\begin{pmatrix} 6 & 0 \\ 2 & 8 \end{pmatrix}$ (d) $\begin{pmatrix} 6 & 0 \\ 2 & 8 \end{pmatrix}$ **19.** Yes
20. (a) $\begin{pmatrix} 31 & 40 \\ 67 & 88 \end{pmatrix}$ (b) $\begin{pmatrix} 31 & 40 \\ 67 & 88 \end{pmatrix}$ (c) $\begin{pmatrix} 66 & -30 \\ -38 & 18 \end{pmatrix}$ (d) $\begin{pmatrix} 66 & -30 \\ -38 & 18 \end{pmatrix}$ **21.** Yes
22. (a) $\begin{pmatrix} 5 & 8 \\ 5 & 6 \end{pmatrix}$ (b) $\begin{pmatrix} 10 & 18 \\ 10 & 12 \end{pmatrix}$ (c) $\begin{pmatrix} 5 & 2 \\ 2 & 2 \end{pmatrix}$ (d) $\begin{pmatrix} 10 & 18 \\ 10 & 12 \end{pmatrix}$, yes **23.** Answers to (b) and (d) are the same
24. (a) $\begin{pmatrix} 1 & 2 \\ 3 & 4 \end{pmatrix}$ (b) $\begin{pmatrix} 3 & 0 \\ 1 & 4 \end{pmatrix}$ (c) $\begin{pmatrix} -4 & 2 \\ 3 & -1 \end{pmatrix}$ (d) $\begin{pmatrix} 1 & 2 \\ 3 & 4 \end{pmatrix}$ (e) $\begin{pmatrix} 3 & 0 \\ 1 & 4 \end{pmatrix}$ (f) $\begin{pmatrix} -4 & 2 \\ 3 & -1 \end{pmatrix}$
 A, B and **C** are unaffected by the multiplication. When any matrix is multiplied by **I** it remains
 unaffected.
25. (a) $\begin{pmatrix} 4 & 5 \\ 4 & 5 \end{pmatrix}$ (b) No (c) No (d) $\begin{pmatrix} -1 & 10 \\ -1 & 10 \end{pmatrix}$, no **26.** (a) $\begin{pmatrix} 3 & -1 \\ -12 & 4 \end{pmatrix}$ (b) No, **BA** $= \begin{pmatrix} 6 & -2 \\ -3 & 1 \end{pmatrix}$
27. For example, $\begin{pmatrix} 2 & -2 \\ -2 & -2 \end{pmatrix}$

Answers to Part 3

I Relations and functions 2

page 306 **Lines and regions** (1.1)
1. (a) Yes (b) No (c) No (d) No 2. (a) Yes, yes (b) Yes, no
3. (a) Yes, no (b) Yes, no 5. Yes, yes 6. $(3,4), (x + y = 7)$
7. $(6,3)$ and $(5,4)$. For $(6,4), x + 3y = 18$ not < 18 8. (a) 7 (b) 2 (c) 5
9. (a) $x + 3y \geq 12, y \geq 2x + 3, x + y \leq 6$ (b) $x + y \leq 6, x + 3y \leq 12, y \leq 2x + 3$
   (c) $x + 3y \leq 12, x + y \geq 6$

page 308 **Linear programming** (1.2)
3. (a) $X + Y \leq 45, 4X + 5Y \geq 200$ (c) (i) Yes (ii) Yes (iii) Yes
4. (a) $2000A + 2400B \leq 18\ 000, 16A + 10B \leq 120$ (c) (i) 4 of each (ii) 5 of A and 3 of B
   (d) (i) Yes (ii) No
5. (c) Yes
6. $5N + 6L = 600, N = 24\ L = 80$, Yes 7. $L = 80, N = 30$ for example.
8. (a) $x + 2y \geq 8, 3x + 12y \geq 12$ (d) $x = 2, y = 3$ (e) $2.70
   (f) $x = 3, y = 4\frac{1}{2}$ for example; $4.05 per kg.
page 310
9. (c) $(3,12)$. $(4,8), (4,9), (4,10)$. $(4,11), (5,6), (5,7), (5,8), (5,9), (5,10), (6,6), (6,7), (6,8), (6,9), (7,6),$
   $(7,7), (7,8), (8,5), (8,6), (8,7), (9,5), (9,6), (10,4), (10,5), (11,4)$ (d) 11, 12, 13, 14 or 15
10. (a) 3 (b) 4 (c) 11 11. (a) Yes (b) 11 12. (a) $x + 2y \leq 18, 3x + y \leq 18$
13. (a) Yes, (d) No whole number values satisfy the two inequalities in 12(a) and $x + y > 10$.
14. (a) (i) $x + y \leq 8$ (ii) $x \geq 2$ (iii) $y \geq 1$ (iv) $15x + 25y \leq 150$
15. (a) Profit $= 4x + 6y$
    (c) Yes No point on the line $4x + 6y = 48$ satisfies the inequalities in 14(a). (d) $38
16. Any values for the areas which are bound within the following values: 4 hectares of A and 2 hectares
    of B; 4 hectares of A and 3.6 hectares of B; 5 hectares of A and 3 hectares of B; 6 hectares of A and 2
    hectares of B.
page 311
17. (a) $5m + 8n \geq 60; 2m + n \geq 15$ (b) 10 boats, $(5,5)$ or $(6,4)$
18. (a) $8L + 3S \leq 72$ (b) $L + S \leq 18$ (c) Cost $= 32L + 8S; L = 4, S = 18$, Cost $= 240
19. $90C + 36P \leq 5400, C + P \leq 100; C = 33\frac{1}{3}$ hectares, $P = 66\frac{2}{3}$ hectares; $10\ 400; 150
20. $(4,12), (3,14)$ and $(2,16)$ for which $2x + y = 20$
21. (a) $v + l \leq 10$ (b) $18v + 45l \leq 270$
    (c) $600v + 1100l \geq 6600$; 5 vans and 4 lorries, 6 vans and 3 lorries, 7 vans and 3 lorries or
        8 vans and 2 lorries

page 312 **Areas under graphs** (1.3)
1. (a) $28.8\,\text{cm}^2$ (b) 3.2 (i) Quite accurate (ii) Quite accurate
2. (b) 123 square units (c) Quite close 3. Split the area up into five trapezia
4. (a) 19.5 square units (b) 17.6 square units

5.
$x =$	0	1	2	3	4	5
$y =$	0	3	12	27	48	75

6. A straight line between a pair of points has a greater area underneath it than that of the
   corresponding part of the curve

7. (b) The equation of the circle is $x^2 + y^2 = 9$ (c) $6.56\,\text{cm}^2$
   (d) A straight line between a pair of points has a smaller area underneath it than that of the corresponding part of the curve
8. 14 square units

9.

$x =$	0	1	2	3	4	5	6	7	8	9	10
$y =$	0	9	16	21	24	25	24	21	16	9	0

   (a) 160 square units   (b) 165 square units   (c) The second method
   (d) Divide it up into a greater number of trapezia
10. (a) 38 square units   (b) $47\frac{1}{2}$ square units   (c) $235\frac{1}{2}$ square units
page 314
11. (a) 250 km   (b) From the area under the graph line
12. (a) 50 km/h   (b) 250 km   (c) From the area under the graph line
13. (a) 240 km/h   (b) 240 km/h, yes

14. (a)

$t =$	0	1	2	3	4	5
$v =$	0	29	52	69	80	85

   (b) 14.5 km/h, 40.5 km/h, 60.5 km/h, 74.5 km/h, 82.5 km/h

   (c) (i) 272.5 km   (ii) 272.5 km   (d) Yes

page 315   **Using tangents and areas** (1.4)
 1. (a) 70 km/h, 50 km/h, 30 km/h, 10 km/h, 10 km/h, 30 km/h, 50 km/h, 70 km/h
   (b) 60 km/h, 20 km/h, 20 km/h, 60 km/h. It decreases for the first four seconds and then increases again
 2. 80 km/h, 60 km/h, 40 km/h, 20 km/h, 0 km/h, $^-$20 km/h, $^-$40 km/h, $^-$60 km/h, $^-$80 km/h. It decreases to reach zero after four seconds and then increases again with the motion in the opposite direction
 3. (a) $t = 4$ seconds   (b) $t = 0$ seconds and 8 seconds
 4. (a) 72 m/s, 56 m/s, 40 m/s, 24 m/s, 8 m/s   (b) 80 m/s, 64 m/s, 48 m/s, 32 m/s, 16 m/s, 0 m/s   (c) $t = 5$
   (d) $t = 10$
 5. (a) 24 m   (b) 9 m/s   (c) 10 m/s   (d) 4 m/s
page 316
 6. (a) $15\,\text{m/s}^2, 13\,\text{m/s}^2, 11\,\text{m/s}^2, 9\,\text{m/s}^2, 7\,\text{m/s}^2, 5\,\text{m/s}^2, 3\,\text{m/s}^2, 1\,\text{m/s}^2$ (b) $14\,\text{m/s}^2, 10\,\text{m/s}^2, 6\,\text{m/s}^2, 2\,\text{m/s}^2$
 7. $16\,\text{m/s}^2, 14\,\text{m/s}^2, 12\,\text{m/s}^2, 10\,\text{m/s}^2, 8\,\text{m/s}^2, 6\,\text{m/s}^2, 4\,\text{m/s}^2, 2\,\text{m/s}^2, 0\,\text{m/s}^2$. It decreases uniformly to zero.
   $t = 8$ seconds
 8. (a) $3\,\text{m/s}^2, 9\,\text{m/s}^2, 15\,\text{m/s}^2, 21\,\text{m/s}^2, 27\,\text{m/s}^2$ (b) $6\,\text{m/s}^2, 12\,\text{m/s}^2, 18\,\text{m/s}^2, 24\,\text{m/s}^2, 30\,\text{m/s}^2$
   (c) $t = 8$ seconds
 9. (a) $0 \leqslant t \leqslant 2\frac{1}{2}$ (b) $t \geqslant 2\frac{1}{2}$ (c) $t = 2.5$
10. (a) 0.4 m/s, 6.8 m/s, 13.2 m/s, 19.6 m/s, 26 m/s, 32.4 m/s, 38.8 m/s, 45.2 m/s   (b) 22.8 m/s
   (c) It is uniform at $6.4\,\text{m/s}^2$
11. 40 m
page 318
12. 600 m, 1125 m, 810 m   **13.** 6.5 m, 12.5 m, 24.5 m, 42.5 m; 66.5 m/s   **14.** 90 m, 18 m/s

15. Question 13

time (s)	2	3	4
acceleration (m/s^2)	12	18	24

Question 14

time (s)	2	3	4
acceleration (m/s^2)	7	9	11

16. (a) 19 m   (b) 19 m   (c) 116 m   (d) (i) $5\,\text{m/s}^2$ (ii) $^-5\,\text{m/s}^2$
17. (a) (i) 5 m   (ii) 5 m   (b) (i) $^-3\,\text{m/s}^2$ (ii) $1\,\text{m/s}^2$ (c) 0.75 m/s   (d) 13 m/s $(t = 6)$ (e) $t = 2\frac{1}{2}$

18. (a) 26.15 m, 29.4 m, 30.45 m, 29.2 m, 26.15 m, 21.4 m, 14.3 m, 5.05 m   (b) 22.8 m/s   (c) 1 m/s^2
    (d) $^-$11 m/s^2 (t = 8)
19. 169 square units

2 Graphs 4

page 319   **More about graphs** (2.1)
1. $\{6,1,^-2,^-3,^-2,1\}$; $^-\frac{3}{4}, 3\frac{1}{4}, ^-\frac{3}{4}$
2. (a) 0 and 4   (b) 1 and 3   (c) $^-$1 and 5   (d) $2 + \sqrt{3}$ and $2 - \sqrt{3}$
4. (a) $\{5,0,^-3,^-5,^-3,0,5\}$, $^-1\frac{3}{4}$ (b) $\{16,9,4,1,0,1,4\}$, $2\frac{1}{4}$ (c) $\{2,0,0,2,6,12,20\}$, $3\frac{3}{4}$
   (d) $\{10,4,0,^-2,^-2,0,4,10\}$, $1\frac{3}{4}$
5. (a) 1 and $^-$3, 2, $^-$1 and $^-$2, 1 and 4   (b) $^-1 \pm \sqrt{6}, 2\pm \sqrt{2}$ and $3, \frac{5}{2}\pm \frac{\sqrt{17}}{2}$
   (c) $^-1 \pm 2\sqrt{2}$, 0 and 4, $^-\frac{3}{2}\pm \frac{\sqrt{17}}{2}$, 0 and 5   (d) 0 and $^-$2, none, none, none
7. (a) $\{^-5,0,3,4,3,0,^-5\}$, $3\frac{3}{4}$ (b) $\{^-10,^-4,0,2,2,0,^-4\}$, $1\frac{1}{4}$ (c) $\{^-5,0,3,4,3,0,^-5\}$, $3\frac{3}{4}$
   (d) $\{^-5,0,3,4,3,0,^-5\}$, $1\frac{3}{4}$
8. (a) $^-$2 and 2, 0 and 3, $^-$1 and 3, $^-$3 and 1   (b) $\pm \sqrt{3}, \frac{3}{2}\pm \frac{\sqrt{5}}{2}, 1\pm \sqrt{3}, ^-1\pm \sqrt{3}$
   (c) $\pm \sqrt{6}, \frac{3}{2}\pm \frac{\sqrt{17}}{2}, 1\pm \sqrt{6}$ (d) $^-$1 or 1, none, 0 and 2, $^-$2 and 0
page 320
9. They are the same shape. $y = 4 - x^2$ is translated through $\binom{1}{0}$ to $y = 3 + 2x - x^2$, and through $\binom{^-1}{0}$ to
   $y = 3 - 2x - x^2$
10. (a) 2 and 3   (b) $^-$4 and 2   (c) $\frac{5}{2}\pm \frac{\sqrt{5}}{2}$ (d) $^-1\pm \sqrt{7}$
11. (a) $^-$3 and 8   (b) $^-$6 and 4
13. (a) $(x-3)(x-1)$. When each factor is put equal to zero the resulting equation gives an intercept on
    the x-axis   (b) $(x-3)(x-2)$. Some explanation as in part (a).
15. (a) 1   (b) 2   (c) 3
16. (a) Yes   (b) Translate through $\binom{0}{-3}$ (c) Translate through $\binom{3}{0}$
17. (a) Yes   (b) Translate through $\binom{2}{-1}$ (c) Translate through $\binom{3}{-4}$
18. (a) $y = (x-2)^2 - 1$ (b) $y = (x-3)^2 - 4$ (c) $y = (x-0)^2 - 0$ (d) $y = (x-0)^2 - 3$
    (c) $y = (x-3)^2 - 0$
19. The coordinates of the minimum point are $(p, ^-q)$
page 321
21. (a) 3, $x = 3$ (b) 1, $x = 2$ (c) 5, $x = 1$ (d) $^-$3, $x = 4$ (e) 7, $x = ^-2$ (f) $^-$2, $x = 1$
    (g) 3, $x = 3$ (h) 1, $x = 2$ (i) 1, $x = 4$ (j) 5, $x = 5$
22. (a) $^-$4, 2, 0, 0, $^-$4   (b) Yes
23. (a) $^-$1, $^-$4, 0, $^-$3, 0   (b) 2, 3, 0, 0, 3   (c) See question 18
    (d) The coordinates of the minimum point are $(p, ^-q)$
24. (b) 3   (c) $y = (x-2)^2 + 3$ (d) Yes   (e) Yes   25. (a) 12   (b) 5   26. $^-$9, 16; 1 and 7
27. (a) $\{^-3,^-4,^-3,0,5,12\}$ (b) $\{5,0,^-3,^-4,^-3,0\}$ (c) $\{^-3,0,5\}$
28. (a) $^-$4, 12   (b) $^-$4, 5   (c) $^-$3, 5
29. (b) $^-$9,7; $\{7,0,^-5,^-8,^-9,^-8,^-5,0\}$ (c) $\{^-8,^-9,^-8,^-5\}$ (d) $^-$9, $^-$5
30. (a) $^-1 < x < 3$ (b) $x \leqslant ^-1$ and $x \geqslant 3$ (c) $0 < x < 2$ (d) $x \leqslant ^-2$ and $x \geqslant 4$
31. (b) 0, 27; $\{9,2,^-1,0,5,14,27\}$ (c) (i) $x < \frac{1}{2}$ and $x > 2$ (ii) $x < 4$ (d) $\{^-1,0,5\}$
page 322
32. (a) $(2x+3)^2 + 2, 2$ (b) $(3x+2)^2 + 1, 1$ (c) $(4x+1)^2 + 0, 0$ (d) $(5x+2)^2 - 4, ^-4$
    (e) $(2x-4)^2 + 4, 4$ (f) $(7x-4)^2 + 3, 3$ (g) $(6x-1)^2 + 0, 0$ (h) $(9x-1)^2 - 1, ^-1$
33. (a) 13   (b) 20   (c) 36   (d) 16   34. (a) 7   (b) 5   (c) 2   (d) 1
35. (a) $2\frac{2}{3}$ (b) $^-5\frac{1}{8}$ (c) $\frac{1}{5}$ (d) $^-19\frac{2}{7}$ (e) $^-5\frac{2}{3}$ (f) $^-2\frac{1}{16}$
36. (a) $7\frac{1}{3}$ (b) $8\frac{1}{3}$ (c) $9\frac{1}{16}$ (d) $15\frac{1}{4}$ (e) 11   (f) $4\frac{1}{24}$

page 323 Quadratic inequalities (2.2)

1. Either $l < 0$ and $m > 0$ or *vice versa* 2. (c) and (d) 3. (b) 4. (b)
5. (a) $x < 1$ or $x > 5$ (b) $3 < x < 7$ (c) $2 \leqslant x \leqslant 4$ (d) $x \leqslant 4$ or $x \geqslant 7$ (c) $1 \leqslant x \leqslant 2$
   (f) $1 \leqslant x \leqslant 3$
6. (a) $x \leqslant {}^-1$ or $x \geqslant 5$ (b) ${}^-7 \leqslant x \leqslant 3$ (c) ${}^-2 < x < 4$ (d) $x < {}^-7$ or $x > 4$ (e) $1 \leqslant x \leqslant 4$
   (h) $x \leqslant 1$ or $x \geqslant 8$
7. (a) $x > 1\frac{1}{2}$ (b) $x < {}^-2$ (c) $x < {}^-2$ or $x > 1\frac{1}{2}$
8. (a) $\frac{2}{3} < x < 4$ (b) $x < {}^-1$ or $x > 4$ (c) $x < {}^-3$ or $x > 2$ (d) ${}^-2 < x < 2\frac{1}{2}$
9. (a) $x < 1\frac{1}{2}$ or $x > 3\frac{1}{2}$ (b) ${}^-3 < x < {}^-1$ (c) ${}^-2 < x < \frac{1}{2}$ (d) $x < {}^-1\frac{1}{2}$ or $x > {}^-\frac{1}{2}$

page 324

10. (a) $x = 3$ or 5 (b) (i) positive (ii) negative (iii) positive
    (d) (i) $\{x : x < 3\} \cup \{x : x > 5\}$ (ii) $\{x : 3 < x < 5\}$
    (e) $1\frac{1}{2}$ and ${}^-\frac{1}{3}$; negative, positive, positive; $\{x : x < {}^-\frac{1}{3}\} \cup \{x : x > 1\frac{1}{2}\}$, $\{{}^-\frac{1}{3} < x < 1\frac{1}{2}\}$
12. (a) $\{x : {}^-2 \leqslant x \leqslant 3\}$ (b) $\{x : x < \frac{1}{2} - \frac{\sqrt{41}}{2}\} \cup \{x > \frac{1}{2} + \frac{\sqrt{41}}{2}\}$
    (c) $\{x : 0 < x < 1\}$
    (d) $\{x : x \leqslant {}^-1\} \cup \{x : x \geqslant 2\}$

13. (a)

x	0	1	2	3	4	5	6
$4x^2$	0	4	16	36	64	100	144
$16x$	0	16	32	48	64	80	96
$4x^2 - 16x + 7$	7	${}^-5$	${}^-9$	${}^-5$	7	27	55

(c) $\{x : \frac{1}{2} < x < 3\frac{1}{2}\}$

page 325

14. (a) $\{x : x < \frac{1}{2}\} \cup \{x : x > 3\frac{1}{2}\}$ (b) $\{x : 1 \leqslant x \leqslant 3\}$
15. (a) $\{x : x \leqslant 1\} \cup \{x : x \geqslant 4\}$ (b) $\{x : {}^-1 < x < 1\frac{1}{2}\}$
16. (a) $0 < x < 2$ (b) $x < {}^-2$ or $x > 4$ (c) All x other than $x = 1$
    (d) $x = 3$ or ${}^-1$; $1 - \sqrt{6} < x < 1 + \sqrt{6}$
17. (a) $x < {}^-3$ or $x > 2$ (b) ${}^-4 < x < 3$ (c) $x < {}^-1$ or $x > 0$ (d) $x = 4$ or 5; $x < {}^-2$ or $x > 1$
18. (a) ${}^-2 < x < 4$ (b) $x < 0$ or $x > 2$ (c) $x < {}^-3$ or $x > 5$ (d) ${}^-1 < x < 3$; all x except $x = 1$
19. (a) ${}^-3 < x < 3$ (b) $x < {}^-1$ or $x > 1$ (c) ${}^-2 \leqslant x \leqslant 2$
    (d) $x \leqslant {}^-4$ or $x \geqslant 4$; $x = \pm \sqrt{2}$, $x = {}^-1.414$ or 1.414
20. (a) $x < {}^-1$ or $x > 3$ (b) 4 or ${}^-2$ (c) $0 \leqslant x \leqslant 2$ (d) $x = 1$; $1 - \frac{\sqrt{14}}{2} \leqslant x \leqslant 1 + \frac{\sqrt{14}}{2}$
21. (a) $2 < x < 3$ (b) $x \leqslant {}^-5$ or $x \geqslant 1$ (c) $x \leqslant {}^-1$ or $x > 5$ (d) $x < 1$ or $x > 4$ (e) ${}^-3 \leqslant x \leqslant {}^-1$
    (f) $1 \leqslant x \leqslant 3$
22. (a) $2 - \sqrt{3} < x < 2 + \sqrt{3}$ (b) $\frac{3}{2} - \frac{\sqrt{13}}{2} \leqslant x \leqslant \frac{3}{2} + \frac{\sqrt{13}}{2}$ (c) $\frac{5}{2} - \frac{\sqrt{17}}{2} < x < \frac{5}{2} + \frac{\sqrt{17}}{2}$
23. $x = 2$ and $x = 4$, $\{x : 2 \leqslant x \leqslant 4\}$ 24. $x = 3$ and $x = {}^-4$, $\{x : x < {}^-4\} \cup \{x : x > 3\}$
25. (a) $\{x : x < 2\} \cup \{x : x > 3\}$ (b) $\{x : {}^-1 < x < 4\}$ (c) $\{x : 3 \leqslant x \leqslant 4\}$

page 326

26. $\{x : x < 2\} \cup \{x : x > 3\}$ 27. $\{x : 1 < x < 4\}$ 28. $\{x : {}^-2 < x < 3\}$
29. $\{x : x < {}^-4\} \cup \{x : x < {}^-3\}$
30. (a) $x > 2$ (b) $x > 5$ (c) $x > 5$ (d) $x < 2$ (e) $x < 5$; $\{x : x < 2\} \cup \{x : x > 5\}$
31. (a) $x > 3$ (b) $x < 4$ (c) $3 < x < 4$ (d) $x < 3$ (e) $x > 4$ (f) None; $\{x : 3 < x < 4\}$
32. $\{x : x < {}^-3\} \cup \{x : x > 4\}$ 33. $\{x : {}^-4 < x < {}^-5\}$
34. (a) When $x > 5$ (b) When $x < 3$ (c) $\{x : x < 3\} \cup \{x : x > 5\}$
35. (a) When ${}^-4 < x < 1$ (b) When $x < {}^-4$ or $x > 1$ (c) $\{x : {}^-4 < x < 1\}$
36. $\{x : x < {}^-2\} \cup \{x : x > 4\}$
37. $\{x : {}^-3 < x < 3\}$

38. (a) $\{x : x < 1\} \cup \{x : x > 6\}$ (b) $\{x : {}^-2 < x < 3\}$ (c) $\{x : {}^-5 < x < 4\}$ (d) $\{x : {}^-1 < x < 2\}$
(e) $\{x : x < 2\} \cup \{x : x > 3\}$ (f) $\{x : x < \frac{1}{2}\} \cup \{x : x > 4\}$ (g) $\{x : {}^-3 < x < \frac{1}{4}\}$
(h) $\{x : {}^-\frac{1}{2} < x < \frac{1}{5}\}$

3 Trigonometry 3

page 328 **Lengths and angles in 3-D shapes** (3.1)
1. Yes (a) $\sqrt{20}$ cm (b) 5 cm (c) $\sqrt{13}$ cm **2.** (a) Yes (b) Yes (c) Yes (d) Yes
3. (a) $\sqrt{41}$ cm (b) $\sqrt{29}$ cm (c) $\sqrt{41}$ cm (d) $\sqrt{29}$ cm **4.** (a) Yes (b) 5 cm (c) $\sqrt{29}$ cm
5. (a) Yes (b) $\sqrt{29}$ cm **6.** (a) Yes (b) $\sqrt{13}$ cm **7.** (a) 5 cm, $\sqrt{29}$ cm (b) $\sqrt{13}$ cm, $\sqrt{17}$ cm
8. (a) 26.6° (b) 21.8° (c) 29.0° 33.7°, Yes
9. (a) $\sqrt{32}$ cm (b) $2\sqrt{2}$ cm (c) $\sqrt{17}$ cm (d) 2 cm (e) $\sqrt{21}$ cm, 64.1°
(f) VN is common to $\triangle$VAN and $\triangle$VMN, but MN $\neq$ AN
10. (a) (i) 90° (ii) 36.9° (iii) 27.9° (iv) 36.9° (v) 56.3° (b) 48.0°
page 330
11. (a) Yes (b) Yes (c) Yes (d) Yes (e) $4\sqrt{5}$ cm, $2\sqrt{5}$ cm, 4 cm (f) 4 cm, 45°
(g) 2 cm, 63.4°; VN is common to $\triangle$VXN and $\triangle$VYN, but NX $\neq$ NY
12. (a) 64.1° (b) PB̂C (part (a)) **13.** 24.4 m **14.** (a) XB tan 65° (b) XB tan 70° (c) 2.30 m
15. 16.7 m **16.** (a) 31.51 m (b) 91.1 m

page 331 **Vectors and the real world** (3.2)
1. 20 km/h **2.** $v_b - v_a = 80 - {}^-60 = 140$ km/h **3.** (a) 550 km/h (b) 650 km/h
4. A bearing of 265.2°. The bearing would be 274.8° **5.** 602.1 km/h, bearing 265.2°
6. (a) 608.3 km/h, bearing 260.5° (b) 602.1 km/h, bearing 274.8° (c) 608.3 km/h, bearing 279.5°
(d) 636.3 km/h, bearing 266.8°
7. 130 km/h, bearing 337.4°; 150 km/h, bearing 323.1° **8.** 608.3 km/h, bearing 054.5°
page 332
9. 1 hour 38 minutes 38 seconds
10. (b) 10 km/h at an angle of 36.9° downstream to the original direction
11. $2\sqrt{7}$ km/h at 90° to either bank
12. Velocity would be 5.67 km/h at an angle of 3.5° downstream to the direction in Q11
13. (a) 27.2 seconds (b) 25.5 seconds **14.** 7.43 km, bearing 061.6°
15. (b) 001.5° (12.165 km)

page 333 **Earth distances** (3.3)
2. (a) Latitude (b) Longitude (c) Longitude (d) Latitude (e) Longitude (f) Latitude
(g) Latitude (h) Longitude
4. (a) New Orleans (b) Toronto (c) Hamilton
5. (a) Australia (b) Great Britain (c) Spain (d) Cuba **7.** (a) 180°W (b) 90°N
8. (a) Yes (b) Yes (c) Cut the sphere in half
(d) Same as the radius of the sphere. Its centre is at the centre of the sphere.
page 334
9. (a) Yes, the Equator is
10. (a) It comes to rest on the surface of the sphere (b) On the vertical axis of the sphere (c) No
11. It was exactly half submerged **12.** (a) At the North Pole (b) White
13. (a) 40 200 km (b) 10 050 km **14.** (a) 5585 km (b) 559 km (c) 5362 km
15. (a) 9556 km (b) 3333 km (c) 2222 km (d) 5000 km **16.** 43°N **17.** (0°N, 140°E)
18. 57°S
page 336
19. (a) 2374 km (b) 5221 km **20.** (a) 10 053 km (b) 6702 km

21. (a) 5178 km (b) 1717 km **22.** (a) 11 705 km (b) 12 238 km (c) 7036 km
23. (a) 111.7 km, 55.85 km (c) 30 nautical miles **24.** (a) 36 682 km (b) 1778 km (c) 6667 km
25. (a) 2234 km, 3491 km (b) Yes, the shorter one is **26.** (a) 1117 km (b) 1935 km (c) 2234 km
27. 3567 km **28.** 221 168 km **29.** 129.8°W **30.** 51.4°W
31. (a) (29°N, 25°E), (29°N, 35.2°E) (b) 6825 km

page 337 **Sines, cosines and tangents in surd form** (3.4)
1. (a) Yes (b) 45° **2.** (a) 1 (b) $\frac{\sqrt{2}}{2}$ (c) $\frac{\sqrt{2}}{2}$ **3.** (a) $\sqrt{2}$ cm (b) 45°, 45°
4. (a) 1 (b) $\frac{\sqrt{2}}{2}, \frac{\sqrt{2}}{2}$ **5.** $\frac{2}{4} + \frac{2}{4} = 1$ **6.** 1, yes
7. (a) The triangle is equilateral and $A\hat{B}C$ is bisected.
8. (a) $\frac{1}{2}$ (b) $\frac{\sqrt{3}}{2}$ (c) $\sqrt{3}$ (d) $\frac{1}{2}$ (e) $\frac{\sqrt{3}}{2}$ (f) $\frac{\sqrt{3}}{3}$ **10.** (a) $\frac{3}{4} + \frac{1}{4} = 1$ (b) $\frac{1}{4} + \frac{3}{4} = 1$
page 338
13. (a) $\dfrac{b}{c}, \dfrac{a}{c}, \dfrac{b}{a}$ **15.** (a) $\frac{4}{5}$ (b) $\frac{3}{4}$ **16.** (a) $\frac{\sqrt{3}}{2}$ (b) $\frac{-1}{2}$ (c) $\frac{-\sqrt{3}}{3}$ **17.** (a) $\frac{2\sqrt{5}}{5}$ (b) $\frac{\sqrt{5}}{5}$

4 Vectors and matrices 2

page 340 **The inverse of a matrix** (4.1)
1. $\begin{pmatrix} 1 & 0 \\ 0 & 1 \end{pmatrix}, \begin{pmatrix} 3 & -4 \\ -5 & 7 \end{pmatrix}$ **2.** (a) $\begin{pmatrix} 1 & 0 \\ 0 & 1 \end{pmatrix}$ (b) $\begin{pmatrix} 5 & 7 \\ 2 & 3 \end{pmatrix}$ (c) $\begin{pmatrix} 3 & -7 \\ -2 & 5 \end{pmatrix}$

3. (a) $\begin{pmatrix} 1 & 0 \\ 0 & 1 \end{pmatrix}$ (b) $\begin{pmatrix} 1 & -3 \\ -2 & 7 \end{pmatrix}$ (c) $\begin{pmatrix} 7 & 3 \\ 2 & 1 \end{pmatrix}$ **4.** (a), (b), (c) and (d) $\begin{pmatrix} 1 & 0 \\ 0 & 1 \end{pmatrix}$

5. $\begin{pmatrix} 3 & -11 \\ -1 & 4 \end{pmatrix}$

page 341
6. (a) $\begin{pmatrix} 2 & 0 \\ 0 & 2 \end{pmatrix}$ (b) $\begin{pmatrix} 2 & 0 \\ 0 & 2 \end{pmatrix}$ (c) No (d) $\begin{pmatrix} 1 & 0 \\ 0 & 1 \end{pmatrix}$, yes (e) $\mathbf{C} = \frac{1}{2}\mathbf{B}$ (f) $\frac{1}{2}\begin{pmatrix} 3 & 2 \\ 5 & 4 \end{pmatrix}$
7. No, yes **8.** $4 \times 2 - 5 \times 1 = 3, 1 \times 8 - {}^-2 \times 3 = 14, {}^-3 \times 1 - {}^-2 \times 1 = {}^-1$
9. (a) 3 (b) 16 (c) $^-1$ (d) 0 (e) $^-1$ (f) 1 **10.** (a) 3 (b) $2\frac{1}{2}$ (c) 2 (d) 0
11. (a) ± 4 (b) ± 5 (c) ± 10 **12.** (a) ± 5 (b) ± 6 (c) ± 8
13. (a) $\begin{pmatrix} 3 & -2 \\ -1 & 1 \end{pmatrix}$ (b) $\begin{pmatrix} 3 & -1 \\ -5 & 2 \end{pmatrix}$ (c) $\frac{1}{10}\begin{pmatrix} 5 & -1 \\ -10 & 4 \end{pmatrix}$ (d) $\frac{1}{2}\begin{pmatrix} 2 & -3 \\ -4 & 7 \end{pmatrix}$ (e) $\frac{1}{3}\begin{pmatrix} 2 & -3 \\ -5 & 9 \end{pmatrix}$

(f) $\frac{1}{10}\begin{pmatrix} 3 & -2 \\ -4 & 6 \end{pmatrix}$

14. (a) $\begin{pmatrix} -4 & 3 \\ 3 & -2 \end{pmatrix}$ (b) $2\begin{pmatrix} -2 & 8 \\ 1 & -3 \end{pmatrix}$ (c) $\frac{1}{5}\begin{pmatrix} -5 & 5 \\ 2 & -1 \end{pmatrix}$ (d) $\frac{1}{20}\begin{pmatrix} 3 & 2 \\ 4 & -4 \end{pmatrix}$ (e) $\frac{1}{4}\begin{pmatrix} 0 & 1 \\ 4 & 1 \end{pmatrix}$ (f) $\frac{1}{2}\begin{pmatrix} 1 & 0 \\ 1 & -2 \end{pmatrix}$
15. Yes

16. (a) 0 (b) $\begin{pmatrix} 0 & 0 \\ 0 & 0 \end{pmatrix}$

page 342

17. (a) Singular (b) Singular (c) $\frac{1}{2}\begin{pmatrix} 1 & -1 \\ 1 & 1 \end{pmatrix}$

18. (a) $\begin{pmatrix} 3 & -7 \\ -2 & 5 \end{pmatrix}$ (b) $\frac{1}{2}\begin{pmatrix} 3 & -2 \\ -5 & 4 \end{pmatrix}$ (c) $\begin{pmatrix} 4 & 3 \\ 3 & -2 \end{pmatrix}$ (d) Impossible (e) $\frac{1}{2}\begin{pmatrix} 0 & -1 \\ -2 & -2 \end{pmatrix}$ (f) $\frac{1}{36}\begin{pmatrix} 6 & 9 \\ 2 & -3 \end{pmatrix}$
19. $\begin{pmatrix} 4 & 0 \\ 0 & 4 \end{pmatrix}, \frac{1}{4}\begin{pmatrix} 8 & -9 \\ 4 & -5 \end{pmatrix}, \frac{1}{4}\begin{pmatrix} 5 & -9 \\ 4 & -8 \end{pmatrix}$

20. $\begin{pmatrix} -1 & 0 \\ 0 & -1 \end{pmatrix}, \begin{pmatrix} -1 & 2 \\ 3 & -5 \end{pmatrix}$

21. (a) $\frac{1}{2}\begin{pmatrix} 8 & 1 \\ -2 & 0 \end{pmatrix}$, $\begin{pmatrix} -1 & 3 \\ -2 & 5 \end{pmatrix}$ (b) (i) $\begin{pmatrix} -2 & 1 \\ 26 & -14 \end{pmatrix}$ (ii) $\frac{1}{2}\begin{pmatrix} -14 & -1 \\ -26 & -2 \end{pmatrix}$ (iii) $\frac{1}{2}\begin{pmatrix} -14 & -1 \\ -26 & -2 \end{pmatrix}$

(c) $\mathbf{B}^{-1}\mathbf{A}^{-1} = (\mathbf{AB})^{-1}$

22. (a) $\frac{1}{2}\begin{pmatrix} -5 & 4 \\ 3 & -2 \end{pmatrix}$, $\frac{1}{3}\begin{pmatrix} 3 & 0 \\ -7 & 1 \end{pmatrix}$, (b) (i) $\begin{pmatrix} 30 & 12 \\ 38 & 15 \end{pmatrix}$ (ii) $\frac{1}{6}\begin{pmatrix} -43 & 4 \\ 23 & 2 \end{pmatrix}$ (iii) $\frac{1}{6}\begin{pmatrix} -15 & 12 \\ 38 & -30 \end{pmatrix}$

(c) $\frac{1}{6}\begin{pmatrix} -15 & 12 \\ 38 & -30 \end{pmatrix}$ (d) (ii)

23. $\begin{pmatrix} 1 & 0 \\ 0 & 1 \end{pmatrix}$, $\begin{pmatrix} 4 & -5 \\ 3 & -4 \end{pmatrix}$ (a) $\begin{pmatrix} 1 & 0 \\ 0 & 1 \end{pmatrix}$ (b) $\begin{pmatrix} 4 & -5 \\ 3 & -4 \end{pmatrix}$

24. $\begin{pmatrix} 4 & 0 \\ 0 & 4 \end{pmatrix}$, $\frac{1}{4}\begin{pmatrix} -2 & 0 \\ 4 & 2 \end{pmatrix}$; $\begin{pmatrix} 16 & 0 \\ 0 & 16 \end{pmatrix}$, $\begin{pmatrix} -32 & 0 \\ 64 & 32 \end{pmatrix}$

25. $\begin{pmatrix} 5 & -8 \\ 3 & -5 \end{pmatrix}$ (a) $\begin{pmatrix} 1 & 0 \\ 0 & 1 \end{pmatrix}$ (b) $\begin{pmatrix} 5 & -8 \\ 3 & -5 \end{pmatrix}$ (c) $\begin{pmatrix} 5 & -8 \\ 3 & -5 \end{pmatrix}$

26. $\frac{1}{4}\begin{pmatrix} -6 & 8 \\ -4 & 6 \end{pmatrix}$ (a) $\begin{pmatrix} 4 & 0 \\ 0 & 4 \end{pmatrix}$ (b) $\begin{pmatrix} -24 & 32 \\ -16 & 24 \end{pmatrix}$ (c) $\begin{pmatrix} 64 & 0 \\ 0 & 64 \end{pmatrix}$

27. (a) $\begin{pmatrix} 1 & 0 \\ 0 & 1 \end{pmatrix}$ (b) $\begin{pmatrix} k & 1-k \\ 1+k & k \end{pmatrix}$ (c) $\begin{pmatrix} k & 1-k \\ 1+k & k \end{pmatrix}$

28. $\begin{pmatrix} -1 & 0 \\ 0 & -1 \end{pmatrix}$, $\begin{pmatrix} 0 & 1 \\ -1 & 0 \end{pmatrix}$, $\begin{pmatrix} 1 & 0 \\ 0 & 1 \end{pmatrix}$, $\begin{pmatrix} -1 & 0 \\ 0 & -1 \end{pmatrix}$, $\begin{pmatrix} 0 & -1 \\ 1 & 0 \end{pmatrix}$, $\begin{pmatrix} 1 & 0 \\ 0 & 1 \end{pmatrix}$

29. (a) 1 (b) $\begin{pmatrix} \frac{1}{2} & \frac{\sqrt{3}}{2} \\ -\frac{\sqrt{3}}{2} & \frac{1}{2} \end{pmatrix}$ (c) $\begin{pmatrix} -\frac{1}{2} & -\frac{\sqrt{3}}{2} \\ \frac{\sqrt{3}}{2} & -\frac{1}{2} \end{pmatrix}$ (d) $\begin{pmatrix} -1 & 0 \\ 0 & -1 \end{pmatrix}$ (e) $\begin{pmatrix} 1 & 0 \\ 0 & 1 \end{pmatrix}$, 6

30. $k = 0, {}^-1$ or 1

31. (a) $\begin{pmatrix} 31 & 18 \\ 30 & 19 \end{pmatrix}$ (b) $\begin{pmatrix} 0 & 0 \\ 0 & 0 \end{pmatrix}$

32. (a) $\begin{pmatrix} -1 & 8 \\ -4 & 7 \end{pmatrix}$ (c) $\begin{pmatrix} -9 & 22 \\ -11 & 13 \end{pmatrix}$

33. $\begin{pmatrix} 4 & 0 \\ 0 & 4 \end{pmatrix}$, $\begin{pmatrix} 0 & 8 \\ 8 & 0 \end{pmatrix}$, $\begin{pmatrix} 16 & 0 \\ 0 & 16 \end{pmatrix}$ (a) $\begin{pmatrix} 0 & 32 \\ 32 & 0 \end{pmatrix}$ (b) $\begin{pmatrix} 64 & 0 \\ 0 & 64 \end{pmatrix}$

34. (a) $\begin{pmatrix} -1 & 0 \\ 0 & -1 \end{pmatrix}$, $\begin{pmatrix} -1 & 0 \\ 0 & -1 \end{pmatrix}$ (b) $\begin{pmatrix} 1 & 0 \\ 0 & 1 \end{pmatrix}$, $\begin{pmatrix} 1 & 0 \\ 0 & 1 \end{pmatrix}$, $\begin{pmatrix} 1 & 0 \\ 0 & 1 \end{pmatrix}$

(c)

$\times$	**X**	**Y**	**R**
X	$\begin{pmatrix} 1 & 0 \\ 0 & 1 \end{pmatrix}$	$\begin{pmatrix} -1 & 0 \\ 0 & -1 \end{pmatrix}$	$\begin{pmatrix} 0 & -1 \\ -1 & 0 \end{pmatrix}$
Y	$\begin{pmatrix} -1 & 0 \\ 0 & -1 \end{pmatrix}$	$\begin{pmatrix} 1 & 0 \\ 0 & 1 \end{pmatrix}$	$\begin{pmatrix} 0 & 1 \\ 1 & 0 \end{pmatrix}$
R	$\begin{pmatrix} 0 & -1 \\ -1 & 0 \end{pmatrix}$	$\begin{pmatrix} 0 & 1 \\ 1 & 0 \end{pmatrix}$	$\begin{pmatrix} 1 & 0 \\ 0 & 1 \end{pmatrix}$

page 343 **Simultaneous equations** (4.2)

1. (a) $\begin{pmatrix} 2x + y \\ 5x + 3y \end{pmatrix}$ (b) $\begin{pmatrix} 4x + y \\ 7x - 2y \end{pmatrix}$

2. (a) $\begin{pmatrix} 5x - y \\ 2x + y \end{pmatrix} = \begin{pmatrix} 5 & -1 \\ 2 & 1 \end{pmatrix}\begin{pmatrix} x \\ y \end{pmatrix}$ (b) $\begin{pmatrix} 2x + 0y \\ 3x - y \end{pmatrix} = \begin{pmatrix} 2 & 0 \\ 3 & -1 \end{pmatrix}\begin{pmatrix} x \\ y \end{pmatrix}$

3. (a) 5 (b) 3 **4.** (a) 10 (b) 4 **5.** $\begin{pmatrix} 4 & 3 \\ -7 & -2 \end{pmatrix}\begin{pmatrix} x \\ y \end{pmatrix} = \begin{pmatrix} 7 \\ -9 \end{pmatrix}$

6. $2x + y = 4, 3x - y = 7$ **7.** $3x = 3, 4y = 8; x = 1, y = 2$ **8.** $4y = 4, 2x = 2; x = 1, y = 1$

9. $x = 2, y = 1$ **10.** $x = 1, y = 3$ **11.** $2x + y = 7, x + y = 3; x = 4, y = 7$

12. $\begin{pmatrix} 2 & 1 \\ 5 & 3 \end{pmatrix}\begin{pmatrix} x \\ y \end{pmatrix} = \begin{pmatrix} 1 \\ 3 \end{pmatrix}; x = 0, y = 1$

13. (a) $(0, {}^-1)$ (b) $({}^-11, 5)$ (c) $(1, {}^-1)$ (d) $(3, 2)$

14. (a) $(2, 7)$ (b) $(3, 10)$ (c) $({}^-5, {}^-20)$ (d) $(1, 1)$

page 344
15. (a) $(^-9,20)$ (b) $(^-\frac{1}{5}, 1\frac{3}{5})$ (c) $(5,^-8)$ (d) $(^-\frac{1}{10}, ^-1\frac{7}{10})$
16. (a) $(\frac{1}{3}, \frac{1}{3})$ (b) $(\frac{7}{9}, 1\frac{4}{9})$ (c) $(\frac{4}{5}, \frac{2}{5})$ (d) $(^-3,5)$
17. (a) $(2,1)$ (b) $(\frac{18}{35}, \frac{11}{35})$ (c) $(^-1,^-2)$ (d) $(5,^-6)$
18. (a) $(4,^-1)$ (b) $(1\frac{1}{2}, \frac{1}{2})$ (c) $(^-3,2)$ (d) $(\frac{1}{4}, \frac{1}{3})$
19. $(^-4,5)$ **20.** $(1,^-1)$ (b) $(3,2)$ (c) $(7,8)$
21. (a) $(1,1)$ (b) $(5,3)$ (c) $(\frac{1}{3}, 1\frac{2}{3})$ (d) $(1\frac{3}{4}, 1\frac{1}{2})$
22. (a) $(2,^-1)$ (b) $(^-3,11)$ (c) $(0.2,0.2)$ (d) $(3,^-2)$
23. (a) $(\frac{1}{4},2)$ (b) $(\frac{1}{5}, \frac{1}{3})$ (c) $(0.1,^-0.3)$ (d) $(^-4,6)$
page 345
25. (a) It is singular   (b) The determinant is zero   (d) The graph lines are parallel
26. (b) $\begin{pmatrix} 1 & -2 \\ 2 & -4 \end{pmatrix}\begin{pmatrix} x \\ y \end{pmatrix} = \begin{pmatrix} 1 \\ -1 \end{pmatrix}$ (c) 0   (d) Yes

27. (i) (a) $\begin{pmatrix} 2 & -1 \\ 6 & -3 \end{pmatrix}\begin{pmatrix} x \\ y \end{pmatrix} = \begin{pmatrix} 5 \\ 10 \end{pmatrix}$ (b) 0   (c) Impossible   (ii) (a) $\begin{pmatrix} 1 & 1 \\ 1 & -1 \end{pmatrix}\begin{pmatrix} x \\ y \end{pmatrix} = \begin{pmatrix} 1 \\ 11 \end{pmatrix}$

   (b) $^-2$ (c) $x = 6, y = ^-5$ (iii) (a) $\begin{pmatrix} 7 & -7 \\ 1 & 2 \end{pmatrix}\begin{pmatrix} x \\ y \end{pmatrix} = \begin{pmatrix} 32 \\ 8 \end{pmatrix}$

   (b) 21   (c) $x = 5\frac{5}{7}, y = 1\frac{3}{21}$ (iv) (a) $\begin{pmatrix} -2 & -6 \\ 3 & 9 \end{pmatrix}\begin{pmatrix} x \\ y \end{pmatrix} = \begin{pmatrix} 5 \\ 1 \end{pmatrix}$

   (b) 0   (c) Impossible
29. (a) The determinant is zero   (b) They are the same
30. They are the same   **31.** $1\frac{1}{2}$ **32.** 9

page 346   **Transformation matrices** (4.3)
 1. (a) Stretch (factor 2) parallel to y-axis, with x-axis invariant   (b) Reflection in the line $y = x$
   (c) Enlargement, scale factor 2, with centre of enlargement at (0,0)
 2. Rotation of 90° (clockwise) about (0,0)
 3. Shear with the x-axis invariant
 4. Yes, $\begin{pmatrix} 1 & 0 \\ 0 & 3 \end{pmatrix}$ **5.** $\begin{pmatrix} 2 & 0 \\ 0 & 3 \end{pmatrix}\begin{pmatrix} x \\ y \end{pmatrix} = \begin{pmatrix} 2x \\ 3y \end{pmatrix}$
 6. (a) (i) 1 square unit   (ii) 10 square units   (b) 10
   (c) The determinant is equal to the ratio of the image area to the object area
 7. (a) 2   (b) $^-2$ (c) The stretch is in the negative x-direction
 8. (a) 2   (b) $^-2$ (c) The stretch is in the negative y-direction.
 9. (a) Right-angled, but not isosceles.   (b) Right-angled, but not isosceles
   (c) Right-angled and isosceles
page 347
11. Yes, $\frac{1}{3}$ **12.** $(0,^-8)$, $(^-12,4),(4,4)$. The image is transformed back to the object.
13. (a) $^-2$ (b) $^-\frac{1}{2}$ (c) $\begin{pmatrix} -2 & 0 \\ 0 & -2 \end{pmatrix}, \begin{pmatrix} -\frac{1}{2} & 0 \\ 0 & -\frac{1}{2} \end{pmatrix}$

page 348
14. (a) $(2,0), (4,^-2), (3,^-3)$ (b) Yes, in the x-axis.
   (c) Evaluate the product $\begin{pmatrix} 1 & 0 \\ 0 & -1 \end{pmatrix}\begin{pmatrix} x \\ y \end{pmatrix}$

15. (a) $\begin{pmatrix} -1 & 0 \\ 0 & 1 \end{pmatrix}$ (c) It is transformed back to the object

16. (c) $y = x$ (d) $\begin{pmatrix} 0 & 1 \\ 1 & 0 \end{pmatrix}$

17. (a) $(x,y) \rightarrow (^-y, ^-x)$ (b) $\begin{pmatrix} 0 & -1 \\ -1 & 0 \end{pmatrix}$

18. (a) $(0,0), (^-2,1), (1,2), (2,4)$ (b) $(k,2k), y = 2x$

19. (a) $(0,0), (2,4), (^-4,2), (^-1,3)$ (c) $y = -3x$

20. (b) $y = 3x$ (c) $\begin{pmatrix} -0.8 & 0.6 \\ 0.6 & 0.8 \end{pmatrix}$

page 349

21. $\begin{pmatrix} -1 & 0 \\ 0 & -1 \end{pmatrix}$ **22.** A rotation of 270° about $(0,0)$

23. $(0,0), (^-3.2,2.4), (4,3), (0,5); 53°$

24. $\begin{pmatrix} ^-\cos\theta \\ ^-\sin\theta \end{pmatrix}$

26. $\frac{1}{2}\begin{pmatrix} \sqrt{3} & -1 \\ 1 & \sqrt{3} \end{pmatrix}$

27. (b) $\begin{pmatrix} 0.8 & -0.6 \\ 0.6 & 0.8 \end{pmatrix}$ (c) $(0,0), (^-0.4,2.2), (0.4,2.8)$

28. (a) $\begin{pmatrix} -0.96 & -0.28 \\ 0.28 & -0.96 \end{pmatrix}$ (b) $(^-12.4,^-6.8),(^-2.8,^-9.6)$ (d) No   (e) 164°

page 350

29. $x = 0, y = 0$

30. (a) $(0,0), (3,1), (4,1), (1,0)$ (b) $(0,0), (^-1,1), (0,1), (1,0)$ (c) $(0,0), (0,1), (1,^-1), (1,^-2)$

31. (a) $y = 0$ (x-axis)   (b) $y = 0$ (x-axis)   (c) $x = 0$ (y-axis)

32. $\begin{pmatrix} 1 & 0 \\ 3 & 1 \end{pmatrix}$ **33.** $\begin{pmatrix} 1 & -2 \\ 0 & 0 \end{pmatrix}$ **34.** $\begin{pmatrix} 1 & 0 \\ 5 & 1 \end{pmatrix}$, yes

35. $(0,0), (3,6), (5,8), (2,2)$ yes, $y = x$

36. $(0,0), (0,2), (^-1,3), (^-1,1)$ Yes, $y = -x$ **37.** $y = x$

38. $(0,0), (2,^-6), (5,10), (3,16); (0,0)$ and $(5,10); y = 2x$ **39.** (b) and (c), (a) is a stretch

page 351   **Combining transformations** (4.4)

1. (a) $\begin{pmatrix} 2 & 0 \\ 0 & 2 \end{pmatrix}$ (b) $\begin{pmatrix} 3 & 0 \\ 0 & 3 \end{pmatrix}$ (c) $\begin{pmatrix} 6 & 0 \\ 0 & 6 \end{pmatrix}$ (d) $(6,6),(6,18),(12,18)$

2. (a) $\begin{pmatrix} 20 & 0 \\ 0 & 20 \end{pmatrix}$ (b) Yes   **3.** $\begin{pmatrix} -8 & 0 \\ 0 & -8 \end{pmatrix}$

4. $\begin{pmatrix} 2 & 0 \\ 0 & 2 \end{pmatrix}$ **5.** $\begin{pmatrix} -2 & 0 \\ 0 & -2 \end{pmatrix}, \begin{pmatrix} -1\frac{1}{2} & 0 \\ 0 & -1\frac{1}{2} \end{pmatrix}, \begin{pmatrix} 3 & 0 \\ 0 & 3 \end{pmatrix}$, yes

6. (a) $^-2$ and $\frac{1}{2}$ (b) Image is inverted   (c) Image is smaller than object by a factor of 2
  (d) $(1,\frac{1}{2}), (1\frac{1}{2},1)$ (e) $(^-2,^-1), (3,2)$
  (f) Not in size, because the image is inverted and is the same size as the object   (g) Yes

7. (a) $\begin{pmatrix} a & 0 \\ 0 & a \end{pmatrix}\begin{pmatrix} \frac{1}{a} & 0 \\ 0 & \frac{1}{a} \end{pmatrix}$ (b) $\begin{pmatrix} -1 & 0 \\ 0 & -1 \end{pmatrix}$

page 352

8. (a) A rotation of 90° about $(0,0)$ (b) $(\frac{1}{3})$, yes   (c) $\begin{pmatrix} ^-1 & 0 \\ 0 & 1 \end{pmatrix}$ (d) $\begin{pmatrix} 0 & ^-1 \\ 1 & 0 \end{pmatrix}$, yes   (e) $\begin{pmatrix} 0 & 1 \\ ^-1 & 0 \end{pmatrix}$, no

9. $\begin{pmatrix} ^-1 & 0 \\ 0 & ^-1 \end{pmatrix}$, a rotation of 180° about $(0,0)$

10. (a) A rotation of 180° about $(0,0)$ (b) Yes   (c) A reflection in $y = x$ (d) No

12. (b) A reflection in $y = -x$, $\begin{pmatrix} 0 & ^-1 \\ ^-1 & 0 \end{pmatrix}$ (c) **XR**   (d) $\begin{pmatrix} 0 & ^-1 \\ ^-1 & 0 \end{pmatrix}$

13. (a) Reflection in y-axis followed by a 180° rotation about $(0,0)$
  (b) Reflection in $y = x$ followed by a 270° rotation about $(0,0)$
  (c) Reflection in $y = -x$ followed by a 90° rotation about $(0,0)$

page 353

15. Rotation of 90° about $(1\frac{1}{2}, \frac{1}{2})$.   (b) Rotation of 90° about $(3,0)$

    (c) Enlargement, scale factor 2, centre of enlargement $(3, ^-2)$

16. (b) Rotation of 90° about $(0,0)$ (c) Reflection in the x-axis, reflection in the y-axis

17. (b) $(^-1, ^-2), (^-3, ^-2), (^-3, ^-3)$ (c) and (d) Rotation of 180° about $(0,0)$

18. (a) $\begin{pmatrix} 3 & 2 \\ 4 & 3 \end{pmatrix}$ (b) $(8,11), (14,19), (16,22)$ (c) It is the same

19. (a) $(2,2), (2,6), (4,6), (4,2)$ (b) 8   (c) 16

20. (a) $(0,0), (3.6, 2.4), (1.2, 6.0), (^-2.4, 3.6)$ (b) 4.33 units, 33.7°   (c) 18.72 square units, 6.12 units

21. (a) $(^-2, ^-3)$ (b) $(^-2, 3)$ (c) $(^-3, 2)$ (d) $(3, ^-2)$ (e) $(^-2, ^-3)$ (f) $(3, ^-2)$ (g) $(3, ^-2)$

22. (a) $\begin{pmatrix} 0 & 1 \\ 1 & 0 \end{pmatrix}$ (b) $\begin{pmatrix} ^-1 & 0 \\ 0 & 1 \end{pmatrix}$ (c) $\begin{pmatrix} 0 & 1 \\ ^-1 & 0 \end{pmatrix}$, 270° rotation about $(0,0)$

    (d) $\begin{pmatrix} 0 & ^-1 \\ 1 & 0 \end{pmatrix}$, 90° rotation about the origin

23. (a) $\frac{3}{4}$ square units   (c) 18.4°

page 356   **Practice Paper A**

1. (b)   **2.** (c)   **3.** (b)   **4.** (b)   **5.** (a)   **6.** (c)   **7.** (a)   **8.** (a)   **9.** (c)   **10.** (b)   **11.** (a)

12. (c)   **13.** (c)   **14.** (c)   **15.** (c)   **16.** (c)   **17.** (b)   **18.** (d)   **19.** (b) **20.** (b)   **21.** (b)   **22.** (c)

23. (a)   **24.** (c)   **25.** (b)   **26.** (b)   **27.** (d)   **28.** (d)   **29.** (a)   **30.** (d)   **31.** (c)

32. (c)   **33.** (d)   **34.** (b)   **35.** (c)   **36.** (a)   **37.** (b)   **38.** (d)   **39.** (a)   **40.** (c)   **41.** (c)

42. (b)   **43.** (b)   **44.** (a)   **45.** (b)   **46.** (d)   **47.** (b)   **48.** (c)   **49.** (d)   **50.** (b)   **51.** (b)

52. (a)   **53.** (b)   **54.** (b)   **55.** (b)   **56.** (a)   **57.** (a)   **58.** (b)   **59.** (d)   **60.** (b)

page 359   **Practice Paper B**

1. (c)   **2.** (c)   **3.** (b)   **4.** (c)   **5.** (a)   **6.** (c)   **7.** (b)   **8.** (d)   **9.** (c)   **10.** (c)   **11.** (a)

12. (b)   **13.** (b)   **14.** (d)   **15.** (b)   **16.** (c)   **17.** (a)   **18.** (d)   **19.** (d)   **20.** (c)   **21.** (d)

22. (c)   **23.** (c)   **24.** (d)   **25.** (d)   **26.** (b)   **27.** (b)   **28.** (d)   **29.** (b)   **30.** (b)   **31.** (c)

32. (b)   **33.** (b)   **34.** (b)   **35.** (c)   **36.** (d)   **37.** (d)   **38.** (a)   **39.** (b)   **40.** (c)   **41.** (d)

42. (a)   **43.** (b)   **44.** (c)   **45.** (b)   **46.** (c)   **47.** (b)   **48.** (c)   **49.** (a)   **50.** (d)   **51.** (a)

52. (c)   **53.** (d)   **54.** (d)   **55.** (c)   **56.** (b)   **57.** (b)   **58.** (c)   **59.** (a)   **60.** (b)

page 363   **Practice Paper 1**

1. (a) 8   (b) $\{a,b,c\}, \{a,b\}, \{a,c\}, \{b,c\}, \{a\}, \{b\}, \{c\}, \{\ \}$

2. (a) 60 m by 30 m   (b) $T^2 = \dfrac{5\pi^2 l}{g}$, 10.82   **3.** (a) (i) 366   (ii) $\frac{5}{8}$ (b) \$24 720, \$32 902

4. (a) $\frac{3}{5}$ (c) $\dfrac{1-x}{1+x}$

5. 5.58 cm, 13.96 cm   **6.** (b) 58.5 kg, 5 kg   (c) $\frac{19}{100}$

7. (a) $y = -\frac{3}{5}x + \frac{11}{5}$ (b) $(1\frac{2}{3}, 0)$ **8.** 4.62 cm   **9.** 1 part "Feed 1" to 3 parts "Feed 2".

10. (a) 68.5°N, 38°E   (b) 56°N, 15.6°E

11. (a) $(0,0), (\frac{-\sqrt{3}}{2}, \frac{1}{2}), (\frac{1}{2}, \frac{\sqrt{3}}{2}), (\frac{1}{2} - \frac{\sqrt{3}}{2}, \frac{\sqrt{3}}{2} + \frac{1}{2})$ (b) $(0,0), (^-1,0), (^-1, ^-1), (0, ^-1)$ (c) 6

12. (a) 3.3 cm   (b) 72 cm³   **13.** (a) $a = 3, b = ^-1, c = ^-1$ (c) 1.58 or 0.42

14. (a) $a = 4, b = 6$ (b) $\frac{1}{2}\begin{pmatrix} 2 & ^-1 \\ 4 & ^-3 \end{pmatrix}; x = ^-1, y = ^-5$

page 364   **Practice Paper 2**

1. (a) 0.256   (b) \$200   **2.** (a) 45.48   (b) 20.1   **3.** (a) 1.77 cm   (b) 704 cm³

4. (a) 0.66 or $^-1.52$ (b) $V = \dfrac{RD - C}{R - 1}$

5. (a) (i) $\frac{1}{221}$ (ii) $\frac{1}{17}$ (iii) $\frac{1}{1326}$ (b) \$955.08

6. (a) 5.144 cm   (b) 48.6°   **7.** (a) $2\frac{1}{5}$ (b) $\dfrac{x - 3}{2 - x}$ (c) Not defined

8. (b) 9 m/s   (c) 35 m   **9.** $-2(x - \frac{5}{2})^2 + 9\frac{1}{8}$ (c) $9\frac{1}{8}$ **10.** (a) 20 106 km   11 705 km
11. At an angle of 60° with the bank in an upstream direction. 8 min 40 s
12. (b) $\frac{1}{84}$ $\begin{pmatrix} -4 & 20 \\ 7 & -14 \end{pmatrix}$ (c) $x = 2, y = {}^-1$
13. (a) (i) $\mathbf{b} - \mathbf{a}$ (ii) $\mathbf{a} + \mathbf{b}$ (b) (i) $(3,0), ({}^-3,3), ({}^-6,3)$
     (iii) A shear with x-axis as invariant line. (The shear is in the negative x-direction)

page 366   **Practice Paper 3**
1. (a) 240   (b) 11   **2.** (a) $x = 11, y = 7$ (b) $-\frac{1}{4} \pm \frac{\sqrt{41}}{4}$ (c) $\{x : x > {}^-3\}$
3. (a) 6.123 cm   **4.** (a) 152.9 cm   (b) 47.5%   (c) $\frac{13}{40}$
5. (a) 43.0 cm^2 (b) $\frac{1}{3}$ of the height of the cone   **6.** (a) $16 200   (b) $1200 or 7.4%
7. (a) 7   (b) $^-11$ (c) 1   (d) $\frac{1}{2}(x - 3)$ (e) $\frac{1}{2}(3 - x)$ (f) $^-1\frac{1}{4}$ **8.** 8 of X and 7 of Y
9. (b) A minimum value   (c) $^-3\frac{1}{4}, x = 1\frac{1}{2}$ **10.** 10°N, 95.1°W   **11.** 86.60 m, 166.1 m
12. (a) $(0, {}^-1), (1, {}^-2), (1, {}^-3); ({}^-3, {}^-1), ({}^-5, {}^-2), ({}^-8, {}^-3)$ (b) $\begin{pmatrix} -3 & 1 \\ -1 & 0 \end{pmatrix}, \begin{pmatrix} 0 & -1 \\ 1 & -3 \end{pmatrix}$
13. (a) Reflection in x-axis   (b) 90° rotation about the origin   (b) (i) $\begin{pmatrix} 0 & -1 \\ -1 & 0 \end{pmatrix}$ (ii) $\begin{pmatrix} 0 & 1 \\ 1 & 0 \end{pmatrix}$
     (c) Reflection in $y = -x$, reflection in $y = x$

page 367   **Practice Paper 4**
1. 19%   **2.** (b) Some dogs do not have long teeth.   **3.** (b) $x = 6$ **4.** (a) 3.22   (b) 2.08
5. (a) $p = 1\frac{1}{7}$ (b) 14 cm and 10 cm   **6.** (a) 20 m, 3600 m^2 (b) 200 000 mm^3
7. (a) $1\frac{1}{2}$ (b) (i) $\frac{1}{9}$ (ii) x^2 (c) 2   **8.** 5.196 cm, 3 cm   **9.** (b) 23 m/s   **10.** $\frac{1}{12}, 1\frac{23}{24}$
11. (c) $\frac{\sqrt{3}}{3}$ **12.** (c) 179.8°W   **13.** (a) $(0,0), ({}^-1,0), (0,{}^-2)$ (b) $\begin{pmatrix} 0 & -1 \\ -1 & 0 \end{pmatrix}$
14. (a) $x = 2, y = 0$
     (b) $\begin{pmatrix} 1 & 0 \\ 0 & 1 \end{pmatrix}$ (i) $\begin{pmatrix} 1 & 0 \\ 0 & 1 \end{pmatrix}, \begin{pmatrix} 1 & -3 \\ 0 & -1 \end{pmatrix}$

page 369   **Practice Paper 5**

1. (a) 8.59 m/s   (b) 200   **2.** (a) 0.0576   (b) $h = \dfrac{V}{d^2}$ (c) $1\frac{1}{2}$ (d) $\{x : 1 < x < 3\}$

3. (a) $\frac{1}{8}$ (b) $\frac{1}{8}$ **5.** (a) $\begin{pmatrix} -3 \\ -1 \end{pmatrix}, \begin{pmatrix} 2 \\ 7 \end{pmatrix}$ (b) $2(\mathbf{b} - \mathbf{a}), \mathbf{b} - 2\mathbf{a}$
6. (a) $y = \frac{3}{5}x + \frac{11}{5}$ (b) $y = -\frac{5}{3}x + 9$ (c) $2\sqrt{17}$ units
7. (b) 7.52   (c) 7   **8.** 6 drinks and 12 cakes
9. (a) $\{x : x < {}^-1 \text{ or } x > 1\frac{1}{2}\}$ (b) $\{x : x \leqslant {}^-2 \text{ or } x \geqslant 2\}$ **10.** (a) 2 radians   (b) 36 cm^2 (c) 2.14 to 1
11. (a) 13 cm   (b) 49.5°   (c) 7.6 cm
12. (b) A rotation of 90° about $(\frac{1}{2}, \frac{1}{2})$ (c) A rotation of 270° about $(\frac{1}{2}, \frac{1}{2})$
13. (a) 3   (b) $\frac{1}{4}\begin{pmatrix} -4 & -6 \\ -2 & 0 \end{pmatrix}, x = {}^-2\frac{1}{2}, y = 2$

page 370   **Practice Paper 6**
1. (b) Intelligent people who are not mathematicians
2. (a) ± 3 (b) $^-5$ (c) 8   (d) $\frac{1}{2}(1 - x), {}^-\frac{3}{4}$
3. (a) (i) 27 : 1   (ii) 3 : 1   (b) (i) 201π cm   (ii) $10\,100.25\pi$ cm^2
4. (a) 20.57 cm^2 (b) 1.77 cm^2 **5.** (a) 0.24 or $^-1.64$ (b) 12 years   **6.** (b) 21.5 minutes
7. (a) 81.8°   (b) $17 147.50   **8.** (b) $N = 5(2^{t/10})$ (c) 1.96 per second   **9.** $6\frac{9}{20}$ **10.** 76.2°
11. (a) 4.038 cm   (b) 57.5°   **12.** (b) Shear with x-axis as invariant line   (c) $\begin{pmatrix} 1 & -2 \\ 0 & 1 \end{pmatrix}$
13. (a) $\begin{pmatrix} 18 & 11 \\ -23 & -14 \end{pmatrix}$

TABLE OF SINES

Angle in degrees	.0	.1	.2	.3	.4	.5	.6	.7	.8	.9
0	0.000	.002	.003	.005	.007	.009	.010	.012	.014	.016
1	0.017	.019	.021	.023	.024	.026	.028	.030	.031	.033
2	0.035	.037	.038	.040	.042	.044	.045	.047	.049	.051
3	0.052	.054	.056	.058	.059	.061	.063	.065	.066	.068
4	0.070	.071	.073	.075	.077	.078	.080	.082	.084	.085
5	0.087	.089	.091	.092	.094	.096	.098	.099	.101	.103
6	0.105	.106	.108	.110	.111	.113	.115	.117	.118	.120
7	0.122	.124	.125	.127	.129	.131	.132	.134	.136	.137
8	0.139	.141	.143	.144	.146	.148	.150	.151	.153	.155
9	0.156	.158	.160	.162	.163	.165	.167	.168	.170	.172
10	0.174	.175	.177	.179	.181	.182	.184	.186	.187	.189
11	0.191	.193	.194	.196	.198	.199	.201	.203	.204	.206
12	0.208	.210	.211	.213	.215	.216	.218	.220	.222	.223
13	0.225	.227	.228	.230	.232	.233	.235	.237	.239	.240
14	0.242	.244	.245	.247	.249	.250	.252	.254	.255	.257
15	0.259	.261	.262	.264	.266	.267	.269	.271	.272	.274
16	0.276	.277	.279	.281	.282	.284	.286	.287	.289	.291
17	0.292	.294	.296	.297	.299	.301	.302	.304	.306	.307
18	0.309	.311	.312	.314	.316	.317	.319	.321	.322	.324
19	0.326	.327	.329	.331	.332	.334	.335	.337	.339	.340
20	0.342	.344	.345	.347	.349	.350	.352	.353	.355	.357
21	0.358	.360	.362	.363	.365	.367	.368	.370	.371	.373
22	0.375	.376	.378	.379	.381	.383	.384	.386	.388	.389
23	0.391	.392	.394	.396	.397	.399	.400	.402	.404	.405
24	0.407	.408	.410	.412	.413	.415	.416	.418	.419	.421
25	0.423	.424	.426	.427	.429	.431	.432	.434	.435	.437
26	0.438	.440	.442	.443	.445	.446	.448	.449	.451	.452
27	0.454	.456	.457	.459	.460	.462	.463	.465	.466	.468
28	0.469	.471	.473	.474	.476	.477	.479	.480	.482	.483
29	0.485	.486	.488	.489	.491	.492	.494	.495	.497	.498
30	0.500	.502	.503	.505	.506	.508	.509	.511	.512	.514
31	0.515	.517	.518	.520	.521	.522	.524	.525	.527	.528
32	0.530	.531	.533	.534	.536	.537	.539	.540	.542	.543
33	0.545	.546	.548	.549	.550	.552	.553	.555	.556	.558
34	0.559	.561	.562	.564	.565	.566	.568	.569	.571	.572
35	0.574	.575	.576	.578	.579	.581	.582	.584	.585	.586
36	0.588	.589	.591	.592	.593	.595	.596	.598	.599	.600
37	0.602	.603	.605	.606	.607	.609	.610	.612	.613	.614
38	0.616	.617	.618	.620	.621	.623	.624	.625	.627	.628
39	0.629	.631	.632	.633	.635	.636	.637	.639	.640	.641
40	0.643	.644	.645	.647	.648	.649	.651	.652	.653	.655
41	0.656	.657	.659	.660	.661	.663	.664	.665	.667	.668
42	0.669	.670	.672	.673	.674	.676	.677	.678	.679	.681
43	0.682	.683	.685	.686	.687	.688	.690	.691	.692	.693
44	0.695	.696	.697	.698	.700	.701	.702	.703	.705	.706
45	0.707	.708	.710	.711	.712	.713	.714	.716	.717	.718

TABLE OF SINES – *continued*

Angle in degrees	.0	.1	.2	.3	.4	.5	.6	.7	.8	.9
45	0.707	.708	.710	.711	.712	.713	.714	.716	.717	.718
46	0.719	.721	.722	.723	.724	.725	.727	.728	.729	.730
47	0.731	.733	.734	.735	.736	.737	.738	.740	.741	.742
48	0.743	.744	.745	.747	.748	.749	.750	.751	.752	.754
49	0.755	.756	.757	.758	.759	.760	.762	.763	.764	.765
50	0.766	.767	.768	.769	.771	.772	.773	.774	.775	.776
51	0.777	.778	.779	.780	.782	.783	.784	.785	.786	.787
52	0.788	.789	.790	.791	.792	.793	.794	.795	.797	.798
53	0.799	.800	.801	.802	.803	.804	.805	.806	.807	.808
54	0.809	.810	.811	.812	.813	.814	.815	.816	.817	.818
55	0.819	.820	.821	.822	.823	.824	.825	.826	.827	.828
56	0.829	.830	.831	.832	.833	.834	.835	.836	.837	.838
57	0.839	.840	.841	.842	.842	.843	.844	.845	.846	.847
58	0.848	.849	.850	.851	.852	.853	.854	.854	.855	.856
59	0.857	.858	.859	.860	.861	.862	.863	.863	.864	.865
60	0.866	.867	.868	.869	.869	.870	.871	.872	.873	.874
61	0.875	.875	.876	.877	.878	.879	.880	.880	.881	.882
62	0.883	.884	.885	.885	.886	.887	.888	.889	.889	.890
63	0.891	.892	.893	.893	.894	.895	.896	.896	.897	.898
64	0.899	.900	.900	.901	.902	.903	.903	.904	.905	.906
65	0.906	.907	.908	.909	.909	.910	.911	.911	.912	.913
66	0.914	.914	.915	.916	.916	.917	.918	.918	.919	.920
67	0.921	.921	.922	.923	.923	.924	.925	.925	.926	.927
68	0.927	.928	.928	.929	.930	.930	.931	.932	.932	.933
69	0.934	.934	.935	.935	.936	.937	.937	.938	.938	.939
70	0.940	.940	.941	.941	.942	.943	.943	.944	.944	.945
71	0.946	.946	.947	.947	.948	.948	.949	.949	.950	.951
72	0.951	.952	.952	.953	.953	.954	.954	.955	.955	.956
73	0.956	.957	.957	.958	.958	.959	.959	.960	.960	.961
74	0.961	.962	.962	.963	.963	.964	.964	.965	.965	.965
75	0.966	.966	.967	.967	.968	.968	.969	.969	.969	.970
76	0.970	.971	.971	.972	.972	.972	.973	.973	.974	.974
77	0.974	.975	.975	.976	.976	.976	.977	.977	.977	.978
78	0.978	.979	.979	.979	.980	.980	.980	.981	.981	.981
79	0.982	.982	.982	.983	.983	.983	.984	.984	.984	.985
80	0.985	.985	.985	.986	.986	.986	.987	.987	.987	.987
81	0.988	.988	.988	.988	.989	.989	.989	.990	.990	.990
82	0.990	.991	.991	.991	.991	.991	.992	.992	.992	.992
83	0.993	.993	.993	.993	.993	.994	.994	.994	.994	.994
84	0.995	.995	.995	.995	.995	.995	.996	.996	.996	.996
85	0.996	.996	.996	.997	.997	.997	.997	.997	.997	.997
86	0.998	.998	.998	.998	.998	.998	.998	.998	.998	.999
87	0.999	.999	.999	.999	.999	.999	.999	.999	.999	.999
88	0.999	.999	1.000	1.000	1.000	1.000	1.000	1.000	1.000	1.000
89	1.000	1.000	1.000	1.000	1.000	1.000	1.000	1.000	1.000	1.000
90	1.000									

TABLE OF COSINES

Angle in degrees	.0	.1	.2	.3	.4	.5	.6	.7	.8	.9
0	1.000	1.000	1.000	1.000	1.000	1.000	1.000	1.000	1.000	1.000
1	1.000	1.000	1.000	1.000	1.000	1.000	1.000	1.000	1.000	0.999
2	0.999	.999	.999	.999	.999	.999	.999	.999	.999	.999
3	0.999	.999	.998	.998	.998	.998	.998	.998	.998	.998
4	0.998	.997	.997	.997	.997	.997	.997	.997	.996	.996
5	0.996	.996	.996	.996	.996	.995	.995	.995	.995	.995
6	0.995	.994	.994	.994	.994	.994	.993	.993	.993	.993
7	0.993	.992	.992	.992	.992	.991	.991	.991	.991	.991
8	0.990	.990	.990	.990	.989	.989	.989	.988	.988	.988
9	0.988	.987	.987	.987	.987	.986	.986	.986	.985	.985
10	0.985	.985	.984	.984	.984	.983	.983	.983	.982	.982
11	0.982	.981	.981	.981	.980	.980	.980	.979	.979	.979
12	0.978	.978	.977	.977	.977	.976	.976	.976	.975	.975
13	0.974	.974	.974	.973	.973	.972	.972	.972	.971	.971
14	0.970	.970	.969	.969	.969	.968	.968	.967	.967	.966
15	0.966	.965	.965	.965	.964	.964	.963	.963	.962	.962
16	0.961	.961	.960	.960	.959	.959	.958	.958	.957	.957
17	0.956	.956	.955	.955	.954	.954	.953	.953	.952	.952
18	0.951	.951	.950	.949	.949	.948	.948	.947	.947	.946
19	0.946	.945	.944	.944	.943	.943	.942	.941	.941	.940
20	0.940	.939	.938	.938	.937	.937	.936	.935	.935	.934
21	0.934	.933	.932	.932	.931	.930	.930	.929	.928	.928
22	0.927	.927	.926	.925	.925	.924	.923	.923	.922	.921
23	0.921	.920	.919	.918	.918	.917	.916	.916	.915	.914
24	0.914	.913	.912	.911	.911	.910	.909	.909	.908	.907
25	0.906	.906	.905	.904	.903	.903	.902	.901	.900	.900
26	0.899	.898	.897	.896	.896	.895	.894	.893	.893	.892
27	0.891	.890	.889	.889	.888	.887	.886	.885	.885	.884
28	0.883	.882	.881	.880	.880	.879	.878	.877	.876	.875
29	0.875	.874	.873	.872	.871	.870	.869	.869	.868	.867
30	0.866	.865	.864	.863	.863	.862	.861	.860	.859	.858
31	0.857	.856	.855	.854	.854	.853	.852	.851	.850	.849
32	0.848	.847	.846	.845	.844	.843	.842	.842	.841	.840
33	0.839	.838	.837	.836	.835	.834	.833	.832	.831	.830
34	0.829	.828	.827	.826	.825	.824	.823	.822	.821	.820
35	0.819	.818	.817	.816	.815	.814	.813	.812	.811	.810
36	0.809	.808	.807	.806	.805	.804	.803	.802	.801	.800
37	0.799	.798	.797	.795	.794	.793	.792	.791	.790	.789
38	0.788	.787	.786	.785	.784	.783	.782	.780	.779	.778
39	0.777	.776	.775	.774	.773	.772	.771	.769	.768	.767
40	0.766	.765	.764	.763	.762	.760	.759	.758	.757	.756
41	0.755	.754	.752	.751	.750	.749	.748	.747	.745	.744
42	0.743	.742	.741	.740	.738	.737	.736	.735	.734	.733
43	0.731	.730	.729	.728	.727	.725	.724	.723	.722	.721
44	0.719	.718	.717	.716	.714	.713	.712	.711	.710	.708
45	0.707	.706	.705	.703	.702	.701	.700	.698	.697	.696

TABLE OF COSINES – *continued*

Angle in degrees	.0	.1	.2	.3	.4	.5	.6	.7	.8	.9
45	0.707	.706	.705	.703	.702	.701	.700	.698	.697	.696
46	0.695	.693	.692	.691	.690	.688	.687	.686	.685	.683
47	0.682	.681	.679	.678	.677	.676	.674	.673	.672	.670
48	0.669	.668	.667	.665	.664	.663	.661	.660	.659	.657
49	0.656	.655	.653	.652	.651	.649	.648	.647	.645	.644
50	0.643	.641	.640	.639	.637	.636	.635	.633	.632	.631
51	0.629	.628	.627	.625	.624	.623	.621	.620	.618	.617
52	0.616	.614	.613	.612	.610	.609	.607	.606	.605	.603
53	0.602	.600	.599	.598	.596	.595	.593	.592	.591	.589
54	0.588	.586	.585	.584	.582	.581	.579	.578	.576	.575
55	0.574	.572	.571	.569	.568	.566	.565	.564	.562	.561
56	0.559	.558	.556	.555	.553	.552	.550	.549	.548	.546
57	0.545	.543	.542	.540	.539	.537	.536	.534	.533	.531
58	0.530	.528	.527	.525	.524	.522	.521	.520	.518	.517
59	0.515	.514	.512	.511	.509	.508	.506	.505	.503	.502
60	0.500	.498	.497	.495	.494	.492	.491	.489	.488	.486
61	0.485	.483	.482	.480	.479	.477	.476	.474	.473	.471
62	0.469	.468	.466	.465	.463	.462	.460	.459	.457	.456
63	0.454	.452	.451	.449	.448	.446	.445	.443	.442	.440
64	0.438	.437	.435	.434	.432	.431	.429	.427	.426	.424
65	0.423	.421	.419	.418	.416	.415	.413	.412	.410	.408
66	0.407	.405	.404	.402	.400	.399	.397	.396	.394	.392
67	0.391	.389	.388	.386	.384	.383	.381	.379	.378	.376
68	0.375	.373	.371	.370	.368	.367	.365	.363	.362	.360
69	0.358	.357	.355	.353	.352	.350	.349	.347	.345	.344
70	0.342	.340	.339	.337	.335	.334	.332	.331	.329	.327
71	0.326	.324	.322	.321	.319	.317	.316	.314	.312	.311
72	0.309	.307	.306	.304	.302	.301	.299	.297	.296	.294
73	0.292	.291	.289	.287	.286	.284	.282	.281	.279	.277
74	0.276	.274	.272	.271	.269	.267	.266	.264	.262	.261
75	0.259	.257	.255	.254	.252	.250	.249	.247	.245	.244
76	0.242	.240	.239	.237	.235	.233	.232	.230	.228	.227
77	0.225	.223	.222	.220	.218	.216	.215	.213	.211	.210
78	0.208	.206	.204	.203	.201	.199	.198	.196	.194	.193
79	0.191	.189	.187	.186	.184	.182	.181	.179	.177	.175
80	0.174	.172	.170	.168	.167	.165	.163	.162	.160	.158
81	0.156	.155	.153	.151	.150	.148	.146	.144	.143	.141
82	0.139	.137	.136	.134	.132	.131	.129	.127	.125	.124
83	0.122	.120	.118	.117	.115	.113	.111	.110	.108	.106
84	0.105	.103	.101	.099	.098	.096	.094	.092	.091	.089
85	0.087	.085	.084	.082	.080	.078	.077	.075	.073	.071
86	0.070	.068	.066	.065	.063	.061	.059	.058	.056	.054
87	0.052	.051	.049	.047	.045	.044	.042	.040	.038	.037
88	0.035	.033	.031	.030	.028	.026	.024	.023	.021	.019
89	0.017	.016	.014	.012	.010	.009	.007	.005	.003	.002
90	0.000									

TABLE OF TANGENTS

Angle in degrees	.0	.1	.2	.3	.4	.5	.6	.7	.8	.9
0	0.000	.002	.003	.005	.007	.000	.010	.012	.014	.016
1	0.017	.019	.021	.023	.024	.026	.028	.030	.031	.033
2	0.035	.037	.038	.040	.042	.044	.045	.047	.049	.051
3	0.052	.054	.056	.058	.059	.061	.063	.065	.066	.068
4	0.070	.072	.073	.075	.077	.079	.080	.082	.084	.086
5	0.087	.089	.091	.093	.095	.096	.098	.100	.102	.103
6	0.105	.107	.109	.110	.112	.114	.116	.117	.119	.121
7	0.123	.125	.126	.128	.130	.132	.133	.135	.137	.139
8	0.141	.142	.144	.146	.148	.149	.151	.153	.155	.157
9	0.158	.160	.162	.164	.166	.167	.169	.171	.173	.175
10	0.176	.178	.180	.182	.184	.185	.187	.189	.191	.193
11	0.194	.196	.198	.200	.202	.203	.205	.207	.209	.211
12	0.213	.214	.216	.218	.220	.222	.224	.225	.227	.229
13	0.231	.233	.235	.236	.238	.240	.242	.244	.246	.247
14	0.249	.251	.253	.255	.257	.259	.260	.262	.264	.266
15	0.268	.270	.272	.274	.275	.277	.279	.281	.283	.285
16	0.287	.289	.291	.292	.294	.296	.298	.300	.302	.304
17	0.306	.308	.310	.311	.313	.315	.317	.319	.321	.323
18	0.325	.327	.329	.331	.333	.335	.337	.338	.340	.342
19	0.344	.346	.348	.350	.352	.354	.356	.358	.360	.362
20	0.364	.366	.368	.370	.372	.374	.376	.378	.380	.382
21	0.384	.386	.388	.390	.392	.394	.396	.398	.400	.402
22	0.404	.406	.408	.410	.412	.414	.416	.418	.420	.422
23	0.424	.427	.429	.431	.433	.435	.437	.439	.441	.443
24	0.445	.447	.449	.452	.454	.456	.458	.460	.462	.464
25	0.466	.468	.471	.473	.475	.477	.479	.481	.483	.486
26	0.488	.490	.492	.494	.496	.499	.501	.503	.505	.507
27	0.510	.512	.514	.516	.518	.521	.523	.525	.527	.529
28	0.532	.534	.536	.538	.541	.543	.545	.547	.550	.552
29	0.554	.557	.559	.561	.563	.566	.568	.570	.573	.575
30	0.577	.580	.582	.584	.587	.589	.591	.594	.596	.598
31	0.601	.603	.606	.608	.610	.613	.615	.618	.620	.622
32	0.625	.627	.630	.632	.635	.637	.640	.642	.644	.647
33	0.649	.652	.654	.657	.659	.662	.664	.667	.669	.672
34	0.675	.677	.680	.682	.685	.687	.690	.692	.695	.698
35	0.700	.703	.705	.708	.711	.713	.716	.719	.721	.724
36	0.727	.729	.732	.735	.737	.740	.743	.745	.748	.751
37	0.754	.756	.759	.762	.765	.767	.770	.773	.776	.778
38	0.781	.784	.787	.790	.793	.795	.798	.801	.804	.807
39	0.810	.813	.816	.818	.821	.824	.827	.830	.833	.836
40	0.839	.842	.845	.848	.851	.854	.857	.860	.863	.866
41	0.869	.872	.875	.879	.882	.885	.888	.891	.894	.897
42	0.900	.904	.907	.910	.913	.916	.920	.923	.926	.929
43	0.933	.936	.939	.942	.946	.949	.952	.956	.959	.962
44	0.966	.969	.972	.976	.979	.983	.986	.990	.993	.997
45	1.00	1.00	1.01	1.01	1.01	1.02	1.02	1.02	1.03	1.03

TABLE OF TANGENTS – *continued*

Angle in degrees	.0	.1	.2	.3	.4	.5	.6	.7	.8	.9
45	1.00	1.00	1.01	1.01	1.01	1.02	1.02	1.02	1.03	1.03
46	1.04	1.04	1.04	1.05	1.05	1.05	1.06	1.06	1.06	1.07
47	1.07	1.08	1.08	1.08	1.09	1.09	1.10	1.10	1.10	1.11
48	1.11	1.11	1.12	1.12	1.13	1.13	1.13	1.14	1.14	1.15
49	1.15	1.15	1.16	1.16	1.17	1.17	1.17	1.18	1.18	1.19
50	1.19	1.20	1.20	1.20	1.21	1.21	1.22	1.22	1.23	1.23
51	1.23	1.24	1.24	1.25	1.25	1.26	1.26	1.27	1.27	1.28
52	1.28	1.28	1.29	1.29	1.30	1.30	1.31	1.31	1.32	1.32
53	1.33	1.33	1.34	1.34	1.35	1.35	1.36	1.36	1.37	1.37
54	1.38	1.38	1.39	1.39	1.40	1.40	1.41	1.41	1.42	1.42
55	1.43	1.43	1.44	1.44	1.45	1.46	1.46	1.47	1.47	1.48
56	1.48	1.49	1.49	1.50	1.51	1.51	1.52	1.52	1.53	1.53
57	1.54	1.55	1.55	1.56	1.56	1.57	1.58	1.58	1.59	1.59
58	1.60	1.61	1.61	1.62	1.63	1.63	1.64	1.64	1.65	1.66
59	1.66	1.67	1.68	1.68	1.69	1.70	1.70	1.71	1.72	1.73
60	1.73	1.74	1.75	1.75	1.76	1.77	1.77	1.78	1.79	1.80
61	1.80	1.81	1.82	1.83	1.83	1.84	1.85	1.86	1.86	1.87
62	1.88	1.89	1.90	1.90	1.91	1.92	1.93	1.94	1.95	1.95
63	1.96	1.97	1.98	1.99	2.00	2.01	2.01	2.02	2.03	2.04
64	2.05	2.06	2.07	2.08	2.09	2.10	2.11	2.12	2.13	2.13
65	2.14	2.15	2.16	2.17	2.18	2.19	2.20	2.21	2.23	2.24
66	2.25	2.26	2.27	2.28	2.29	2.30	2.31	2.32	2.33	2.34
67	2.36	2.37	2.38	2.39	2.40	2.41	2.43	2.44	2.45	2.46
68	2.48	2.49	2.50	2.51	2.53	2.54	2.55	2.56	2.58	2.59
69	2.61	2.62	2.63	2.65	2.66	2.67	2.69	2.70	2.72	2.73
70	2.75	2.76	2.78	2.79	2.81	2.82	2.84	2.86	2.87	2.89
71	2.90	2.92	2.94	2.95	2.97	2.99	3.01	3.02	3.04	3.06
72	3.08	3.10	3.11	3.13	3.15	3.17	3.19	3.21	3.23	3.25
73	3.27	3.29	3.31	3.33	3.35	3.38	3.40	3.42	3.44	3.46
74	3.49	3.51	3.53	3.56	3.58	3.61	3.63	3.66	3.68	3.71
75	3.73	3.76	3.78	3.81	3.84	3.87	3.89	3.92	3.95	3.98
76	4.01	4.04	4.07	4.10	4.13	4.17	4.20	4.23	4.26	4.30
77	4.33	4.37	4.40	4.44	4.47	4.51	4.55	4.59	4.63	4.66
78	4.70	4.75	4.79	4.83	4.87	4.92	4.96	5.00	5.05	5.10
79	5.14	5.19	5.24	5.29	5.34	5.40	5.45	5.50	5.56	5.61
80	5.67	5.73	5.79	5.85	5.91	5.98	6.04	6.11	6.17	6.24
81	6.31	6.39	6.46	6.54	6.61	6.69	6.77	6.85	6.94	7.03
82	7.12	7.21	7.30	7.40	7.49	7.60	7.70	7.81	7.92	8.03
83	8.14	8.26	8.39	8.51	8.64	8.78	8.92	9.06	9.21	9.36
84	9.51	9.68	9.84	10.0	10.2	10.4	10.6	10.8	11.0	11.2
85	11.4	11.7	11.9	12.2	12.4	12.7	13.0	13.3	13.6	14.0
86	14.3	14.7	15.1	15.5	15.9	16.3	16.8	17.3	17.9	18.5
87	19.1	19.7	20.4	21.2	22.0	22.9	23.9	24.9	26.0	27.3
88	28.6	30.1	31.8	33.7	35.8	38.2	40.9	44.1	47.7	52.1
89	57.3	63.7	71.6	81.8	95.5	115	143	191	286	573